SAP PRESS e-books

Print or e-book, Kindle or iPad, workplace or airplane: Choose where and how to read your SAP PRESS books! You can now get all our titles as e-books, too:

- By download and online access
- For all popular devices
- And, of course, DRM-free

Convinced? Then go to www.sap-press.com and get your e-book today.

SAP® Commerce Cloud: Commerce with SAP C/4HANA®

SAP PRESS

Seema Vishnoi, Sietse Verhoog, Drew Messinger-Michaels

SAP® Commerce Cloud: Commerce with SAP C/4HANA®

Rheinwerk Publishing

Editor Meagan White
Acquisitions Editor Emily Nicholls
Copyeditor Melinda Rankin
Cover Design Graham Geary
Photo Credit Shutterstock.com/66946150/© Natali Glado
Layout Design Vera Brauner
Production Hannah Lane
Typesetting SatzPro, Krefeld (Germany)
Printed and bound in the United States of America, on paper from sustainable sources

ISBN 978-1-4932-1699-4

1st edition 2019

Library of Congress Cataloging-in-Publication Data
Names: Thomas, Seema, (SAP consultant), author. | Verhoog, Sietse, author. | Messinger-Michaels, Drew, author.
Title: SAP Commerce Cloud: Commerce with SAP C/4HANA/ Seema Thomas, Sietse Verhoog, and Drew Messinger-Michaels.
Description: 1st edition. | Bonn ; Boston : Rheinwerk Publishing, [2018] | Includes index.
Identifiers: LCCN 2018024378 (print) | LCCN 2018028908 (ebook) | ISBN 9781493217007 (ebook) | ISBN 9781493216994 (alk. paper)
Subjects: LCSH: Selling--Data processing. | Marketing--Data processing. | Electronic commerce--Computer programs. | SAP ERP.
Classification: LCC HF5438.35 (ebook) | LCC HF5438.35 T46 2018 (print) | DDC 658.8/72028553--dc23
LC record available at https://lccn.loc.gov/2018024378

Contents at a Glance

Dear Reader,

These days, many of us do a large portion of our shopping online. As a result, we all know what makes a good online shopping experience, and what doesn't. A discount code automatically applies when you put eligible products in your cart? Score! The website forgets what's in your cart if you switch between tabs? On second thought, maybe you didn't really need that item anyway.

If you're implementing or using SAP Commerce or SAP Commerce Cloud, you've already taken steps to improving your customers' online shopping experiences. With that software—and this comprehensive resource as your guide—you're on your way to better commerce workflows! From the all-important online storefront to order management, search, and backend integration, expert authors Seema Vishnoi, Sietse Verhoog, and Drew Messinger-Michaels have dug around in SAP Commerce to give everything you need.

What did you think about *SAP Commerce Cloud: Commerce with SAP C/4HANA*? Your comments and suggestions are the most useful tools to help us make our books the best they can be. Please feel free to contact me and share any praise or criticism you may have.

Thank you for purchasing a book from SAP PRESS!

Meagan White
Editor, SAP PRESS

meaganw@rheinwerk-publishing.com
www.sap-press.com
Rheinwerk Publishing · Boston, MA

Contents

Foreword

Disruption has always been a concept I have been passionate about.

When I co-founded hybris in 1997, the very notion of e-commerce was itself still disruptive in many, if not most, industries. More than two decades later, hybris has become SAP Commerce Cloud, and the team behind it, myself still included, has worked to make sure that it has *stayed* disruptive. Artificial intelligence, machine learning, and the Internet of Things might sound as abstract and future-facing now as e-commerce itself did in 1997, but that's exactly the point: Being ready to face the future means being willing to go there first. It means looking at your industry, seeing what new ideas *aren't* being applied across the board, and asking what would happen if they were. That's what disruption is all about.

Traditional businesses, regardless of size, are changing—and doing so within just a few years. Entirely new business models are emerging. We're in a period of rapid innovation. Big data, integration, and predictive analytics are here, but they're only parts of the whole when it comes to digitization. It's not really about any one technology. It's about a customer-first mindset when designing an experience and a cloud-first mindset when you're delivering that experience.

Yet the technology that you choose still matters. It matters a great deal, and SAP Commerce Cloud is one example of a technology that has managed to stay relevant and disruptive throughout its history, to the point that, today, it is more so than ever before. SAP Commerce Cloud has been a market leader for many years now, and we have achieved that by keeping in mind the evolving expectations of businesses and end customers alike.

This book explains how and why.

Although SAP provides a good deal of information on functionality and methodology, this is the first time that this information has been collected into a straightforward, narrative form that can be consumed from cover to cover. This is the first time that there's been resource of the kind that implementation partners, project stakeholders, program managers, architects, business analysts, developers, and end users alike have been saying they want.

To put this book together, Seema, Sietse, and Drew have drawn not only on their own expertise in SAP Commerce Cloud and on-the-ground experience with customers, but also on their colleagues' technical expertise and the wealth of project best practices that have emerged as the SAP Commerce ecosystem has grown. They have put together a text that will be useful to technical and not-so-technical readers alike and a valuable read for customers at every stage of their commerce journeys.

I hope that you find this book informative and useful, but more than that, I hope that it inspires you to try something new for your business. Specifically, by using established best practices, you can open up unexplored possibilities where they count most. Your customers expect it, and in SAP Commerce Cloud you have a platform that is uniquely equipped to anticipate and answer those expectations, as well as the constant change that shapes them.

We live in a time of immense opportunities. Let's work together, grow together, and build something new.

Moritz Zimmermann,
Co-founder of hybris, chief technology officer
for SAP Customer Experience

Preface

You're reading this book because you want to learn about SAP's commerce offering, currently known as SAP Commerce Cloud (cloud offering) and SAP Commerce (on-premise offering). Maybe you've heard about SAP Commerce Cloud as one of the key pillars of customer experience within SAP's intelligent enterprise. Maybe you know it by one of its previous names, like SAP Hybris Commerce Cloud, or from its earlier days. Maybe you know it only by reputation, or in the context of integrating it with other SAP products. Maybe you don't know it at all.

Regardless, this book exists to offer an overview of SAP Commerce, aimed both at those who know the solution and want to know more, and those who are encountering it for the first time. We take the time to introduce the vocabulary used both in the code and in the documentation, but having established that, we make sure to share technical details and general best practices that you probably have not encountered, even if you have taken some training on SAP Commerce in the past.

Target Audience

We want to offer a text that is useful to both technical and non-technical audiences. Developers and architects will gain an understanding of data models, process flows, and the format and location of key pieces of code. Business analysts and business stakeholders will gain an understanding of methodologies, planning, and the system's toolset for permissions and organization management.

Hopefully, each group will also learn a bit about how the other views the SAP Commerce stack and will therefore be able to move into future projects with a shared language, as well as a shared sense of purpose and a shared understanding of how their goals should be defined, refined, prioritized, perused, and achieved. In short, we as experts want to provide you with a text that we wish we'd had access to when *we* got started.

Structure of This Book

This volume focuses entirely on the SAP Commerce solution, with other books in this series outlining the other pillars of the Intelligent Enterprise, and another overview text outlining the entire SAP C/4HANA big picture. In this preface, as well as the introduction contained in Chapter 1 we will lay out some of the background for the outline of this book, the technologies it describes, and the larger market to which those technologies address themselves.

In Chapter 2, we'll walk you through the process of getting started with a new Commerce project, outlining best practices around team composition, planning, scoping, design, and development—and continuing on through testing, deployment, cutover, go-live, and post-go-live management. We'll then explain how to operate in the cloud, and how to employ and *land-and-expand* approach to building out your system for future improvements and upgrades.

Note

Throughout this book, we will frequently use the term *SAP Commerce* in place of *SAP Commerce Cloud*. The reason for this is that our audience includes businesses that already have SAP Commerce deployments as well as those that are starting fresh, and a majority of these existing customers currently run SAP Commerce on-premise. While moving to the cloud is a key element to our strategy, we do not want to ignore the significant number of projects that are not currently cloud-based. We therefore use the broader term to cover SAP Commerce on-premise, SAP Commerce Cloud, and hybrid implementations holistically, and call out cloud-specific design patterns, project methodologies, integrations, and functionalities, where appropriate.

After telling you how to get started, we will dive into a functional overview, configuration guide, and customization framework for the entire SAP Commerce suite, starting in Chapter 3 with commerce management. This covers sales organization management, carts, wish lists, checkout processes, promotions, coupons, campaigns, and the SAP Commerce accelerators storefronts. This chapter, in other words, covers the basic functions of *transnationality*. (If any of these terms are currently ambiguous, then do feel free to refer to the chapters in question—but also, do expect to have a basic understanding of how these concepts all fit together by the time you have finished with this introduction).

In Chapter 4, we will address product content management, by which we mean the creation, approval, maintenance, and improvement of any data specific to products. We will go over the structure of product data in SAP Commerce, the importance of *catalogs* for structuring this data, and your ability to change the product data model as your business requires.

We will also go over the employee-facing tools for working with this product data, both from the perspective of end users and those who run their teams, and from the perspective of a developer altering this experience and these groups. Finally, we will cover important but non-standard ways of selling, such as configurable products and bundles.

Chapter 5 will focus on customer experience management. Here we do not mean anything quite so broad as customer experience in the intelligent enterprise, but neither do we mean anything so narrow as *user interface (UI)* or *user experience (UX)*. While these terms tend to refer exclusively to the design and flow of user-facing instrumentation, and while customer experience in the intelligent enterprise is as much a philosophical approach as anything, in this book we think of customer experience as the *reflection* or *application* of those core principles to design and management within an omnichannel commerce experience.

After that, we'll turn to order management in Chapter 6. This includes sales organization management and cart and checkout processes from a backoffice perspective, as well as the process for managing and negotiation quotations. Just as importantly, this chapter covers *order orchestration, or the* process of receiving, picking, packing, shipping (or preparing pickup for) and order, and troubleshooting any part of the process that does not proceed as planned.

We will then describe these same processes from a support and service perspective, and from a customer self-service perspective. Chapter 7 will include the process of placing an order, checking its status, and initiating and completing a return. For each of these steps, we will explain what customers on the storefront can do for themselves, and what a customer support agent can do for them.

Having done that, we will next talk about search and navigation in Chapter 8. Here we will talk about the design and flow of customer journeys within your storefronts, with a special emphasis on configuring and optimizing your onsite search. You'll learn about the best practices for search index creation and configuration, as well as the tooling for both coarse-grained and fine-grained changes to customer-facing search results. The goal will be to craft engaging selling experiences, both within the Accelerator Storefronts (shown in Figure 1) and beyond them.

Having gone over all of these key areas or *modules* of the suite—more on the concept of modules in just a moment—we will turn to some important cross-module topics. Chapter 9 covers functionality, terminology, and concepts that are key to building and running Commerce, but that do not fit neatly into any of the other categories, generally because they are applicable to all of them. Here we will discuss internationalization (including currencies, languages, and regions), permissions management for both customer and employee accounts, and search engine optimization.

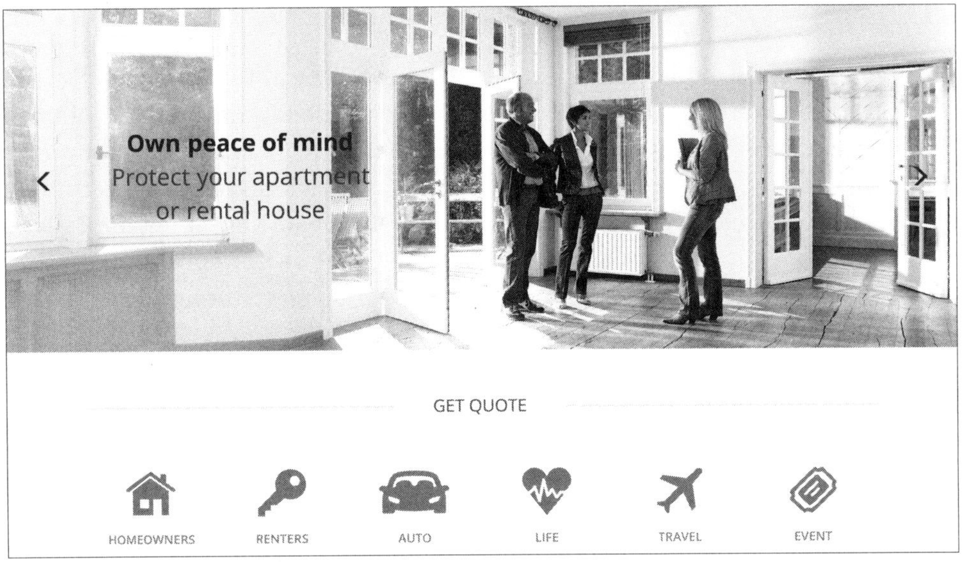

Figure 1 An SAP Commerce Accelerator Storefront

On a similar note, in Chapter 10 we will then go into some additional detail about the overall SAP Commerce platform, from the architecture of the system, to its data model, to the platform's processes for importing, exporting, and workflow. This chapter also covers the security principles in the system and recommended practices around them, taking full benefit of the flexibility and extensibility of the architecture and platform without sacrificing security.

Continuing in that same vein, we will then outline integrations in Chapter 11. This chapter explains how SAP Commerce fits into the larger SAP landscape strategy that allows you to move data from one system to another, leveraging SAP Cloud Platform Integration or SAP Commerce, data hub to integrate with other SAP cloud solutions. We then discuss specific integration points with other SAP products and functionality, including on-premise SAP ERP and SAP S/4HANA, SAP CRM, SAP Marketing Cloud, SAP Sales Cloud, SAP Service Cloud, and SAP Customer Engagement Center. Finally, we walk you through the upcoming integration strategy with SAP Cloud Platform Integration, as well as the overall application programming interface (API) framework and OData services.

In Chapter 12, we will then discuss how all of this functionality can be deployed to the cloud, and how you can take advantage of self-service capabilities in SAP Commerce Cloud portal. This includes the process of *cloud onboarding*, the infrastructure of SAP Commerce Cloud, and deployment services, unfractured and database services, as well as processes for monitoring, response, and security compliance.

This book can serve as a reference guide, there for you need information at the ready. It can also serve as a broad-but-deep introduction to SAP Commerce overall, ideal for when product documentation and best practices documents just don't seem to be arranged to tell digestible *stories*.

We want to provide you with a story that makes sense, supported not only by our expertise in the product itself, and by our experience with customers in the field, but also by our understanding of what you need to know before you start.

We've seen what happens when a project starts from a strong set of knowledge and an equally strong vision, and frankly, we've seen the opposite as well. Whatever your plans and whatever your goals, let us help you to build—and to be—one of the exemplary cases of success in the SAP Commerce space.

Acknowledgments

Writing a book is no small step, and being asked to take on the project of an SAP Commerce book was a big deal for me, both professionally and personally.

I have been fortunate to have a team of people who helped me get this project completed. My co-authors, Sietse and Drew, took this on knowing that they would have to burn quite a bit of midnight oil since their days were already full. Adam Davis, a good friend and master of order management, helped write the order management chapter. Karsten Hartmann, the integration guru, helped write the integration chapter. Thanks to Robert Dutoit and Krupa Singhampali for reviewing the content of the SAP Commerce portal chapter. I would like to thank Laryssa, who researched and pulled together critical content. I would like to give a shout out to Volker Hildebrand, a friend and a fellow author, whose guidance and support was priceless.

Last, but not the least, I would like to thank my family for cooking dinner, providing caffeine, and playing the right music to create the writing environment. (My daughter, Samara, even edited four pages of one of the chapters!) I am very thankful for their encouragement to take on this project and for their continuous support throughout.

—Seema Vishnoi

Thanks to the following people for helping review and putting the dots on the i's in specific chapters by sharing their thoughts and experience as subject matter experts: Bonny Lee for sharing her experience on methodology and project best practices, Rafael Tabosa for providing his insight into and experience with the platform and architecture, and Bruno Siqueira and Christian Muench for their expert contributions and feedback on the product content management chapter. I'd also like to share a special thanks to my co-writers Seema and Drew for the great teamwork. Finally, thanks to my wife, Anita, for the support during the writing and reviewing process, as this was a new experience for me.

—Sietse Verhoog

Thanks to Bonny Lee for her invaluable insights on methodology and best practices, to Laryssa Fonzo for helping us to widen our net as we researched past projects and engagements, and to Jeff Ellsworth for being a solid collaborator and an equally solid friend.

Thanks as well to Lauren Villegas for helping us ensure that the more technical aspects of this book were as clear as possible to less technical audiences—and even more importantly, for the kind of love that makes impossible things stubbornly possible and difficult things surprisingly easy.

—Drew Messinger-Michaels

Chapter 1
Introduction

SAP Commerce is only one part of the intelligent enterprise, but it contains an enormous amount of functionality in its own right. This introduction will explain the history and purpose of these features and put them in the context of the history of the broader commerce ecosystem.

SAP Commerce, in various versions and under various names, has been around for more than 20 years now. To understand why it looks and functions the way it does today, we should take a moment to explain its history and the broad outlines of its development—and perhaps even more importantly, we should talk briefly about how commerce more generally has changed and why it is continuing to change.

Here we will look both at customer expectations (what your customers want from your offering) and at vendor expectations (what we have seen that vendors want from SAP—or from any other enterprise software company, for that matter, when pursuing a commerce project). Having done that, we will briefly discuss the history of SAP Commerce and explain how the current version addresses these rapidly changing market conditions.

1.1 The Commerce Market

Before we talk about SAP Commerce itself in any greater detail, let's take a moment to define the context of the current commerce marketplace. What do customers expect? What do businesses need? How have these circumstances changed while SAP Commerce has existed, and how is it still changing right now?

The changes that have been made to the platform have not been arbitrary. Rather, they've been attempts to respond to current market conditions and prepare for future ones. So what are those conditions, and what has SAP done to ensure that SAP Commerce is ready to help you thrive within them?

1.1.1 Customer Expectations

It shouldn't be too controversial to say that a great deal has changed since 1997 or that this statement holds especially true when it comes to the internet, and *especially* true when it comes to buying and selling online. Even the very notion of being online has changed, with social media and smart devices being so ubiquitous that we don't even necessarily think of using them as *being online* in the same way that we did in the days of dial-up modems. The distinction between being online and offline has blurred for many of us, and in some situations it has become a distinction without a difference.

The effect of this change on commerce cannot be overstated. First and foremost, customers expect the experience of shopping on a mobile device to be comparable to that of shopping on a traditional web storefront; beyond that, they expect the experience of shopping in a brick-and-mortar store to integrate seamlessly with those other flows. They expect their account and order data to cross channels. They expect their shopping experience to *transcend* channels.

A few years ago, we were talking about the broader acceptance of shopping online and the need for businesses to adapt to that reality. Business-to-business (B2B) vendors that have spent decades (perhaps even more than a century) relying on face-to-face communication with their buyers at brick-and-mortar locations have had to consider selling online as well.

But now, framing the situation even in those terms seems a little naïve and insufficient. Those B2B vendors don't just need to set up a web-based storefront. They need to show their customers how web-based storefronts can enhance their brick-and-mortar experiences and vice versa. For example, Figure 1.1 shows a feature via which customers can check in-store availability online, purchase an item online, and then pick it up in a local store.

This is why we now talk less about simply *selling online*, or even doing *digital business*, and talk much more about *digital transformation*. A large network of brick-and-mortar stores is not a liability. Indeed, it's a resource that, sticking with our B2B example, upstart competitors (up to and including Amazon) simply do not have.

If you can offer unparalleled buy online, pick up in store (BOPIS) capabilities in otherwise underserved areas, then your brick-and-mortar stores are a *significant* asset to your customers, and therefore to you.

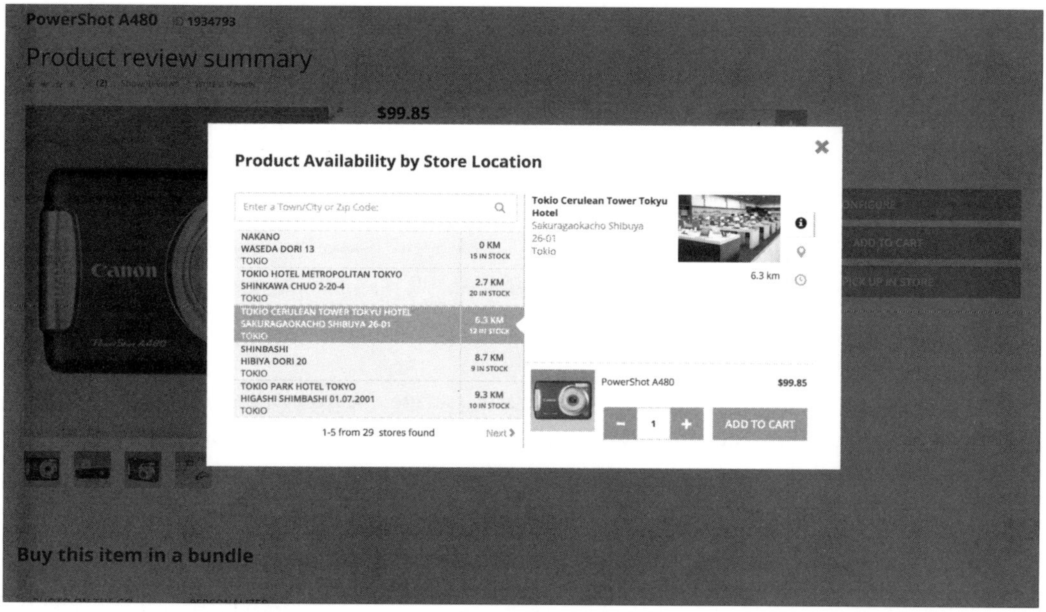

Figure 1.1 Buy Online, Pick Up in Store Functionality

So if your new storefront or your new mobile app or your newly introduced chatbot can provide availability information to your customers more quickly than a human can, then that can free your existing staff up to do what they do best: interact with customers on a one-to-one level, provide hands-on service and support (perhaps enhanced by readier access to customer and product information), and keep your brand relevant to your most important customers, who in turn will take your business where you want it to be.

That's digital transformation. That's a business running better, and thriving, by rising to meet its customers' changing expectations.

1.1.2 Vendor Requirements

SAP's overall strategy is, of course, focused on the cloud—and in that aspect, SAP Commerce is no exception. As we will discuss later in this introduction, cloudification has been a key principle in SAP Commerce development for several years now, and SAP Commerce Cloud is first and foremost a piece of a larger customer experience picture, a pillar of the intelligent enterprise.

The *intelligent enterprise* is a business that effectively leverages data to achieve desired outcomes while maximizing efficiency and minimizing risk. When SAP says that it wants *to make the world run better*, this is what it concretely means: it wants to empower every business to run the best that it can. The more businesses can do so, the happier SAP customers can make *their* customers, and the better the world will run as a whole.

To meet the changing customer expectations outlined thus far, businesses need to adapt. In the same way that a few years ago the received wisdom was to simply *go online*, the knee-jerk digital strategy of the recent past was to simply collect data—big data, bigger data, *all available data*.

Recently, two things have changed this narrative. Narrowly, the European Union's General Data Protection Regulation (GDPR) has ushered in a new era of consumer protections surrounding privacy, consent, and bounded data retention. This is going to be a tremendously good thing in the long run for customers' trust in the businesses from which they buy and the systems in which they put their trust—but in the short term, it means that for the first time since the data gold rush began, *data can be a liability as well as an asset*. This is a huge shift in thinking, and it also leads us naturally to the second large change surrounding the culture of customer data.

More broadly, it's become clear that a great many businesses were collecting data without really knowing what they planned to do with it. If you are selling advertising, and if you have your customers' demographic information readily accessible, then this catchall approach to data retention likely has served you well. If you do just about anything else—that is to say, if you are neither Google nor Facebook—then you might be sitting on a large quantity of unstructured data, struggling to put it to good use, and wondering why.

If you have been collecting enormous amounts of customer data, then the good news is that SAP provides vastly improved best practices for organizing it and putting it to use—and for providing customers the transparency they need in regard to what you have and what you plan to do with it. If you have not been collecting this sort of customer data, then the good news is that SAP now allows you collect it *better*, in a fashion that is more intelligent, focused, and aligned with customers' expectations.

Any business' digital transformation has to include some serious thinking about customer *personas* (the meaningful groups into which you will subdivide your customers for the purposes of personalization, marketing, and communication) and about the goals of data use. As you'll see, SAP Commerce provides some of the most important tools for making that leap, including consent management, which is shown in Figure 1.2 and described in more detail in Chapter 8.

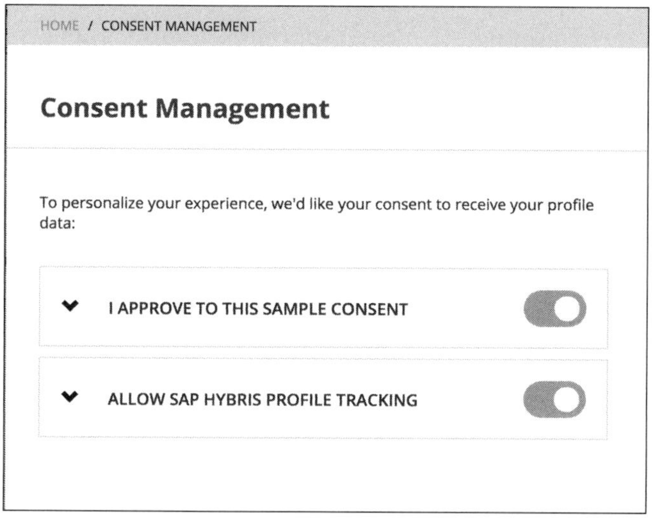

Figure 1.2 Some Native Consent Management Features in SAP Commerce

Of course, this is not the only change facing vendors across all verticals, or even the only one to do with data. To put it simply, businesses need to make intelligent decisions about how to show and sell their products, and this means finding the right balance between manual tooling and automation.

As we discuss in more detail in our chapter on service and support, no business can possibly get by only on one-to-one interactions between employees and customers—that simply doesn't scale—nor can any business get by without *some* such interactions. You want to empower your customers to take care of simple issues such as password resets and order inquiries (not to mention somewhat more involved issues, such as returns processing and ticketing) themselves, specifically so that your human support team can focus on the cases for which they are needed most.

This same principle applies to nearly every aspect of your business, during and after digital transformation. You should absolutely use some form of business intelligence to divvy up your customers and personalize their experiences, but there is no automated process for deciding which factors are most important to personalize on. That requires intentional, manual action from your team.

There is a tendency—among software vendors, project architects, and futurists, along with anyone else prone to being overcome with enthusiasm—to treat automation as a switch that, once flicked, removes human decision-making from a given aspect of business. Although automation *can* be used this way, anyone who *has* used it this way knows that there are far more effective ways to approach automation.

Just as customer self-service does not replace your support and service team members but rather allows them to focus their efforts where they are actually needed, so too does business intelligence enhance your ability to make decisions rather than simply outsourcing the need to do so.

We will touch on some concrete examples of this balance not only when we talk about support and service in Chapter 7, but also when we talk about customer experience management and context-driven services in Chapter 5, search and navigation management in Chapter 8, and personalization in Chapter 9. For now, we just want to get you thinking about the role that business intelligence can and should play in your digital transformation.

What problems do you want to solve? What decisions do you want to keep in your own hands, and which day-to-day ones should you offload to automation?

1.2 The SAP Commerce Story

What we now call *SAP Commerce Cloud* is the most recent and most advanced version of what used to be called *SAP Hybris Commerce*, and what before that was simply called *hybris* (styled with a lowercase *h*). Specifying hybris *Commerce* was not initially necessary, because hybris was a commerce product and a commerce platform through and through.

The company called *hybris* was founded in 1997 by Carsten Thoma, Moritz Zimmermann, and Klaas Hermanns. The collaborators named their new venture after a German rendering of the Greek word *hubris*, which roughly translates to *pride* or *extreme self-confidence*, as well as to *defiance of the powers that be*. The idea was that these upstarts thought they could make something good enough to take on the "gods" of the field, principally IBM and Oracle. The plan was audacious and ended up being successful, first throughout Europe and then elsewhere.

In 2011, the private equity firm HGGC, which held a majority stake both in hybris and in the Canadian commerce company iCongo, merged the two companies. iCongo's team became a key part of hybris' presence in the Americas (perhaps most notably forming the earliest version of their cloud hosting and infrastructure team), and iCongo's suite of order management and warehouse management features became key parts of the hybris suite.

Then, in 2013, SAP acquired hybris. This kicked off a new era in which hybris had access to more and more high-profile customers, built new functionality throughout and beyond the purview of commerce, and, increasingly, collaborated and integrated with other parts of SAP. To a certain degree, this process continues to this day—but the current incarnation of SAP Commerce Cloud represents the culmination of this process, which brought the strengths of hybris to SAP and leveraged the considerable strengths and unique position of SAP to transform hybris.

This transformation began with integrations between hybris and SAP ERP and SAP S/4HANA and over the past few years has extended to the point of SAP Commerce (as it is now called) being a core component of the SAP C/4HANA suite, intended as an end-to-end, cloud-based solution for intelligent enterprises. SAP Commerce has retained the functionality that it acquired throughout its pre-SAP growth but has expanded its scope as it has become a single key piece of a much larger whole.

This history is worth recounting briefly, both because it will make some of the technical details a bit clearer—especially regarding how and why SAP Commerce Cloud differs from other SAP products—and because words like *hybris* (and as you will see, *cockpit* as well) recur throughout the code itself. Branding aside, it's worth knowing what those terms are doing there.

1.2.1 The Platform and Its Evolution

The original hybris began its life as a product content management (PCM) solution and gradually grew into an end-to-end commerce platform. This process was relatively natural, arising from customer needs. Businesses that sell tend to sell online; businesses that sell need to offer service and support during and after doing so; businesses that sell online through a traditional, desktop-facing, single-channel web storefront tend to also sell through other channels—and, increasingly, such businesses need to offer a consistent, seamless experience across all of their channels. To meet these needs, hybris added its accelerator storefronts and its attached content management system, its support and service functionality, and, eventually, its omnichannel capabilities.

Because of this approach, the platform's core strength lies in its interconnectedness. As you will see throughout this book, product and web content share a data structure, customer and employee accounts share a permissions structure, and as a general design principle, each module is closely coupled to the others.

This is not to say that individual features or functionalities cannot be customized or switched out for other solutions or for entirely custom technology. They absolutely can. But the interconnected nature of modules means that when doing so, you will need to plan holistically and consider potential dependencies. More than that, it means that customers who do *not* plan to heavily customize these features can benefit from a shared set of underlying data objects, design principles, and shared tools.

No integration is necessary, for example, to connect a standard carousel of recommended products to the products themselves. Employees can simply plug a list of unique identifiers for the products into the carousel in the content management system and see the results immediately (see Figure 1.3). Any product details shown in the carousel, from the product names and imagery to prices and short descriptions, will automatically stay up to date in the carousel so long as they're kept up to date in the product catalog.

Figure 1.3 Product Carousel in Accelerator Storefronts

It is this unusual combination of configurability and customizability on the one hand and robust out-of-the-box interconnection on the other that most defined SAP Hybris Commerce throughout its initial development—and that most defines SAP Commerce as it exists today. There are solutions on the market that require less setup, but these tend to offer far less adaptability and room to grow. Conversely, there are solutions on the market that offer equally robust platforms for future development, but they tend not to offer a speedy time to value via market-tested default functionality.

With that said, there is another sense in which SAP Commerce is if not unique within the SAP ecosystem, then certainly unusual and notable—namely, the language and stack that undergirds it. This is true of the entire SAP Commerce solution, which emerges directly from what used to be called the SAP Hybris platform, but not, for example, of the SAP Marketing Cloud solution (formerly known as SAP Hybris Marketing), which was developed after the SAP acquisition.

SAP Commerce was coded in Java—more specifically, in the Spring framework. From a technical perspective, and in the context of this book, the most important implication of SAP Commerce being based on Java and Spring is simply that it is *not* based on ABAP, SAP Fiori, or other elements common to most SAP products. It was developed entirely independently of those technologies, and no effort has yet been made to move it onto any of them.

This does not mean, of course, that SAP Commerce is somehow incompatible with the rest of the SAP ecosystem. As you will see in our chapter on integrations, that is not the case at all. What it *does* mean is that working in SAP Commerce requires a significantly different skillset than working in, say, SAP S/4HANA. We will discuss team composition and skillset in greater detail later in this book, but the broad point is important to keep in mind when selecting architect and building teams.

For less technical readers, the most important thing to understand is that Java is an object-oriented language, meaning that it defines simple objects and then iterations on those objects, adding layers of complexity. As you will see when we discuss the SAP Commerce product data model, this concept is core to the platform's approach to data. The *type system* works in about this same way, starting with a fairly simple type, such as `user`, and then defining more specific subtypes, such as `customer` and `employee`.

All these types have some qualities in common—they will all have user IDs, for example—but customers will have different attributes, not to mention different access within the system, than employees will. Other types in the system, such as `product` and `page`, follow this same pattern.

Although this core technological basis has not changed throughout the history of SAP Commerce, a great deal *has* changed. Aside from the greatly expanded scope of functionality in the suite, perhaps the most important change was the introduction of accelerator storefronts. During the hybris 4 release cycle, hybris released the first version of the accelerators, built-in storefronts to go with the suite's commerce tooling, a current deployment of which is shown in Figure 1.4.

Prior to the SAP Commerce accelerator storefronts, all customers were responsible for building their own storefronts. The accelerators allowed businesses with relatively simple cases to achieve considerably faster time to value and businesses with more complicated cases to leverage accelerator storefronts as a basis for building their own solutions—or, even better, to launch with something very close to the accelerator, then land and expand into their own solution.

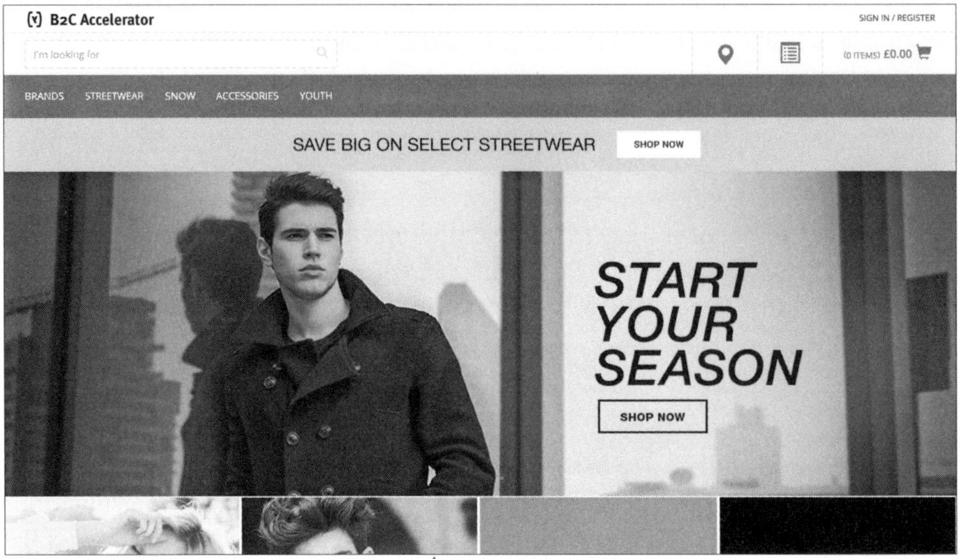

Figure 1.4 Current Example of B2C Accelerator Storefront

The first release of the SAP Commerce accelerators only included a B2C storefront, but soon after a B2B storefront was released, which included support for purchase order numbers and cost centers. Next came the telco accelerator storefront (now SAP Commerce, telco and media accelerator), which included bundling and guided selling, as well as the ability to sell products and services together. This was the first industry-specific solution. In later versions, what are now known as the SAP Commerce, financial services accelerator; SAP Commerce, citizen engagement accelerator; and SAP Commerce, accelerator for China were introduced. During the hybris 5 release cycle, all these accelerators were brought together into a single accelerator framework, allowing developers to mix and match functionality from different storefronts more easily. (We go into more detail about each, and about the general concept of accelerators, in Chapter 3.)

The other important changes and enhancements in the platform fall into three important categories: modularization, cockpits, and cloudification. Before we get into the main body of this book, we'll take a moment to go over the history, intent, and current state of each.

Note that we are summarizing these changes and the thinking behind them; for specific version-to-version and patch-to-patch changes, you should refer to the product documentation available at SAP Hybris Help (*https://help.hybris.com/*), a searchable, up-to-date tool available to vendors and implementation partners alike. Including the differences among all versions is out of scope here. At the time of writing, this tool's name has not been updated to reflect the new branding of SAP C/4HANA.

On that same note, be aware that most of this book will assume that you are using the most recent version of the SAP Commerce suite. Knowing that not everyone will be on the newest version, we do call out important version differences and deprecated features where necessary, but, for the most part, everything from screenshots to code snippets to feature descriptions will be taken from the most recent release.

1.2.2 Modularizing

The idea of modules is built into the core structures of SAP Commerce. In the system, discrete pieces of functionality are deployed as extensions, and these extensions are organized into modules. For example, payment processing functionality lives primarily in (appropriately enough) the `payment` extension, which is part of the cart and checkout module.

These modules allow you to more effectively manage dependencies. Some extensions rely on extensions from other modules (with most storefront extensions, regardless of what they do, typing back to the core facades extension, for example), but specific functionality will generally stay within a module. This means that as new functionality is added, the relationships of extensions within modules, and of one module to another, remain fairly clear.

This also means that if you introduce custom functionality to your SAP Commerce system, you can keep it bounded within a module using the modulegen tool (for modules) and the extgen tool (for extensions). Extensions provide a framework not only for understanding and organizing existing functionality, but also for adding new functionality cleanly.

1.2.3 Cockpits

When hybris first launched as a PCM-focused solution, and as it made its first steps toward a broader set of commerce functionality, it relied on a single employee-facing user interface for most of its functions: the hybris Management Console (hMC). This interface was powerful, but not especially friendly to nontechnical users. The hMC stuck around for many years—increasingly as an exclusively developer-facing option—but general tooling in hybris began to move more and more toward cockpits, an example of which is shown in Figure 1.5.

Figure 1.5 Product Cockpit

Cockpits were so named because the idea was to offer interfaces that would look to specific subsets of business users the same way a plane's cockpit looks to a pilot: everything necessary for the task at hand, and nothing *unnecessary* for the task at hand. Cockpits were conceived as narrowly targeted, purpose-built UIs for product managers, web content managers, customer support teams, and so on.

Although this worked well for some vendors' needs, others found that some or all of their key employees needed to hop from cockpit to cockpit, logging in and out of each. To address this issue, SAP moved away from individual cockpits and toward a single, unified backoffice UI with role-specific perspectives.

Figure 1.5 showed the Product Cockpit; Figure 1.6 shows the perspective that offers equivalent functionality in the backoffice. Both interfaces allow users to create and edit products, organize them into categories, associate them with digital assets such as images, and apply workflows to all those processes (e.g., having one employee create the product, another add a description, another translate that description into additional languages, and yet another approve the work and activate the product).

The backoffice version of the interface—besides being easier on the eyes, especially on mobile devices—allows for easier editing of multiple products and allows product managers to search for products in an indexed, faceted search (shown here), similar to the one available to customers on the storefront.

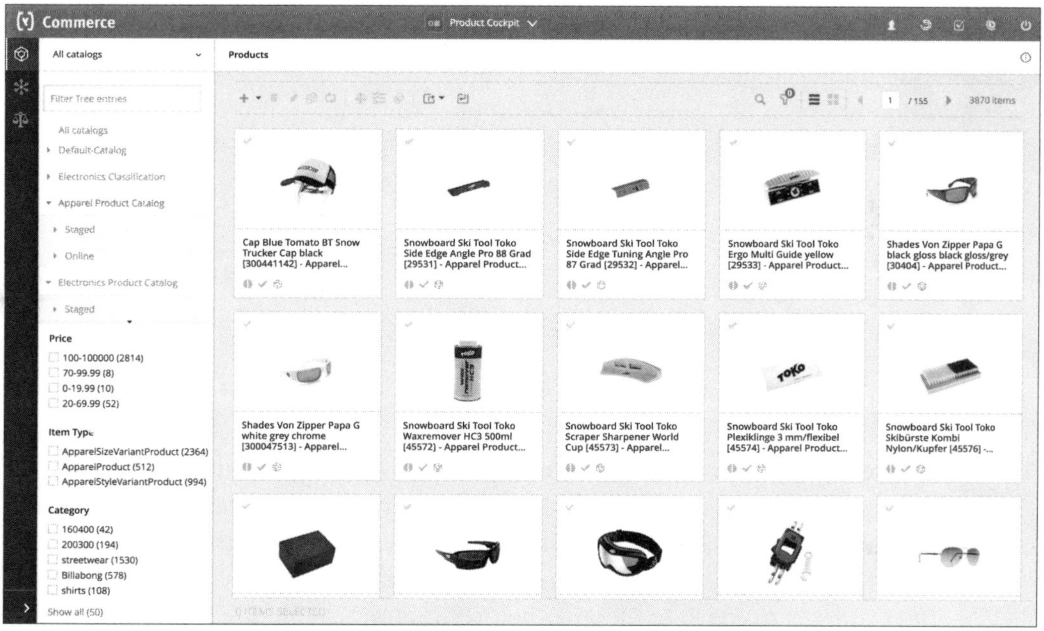

Figure 1.6 Backoffice Product Cockpit Perspective

Figure 1.6 shows just one example of the enhancements present in the backoffice equivalents of the older cockpit UIs, and we will go into more detail about each as we talk about their specific functionality. Eventually, the backoffice replaced not only the cockpits but the hMC as well, providing administrative and technical tooling (and, just as importantly, a single view of *all* functionality) via the administration perspective, thereby completing the unification of the employee-facing tooling into a single, configurable tool (shown in Figure 1.7).

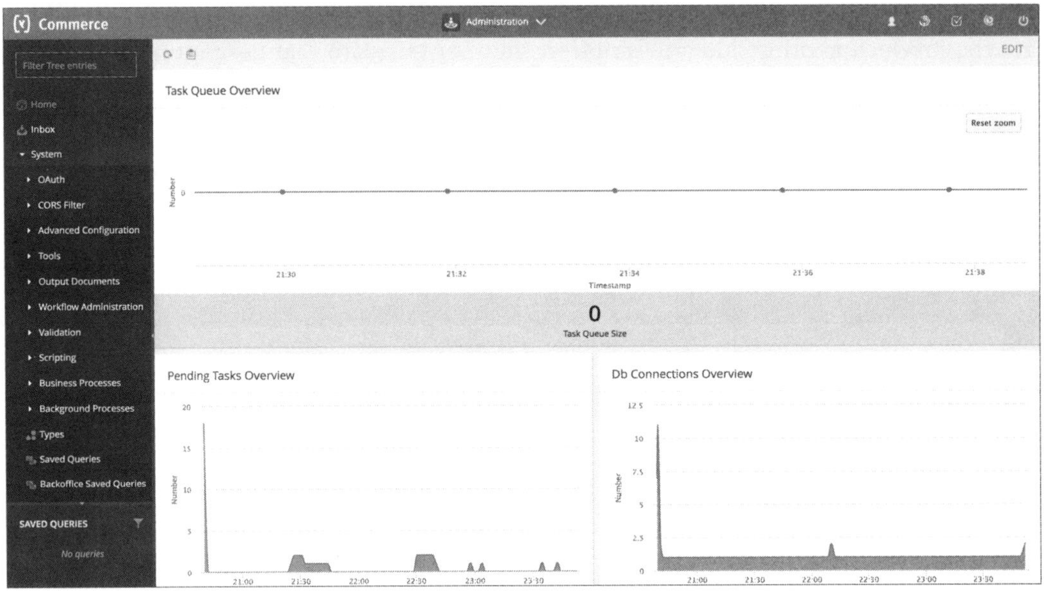

Figure 1.7 Admin Perspective in Backoffice

1.2.4 Cloudification

Because SAP Commerce offers an unusually robust set of functionality out of the box, and also because of its interconnectivity to other systems, the solution is well-suited to cloud strategies. Beyond that, to take full advantage of the rest of the SAP C/4HANA suite and of the SAP Commerce Cloud platform, we have been encouraging our customers to consider moving their solutions into the cloud. We go into more detail about the platform, its advantages, and the other solutions to which it connects in Chapter 12.

1.3 Summary

From the earliest days of hybris to the current momentum of the SAP C/4HANA suite, the team behind SAP Commerce always has attempted to address its work to the expectations of customers and vendors alike. These expectations have changed enormously and are always changing more; so too has and is the product. Some of the key concepts and vocabulary outlined here will help you make sense of the domain- and platform-specific references throughout the core chapters of this book.

With all that said, let's dive in! You now have a basic overview of what SAP Commerce is and where it came from, so we'll now focus on how to begin applying that knowledge to your projects and your goals.

Chapter 2
Getting Started with SAP Commerce

In this chapter, we will introduce recommended practices that should be considered before starting an SAP Commerce project. We will discuss the different kinds of methodologies that can be considered when executing an SAP Commerce project, as well as the different phases of implementation projects.

The SAP Commerce solution comes with many capabilities and features for different kinds of business in different markets across the globe. The possibilities offered by the software are many: to make sure the solution attends to the needs of your organization and market, it's important to prepare and involve the entire organization from an early stage. Make sure the objective of the project is known and expectations are set within the organization for timelines, return on investment, goals, success, and how to measure the same.

Although most commerce solutions in the market share a lot of similar functionalities, as well as similar base processes and concepts, each business is unique and has its own competitive characteristics to be reflected in the solution. Furthermore, technology keeps evolving and our markets growing, and the needs and expectations of your customers grow with them. Therefore, it is good to say that an SAP Commerce solution keeps evolving over time and in response to feedback from the market.

In this chapter, we'll introduce the various topics that should be considered before, during, and after the execution of an SAP Commerce project. From technical perspectives (like infrastructure and architecture) and how the business expectations impact these to other topics like project execution, teams, methodology, and an operational model to support your business, these points and others will be covered throughout the chapter and linked to a project delivery framework to structure and give guidelines for how these topics should be covered during a project.

2.1 Before You Begin

SAP teams have defined a framework of recommended practices and structures to guide you during your project and afterwards, which is called the application lifecycle framework for SAP Commerce (formerly the SAP Hybris Application Lifecycle Framework for Commerce). Within this framework, the project delivery framework is a set of practices and structures focused on the project aspects within your lifecycle.

In this section, we will cover an introduction to the application lifecycle framework for SAP Commerce, a subset of recommended practices focused on the whole lifecycle of your organization with the SAP Commerce suite. Next, we'll discuss the technical requirements and infrastructure to run SAP Commerce to give you an idea of what's needed to install and run SAP Commerce in your organization. We'll also discuss recommended practices and methodology for SAP Commerce implementations to share possible approaches and the differences between methodologies and what are considered recommended practices (e.g., land and expand strategies, as well as project methodology examples).

2.1.1 Application Lifecycle Framework

The *application lifecycle framework* is a set of practices and structures focused on the whole lifecycle of a solution, including project delivery, and it's structured into four main areas:

1. **Business execution**
   This section includes business topics that are relevant throughout an SAP Commerce project lifecycle. Examples and guidance are provided on topics like business operations and business readiness for e-commerce projects.
2. **Project delivery frameworks**
   This section explains the different types of projects within the context of an SAP Commerce solution and provides frameworks and approaches for delivering and managing SAP Commerce projects.
3. **Discipline recommended practices**
   This section focuses on recommended practices that are applicable within any stage of the lifecycle. Topics included in this chapter are architecture and development, business requirements (e.g., pricing, stock, search engine optimization), quality management (e.g., performance testing, test automation, package delivery), application management (e.g., maintenance topics), and project management (e.g., governance models, distributed teams).

4. **SAP Customer Experience Expert Services**
   This section contains information on how and when to involve the SAP Customer Experience Expert Services teams, including information about the success-guarding services (quality-focused services that are focused on reducing risk and increasing the success of projects) and solution add-ons and optimization services (workshops and other services to optimize the solution). The SAP Customer Experience Expert Services teams focus on supporting SAP's customers throughout their lifecycle with services focused on time to value, adoption, and transformation.

Note

More information about the framework can be found on the SAP Customer Experience site, including more details about the topics discussed in this chapter. Visit *http://cx.sap.com/alf* for more details.

In the following sections, we will focus on recommended practices within the project delivery framework of the application lifecycle framework throughout the different stages of SAP Commerce projects.

2.1.2 Technical Requirements and Infrastructure

The infrastructure required for deploying SAP Commerce exists in several components. Hardware sizing is a key factor during the initial project estimates and needs to be determined as soon as possible. Components like hardware, operating systems, storage, and network contribute to the hardware sizing needed for a project. For SAP Commerce Cloud, the infrastructure will be the responsibility of SAP.

Sizing

An initial sizing (which occurs during the presales phase) is a combination of assumptions and project-specific metrics that need to be validated and refined later in the project. During the engineering phase, performance tests can be executed to validate and refine the sizing.

Infrastructure sizing can be defined once there is a clear understanding of the logical architecture and the number of page requests and/or orders that need to be processed.

The sizing of logical architecture is determined by considering the peak point of choices to meet nonfunctional requirements (NFRs) such as scalability, high availability, and performance. Together with the technical capabilities of the underlying supporting software and hardware, the deployment architecture needs to be defined before the size of each infrastructure component can be defined. The main factors that influence the size and cost of the infrastructure are the number of CPUs, amount of RAM, and amount of disk space available for each component. The minimal required components that are recommended for an SAP Commerce infrastructure are as follows:

- Load balancer layer
- Web server
- Application server layer
- Search engine layer
- Database layer

Installing SAP Commerce

To start using SAP Commerce, it must be downloaded and initialized by the user. There is no need to install a separate database if the purpose is a demonstration or try-out of the software. The solution comes with a preconfigured lightweight database that is usually sufficient for preliminary tests. For implementation purposes, we recommend using a professional database system such as SAP HANA, Oracle, MySQL, or Microsoft SQL Server.

SAP Commerce is a lightweight and completely Java-based application. It can run on a standard web browser for demonstration and development purposes. Table 2.1 shows the minimum system requirements (for demos) and recommended requirements (for development).

	Minimum	Recommended
CPU	Dual core (e.g., i5)	Quad core (e.g., i7)
RAM	8 GB	16 GB
Hard disk	7200 rpm IDE	SSD
Hard disk space	10 GB	20 GB

Table 2.1 SAP Commerce Requirements

The requirements for RAM, CPU, and hard disk shown in Table 2.1 are needed to locally run the SAP Commerce suite and development tools like Eclipse and IntelliJ. To install SAP Commerce on your local machine, SAP Commerce installer recipes have been made available. A *recipe* is an automated, preconfigured installation script that creates directories, moves files, updates configuration files, and initializes the system. Java must be downloaded and installed to run the recipe.

Development Tools

In addition to the hardware recommendations, the following tools and functionalities help developers work more efficiently in their projects:

- **Java integrated development environment**
  Eclipse, an integrated development environment (IDE) used by most Java developers, is often used with SAP Commerce. All SAP Commerce extensions can be imported easily into Eclipse. Other IDEs include Spring Tool Suite and IntelliJ.
- **Import and export**
  For importing and exporting data (common activities during a project), ImpEx is the standard within SAP Commerce. For more details, see Chapter 10, Section 10.3.
- **Issue management**
  Issue management can be handled in a tool like Jira, in which development tasks can be managed and defects reported.
- **Source control management**
  There are two recommended tools for source control management: Apache Subversion and Git. IntelliJ has native support for both tools, for which Eclipse plugins exist.
- **Project documentation**
  It is important to have a centralized project knowledge base in which project documentation is stored and accessible for the SAP team, your team, and anyone else who needs access.

2.1.3 Methodology and Recommended Practices

You can extend the SAP Commerce platform by building your solutions on top of it to extend existing behavior or develop new functionality within the different modules.

As during any software development, there is a certain degree of complexity and uncertainty that you and delivery teams must manage in a project. This cannot be entirely eliminated but can be significantly reduced by developing on a stable and robust software platform such as SAP Commerce. The remaining complexity and uncertainty can be managed during the project by using an appropriate software development lifecycle method.

In the following sections, we will look at what should be considered as you begin your project, discuss how to select the approach that is right for your company, and explain the idea of land and expand.

Getting Started

Companies and organizations are different in various aspects, and these differences mean that there is no one right approach for executing SAP Commerce projects. Every organization is different: they have different requirements, different ways of working, different standards, different internal governance processes, and so on. Therefore, there are multiple approaches and methodologies for delivering implementation and upgrade projects, each with its advantages and disadvantages, and the right approach might differ depending on the project context. Some of the major factors that can influence behavior and the use of a certain methodology are as follows:

- **Governance processes and policies**
  What is the cultural and organizational setup for governance and policies? Are there strict sign-off or other corporate project governance requirements that need to be considered?
- **Decision-making processes**
  Who within the organization is empowered to make project-related decisions? How is this process set up, and how quickly can decisions be made?
- **Levels of collaboration**
  Can the people involved in the project collaborate in real time during the project?
- **Availability of skills and relevant experience**
  Do relevant technical skills and experience exist within the organization, or should third parties be hired? What project (management) experience does the team have, and is the organization used to certain methodologies?
- **Certainty of requirements**
  What is the likelihood of changing requirements? What flexibility is required to control this?

- **Language and location**
  Where are the teams located? Is the project managed via a centralized approach or does each location have its own project team or is there a hybrid model? Do the teams speak the same languages and are they in the same time zones?

As the context variables can vary for each project, these projects need to be managed differently; no two projects will be the same. The scope, size, and duration of these projects will also vary significantly from project to project and organization to organization.

Therefore, it is important to define what to control in a project. This is demonstrated by the well-known project management triangle (also known as the iron triangle), as shown in Figure 2.1.

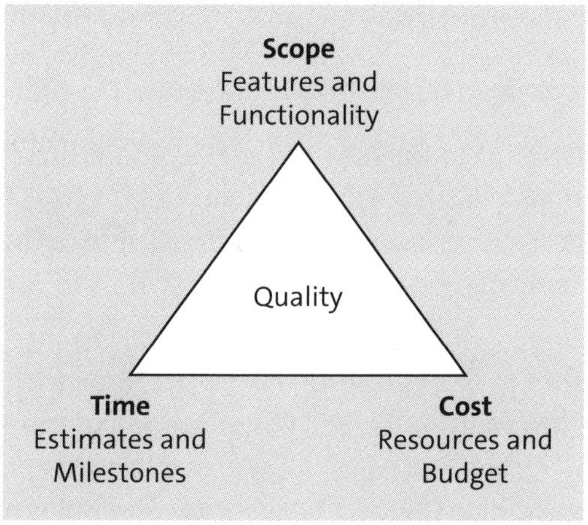

Figure 2.1 Iron Triangle for Project Management

The project management triangle shows the relationships among a project's scope, time, and cost. These three fundamental aspects of any project are all dependent on each other and tightly related. Adjustment to one will have implications for the other two. Quality, in the middle, must always be considered too, although unfortunately it's often overlooked and assumed because there is no specific direct dependency.

In an ideal world, all scope is delivered on time, on budget, and with high quality, and the four aspects are managed by the team. However, in a project environment, no matter how good the planning, something unexpected will always happen, so the plan must be adjusted. It usually won't be possible to manage and fix all four.

For SAP Commerce projects, the rate of change during a project typically can be very high as not everything is known beforehand, and what is known can change—for example, how the solution should work functionally and nonfunctionally (e.g., expected traffic, peak times, etc.). This makes it even more challenging to fully control scope, time, cost, and quality throughout the project.

Elements that often change during an SAP Commerce project include the following:

- Specific integrations with an external system can be subject to change (projects often integrate and have dependencies with multiple external systems that are not part of the project scope).
- The competitive environment can be very fast changing. If a leading competitor makes significant changes to its commerce website to offer new features, often other competitors want to react very quickly.
- Technology changes very quickly, such as social media, web technologies, mobile technologies, new releases of the SAP Commerce platform, and so on.

Because commerce is fast changing and it's hard to fully control these variables, SAP Commerce projects often operate in a very high change environment, and it's critical that the rate of change is considered properly when selecting an approach and deciding which aspect of the project management triangle will be flexible.

Of the four aspects in the triangle, it is not recommended to allow quality to be flexible. A poor-quality implementation can lead to issues during the project implementation and to much greater issues once the solution is live. Issues are much more expensive to fix later than during the project, and end users are exposed to problems that can lead to lost sales, long-term brand damage, and reductions in employee morale. These losses often will far outweigh any perceived upfront savings.

That leaves scope, time, and budget as the three variables that can be flexible. Because time and budget are factors that are significantly related and determine the success of a project in terms of return on investment or speed to market, there are typically two approaches for managing SAP Commerce implementation projects:

1. **Variable scope**
   The project control is focused on time and cost, allowing scope to vary. Often risk is managed by reducing the scope.
2. **Fixed scope**
   The project control is focused on scope, allowing cost and time to vary. Risk is managed by including an extra risk buffer in planned time and costs.

The business and project team need to agree on this choice before the project starts, and if there are contracts between the parties, these contracts need to be set up accordingly because they will drive relevant behavior.

Within the project delivery framework, there are methodologies leaning both towards agile (developed for variable-scope implementation projects) and iterative (developed for fixed-scope implementation projects) approaches.

SAP Commerce project delivery teams use and recommend the agile framework if possible: successful projects are more often measured on whether they were delivered on time and on budget, not whether every scope feature was delivered irrespective of value. Considering the naturally high rate of change in commerce, projects require an approach that supports very flexible scope changes, which the variable-scope approach does by design.

The iterative (fixed-scope) approach can be equally valid in the appropriate context if managed correctly, and many organizations prefer this more traditional approach. If the requirements and exact scope/deliverables need to be agreed on and signed-off on before the build begins to avoid any ambiguity later in the project, then the iterative project delivery framework can be used or adapted. In this case, it is extremely important to make clear the level of detail of the requirements that are considered part of the fixed scope.

For both the iterative and the agile methods, the following project phases can be considered:

1. Initiation
2. Foundation
3. Engineering
4. Deployment
5. Cutover

In Section 2.2, we will explore these phases deeply and elaborate on their characteristics for both the iterative and agile project methodologies.

Selecting Your Approach

As discussed earlier, the right approach or method to deliver a successful SAP Commerce implementation project depends on the particular context of each project. Every project is different and trying to force a method on a project where it doesn't fit will create problems and hugely increase risks.

For example, applying a waterfall (iterative) approach with fixed up-front requirements and design to a project with very fluid or uncertain requirements in a very changeable environment will be challenging. Instead, an agile approach would be much better suited for this project to allow for flexible scope changes throughout as requirements change. However, this very flexible agile approach might not be suitable for other reasons.

It's critical to design the approach for a specific project by considering the needs of the project first. After selecting the most appropriate method, it can be fine-tuned as necessary. There is no one right approach for all projects across all organizations. The key is understanding the options and how to apply them without compromising the underlying factors that form the foundation and underpin the benefits of that method. Therefore, we will not make a distinction between the two approaches in this chapter but will describe the recommended practices of both approaches; you can mix and adjust methodologies as need to meet your project's needs and characteristics.

Land and Expand

Land and expand is an often-discussed concept in projects, especially in customer experience projects. When you split a project or a program into different smaller projects, this is often considered a land-and-expand approach. Commerce is fast changing; competition never stops evolving their customer experience. Therefore, it's often recommended to split your project into smaller releases, often designed as minimal viable products (MVPs) or pilots (presented to select groups of customers or friends and family first). Some of the benefits are as follows:

- Get quick wins. The earlier you go-live, the earlier you can show results to your stakeholders.
- Validation of functionalities in a short time frame. The market grows fast; something that is innovative or a good idea at the beginning of the project might be less of a good idea after a couple of months.
- Often the real (customer) feedback comes after go-live. It is less costly when you have a smaller implementation to adjust in the next release than to do so after a full implementation. This feedback is often great input for a backlog.
- You can minimize the risk of delays with smaller scopes.
- Test environments let you see how the solution behaves under real customer traffic and (unforeseen) peaks or load.

Figure 2.2 shows an example of an implementation project with the different phases that are applicable for both the iterative and agile approaches. Independent of the methodology, it's a good practice to split a project into shorter releases (the example in Figure 2.2 has three releases), each with its own characteristics, scope, timeline, and application management workstream. We recommend splitting big projects into several smaller ones to improve time to market, adjustment to feedback (each go-live will give an organization real customer feedback), and understanding of possible new requirements due to business or organizational changes. Ideally, releases shouldn't be longer than five months.

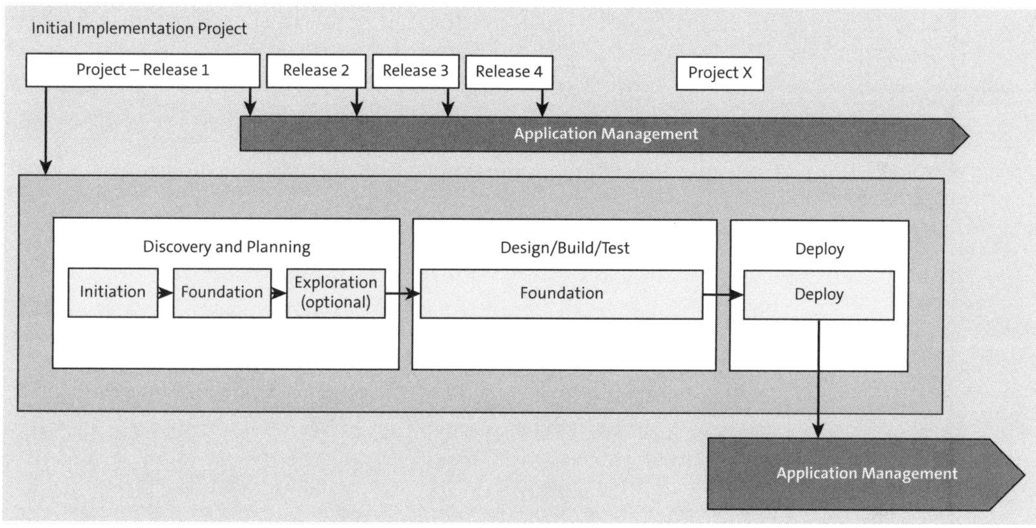

Figure 2.2 Example Implementation Project Framework

2.2 Running Your Project

In this section, we'll go into more detail on the different phases to be considered for an implementation and give you the tooling and insights that can be used for your project independent of the methodology chosen for your organization.

2.2.1 Defining the Scope

As mentioned earlier, all projects can follow similar phases independent of the methodology chosen. The methodology often is defined during the initiation phase of a project. One concept that is important to understand beforehand is the scope of the project. *Scope* includes all activities and tasks that are needed to complete a project implementation. Although a functional requirement is the most commonly known scope item, and it's important to agree on the requirements, it's also important to agree on all activities for each phase of the project beforehand to avoid conflicts during execution.

For each phase, the scope can contain various tasks and activities. For each activity per phase, it's important to determine and document the activities, the deliverables, and who is *responsible*, who *approves*, who is *consulted*, and who is *informed* (RACI).

Table 2.2 shows an example of scope activities that result in specific deliverables per phase.

Phase	Activities	Deliverable
Foundation	Define, review, estimate, and prioritize requirements	Functional requirements
	Define nonfunctional requirements	Nonfunctional requirements
	Define architecture, system integration, and logical/physical architecture	Solution architecture design (SAD)
	Define project quality management and testing strategy, defect management process, and responsibilities	Quality assurance deliverable (QAD)
	Define project governance, structure, roles, and responsibilities	Project governance and team structure
	Define infrastructure, environment, and tools required	Infrastructure and tools requirements
	Provision infrastructure and tools	
	Define project roadmap, project planning, release planning, data migration strategy, cutover strategy, cost planning, and risk analysis	Project plan, prioritized requirements list, cost plan, and risk register

Table 2.2 Scope Deliverables Examples per Phase

Phase	Activities	Deliverable
	Define documentation and training requirements (user guide, training material, knowledge transfer to application maintenance team, end user training, etc.)	
	Define UX wireframes and media	
	Project scope review and sign off	
Engineering	Set up sprint	Tools and environment setup
		Development environment guide
		Set up access to environments, repositories and tools
	Refined user stories and acceptance criteria	Approved sprint backlog
	Sprint planning, execution, review, and demos	Completed user stories
	Create automated tests, execute tests, and regression testing	
	Provide test data	
	System integration testing	
	Performance and security testing	
	Defect resolution	
	End user training	
	User acceptance testing and sign-off	
	Content creation	
Deployment	Verification of data on production environment	
	Production deployment	

Table 2.2 Scope Deliverables Examples per Phase (Cont.)

Phase	Activities	Deliverable
	Final end-to-end testing	
	Definition of backup processes and restore mechanisms	
	Post-go-live support	

Table 2.2 Scope Deliverables Examples per Phase (Cont.)

These definitions are made on a high level during the initiation phase. This phase has an objective to create a high-level alignment and understanding of the why/what/how/when and cost and risks of a project before moving into the foundation or design phase. Subsequently, scope is further detailed and documented in the foundation phase. Depending on the project methodology chosen (iterative or agile), detail is greater and scope is more fixed in the iterative approach, whereas the agile approach scope is less fixed and detail is elaborated in each different sprint setup.

2.2.2 Initiation Phase

The initiation phase is the first part of the discovery and planning activity of a new project. During the initiation phase the objective is to explore and come to a shared understanding of the following:

- **The why**
  Business goals and objectives of the project
- **The what**
  High-level scope, prioritization, and estimated effort
- **The how**
  Approach, methodology, and ways of working
- **The when**
  High-level project plan, milestones, and resource planning
- **The cost**
  Estimated project costs, including project team, infrastructure, licensing, and so on
- **The risks**
  The business/project/technical risks of the project

The initiation phase usually consists of three steps—qualification, workshop, and planning—as we'll discuss in the following sections.

Qualification

It's essential to qualify potential projects as early as possible to ensure the fit of all aspects. As a project proceeds through the phases, greater investments are made with each phase, in terms of time and resources and therefore also greater costs. It's therefore very important to establish as early as possible whether the project is viable and to determine that the relevant parties can work together and succeed in meeting the project goals.

Often qualification occurs during the software license sales process—for example, during the vendor selection process. Sometimes it happens afterward—for example, when the organization has already purchased SAP Commerce and needs to decide how to implement it.

During qualification, high-level discussions are held on topics like project goals, methodology, concurrent projects, timelines, project size, long-term ownership, and responsibilities, as well as partners, infrastructure, location, culture, and licensing.

Initiation Workshop

The initiation workshop involves all stakeholders and project teams discussing and exploring on a high level the why/what/how/when and cost and risks of the project, with a specific focus on the initial high level and functional and nonfunctional requirements.

Executing the workshop with all the teams physically present in the same location minimizes misunderstandings, stimulates clear communications, and increases dedication to the workshops from all involved teams (by limiting distractions from email, phone calls, etc.).

It's important to have experts on the topics to be covered in the room from both the business and the project team. If demos have been shown during a presales phase, analyzing these can be helpful to determine the expectations that have been set within the organization.

The workshop typically lasts one or two days, but this time can be reduced or extended based on the project size and complexity. The topics to be covered to achieve the objectives must be set beforehand and time boxed in the agenda to make sure all topics will be covered with the right amount of depth.

Typical topics to consider in the initiation workshop agenda are as follows:

- Organization's vision of its business and goals for the project
- Project delivery framework introduction and methodologies
- Phased releases approach versus big-bang go-live strategy
- High-level functional requirements and priorities, ideally with a list of requirements or wish list shared up front to prepare the functional topics
- Nonfunctional requirements (e.g., performance, scalability, security)
- High-level system landscape and integration points
- Key milestones: project start, release roadmap, and go-live dates
- Third-party dependencies and project and technical risks
- Data requirements and dependencies
- Tooling and ownership
- Hosting, infrastructure, and environments
- Organizational/team structure
- Testing activities and responsibilities
- Stakeholder analysis and identification of all involved parties and their responsibilities
- Long-term ownership of solution, including development, maintenance, and support
- Responsibility for user experience and creative designs
- Any open qualification topics

During the workshop, it's important to moderate time to ensure all topics are covered to a level that enables high-level understanding and estimating. It happens often that certain topics generate more discussion by involved teams. Any internal discussion should be encouraged to be picked up after the workshops in preparation for the actual design or foundation phase. It's important to take notes of these topics as they will probably require more time and attention during the foundation phase.

Furthermore, when discussing features, timelines, and important dates for the organization, expectations around meeting these dates and features in the project should be managed, and no commitment can be made until proper planning is done and estimations are made.

Planning

After the initiation workshops, enough (high-level) information should be available on the why/what/how/when to plan the project, estimate the effort required, and provide a high-level rollout strategy.

The final step of the initiation phase is to take all information gathered during qualification and workshops and present a proposed high-level timeline and estimate of effort and costs. It's important to leave space in this presentation for further discussion and have time to revise and replan certain details. The following topics must be elaborated during planning in the initiation phase:

- **Estimation**
  All appropriate people from the project should have been involved in providing estimates for the feature requirements identified during the workshops. Follow-up questions should be directed to the respective teams to clarify outstanding uncertainties and assumptions should be clearly documented. Low-/medium-/high-effort estimation should be used to enable estimates and costs to be provided as a range.
- **Sizing**
  Nonfunctional requirements, architecture, integrations, and so on define the minimal infrastructure setup, which has direct impact on the cost of the project from operational, infrastructure, and eventual licensing perspectives. Also, the team responsible for setup of the environments can be defined and lead times for environment setup estimated.
- **Planning**
  By combining the high-level estimates (low/medium/large) with the prioritized requirements during the workshops, a requirements backlog can be created. In the backlog, features can be assigned to each planned release, and the total high-level effort per release (as a range) can be defined.

If the organization decides that the project is still within the expectations and feasible, the subsequent foundation phase can be kicked off.

2.2.3 Foundation Phase

The primary objective of the foundation phase is to establish a foundation for the project to be implemented, from technical, business, and project management perspectives.

This is also the phase in which detailed requirements are documented and signed off on to move forward into the engineering phase. As we mentioned earlier, we recommend dividing an SAP Commerce project into multiple releases. Whereas the initiation phase usually is executed only once for a project, a foundation phase can be executed once every release. The foundation phase is ideally conducted with on-site workshops with the project team and stakeholders, and five steps can be identified: preparation of the workshops, execution of the workshops, defining roles, project planning, and documentation and sign-off. We will discuss each of these steps in the following subsections.

Preparation

Without proper preparation, the foundation workshops can lose their strength and effectiveness. The agenda must be planned (based on input from the initiation phase), and the attendees should be assigned for each session. It's important that all teams work together on this planning order to guarantee the right topics are discussed and all required participants are available.

Workshops

The workshops are requirement-gathering sessions in which the main goal is to understand the project as a whole. The foundation workshops can last for a couple of weeks based on the project size. Definitions are set for the following topics during these workshops:

- **Project governance, organization, and structure**
  Roles and responsibilities should be documented, as well as the regular project meetings (weekly, steering committee, etc.) and communication channels (Skype, Slack, etc.).
- **Solution goals**
  These are usually centered around current pain points, revenue, and KPIs, as well as competitive advantage in the market. Pain points of an existing solution can be things like performance, scalability, integration issues, or lack of functionality. Revenue targets and KPIs go hand in hand with goals and objectives. Typical key metrics to establish include sales targets, conversion rates, margins, site visits, and so on.
- **Functional requirements**
  These can be further elaborated and should be defined in sufficient detail to have a business sign off, to enable the architect to define a solution design, to allow

testers to create the test cases, to help developers to understand the acceptance criteria, and to allow the project manager to plan the subsequent phases.

- **Nonfunctional requirements**
  These are as important as the functional requirements. If the solution is not accessible for the customer due to low performance, this can you're your organization revenue and lead to serious impact on brand perception. These requirements should be covered separately as they often overarch all individual functional requirements. Nonfunctional requirements are vital input for the architecture and infrastructure workshops and can have additional impact on planning and cost.
- **Architecture and integration design**
  The high-level architecture should be discussed during the workshops. Topics like integrations with other systems and early data modeling can be addressed. If systems that are managed by other parties need to be integrated, participants should be invited that can explain the integrations or the other systems.
- **Environments and tooling**
  Environment definition and planning around availability are important to consider in the project plan. Tooling definition for project management (e.g., Jira), development tools, testing tools, and so on also need to be defined because they require effort and time for setup and operations.
- **Quality management and testing strategy**
  It's crucial for a project to define and agree on how the solution will be tested throughout the project to make sure quality goals are met. Specific workshops should be set up to cover different forms of testing, and a RACI matrix should be created to be included in the quality assurance definition document.
- **Planning and prioritization**
  When an iterative methodology is used, usually the planning or prioritizing is not something to be covered in a workshop because all functionality will be delivered and tested at the end of the build phase. In a more agile approach, features and activities will be collaboratively prioritized and planned for the coming sprints.

Defining Personas and Roles

One of the major topics that drives the solution design, and which should explored with care, is the roles and responsibilities of the teams involved, as well as what kind of functionality will attend certain customers (personas). During the design phase, this definition is translated into a clear description of the personas that will be supported within the commerce solution and the roles and permissions that should be considered for these personas and for the business users.

Personas are the potential users of the platform after implementation. Different types of personas can include external personas, like consumers and organizational managers (buyers), as well as internal personas (sales representatives, call center operators, product managers, content managers, etc.).

When defining personas, it's important to think about their interactions with the solution. Workshop discussions can center on the following topics:

- **Touchpoints**
  This defines the touchpoints the persona will use (e.g., tablet, mobile, point of sale machine, store clerk, etc.).
- **Top tasks**
  These are tasks the persona will execute 80% of the time.
- **Domain context**
  This defines in which domain or industry the persona is active (e.g., B2B, B2C, telco, etc.).
- **Physical context**
  This is location and context in which the persona usually operates (e.g., in the office, at home, with a keyboard rather than mouse, etc.).
- **Emotional context**
  This is emotional location of the persona (e.g., busy, multitasking, attending customers, in traffic, etc.).
- **Expectations and values**
  For this item, you take into account the expectations and values of the persona in relation with its interactions (e.g., ease of use, consistency, comfort, freedom, etc.).
- **Motivations**
  This is the motivation of the persona when interacting with the solution (e.g., fun to use, socializing, productivity, etc.).
- **Deal breakers**
  Attention should be paid to the deal breakers for the interaction of a persona. Things like inconsistency, slowness, errors, and complexity can make a persona not want to interact with your organization.

A logical step that derives from defining the possible characteristics of the interaction of the persona with the solution is the definition of permissions and access rights each persona should be granted in the system. Poorly defined access permissions can have impacts like reduced end user satisfaction or even possible security breaches. Allowing too much visibility and too many permissions to extract key information may also become a potential threat. How to set up these authorizations will be further discussed in Chapter 9.

Project Planning

After the workshops, all outputs need to be consolidated to create a final project plan with milestones, a prioritized requirement list, a cost plan, and a risk register. Typical activities during this step involve project planning, cost planning, and risk analysis. During this activity, all activities are listed that are needed to complete the entire project, like user acceptance testing (UAT) dates.

Documentation and Sign-Off

During the foundation workshops, the scope is documented by the team and further translated into certain deliverables (e.g., scope definition, scope description, and proposed solution design). The design represents the understanding of the business requirements and how these will be translated into a solution. Furthermore, the documentation represents an agreement on how development and implementation will be managed from technical and project management perspectives. You'll sign off on the (detailed) documented requirements before you move to the engineering phase.

2.2.4 Development and Engineering

After the definition of the detailed scope for the project in the foundation phase, the project will move on into the engineering phase. During this phase, the software is built and configured to meet the functional and nonfunctional requirements as set in the foundation phase. Depending on the methodology used, the scope is more fixed and detailed at the start of the engineering phase, but for projects that are using an iterative approach, we recommend adopting some of the agile methods during this phase—specifically, the concept of sprints and related activities. Therefore, we won't make a distinction here between the two methodologies but will indicate when a certain recommended practice is specifically for iterative or agile approaches.

For software development projects such as SAP Commerce projects, we recommend creating iterations of development cycles throughout the phases of a project. In the Scrum methodology, these are called *sprints*.

The sequential activities of the engineering phase are as follows:

- Single sprint 0, which is a setup (of environment and tooling) sprint at the start of the building phase and usually takes one to two weeks depends on the size of the project.
- Multiple implementation sprints to develop the software. The duration can be between one and four weeks, but the recommended duration is two to three weeks, depending on the project-specific factors.
- Single hardening sprint (one- to two-week duration) after the implementation sprints to prepare the software for user acceptance testing.
- User acceptance testing.

There are various parallel activities that also can be executed during this phase that should be considered. Each of these activities happens at a specific moment in time and can be divided into different steps, which will be covered in the following sections.

Sprint 0

Sprint 0 or the startup sprint is the sprint that is the first step in the engineering phase. Ideally sprint 0 starts immediately after the foundation phase is finished to avoid impacting the execution of the planned implementation sprints. This step is usually only needed for the first phase of a project if the phases are executed after each other and the teams don't change. Some of the activities to be executed in sprint 0 are as follows:

- **Infrastructure**
  Set up the environments and establish the network and connectivity.
- **Development setup**
  The team sets the base configurations of the platform, creates the core data model, and sets up the tools that are needed to execute the development tasks.
- **Tooling setup**
  During the project, various tools should be used to manage code, documentation, testing, quality, defects, and so on. These tools need to be set up and ready to use before starting the implementation sprints. Not all team members might be skilled, so sometimes training is necessary. There are no specific rules for the tooling, so long as the team knows how to use the tools correctly for the specific tasks. Specific tools should include the following:

  - Project task tracking tools
  - Code repository management tools
  - Development IDE tools
  - Project file sharing repository
  - Project knowledge sharing tools
  - Continuous integration and deployment
  - Code review and static code analysis
  - Unit testing tools
  - Defect management tools
  - Performance testing tools
  - Test automation tools
  - Communication tools (in particular, with distributed teams, efficient tools for internal communication, such as Skype, Slack, and so on)
- **First sprint preparation**
  The team prepares for the first couple of implementation sprints that will come next. The team divides the tasks and set the prioritization for the first two sprints and decides how the tests will be done (preparation and process setup). Acceptance criteria must be defined and signed off on, test data made ready, and technical design discussions held and documented. Sometimes a proof of concept must be defined for certain functionality to see how it would work.

Implementation Sprint

The implementation sprints occur after sprint 0 and usually have a duration of two to three weeks. This is when the team will build, design, analyze, and test to build the solution. The number of sprints and the duration must be carefully planned as these drive the possible go-live dates of the project. The more sprints, the more development, the more software building, and the more time needed for a deployment phase. There is no fixed duration for sprints, but we recommend two to three weeks depending on the characteristics of the project. For each implementation sprint, there are five mandatory main activities to be considered, along with two optional activities, as follows:

1. **Sprint preplanning**
   The sprint planning occurs one sprint ahead the actual sprint, and the objective is to be prepared for the actual sprint. Preplanning activities usually include reviewing sprint capacity based on team capacity and velocity, guaranteeing that the

backlog items meet the agreed-upon definition of ready before entering sprint planning, and preassigning tasks to individual team members.

2. **Sprint planning**
   Once preplanning is completed, the team is ready for the actual start of the sprint, starting with its planning. The purpose of sprint planning is to discuss as a group all tasks and guarantee there is a shared understanding within the team of the work to be done during the sprint. Sprint planning is usually a one- to two-hour meeting with the whole team.
3. **Sprint execution**
   This step takes up most of the time during the sprint. The team works on completing the work defined during the sprint planning. Completion means that each task or user story is considered done as per the agreed-upon definition of done. It's important to track progress during sprint execution using tools like physical task boards or project tracking software like Jira. This helps the project teams and other teams involved in the project to track progress. Tasks that are not ready by the end of the sprint need to be refactored in the next sprint. Within the teams, progress and difficulties are discussed in short daily (stand-up) and weekly working group meetings. After these meetings, the teams review the risk log and update the status, track new risks, review existing actions, and document new actions.
4. **Sprint review**
   At the end of the implementation sprint, the development team holds a sprint review. Development team members show completed user stories and tasks to the rest of the team. This is an internal meeting and usually stimulates quality work and increases motivation of the team members to show good results.
5. **Sprint retrospective**
   During this meeting, the whole project team (including partners, and other stakeholders) comes together for a maximum of one hour. The sprint retrospective marks the end of the implementation sprint. During the retrospective meeting, successful actions and approaches are discussed and plans are made to keep success in the next sprints. Lessons learned will be discussed and actions defined to avoid similar pitfalls in the next sprints, and actions defined from last sprints are reviewed. All of this is documented and available in the general repository for the project team.
6. **Postsprint demo (agile; optional for iterative)**
   In an agile methodology, the business analyst presents the completed user stories and tasks to the organization. Each story will be presented together with its

acceptance criteria. This presentation is similar to the one in the retrospective, but the actual test data and the presentation can be given in the form of a demo on the test environment (QA). In an iterative methodology, this step is optional and should be used carefully as it can cause unwanted feedback and be confusing if an unfinished build is shown without the context of the full build.

7. **Postsprint testing (agile only)**
   In an agile project approach, the project team makes the build software available for testing in your testing environment. The in-house team should test the software functionally. By doing these tests at the end of each sprint, possible issues are identified earlier and can be included in the next sprint's backlog. Furthermore, the in-house team gets a feeling for the software before the actual user testing phase later in the project. The business user can adjust priorities and add or change functionality planned for upcoming sprints. This has to be managed correctly to avoid delays on go-live dates. During postsprint testing, there is not necessarily a formal sign-off on functionality because some of the features will not be 100% ready and signed-off user stories can be touched again in another sprint.

Hardening Sprint

The hardening sprint occurs once at the end of the last implementation sprint of the release and is considered the last sprint in the engineering phase. This is the final step before user acceptance testing. The purpose of the hardening sprint is to finalize the software created for a testing step and sequential deployment phase. All activities during this step are finalization activities that should have been planned and mostly started already during the implementation sprints. During the hardening sprint, the completion of these activities will be guaranteed. The hardening sprint usually is not longer than the duration of an implementation sprint. During the hardening sprint, the project team focuses on the following tasks:

- Finalization of the code and clean-up of the code.
- Finalization of nonfunctional requirement testing. This usually includes software security scans, penetration testing, PCI compliance review, and other regulatory tests that are mandated within the project's industry.
- Finalization of defect fixing.
- Finalization of software configuration.
- Finalization of documentation.
- Finalization of the environment setup for UAT and the test data creation for UAT.

User Acceptance Testing

During user acceptance testing, the delivered solution is formally accepted by the end/business user. This is a period of several weeks of testing after the hardening sprint in which your organization executes end-to-end testing. This is preferably executed by business users who will use the solution after go-live.

It's important to have the code ready and integrations built (and tested) before starting UAT. If users are starting to test in areas that are not necessarily ready, defects will be raised and users might become distracted and demotivated. Before starting UAT, it's important that integration testing has taken place. The code may integrate with other systems directly or through middleware that needs to be tested. Most of the integration testing is done during development sprints but is only fully completed at the end of the engineering phase.

The duration of the UAT is usually proportional to the duration of the implementation sprints, and the logistics and test criteria are discussed and documented during the foundation phase in the quality assurance definition and project management definition. During UAT, you test the solution and report issues that are then evaluated and labeled as defects or scope items. The UAT is not for development of new features, and a feature freeze occurs at the end of the last implementation sprint before starting the UAT phase. Acceptance testing only ends when the solution is formally accepted by the business user team.

The following testing activities can be considered during UAT:

- **Acceptance testing and acceptance criteria**
  Ensure that the delivered user stories meet the acceptance criteria agreed on during the implementation sprints. We recommend creating automated test scripts to validate these criteria during the implementation sprints. This increases the speed of testing during UAT and decreases the chances of issues being found during UAT.
- **Performance testing**
  During the foundation phase, performance-related nonfunctional requirements acceptance criteria are defined and documented. These need to be tested beyond the functional testing during the UAT phase. Performance testing should be done in a production-like environment, and successful performance testing depends on the readiness of the test environments and quality of the test data. More performance testing will be described in the following section.

- **Security testing**
  During this activity, security-related NFR acceptance criteria are tested. Often, external parties specializing in security testing are involved in this testing.

Parallel Activities

During the engineering phase, there are some parallel activities to be executed. As mentioned in the previous two subsections, there are many activities that start or are ongoing and are finalized during these moments in the engineering phase. We recommend that these activities be planned together with the sprints and start as early as possible with these activities to allow appropriate time for feedback and adjustments being incorporated in implementation sprints. Some activities that should be executed in parallel with the implementation sprints are as follows:

- **Performance testing**
  The earlier in the project these tests are executed, the more time can be reserved to make adjustments in subsequent sprints.
- **System integration testing**
  Test integrations and validate touchpoints with external systems.
- **Code testing**
  The recommended practice is that a code unit test is executed before a developer merges the code into a shared code branch. Reviewing code is an important practice that helps to improve code quality and identify bugs. Continuous integration includes tools for code testing and automatization of this process during the engineering phase.
- **Security testing**
  This includes penetration and cross-site testing.
- **Training**
  This includes of business users to use the solution, or train-the-trainer programs.
- **Content creation**
  Prepare web content images and other content, such as text.
- **Data loading and enrichment**
  Prepare product images, pricing, text, and so on.
- **Data migration**
  Customer and order data should be imported/migrated from other systems.
- **Knowledge transfer**
  Knowledge is transferred from the project to the operational and support teams.

2.2.5 Deployment and Cutover/Go-Live

After the engineering phase has been completed and all testing activities have been started, the deployment phase begins, in which the objective is the successful testing and deployment of the solution into a production environment so that it is accessible for the final end users.

Cutover is the moment during then deployment phase when the solution goes live, also called go-live.

Deployment

The purpose of the deployment phase is to test what has been produced during the engineering phase successfully, support the transition into the live environment, and provide post-go-live support. The deployment phase can be split into two distinct activity groups—pre-go-live and post-go-live activities—and starts a couple of weeks before actual go-live and continues for a period of time after go-live for post-go-live support.

Depending on the methodology used, the deployment phase can be longer or shorter in duration. In an agile methodology, the testing has been mostly done during the engineering phase and little testing is left, whereas in an iterative methodology, the end user testing has been limited until this phase. Most of the activities are the same, however.

The main activities to be considered in the deployment phase prior to go-live are as follows:

- **Testing of the delivered solution**
  Test activities should be continued from the previous phase or started during the deployment phase in a productive (or production-like) environment. Does the solution work and attend to the functional requirements? Think about full end-to-end user acceptance testing, integration testing, performance testing, security testing, and operational and failover testing.
- **Data migration into the productive environment**
  Although data migration has to be considered as a parallel activity, as described for the deployment phase, during deployment the final data migration will take place.
- **Training and handover**
  User training and handover to the business as usual (BAU) team, which will take responsibility going forward. Preparation of support teams in terms of training and processes.

- **Go-live preparation activities**
  This includes final checks of production environment infrastructure and operating systems, verification of the production data, and testing the backup and restore process. For a full list, check the go-live checklist on the wiki (*wiki.hybris.com*).

The main activity in the deployment phase after go-live is post-go-live support. Resources are dedicated to support the first-, second-, and third-level customer support teams to provide expert knowledge and fast responses to incidents.

Sometimes a customer may decide not to go through with a go-live, or sometimes a deployment phase is not necessary. Therefore, this phase is optional and might not be required if there is no go-live, there is a soft go-live, or the go-live overlaps with a subsequent engineering phase.

Cutover and Go-Live

The cutover is the point when the project goes live in the production environment and is opened to the public during the deployment phase. To avoid issues during the go-live or right after, several steps and actions need to be defined and planned in an early stage of the project. Although cutover takes place at the end of the project, the planning and definition should start at the very beginning of the project during the initiation phase. Therefore, we make a distinction between preparation and execution activities.

Cutover preparation activities need to be completed before a go-live decision (go or no-go) can be made when the execution activities are completed around go-live itself.

Cutover preparation activities will vary depending on the specific context of the project, but in general the following activities can be considered:

- **Define the cutover strategy**
  Because it can impact the timeline, resource planning, prioritization, and other decisions, it is important to agree on the strategy with all project stakeholders. Think about things like key sales periods during the year during which no cutover activity should be planned or a soft-launch versus hard-launch approach for go-live (launch for family and friends first or in small releases instead of a big bang for the public).
- **Identify cutover resources**
  Who will be necessary from the business and project teams during the cutover?

Sometimes these activities occur outside business hours, and this must be planned and scheduled. Escalation paths and decision makers in case of emergencies need to be defined and documented.

- **Prepare the business for the new solution**
  Change management is an important part of cutover planning. A strategy needs to be defined to enable acceptance of the solution, and the number of change management activities varies per organization. Promoting new functionalities and processes, defining a communication strategy, and end user enablement through training are some of the activities to promote change management and acceptance in an organization. The project team ideally provides the training because it has knowledge of the implemented solution.
- **Transition planning**
  The solution must be handed over from the project team to long-term application management after go-live. The model must be defined during the foundation phase, and the knowledge transfer to the other teams can be planned on an ongoing basis during engineering and testing. Typical topics to be included usually are related to development and architecture practices (e.g. coding standards), project management, quality management (e.g., test automation and performance testing), and operations (e.g., release management).
- **Backup and restore process**
  It's essential to have a backup and restore process to recover from failed deployments. It's very costly to have any problem during deployment that can cause downtime or interruptions in the production environment. Definition of these processes should be handled during the engineering phase and repeatedly tested and improved.
- **Data readiness**
  Data is essential for the success of the project because it can impact many things (performance, user experience, application behavior, etc.) and any impact can create frustrating experiences and issues. To avoid these problems and make sure your data is ready, there are three main topics to consider: data migration to move data from one system to another (legacy systems, databases, etc.); data creation (creation and enrichment of product data, customer data, etc.), which often has resource and data dependencies for which we recommend planning ahead; and data cleansing, in which the quality of the data needs to be checked, validated, and adjusted to make sure no inconsistent data is used in the solution (e.g., navigation and search is 100% dependent on clean and consistent data).

- **Go-live checklist**
  This checklist should be used to guarantee that no steps are missed during deployment to the live production environment. It contains task descriptions, dependencies, owners, and statuses.
- **Cutover execution activities**
  These activities are completed around go-live once all preparation is done and go-live is confirmed and are executed during the deployment phase. Some of the tasks that should be considered as cutover execution tasks are as follows:
  - Preparation tasks that will move into execution tasks throughout go-live day, like validating the go-live checklist, final testing of integrations points, and so on
  - Preliminary go-live tasks on the go-live day, such as stopping business transactions that will be replaced by the new solution
  - Post-go-live activities, such as testing the end-to-end transactions, monitoring the application and system resources, and resolving post-go-live issues as quickly as possible

2.2.6 Application Management

After go-live, the solution is handed over to the business and application management teams. Every solution needs activities and support to ensure it's maintained; if not managed correctly, performance can decline after go-live. Some important things to consider when taking on the application management of a solution are as follows:

- Review and understand the architecture design.
- Create a team that reflects the different specialties that are in the project team.
- Create a training plan for the team members, including meetings and trainings with subject matter experts (SMEs) from the project implementation. If the team can take on some tasks during the engineering phase, its ramp-up time might be reduced significantly.
- Create a common ticketing system and knowledge base for the project and the application management team.

The application management team will have to address various topics, such as support, release management (including continuous integration and platform release management), maintenance topics like content and password maintenance, performance and application monitoring, disaster recovery, analytics, and eventually third-party technology stack topics.

2.3 Building Your Team

During the different phases of an SAP Commerce project, teams will change and evolve. In this section, we'll focus on three main teams that should be considered during a project implementation:

1. The *client team*, which owns and is implementing the software.
2. The *project team*, which is contracted by the client team to implement and customize the software. Sometimes client teams want to be able to execute some of the project activities and resources are mixed between partners and clients, or a client builds its own implementation team.
3. The *SAP Customer Experience team*, formed of professionals from SAP Customer Experience lines of business that can be involved during various stages of the lifecycle. We recommend having an SAP Customer Experience Expert Services team involved to ensure success, provide quality assurance, and ensure that out-of-the-box features are being leveraged to provide smooth upgrade paths in the future.

These teams will need different skills to fulfill different roles throughout the different stages of a project. Depending on the size of the project, multiple roles may be filled by one or more people (big projects) or one person may fulfill multiple roles (smaller projects). In the following sections, we'll discuss these roles in detail per project phase.

Note

Some of the roles have quite a bit of overlap between the different phases. For the sake of completeness, we have included roles in each phase in which they are relevant—even if, for example, the role of the customer engagement executive is nearly identical in the engineering phase and in the deployment phase.

2.3.1 Initiation Phase

As mentioned in Section 2.2.2, the objective of the initiation phase is to assess whether to move forward with the project. The team involved in this phase will align on the why/what/how/when and cost/risks to move forward, and the individuals will form the foundation of the project team when moving forward in the project.

Client Team

The client team will have a couple of roles involved in this phase, overseeing different areas and different responsibilities. Some typical roles to consider are as follows:

- **Executive sponsor**
  This professional will have oversight and is a decision maker. The executive sponsor will have ultimate responsibility over the project, mainly related to budget, vendor evaluation, schedule, and any final decision to be made.
- **Project lead/program manager**
  This professional will be in charge of day-to-day activities and responsible for assisting the executive sponsor in the vendor selection, coordination of the SMEs, and providing scope and business objectives during this phase.
- **Subject matter experts**
  These professionals are contributors to the initiation phase. The SMEs will provide input and opinions based on their expertise within the organization. They represent various areas (IT, business, operations, etc.) and can identify requirements.

Project Team

The project team can be an internal team, be from an implementation partner, be from SAP Customer Experience, or a mix of all three. The roles in the team are delivery-oriented and their objective is to support the client team and gather enough information to provide a high-level solution design and understanding of effort (and price) for an eventual project:

- **Engagement manager/delivery director**
  This person will have oversight from the project team and is mainly responsible for selling an eventual project. His key responsibilities are delivering a proposal, negotiations and resource allocation.
- **Project manager**
  This person mainly will look over the budget scope and cost; her principal priority is to create and present a project proposal. Her main activities are focused on creating project estimations, coordinating the logistics of the team, and delivering the phase deliverables, such as a project plan and the foundation agenda for the next phase.

- **Business analyst/product owner**
  The business analyst or product owner will cover the functional requirements; his main priorities are focused on capturing and analyzing functional requirements to create a project scope. His main activities are focused on reviewing the requirements and creating phase deliverables, such as the foundation workshop agenda for the next phase and an initial ballpark estimate.
- **Solution architect**
  The solution architect is focused on the technical solution for the project; this person's main priority is to capture nonfunctional and technical requirements to create a technical solution. Their key responsibilities during this phase include high-level technical solutions, as well as the initial ballpark estimate.

SAP Customer Experience Team

The SAP Customer Experience team involves the sales and presales teams, as well as someone from SAP Customer Experience Expert Services to help design the proposed software proposal for the project and the success services for the project:

- **Account executive or solution sales specialist**
  This person is mainly focused on software sales; his main priority and activity is license sales during this phase.
- **Presales engineer**
  She supports the account executive in the license deal by identifying the complexity of a possible project and recommending possible modules and solutions. Her key priorities are product demos to support sales.
- **Service delivery manager or engagement manager from SAP Customer Experience Expert Services**
  The service delivery manager is mainly focused on services. By understanding the project context and complexity, a service plan is defined by the service delivery manager or engagement manager.

2.3.2 Foundation Phase

During the foundation phase, a foundation is established for the project from business, technical, and management perspectives. In this phase, the detailed documented requirements and project approach are defined.

Client Team

Because this is the phase in which the requirements are further detailed (both functional and nonfunctional), more areas from the client side need to be involved to guarantee all input is captured and considered by all teams involved in this phase:

- **Executive sponsor**
  As in the initiation phase, this person has the oversight over the whole phase. The executive sponsor is the ultimate approver for critical decisions, is an escalation point when things need to be escalated, determines the objectives and success criteria, and controls the budget and schedule.
- **Project lead/program manager**
  This professional has the day-to-day oversight of the foundation phase. The project lead manages day-to-day activities with the project manager and is the approver of daily activities. This role's main priorities are an overall view of scope, budget, and timeline, and the project lead is the first point of escalation in case of project issues.
- **Project manager**
  Depending on the project size, the project manager is an additional level of management below the project lead and maintains a close working relationship with the project lead and the associated activities and tasks.
- **Stream leads**
  For complex projects, stream leads are defined to participate on a day-to-day basis in the foundation phase, to interact with the SMEs and simplify project management (think about stream leads for master data, fulfillment, product catalog, etc.).
- **Business representative**
  On larger projects, the business representative works side by side with the project team business analyst on requirements.
- **Architect**
  The architect is involved on a day-to-day basis; her main priority is to own the overall technical solution across all systems and help in the technical definition of integrations and interfaces.
- **Commerce manager**
  His overall focus is to be an SME in the (e-)commerce business and provide details on the business rules of commerce, such as promotions and pricing, and the expected capabilities of the solution.

- **Subject matter experts**
  Depending on the type of organization and scope of the project, different types of SMEs should be involved. They are responsible for providing detailed requirements in their specific areas. Some SME areas to consider are as follows:
  - **Marketing**
    Provides detailed requirements of the marketing needs of the organization.
  - **CRM**
    Provides detailed requirements of customer relationship needs.
  - **Merchandiser**
    Provides detailed requirements that pertain to the merchandising needs of the organization.
  - **Finance**
    Provides detailed requirements of finance-related needs of the organization, such as fraud, reporting, and statements.
  - **Business intelligence**
    Provides detailed requirements for business intelligence, data, and reporting.
  - **Operations/support**
    From this part of the organization, detailed information is provided for analytics, service-level agreements, and so on.
  - **Fulfillment/inventory**
    All logistics needs and requirements, as well as requirements for stock management, will be provided by this SME during this phase.
  - **Brand management**
    Brand management defines the expected user experience based on brand guidelines and often works together with digital agencies on UI screens.
  - **Data protection**
    Depending on the complexity, various SMEs for data protection can be included in the foundation phase. Because data protection is an important topic, the right people should be assigned to provide detailed requirements and guidance on data privacy topics.

Project Team

The project team remains mostly the same in the foundation phase as it was in the initiation phase, but the team on the client side grows. The following roles should be considered:

- **Engagement manager/delivery director**
  The delivery director or engagement manager has oversight over the project team for the whole program and phase. This professional is responsible for top-level leadership alignment with the client and the SAP Customer Experience service delivery manager.
- **Project manager**
  The project manager is involved on a day-to-day basis and responsible for the on time and on budget delivery of the project. This professional's main priorities are the phase deliverables (e.g., project management plan definition, cost plan, project plan).
- **Business analyst/product owner**
  The business analyst is involved daily and responsible for gathering the project requirements and is the expert in SAP Commerce and SAP C/4HANA. Also within the priorities of this role are the feature roadmap and prioritized requirements deliverables, as well as the translation of requirements in so-called "epics" and user stories. The business analyst is the link between the business and technical team.
- **Solution architect**
  Another role to be considered daily in the foundation phase, the solution architect is responsible for the overall technical solution. His main priority is to take the functional and nonfunctional requirements and translate them to a solution design (data model, design, integration points, etc.). The solution architect also performs an initial sizing and creates the foundation deliverables as the software architecture definition and nonfunctional requirements.
- **Development lead**
  The development lead is also involved daily during the foundation phase to assist the architect with some of the overall design activities. The development lead can act as a scrum master, leads the development team, and handles code management.
- **Quality assurance lead**
  Another role to be considered daily in the foundation phase, the QA lead is responsible during the project for the testing strategy and code quality. During the foundation phase, the QA lead is responsible for the test plan and test cases, automation of testing (if applicable), and the delivery of the QA definition and test strategy plan.

SAP Customer Experience Team

During the foundation phase, the SAP Customer Experience team grows to provide the right amount of support to the project throughout this phase with success managers and specific SAP Customer Experience Expert Services:

- **Customer engagement executive (success manager)**
  The customer engagement executive (CEE) is the main contact point for all things related to SAP C/4HANA (licenses, maintenance, escalations, events, etc.) and is responsible for account management throughout the customer lifecycle.
- **Service delivery or engagement manager**
  The service delivery manager is responsible for delivery of SAP Customer Experience Expert Services and quality assurance services. His main responsibility is to provide commerce and delivery experience in this phase and deliver quality services.
- **Technical and functional consultants**
  The technical and functional consultants provide technical and functional consulting when engaged through a success services plan for SAP Customer Experience Expert Services. Typical services during this phase include design workshops, capabilities workshops, and design reviews to guarantee the use of recommended practices in the project and solution.
- **Enterprise architect**
  The enterprise architect is involved during the foundation phase to help the project and client team define target architecture and infrastructure within an SAP Customer Experience Expert Services success services plan.

2.3.3 Engineering Phase

During the engineering phase, the software is built as defined during the previous foundation phase. Because the main focus is to develop software in this phase, the client team shrinks and the project team grows to its maximum size.

Client Team

After the foundation phase, the client team shrinks because the focus of this phase is on software development. The following roles should be considered:

- **Executive sponsor**
  The executive sponsor keeps the oversight during this phase and remains the

escalation point for the project. Furthermore, the executive sponsor organizes the steering committee calls and approves any change request.

- **Project lead**
  The project lead keeps oversight as well and is involved daily in the engineering phase. Her main priority is the approval of daily and sprint-based activities and unlocking any project issue.
- **Project manager**
  Depending on the size of the project, this professional supports the project lead in the daily activities.
- **Business representative**
  The business representative is involved daily in the project and has your organization's business knowledge. This professional is the single point of contact (SPOC) when the project team needs clarification on business requirements. His main priorities are to work with the business analyst from the project team to refine functional requirements, prioritize requirements, and approve sprint acceptance criteria. The business representative works with business users to perform user testing and provide support during user acceptance testing.
- **Architect**
  The architect continues as the point of contact for the project team for system integration and interface decisions.
- **System/network administrator**
  This is a specialist role and the focus of this role is on technical infrastructure.
- **Database administrator**
  This is another specialist role, focused on database setup and maintenance.
- **Change management**
  The change management role is a specialist role that oversees the business transformation within the organization and creates plans to communicate with, prepare, and train employees and other stakeholders that will be impacted by the change of process/solution.
- **Test lead**
  The test lead role is focused on the testing during this phase. The test lead is responsible for the execution of system integration testing, user acceptance, and performance and security testing.
- **Developer**
  Depending on the structure and size of the project, a developer is available from the client side.

Project Team

As mentioned earlier, the project team grows to its maximum size during this phase. The following roles and responsibilities can be considered for the project team:

- **Engagement manager**
  The engagement manager keeps oversight and is the escalation point from the project team side. The engagement manager participates in steering committee calls.
- **Project manager**
  The project manager is involved daily in the management of the project, handling risks and addressing issues that can block the project.
- **Business analyst/product owner**
  The business analyst is involved in the project daily and is the connecting point between the business and technical teams.
- **Solution architect**
  The solution architect is responsible for the technical solution.
- **Development lead**
  This role is responsible for overall delivery of custom code. The development lead leads the development team, handles most complex development tasks, manages the peer code reviews, and handles code management.
- **Quality assurance lead**
  This role is focused daily on testing and quality of the code. If possible, the quality assurance lead makes sure that the test automation or framework is in place.
- **Performance analyst**
  This is one of the specialist roles to be considered during the engineering phase. The performance specialist's priorities and responsibilities are the creation and execution of performance test scripts and performing performance testing against the system during this phase (e.g., load, stress, capacity, spike, and soak testing).
- **Release engineer**
  This specialist role is focused on automated builds and deployments during this phase. The release engineer owns the source code repository.
- **Technical writer**
  This is a specialist whose responsibility is to create the solution documentation that will be handed over to the client team.

- **Security engineer**
  The security engineer is responsible for security testing and penetration testing. This is a specialist role with the responsibility to test the overall strength of the solution and its ability to resist external attacks.
- **Operations engineer**
  The operation engineer is a specialist role that gets involved towards the end of this phase and will set up the operations process.
- **Optional roles**
  The following roles are optional and might be staffed from external parties because sometimes other software is involved or because specific experience or skills are needed that are not available in house:
  - **Analytics and business intelligence specialist**
    This specialist role focuses on big data analytics and reporting.
  - **Graphic design specialist**
    This role is responsible for graphic content and design.
  - **Payment and risk specialists**
    Their responsibility is to assist with payment integrations and antifraud tooling, as well as the payment certification process.
  - **Search engine optimization specialist**
    This specialist is responsible for optimizing search engine results.
  - **UI/UX designer**
    This role is dedicated to user experience, user interaction, and design.

SAP Customer Experience Team

During this phase, the SAP Customer Experience team remains involved to give the right amount of support to the client project:

- **Customer engagement executive (success manager)**
  The customer engagement executive is the main contact point for all things related to SAP C/4HANA (licenses, maintenance, escalations, events, etc.) and is responsible for account management throughout the lifecycle.
- **Service delivery or engagement manager**
  The service delivery manager is responsible for delivery of SAP Customer Experience Expert Services and quality assurance services. His main responsibility is to provide commerce and delivery experience in this phase and deliver quality services and recommendations related to quality.

- **Functional consultants**
  Functional consultants provide functional consulting through a success services plan for SAP Customer Experience Expert Services. Their responsibility is to provide recommendations related to the right usage of the software.
- **Technical consultants**
  Technical consultants provide technical consulting. Typical services during this phase are code reviews to help guarantee good code quality, system reviews, and go-live readiness checks.
- **Performance specialist**
  The performance specialist delivers performance tuning for a project if included in the success services plan. Her activities are focused on the performance tuning of the system to attend to nonfunctional requirements and prepare the solution for high performance. Performance tuning should be executed before go-live but can be repeated for specific occasions, such as Black Friday or Christmas.

2.3.4 Deployment Phase

During the deployment phase, the built software is tested and deployed into a production environment to make it available to end users. Besides testing, which will need a lot of client team involvement, the project will shift from project mode to actual operations mode after go-live. The client team will increase, and the project team will become smaller in size.

Client Team

The client team will ramp up to transition to operations mode in this phase. Although some training can be done during the engineering phase, some of these activities have to wait for the deployment phase when the software is ready to be effective. The team members during this phase are as follows:

- **Executive sponsor**
  The executive sponsor keeps oversight during this phase and remains the escalation point for the project. Furthermore, the executive sponsor organizes the steering committee calls and approves any change request.
- **Project lead**
  The project lead keeps oversight and is involved daily and oversees the deployment phase. Her main priority is unlocking project issues, seeking approval for go-live, and providing project sign-off.

- **Project manager**
  Depending on the size of the project, this professional supports the project lead in daily activities.
- **Business representative**
  The business representative is involved daily in the project and works with the client's business units on training and onboarding.
- **Architect**
  The architect is responsible for approving the technical cutover plan and makes decisions on technical, system, and integration topics.
- **Test lead**
  The test lead is responsible for the final end-to-end testing before go-live.
- **Change management**
  He continues oversight and administration of change management topics and facilitates in the transition from project to operations.
- **Training**
  The training role is an optional role to support the project team trainer.
- **Data protection**
  This role is responsible for data protection policy and regulation compliance.

During this phase, the transition takes place from project to operations and various operational roles start onboarding and participating in (training) activities and running day-to-day operations. The following roles either transition from previous roles in the project, onboard as new team members, or roll over from the project team:

- **Online store manager**
  The online store manager will begin onboarding and perform training for the execution of operational tasks after go-live.
- **Operations manager**
  The manager of the operations team will begin onboarding and training to prepare for day-to-day operation and support activities.
- **Warehouse manager/shipper**
  The manager and team will be trained and onboarded to run day-to-day fulfillment activities.
- **Accounting/finance manager/team**
  The accounting team and the finance department will be prepared to run day-to-day financial activities.

- **Content manager**
  The content team will be prepared to run day-to-day content management tasks.
- **Pricing manager/team**
  This team, which works on a daily basis with price management, will be onboarded and trained.
- **Marketing manager/team**
  Onboarding and training of the marketing team is initiated to prepare for day-to-day marketing activities.
- **Customer support**
  The customer support team will be onboarded and trained to start day-to-day customer support activities.
- **Technical support**
  Define support protocols and service-level agreements and train for first-level troubleshooting on the application.
- **Developer**
  The developer may roll over from the project team and is the internal technical lead for code analysis, troubleshooting, and patches/fixes.
- **Database specialist**
  This role supports testing and troubleshooting on the database level.
- **Network administrator**
  This role supports testing and troubleshooting pertaining to infrastructure.

Project Team

As mentioned earlier, the transition from project to operations means a decrease in responsibilities and team members of the project team during the deployment phase compared to the engineering phase, as follows:

- **Engagement manager**
  The engagement manager closes the engagement and is responsible for official project sign-off.
- **Project manager**
  He oversees the project team roll-off (i.e., when the project team leaves the project) and manages defects and warranty topics.
- **Business analyst/product owner**
  The business analyst provides training during this phase to end users on the customer software and is responsible for user guides.

- **Solution architect**
  She is responsible for the technical runbook, which contains the procedures that are regularly undertaken by the team members.
- **Development lead**
  He is responsible for bug fixes. If this is a multimember team rather than an individual, the team size goes down shortly after launch until the end of the post-go-live support.
- **Quality assurance lead**
  She is responsible for bug handling and defect prioritization and resolution. If this is a multimember team the team, the size goes down shortly after launch until the end of the post-go-live support.
- **Performance analyst**
  The performance specialist is responsible for the test scripts and execution of performance testing (e.g., load, stress, capacity, spike, soak testing) against the system.
- **Trainer**
  The trainer is responsible for training the client project team on the solution to guarantee a smooth transition. Training topics include business, technical, and administration tools and user cockpits.

SAP Customer Experience Team

During this phase, the customer experience team remains involved to give the right amount of support to the client project. Especially during deployment, communication within SAP is important to make sure all involved teams are aligned and set up for success:

- **Customer engagement executive (success manager)**
  The customer engagement executive is the main contact point for all things related to SAP C/4HANA (licenses, maintenance, escalations, events, etc.) and is responsible for account management throughout the customer lifecycle. During deployment, the CEE can be a strong point of contact with the cloud operations team or other SAP teams that need to provide support during deployment and go-live.
- **Service delivery or engagement manager**
  The service delivery manager is responsible for delivery of SAP Customer Experience Expert Services and quality assurance services. His main responsibility is to deliver quality services and recommendations related to quality.

- **Functional consultants**
  The functional consultants provide functional consulting through a success services plan for SAP Customer Experience Expert Services. Their responsibility is to provide recommendations related to the right usage of the software and recommended practices for SAP Commerce.
- **Technical consultants**
  The technical consultants provide technical consulting. Typical services during this phase include system reviews, go-live readiness reviews, or performance tuning.
- **Performance specialist**
  The performance specialist delivers performance tuning to a customer project if included in the success services plan. Her activities are focused on the performance tuning of the system to attend to nonfunctional requirements and prepare the solution for high performance.

2.3.5 Application Management

This section will go into detail on the team involved after site go-live and the activities that are needed to manage the application.

Client Team

In the client team, the activities related to day-to-day operations continue after the deployment phase, as follows:

- **Executive sponsor**
  The executive sponsor remains involved with the solution and receives weekly reports on site performance (sales, returns, stability). One of his priorities is to define the upcoming roadmap for future features.
- **Commerce manager**
  The (e-)commerce manager oversees daily activities related to the site and is responsible for following up on change requests and issues raised.
- **Business representative**
  The business representative works with other business units on the roadmap.
- **Architect**
  The architect is responsible for monitoring the daily technical activities on the site and following changes and issues raised.

- **Data protection**
  This role is responsible for data protection policy and regulation compliance.
- **Translator**
  The translator provides translations for language-specific content (e.g., product descriptions).
- **Online store manager**
  The online store manager runs day-to-day operations of the online store.
- **Operations manager**
  This person is in charge of day-to-day operations.
- **Warehouse manager**
  The warehouse manager runs day-to-day fulfillment activities.
- **Accounting/finance manager/team**
  This team manages risk and financial activities.
- **Content manager**
  The content manager oversees day-to-day content management activities.
- **Pricing manager/team**
  The pricing manager and team execute daily price management activities.
- **Purchasing manager/team**
  This team executes daily procurement activities.
- **Marketing manager/team**
  The marketing team works on a daily basis with the platform to execute marketing activities.
- **Customer support**
  The customer support team performs day-to-day customer support.
- **Technical support**
  They monitor support protocols and service-level agreements and are responsible for first-level troubleshooting on the application.
- **Developer**
  The developer is responsible for code analysis, troubleshooting, and patches/fixes.
- **Database specialist**
  This role supports testing and troubleshooting on the database level.
- **Network administrator**
  He supports testing and troubleshooting pertaining to infrastructure.

Project Team/Maintenance Team

During application management, the project/maintenance team can be from the client side, a third party, or SAP, as follows:

- **Engagement manager**
  The engagement manager is responsible for account management and oversees maintenance activities.
- **Project/support manager**
  The support manager is responsible daily for managing warranty topics and defects. This person manages the maintenance team (defines team setup and activities).
- **Business analyst/product owner**
  The business analyst reviews functional change requests and functional defects that have been raised.
- **Solution architect**
  This role is responsible for reviewing technical change requests and qualifying technical defects that have been raised.
- **Development lead**
  He is responsible for bug fixes and the development of change requests.
- **Quality assurance lead**
  She is responsible for bug handling and testing (e.g., smoke and integration and regression testing).

SAP Customer Experience Team

During this phase in the customer lifecycle, the SAP Customer Experience team will be involved with the following roles:

- **Customer engagement executive (success manager)**
  The customer engagement executive is the main contact point for all things related to SAP Commerce (licenses, maintenance, escalations, events, etc.) and is responsible for account management throughout the customer lifecycle.
- **Service delivery or engagement manager**
  The service delivery manager is responsible for delivery of SAP Customer Experience Expert Services and product-related services. During this phase, the service delivery manager can support you as you look at future requirements. When new functionality is released, reviews from SAP Customer Experience Expert Services can help guarantee the quality of the solution (e.g., performance or architecture reviews).

- **Technical and functional consultants**
  The technical and functional consultants provide technical and functional consulting to customers of SAP Customer Experience Expert Services.

2.4 Operating in the Cloud

The SAP Commerce Cloud subscription is provisioned by SAP to the customer within three business days after the contract start date. The person responsible within the customer team for technical topics and the cloud operation (the customer system administrator) is contacted with instructions to register within the cloud portal. Furthermore, access to documentation and support materials to use the cloud portal and SAP Commerce Cloud is provided.

In this section, we'll share more information about services and activities that can be considered to operate in the cloud during a project lifecycle.

2.4.1 Cloud Portal

A self-service portal is available for customers and/or their nominated partners to operate and manage the cloud solution. This self-service portal is the main tool for the customer, and the following tasks are considered the customer's responsibility:

- Connecting the code repository to SAP Commerce Cloud (e.g., configuring and enabling access and connectivity)
- Triggering the build process and configuring/initiating the deployment of builds to the productive environment
- Management of environments, including their creation, configuration, and termination
- User management
- Configuring firewall rules and VPNs

Chapter 12 will go into more detail on using the portal and managing the cloud solution as a user.

2.4.2 Cloud Readiness Check

The *cloud readiness check* is a set of quality gates provided by SAP to ensure that custom extensions to the SAP Commerce Cloud application do not degrade the performance profile of the application. Currently, there are two milestones identified for executing the cloud readiness check. The second check needs to be executed before go-live.

The cloud readiness check does not replace the quality assurance services of SAP Customer Experience Expert Services, such as advanced review of design and architecture throughout the project (e.g., application architecture, integration review, order management, cart, search, etc.) or actual performance tests (e.g., profiling, bottleneck analysis, system tuning, etc.).

The cloud readiness check includes a review of the following topics:

- Architecture design
- Technology design
- Code quality
- Test execution
- Performance metrics

2.4.3 Platinum Upgrade Program

Customers that are on the professional or enterprise edition of SAP Commerce Cloud can count on the platinum upgrade program. This service ensures that SAP customers stay on the latest SAP Commerce Cloud product release by executing annual platform upgrades. Customers who contracted the standard edition of SAP Commerce Cloud are responsible for ensuring upgrades to appropriate versions of the platform.

This set of services provides the customer with a temporary development environment upgraded to the target version of the SAP Commerce Cloud application, including SAP-supported extensions. SAP will deploy the configurations and extensions provided by the customer to the target platform. This upgrade needs to be planned carefully with the customer engagement executive and SAP Customer Experience Expert Services service delivery manager to guarantee that the activities are in line with the customer's plans and roadmap.

The platinum upgrade program is composed of the following components:

- **Upgrade benefits assessment**
  A summary report detailing customer benefits for upgrading in terms of functionality, innovation integration, support, and so on.

- **Technical upgrade analysis**
  This is a deep technical investigation of your current implementation, which produces an estimate of the total effort required to execute the platform upgrade.
- **Platform and database upgrade**
  This activity delivers the actual technical upgrade and any necessary dependencies.
- **Go-live quality review**
  During this engagement, SAP application consultants will review your specific customizations that could impact the stability, performance, or security of the SAP Commerce Cloud environment. Static source code analysis, data model analysis, and correct usage of the SAP Commerce Cloud APIs are verified. This does not replace actual system architecture or performance reviews.

The upgrade doesn't include your specific refactoring of custom code (identified during the technical upgrade analysis), nor does it include user acceptance, regression, or performance testing.

2.5 Upgrade Projects

SAP is consistently releasing new code, either through patches or via feature and large-scale releases. The recommended practice is always to be on the latest version to take advantage of all new features, bug fixes, and improvements. That said, depending on how far behind you are from the latest release or how much your solution has been customized, it can be difficult to remain up to date. There are two main drivers for you to perform an upgrade project:

- Ensure supportability; that is, make sure you're on the latest supported version and guarantee continuity of product support.
- Enable new features that were released in the target version of the product.

Before discussing how to upgrade, it's important to understand *why* you should upgrade. Each new release of SAP Commerce may include the following:

- **Improvements and bug fixes**
  Take advantage of bug/security fixes and performance improvements as part of new releases.

- **Innovation and new functionality**
  New functionality is available with every new release, and enhanced functionality can be used to transform your business.
- **Simplification**
  Replace custom code with out-of-the-box functionality in new releases.
- **Integration**
  Enjoy increased ease of integrations with other systems.
- **Support**
  Run on a fully supported version (product support generally ends two years after a version's release).
- **Deprecation**
  Some of the features your solution relies on can include partly deprecated code. Moving to the functionality that replaces it takes away this dependency on deprecated code.

2.5.1 Upgrade Considerations

When considering an upgrade, it's important to review the **SAP Commerce Upgrade Services** page on the wiki, which includes a self-assessment tool to help you understand your possible upgrade journey. The following main topics should be investigated when considering an upgrade:

- **Roadmap**
  "When is feature X going to be ready?" is a question that's asked a lot. With access to the wiki, you should also have access to the **Roadmap** page, which outlines (at a high level) potential new features and functionality that are planned for future releases. Before upgrading, you may want to understand what's planned for upcoming releases and think about how that could affect your application. Although the information on this page is subject to change, it can provide insight into the general direction that SAP Commerce suite is going and may help you understand when the best time to upgrade is.
- **Deprecation**
  It's also important to understand the deprecation process. Each major or feature release could include the deprecation of a particular functionality within the SAP Commerce suite. It's best to look at what's been deprecated and evaluate how the removal of that functionality will affect your requirements.

- **Compatibility**
  With each new release, the supported compatibility with third parties may change. This could mean the version number has changed, or it's possible that something previously supported may no longer be supported. When evaluating an upgrade, it's important to review the **Third-Party Compatibility** page for the version you're upgrading to, as it may require you to upgrade things like your database or Java version.

When executing an upgrade project, there are three approaches to be considered. Independent of the approach, the previously discussed considerations should be taken into account. The three approaches are as follows:

1. **Like for like**
   Also known as a *technical upgrade*; all features are moved from the source version to the newer version, including custom features. Only new, out-of-the-box features that require minor configuration would be considered in this kind of upgrade. This method is mostly used when the upgrade is driven by security and support requirements. Effort is needed to guarantee that the solution functions the same way it did before the upgrade.
2. **Extended upgrade**
   This kind of upgrade considers all desired functionality from the source version, as well as all desired features that come with the new version. This kind of upgrade is driven by the objective to take advantage of one or more large new features. This kind of upgrade can result in a solution that differs significantly from the previous version.
3. **Functional upgrade**
   This method uses a template approach in which the latest accelerator template is used as a basis for the new solution. After creating the new custom extensions for the project on the new template, the custom logic is migrated from the old code base into the new code base. This kind of upgrade is usually driven by a desire to take advantage not only of large new features but also the newest accelerator templates. Depending on the quantity of custom code to be reused, this could result in a full implementation project. In this case, all recommendations for full implementation projects should be considered.

2.5.2 Roles and Responsibilities

To have a successful upgrade project, it's essential that there be specific roles within the team to support that process and the activities and the corresponding deliverables. Just as in implementation upgrades, we consider the client team, the project/upgrade team, and the SAP team. The roles described in the following sections need to be clearly defined and responsibilities need to be defined to support the activities and deliverables of this phase.

Client Team

From the client team, the following roles should be considered in this phase:

- **Lead manager**
  This role is responsible for the upgrade on the client side by overseeing and making adjustments to the project. The lead manager is part of the steering committee and is the point of escalation.
- **Project manager**
  The project manager is responsible for the project organization on your side.
- **Deployment manager**
  The deployment manager is responsible for deployment to the test and production environments. The deployment manager assists with environment troubleshooting.
- **QA manager**
  This person leads the QA team that is responsible for executing and reporting all tests of the upgraded application.
- **Lead business analyst**
  This role represents the business and is responsible for defining how the application works functionally after the upgrade.
- **Technical architect**
  Any technical-oriented questions related to the platform or upgrade are handled by the technical architect. This person supports the upgrade lead during the upgrade project.

Project/Upgrade Team

The project/upgrade team can be a partner team, an internal team, or an SAP team, with the following roles:

- **Lead manager/delivery manager**
  The lead manager is part of the steering committee and oversees and reports on the direction of the project. This professional works with the client lead manager to act upon escalations.
- **Project manager**
  The project manager is responsible for managing the upgrade project in terms of cost, resources, and progress. The main activities are related to people management, risk management, escalation management, and cost management.
- **Upgrade lead**
  The upgrade lead is an experienced upgrade engineer who completes the technical responsibility. The main tasks are related to the installation, engineering, tests, and documentation.
- **Upgrade engineer**
  This is a developer with experience in SAP Commerce who executes the upgrade plan.
- **QA manager**
  The QA manager leads the QA team and is responsible for all quality-related tests on the upgraded application prior to delivery.

SAP Customer Experience Team

The following roles can be considered in this phase of the customer lifecycle:

- **Customer engagement executive (success manager)**
  The customer engagement executive is the main contact point for all things related to SAP C/4HANA (licenses, maintenance, escalations, events, etc.) and is responsible for the account management throughout your lifecycle. During deployment, the CEE can be a strong point of contact with the cloud operations team or other SAP teams that need to provide support during deployment and go-live.
- **Service delivery or engagement manager**
  The service delivery manager is responsible for delivery of SAP Customer Experience Expert Services and quality assurance services. His main responsibility is to deliver quality services and recommendations related to quality.
- **Functional consultants**
  The functional consultants provide functional consulting. Their responsibility is to provide recommendations related to the right usage of the software and recommended practices for SAP Commerce.

- **Technical consultants**
  The technical consultants provide technical consulting. Possible services during this phase are system reviews, go-live readiness reviews, and performance tuning.
- **Performance specialist**
  The performance specialist delivers performance tuning to your project if included in the success services plan. Her activities are focused on the performance tuning of the system to attend to nonfunctional requirements and prepare the solution for high performance.

2.6 Summary

In this chapter, we covered the basic information that should be known before getting started with SAP Commerce. As mentioned earlier, it's important to have a clear idea of what methodology to use. Methodologies need to be in line not only with an organization's culture but also need to give space for SAP Commerce projects to have a quick win. It's better to have a land-and-expand strategy in place to make sure the project grows with the business and adjusts to market or organizational changes in an organic way that avoids risks, rather than go with long, big-bang-approach projects.

We also provided insights into and examples of how the different recommended projects (phases) are structured and what kinds of activities, tasks, and teams should be considered for each phase and type of project (implementation and upgrades), as well as an introduction into how to operate in the cloud.

In the next chapter, we'll introduce and explain commerce management and out-of-the-box accelerators.

Chapter 3
Commerce Management

Whether you sell directly to customers, to other businesses, to both, or to neither—or whether your business isn't quite covered by any of those descriptions—there are certain common elements to most, if not all, SAP Commerce projects. Let's look at some of the most important ones.

Because the SAP Commerce platform serves such a wide variety of verticals—sometimes simultaneously and even within the same implementation—there are a relatively small number of concepts and data structures underlying all SAP Commerce functionality. By their nature, these are flexible concepts, and any project should begin with a thorough understanding of their nature and of how they fit together.

In this chapter, we will explore some of these concepts, paying special attention to those that enable business-to-customer (B2C) and business-to-business (B2B) ways of working, as well as specific verticals—while also demonstrating how much of what's happening under the hood in SAP Commerce is applicable to just about *every* commerce scenario.

We'll start by looking at sales organizations and the management of carts, products, wishlists, and checkout processes. Then we'll dive into promotions, beginning with an overview of the architecture behind the engine, the mechanics of rules and planning, and the creation and management of coupons—after which we will go into detail about the rule engine, which drives promotions functionality but can also be used for other, more custom forms of conditional logic.

Finally, we will take a closer look at the SAP Commerce accelerators, which we mention throughout this book. We'll talk about what the different accelerator storefronts have in common, as well as what fits each of them to specific businesses' purposes, whether that means the industry-specific features of SAP Commerce, telco and media accelerator, SAP Commerce, financial services accelerator, and SAP Commerce, citizen engagement accelerator; the regionally specific layouts in SAP Commerce, accelerator for China, or the organization management tools in SAP Commerce, B2B accelerator.

Not every project will use every single one of these features, but every implementation team should consider how these concepts relate to the requirements at hand. Our goal is to make sure that you are acquainted with the foundational elements of commerce, *especially* when those building blocks can support a great many different structures.

3.1 Sales Organization

Just as important as what you sell is who sells it and how. Your sales organization is the group responsible for this process. Empowering them is key to your success. In B2C scenarios, this organization is typically divided into three groups: *merchants*, *marketers*, and *support*. Although this division of labor is not universal, it is common enough in the broad strokes to warrant summarizing in an SAP Commerce context, as follows:

- Merchants are responsible for creating and maintaining product information and for surfacing it to the channels from which customers can purchase the items in question. This generally means enriching product information in PCM and setting base and/or customer-specific prices, either in an integrated ERP system or in SAP Commerce itself.
- Marketers are responsible for making the products accessible and appealing to customers—or, put another way, their job is to manage everything about products that merchants don't. They are typically responsible for promotions, campaigns, banners, creative—often managed via the SAP Commerce content management system (CMS)—and onsite search optimization, including boost and bury (which we will discuss in more detail in Chapter 8).
- Your internal support team is responsible for the nonautomated portions of the customer experience. Merchants and marketers are of course concerned with customer experience as well, insofar as the ways that products are presented and promoted should always put the customer at the center. But support goes beyond that, assisting the customer with order placement, account management, and potentially postorder workflows, such as returns.

In a B2B scenario, all these roles may still exist, though marketers' roles are typically a bit less concerned with campaigns and marketing in the traditional sense. They may be more involved in buyer-specific catalogs, frequent pricing changes, and contract management.

In addition, B2B SAP Commerce projects will require an internal team to manage purchasing organizations, from order approvals to quotes and invoicing to (once again) contracts. We will describe these groups and their relationship to customer purchasing organizations more thoroughly in Chapter 9, Section 9.1.

It is important to keep in mind that not every sale will involve a direct interaction between your sales team and the customer making the purchase. A sale made through a web storefront that goes smoothly and gets fulfilled to the customer's home may not involve a human salesperson, a customer support representative, or anyone else. This is the essence of automation, it's an enormous part of the value of going omnichannel in the first place, and it frees up your team members to go where they are most needed and to work with maximum efficiency.

Next, let's talk about some topics that fall outside the notion of a sales organization, but that nonetheless are vital to *organizing your sales* and the process of selling. When the automated flow described previously is working as intended, these are the features making it work—and when the process does require human intervention, these are the features that empower the team to make that intervention effective.

3.2 Cart Management

Carts are a key unit in customer interactions in almost any SAP Commerce storefront. In a more traditional B2B or B2C storefront, carts are absolutely central to the customer experience—and even in a vertical that does not rely on finished goods, such as insurance or banking, a "product" still gets added to a "cart" somewhere behind the scenes, to apply prices, check for promotion eligibility, and eventually convert the product or products into an order for fulfillment. Indeed, during the standard checkout process in SAP Commerce, a cart is converted directly into an order, as we will discuss in Section 3.4.2.

In the most basic sense, a cart is an object that contains one or more products and is attached to an account. If the user is currently shopping anonymously, and/or then checking out as a guest, the cart is still associated with her provisional account.

The customer does not necessarily know that, of course. The name of the provisional account will be a long, system-generated string that the customer does not know—so if customer support needs to look up the customer's current cart, either in the back-office or in assisted service mode, they would generally do so using the *cart ID*, a unique identifier attached to each cart and fully visible to the customer on the front-end.

The behavior of a shopping cart is enormously extensible, as we will discuss in just a moment. But for most projects, something close to the default SAP Commerce accelerators settings is appropriate: customers generally should be able to add a product to a cart, remove a product from a cart, apply a coupon code, save a cart, and initiate the checkout process. Customers can generally see the current contents of their cart in the form of a *mini cart* page component, usually surfaced by hovering over the cart icon while shopping.

The cart is sometimes presented as a "bag" or "basket," but the underlying concept is not different from a technical or functional standpoint, important as the choice of words might be within a given organization from a brand identity point of view. The real differences come into play when you begin to think about how these behaviors, which are fairly universal, apply to your project. We'll begin by looking at the extensions and configurations behind carts, and then move on to the mechanics of cart behavior.

3.2.1 Extensions and Configurations

Cart behavior is governed by the `CommerceCartService` extension. In most projects, developers will only edit a single parameter to alter the cart: `CommerceCartParameter`, which resides in the commerceservices-beans.xml configuration file.

This file determines what happens when the appropriate cart method is called, in accordance with one or more default strategies. For example, then `DefaultCommerceAddToCartStrategy` adds a certain quantity of a certain unit of a certain product, based on the properties defined in the parameter.

Because pricing and promotions are confirmed at the cart level, API hooks for order placement rely heavily on carts in SAP Commerce by default. Out of the box, the `de.hybris.platform.commerceservices.order.hook` package offers the following hooks for other applications:

- `AthorizePaymentMethodHook`
- `CommerceAddToCartMethodHook`
- `CommerceCartCalculationMethodHook`
- `CommercePlaceOrderMethodHook`

In addition to defining the data flow between SAP Commerce and the other system or system with which it is communicating, these hooks invoke parameters and define error handling behavior for that communication. Listing 3.1, for example, shows the `CommerceAddToCartMethodHook` method hook, as implemented in `de.hybris.platform.commerceservices.order.hook.CommerceAddToCartMethodHook`.

```
public interface CommerceAddToCartMethodHook
{
void beforeAddToCart(CommerceCartParameter parameters) throws
  CommerceCartModificationException;
void afterAddToCart(CommerceCartParameter parameters,
  CommerceCartModification result) throws CommerceCartModificationException;
}
```

Listing 3.1 CommerceAddToCartMethodHook Method Hook

3.2.2 Cart Merging

Let's say that a customer has begun shopping on his laptop, added some products to his cart, and then walked away from the transaction. Let's assume that he already has an account and that he was logged in while shopping, but that he then had to leave to house.

Now, let's say that while the customer is on the bus or the train, he accesses the same storefront from his mobile device. He starts shopping again, and once again he adds some products to his cart. Then he realizes that he's not logged in to his account. Perhaps he remembers that he was shopping at home earlier. So he logs back in.

What behavior should we expect from the cart in this case? And more to the point, what behavior does the customer probably expect? Recall that the customer already had some products in his cart, attached to his account. Now he has some additional products in his cart, attached to his browsing session.

In most B2C settings, the customer will expect to see the two carts merge—that is, to keep the products from the anonymous browsing session *and* keep the products from the earlier, logged-in browsing session, and to see the combination of both reflected in his cart once he's logged back in. This is considered a best practice, and it is enabled by default in some configurations of SAP Commerce.

However, this is not the right cart merging strategy for every situation. In industries in which products very frequently go in and out of stock—and especially in those in which inventory is therefore reserved when the customer adds a product to his cart, as opposed to when he checks out—it may be preferable to wipe out the old, possibly stale cart and replace it completely with the new one. Customers of those sorts of businesses might in fact expect that behavior and might be put off (or at the very least, surprised) by a merge. In cases such as these, you will most likely want to alter the system's default cart merging strategy.

Cart merging behavior is configurable in SAP Commerce, via the `mergeCarts` method in `CommerceCartMergingStrategy`, which is located in the `commerceservices` extension.

This method determines which cart's contents will be moved into which of the two carts and what modifications might be made to the cart itself during the process. To these ends, it contains three parameters:

- `fromCart`, which indicates which cart to remove products from
- `toCart`, which indicates which cart to move those products into
- `modifications`, which lists the possible changes to the cart or the display thereof, such as a message box explaining that the two carts have been merged and that the customer is now seeing the combined contents of both

These parameters can be set in the *commercecartmergingstrategy.java* file, as shown in Listing 3.2.

```
/**
 * A strategy for merging carts.
 */
public interface CommerceCartMergingStrategy
{
    /**
     * Merge two carts and add modifications
     *
     * @param fromCart
     *          - Cart from merging is done
     * @param toCart
     *          - Cart to merge to
     * @param modifications
     *          - List of modifications
     * @throws CommerceCartMergingException
     */
    void mergeCarts(CartModel fromCart, CartModel toCart,
```

```
  List<CommerceCartModification> modifications) throws
    CommerceCartMergingException;
}
```


Listing 3.2 Cart Merging Parameters

Within the commercefacades extension, `CommerceAddToCartStrategy` executes this merge by two methods, `restoreCartAndMerge` and `restoreAnonymousCartAndMerge`, both targeting the `CartModel` object. The former requires the two carts being merged to belong to the same user, whereas the latter merges an anonymous user's cart into a known customer's, as in the scenario described earlier.

3.3 Product Recommendation

Whether your goal is to cross-sell (as shown in Figure 3.1), upsell, or simply make customers aware of products they might not have considered, product recommendations are a key element of any online shopping experience—but using them well, so that they come off as relevant and helpful rather obnoxious and obtrusive, requires some thinking, some skill, and some decisions about what kind of automation is right for a given situation.

Machine learning is advancing rapidly and is a tremendously exciting field of study and an equally exciting space for practical business opportunities.

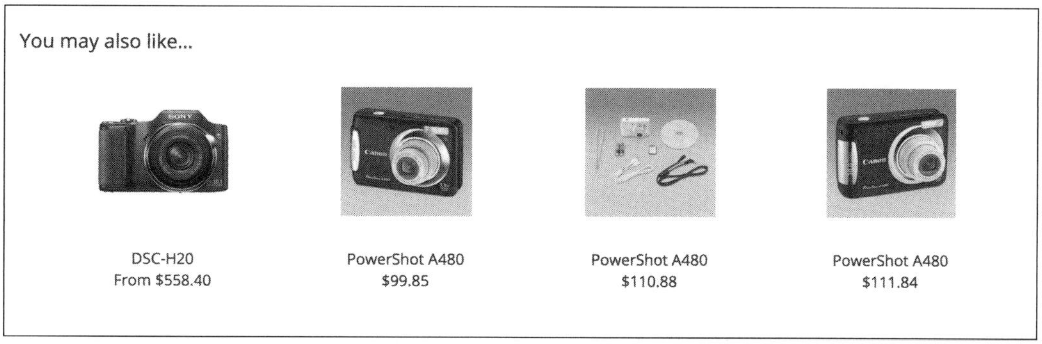

Figure 3.1 Cross-Sell Product Carousel in Electronics Store

But we do not want to take for granted that more automation is automatically better in every situation. If you have a large product set and a large amount of data about your customers, and you are having a hard time matching the one to the other, then machine intelligence is often the most efficient way to bridge the gap and match products to buyers. If you do not have a large data set, however, or if you already have some clear ideas about what kinds of products you want to recommend to which kinds of customers, then a more manual, hands-on approach may be preferable.

SAP Marketing Cloud is one example of a product that focuses on automating business intelligence and presenting product recommendations to customers with a minimum of direct human input. The toolset takes customer data from the SAP Commerce channel, the golden customer record, social media, and any other integrated channel and maps that data to customer segments, then maps those segments to products based on machine learning. If you have both SAP Marketing Cloud and SAP Commerce in place and integrated with one another, then you can surface these recommendations in SAP Commerce and/or use these segments to trigger SAP Commerce content.

If you do not have SAP Marketing Cloud, or any third-party tool that serves a similar purpose as far as automated product recommendations, then you can still recommend products in SAP Commerce. The process will, however, be a considerably more manual one, relying on hand-selected recommendations. Business users will need to map products to one another in the Product Cockpit perspective in the backoffice and map different product carousels to different users and user groups using SmartEdit. (For more details on the latter, see the sections on components and SmartEdit in Chapter 5 and the sections on user and user group restrictions in Chapter 9.)

As mentioned earlier, this manual curation may be a better approach for some organizations. The beauty of automation, in a sense, is that the results can surprise you: customers might see products they didn't know they wanted, and you might see customers buying products that *you* didn't know they wanted. But the other side of this coin is that you give up some direct control over what customers do, in fact, see when they shop. Organizations with teams dedicated to marketing and merchandizing—though they can of course benefit from machine learning insights—may prefer a more hands-on approach.

Each product in SAP Commerce has a list of product references, along with its classifications and categories (both of which we will explain in depth in Chapter 4). The mappings between products in SAP Commerce are called *product references*. Each reference is simply a one-to-one relation between two specific products, with a parameter to determine how the two products are related.

In SAP Commerce accelerators' sample data, the preconfigured types of product references include the following:

- **Cross-selling**
  This is for products that are recommended to be bought together (also referred to as "You may also like...").
- **Upselling**
  This is for upgraded, improved, or more full-featured versions of products already in the cart.
- **Similar**
  This is for products that the customer might consider instead of those in the cart, but which are not necessarily upsells.
- **Spare part**
  This is for products that might be used to maintain or repair the product in the cart.
- **Alternative order unit**
  This is for different amounts of the product in the cart (e.g., different packs of the same types of batteries).
- **Accessories**
  This is for products that might compliment the product in the cart (e.g., a case or protector for a portable electronic device).
- **Follow-up**
  This is for products that the customer might want to order after ordering the product in the cart (e.g., a warranty or protection plan).
- **Mandatory**
  This is for products that *must* be ordered along with the product in the cart (e.g., safety equipment that ships with regulatory goods).
- **Consists of**
  This is for products that are essentially kits, composed of other products that may or may not be individually purchasable.
- **Others**
  This acts as a catch-all for product references to do not fit into any of the other default categories.

Out of the box, none of these parameters have any business logic attached to them. They are simply categories, or tags, to be used in whatever way the business finds most useful—and as the presence of the *others* options suggests, the list is easily extensible. Business users can easily add their own product reference types, with one common addition being *replaces*, for products that are available in place of some other, recently discontinued SKU. If there are multiple products now taking the place of the old one, then all of them can be easily displayed wherever the old product once lived or continues to live on the site.

3.4 Wishlists and Checkout

Sometimes, customers research and select without necessarily being ready to transact. You can and should try to get them to transact in the moment: their saved cart will persist as described previously, and you can consider following up on their abandoned carts as well—but the simplest way to get customers to return to the list of products they were looking at is to simply *let them make a list*. You don't need to infer their interest if they have explicitly expressed it, and they don't need to go looking for the products they're interested in if they've already assembled them into a list. In this section, we will describe the wishlist functionality that makes this possible.

Then we will discuss the checkout process that begins when a customer *is* ready to transact. We'll discuss the default checkout flows built into the accelerators and the processes for guiding customers to the correct one, for combining them or introducing your own custom ones, and for keeping all of your checkout flows efficient, secure, and compliant.

3.4.1 Wishlists

Customers frequently expect to be able to save the contents of their carts and come back to them later. As discussed in the previous section, SAP Commerce natively allows them to do exactly that by persisting one active cart to each customer account at any given time. For some customer experiences, however, you will need to go beyond simple cart persistence. Customers might want to save multiple carts to their accounts and restore the entire list later on, or even share the list with others, as in the case of a wedding registry. These sharing features are not native to SAP Commerce, but the notion of a wishlist is—and it can serve as the basis for other, more business-specific cases.

Wishlists are, fundamentally, saved carts. Whether they are presented as such will vary from vertical to vertical—but behind the scenes, SAP Commerce always saved a wishlist as a saved cart, which can then be retrieved, renamed, edited, or merged with an existing cart. By default, only customers with full accounts can save carts, and so only they can create wishlists.

From the cart summary page in an accelerator storefront, a customer can save a cart (and thus create a wishlist) by clicking **New Cart**. At that point, as shown in Figure 3.2, anonymous or guest users will be prompted to log in or create an account. Logged-in customers will be promoted to enter a name and (optimally) a description for their wishlist. At any later point, they can then select a particular cart from a listing of all their saved carts and restore it, turning carts one at a time into an active cart.

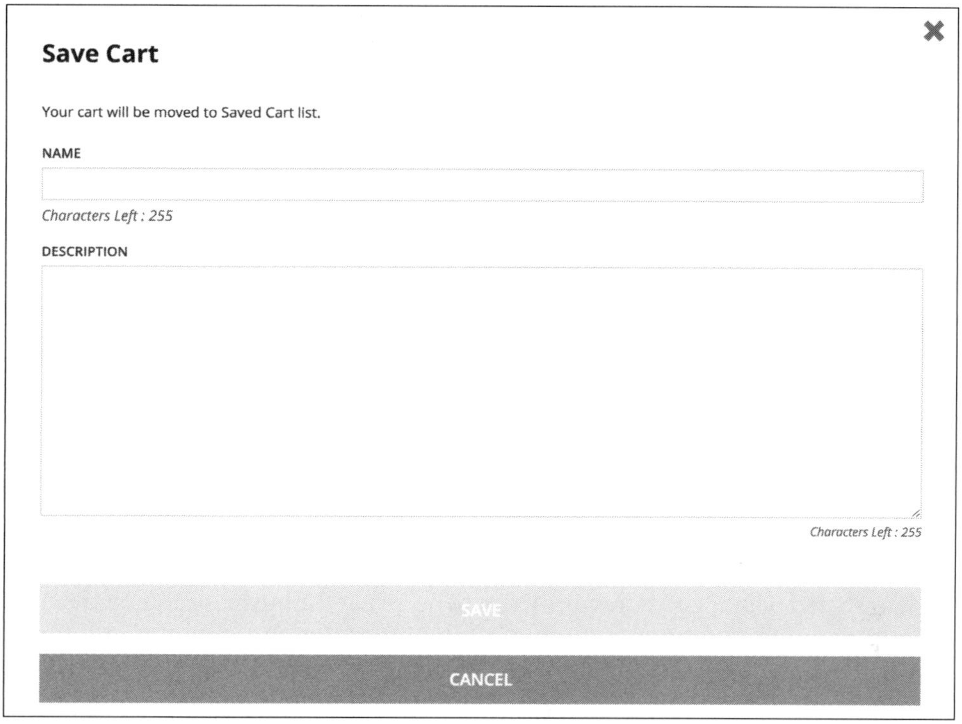

Figure 3.2 Customer Creates New Wish List in Electronics Store

In general, the cart merging logic described in Section 3.2.2 will not apply to restoring saved carts. Rather, the contents of the wishlist will become the new active cart; if the customer already had an active cart, she will be offered the option to save those contents to a new, additional wishlist.

In addition to its contents, each wishlist holds attributes for the date that it was originally saved, the date that it was last modified, its cart ID, its name, its description, and the total calculated cost of the cart at the time of saving. The customer will not necessarily get the same prices if she restores the cart—the system will check for the current prices on the products once the wishlist once again becomes an active cart—but the customer can nonetheless store the context in which she was shopping.

Saved cart functionality lives within the `commerceservices` extension. It is enabled by default in SAP Commerce, B2C accelerator and SAP Commerce, B2B accelerator storefronts using the following two methods:

1. `getSavedCartsCountForSiteAndUser`
   This leverages `BaseSiteModel` and `UserModel` to enumerate the carts currently saved to a customer account.
2. `getSavedCartsForSiteAndUser`
   This retrieves the saved carts and allows them to be sorted, modified, and restored, by leveraging `PagableData`, `BaseSiteModel`, `UserModel`, and `List<OrderStatus>`.

You can enable wishlists on other storefronts by setting these two parameters in your *local.properties* file:

- `acceleratorservices.commercesavecart.sessioncart.hook.enabled.<storefront>=true`
- `acceleratorservices.commercesavecart.restoration.savetime.hook.enabled.<storefront>=true`

If you do not specify a storefront in these parameters, then wishlist functionality will be enabled for all the storefronts currently running in your SAP Commerce system.

Note that saved carts persist at the customer level by default. Certain B2B use cases, such as shared bills of goods, require them to persist at the business unit or organization level instead, and this requires some customization to the cart object to share it between customer accounts. In such cases, extending the cart object constitutes the bulk of the work, and leveraging saved cart options *on* those now-shared carts then becomes relatively straightforward.

As described earlier, carts are essentially provisional orders. Branching out from that topic, let's talk next about the checkout process, wherein a cart becomes an order—and a customer generally has to enter a significant amount of information, much of it quite sensitive, to make that process happen. Checkout can be an enormously tricky process to design and configure, both from a customer experience perspective and from a security and compliance perspective, and getting it right can be the difference between a frustratingly low conversion rate and a truly excellent one. So here's how to get it right.

3.4.2 Checkout

SAP Commerce supports multiple checkout flows within a single storefront, allowing for a single-page or multipage checkout experience that can be dynamically selected based on, for example, the line of business.

In the standard B2C flow, the customer begins by entering shipping information. If the customer has an account, then she can select a saved address from her address book. If the customer does not have any saved addresses or is checking out as a guest, or if she simply wants to ship to a new address, then she can enter the address and decide whether or not she wants to save it for future use.

Next, the customer selects a shipping method. In the SAP Commerce, B2C accelerator storefront sample data (which we will discuss in more detail later in this chapter), the available shipping options are *standard* and *premium*, with the latter generally being more expensive but providing faster fulfillment. These shipping types are configurable and extensible, with one very common addition being one or more promotional shipping rates that are cheaper or faster and that the customer can access by qualifying for a promotion. (For more on promotions, Section 3.5.)

If the order contains items that will be bought online but picked up in store, then at this step, rather than (or in addition to) entering a fulfillment address, the customer will select the store or stores where she will pick up her order. (If the order has to be split for fulfillment at two different locations or if part of the order is being shipped while part of it is picked up or if it needs to be fulfilled from multiple warehouses, then it will be split into multiple consignments.)

In the next step, the customer enters payment information. As with the shipping information step, if the customer has a saved payment method, then she can select it. Otherwise, she can enter a new one. In general, when the customer moves on from this step, the payment gateway will perform a preauthorization on the customer's method of payment before moving ahead to the order summary.

In the final review step (as shown in Figure 3.3), the customer sees a summary of the shipping, billing, payment, promotion, and cart information that comprises her order. Here she can return to any previous step, or she can agree to the site's terms and conditions and proceed with the order. At this point, the payment gateway authorizes payment, and after this is done the SAP Commerce storefront sends the customer to an order confirmation page.

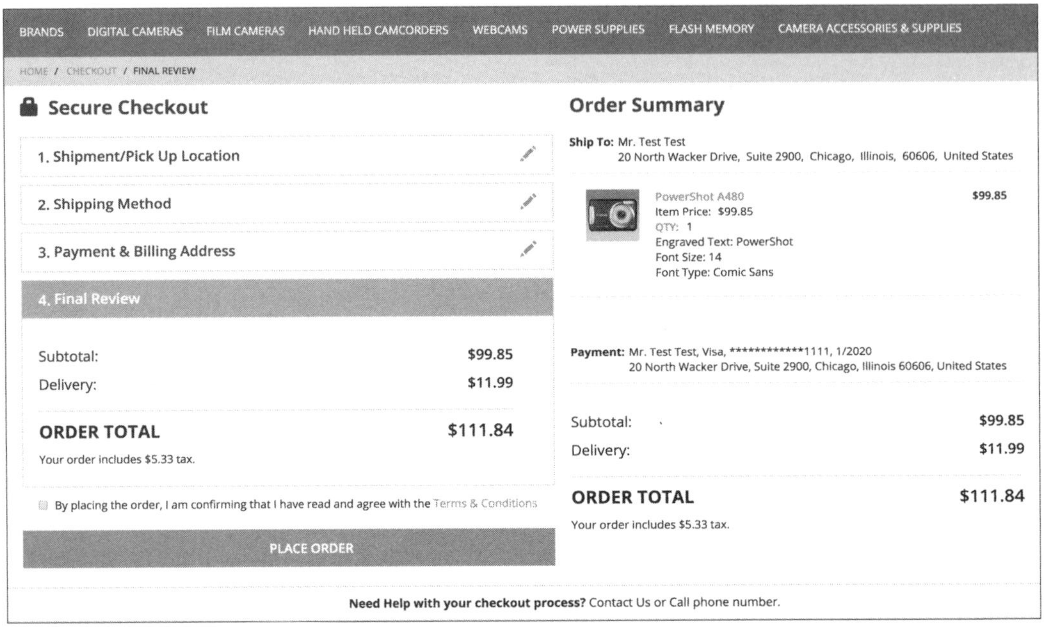

Figure 3.3 Final Review Step of Standard, Multipage Checkout Flow

If the customer has checked out as a guest, then at this point she will be offered the opportunity to create a password and turn her guest account into a full customer account, giving her the ability to track her order and initiate communication with customer support—and giving you the ability to tie the customer's activity to a single golden record and market to her accordingly.

If the customer already has an account and has saved payment and shipping information in the system, then she can use the *express checkout* flow, which skips her directly to the final review step with her default settings applied to the order. This option offers a speedy checkout flow, as well as an incentive for customers to create full accounts (and therefore to opt-in to some form or other of profile tracking so that you can market to her more effectively).

In a B2B checkout flow, there is often no payment information to enter because the order might be billed to a cost center and settled after the fact, through some sort of invoicing process. For this reason, B2B checkout flows in SAP Commerce allow the customer to select cost centers and enter invoice numbers. In addition, B2B orders can be submitted as replenishment orders, which repeat the order daily, weekly, monthly, and so on.

Critically, any of these steps can be freely reordered, disabled, or customized. If the customer's order is going to be picked up in store, in whole or in part, then the step for selecting a pickup location will be included automatically. If you have a payment method such as PayPal Express that requires a punch-out to a hosted ordering page, that punch-out will be added dynamically as well.

Other checkout flow changes might be more business-specific. If you only sell digital goods, for example, then you can turn off the shipping information step. In the insurance or banking spaces, the process of opening an account, purchasing a policy, or filing a claim might involve one or multiple forms, and these too can be included in the checkout process.

To better understand how to configure and customize checkout flows, let's take a closer look at a basic one and at how it's working behind the scenes.

The basic B2C flow described earlier—with its standard progression through shipping information, shipping method, billing information, and confirmation—is based entirely on `defaultMultiStepCheckoutGroup`, the out-of-the-box `CheckoutGroup` for the accelerator storefronts. Any variations on this flow or mappings to other flows based on the customer's preferences or order type will generally branch out from a basic configuration such as this one.

`CheckoutGroup` is composed of one or more `CheckoutSteps`, each tied to a `Validator` that determines that the necessary information has been entered and that it is valid by checking it against `ValidationresultsMap` before proceeding to the next `CheckoutStep`.

This same logic can be used to dynamically present multiple checkout flows to the customer, as in the case of a default multistep checkout flow incorporating a punch-out for a payment method. For example, the XML configuration for our branching B2C checkout flow would appear as shown in Listing 3.3.

```
<alias name="defaultMultiStepCheckoutGroup" alias="defaultCheckoutGroup" />
<bean id="defaultMultiStepCheckoutGroup"
  class="de.hybris.platform.acceleratorstorefrontcommons.
         checkout.steps.CheckoutGroup">
<property name="groupId"  value="defaultGroup"/>
<property name="checkoutStepMap">
<map merge="true">
<entry key="multi" value-ref="defaultMultiStepCheckout"/>
<entry key="delivery-address" value-ref="deliveryAddressCheckoutStep"/>
<entry key="delivery-method" value-ref="deliveryMethodCheckoutStep"/>
```

```
<entry key="pickup-location" value-ref="pickupLocationCheckoutStep"/>
<entry key="payment-method" value-ref="paymentMethodCheckoutStep"/>
<entry key="summary" value-ref="summaryCheckoutStep"/>
</map>
</property>
<property name="validationResultsMap">
<map merge="true">
<entry key="FAILED" value-ref="REDIRECT_TO_CART"/>
<entry key="REDIRECT_TO_DELIVERY_ADDRESS"
       value-ref="REDIRECT_TO_DELIVERY_ADDRESS"/>
<entry key="REDIRECT_TO_PICKUP_LOCATION"
       value-ref="REDIRECT_TO_PICKUP_LOCATION"/>
<entry key="REDIRECT_TO_CART" value-ref="REDIRECT_TO_CART"/>
<entry key="REDIRECT_TO_PAYMENT_METHOD"
       value-ref="REDIRECT_TO_PAYMENT_METHOD"/>
<entry key="REDIRECT_TO_DELIVERY_METHOD"
       value-ref="REDIRECT_TO_DELIVERY_METHOD"/>
</map>
</property>
<property name="checkoutProgressBar">
<map merge="true">
<entry key="1" value-ref="deliveryAddressCheckoutStep"/>
<entry key="2" value-ref="deliveryMethodCheckoutStep"/>
<entry key="3" value-ref="paymentMethodCheckoutStep"/>
<entry key="4" value-ref="defaultSummaryCheckoutStep"/>
</map>
</property>
</bean>
```

Listing 3.3 XML Configuration for Branching B2C Checkout Flow

Note that each step has a numerical value, determining the order in which the steps will appear to the customer within the active checkout flow and how the progress bar at the top of the page will be drawn, as well as references redirecting the customer to the next appropriate step. Note as well that these redirects are the mechanism by which a checkout flow can essentially have multiple branches, applying different processes to different customers as a result of the products they are buying, the payment method that they are using, or their own manual selection of a specific checkout flow option.

If you want to make deeper changes to these checkout options, you can do so using `CommerceCheckoutParameter` in the `CommerceCheckoutService` extension, as configured in the */resources/commerceservices-beans.xml* bean, which appears as shown in Listing 3.4.

```
<bean class="de.hybris.platform.commerceservices.service.data.
  CommerceCheckoutParameter">
<property name="cart" type="de.hybris.platform.core.model.order.CartModel">
<description>The CartModel</description>
</property>
<property name="address"
          type="de.hybris.platform.core.model.user.AddressModel">
<description>the Address</description>
</property>
<property name="isDeliveryAddress" type="boolean">
<description>Delivery address flag</description>
</property>
<property name="deliveryMode"
          type="de.hybris.platform.core.model.order.delivery.
                DeliveryModeModel">
<description>The delivery mode</description>
</property>
<property name="paymentInfo"
          type="de.hybris.platform.core.model.order.payment.PaymentInfoModel">
<description>payment information</description>
</property>
    ...
</bean>
```

Listing 3.4 Parameters for Custom Checkout Flow

3.4.3 PCI Compliance

All these checkout flows are designed to comply with the guidelines set forth by the Payment Card Industry Security Standards Council, guidelines generally referred to simply as *PCI compliance*—a cascading set of requirements and certifications for any organization that takes responsibility for storing, transmitting, and/or processing credit card information. An SAP Commerce storefront, if it has been set up according to best practices, should not in principle be doing any of those things per se.

This is because it is the payment gateway, not SAP Commerce, that stores, transmits, and processes the customer's credit card information and connects the transactions to the customer's cart, order, and account via tokenization.

In this process, the payment gateway generates a non-human-readable code, referred to as a *token*, and passes this to SAP Commerce for storage. SAP Commerce then passes this token back to the payment gateway to capture payment (usually when the order ships or is picked up), issue a refund (if necessary), or make any other necessary adjustment. Because SAP Commerce stores only this token (and sometimes the card type and/or last four digits of the card number so that the customer can easily identify a given saved payment method), SAP Commerce accelerator storefronts avoid the burden of having to be PCI-compliant from end to end.

With that said, there are still some design best practices that you will need to follow to comply with PCI standards. One key rule of thumb is that credit card information cannot be entered on any page with scripts for which you, the seller, are not responsible. Payment gateways transmit such sensitive information securely, either with fields on your page that connect directly to the gateway itself or with entire hosted pages to which the customer will punch out during the checkout process (familiar to most customers as the flow used by PayPal Express). But something as simple as a Facebook **Like** button on one of these pages introduces a call to a remotely hosted and ultimately unaccountable external script and can therefore endanger PCI compliance.

It is therefore advisable to keep your checkout page or pages streamlined and focused. This also carries some business benefits. You can and should attempt to cross-sell and upsell the customers while they are browsing and while viewing their cart—but once they have crossed the threshold into beginning the checkout process proper, your goal should be to have them complete that process. Removing superfluous elements from the page makes the intent of the page clearer while simultaneously improving performance.

3.5 Promotions

When you want customers to receive some special price or some other special offer, based on limited time, limited availability, or some other personalized parameters, you want to consider using promotions. In this section, we will discuss the *promotion engine*, which allows business uses to create and publish not only promotions but also the messaging and media associated with them. Creating an effective promotion means thinking in terms of a promotional campaign, and the promotion engine offers the tolls to help backoffice users do just that.

Once we have gone through the core promotion functionality in SAP Commerce, we will then discuss the rule engine that enables it. This engine represents an additional and substantially more flexible—though also somewhat more technical and potentially somewhat daunting—layer of configurability, and its potential goes well beyond the specifics of promotions. Before we discuss those more general points, however, let's get into the details of the promotion engine, both from a technical perspective and from that of an end user.

3.5.1 Promotional Pricing

There are numerous ways to offer a specific customer a specific price in SAP Commerce. You could establish different prices for different channels or make your prices time-sensitive or even dynamic, as described in Chapter 4. You could leverage B2B price lists to give different contracted customers different enumerated prices and/or standing discounts. Or you could offer specific prices to specific users or user groups, or to specific countries or regions, as explained in Chapter 9.

But this functionality does not cover every case. In fact, it does not perfectly cover the most common sort of temporary pricing case in B2C retail scenarios, wherein the customer should receive a discounted price—or a free gift or a future discount or a change in shipping class—after meeting certain conditions. For this wide range of important possibilities, we have promotion functionality.

The business value of promotions should be clear enough, but they are so ubiquitous a part of the shopping experience, online and off, that the philosophy behind them bears explaining. Promotions do not exist simply because customers expect them, though customers do undoubtedly expect them. Rather, promotions exist to achieve three major goals, ideally all at once.

First and foremost, promotions can drive conversion. Charging a lower amount on each individual product can make a customer more likely to buy, and furthermore, more likely to buy more and more expensive items than they would have otherwise. This generally means accepting a lower margin on each individual product, but it often increases profit overall over the course of days, weeks, months, or quarters by increasing conversion rates, often quite significantly.

Second, promotions help with the controlling and planning of stock. They can help to clear warehouses of unsold goods—especially goods that could expire or that are seasonal and therefore temporal despite *not* expiring per se—or direct customers toward products they might not have otherwise considered.

Third, and perhaps just as importantly as driving up conversion, promotions make customers engage with your brand. A regular cadence of promotions can encourage customers to check back in at regular intervals. Surprise promotions can drive them to your purchasing channels at times when they might not otherwise have thought to check in. The expectation of ongoing (but not continuous) discounts can keep you in your customer's mind in between transactions.

When planning promotions, then, it is important to keep these three goals in mind. If you're not driving conversion, controlling stock, and/or increasing your customers' engagement with your commerce channels specifically or your brand more generally, then at the very least you might not be using your resources—from the budgets behind the discounts to the time and skills of your marketing and merchandizing teams—nearly as effectively as you might be.

Again, this may seem obvious. But many organizations run promotions mostly out of habit, without necessarily stopping to align their strategy with clear objectives. Here we'll discuss how to align the functionality with the goals, as you should on any project, as early in the process as possible.

Promotions in SAP Commerce are essentially an extra layer of price and/or shipping adjustment with some conditional logic attached. Discounts can be applied at the product level and/or the cart level, and conditions for activation include the presence of specific products or categories of products in the cart, the total value of the cart, a range of valid dates and times, the customer's user group or segment membership, and whether the customer has already activated some other rule and therefore received some other promotion.

Marketers can configure promotions in the backoffice, under the **Marketing** node. Here they can view and edit the basic attributes of each promotion, including its name, description, and unique code—as well as, most importantly, the conditions and actions that define the promotion. Promotions are fundamentally if/then statements wherein one, several, or all of the conditions being met means that the actions will take place.

These actions can include fixed and percentage discounts (both at the product level and at the cart level), changes in delivery mode (for a free, cheaper, or faster class of shipping), free gifts (for incentive products, free samples, or appeasement offers), and, of course, triggered messages to describe what the customer has received as a result of qualifying for the promotion. These messages can be internationalized into the local language and can contain variables that, for example, calculate how much the customer has saved by qualifying for the promotion—or how much they *would* save if they *did* qualify and precisely what they would need to do or buy to do so.

Marketers can add or remove these conditions and actions from a given promotion template via drag and drop, as shown in Figure 3.4. (We will discuss this process in more detail in the next section.) Because individual conditions and actions can be freely combined, the preconfigured default promotions are nothing more or less than that: the default.

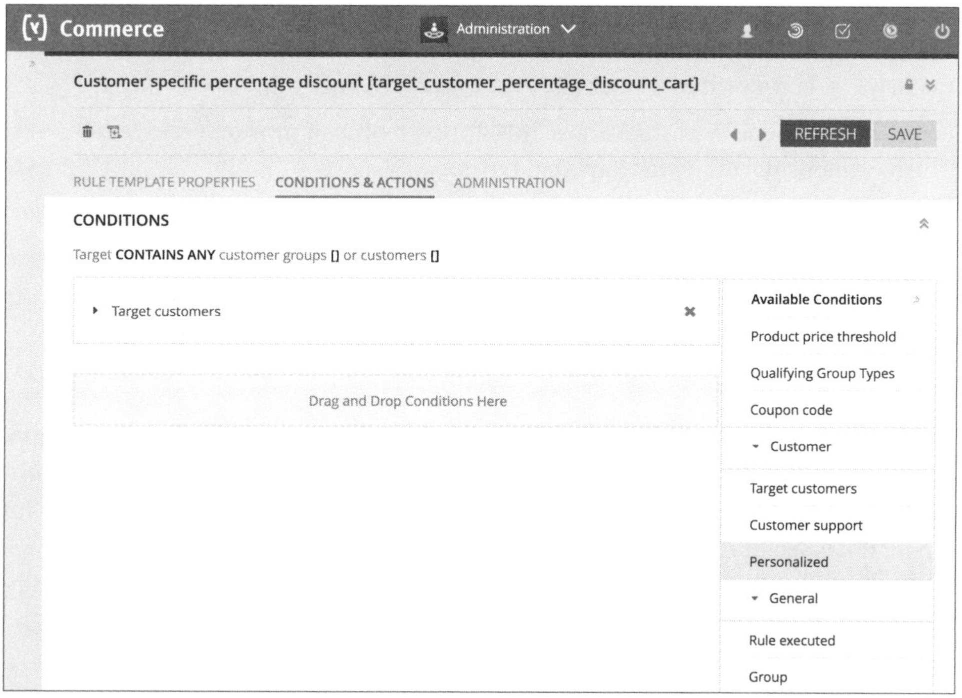

Figure 3.4 Conditions and Actions for Customer-Specific Discount in Backoffice

Even without doing any customization whatsoever, your project can include a wide variety of promotion types, from simple temporary discounts to buy one, get one free offers to "perfect partners" (when buying one product at full price gives the customer access to some other product for free or at a discount) to basic loyalty tiers. Most of these are at least partially templatized in the SAP Commerce accelerators' sample data, but they may not align perfectly with your project's needs—which is fine because adjusting them is a straightforward process.

3.5.2 Promotions Engine

The heart of the SAP Commerce promotion engine is the rule engine, which we will discuss in detail in the next section. Before doing that, however, we will look at the layer of SAP Commerce-specific functionality that sits on top of it, both from a technical perspective and from a functional perspective.

Technical Overview

Promotions essentially sit a layer above rules, being created and stored in the running system as abstract rules, rather than the intermediate representations that they will eventually become before being compiled and executed (a process that, once again, we will cover when we talk about the rules engine).

The primary module that enables this functionality is `promotionengineservices`, which contains the following key item types:

- `PromotionSourceRule`, which extends the rule engine `SourceRule` extension
- `PromotionSourceRuleTemplate`, which extends the rules engine `SourceRuleTemplate` extension
- `RuleBasedPromotion`, which extends `AbstractPromotion`
- `AbstractRuleBasedPromotionAction`, which extends `AbstractPromotionActionModel`

`AbstractRuleBasedPromotionAction` has subtypes that map to the more granular units of promotion calculation and execution—and, just as importantly, for reversing promotion actions if the customer removes something from his cart or otherwise no longer qualifies for the promotion. For example, `RuleBasedOrderChangeDeliveryModeAction` keeps track of the shipping method that the customer was using before a shipping-related promotion was applied, so that said method can be reapplied after the promotion is removed.

Next, there is `ruleengineservices`, which stores and transmits details for the abstract rules, using these key item types:

- `SourceRule`, which extends `AbstractRule` to add conditions, actions, and other attributes such as start date and end date, which are then passed to the rule engine
- `SourceRuleTemplate`, which extends `AbstractRuleTemplate` to provide starting points and formats for new rules
- `RuleToEngineRuleTypeMapping`, which maps a subtype of abstract rules (such as `PromotionRule`) to its equivalent in the rule engine, and specifically in the KIE object described in the next section

In addition, within `ruleengineservices` there are item types that allow you to set parameters for the rules you are building, such as the total value of the cart. To achieve that, you would pass the `<cart.total>` condition to `RuleConditionDefinition`, along with its three required parameters: `<operator>`, `<value>`, and `<currency>`.

The other relevant item types, which work similarly, are as follows:

- `RuleConditionDefinitionParameter`
- `RuleConditionDefinitionCategory`
- `RuleActionDefinition`, `RuleActionDefinitionParameter`
- `RuleActionDefinitionCategory`

Finally, there is ruleengine, which connects the abstract rules in the promotion engine to their equivalent intermediate representations in the rule engine, using these key item types:

- `AbstractRuleEngineRule`, a type for the abstract rules themselves
- `AbstractRulesModule`, a type for a container that holds reference to several abstract rules
- `AbstractRuleEngineContext`, a type for the parameters attached to abstract rules, checked when the rule is compiled or evaluated

The complete picture, from a type and extension perspective, looks like Figure 3.5 and Figure 3.6.

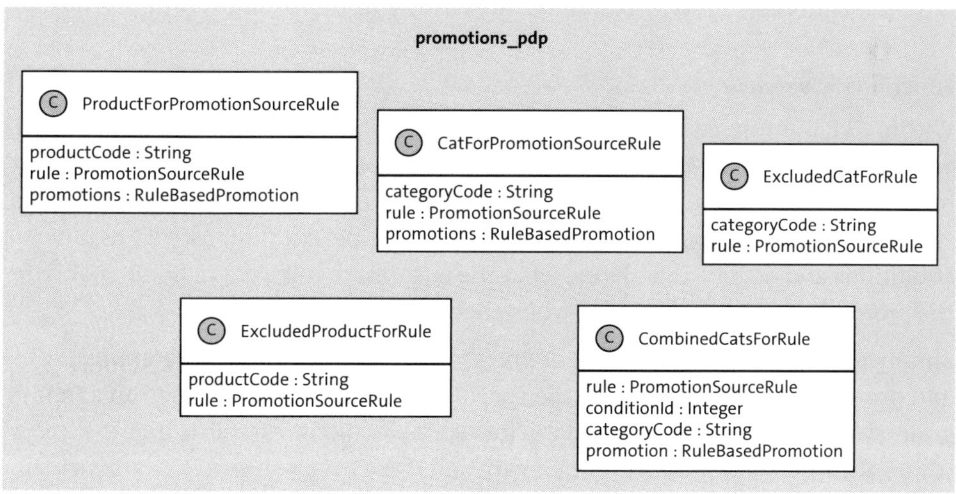

Figure 3.5 Data Model for Promotion Engine and Rule Engine: Part I

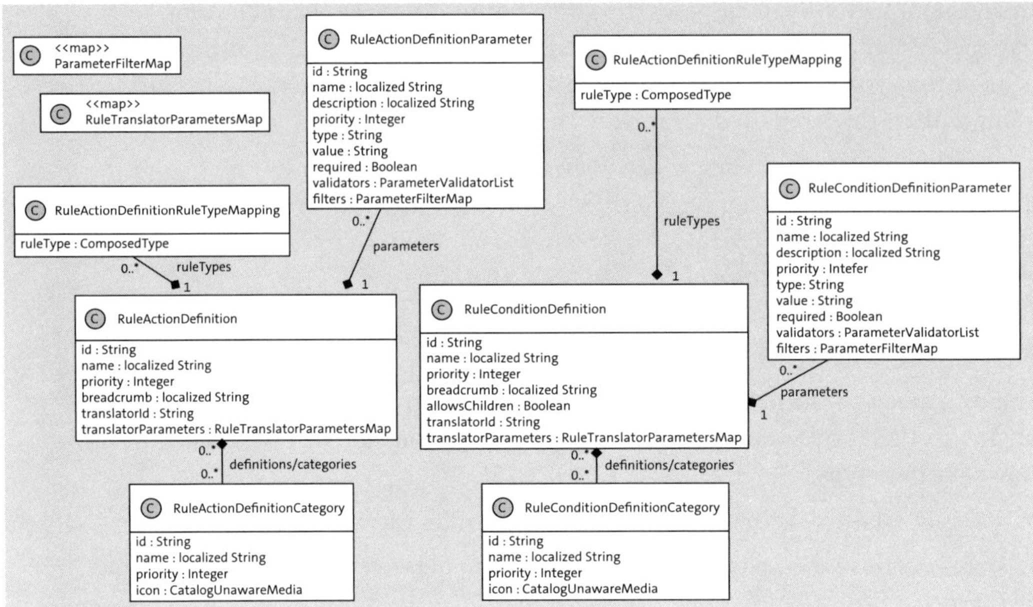

Figure 3.6 Data Model for Promotion Engine and Rule Engine: Part II

Of course, marketers can engage with the promotion engine without understanding any of that. From their point of view, there is no need to worry about the intermediate representations at all because they will be building abstract rules and then allowing the architecture described previously to do the rest.

Functional Overview

Within SAP Commerce itself, promotions come in two parts: promotion templates and promotion rules. Marketers begin the process of creating a promotion by creating a new promotion template or working from an existing one. This template contains some base attributes, such as a name and a description, as well as a set of conditions and actions that define what the customers will have to do to qualify for the promotion and what happens when they do.

Simply put, promotion templates define promotion types at a coarse-grained level, and promotion rules then define the specifics of an individual promotion at a fine-grained level. A promotion template, for example, might establish that if the customer adds a certain product to their cart, and if the total value of the cart is greater than a certain number, then they will receive a percentage discount on their entire order. A marketer would set these parameters and then click the **Create a Promotion Rule Based on This Template** button.

The promotion rule based on that template would then establish *which* product the customer would need to add to the cart, and exactly *what value* the cart would need to be greater than or equal to. Starting from the preceding example and referencing some SAP Commerce accelerators' sample data, we might say that if a customer buys the PowerShot 480 digital camera, and if the total value of his cart is greater than $200 (which would mean buying something else in addition to that camera), then he will receive 20% off of his order.

Here the marketer has a great deal of freedom in determining how the promotion will work and how it will be presented. She can drag and drop individual conditions and actions into the two appropriate fields in the *rule builder*, combining them in whatever way makes the most sense for the promotion being enabled. There is no hard, systemic limit on how many conditions or actions a marketer can add to a promotion—though as a matter of best practices, she should not complicate the offer any more than is necessary, both because it will increase the possibility of keystroke error when building the rule and because complicated promotions can be confusing to customers.

If the marketer wants to create some *and* or *or* logic within the conditions she's building, then they can do so using containers. Let's say that, in the preceding example, the customer should be able to qualify for the promotion by purchasing the PowerShot camera and spending $200 total, as described (in a simple example of *and* logic)—but that they could also qualify by purchasing a slightly more expensive camera, and that this would remove the cart value requirement (whether or not the cost of the upsell would put him above that original threshold). The marketer could achieve this by creating a container for the first set of conditions and a separate container for the second. The marketer would then set the actions to activate if the conditions in *either* container were to be met, effectively creating *or* logic.

Especially if the promotion is somewhat more complicated or conditional—as in the new version of our example, which is probably already skirting the edge of how much complexity most businesses will want to introduce—the marketer might also want to add a message to the promotion, as described earlier in this chapter. This message explains why the customer has received the deal or else what he would have to do to receive it.

In that latter case, which can be enormously powerful from the perspective of motivating customers to shop more or shop differently, the marketer would want to add a potential promotion to the promotion rule. To do this, they would add a *rule executed* condition to the rule.

This condition can check whether the customer has already qualified for some *other* promotion, to control stacking or encourage repeated transactions, but here we are instructing the system to check for whether the customer has already qualified for the promotion by entering the name of the promotion rule that we are currently working on and selecting **False** as the condition to check for, as shown in Figure 3.7. This allows us to tie an action to the state of a customer currently not qualifying for the promotion in question.

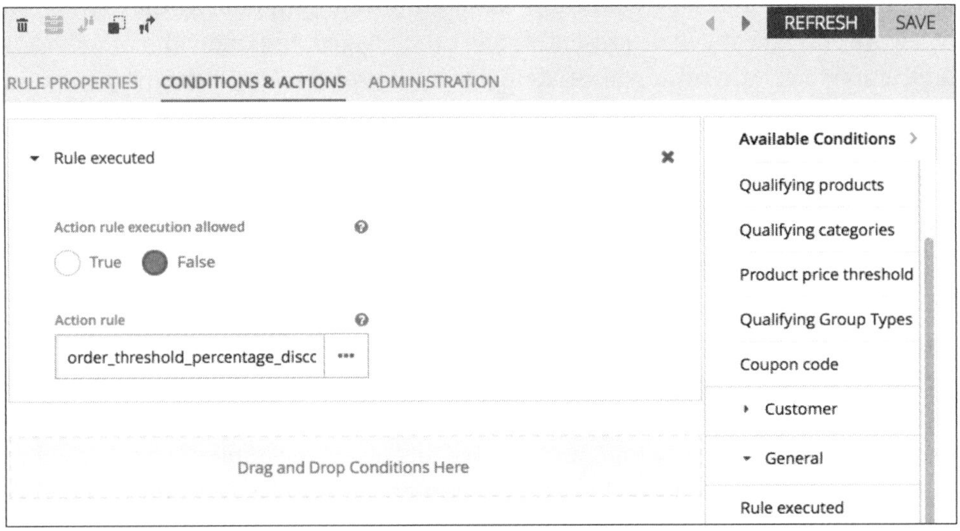

Figure 3.7 Adding the Condition for Potential Promotion to Promotion Rule in Rule Builder

The marketer would then add a trigger rule message action and enter a message explaining what the customer would need to do to qualify for the promotion. As discussed earlier, this message can contain numerical variables and can therefore be exact about the additional cart value and/or additional quantities of specific products needed to qualify.

When the marketer is ready to send the promotion live, she can click on the **Publish Promotion Rule for Module** button. Before publishing a promotion rule, however, the marketer will want to add it to a promotion group. These are simple functional groupings of promotions, most commonly used to associate a given storefront's promotions with that storefront to ensure that your apparel customers do not receive offers intended for your electronics customers, or vice versa. Promotions groups also can be used in a more targeted fashion, however. Promotions that use coupon codes, for example, are grouped under `couponPromotionRuleGroup` in the SAP Commerce, B2C accelerator storefronts.

Marketers with more data to work with and more specific ideas for segmentation might also use promotion groups to assign multiple promotion rules (and thus multiple promotions) to specific lines of business or groups of customers. They might, for example, have a group of promotions that is meant specifically for the members of a loyalty program or, more specifically still, for the gold tier members of that loyalty program. To achieve this, marketers would create that promotion group and then associate it with the user group that aligns with that program, tier, or other relevant segment.

If the marketer wants to create a new rule that is very close to an existing one but distinct in some specific aspect, then she can do so in one of two ways. First, she can clone the rule using the **Clone Promotion Rule** button. This will create a new promotion rule with a new name while keeping the old one exactly as it is. Alternately, she can save the current rule as an old version of the promotion by clicking the **Archive Rule Version** button.

This is useful if different iterations of the same promotion will run at different times throughout a marketing campaign, or if the business runs similar (but not identical) promotions annually or quarterly, or if the business simply wants to keep close track of which iteration of a given promotion was attached to a specific set of customer orders.

If the marketer has already published a rule and needs to remove it from the active storefront—either because it contains an error of some kind or because the business simply wants to discontinue it and did not set an end date in advance—then she can do so by clicking the **Undeploy Promotion Rule from Module** button.

These concepts of publishing and undeploying give the marketer or marketing department control of which rules are converted and compiled, moving from the promotion engine to the rule engine while explicitly exposing them only to the more user-friendly and abstract versions of the objects they are creating. In other words, it gives them access to the flexibility of the rule engine without asking them to engage with the full complexity of the rule engine.

Promotion Planning

Marketers can deploy groups of promotions on a schedule and, in accordance with a broader campaign plan, using the promotion planning tool in the backoffice. Promotion plans are also known as *campaigns* within the system, and they consist of one or more promotion rules (here also referred to as *source rules*), as well as a validity period and one or more restrictions. At its simplest, this feature allows marketers to set up several related promotions ahead of time and to schedule them centrally rather than having to set each promotion rule's validity period individually (and manually make sure that they are all synchronized to a single schedule).

Beyond this, however, campaigns in the promotion planning tool are campaigns in more than name. They allow marketers to introduce content and business logic within the same centralized, time-sensitive framework used for grouping promotion rules. In the SAP Commerce accelerators sample data, for example, there is an example called the Enjoy the Winter campaign, which has some promotion rules associated with winter apparel and adds a restriction called `[enjoy_winter_campaign]`. This restriction can be used in the same way that category or user group restrictions can, as described in Chapter 9. That is, they can be used to show or hide page components—or to make other business objects in SAP Commerce accessible or inaccessible—dynamically, based on whether a given customer qualifies for the promotions used as sources in the campaign.

If you have SAP Marketing Cloud, then these campaigns can and should be aligned to the campaign management tooling there. But if you are using SAP Commerce on its, own this feature still allows for a significant amount of segmentation, planning, and control from within the backoffice.

Coupon Management

If you are familiar with older versions of SAP Commerce, then you might remember the legacy promotions and coupon engines, which were indeed two separate extensions, each running its own logic for discounts—and you might remember the care necessary in making them work well together. In more recent versions of SAP Commerce, this is no longer the case, and coupons are simplified; they are simply one kind of condition that the marketer can add when creating promotion templates and promotion rules. In addition to checking for cart totals or products included in the order (or instead of doing so), the promotion engine can check for a valid coupon code.

Coupon codes come in two varieties: single code and multi code. *Single-code coupons*, as their name implies, are codes that can be used multiple times. As such, this can be an arbitrarily set and easily memorable code, commonly called a vanity code. Marketers can set how many times these codes can be redeemed on a given customer account and how many times they can be redeemed *total*, effectively setting a budget for the promotion to which they are attached.

Multicode coupons, as their name implies, are series of codes, each of which can only be used once. As such, the codes themselves are system-generated in whatever quantity the marketer specifies. The marketer can set a prefix for the series of codes—so that they are easily identifiable to customer support—and also can set the rules for the actual generation of the codes, determining the length of the code, as well as the number of segments in it and the character separating those segments (such as a dash), as shown in Figure 3.8.

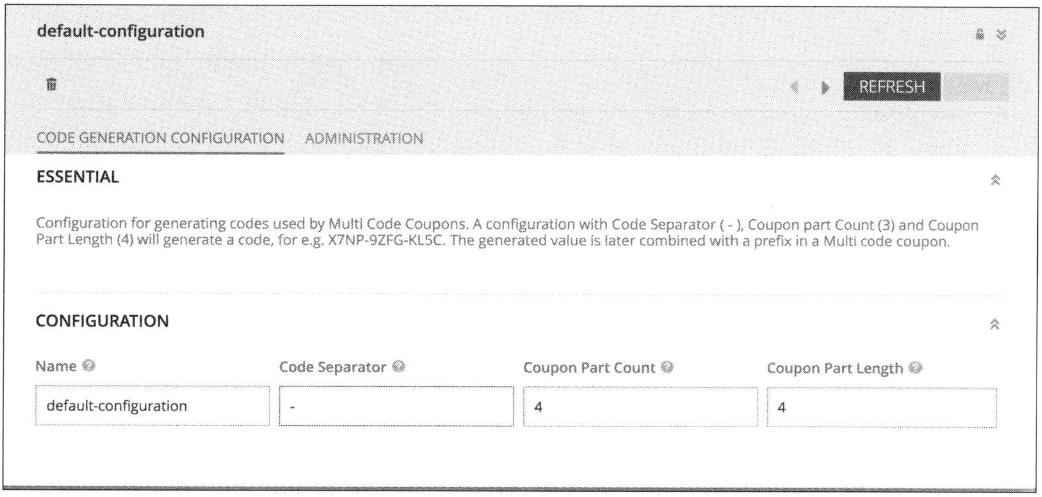

Figure 3.8 Multicode Generation Settings in Backoffice

Coupon functionality resides in the `commercefacades` extension, which uses `OrderAppliedVouchersPopulator` to retrieve the list of applied coupons in a given cart. `AcceleratorVoucherController`, meanwhile, interprets requests from the frontend JSP and invokes the `couponfacades` extension, as reflected in the data model shown in Figure 3.9.

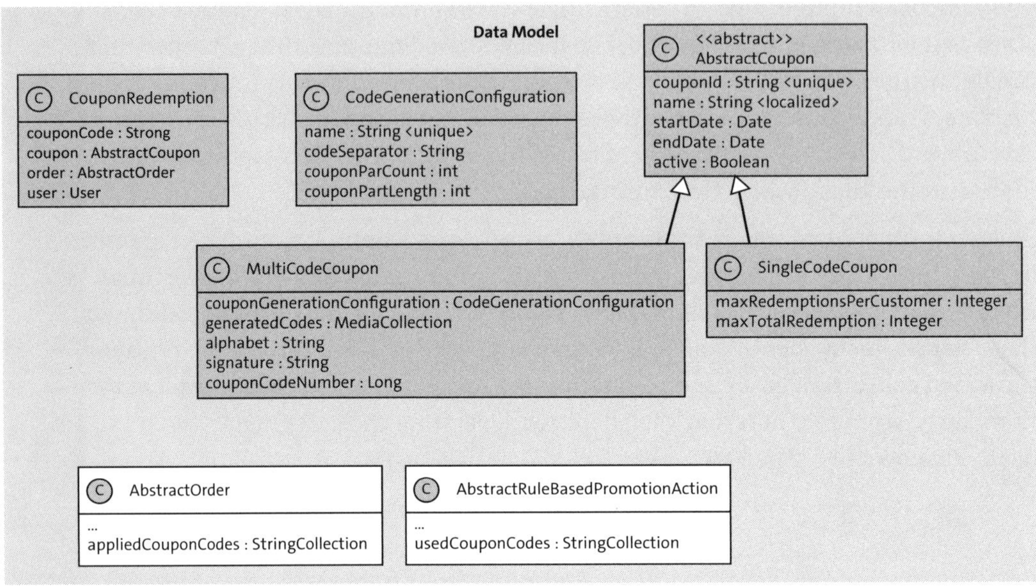

Figure 3.9 Data Model for Coupon Management

In the **Coupon Redemption** node of the **Coupon Management** settings in the backoffice, marketers can (if they have the appropriate permissions) see the orders that redeemed a particular coupon so that they can keep track.

Customer support can see this same information from the opposite direction, when viewing any orders that used a coupon code or received a promotional discount. This visibility is enormously useful when auditing the success rate of a promotion, and equally useful in scenarios in which, for example, each member of the customer support team is given a stack of multicode coupons for the purposes of appeasement, in which case knowing who used how many and why becomes vital.

3.5.3 Rule Engine

As we have discussed, rules in SAP Commerce exist primarily to enable promotions functionality. That was the reason that the new engine was introduced, and all the promotions and coupons that came preconfigured in older releases of SAP Commerce (along with several new ones) now come preconfigured in the rule engine.

With that said, however, the rules engine is a robust, flexible, and highly extensible framework in its own right. Much like SAP Commerce adaptive search, which is based on the open-source Solr search engine, the SAP Commerce rule engine is based on an open source, Java-based rules framework called Drools. Drools is capable of both forward chaining and backward chaining and supports the JSR-94 standard to facilitate enterprise-wide consistency and compliance.

Technical Overview

At the most abstract level, a Drools rule is composed of *conditions* and *actions*, which you can think of as the two halves of an if/then statement: If *x* happens, then *y* should happen. Whereas the *rule builder* is the interface, described earlier, in which business users can create and modify rules (promotional or otherwise) in the running SAP Commerce system, the *rule processor* is the component that executes those rules.

It should be clear why the concepts of conditions and actions and the relationship between them maps so well to promotions in SAP Commerce—and also why, natural as that fit may be, the underlying concepts and technologies need not be limited to that single use case within the system. Hopefully it's now *also* clear that when you are using the rule engine in a more expansive or project-specific way, you are necessarily moving away (but hopefully not too far away) from the structures already present in the SAP Commerce accelerators.

As shown in Figure 3.10, promotion rules in SAP Commerce are separated from the execution process by a layer of abstraction. That is, a backoffice user would never need to understand the finer points of Drools, nor indeed have any idea that the Drools engine is involved in promotion execution, to set up and maintain promotions and their templates.

It also means that Drools rules can be used on just about *any* SAP Commerce type, so long as that type is connected to a rule-aware object (RAO) in the rules engine. You don't need to limit yourself to products, prices, promotions, and carts because Drools can also act on customers and business units, pages and components, segments, and search profiles. These nonpromotion examples do not come out of the box, to be clear. But they involve leveraging the framework that is already in place for promotions, rather than introducing some other set of conventions to layer on top of the existing one.

As such, extensions to the rule engine will likely use the rule-aware objects already in the system—the ones built and configured around promotions—as their basis in terms of design, even when the goal has very little to do with promotions, pricing, or even products.

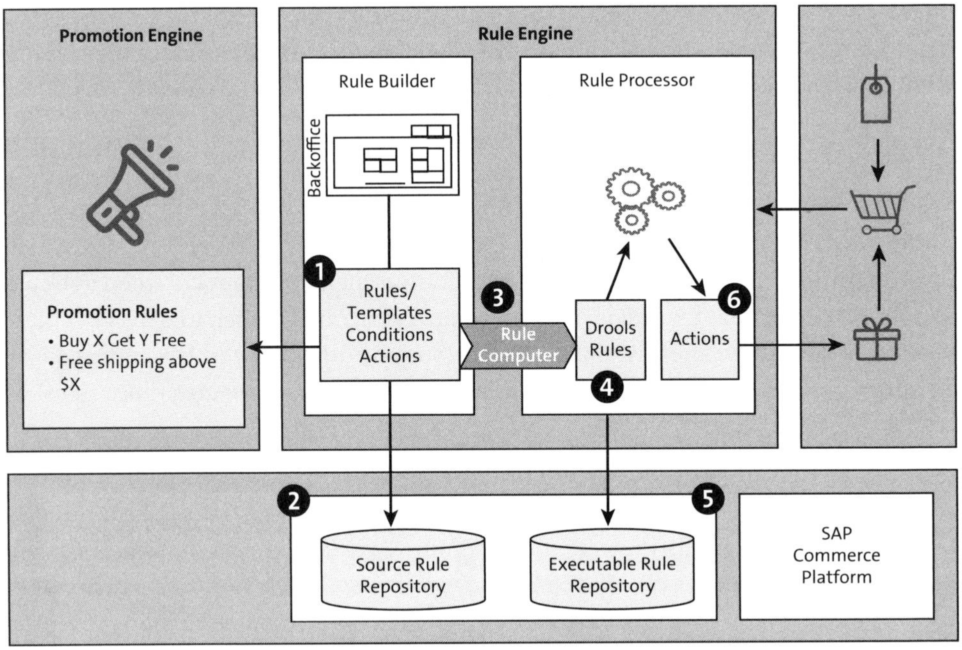

Figure 3.10 Data Flow of Promotions through Drools-Based Rule Processor

With that in mind, let's look at how Drools interacts with SAP Commerce from a technical perspective. The relations among rule-aware objects in the promotion engine appear as shown in Figure 3.11.

To break that monster of a diagram down a bit, rule-aware objects are *plain old Java objects* (POJOs) generated using beans.xml in a process common to bean and enum generation in many areas of the SAP Commerce suite. Rule-aware objects in SAP Commerce use Drools' `RAOProvider` approach, extending `AbstractActionedRAO` to deliver subclasses such as `ProductRAO` and `CartRAO`.

To make this process work well in an SAP Commerce context, you will want to implement your own `equals()` and `hascode()` methods, rather than using the Drools defaults. This allows you to retain control over runtime behavior and improves performance by avoiding the reflection-based approach of the default `equals()` and `hascode()` methods.

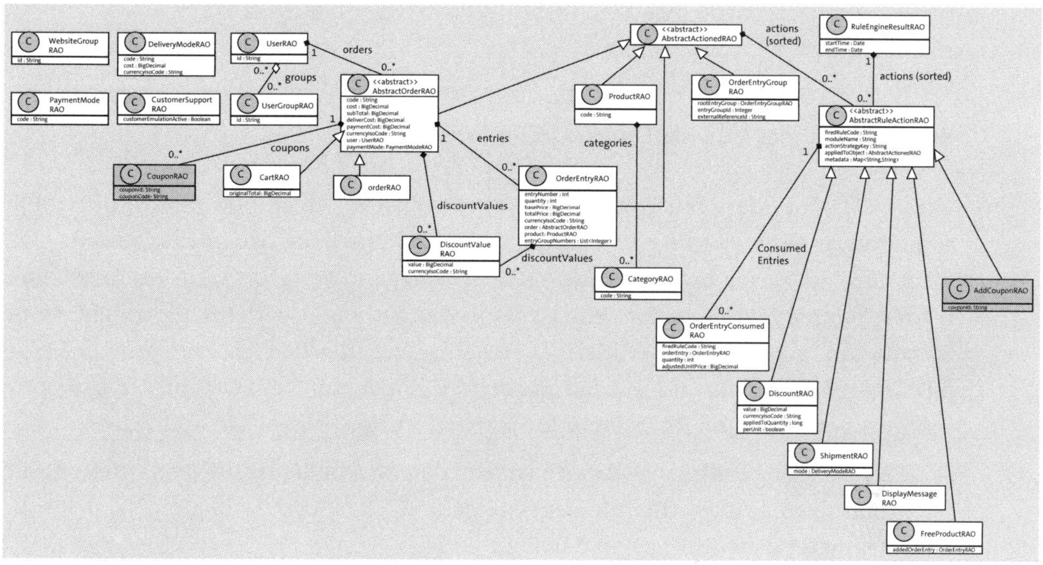

Figure 3.11 Rule-Aware Objects in Promotion Engine

You can set your `equals()` and `hascode()` methods for a given object in the *ruleengine-services-beans.xml* file. Listing 3.5 shows the appropriate settings for the promotions-centric `OrderEntryRAO` rule-aware object.

```
<bean class="de.hybris.platform.ruleengineservices.rao.OrderEntryRAO"
      extends="de.hybris.platform.ruleengineservices.rao.AbstractActionedRAO">
<property name="entryNumber" type="java.lang.Integer" equals="true"/>
<property name="quantity" type="int" />
<property name="basePrice" type="java.math.BigDecimal" />
<property name="totalPrice" type="java.math.BigDecimal" />
<property name="currencyIsoCode" type="String" />
<property name="order"
          type="de.hybris.platform.ruleengineservices.rao.AbstractOrderRAO"
          equals="true"/>
<property name="product"
          type="de.hybris.platform.ruleengineservices.rao.ProductRAO" />
<property name="discountValues"
          type="java.util.List&lt;de.hybris.platform.ruleengineservices.rao.
                DiscountValueRAO>" />
<property name="orderEntryGroups"
```

```
type="java.util.List&lt;de.hybris.platform.ruleengineservices.rao.
      OrderEntryGroupRAO>" />
</bean>
```

Listing 3.5 Settings for OrderEntryRAO Rule-Aware Object

These RAO providers retrieve the rule-aware objects (which you might think of as *condition RAOs*) according to the parameters defined in two files, *de.hybris.platform.ruleengineservices.rao.providers.RAOProvider* and *de.hybris.platform.ruleengineservices.rao.providers.ExpandedRAOProvider*, and then use them to trigger some activity on action RAOs, which are themselves defined in the *de.hybris.platform.ruleengineservices.rule.evaluation.actions.RAOAction* file. Out of the box, promotions-centric action RAOs include `DiscountRAO`, `FreeProductRAO`, and `ShipmentRAO`.

With that understanding, we can revisit the diagram in Figure 3.11 and differentiate (in Drools terminology) the rule runtime data (RRD), shown in Figure 3.12, from the rule parameter data (RPD), shown in Figure 3.13.

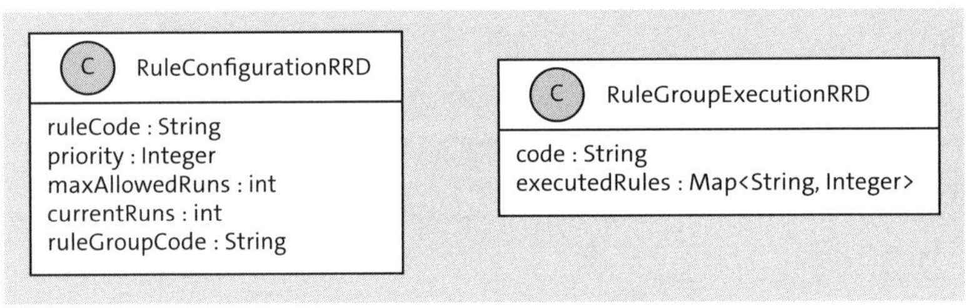

Figure 3.12 Rule Runtime Data in Rule-Aware Objects Diagram

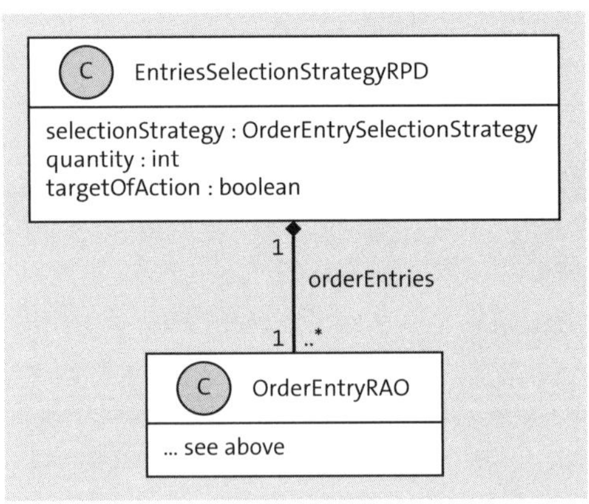

Figure 3.13 Rule Runtime Data in Rule-Aware Objects Diagram

That is, you should now be able to differentiate an RAO referring to a condition from one referring to an action and to understand how each RAO relates to an SAP Commerce type or business object.

Rule Builder and Compiler

To manage its relevant data objects, Drools uses an overall framework called *knowledge is everything* (KIE). An interface called KieBase manages Drools' knowledge definitions, which encompass the processes and internal types that drive rules in the system, as well as the rules themselves.

Different rules run on different KIE modules, which we can invoke in SAP Commerce using the `RuleType` attribute in the `AbstractRulesModule` extension. The four most important objects to keep in mind when working with this extension are as follows:

1. `DroolsKIEModule`, an SAP Commerce representation of `KIEModule` in Drools, which holds the resources necessary to define a set of `KIEBases`
2. `DroolsKIEBase`, an SAP Commerce representation of `KIEBase` in Drools, a repository for all your applications' knowledge definitions
3. `DroolsKIESession`, an SAP Commerce representation of `KIESession` in Drools, which (as the name implies) creates a running session for retrieving, evaluating, and executing rules
4. `DroolsRuleEngineContext`, which provides input to the SAP Commerce `ruleengineservice` extension as to what rule evolution should be done during the current `DroolsKIESession`

As you can see, most of these extensions serve to bridge the gap between SAP Commerce objects and corresponding Drools objects. This same concept extends to the two most important tools that SAP Commerce uses to manage Drools rules: the rule compiler and the rule builder.

Rule builder is the drag-and-drop interface provided in SAP Commerce for building promotions. Once other objects have been made rule-aware, this same tool can be used similarly with those objects. Once again, however, our examples will focus on promotions because their data types are the ones that come enabled out of the box.

A rule evaluates conditions in the context of one or more parameters and then executes actions accordingly, as shown in Figure 3.14.

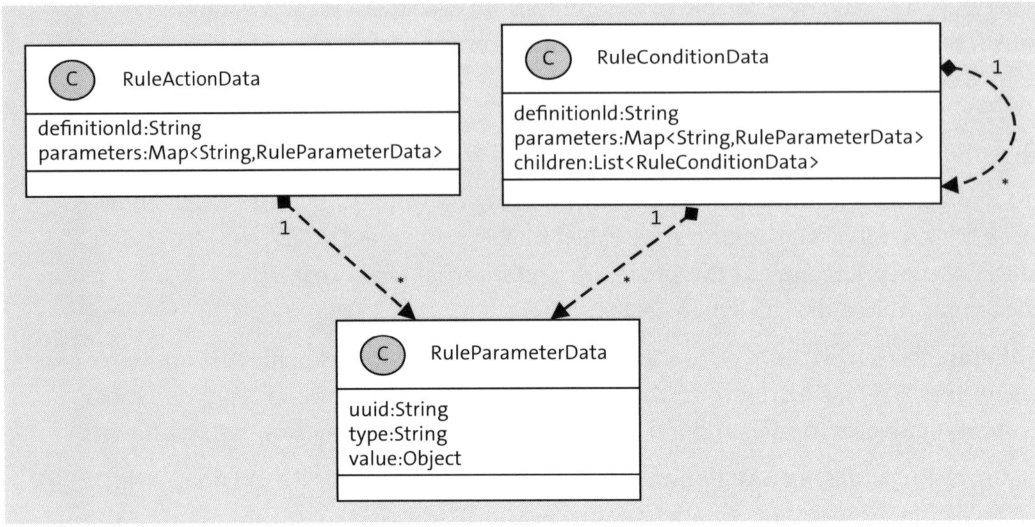

Figure 3.14 Relations between Types for Condition and Action Data Model

As you can see, this data flow involves three major SAP Commerce objects. First, there is `RuleConditionData`, which defines the conditions of the rule. As an example, Listing 3.6 shows the "the total value of the cart must be greater than or equal to $100" condition, expressed in JSON.

```
[
  {
    "definitionId": "cart_total",
    "parameters":{
          "value":{
                "uuid":"b07060b4-bcb0-4016-b778-e3c566051df4",
                "type":"Map(ItemType(Currency),java.math.BigDecimal)",
                "value":{
                   "USD":500
                }
          },
          "operator":{
                "uuid":"c3217773-9e3b-4b22-8251-c4626251d854",
                "type":"Enum(de.hybris.platform.ruledefinitions.AmountOperator
)",
                "value":"GREATER_THAN_OR_EQUAL"
          }
```

```
    },
     "children": [

    ]
  }
]
```

Listing 3.6 Condition Expressed in JSON

Next there is `RuleAction`, which defines what should happen as a result of the conditions being met. Listing 3.7 shows "apply a 50% discount to the cart total," once again expressed in JSON.

```
[
   {
        "definitionId":"change_delivery_mode",
        "parameters":{
                "delivery_mode":{
                          "uuid":"f24a89ee-b418-4418-b8a9-30738728f9f9",
                          "type":"ItemType(DeliveryMode)",
                          "value":"free-standard-shipping"
                }
        }
   }
]
```

Listing 3.7 Action Expressed in JSON

Finally, there is `RuleConditionValidator`, which allows you to set parameters on the evaluation of the conditions and the execution of the actions. These parameters are most commonly used to check for bad data, prevent erroneous transactions, and provide messaging when errors occur. In Listing 3.8, for example, `RuleQualifyingCategoriesConditionTranslator` and `RuleQualifyingProductsConditionTranslator` are ensuring that all the required attributes have valid values and that all numbers being evaluated are positive integers.

```
public void validate(final RuleCompilerContext context, final RuleActionData
  action, final RuleActionDefinitionData actionDefinition) throws
  RuleCompilerException
    {
```

```
        ...
        ruleContainerValidator.validateContainerId(context, containerId,
          errorMessage, actionDefinition, qualifyingContainerParam,
          qualifyingContainerParamDef);
        ruleContainerValidator.validateContainerExists(context, containerId,
          errorMessage, actionDefinition, qualifyingContainerParam,
          qualifyingContainerParamDef);
        ...
    }
```

Listing 3.8 Example of RuleConditionValidator

This is what is being called behind the scenes when a backoffice user drags and drops a condition or action into place. Conditions and actions in the backoffice become conditions and actions in Drools, fairly directly.

There is, however, one important intermediate step—namely, the rule compiler. Simply put, the rule compiler converts high-level, easily editable representations of rules, as built in SAP Commerce, into a representation that Drools can actually run behind the scenes.

The rule compiler translates the high-level rules into what is called an *intermediate representation* (IR). The terminology here is frankly a bit confusing, so stick with us. The `RuleConditionsTranslator` helper interface calls the `RuleConditionTranslator` interface (note the change in pluralization from *conditions* to *condition*) and uses the parameters in `RuleConditionData` to evaluate and translate the condition data. Likewise, the `RuleActionsTranslator` helper interface calls the `RuleActionTranslator` interface (once again, note the very subtly different name) and uses the parameters in `RuleActionData` to evaluate and translate the action data. Next, the compilation is validated by the `RuleCompilerContext` extension. This step is in fact what you are seeing in the code snippet in Listing 3.8, in which the system checks for errors in the rule based on the established parameters.

If you want to alter or extend the rule compiler's logic, then you can do so in `RuleCompilerContext.class` by generating a new `PromotionRuleCompilerListener` and making sure that the `beforeCompile` method is registered in the system. In Listing 3.9, we are doing so for the cart, website, and a few other promotional attributes.

```
public class PromotionRuleCompilerListener implements RuleCompilerListener
{
    @Override
```

```
    public void beforeCompile(final RuleCompilerContext context) throws
      RuleCompilerException
    {
        if (context.getRule() instanceof PromotionSourceRuleModel)
        {
            context.generateVariable(CartRAO.class);
            context.generateVariable(RuleEngineResultRAO.class);
            context.generateVariable(WebsiteGroupRAO.class);
        }
    }
    ...
}
```

Listing 3.9 Example of Extending Rule Compiler's Logic

Rule Engine Extensibility

Extending the rule engine beyond its defaults, and especially extending it beyond its primary purpose in the SAP Commerce accelerators—namely, defining and executing promotions—means understanding a bit about how Drools applies logic to objects. More importantly, it means understanding how a business object in SAP Commerce relates to the data handling in Drools and what adjustments the SAP Commerce product team has elected to make in order to make Drools run better in the technical and functional context of an SAP Commerce implementation. Hopefully you now have a better grasp of those features; now, let's look at the extensions driving them.

The key extensions included in the Drools framework for SAP Commerce are as follows:

- **`droolsruleengineservices`**
  This defines Drools-specific item types to run on top of the `ruleengineservices` extension.
- **`ordercalculation`**
  This processes order calculations in memory (to avoid database operations and optimize performance).
- **`rulebuilderbackoffice`**
  This enables and defines the user interface for creating and editing rules.
- **`ruledefinitions`**
  This implements the strategies, translators, and wrappers from the source rule

format to intermediate rule representations, which can then be compiled in Drools syntax and run.

- **droolsruleengineservices**
  This defines Drools-specific item types to run on top of the ruleengineservices extension.
- **ruleengine**
  This includes definitions for the basic item types needed for running Drools (but no SAP Commerce functionality whatsoever).
- **ruleengineatddtests**
  This contains the acceptance test-driven development (ATDD) files for testing sample data related to rules (with dependencies on the atddimpex and drulesruleengineservices extensions).
- **ruleenginebackoffice**
  This defines actions for compiling and deploying rules, as well as customizations for the ruleengine, ruleengineservices, and droolsruleengineservices extensions.
- **ruleengineservices**
  This defines and implements SAP Commerce-specific functionality on top of the base Drools functionality.

Most rule-aware objects are implemented in ruleengineservices; if you plan on customizing rule behavior, then your efforts will be focused largely on this extension, keeping in mind the dependencies shown in Figure 3.15.

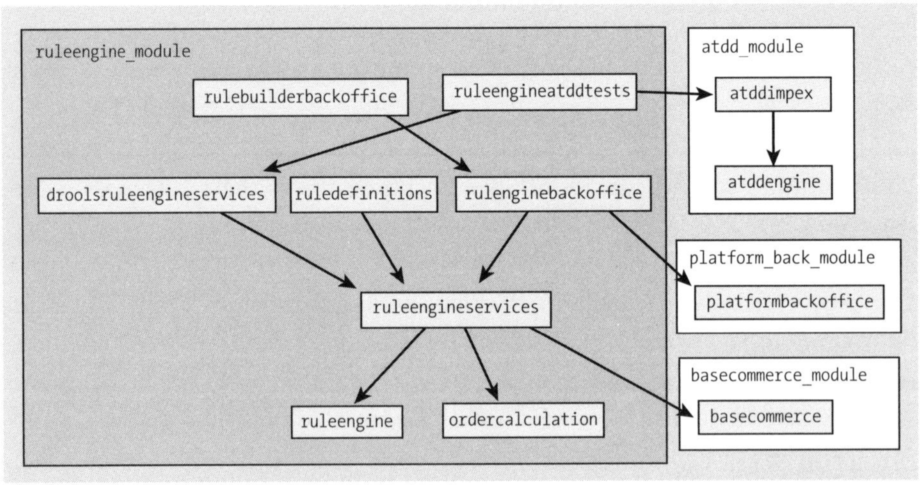

Figure 3.15 Extension Dependencies in Rule Engine

3.6 SAP Commerce Accelerator Storefronts

The SAP Commerce accelerators are a sample instance that ships with the SAP Commerce suite. The idea is to give you roughly 80% of what you need to get an SAP Commerce storefront up and running on the web—from homepages to product listing pages and product detail pages, from search functionality to cart functionality, from banners to carousels to text to menus.

The remaining 20% comes from the fact that the SAP Commerce accelerators do need to be hooked up to a payment gateway, for example—and more importantly, the SAP Commerce accelerators still need your configurations and data. Having an SAP Commerce website is of limited use if it doesn't function well as *your* SAP Commerce website, after all. Getting your product data entered into the system, setting up the account and checkout processes to align with your internal processes and expectations and configuring the site to look and feel the way your business wants it to look and feel is a necessary step even in those projects that launch with a feature set very close to that of the SAP Commerce accelerators. The SAP Commerce accelerators are a rapid and effective way of getting started and of staying close to the SAP Commerce product roadmap—and the SAP Commerce accelerators achieve this balance between speed and flexibility by offering a variety of storefronts.

SAP Commerce accelerator storefronts are different configurations of this sample instance, the SAP Commerce accelerators, covering use cases and verticals that range from B2C retail to B2B distribution to subscription-based telco and digital media packages. All these storefronts share a codebase and a set of base extensions, but each has one of more of its own storefront-specific add-ons, as well as its own sample data. These storefronts are sometimes referred to simply as SAP Commerce accelerators, despite there technically being only one "accelerator" underlying them all.

Some of these configurations are quite specific to the verticals that they serve. The forms functionality for financial services projects are unlikely to be of much use when selling apparel. But most of the SAP Commerce accelerators' functionality is broadly applicable and useful, and even some of the more particular functionality can and should be used in projects for which it was not originally intended. We thought of replenishment orders as particular to B2B until we discovered that B2C customers like a "subscribe and save" model just as much. If you are willing to be inventive, then you might be surprised just how much of the SAP Commerce accelerators functionality you can use and equally surprised about who that functionality was originally built for.

In this section, we will discuss the SAP Commerce accelerators codebase, the different storefronts that sit on top of it, and the roles that different SAP Commerce accelerators configurations and different sets of SAP Commerce accelerators sample data should play in your implementation.

3.6.1 Extensions and Add-Ons

SAP Commerce accelerator storefronts are built on Spring's model-view-controller (MVC) framework, which itself is built on the Java platform. As discussed in Chapter 2, this means that the core concepts of Java-based application development (such as object orientation, as reflected in the SAP Commerce type system) and many of the specifics of Spring (such as inversion of control) underlie the SAP Commerce accelerators framework. A working knowledge of these technologies will go a long way toward empowering developers to extend the platform. SAP Commerce–specific development knowledge is required, but Java and Spring experience on your team will mean having to learn fewer of the basics.

Accelerator storefronts are closely coupled with the core platform in SAP Commerce and, following the MVC model, they are composed of extensions for customer frontends, backend configuration, and underlying logic—all working together while remaining, to a certain degree, operationally distinct. It is important to assign the correct functionality to the correct level, rather than, for example, placing important business logic at the view level.

All the accelerator storefronts run on a common set of shared extensions:

- `acceleratorstorefrontcommons`, which governs automated data import, email generation, payment, and fulfillment
- `yacceleratorfulfilmentprocess`, which manages the process of order fulfillment (discussed in more detail in Chapter 6)
- `yacceleratorcockpits`, which provides storefront-related functionality in the employee-facing backoffice interface
- `acceleratocms`, which specifically controls the creation and editing of web pages within the built-in SAP Commerce CMS
- `yaddon`, which enables other functionality in the selected accelerator storefront via add-ons

The dependencies associated with these core dependencies are shown in Figure 3.16.

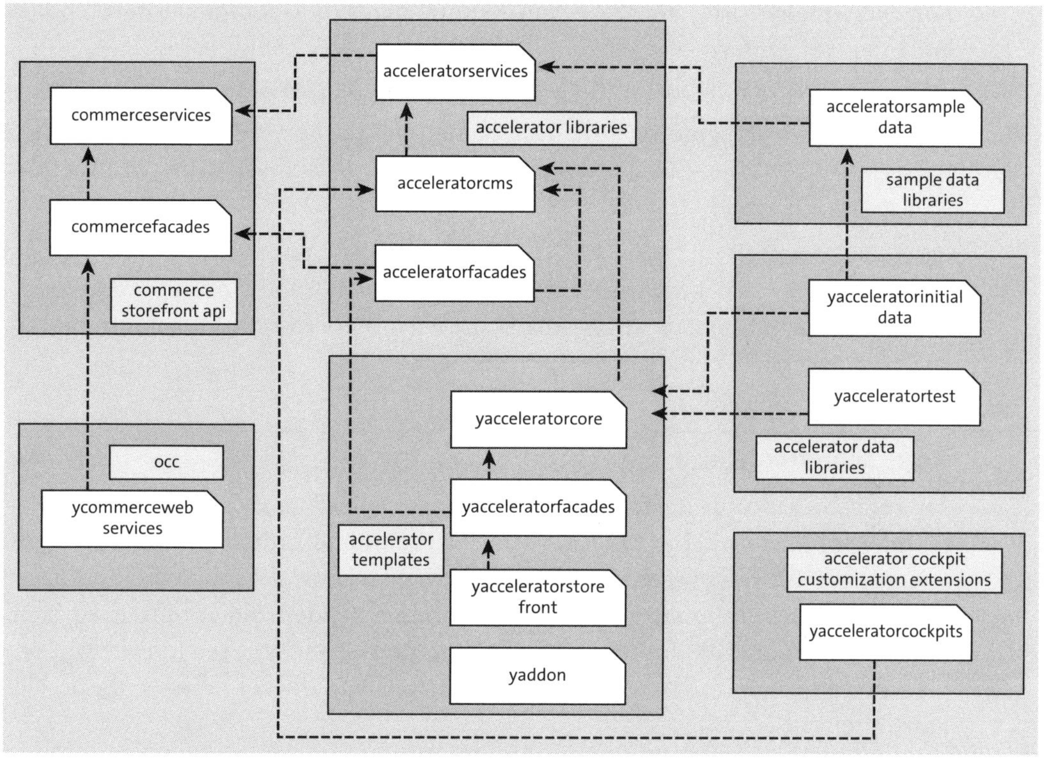

Figure 3.16 Extension Dependencies in SAP Commerce Accelerators

As discussed in Chapter 1, Section 1.2.3, *add-ons* are lightweight SAP Commerce extensions built to be deployed with as few dependencies as possible. Accelerator storefronts use add-ons to build on top of the shared base of accelerator extensions: `yacceleratorstorefront` for B2C storefronts and `yb2bacceleratorstorefront` for B2B storefronts, for example. Two additional extensions enable the add-on structure: `yaddon` and `addonsupport`. These, along with captchaaddon for reCAPTCHA support, are included in every accelerator storefront in addition to the extensions listed previously.

SAP Commerce is frontend-agnostic in principle; customers have successfully integrated third-party frontend/content management solutions such as Adobe Experience Manager and created their own frontends in AngularJS, Ruby on Rails, .NET, or pure HTML5. In each of these cases, SAP Commerce communicates with the frontend via an API, Omni Commerce Connect (OCC), for transactions. This means that any non-accelerators-based approach will require significant additional development and integration effort.

These other frontends are sometimes legacy websites that are replaced by the SAP Commerce accelerators in a later phase. Sometimes they exist alongside an accelerator storefront. In other cases, however, they are indeed deployed in lieu of an accelerator storefront.

Based on your project, a non-SAP Commerce accelerator storefront can be the right approach if the project requirements do not overlap well with any of the accelerator storefronts on offer—so next we will discuss what these storefronts contain, and the key differences between them.

3.6.2 Storefronts

All storefronts include default page templates, sample data, and some form of transnationality, but browsing, search, carts, checkout, and orders are tailored to the appropriate verticals of each in terms of structure and flow. Although this book is not intended to serve as product documentation, it *is* intended to help you make useful decisions in your SAP Commerce implementation—so in this section, we will provide an overview of the key features and functional differences between the accelerator storefronts.

Although it is entirely possible to mix and match functionality from various accelerator storefronts—and the process for doing so is often as simple as knowing which add-ons enable which functionality—most projects will select a single storefront as a starting point. Selecting the right one will save you a great deal of rework later on.

There are two categories of accelerator storefronts: core and additional.

Core Accelerators

Core storefronts are generally designed to cover a wide variety of business requirements and are built, upgraded, and maintained internally by the SAP Commerce Cloud product team. These include two B2C storefronts (the electronics store and the apparel store), as well as one B2B storefront (the powertools store), and one storefront focused on subscriptions and digital goods (the telco and media accelerator).

The B2C storefronts allow customers to create accounts for themselves and to transact via integration with a payment gateway (CyberSource by default). They prominently feature cross-sells, upsells, and featured product carousels, as well as page layouts conducive to media-heavy promotion campaigns. They also feature a customer support self-service interface, in which customers can check an order's status, initiate returns, or request support (which will create a ticket behind the scenes).

The electronics store and the apparel store demonstrate two different modes of B2C product modeling. In the electronics store, most products are base products with no variants, and their attributes come from the type system. In the apparel store, most purchasable products are variants—when you buy a T-shirt, you generally buy a T-shirt in a specific color and size, after all—and the attributes come largely from the classification system. (For a more detailed explanation of these two attribute structures, please see Chapter 4, Section 4.1.4.)

The B2B storefront, by contrast, incorporates purchase orders, replenishment orders, quote negotiation, quick cart building via SKU entry or spreadsheet upload, order approval via workflow, and payment via purchase orders and cost centers. To enable this functionality, the powertools store also introduces a user account self-administration interface for purchasing organizations, as we will discuss in Chapter 9 when we dig into user permissions and authorization. In short, the B2B storefront allows administrators within a purchasing organization to manage their own buyers, budgets, and cost center associations, thereby reducing the management burden on the selling organization and increasing value for the end users of the site.

There are two notable variations on the B2C storefronts, generally considered storefronts in their own right. First, there is *SAP Commerce, accelerator for China*, a variant of the electronics store with native integration for social networks such as Weibo and payment providers such as Alipay, as well as a denser layout and an emphasis on flash sale promotions. The changes are intended to conform with the design expectations of Chinese customers and, just as importantly, to enable the functionality that customers and business owners alike have come to expect on what is, in some ways, a parallel internet—all without abandoning the base extensions that underlie the other accelerator storefronts.

Second, there is the *marketplace store* (shown in Figure 3.17), a business-to-business-to-customer (B2B2C) solution that includes electronics and apparel products in a single storefront managed by multiple product managers in the backoffice vendor portal. In addition to surfacing a combined product catalog for customers on the marketplace storefront, this storefront models secure, manageable access for vendors or other partner organizations that need to add or edit certain key product data—but who are external and therefore should not be provided with full employee accounts.

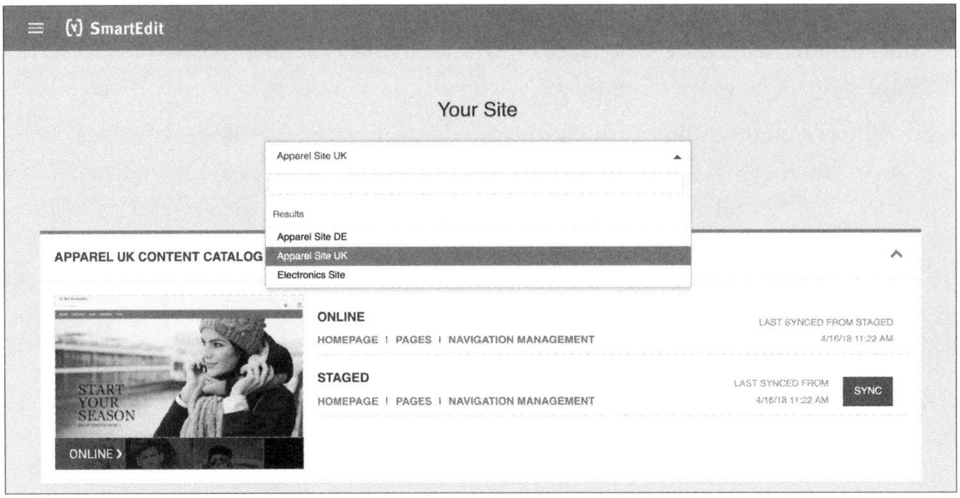

Figure 3.17 SmartEdit Showing Multiple Core Accelerator Storefronts

SAP introduced this configuration after seeing numerous B2B2C customers simply giving their vendors access to their backend interfaces, which is not an especially safe idea in any case but is especially problematic because it required them to let vendors into their office network via VPN, thereby increasing the number of potential points of failure for the security of the site and its data. As with so many of the features in the accelerator storefronts, the product team introduced this feature with a relatively narrow use in mind but is quickly discovering that it has broader appeal to any organization that has multiple semi-autonomous brands or that is looking to update or replace an old, spreadsheet-based system of product creation and enrichment involving multiple vendors.

Additional Accelerators

Additional SAP Commerce accelerators generally focus on more specific use cases and/or industries that display, sell, or fulfill products in ways not covered by the core SAP Commerce accelerators. This is not to say that their functionality is useful *only* in the vertical for which they were built, but it does mean that their added value tends to be a bit less broadly applicable than that of the core SAP Commerce accelerators.

Additional SAP Commerce accelerators are built, upgraded, and maintained by SAP's implementation partners, rather than by the internal SAP Commerce Cloud or SAP C/4HANA product team; as such, they generally incorporate lessons learned on real projects in the applicable verticals.

The SAP Commerce, financial services accelerator (shown in Figure 3.18) is built for businesses such as insurance companies and banks that need to consume a large amount of customer information before providing a quote. They use *yForms*, a set of functionality based on Orbeon Forms, to consume this information and offer what you see is what you get (WYSIWYG) editing tools to business users in the backoffice. yForms allows for dynamic form filling based on known customer information and is dynamic in the sense that it can show or hide fields based on previous answers in the process.

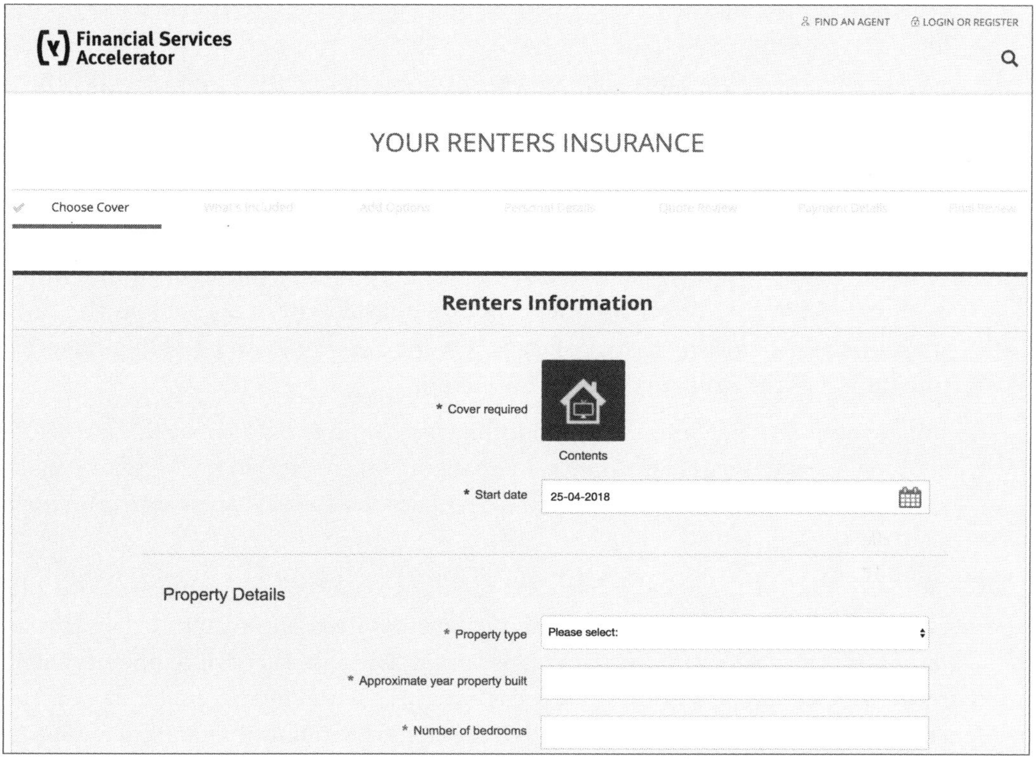

Figure 3.18 yForms in Insurance Store in SAP Commerce, Financial Services Accelerator

This accelerator actually comes with two storefronts, the insurance store and the banking store, with the former focusing on policies and claims and the latter focusing on accounts and inquiries. In addition, the insurance store offers *find an agent* functionality for searching for selling representatives and customer support agents, as well as store locations and products, and storing and surfacing information about these individuals.

The SAP Commerce, citizen engagement accelerator is built for government agencies at the state, city, or local level and those who work with such agencies. Like the financial services accelerator, the citizen engagement accelerator uses yForms to securely consume and store user information. It allows individual citizens to make service requests or pay bills within the web storefront—for themselves or on behalf of someone else—and comes with bespoke integrations for SAP ERP and SAP CRM, along with API hooks specific to billing and receipts.

The SAP Commerce, travel accelerator is built for airlines, railway companies, and other businesses that sell tickets tied to time and place. Like the SAP Commerce, financial services accelerator, the travel accelerator ships with multiple separate storefronts. The airline store sells tickets, the hotel store rents rooms, and the travel store does both—presenting the opportunity for packaged deals and offering a flexible data model for other businesses that traverse those lines, such as event planners and cruise lines.

In addition to enabling recurring charges and conditional authorization via the subscription billing gateway, the SAP Commerce, telco and media accelerator allows a user to order digital or subscription goods alongside physical goods in the same transaction—by creating a "cart of carts" behind the scenes and dividing the order into multiple consignments prior to fulfillment.

Unlike the core accelerators, these additional accelerators do not necessarily include a faceted product search. Insurance and banking businesses do not generally maintain product catalogs as such, for example—hence the use of yForms for the financial services accelerator.

Similarly, the SAP Commerce, telco and media accelerator uses a guided selling process in place of a traditional search and navigation flow. The customer selects a cell phone, say, and then sees the data plans compatible with that cell phone—followed by additional options, followed by accessories. Each step in this guided bundle can change the availability and/or pricing of the steps that follow it, thereby allowing for a significant amount of steering for the customer.

3.6.3 Sample Data and Configurations

Accelerator storefronts should be considered examples of best practices in terms of development, but not necessarily in terms of configuration. The electronics store, for example, has four languages enabled by default—English, German, Chinese, and Japanese—and its search index contains all four of these languages, configured so that the internationalized data is maintained centrally and a customer only sees search results in the language in which she is currently browsing.

The multilingual search index has been set up in accordance with best practices, but the index itself is simply a sample, not a best practice. Customers who do not have data in German or Chinese or Japanese, do not need their Solr index to include values in German, Chinese, or Japanese—and though this may seem like an obvious point, we've seen multiple customers whose search performance was suffering specifically because they had the default accelerator indexes in place and were therefore indexing thousands of valueless attributes.

Likewise, the SAP Commerce, B2C accelerator storefronts include a wide variety of customer self-service widgets, covering account management, consent management, password changes, order status, returns, and so on. (A top-level menu for these features is shown in Figure 3.19.) Most projects will use some of these, but not all of them. Even if your project uses every one of these out-of-the-box features—and it very well might—it probably would not display the options in the way that they are displayed by default. Screens might be combined, for example. Again, the features are enabled and offered according to best practices, but the frankly overstuffed menu showing *every* possible option is not itself considered a best practice.

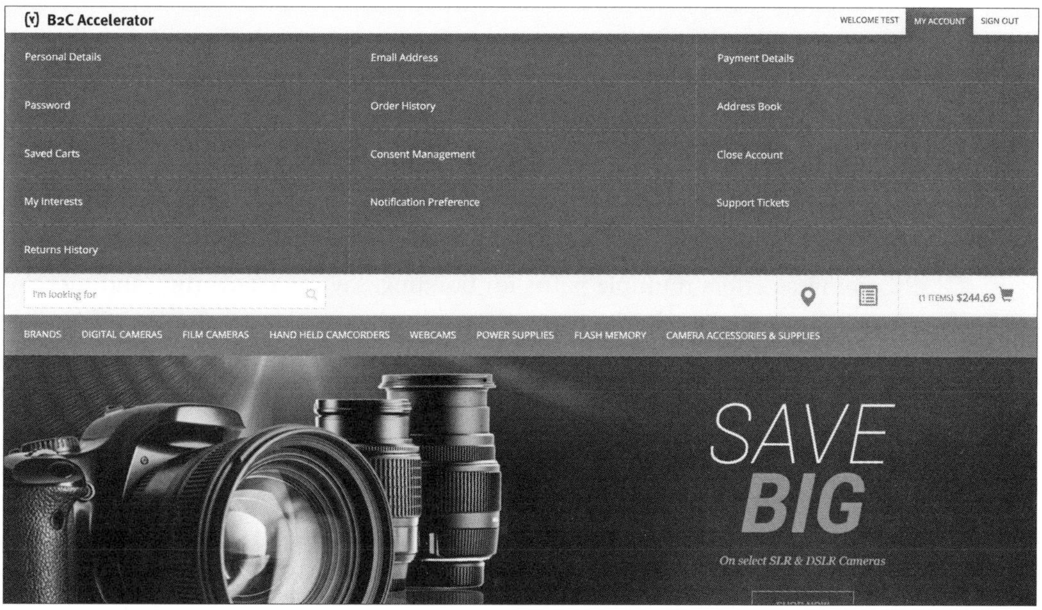

Figure 3.19 Customer Support Self-Service in Electronics Store

Accelerators' sample data also includes some default user groups and sample users. These are intended as examples of good user group modeling and as a means to begin testing as quickly as possible. However, you will almost certainly want to remove all the sample users from the system before launch, and you will most likely remove or significantly alter most of the default user groups as well.

As we will discuss in Chapter 9, your user groups should align with the segments into which your business sorts customers and the roles that your team members take on in day-to-day operations—and it is rare for these to align perfectly with default settings. B2C accelerator sample data takes it for granted, for example, that product content management and web content management are the responsibilities of two separate teams, and the sample user groups reflect this.

If your project involves users who frequently work with products *and* pages, promotions *and* search ranking, then you will probably want a user group that reflects this rather than adding a large number of users to a large number of overlapping groups, each with its own potentially conflicting permissions. Multiple user group memberships are not an issue. What presents an issue is creating a data structure that does not reflect the organization it was intended to serve.

Personalization is a major topic of its own—and to begin discussing it, in the next chapters we will dive into product management and then into customer experience management. Here the core SAP Commerce functionality we've been discussing will allow us to go into greater detail about the lifecycle of product data, the customer journey you want to enable, and the data flow that links the two.

3.7 Summary

SAP Commerce offers multiple paths for building, saving, recovering, and merging carts, as well as multiple checkout flows. These paths, which cover the most common commerce use cases fairly thoroughly, can nonetheless be turned on or off, combined, or replaced with custom functionality should the project require a less common approach.

Meanwhile, the rule engine provides a robust, configurable, and customizable approach to creating conditional logic within SAP Commerce—but just as importantly, out of the box it provides the basis for the promotion engine, which itself can be configured and customized to your specifications but which also provides tremendous flexibility for building, planning, and publishing promotional campaigns via a backoffice-based drag-and-drop interface.

The SAP Commerce accelerators bring these functions—as well as numerous others discussed throughout this book—together into an easily configurable frontend. For some projects, accelerator storefronts can serve as nearly ready-made responsive websites, markedly reducing the time necessary for development and testing.

For other, more complicated projects, accelerator storefronts can serve as the basis for what you plan to build. This can mean using the SAP Commerce accelerators framework to build something more complex, and/or it can mean launching with something fairly close to an accelerator storefront (therefore reducing your time to value) before landing and expanding into a more business-specific solution. In all these cases, the SAP Commerce accelerators let you focus on your business differentiators rather than on creating table stakes commerce functionality from scratch.

Of course, for virtually any commerce project, storefronts, carts, wishlists, checkouts, and promotional campaigns all exist in relation to a product catalog. Products, as well as the categories into which they are organized, form the backbone of commerce design. In the next chapter, we will look at product content management, examining both the core data model in SAP Commerce and some best practices for designing the product data model specific to your project.

Chapter 4
Product Content and Catalog Management

In the previous chapter, we introduced commerce management concepts, including the different accelerators available and how to manage them. In this chapter, we'll cover the product catalog and content, functionality that is core to SAP Commerce and that contains tools to manage products and get them in front of customers.

Getting the right products in front of the right customers at the right time and guaranteeing branding, sales, and marketing campaigns aligned around such offerings are practices that have become increasingly relevant and challenging in a world in which organizations are more and more present across multiple channels, brands, and business models in different regions of the globe. Product content management helps organizations consolidate product content and business information on a single platform and ensure data consistency across channels and systems.

With product content management, the business user is given control of the customer experience by providing tools to business users to easily manage and access product-related data and gather all customer-facing content into a common repository. Because product content management can be set up to absorb data from different sources (online, offline channels, external data sources, users, etc.), it makes consistent production information available across all channels and touchpoints and presents a uniform view to users on different devices throughout the channels. Product content management is a flexible and agile tool that suits B2C strategies and can be suitable for B2B customers as well, complementing or replacing classic master data management tools. The key functionalities of the product content management module are as follows:

- Consolidate product-related data and content and make it easily accessible and manageable for business users. This makes it possible to create a single source of truth for product content.
- Control all product content for all channels in one place.
- Classify and categorize products, manage catalog versions, and import multiple supplier catalogs.
- Get products validated and online quickly thanks to coordinated content creation and approval processes.
- No need for IT intervention to add new products as complex as bundled offers.
- Create a consistent appearance for content across all channels.
- Provide rich and engaging content at the core to create compelling experiences for customers.

In this chapter, we'll discuss the strength of the product content management module and how to execute product content management–related tasks as a core component of SAP Commerce. We'll discuss the management of the product catalog and how to set up catalogs and categories, as well as how to manage different catalog versions and recommended practices for catalog management. We'll also discuss how to use the Backoffice Product Cockpit and the legacy Product Cockpit and how to work with configurable products, bundles, and digital asset management.

4.1 Product Catalog Management

Catalogs are one of the main features in the SAP Commerce suite. They are used to structure data in a hierarchal matter. In SAP Commerce, we distinguish two types of catalogs: product catalogs and content catalogs. The product catalog contains structures and manages products and categories. The product entity is its basic entity, and the product is managed through the Backoffice Product Cockpit. Content catalogs are used to hold, structure, and manage information related to websites, such as web pages and their templates and components. A component is the basic entity of the content catalog. Content catalogs are managed with the Web Content Management System (WCMS) Cockpit, with SmartEdit, or through the backoffice administration. In SAP Commerce, there is no overlap between information stored in product and content catalogs. They interact with each other in the WCMS Cockpit. Each catalog contains one or more product catalog versions, which contain products and categories organized into logical and hierarchical groups.

Content catalogs are containers that hold all the information about the components of the presented website. In Chapter 5, we'll go into more detail on user experience and how to create and maintain content catalogs using SmartEdit, WCMS Cockpit, or the backoffice administration.

Product catalogs allow organizations to automate content modification and maintain a logical hierarchy of products and categories with specific information types, like metadata, localizations, views, restrictions, and so on. Restrictions can be set up for catalogs for purposes such as showing or hiding products from certain users and granting editing permissions to one or more user groups.

In this section, we'll discuss the structure of products and categories, how to work with catalog versions, how to manage multiple catalogs, and recommended strategies, before discussing the synchronization process for catalogs.

4.1.1 Structuring Products and Categories

Products are the core of commerce and the basic elements of any catalog. They're both data structures and items of merchandise (e.g., a shirt or camera).

The product guides everything on the website, from navigation to product display to checkout and order history.

Because the product drives the design of the product, category, and data model, which underpins the entire architecture, it's important to discuss an organization's products and services for sale in an early design stage.

To organize products, they can be grouped into product categories that represent logical groups. This enables organizations to bring related products together, like departments do in a traditional store. Categories can hold other categories and can be used to assemble corresponding categories into supercategories. A product can be assigned to one or more categories or assigned directly to the catalog version. On the storefront, all the products are shown that are assigned to the category. If a product belongs to more than one category, it will be shown under each category it belongs to.

Categories are often organized hierarchically, and the end user's navigation is mainly driven by this hierarchy, called the *selling hierarchy*; it represents the category structure, the hierarchy of categories, and the organization of products under the same categories. A complete selling hierarchy doesn't need to be channel-specific, and usually the online selling hierarchy mirrors or can even be the replication of the in-store selling hierarchy. A selling hierarchy consists of multiple levels; five to six levels is typical, but this varies by industry. Not all levels are necessarily visible to the end customer.

The SAP Commerce accelerators come by default with predefined product hierarchies:

- The apparel store comes out of the box with a three-layer-deep category hierarchy for products, as well as additional hierarchies for brands and collections.
- The electronics store uses a five-layer-deep category hierarchy, as well as smaller brands hierarchies.
- The powertools store comes with a five-layer-deep category hierarchy, as well as additional hierarchies for building multidimensional product variants.

After defining a selling hierarchy, some definitions can be set for categories and products:

- A product manager can define top categories using the selling hierarchy and categories to define the categories that are visible in the upper navigation for the customer. These categories usually have their own landing pages.
- You can create product listing pages, which can be the lowest levels just above the products in the selling hierarchy.
- Some organizations define *invisible categories*. These are categories that will be used for internal grouping but not shown to the end customer.
- Explicit and implicit (e.g., boost and bury) rankings of certain products on the product listing and/or landing pages can be set.
- Categories can be created in the Backoffice Product Cockpit.

The product data model is a part of data modeling, and to model data effectively in SAP Commerce, an understanding of the SAP Commerce type system is required. The SAP Commerce type system is used to model products, users, and orders, as well as processes related to them. In addition, SAP Commerce provides a classification system for modeling products. Both the type system and the classification system can be used to model or extend products and variants.

The following characteristics, among others, are important when defining the data model for the organization:

- **Product visibility**
  Defining whether product visibility should be restricted is mostly relevant for B2B organizations, in which the products in the catalog often are restricted by customer (group). In B2C, usually there is one catalog view for every customer, unless there is some specific target group marketing or merchandising. Organizations can classify products as internal/external/local/global or as equally visible to every customer on the site. It's important to establish whether different views of the catalog are needed for different user bases or different countries/markets.
- **Product attributes**
  Organizations should define the attributes of products and broadly identify the mix of common versus specific attributes per product family. Because some attributes might apply to all or most products, other sets of attributes may exist specific to product families.
- **Product variants**
  Some attributes of products will be variants, for which a difference in the base product's attributes makes it a distinct stock-keeping unit (SKU). These attributes are sometimes called *dimensions* (e.g., color and size). These will be rendered in the SAP Commerce data model as either type variants or using multidimensional variants. For example, the base product *pants* might have style variants (e.g., colors), and each of the style variants might have size variants (e.g., small, medium, large). In the B2B accelerator, up to three variants are available out of the box for a specific product.

4.1.2 Catalog Versions

A catalog usually has one or more catalog versions. Out of the box, SAP Commerce catalogs are configured with two catalog versions, staged and online. The staged catalog is managed and modified internally by the website's employees, and the online version contains data the site's customers will see.

After the data has been modified or added by employees in the staged version of the catalog and it's ready to be published to the customer, the staged catalog should be synchronized with the customer-facing online catalog.

Figure 4.1 shows an out-of-the-box configuration with one staged and online version of the catalog. This is one of the many implementation strategies to structure SAP Commerce catalogs.

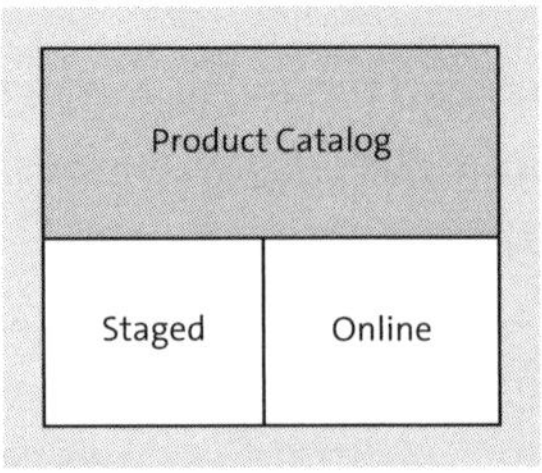

Figure 4.1 Simple One-Catalog Structure

The SAP Commerce suite comes with a predefined implementation for B2C and B2B scenarios with one staged and online catalog version. This is the most basic setup; organizations usually implement more advanced strategies for their business.

When evaluating the product catalog design, an organization should consider the following:

- Business requirements (e.g., regional product assortments)
- Maintainability
- Who will maintain the data and in which catalogs
- Potential duplication of effort in maintaining data for business users
- Data volumes
- Effect on performance and scalability

4.1.3 Managing Multiple Catalogs

In this subsection, we'll discuss how to manage multiple catalogs and create a catalog strategy to implement for an SAP Commerce project. We'll discuss the catalog system and maintenance processes that usually reflect the operations of an organization, then we'll discuss implementation strategies.

Catalog Systems

A catalog system is a group of SAP Commerce catalogs. It provides a framework to manage multiple output catalogs and helps manage the changing content of several catalogs. It can also handle multiple input catalogs. A catalog system is usually set up around a master catalog, which holds the leading versions of catalog data. The different catalog content is synchronized among defined catalog versions that reflect the catalog maintenance process. Multiple catalogs in a catalog system allow you to synchronize to multiple frontends simultaneously—for example, if an organization has a website that features various countries or channels or if there is special sale catalog to support a specific sales event.

Catalog Maintenance Process

SAP recommends that before you define the catalog system for the solution, you should define a catalog maintenance process that reflects your organization's structures and responsibilities.

For example, if your organization has a foreign subsidiary that has its own product line and/or storefront and it manages its own data, merchandising, product strategies, and so on, you can set up the catalog system to reflect that. A subsidiary would be able to manage its data in a separate catalog that receives the basic collection catalog data from a master catalog edited and approved locally. Such a country-specific catalog can have its own local staged and online versions. Permissions and access rights can be given to the local team to edit and manage, and several representatives from headquarters can have read and/or write permissions for supportive tasks. Therefore, when designing the catalog system, we recommend that you take the following into consideration:

- Only have one master catalog.
- Separate the subordinate catalogs that contain actively managed content that differs up to a certain degree.
- Separate input catalogs for different collections, suppliers, content types, or source systems, like ERP systems, product information systems, or file-based imports.
- Separate the data and corresponding process steps before merging them into a master catalog.
- Set up at least one output product catalog that receives its content from a master catalog.
- Define catalog versions for subordinate process steps that can be organized within a catalog because only one catalog version can be active. For example, consider season-specific catalogs and catalog versions that need synchronizations between the two catalog versions to indicate the data flow between catalogs.

Implementation Strategies

Because catalog systems can be as complex as a company's procedures and structures, SAP Commerce provides tools to create these complex catalog systems. Here we'll discuss some implementation strategies based on some example scenarios. Specific project requirements lead to different approaches to product catalog design, and there is no one-size-fits-all configuration for product catalog design. The examples ahead therefore can be used as a starting point but do not represent the only possible scenarios.

When a business has either a single channel, region, or brand, a single staged and online catalog can be used.

In reality, scenarios are often more complex than one staged and one online catalog version. For example, sites in the fashion industry often maintain different staged catalog versions for each season—spring, summer, fall, and winter—with a single online catalog version for the customer-facing channel. In that way, business users can easily switch seasonal catalogs by selecting the season that needs to synchronize with the single online catalog version. Although there are multiple catalog versions, only one can be active at a time, which is the online catalog version. Some typical use cases for multiple catalogs are as follows:

- Multiple regions, channels, brands, or seasons
- Different assortments per region, brand, channel, or season
- Different availability dates for products per region, brand, channel, or season
- Different product attribute values for some products per region, brand, channel, or season (see Figure 4.2)

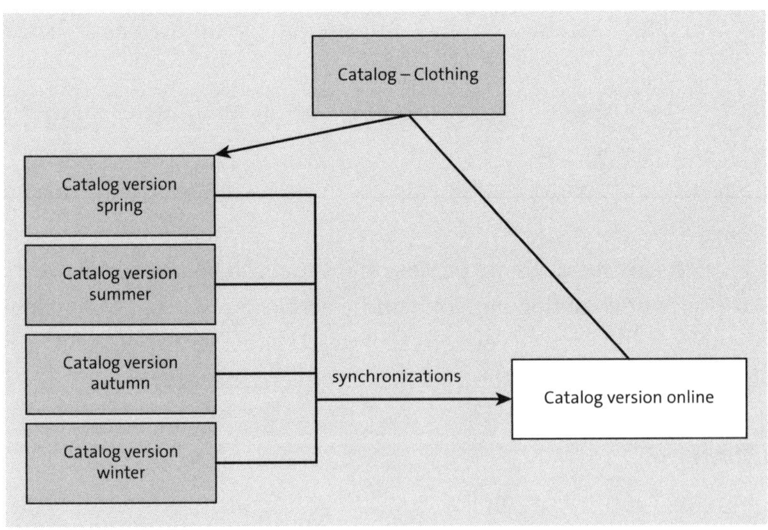

Figure 4.2 Seasonal Catalog

If products and other information is imported from other source systems, this is consolidated in the master catalog. When more than one input source exists, these catalog systems often consist of different catalog versions based on content types that are populated by different input sources. Different sources like suppliers, advertising agencies, ERP systems, and other sources populate the catalog, which synchronizes a master catalog with all the information consolidated into a single source of truth. Figure 4.3 shows how such a multiple-source catalog would be set up.

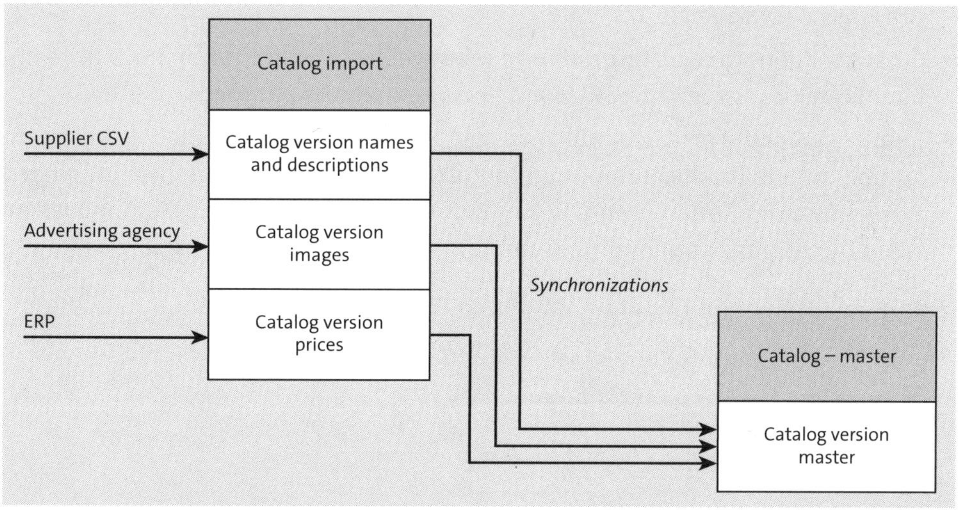

Figure 4.3 Multiple-Source Catalog

The most common catalog design used is a catalog system with one master product catalog that includes different underlying catalogs—for example, when an organization has different catalogs for each region, brand, channel, or season and at least two catalog versions (typically staged and online). Prices would in this case typicially be managed in the these catalogs because managing them in the master product catalog won't provide the flexibility needed to set prices per region, brand, or season.

Having a multiple-catalog approach brings various benefits for the business:

- This works especially well when catalog management is decentralized.
- Category hierarchies can be defined on the local level.
- Works well when organizations want to define product strategies (e.g., prices, promotions, cross/up-sells) at the regional, brand, or seasonal level.

When implementing a multiple-catalog strategy, the following should be considered:

- Having multiple catalogs most likely means a much larger number of products representing a single SKU and more rows in the database. This can lead to performance and scalability issues.
- Small changes may need to be copied many times—and imagine changing an attribute of a product for a system supporting 40 countries!
- Search engine indexing and store requirements will increase significantly, which can affect performance.
- Customizations to reporting might be required if you want to treat a SKU from different catalogs as the same SKU for reporting/analytics purposes.
- Items referencing products will also need to be duplicated for each downstream catalog, such as product promotions and CMS components when these are shared among catalogs. When each country defines its own strategy, this provides an advantage (Figure 4.4 shows an example of such a multicountry catalog).

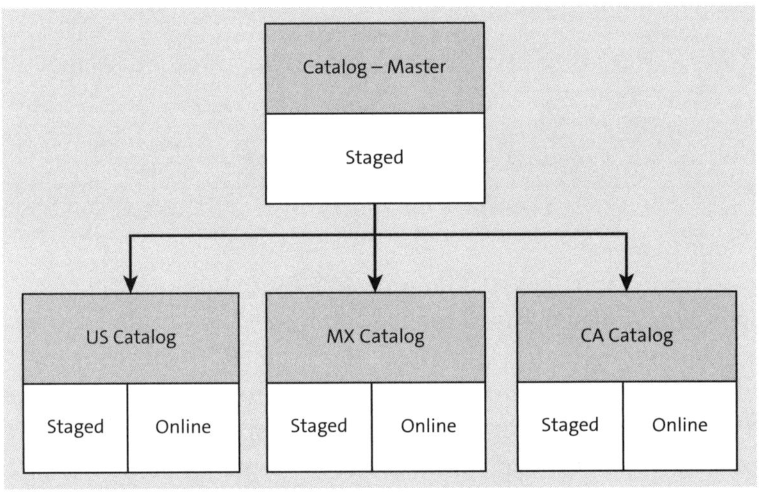

Figure 4.4 Multicountry Catalog

4.1.4 Synchronizing Catalogs

Synchronization is an important concept in SAP Commerce. It's applicable to both products and content catalogs. Synchronization is the mechanism of copying content from a source to a target catalog version while overwriting current catalog data. Synchronization is unidirectional, which means that from the moment the source and target are defined, the system will move the data from the source to the target and can't synchronize back from the target to the source.

Within SAP Commerce, data is not stored in a version-control system but in catalog versions. Catalog versions allow data to be maintained in different stages, preparing it for the final stage, which is the online catalog version. Once the data synchronization is completed, it isn't possible to roll back the changes. Synchronizing data can be automatic through CronJobs or manual through different backoffice tools, as well as the Backoffice Product Cockpit and SmartEdit.

Because synchronization has the potential to significantly influence system performance, it should be set up correctly and controlled. Depending on the size of the data to be synchronized and the frequency of sync tasks, there can be a significant impact on website response time. Also, there can be an impact on other (backend) operations that are in a waiting state for the duration of the synchronization process. Therefore, we recommend giving synchronization permissions only to a small set of users.

Further, we recommend scheduling synchronization tasks during the night or at other times that lower website traffic is expected to minimize impact on user experience. Most companies have scheduled synchronization jobs overnight to push changes to their product catalog to the online version. Departments authorized to execute changes, like product or marketing managers, use the staged catalog during the day to manage product merchandising, set promotions, and so on.

It's possible to manually synchronize data, but usually manual synchronizations are limited to individual products and used only to make minor adjustments or emergency updates. Only selected users should be allowed to manually synchronize items in the product catalog or in any other user interface. Managing such permissions is done easily by defining user restrictions and workflows. Workflows can be used to allow only product or content managers to synchronize data after other team members (e.g., media managers and translators) have updated and edited product information. Using restrictions and workflows also prevents users from overriding each other's work. Restrictions and workflows can be defined in the backoffice administration cockpit.

4.2 Product Cockpit

Today there are two ways of managing catalogs and products within SAP Commerce. Since the backoffice tool was introduced, more functionality has been included in this centralized tool. And as of version 6.4, the Product Cockpit lives in the backoffice. In this section, we'll focus on the new Product Cockpit as the way the product is moving forward, but we'll also cover the functionality in the legacy cockpit still available in older versions of SAP Commerce. We'll refer to the new version as the Backoffice Product Cockpit and to the legacy version as the legacy Product Cockpit. We will use Product Cockpit alone to refer to both simultaneously.

The Product Cockpit is a highly customizable graphical user interface that makes product data maintenance more efficient, process-oriented, and user-friendly. It offers a single user interface to administer information for different product lines. It's used by merchandisers within the customer organization to enrich products and catalogs. The Product Cockpit is ideal for businesses with distributed product content responsibilities. Employees across the organization can access centralized information and then view or edit content that is relevant to them. This access is managed by rule-based restrictions, and workflows can be used to orchestrate these activities across teams.

It offers the following key features:

- Search interface based on Solr for simple and advanced search (in the backoffice)
- Data quality groups for easy and user-focused validation (backoffice)
- Facets to improve search of products (backoffice)
- A product perspective in which a business user can manage product categories and variants directly
- A catalog perspective that allows for managing product categories and variants
- References to product-related business objects like units, media, catalog versions, prices, and more
- A customizable view for users to add sections or fields at runtime to personalize their view
- Seamless workflow management, supporting features like tracking, status changing, and commenting
- Ability to dynamically build validation rules or constraints that can be associated with products

In this section, we'll discuss how to start working with the Product Cockpit to create categories, add and enrich products, and synchronize products.

4.2.1 Getting Started with the Product Cockpit

The Product Cockpit can be accessed through the backoffice. Based on the predefined user profile, different views are available (e.g., admin, product manager, pricing manager, etc.) to support the user's activities with the right information and available tasks on the screen. Figure 4.5 and Figure 4.6 show the cockpit login screen, as well as the login for a specific product manager user profile.

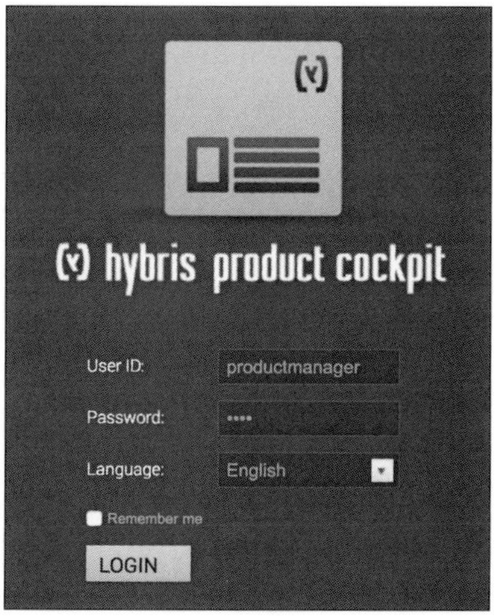

Figure 4.5 Legacy Product Cockpit Login Screen

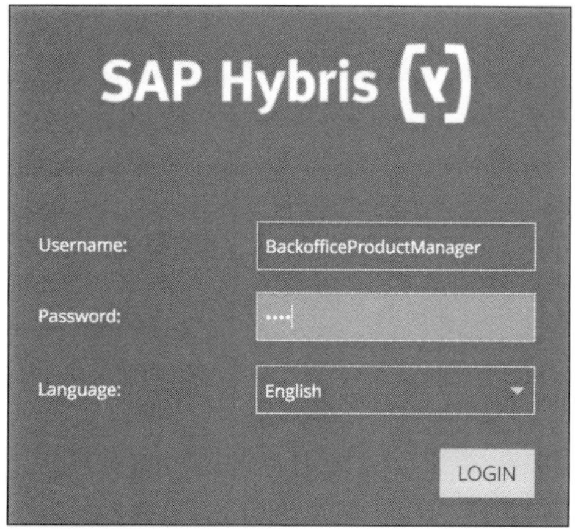

Figure 4.6 Backoffice Product Manager Login

Out of the box, within the Backoffice Product Cockpit, a business user has access to the following three views:

1. Product view
2. Assortment view
3. Compare view

The legacy Product Cockpit has the following two views:

1. Product perspective
2. Catalog perspective

We'll discuss each of these views in the following subsections.

Product View

The *product view* or *product search and browse view* enables users to manage products graphically. Marketers or other business users can modify product attributes such as the name, description, and approval status. This view allows you to easily search for products and manage them. Product properties can be edited, a preview shown, and synchronization between versions initiated. Within the product view, the user can choose different views of the product and how they are organized. You can access the grid view and the list view. Figure 4.7 shows an example of a list view.

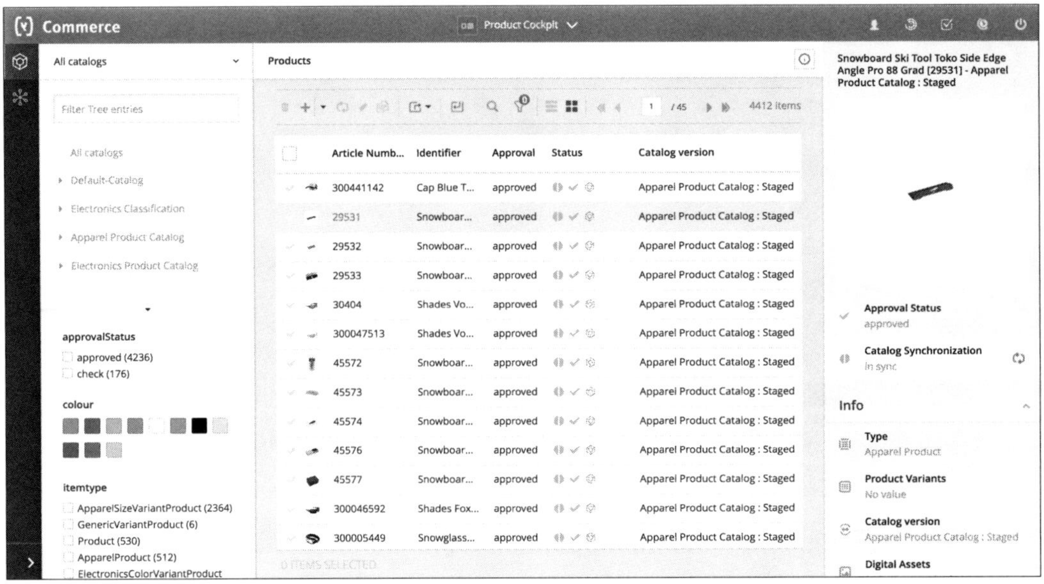

Figure 4.7 Product List View

In the default view of the products view, the following widgets can be found:

- **Explorer tree**
  Within the explorer tree (Figure 4.8), the different catalogs are shown. By selecting a catalog, the products of that specific catalog will be shown. The user can navigate and switch between catalogs in this tool, and synchronization can be initiated from here.

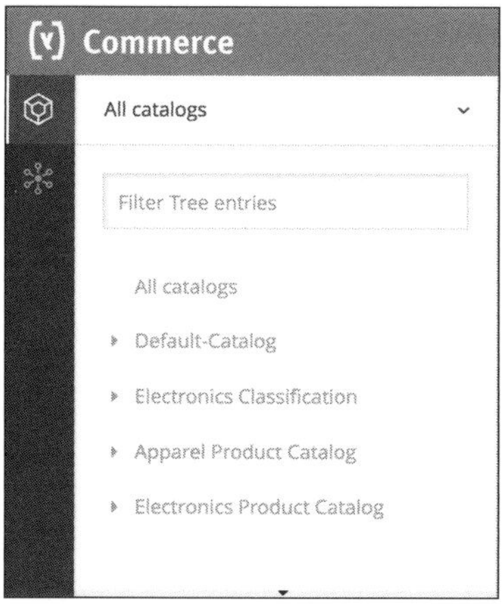

Figure 4.8 Explorer Tree

- **Facets**
  Facets (Figure 4.9) are available in this view to narrow the search results when selecting relevant properties of products. The facets can be configured to improve usability for a specific user of the product catalog.

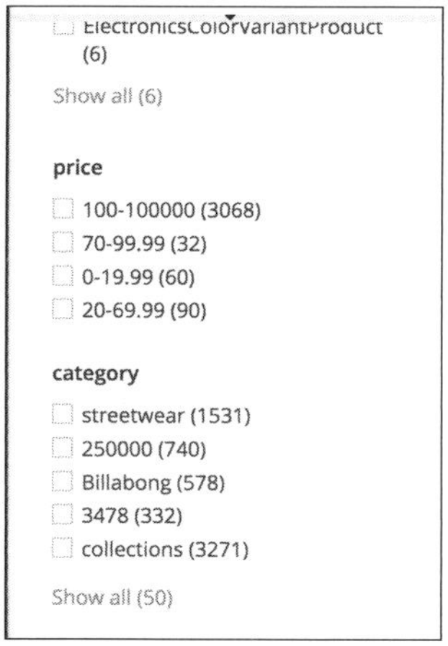

Figure 4.9 Facets Search

- **Simple search and filters**
  By using the simple search (Figure 4.10), a user can search for specific products. Search results can be narrowed by selecting specific filters and adding these to the search (Figure 4.11).

Figure 4.10 Simple Search Bar

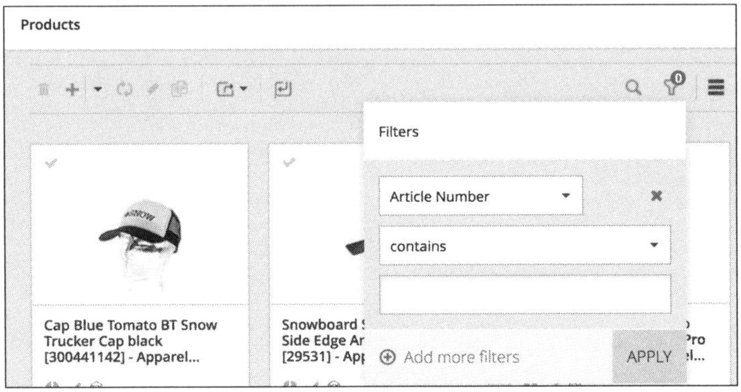

Figure 4.11 Search Filters

- **Browser area**
  Products are shown in the browser area (Figure 4.12). On the toolbar on top of the product browser area are icons to choose a specific view (list or grid view).

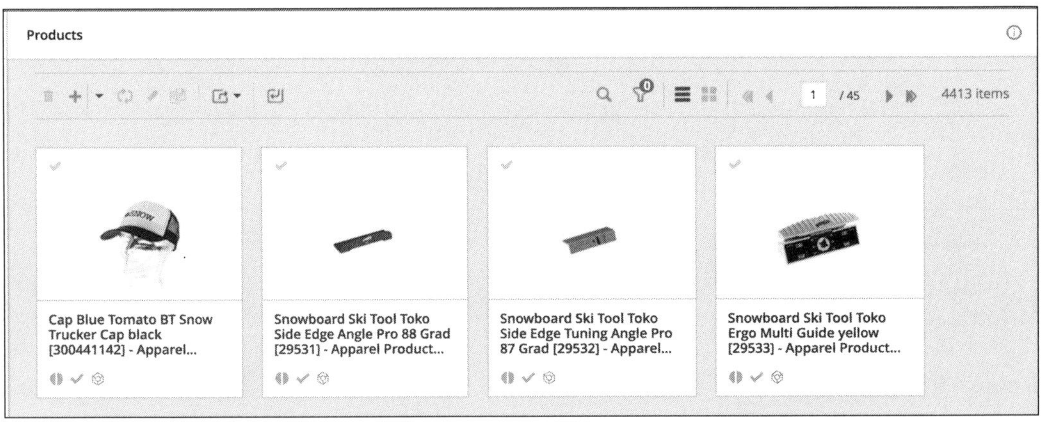

Figure 4.12 Browser Area: Grid View

- **Summary view**
  The preview of a selected product (Figure 4.13) is shown when clicking on the **Information** icon at the top right of the browser area.

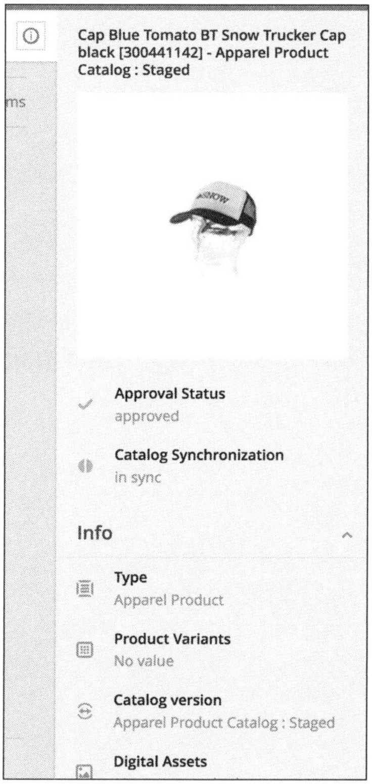

Figure 4.13 Product Summary View

- **Processes**
  The status of synchronization or other processes are shown in the process widget (Figure 4.14). Click the **Process** icon at the top right of the screen to access the processes view.

Figure 4.14 Process Status Bar

- **Product browser toolbar**
  The product browser toolbar (Figure 4.15) shows the options available for quick actions when selecting one or more products. The following actions are available: **Create New**, **Delete**, **Edit**, **Clone**, **Synchronize**, **Compare**, **Bulk Edit**, **Bulk Approval**, **Import**, or **Export** (CSV or Excel), as well as search and filter options for the products shown in the browser area.

Figure 4.15 Product Browser Toolbar

- **Aggregated view**
  By selecting one or more products in the browser area the inspector area on the right will show the aggregated view (Figure 4.16) of the product in the right part of the screen. In this aggregated view, an overview of the product is shown.

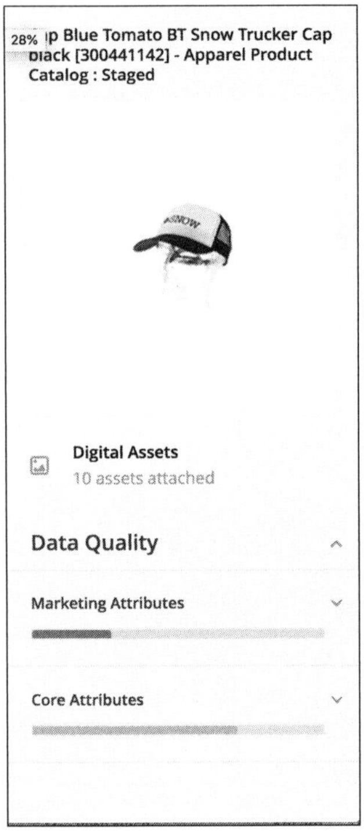

Figure 4.16 Aggregated View: Data Quality Indicators

One of the fields shown is the **Data Quality** field, which indicates the quality of specific data for a product. For example, the marketing data quality indicator shows if the marketing attributes of a specific product are maintained and complete. A product with incomplete marketing data and/or core attributes attached will show a low score on the marketing or core attribute quality indicator.

Assortment View

The assortment view is a feature that offers product managers intuitive and effective management of the product catalog through a visual user interface in the backoffice.

In the assortment view (shown in Figure 4.17), the product manager can easily and quickly browse through catalogs, catalog versions, and categories. In this view, the product manager can also create new catalogs, catalog versions, and categories easily.

Moreover, the product manager can manage the product content by dragging and dropping selected data or by rearranging, creating, and finally removing selected items. The product manager can also access the edit view to quickly work on the selected item.

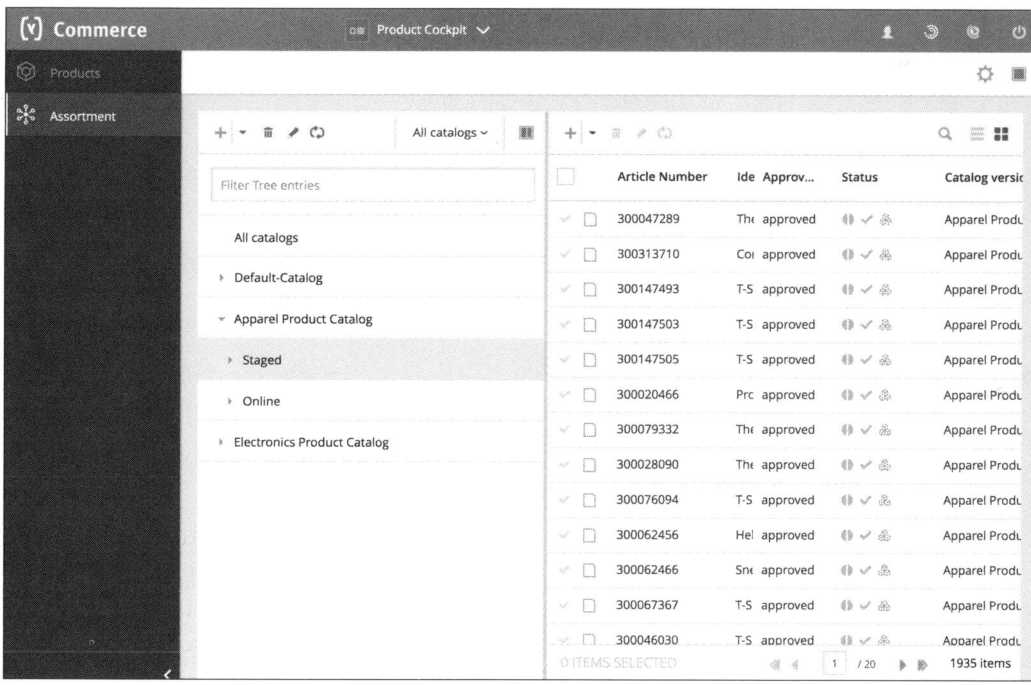

Figure 4.17 Assortment View (Backoffice)

Compare View

On the left side of the screen shown in Figure 4.18, below the **Assortment** icon, is the **Compare** icon. Within the compare view, a business user can visualize various products next to each other to compare them in the backoffice.

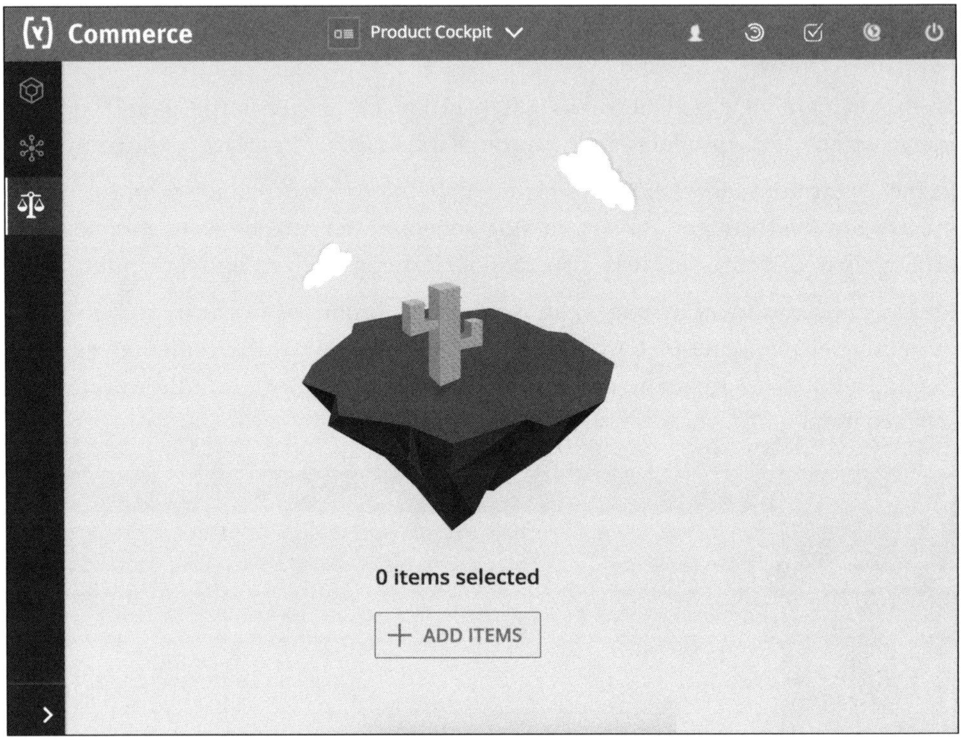

Figure 4.18 Compare View (Backoffice)

In the compare view (shown in Figure 4.19), the user can select two or more products to compare. Details that are different are shown in red and details that are the same in black. The user can decide to show differences only by toggling **Show Diff Only**.

Product Perspective

The product perspective (Figure 4.20) in the legacy Product Cockpit aims to offer a graphical interface for users managing and merchandising products. When logging into the legacy Product Cockpit, the product view is the default landing page for product managers.

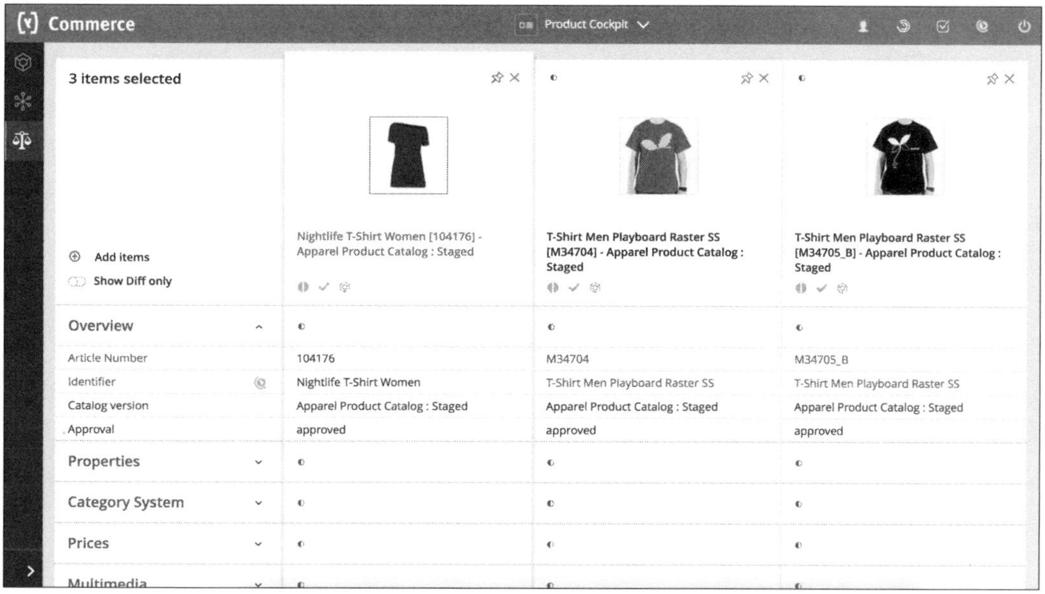

Figure 4.19 Compare Products in Compare View (Backoffice)

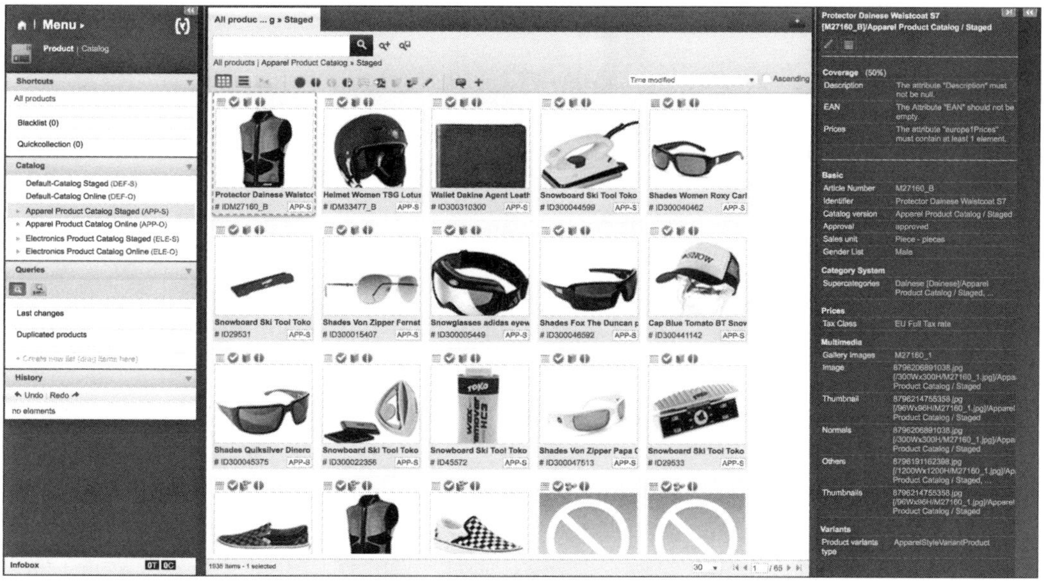

Figure 4.20 Product Perspective (Legacy Product Cockpit)

The product perspective has different tools for users, as follows:

- The navigation area (Figure 4.21) allows users to select a view (product or catalog) and catalog with products to edit.

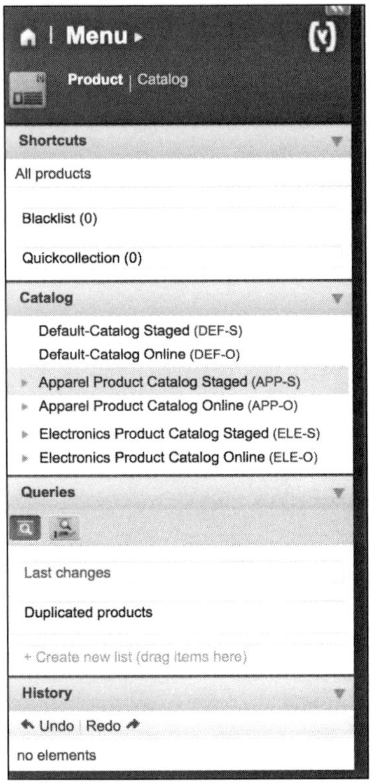

Figure 4.21 Navigation Area (Legacy Product Cockpit)

- The browser area lets users browse for products and categories to edit.
- The editor area lets users edit product information.
- The context area shows contextual information and lets the user add and edit information like product attributes.
- The inspector area shows an aggregated view of the business item and its core attributes, including validations.

Within the product view of the legacy Product Cockpit, the user can choose different views of the products and how they're organized. He can choose the grid view, the list view, or the compare view.

The grid view mode is the default view mode (as shown in Figure 4.22). It displays products in a grid of square boxes and shows users the following:

- Product coverage percentage, which shows the percentage of (obligatory) fields that are missing or not complete for a specific product. The color of the icon indicates if the coverage is sufficient within the set limits (red for not enough; yellow to green for good coverage). Hovering over the icon reveals a percentage indicating exactly how much of the coverage is for that specific product.
- Product approval status, for which an indicator shows whether a product is approved or not. The different statuses are check, approved, or unapproved.
- What product type the product belongs to, either base or variant.
- The synchronization status of a product, either synchronized or not synchronized.
- A thumbnail of the product.
- The product article number.

Figure 4.22 Product Detail Grid View (Legacy Product Cockpit)

In the grid view, there are several actions that can be executed for a product:

- Change the approval status
- Start synchronization
- Sync with source
- Show synchronization sources or targets
- Open a PDF preview

In the list view mode, products are displayed in a linear way. This is useful to edit more than one product at the time. By selecting more than one row, the actions noted for the grid view can be executed for more than one product at a time. Figure 4.23 shows the list view in the legacy Product Cockpit.

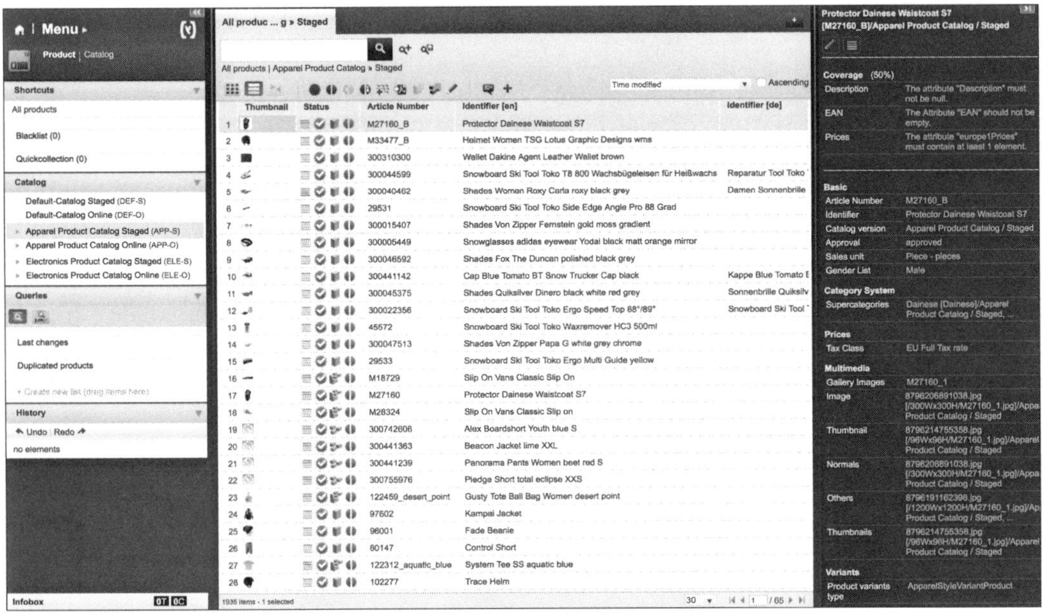

Figure 4.23 List View Product Perspective (Legacy Product Cockpit)

By selecting more than one product in the grid view or more than one line in the list view mode, the compare view for selected items can be used. In this view, a user can easily compare products and see what the differences are for each characteristic. Figure 4.24 shows the product compare view in the legacy Product Cockpit.

Catalog Perspective

The catalog perspective (Figure 4.25) of the legacy Product Cockpit enables a user to structure catalog versions and the related category structures using a graphical interface. The main purpose of the catalog perspective in the product catalog cockpit is not to create catalogs or catalog versions. In this view, a user can use the catalog perspective of the legacy Product Cockpit to assign products to categories, move categories within a catalog version, remove categories from a catalog version, edit product data and product categories, or manage classification categories.

Figure 4.24 Product Compare View, Product View (Legacy Product Cockpit)

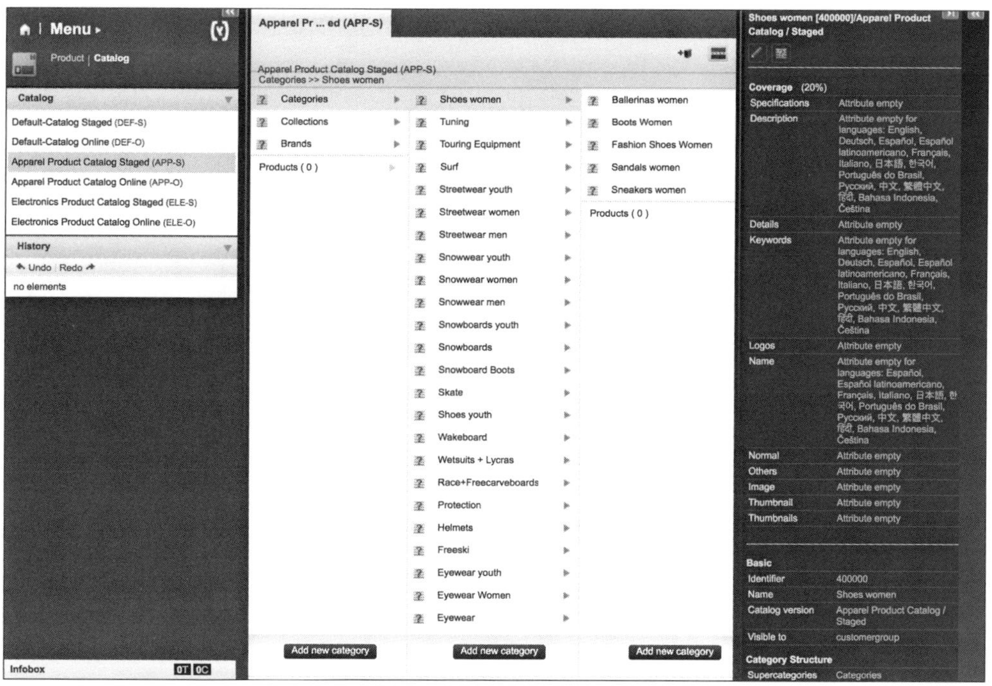

Figure 4.25 Catalog Perspective (Legacy Product Cockpit)

4.2.2 Creating Categories

In both the backoffice (assortment view) and the legacy Product Cockpit (catalog view), a user can create categories. The processes are similar, but we will explain how to create categories in each tool in the following sections.

Backoffice

When you login to the backoffice, the product view is loaded automatically. To begin, follow these steps:

1. Click **Assortment** to select the assortment view in the backoffice (Figure 4.26).

Figure 4.26 Assortment View Selection in Navigation Bar in Backoffice

2. In the assortment view (Figure 4.27), select the category structure to which the new category will belong.

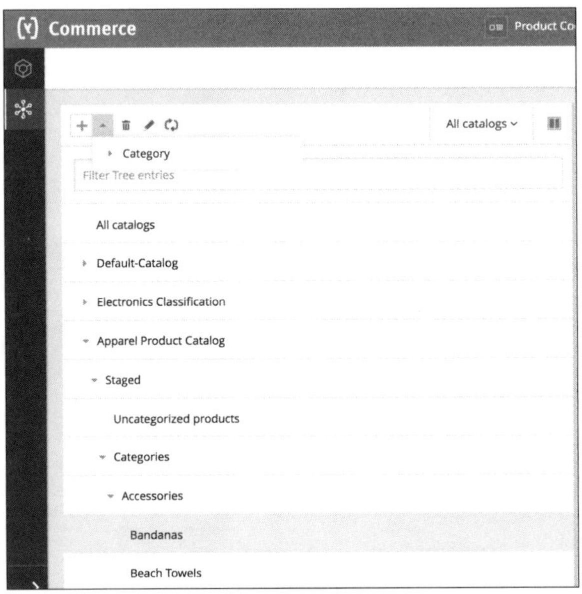

Figure 4.27 Category Structure Assortment View in Backoffice

3. Click **Create Category** and a **Create New Category** screen will appear (Figure 4.28). On this screen, basic information can be defined: the **Identifier**, **Name**, **Catalog Version**, and **Supercategories** the category belongs to.

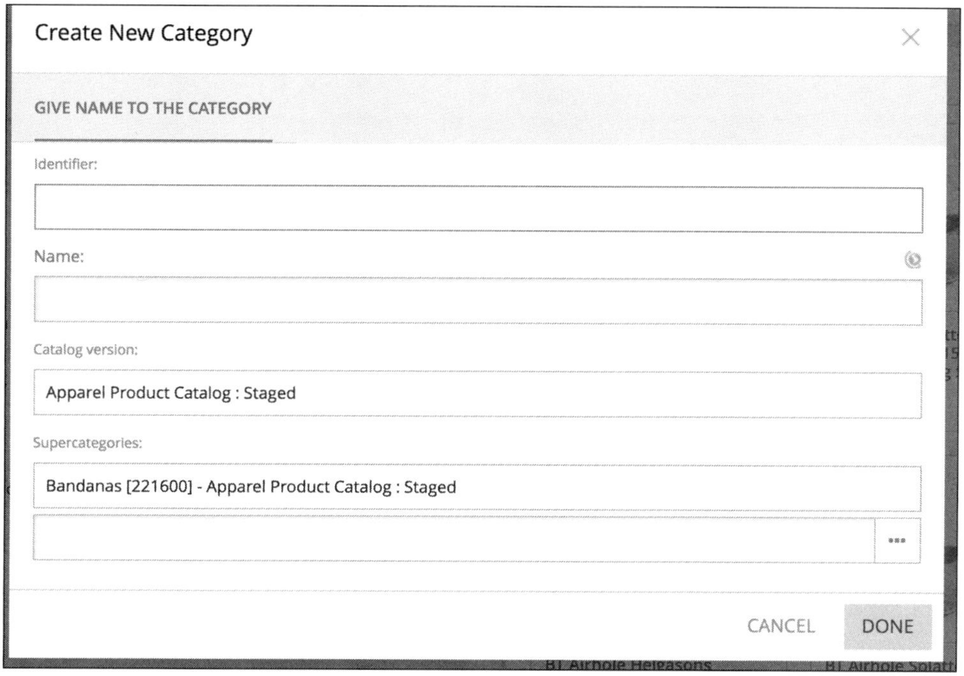

Figure 4.28 Create Category Pop-Up (Backoffice)

A supercategory can be selected if the category should be grouped together with comparable categories below one or more supercategories.

4. When the new category is created, drop and drag products into the new category or create a new product to assign it to this category.
5. In the edit category screen (Figure 4.29), you can manage different attributes in the different tabs.
6. In the **General** tab, the following information must be filled in:
   - An identifier of the category.
   - The catalog version the category will be tied to.
   - A description for the category.

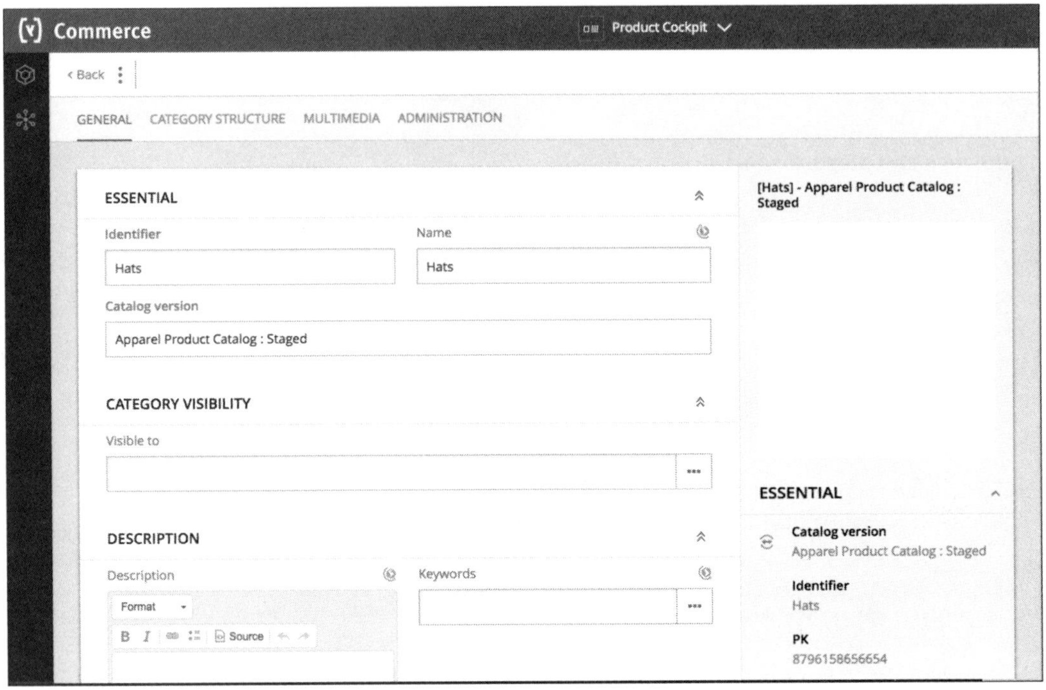

Figure 4.29 Edit Category Screen (Backoffice)

- The category visibility. To make a category visible in a web frontend like a storefront, you must explicitly define the user groups or individual users that are allowed to view the category. The visibility of a category also controls the visibility of all subcategories, products, and other objects that are related to it. On the other hand, a category is not visible if it doesn't contain any visible products.
- Keywords for search engine optimization.

7. In the **Category Structure** tab, the following information can be filled in:
   - Select supercategories, subordinate categories, and included products.
   - Select one or more content blocks that represent reusable content such as general information, corporate visuals, or tables.
8. In the **Multimedia** tab, you can define additional media objects for the category, such as containing media, logos, and thumbnails.

Legacy Product Cockpit

Creating categories in the legacy Product Cockpit is not much different than in the backoffice. Within the legacy Product Cockpit, you can choose the catalog view and then select the catalog the new category should be created in. Figure 4.30 shows the create category pop-up as it appears in the legacy Product Cockpit.

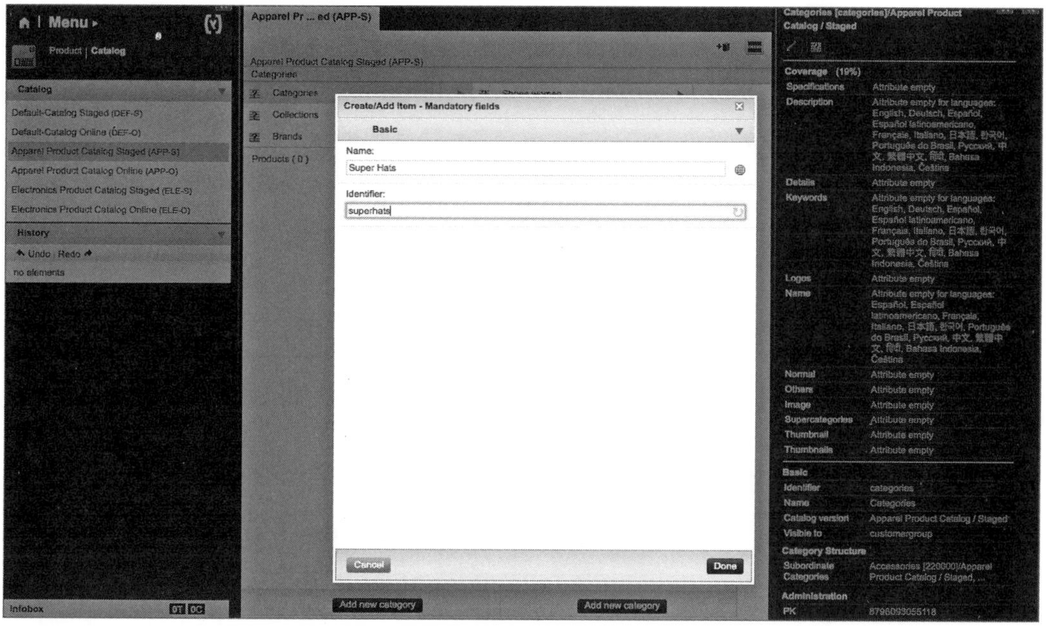

Figure 4.30 Create Category Pop-Up (Legacy Product Cockpit)

When the category is created an edit screen will offer similar tabs as those in the backoffice to fill with relevant information (Figure 4.31). Here you'll fill out similar information again:

- On the **Basic** tab, set the identifier, category visibility, and keywords.
- On the **Category Structure** tab, select supercategories and subordinate categories.
- On the **Multimedia** tab, define additional media objects for the category, such as containing media, logos, and thumbnails.

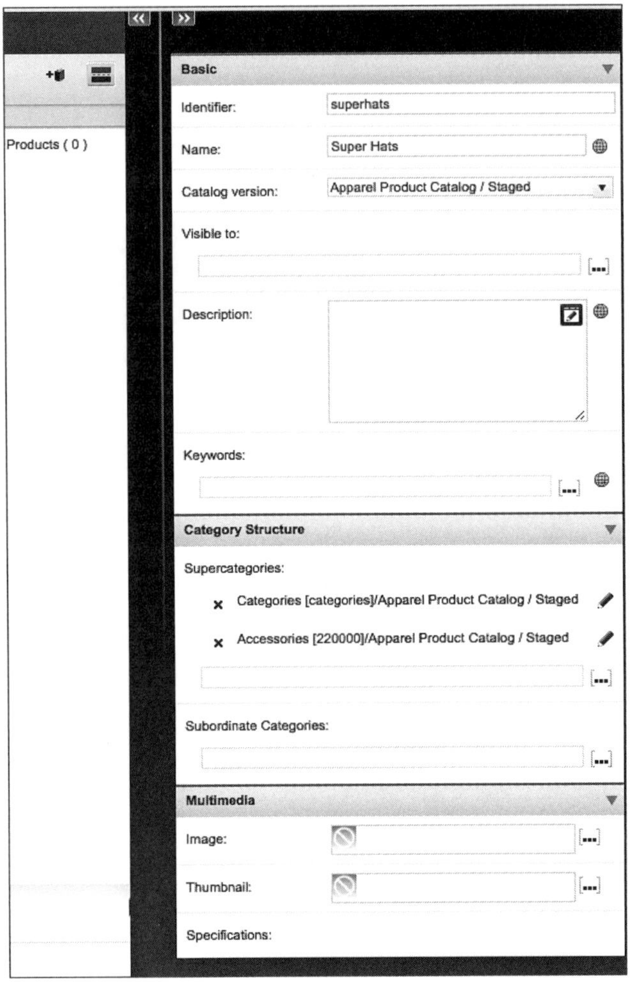

Figure 4.31 Create Category Fields (Legacy Product Cockpit)

4.2.3 Creating and Enriching Products

A product is the basic element of any catalog; it's both a data structure and an item of merchandise (e.g., a hat or camera). A product will have certain attributes, such as SKU, description, prices, media, and so on.

Typically, products are imported from other systems like SAP ERP using ImpEx and will be prepared for commerce (enriched and merchandised) by the business user of an organization using the Product Catalog Cockpit or backoffice (as of version 6.4).

In addition, the Backoffice Product Cockpit supports Excel imports to onboard data and Excel exports to analyze or bulk-change product data, allowing for reimport. During the reimport process, the validations defined in SAP Commerce will be applied, ensuring that the right data quality will end up in the catalog. When you click the **Import** icon, a pop-up appears to drag and drop or select a file to import (as shown in Figure 4.32).

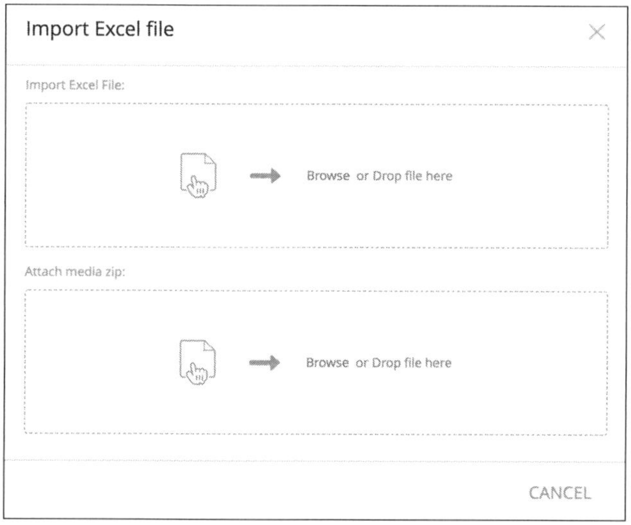

Figure 4.32 Import Excel File (Backoffice)

In this section, we'll show you how to create and enrich a product using both the backoffice and the legacy Product Cockpit.

Backoffice

In the backoffice, enter the product view and click a new product in the browser area of the screen. A pop-up will open (see Figure 4.33), and you're asked to fill in the essential data of the new product (**Article Number**, **Approval Status**, and **Catalog Version**).

On the next screen, fill in the description and identifiers for each language considered for this product; on the final screen, select the supercategories the product belongs to.

In the product view in the Backoffice Product Cockpit, choose either the list or grid view (shown in Figure 4.34). In addition, there are various widgets available to find the right product or sets of products.

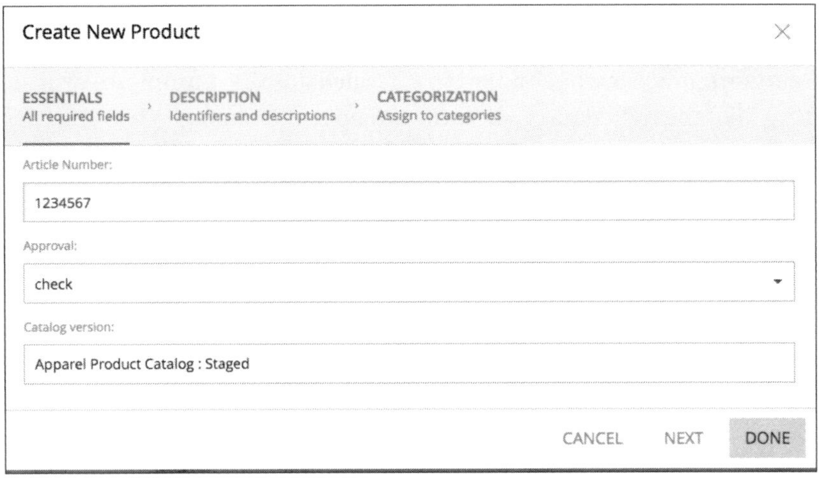

Figure 4.33 Create New Product Pop-Up (Backoffice)

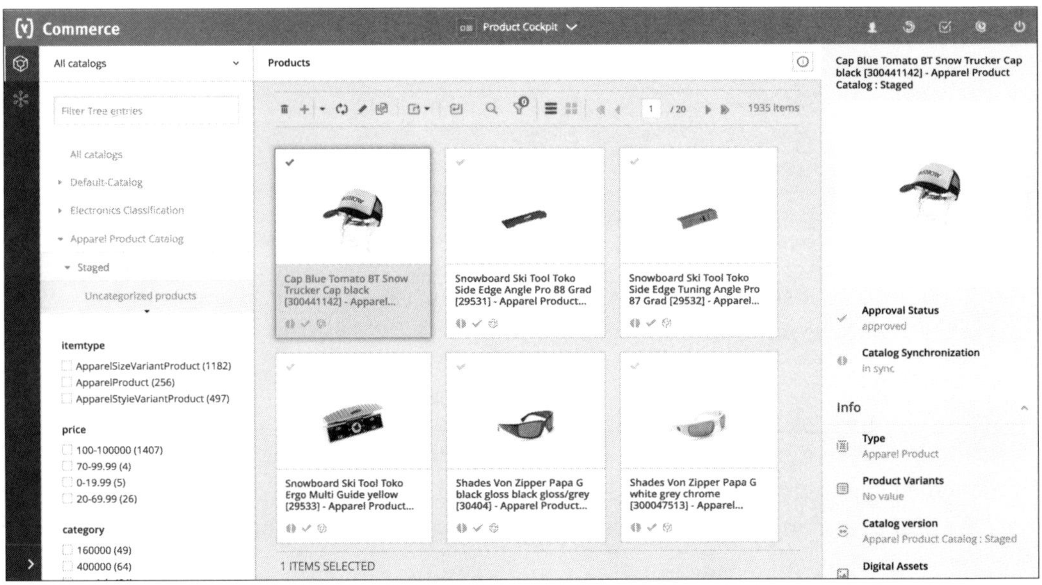

Figure 4.34 Product Grid View (Backoffice)

The **Catalog** widget at the left top helps you select the catalog the products are in, and the **Facet** widget lets you use facet search to narrow the search results. And at the right, the **Information** widget shows the overall view of a selected product (approval and synchronization status, general information, and data quality indicators).

When you enter edit mode in the product, various tabs are available to enrich the product (see Figure 4.35). Specific tabs can be shown or hidden based on user authorization rights. The following tabs and corresponding fields are available to edit:

- **Properties tab**
  General product information is maintained here (e.g., article number, catalog, etc.), as well as validity periods and descriptions.
- **Category System tab**
  Here categories can be assigned and product references can be made. This is useful for cross-selling.
- **Prices tab**
  Here you can assign prices and discounts and define minimum and maximum order quantities.
- **Multimedia tab**
  Here media can be assigned to a product, like images, logos, and thumbnails.
- **Variants tab**
  Use this tab to define the product as a base template to create a family of variants.

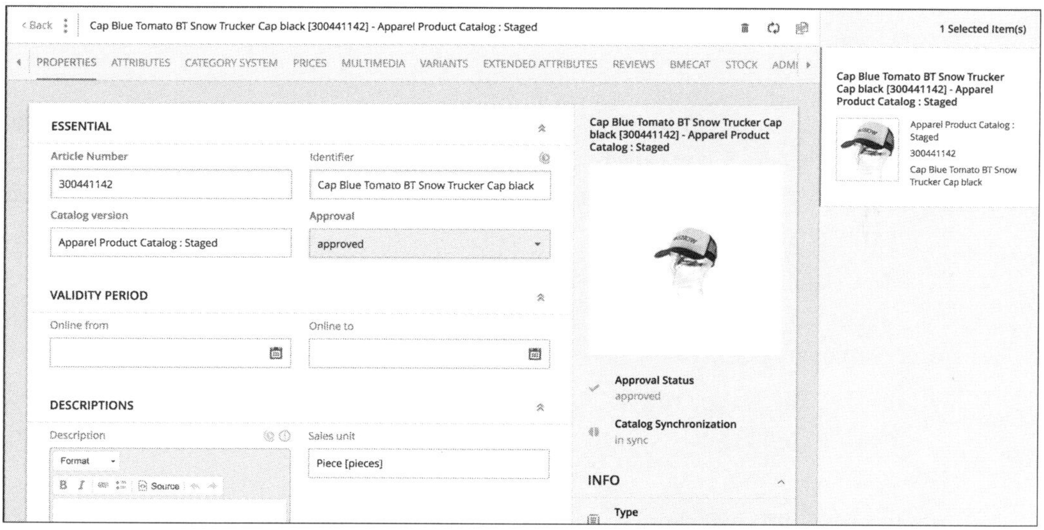

Figure 4.35 Edit Product Details (Backoffice)

Another option to edit products is the bulk edit mode. With this option, more than one product can be edited at the same time, which facilitates the mass editing of a group of products by a user. After editing and enriching products, you can select multiple products to synchronize to the target catalog version. Click the **Synchronization** icon to open a pop-up (as shown in Figure 4.36).

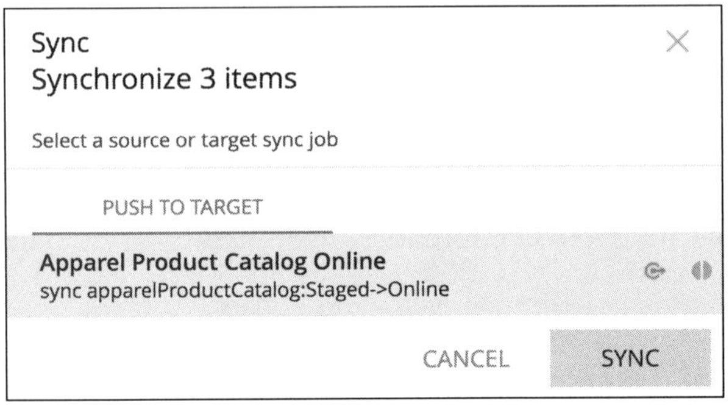

Figure 4.36 Synchronization Pop-Up (Backoffice)

We recommend scheduling synchronization of products at a time where there is less traffic on the website to minimize impact on customer experience.

Legacy Product Cockpit

In the legacy Product Cockpit, enter the product view to see all products. In the legacy Product Cockpit, there are three views here: grid, list, and compare views.

To create a new product manually, click the **New Product** icon. A pop-up will appear (Figure 4.37) in which you can choose the type of product that should be created (**Variants** or **Base**). On the next screen, basic data such as article number, catalog version, and identifier can be added.

Click **Done** and the product is created and the content editor for editing is automatically opened (Figure 4.38). Next to the editor screen, general data is shown about the product (**Coverage** and **Basic** information).

Within the edit mode, similar fields as in the backoffice can be found, which are grouped into topics such as **Basic**, **Attributes**, **Category System**, **Multimedia**, and **Variants**.

To enrich the product data for localization, certain fields have a globe icon next to them. This icon indicates that localization managers—for example, from a specific region or country—can add local translations to the product.

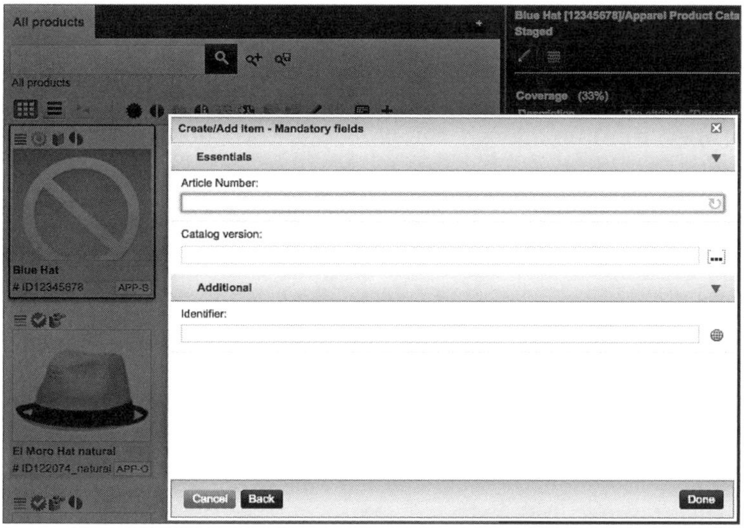

Figure 4.37 Create Product Pop-Up (Legacy Product Cockpit)

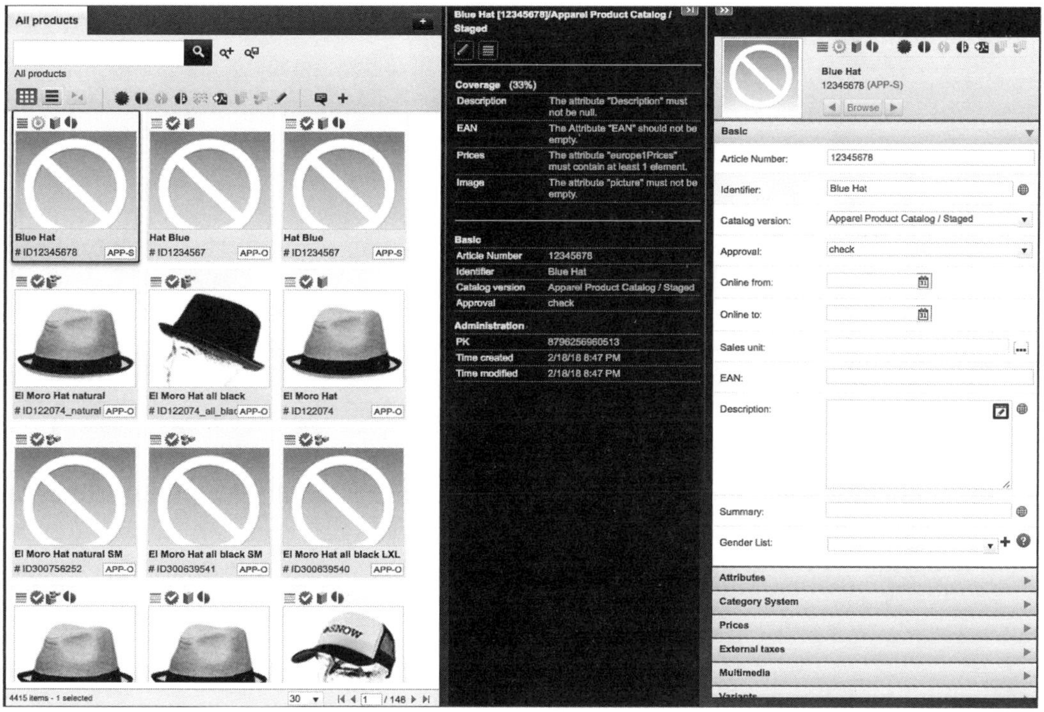

Figure 4.38 Edit Product Details (Legacy Product Cockpit)

4.2.4 Synchronizing Products

Synchronization is a process of propagating data from a staged to an online catalog version. This can be performed easily in the Product Catalog Cockpit for one or more products, categories, or even entire catalog versions. Because synchronization affects performance, permissions to synchronize should be assigned to the right people only and synchronization of large amounts of data should be avoided, as well as synchronization during peak times.

Backoffice

In the backoffice, there are different ways of manually synchronizing a product. Depending on the view you're using and the permissions assigned, a **Synchronize** button is available on the screen. Within the product view, you can select the product(s) that needs to be synchronized. Or, within the grid view, you can select the product(s) and click the **Synchronize** icon in the toolbar.

A pop-up (see Figure 4.39) will appear in which you will choose the destination for synchronizing the products. Click **Sync** to initiate the synchronization process. The status of synchronization jobs is shown in the process view within the backoffice.

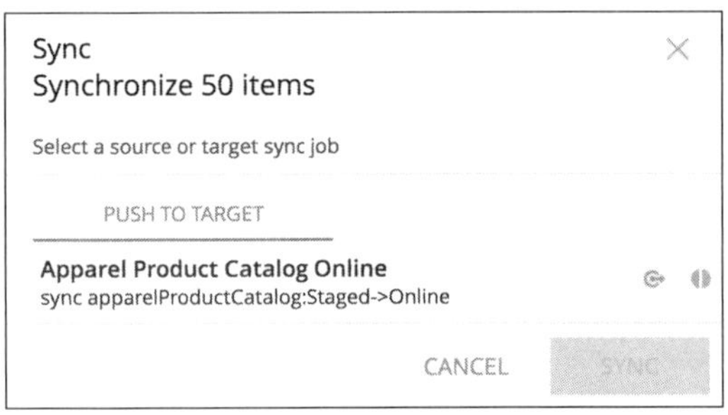

Figure 4.39 Synchronization Pop-Up List View (Backoffice)

Legacy Product Cockpit

In the legacy Product Cockpit, you select products that should be synchronized in the product view. When the products are selected, you can begin synchronization by clicking the **Synchronize** icon .

4.3 Configurable Products

Because SAP Commerce is used in different industries and supports various more complex selling scenarios, customers are using the platform to sell products that require configuration before purchase.

A configurable product is a single product or service with many options or variations that can be configured by a customer before purchase. The category configuration functionality enables a user to define different variants of a product. SAP Commerce supports various configurable products out of the box, which can be modified via configurable bundles.

Customers can use SAP Product Configuration add-on for SAP C/4HANA for complex configurations, product-associated yForms (like in the financial accelerator), bundles configured with the configurable bundle module, or custom product configurators. A mix of products is supported to be made configurable by different configurators in the same catalog, in the same cart, or in the same order.

Depending on the configuration for product variants, a variant category can inherit, override, or combine the configuration from a base product category. In the accelerator storefronts, all configurable products have a **Configure** button next to them (Figure 4.40) that navigates the customer to the **Configure Product Options** page (Figure 4.41). At checkout, the configuration of a product is validated before proceeding to checkout.

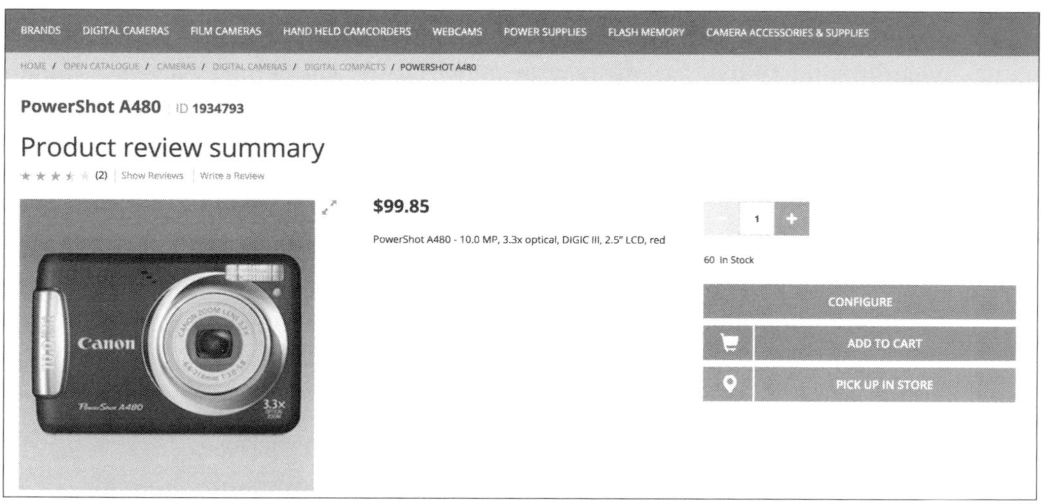

Figure 4.40 Configure Button Product Page

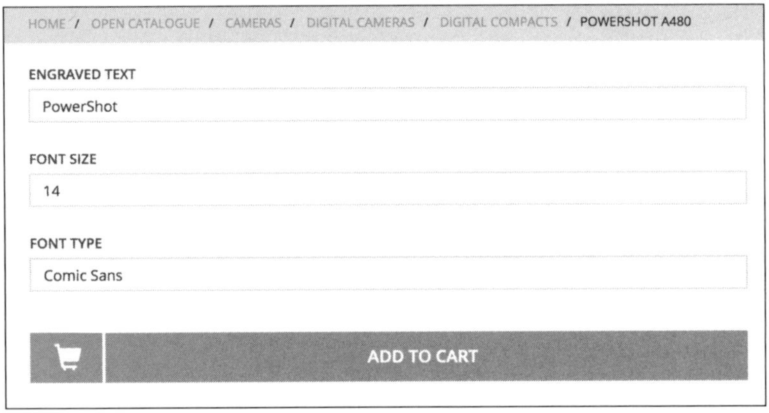

Figure 4.41 Configuration for Engraved Text Product

4.4 Bundling

The bundling module contains features specifically designed to address the needs of businesses that market and sell digital products and services, as opposed to or in addition to physical goods and services. The focus of the solution is to enable organizations to build and sell configurable product bundles and packages.

A product bundle/package is a combination of different products that are sold as a whole. The bundled items can be tangible products, services, or contract items. A package has a superordinate product that bundles the package components and is typically composed of various relationships at different hierarchy levels. A bundle can be composed of both standard and configurable products.

Product packages are used to combine different products into a package that is designed to meet certain customer requirements. Using product packages provides the following benefits:

- Different products can be combined based on specified rules.
- Packages can contain optional components, as well as alternative components.
- Products can be offered as whole but processed via different follow-up processes (e.g., contracts, sales orders, and service orders).
- Products can have special prices when offered within a package.

The option for bundles is available in the backoffice as of version 6.X and available in the legacy Product Cockpit. When a version of SAP Commerce that contains bundling (e.g., SAP Commerce, telco and media accelerator or SAP Commerce, B2C accelerator) is installed, the option for bundles is available as another perspective in the legacy Product Cockpit, in addition to the previously described product and catalog perspectives.

The module also features guided selling functionality, conditional availability of certain products depending on already selected items, and flexible product pricing depending on package contents. Figure 4.42 shows an example of the bundles view from the legacy Product Cockpit.

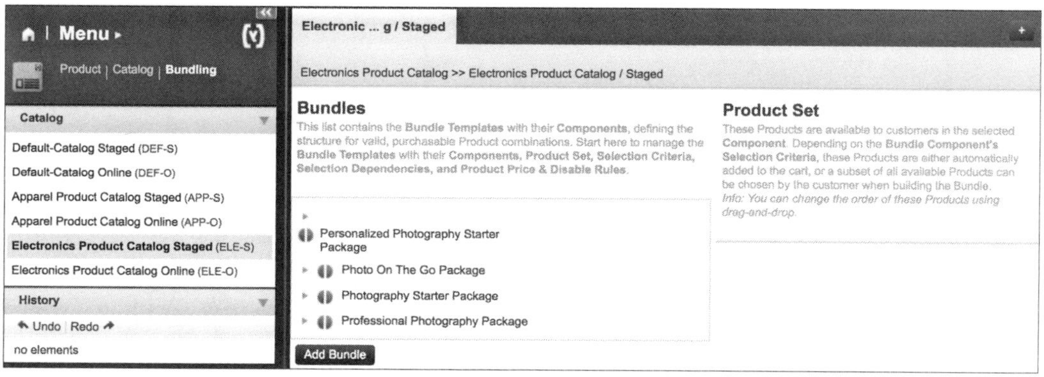

Figure 4.42 Bundles View (Legacy Product Cockpit)

In the legacy Product Cockpit, click **Bundling** on the left side in the navigation area. A bundle consists of the following information:

- **Basic Information**
  As shown in Figure 4.43, this includes information like the ID, name, description, version, parent template, and approval status. If the component is a child template, a parent template would be shown here.

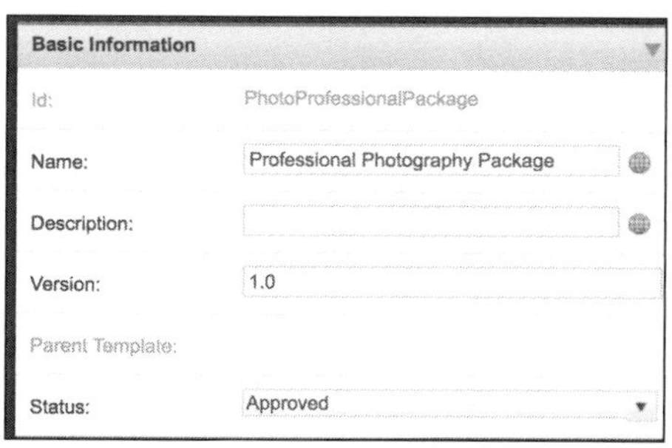

Figure 4.43 Bundle Basic Information (Legacy Product Cockpit)

- **Bundle Template Components**
  As shown in Figure 4.44, this is where child templates can be included by selecting an existing reference or adding a new item by selecting from the dropdown after clicking the **Add Reference** button next to the entry field.

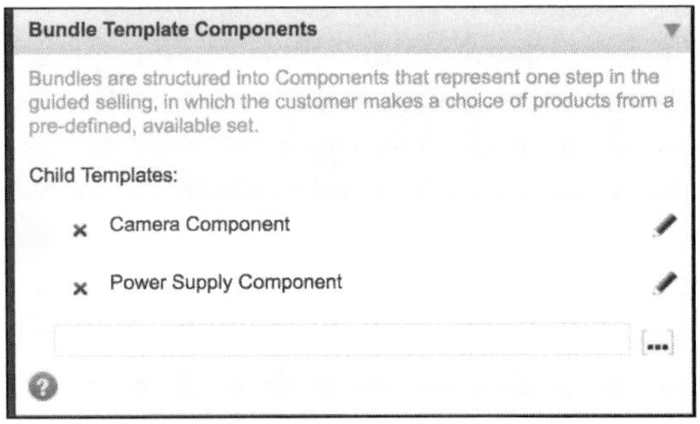

Figure 4.44 Bundle Template Component

- **Selection Criteria and Dependencies**
  As shown in Figure 4.45, the bundle section criteria define how many products a customer can or must choose in this bundle component and whether the selection is to be made automatically. By configuring required components, dependencies can be defined for this component.

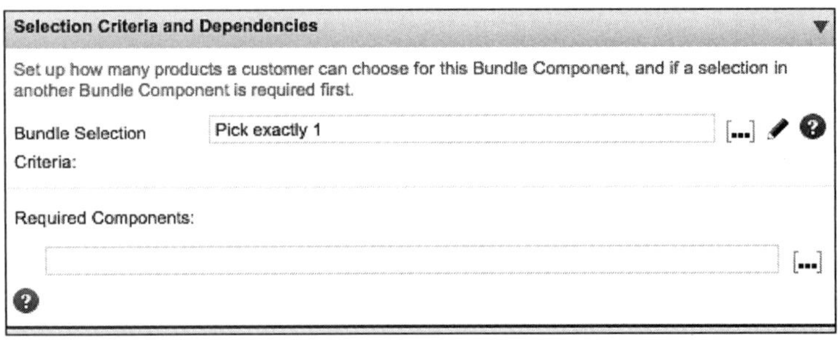

Figure 4.45 Selection Criteria and Dependencies

- **Component Product Set**
  As shown in Figure 4.46, these products are available to customers in the selected component. Depending on the bundle component's selection criteria, either these products are automatically added to the cart, or a subset of all available products can be chosen by the customer when building the bundle.

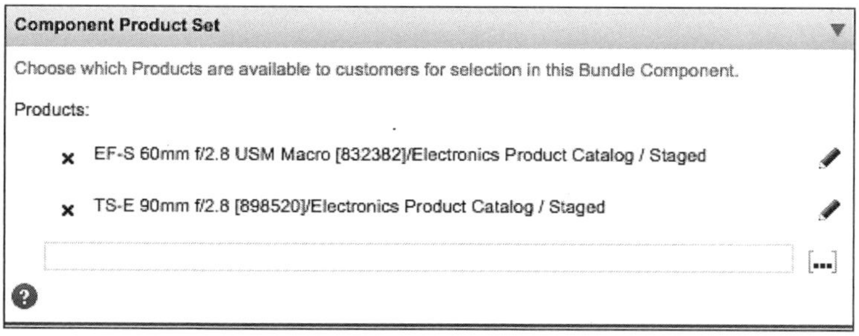

Figure 4.46 Component Product Set, Bundle Template

- **Product Price & Disable Rules**
  As shown in Figure 4.47, here the user can create conditional discounts for products purchased in bundles or set up disable rules to prevent customers from purchasing certain combinations of products.

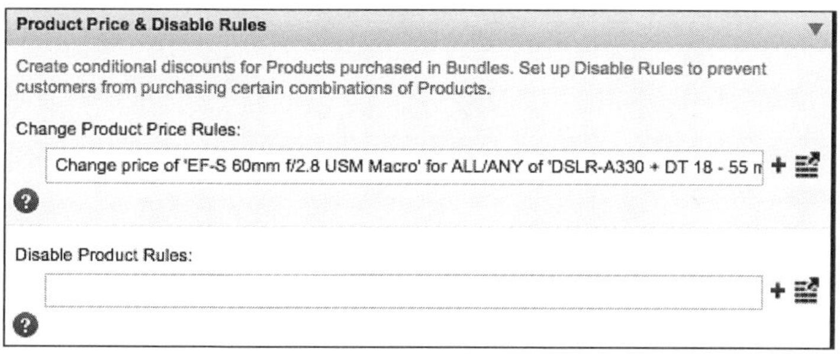

Figure 4.47 Product Price and Distribution Rule, Bundle Template

To add conditions for prices, the user can click **Add Condition** as shown in Figure 4.47, opening a screen (Figure 4.48) to add conditions to the pricing of the bundle. To disable specific rules for products, the user can click **Add Rule** as shown in Figure 4.47, opening a screen (Figure 4.49) in which rules can be applied to disable rules for specific bundle templates.

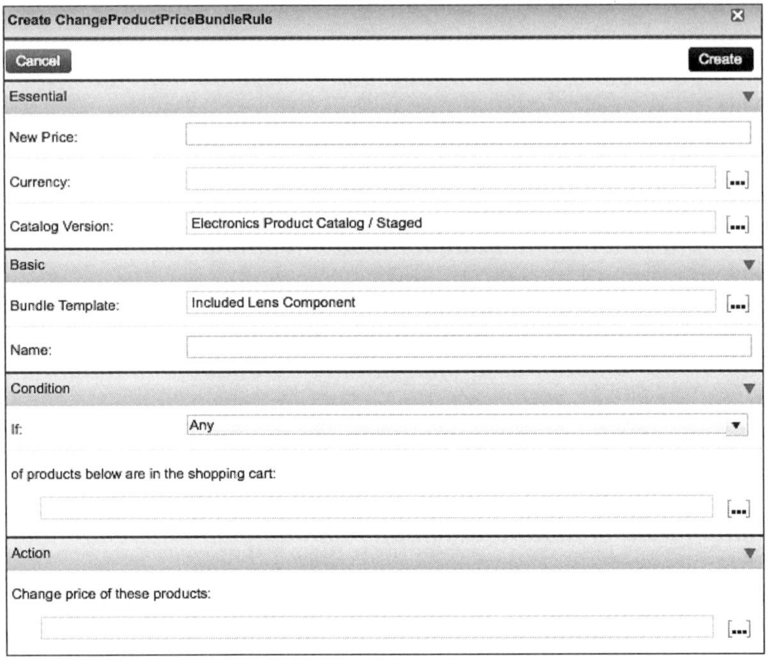

Figure 4.48 Conditional Pricing Definition, Bundle Template

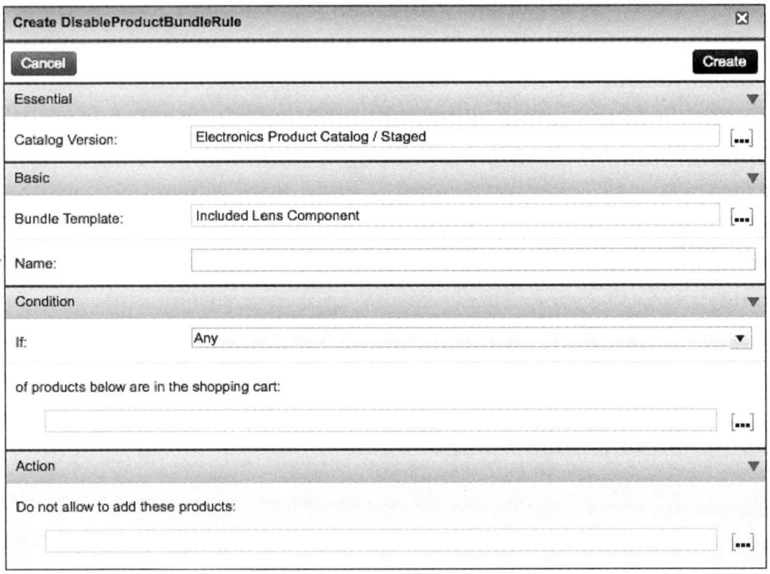

Figure 4.49 Disable Rules for Bundles, Bundles Template

Bundles can be added by clicking **Add Bundle** in the browser area. A pop-up will appear to create the bundle, as shown in Figure 4.50.

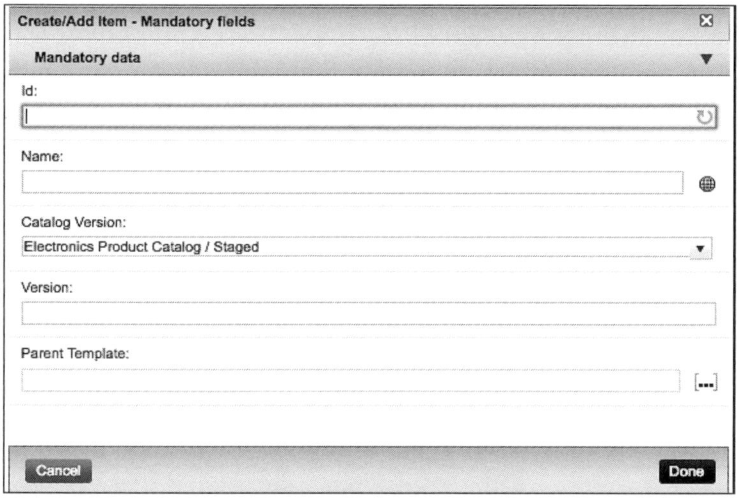

Figure 4.50 Add Bundle Pop-Up, Bundle Template

4.5 SAP Digital Asset Management

SAP Commerce allows users to unify and coordinate every aspect of media management using media conversion or SAP Digital Asset Management by OpenText. An *asset* is anything that adds value to an item managed in SAP Commerce. For example, if an item is a product, the asset can be a product attribute such as description, name, code, approval, or a reference to another business item, like a customer review, upselling product, or category. If an asset is a binary file, like an image or a movie, the asset is a digital asset. Typical digital assets for a product are images, logos, illustrations, audio and video files, presentations, layout page files, office documents and spreadsheets, CAD files, and other digital files in different formats.

Making digital assets more easily and consistently available and manageable in all distribution channels is the key for success in today's business. Growing customer requirements driven by print catalogs, websites, and convergent brand management are rapidly increasing the volume of digital media assets and the management overhead associated with the same. The major challenge is to manage digital assets as well as product data in a centralized and consistent manner. This typically fails because images, graphics, and videos need to be held in many different formats, sizes, and versions, resulting in an abundance of assets and repositories. Multichannel publishing increases the requirements for digital assets. A digital asset needs to be delivered to meet different strategies (e.g., on-demand or scheduled), in different formats depending on distribution channel (e.g., B2B or B2C), and with a specific purpose (e.g., online or offline).

SAP Commerce integrates out of the box with digital asset management solutions like CELUM's Digital Asset Management, SAP Digital Asset Management by OpenText, and Amplience. You can use ImageMagick, an open-source software product, to manage media in your project. With media conversion, you can create, edit, compose, or convert almost any available bitmap image format and extract the metadata of a bitmap image. Figure 4.51 shows an example of how the conversion of images can be defined for different sizes.

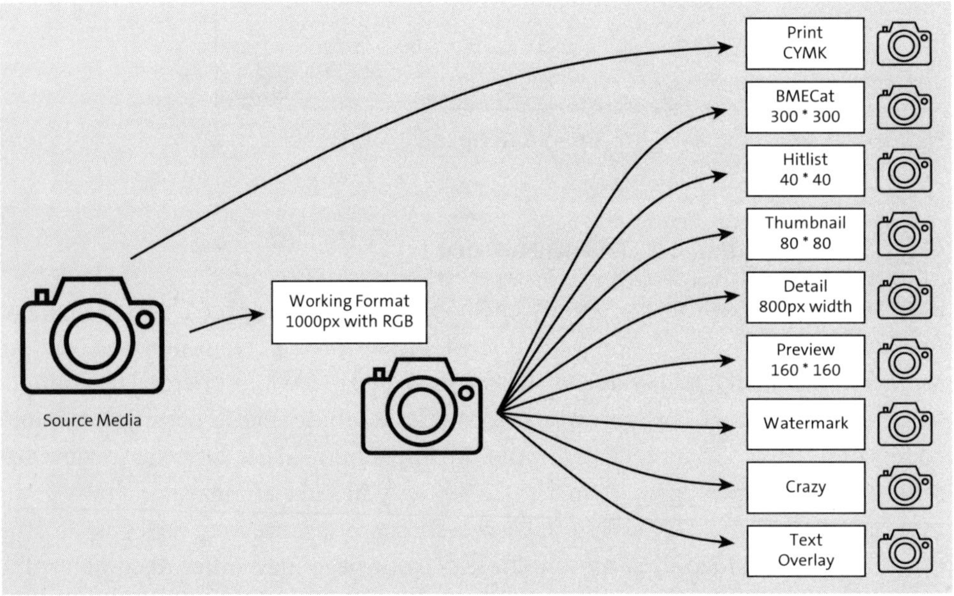

Figure 4.51 Media Conversion of Images

The media containers that will be created can be used as a business representation of a digital asset that contains all required media derivatives and source media. In this way, SAP Commerce becomes a multichannel content distribution platform in which all digital assets can reach any B2B or B2C touchpoint.

4.6 Summary

In this chapter, we discussed the product content and product catalog management functionality of SAP Commerce from different perspectives. SAP provides the product content and catalog module, offering tools to manage and set up catalogs in such a way that they reflect an organization's operating model. We shared recommended practices for setting up catalogs, as well as how to manage catalogs using the Product Cockpit and backoffice. We also introduced concepts such as configurable products, bundles, and digital asset management.

Now that you know how to manage products (content), the next chapter will dive deeper into the customer experience management functionality of SAP Commerce to retain and acquire customers for your SAP Commerce website.

Chapter 5
Customer Experience Management

From the moment that an end customer arrives at your storefront, every moment that he interacts with what you've built will fall to some degree under customer experience, the topic of this chapter. What do you want to enable him to do, and how will the experience look and feel? How will you encourage him to return?

Customer experience (CX) refers not only to the design and flow of a customer-facing web frontend—what we generally call *user experience (UX)*—but also to the way that experience extends beyond any one channel and to the features and functions that enable that omnichannel experience. A given customer-facing user interface is simply the frontend toolset with which your customers will interact. Customer experience includes that UI but also incorporates the functional flow from one UI or channel to another, the data and media strategies that support those interfaces, and, most importantly, the broader philosophies and principles that drive the design. Everything that affects your customers' interactions with what you've built, from the moment you begin designing it, falls within the purview of customer experience.

When we talk about managing customer experience within SAP Commerce, some of that more abstract philosophical work has of course been done for you. As we will discuss, there are omnichannel strategies built into the platform, as well as a set of features and functions that will allow you to innovate beyond the current standard of omnichannel and, in some cases, beyond the boundaries of standard commerce.

SAP Commerce draws a distinction between product content management (which we discussed in the previous chapter) on the one hand and customer experience management on the other. Data, media, design, and rules directly related to products or categories belong to your website's product catalog, whereas the rest of your content, from pages and page components to any media that is independent of structured product data, belongs to your content catalog, which is versioned much like the product catalog (with staged and online versions) but handled separately.

In this chapter, we'll discuss the design and management of content catalogs in SAP Commerce, as well as the suite's tools for personalization, including the newest addition to customer experience in SAP Commerce, *context-driven services*, the robust personalization and conversion optimization solution that lives alongside these core management tools.

5.1 Page Templates for All Channels

SAP Commerce uses *responsive technology* to deploy to multiple devices from a single set of page elements. This means that rather than detecting the browser or operating system that the customer is using and then serving up a page template accordingly (an approach called *adaptive design*), SAP Commerce accelerator storefronts detect the number of pixels being displayed and then select and size their content accordingly.

Note

If you ever want to see whether your favorite site—or, for that matter, your least favorite site—uses responsive design, just resize your browser window; if the layout of the page changes, then you're looking at something responsive.

The pixel counts are typically divided into breakpoints, which allow the responsive frontend to determine whether it is likely displaying for a desktop/laptop, a tablet, a mobile device, and so on. In principle, this approach can extend to any number of devices, if some new screen size standard comes into play (perhaps, say, as wearable technology continues to develop).

As an example, Figure 5.1 shows a block of content as displayed on the desktop breakpoint of the responsive homepage in the apparel store of the SAP Commerce accelerators.

Figure 5.2, by way of contrast, is part of the same set of content, resized for a mobile device breakpoint.

Figure 5.1 Full-Width Desktop Layout of Apparel Storefront

Figure 5.2 Vertically Oriented Mobile Layout of Apparel Storefront

Here we see two different approaches to adjusting content for different devices. In the case of the **Shop Women** banner, the image has simply been resized, making it more prominent in the more vertically oriented mobile layout. The **Start Your Season** banner, however, is a different crop of the source image, which preserves the model as the focal point of the image, as well as the slogan and the call to action, in a way that simply resizing a full-width banner intended for desktop screens would not.

It is up to an individual content team to decide which content should be resized and which should be swapped out for different imagery entirely. In general, you should keep the horizontality of mobile screens in mind and avoid visuals or elements or (especially) text or buttons that will be difficult to interpret when displayed at a smaller size.

In addition, any design elements that require the user to hover over an image should be eliminated for mobile and tablet designs because there is effectively no way to hover over an element on a touch screen. Indeed, this fact means that hover-overs have fallen out of favor in general for SAP Commerce accelerator storefronts. Customers generally want a consistent experience across channels in terms of the basic actions that are possible through the user interface.

So if customers on mobile devices are not going to be able to hover over an image of the front of a dress to see the back of it, for example, then you may not want to set that convention on your desktop site. This is not to say that hover-over is outside of best practices in and of itself, of course. It's simply a question of starting from what your customers expect on mobile and then fostering consistency. This point of caution ties into the larger principle of mobile-first design. The earliest mobile web pages essentially took existing desktop pages and shrunk down as many elements as possible to fit on a smaller screen—which, from a design philosophy perspective, is precisely backwards. That approach can easily result in page elements that are unwieldy, unclear, or otherwise unoptimized.

To avoid that, a *mobile-first approach* reorients your thinking in just the way that the term implies, by challenging you to first consider the smallest screen on which your content will ever be displayed, deciding which page elements are essential in that context, and then building out from there.

Searching and Browsing

Optimized mobile design is beneficial throughout SAP Commerce experiences, but it's more important in some areas of your storefront than in others. Some customers, especially older customers, tend to be reluctant to convert while using a mobile device—but these customers *do* tend to search, research, learn, select, and even build shopping carts or builds of materials on mobile devices. This means that it's tremendously important to let such customers continue their purchasing processes on other devices, as discussed in Chapter 3, Section 3.2. It also means that mobile-optimized content, and therefore mobile-first design, is even more important on product detail pages, product listing pages, and content pages than it is for checkout or account management pages. Even if you have a complex purchasing process that cannot be entirely optimized for mobile, it is very much in your interest to optimize the search and browsing experience for mobile.

Elements that are vital to a customer's initial interactions with your storefront should be initially visible upon arriving at the storefront. Elements that are necessary but may not be immediately necessary, such as account management tools, are typically hidden behind an icon composed of three or four horizontal lines (usually called a hamburger) on the mobile site, as shown on the left in Figure 5.3.

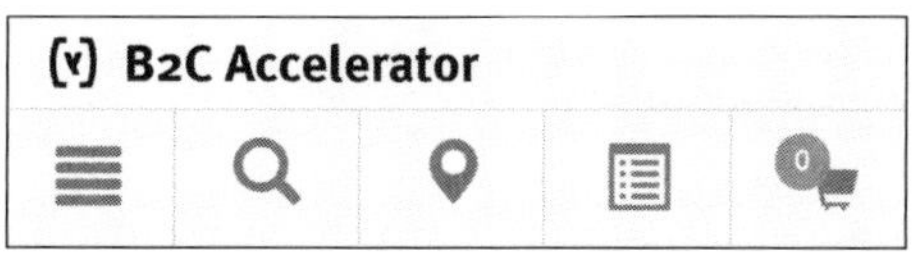

Figure 5.3 Compressed Mobile UI Elements, Including Hamburger, in the Electronics Storefront

The responsive technology in SAP Commerce accelerator storefronts works by compiling Leaner Style Sheets (LESS) into standard Cascading Style Sheets (CSS) for each breakpoint-specific layout. The system also makes use of *resource minification*, meaning that in the cases of media and code and scripts, the system will try to reduce the size of resources as much as possible without losing vital information.

In the specific case of images in a responsive SAP Commerce accelerators storefront, breakpoints are interpreted via *image populators*. Whereas a standard `imagecomponent` element simply holds and displays a single image, responsive components such as the `SimpleResponsiveBanner` component (which is a concrete implementation of the `AbstractResponsiveBannerComponent` abstract class) map individual image files to their respective breakpoints. These mappings are stored in the `Imager.min.js` script library—and they are not necessarily one-to-one; a tablet-sized image may or may not also work for desktop or for mobile, depending on the design.

This more conditional, keypair-based mapping is where image populators come in. The SAP Commerce Accelerator provides two, ResponsiveMediaContainerPopulator and ResponsiveImagePopulator. The former sends image-size parameters, and the latter populates the appropriate components with the appropriate images.

ResponsiveMediaContainerPopulator then passes the sorted results to Imager.min.js, which looks for any and all <img> elements that have the js-responsive-image class attribute in the web browser's Document Object Model (DOM). When it finds one, it renders images using the parameters in Imager.min.js, such as those shown in Listing 5.1.

```
<img class="js-responsive-image" data-media=
'{"100":"Image of width 100x50",
"200":"Image of width 200x50",
"400":"Image of width 400x50",
"600":"Image of width 600x50",
"800":"Image of width 800x50",
"1000":"Image of width 1000x50"}'
alt="">
```

Listing 5.1 Responsive Image Sizing Parameters in Imager.min.js

By default, the system maps and populates images by means of naming conventions, with filenames ending with the size of the images: _800x300, for example. Imager.min.js checks for these suffixes first. The system also offers a fallback mechanism, leveraging the mediaFormat qualifiers defined in the *spring.xml* file of the acceleratorfacades extension. Here the breakpoint is based on width because, as you can see in Listing 5.1, Imager.min.js uses image width to map images to breakpoints. The named breakpoint widths appear as shown in Listing 5.2 in *spring.xml*.

```
<alias alias="responsiveImageFormats" name="responsiveImageFormats" />
    <util:map id="responsiveImageFormats" map-class=
"java.util.LinkedHashMap" value-type="java.lang.Integer">
        <entry key="widescreen" value="1200"/>
        <entry key="desktop" value="992"/>
        <entry key="tablet" value="768"/>
        <entry key="mobile" value="480"/>
    </util:map>
```

Listing 5.2 Named Breakpoints for Responsive Pages

An ImpEx job for `SimpleResponsiveBanner` and its associated types and media items, then, would appear as shown in Listing 5.3.

```
INSERT_UPDATE Media;mediaFormat(qualifier);code[unique=true];@media[
translator=de.hybris.platform.impex.jalo.media.MediaDataTranslator][
forceWrite=true];realfilename;altText;mime[default='image/jpeg'];$contentCV[
unique=true];folder(qualifier)[default=images];
;mobile;Elec_480x320_HomeSpeed_EN_01_480W.jpg;$siteResource/images/banners/
homepage/responsive/Elec_480x320_HomeSpeed_EN_01_480W.jpg;Elec_480x320_
HomeSpeed_EN_01_480W.jpg;"Fast Precise";
;tablet;Elec_770x350_HomeSpeed_EN_01_770W.jpg;$siteResource/images/banners/
homepage/responsive/Elec_770x350_HomeSpeed_EN_01_770W.jpg;Elec_770x350_
HomeSpeed_EN_01_770W.jpg;"Fast Precise";
;desktop;Elec_960x330_HomeSpeed_EN_01_960W.jpg;$siteResource/images/banners/
homepage/responsive/Elec_960x330_HomeSpeed_EN_01_960W.jpg;Elec_960x330_
HomeSpeed_EN_01_960W.jpg;"Fast Precise";
;widescreen;Elec_1400x440_HomeSpeed_EN_01_1400W.jpg;$siteResource/images/
banners/homepage/responsive/Elec_1400x440_HomeSpeed_EN_01_1400W.jpg;Elec_
1400x440_HomeSpeed_EN_01_1400W.jpg;"Fast Precise";

INSERT_UPDATE MediaContainer;qualifier[unique=true];$medias;$contentCV[unique=
true]
;electronics-homepage-spalsh-en;Elec_480x320_HomeSpeed_EN_01_480W.jpg,Elec_
770x350_HomeSpeed_EN_01_770W.jpg,Elec_960x330_HomeSpeed_EN_01_960W.jpg,Elec_
1400x440_HomeSpeed_EN_01_1400W.jpg

INSERT_UPDATE SimpleResponsiveBannerComponent;$contentCV[unique=true];uid[
unique=true];$mediaContainer
;;ElectronicsHompageSplashBannerComponent;electronics-homepage-spalsh-en
```

Listing 5.3 ImpEx Job for Responsive Banner

Finally, it bears mentioning that SAP Commerce accelerator storefronts allow for *themes*, which allow the user to set global colors and typography for their storefronts in the variables.less (for global settings) and theme-variables.less (for theme-specific settings) files. For example, the `@link-color` variable sets the color of links, and the `@text-color` variable sets the default color of text. You can also set variables for brand-specific colors (primary, secondary, and tertiary) within a theme to create brand-specific experiences within a shared responsive storefront.

With the key points of responsive web layouts now clear, and before we move on to SAP Commerce's tools for managing web content, let's take a closer look at the structure of an SAP Commerce accelerator storefront web application.

5.2 Web Content Management System

SAP Commerce uses the terms *content management system* and *web content management system* somewhat interchangeably, both because much if not all of the content you are managing will be deployed to the web in some manner or another and because the management tools themselves are web-based. In this section, we'll discuss these tools, as well as the overall content strategies and structures that they enable.

There are two interfaces for web content management in SAP Commerce—the CMS Cockpit and SmartEdit—as well as some relevant functionality in the administration perspective in the backoffice (as shown in Figure 5.4).

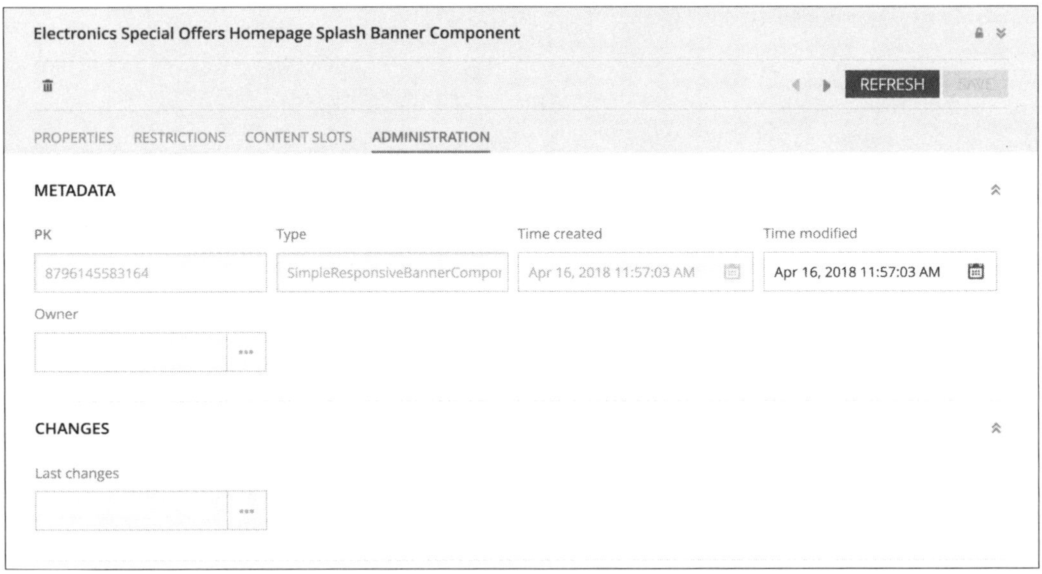

Figure 5.4 Attributes of Banner Component for Electronics Store

Business users creating and editing pages from day to day will do so primarily in SmartEdit, which we will cover in the next section. Here we will focus on the other two interfaces, but before we can do that, we'll discuss the overall structure of web content in an SAP Commerce accelerator storefront. After all, we can't talk about managing content until we understand what we're managing.

Individual elements in an SAP Commerce accelerator storefront—banners, product information, forms, search results, buttons, and so on—are components, defined in their purposes and behaviors by different component types. Components are modeled as individual, modular, reusable parts that can be managed centrally and used repeatedly throughout the customer experience. If your footer links and terms and conditions, for example, are modeled as components, then you can easily include them in your promotional communications or in new pages you create; just as importantly, you can update them a single time in your content management system and see the changes reflected in every location where the content appears.

Components are flexible in terms of the amount of information, visual or otherwise, that they communicate; as such, customers do not necessarily know where one component ends and another begins. In the electronics store, for example, the image carousel at the top of the page houses multiple images within a single component, whereas the content blocks lower on the page are multiple components, each holding a single image, as shown in Figure 5.1 earlier.

But this component-based approach does not mean simply transcluding your header and footer content on each page. It also means reusing banners, product imagery, and other assets on, for example, your homepage, your product listing page, your product detail page, and your promotional pages.

When developing new elements or pages for your site, you want to make sure, whenever possible, to *componentize* them; that is, you want as many elements as possible in your storefront to be modular components rather than static, hard-coded web content. This is helpful if you want to manage these elements centrally and deploy them to multiple areas of your storefront, and it is *necessary* if you want to take full advantage of personalization: swapping out some specific asset for some other asset for a specific group of customers or when a customer adds a certain product to his cart.

In practice, this principle tends to go by the wayside when project timelines get tight or other areas of the project require more attention than you'd originally planned. Although not ideal, this compromise can work so long as you are intentional about which parts of your customer experience need to be componentized and which do not. Perhaps your header and footer will be fairly static and therefore can be hard-coded. Perhaps your checkout experience is specific enough to your line (or lines) of business that you will not be changing or personalizing it. In such cases, leaving some components static may be perfectly acceptable, at least during your first phase of deployment. If too much (or all) of a given page becomes too static, however, you will be missing out on many of benefits of SAP Commerce's personalization features, which we will discuss in Section 5.4.

Components are vital to the structure of your storefront, but they are not the navigational unit that customers most readily think of when they interact with your website. Rather, most customers imagine your site's structure in terms of *pages*, the effectual combination of structured content (componentized or not) that appears when a customer arrives at a certain URL. To understand pages, we will first need to understand page templates and page types, which are themselves divided into five important page types:

1. **Content pages**
   These are built primarily by hand by content managers (though they can be personalized for specific users, as we will discuss later).
2. **Category pages**
   These list products for a given category or a given set of search parameters and are therefore built partially by Solr search (which we will discuss more thoroughly in Chapter 8).
3. **Product pages**
   These show individual products or bundles and are therefore built partially by your product content catalog(s).
4. **Abstract pages**
   These hold functionality such as checkout, managing saved carts, creating returns, initiating password resets, and creating support tickets.
5. **Document pages**
   These generate emails and forms to keep them in line with the look, feel, and functionality of the rest of your storefront.

It is important to emphasize that you have the highest degree of direct, day-to-day control over content pages, such as the homepage. You can add personalized or promotional content to checkout pages, product detail pages, product listing pages, and so on—but these have certain elements that need to be structured and built by the system, whether that means ordered search results in the case of a product listing page (as discussed in Chapter 8) or address and payment forms in the case of a checkout page (as discussed in Chapter 3). Content pages do not necessarily have any of these more system-assembled or instrumental elements, and content pages are therefore the best place to start when you begin to create new pages in the content management system.

The SAP Commerce accelerator storefronts come bundled with some page templates for each of the page types: landing page templates for homepages, product detail pages for product listings, and even prebuilt layouts for frequently asked questions and account management pages. Page templates include JSP-based layouts, sizing information for each slot into which components can be placed, and rules for which component type can be placed into which slot.

This can be as general as saying that a given component slot must contain an image or as specific as saying that a given component slot must contain an image of a type that specifies size, format, and origin. It's up to you to curate your media types, but your inclusion and exclusion rules can be as intentional and proscriptive as you like, so long as your media items are organized and tagged accordingly. Being proscriptive about your template and slot rules can prevent content managers from inadvertently breaking the page but also can limit their ability to be inventive within the rules you've set.

Your goal always should be to balance these two factors because without explicit exclusion or inclusion rules, the system will always tend toward adaptability. If you have a slot for a full-width image, for example, and you do not specify some media type that contains images of the correct dimensions, then a content manager will be able to insert *any* image to which they have access into that slot, which would result in a stretched, blurred, or otherwise suboptimal asset.

This same flexibility means that an attentive and inventive content manager can achieve a large number of discrete looks and feels from a relatively small number of page templates. Removing that full-width banner entirely will not result in a large field of blank white space but rather in the components below that one rising to meet the header, thereby creating an effectually different page layout, as shown in Figure 5.5.

Page templates govern much of the layouts that customers see when they browse your storefront, but again, it is the pages themselves that customers will interact with, moment to moment, and that content managers will build during and after development. An active, potentially browsable instance of a given page template, with one or multiple URLs to reach it, is a page. Where a page template says an image goes here, a page says *this* image goes here. Landing page 2 is a page template; the homepage is a page.

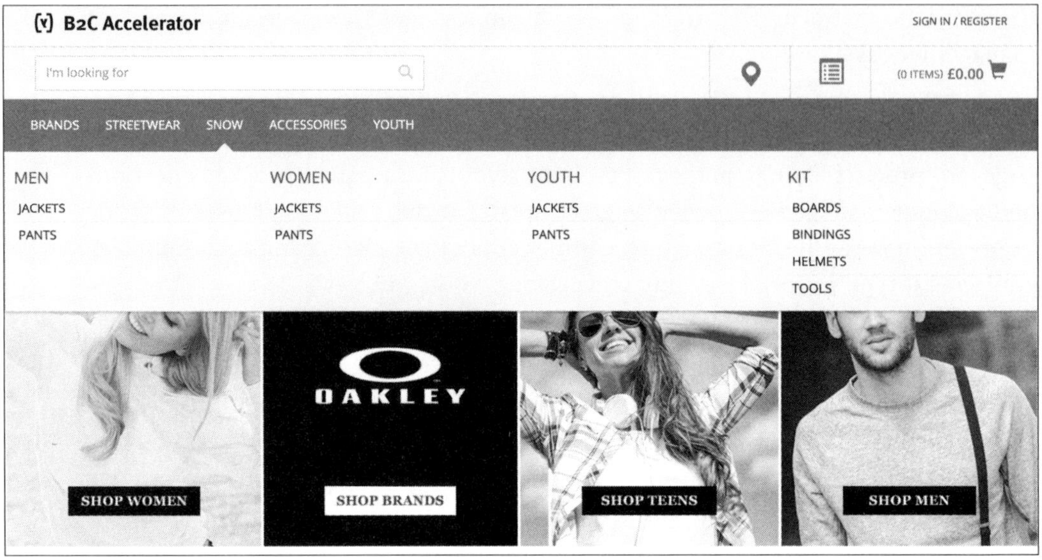

Figure 5.5 Dynamically Altered Layout for Store

That's in the case of content pages. In the case of product pages, even the page says the product content goes here rather than *this* product's content goes here. There is generally only a single product page on a given SAP Commerce accelerator storefront, and, as described earlier, the specific product information being displayed will originate in the product catalog rather than the content catalog.

With all of that said, we can move on to the admin perspective in the backoffice and the Web Content Management System (WCMS) Cockpit, beginning with the former—a view for your content catalogs, data model, and overall structure. You can see this data set under the **WCMS** node (see Figure 5.6) when logged in as an administrator or as any other backoffice user with access to content catalogs and their associated types.

Some important functions that are not available in SmartEdit are available here, as follows:

- Creating content catalogs (and catalog versions)
- Creating homepages
- Restoring deleted pages
- Permanently deleting pages "deleted" in SmartEdit

- Adding actions to components
- Creating and editing page templates

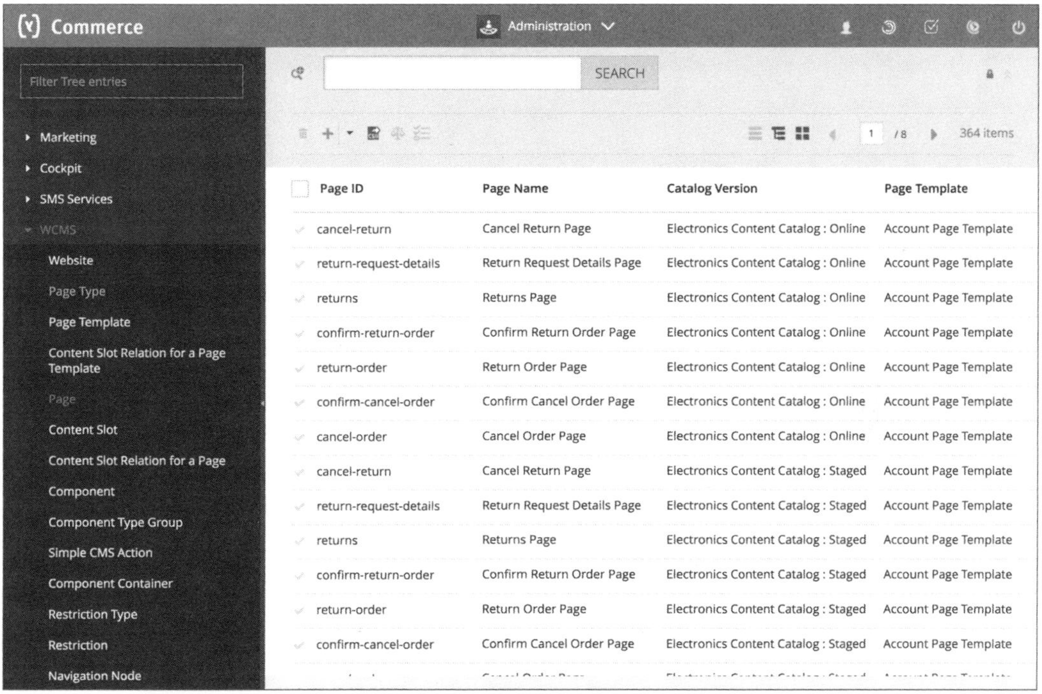

Figure 5.6 WCMS Node, Viewed in Admin Perspective in Backoffice

It is also generally here that more senior or more technical content managers can edit the details of catalogs, catalog versions, and page templates, as well as view restrictions more holistically. (We'll discuss restrictions in Section 5.3.4, as well as in Chapter 9).

You may have noticed that this view does not cover intuitive, what-you-see-is-what-you-get (WYSIWYG) page editing. That functionality is covered by SmartEdit—as well as by the CMS Cockpit, the original purpose-built interface for content catalogs in SAP Commerce. The CMS Cockpit has three important perspectives: WCMS page view, live edit, and navigation. In the *WCMS page view*, shown in Figure 5.7, content managers can edit pages in a wireframe-like view.

Live edit is essentially an earlier iteration of SmartEdit, allowing users to preview pages (with personalization rules if desired) and edit those pages in place. In a system that has SmartEdit running, there is no reason to prefer live edit: though SmartEdit has not yet achieved full feature parity with the old cockpit, the features that it lacks are covered by the admin perspective in the backoffice, as described previously.

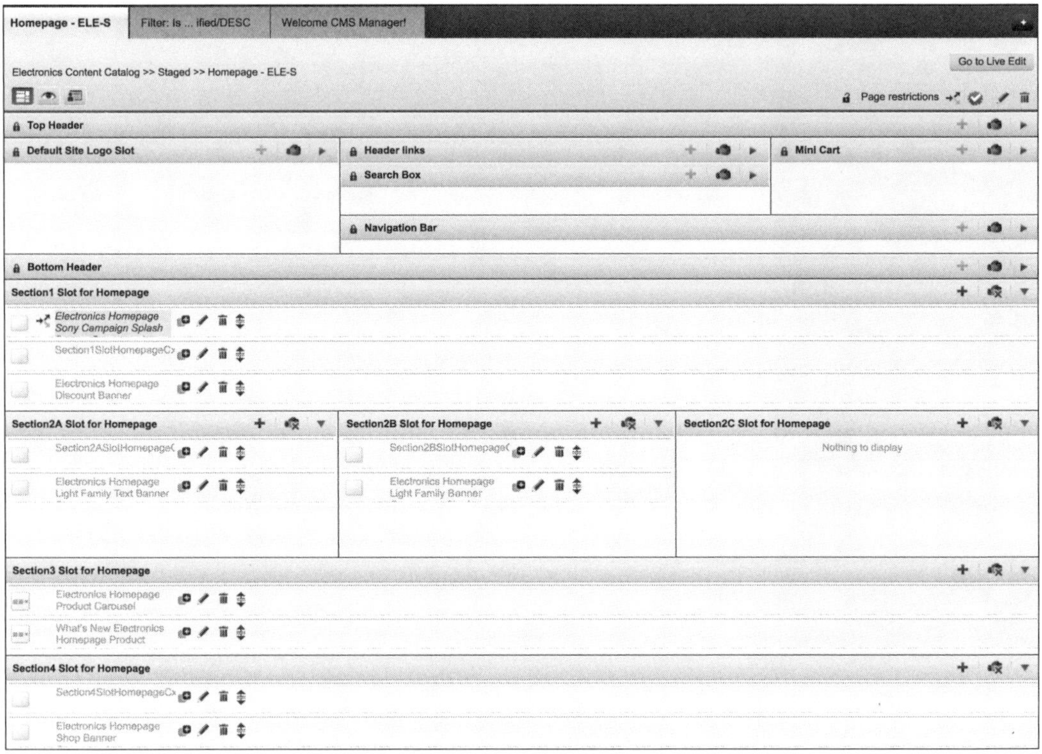

Figure 5.7 WCMS Page View in WCMS Cockpit

Navigation, meanwhile, allows content managers to create and edit the navigation nodes that make up the headers and footers of pages. Although the header nodes typically mirror top-level product categories and/or page hierarchies, it's important to keep in mind that they are in fact entirely independent of these. They are purely content catalog items, even if they link to items in the product catalog.

Because navigation nodes also can be created and modified in SmartEdit, let's now move on to what is, for most users, the primary content manager interface in SAP Commerce. Let's talk about SmartEdit, both in terms of day-to-day use and in terms of configuration and customization.

5.3 SmartEdit

SmartEdit allows content managers to create new pages from existing templates, add, edit, and remove those components via drag and drop, and test personalized experiences within those pages, all from a single scalable user interface. In this section, we'll discuss the technology behind SmartEdit, its core features and functions, the steps necessary to customize the tool, and, perhaps most importantly, the groundwork that SmartEdit lays for personalized customer experiences.

From a technical perspective, SmartEdit is a UI for managing web pages and a JavaScript framework that allows developers to connect pages to that UI, following a model-view-controller (MVC) approach and using AngularJS modules to compose HTML, CSS, and JavaScript fragments.

This UI and this framework are both natively and automatically connected to SAP Commerce accelerator storefront pages, but in principle they can be connected to other web frontends as well.

5.3.1 Framework and Architecture

Before we discuss SmartEdit in greater technical detail, let's take a moment to discuss *Grunt*, third-party software used to build SmartEdit extensions. Grunt organizes and executes plugins, configuring, ordering, and grouping them via the settings in Gruntfile.js, located in the root folder of all SmartEdit extensions that make use of JavaScript.

Grunt plugins format JavaScript and HTML files (often adding semicolons, which are easy to accidentally exclude), analyze JavaScript syntax, translate HTML templates to JavaScript modules, minify Angular JS JavaScript files, and manage source concentration, unit and integration testing, and generation of CSS files via LESS.

The primary function of Grunt in a SmartEdit context is for building extensions, but you can also use plugins that watch for changes in the running system (the `watcher` plugin) and integrate your system with other systems for debugging and testing (the `connect` plugin). To add these plugins to your *Gruntfile.js*, add the code in Listing 5.4.

```
watch: {
          xyz: {
              files: ['Gruntfile.js', 'web/features/**/*', 'jsTests/**/*'],
              tasks: ['dev'],
              options: {
```

```
                atBegin: true
            }
        }

connect: {
        "dev": {
            "options": {
                "hostname": "0.0.0.0",
                "port": 8080,
                "keepalive": true,
                "open": true
            }
        },
        "test": {
            "options": {
                "hostname": "0.0.0.0",
                "port": 7000
            }
        },
        "debug": {
            "options": {
                "hostname": "0.0.0.0",
                "port": 7000,
                "keepalive": true
            }
        },
        "docs": {
             "options": {
                 "hostname": "0.0.0.0",
                 "port": 9090,
                 "keepalive": true,
                 "open": true,
                 "base": "./jsTarget/docs"
             }
...
```

Listing 5.4 Adding Watcher and Connect Plugins to Gruntfile.js

You call Grunt using the `nomancillary` extension of the `npm-ancillary` module. You'll need to include this extension in the *extensioninfo.xml* file for each relevant JavaScript extension. The *extensioninfo.xml* file in the `cmssmartedit` extension, for example, contains the parameters from Listing 5.5.

```
<extensioninfo xmlns:xsi="http://www.w3.org/2001/XMLSchema-
instance" xsi:noNamespaceSchemaLocation="extensioninfo.xsd">

   <extension  name="cmssmartedit"
               abstractclassprefix="Generated"
               classprefix="CmsSmartedit"
               managername="CmsSmarteditManager"
               managersuperclass="de.hybris.platform.jalo.extension.Extension"
               >

      <requires-extension name="npmancillary" />
      <requires-extension name="smartedit" />

      <coremodule     packageroot="de.hybris.cmssmartedit"
                     manager="de.hybris.cmssmartedit.jalo.CmsSmarteditManager"
                     generated="true"
                     />
       <webmodule jspcompile="false" webroot="/cmssmartedit"/>

   </extension>

</extensioninfo>
```

Listing 5.5 Relevant Additions to extensioninfo.xml

This connects your extension to the *extensioninfo.xml* file, which in turn contains and calls the `gruntBuild` macro. This macro creates a symbolic link (called `node_modules`) between the `nomancillary` extension and your own, as shown in Listing 5.6.

```
<?xml version="1.0"?>
<project name="cmssmartedit_buildcallbacks">
<macrodef name="cmssmartedit_before_build">
    <sequential>
        <linkToSELibraries path="${ext.cmssmartedit.path}"/>
```

```
    </sequential>
</macrodef>
</project
```

Listing 5.6 Making Relevant Additions to cmssmartedit

With an understanding of Grunt, we can now move on to the data model and configuration options of SmartEdit itself.

SmartEdit modules contain three key types of features, as shown in Figure 5.8:

1. Decorators, which add rendering and/or behavior to components. (In the code, these behavior triggers are sometimes referred to as *directives*.)
2. Contextual menu items, which are added to the core `contextual menu` decorator, with each item performing a different action.
3. Toolbar actions, which enact behavior when triggered by contextual menu items.

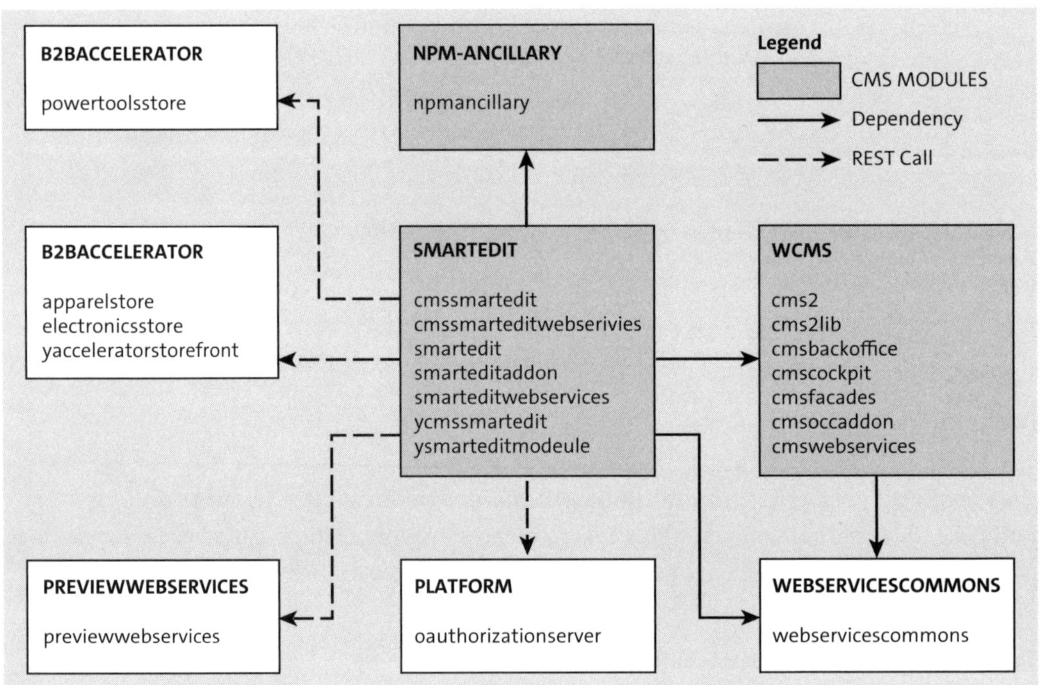

Figure 5.8 Key Modules Used by SmartEdit and Their Dependencies

To add a new decorator, start by creating an AngularJS module. In this example, let's name it `SampleDecorator`; call the decorator (or directive) itself `sample`. (Note that the name of your module must end in the `Decorator` suffix.) Save the new module in the *web/features/sampleDecorator* directory. Our goal will be to create a new decorator activated by the customer's mouse moving over the attached SmartEdit element. In the code, these steps would appear as shown in Listing 5.7.


```
angular.module('sampleDecorator', ['myModuleTemplates'])
    .directive('sample', ['$timeout', function($timeout) {
        return {
            templateUrl: 'web/features/sampleDecorator/
sampleDecoratorTemplate.html',
            restrict: 'C',
            transclude: true,
            replace: false,
            scope: {
                smarteditComponentId: '@',
                smarteditComponentType: '@',
                active: '='
            },

            link: function($scope, element, attrs) {
                $scope.visible = false;
                $scope.mouseleave = function() {
                    $timeout(function() {
                        $scope.visible = false;
                    }, 1000);
                };
                $scope.mouseenter = function() {
                    $scope.visible = true;
                };
            }
        };
    }]);
```

Listing 5.7 AngularJS Module for New Decorator

Let's break down the results of that snippet. First, the code sets the value for `templa-teURL` so that the compiled directive can locate the decorator template, as shown in Listing 5.8.

```
angular.module('sampleDecorator', ['myModuleTemplates'])
    .directive('sample', ['$timeout', function($timeout) {
        return {
            templateUrl: 'web/features/sampleDecorator/
sampleDecoratorTemplate.html',
```

Listing 5.8 Setting Value for templateURL

The code also sets the value for the `restrict` property to `C`, which will cause the directive to invoke only the `CSS` class type:

```
            restrict: 'C',
```

Further, the code sets the `transclude` property to `true` and the `replace` property to `false`. This means that the decorator will append the existing DOM rather than replace it. In other words, this decorator will not override the entire UI but will simply add to it:

```
transclude: true,
            replace: false,
```

The code in Listing 5.7 also adds the following three parameters, which we show again in Listing 5.9:

1. `smarteditComponentType`, which defines the type of component being extracted from the DOM
2. `smarteditComponentId`, which defines the ID of the specific `smarteditComponent` being extracted
3. `active`, which acts as a toggle to activate or deactivate the decorator

```
scope: {
                smarteditComponentId: '@',
                smarteditComponentType: '@',
                active: '='
            },
```

Listing 5.9 Adding Parameters and Enabling Transclude

Finally, the code sets the `link` function, which attaches event listeners to DOM elements, watches model properties for changes, and updates the DOM. When the directive is called, it acts as a controller. Listing 5.10 sets three values for the `link` function:

1. *visible* is set to *false*, meaning that the decorator is not initially active.
2. When the customer's mouse hovers over (mouseenter), the decorator becomes visible.
3. When the customer's mouse is no longer hovering over (mouseleave), the decorator is no longer visible.


```
link: function($scope, element, attrs) {
                $scope.visible = false;
                $scope.mouseleave = function() {
                    $timeout(function() {
                        $scope.visible = false;
                    }, 1000);
                };
                $scope.mouseenter = function() {
                    $scope.visible = true;
                };
            }
        };
    }]);
```

Listing 5.10 Adding Link Function and Its Associated Values

Note that any module you create for a decorator will need to contain the `<div data-ng-transclude>` tag, which tells the directive where to inject its appended—or, more exactly, transcluded—content. (We say that this content is *transcluded* because it exists in a content repository and can be called in multiple contexts, and because it is one part among several in a componentized presentation layer.)

Now, with all of this done, we can create a template. Call it sampledecoratorTemplate.html (decorator template names should always end in the suffix *Template.html*, for a reason that will be clear in a moment) and place it under *web/features/sampleDecorator/SampleDecoratorTemplate.html*. This template will define mouseenter and mouseleave event handlers to properly control the visibility of the decorator, which would appear in the code as shown in Listing 5.11.

```
<div>
<div data-ng-mouseleave="mouseleave()" data-ng-if="active">
<div data-ng-mouseenter="mouseenter()">
<div data-ng-transclude></div>
<span id='decoratorText'>decorator wired</span>
```

```
</div>
</div>
<div data-ng-mouseleave="mouseleave()" data-ng-if="!active">
<div data-ng-transclude></div>
</div>
</div>
```

Listing 5.11 New Template: sampledecoratorTemplate.html

With this done, next write the decorator to the module you created in the *web/features* folder. Create a module called `myModule` and add the decorator as a dependency—while also adding `decoratorServiceModule`, which will allow you to wire the decorator to a component type in the next step, as shown in Listing 5.12.

```
angular.module('myModule', [
        'sampleDecorator',
'decoratorServiceModule'
    ])
```

Listing 5.12 Writing New Decorator to Module

You can now use the `addMappings` method of `decoratorService` to wire the decorator to one or more components, as shown in Listing 5.13.

```
.run(function(decoratorService) {
decoratorService.addMappings({
                'sampleComponent': ['sample']
        });
 });
```

Listing 5.13 Wiring Decorator to Component

If you want to wire decorators to multiple components, you can do so by listing the exact decorator names:

```
'componentType1': ['decorator1', 'decorator2']
```

You can also specify a component type and apply the decorator to all components of that type:

```
'.*Type1': ['decorator1']
```

Or you can wire the decorator to all components, but with exceptions (the exception here being any component with "Type1" in its name):

```
'^((?!Type1).)*$': ['decorator1']
```

Next, let's use *Gruntfile.js* to create an AngularJS module for the decorator templates, converting the HTML JavaScript modules as shown in Listing 5.14.


```
ngtemplates: {
            options: {
                standalone: true, //
to declare a module as opposed to binding to an existing one
                module: 'myModuleTemplates'
            },
            run: {
                src: ['web/features/**/*Template.html'],
                dest: 'jsTarget/web/features/templates.js'
            }
        }
```

Listing 5.14 Creating AngularJS Module for New Decorator Template(s)

On execution of this task, the system will find all templates with names that end in *Templates.html* (which is why you used that suffix on your own new template) and load them into the *templates.js* file. The templates will reside in an AngularJS module called `myModuleTemplates`. You can then wire your decorator modules to the myModule.js module, thereby integrating your templates into the SmartEdit experience and eliminating the need for real-time AJAX calls.

Note that this step is only necessary if you have created your own new module. If you have an extension generated from the out-of-the-box `ysmarteditmodule` template, then this wiring will be complete as soon as you have activated Grunt. The same caveat applies to the next step, in which we will (at last) expose the module to the SmartEdit application.

If you are dealing with a newly added module, then you will need to create a unified JavaScript file to expose it. This file will live in the *web/webroot/js* directory. We will concatenate a file using the Grunt build plugin and save it in *myModule.js* by adding the contents of Listing 5.15 to *Gruntfile.js*.

```
concat: {
         options: {
            separator: ';'
         },
         dist: {
            src: ['web/features/features/**/*.js', 'some other pattern'],
            dest: 'jsTarget/myModule.js'
         },
      },
```

Listing 5.15 Concatenating New File Using Grunt Build Plugin

5.3.2 Content Management

SmartEdit offers four main perspectives for content managers:

1. Preview, which allows the user to view pages as they would appear to a customer without any personalization
2. Basic edit, which allows for quick, drag-and-drop changes to the positions and properties of simple components such as banners
3. Advanced edit, which allows for the editing and movement of all components, including navigation
4. Personalization, which allows the user to view the page as a customer would, with personalization rules in place

You can and should restrict these different perspectives to different content managers (and in the case of preview and personalization, perhaps testers or business stakeholders, who are not interested in making changes but who would like to see new or updated content before it goes live). By doing so, you can offer basic editing to those who are building simple pages, advanced editing to those who are making more complicated, more custom, or more conditional changes, and so on.

While building and testing your storefront, you should be careful to properly componentize your content, as discussed earlier in this chapter. None of the page elements or other components that you have hard-coded will be editable via SmartEdit or personalizable via restrictions.

A common symptom of insufficiently componentized storefronts is the overuse of paragraph components. These are intended for rich text (perhaps with tables, hyperlinks, or embedded images) and can be edited via a WYSIWYG interface in SmartEdit—but because they can contain rich formatting such as tables and hyperlinks and because they can be edited directly in HTML format as well as via WYSIWYG, paragraph components can also include more complicated HTML or scripts. Some developers and content managers will therefore insert custom “components” as large blocks of arbitrary HTML in paragraph components.

This is not a best practice, for three important reasons. First and foremost, this practice is intensely sensitive to keystroke error, which could result in broken components, poorly optimized scripts, or soft security practices. Second, should you notice these issues, it can be very difficult to track down the offending code or even to deactivate only the part that is malfunctioning without also deactivating some other, perhaps critical, piece of functionality or content. Third, and just as importantly, overusing paragraph components in this way denies the business the opportunity to define, design, and refine the component types that they *should* have. If there is some storefront element that is critical to your business but that is not represented or accounted for in the accelerator storefronts, then your project should include building it. The results will be better, you will have more management and personalization options, and you will save yourself a good deal of stress during testing and deployment.

SmartEdit is at its most useful when content managers are empowered to build new pages and variations on existing ones without having to involve developers or internal IT—and the interface allows this, so long as your design and implementation does as well.

5.3.3 Components

Accelerator storefronts ship with components, pages, and page templates prebuilt. As discussed earlier in this chapter, these components can be added, edited, and rearranged using SmartEdit. Developers will frequently create their own new component types, sometimes using the SAP Commerce accelerators components as bases and sometimes starting from scratch. These new components will need to be enabled for SmartEdit, as described earlier in this chapter.

The component types enabled for SmartEdit by default, as well as their functions, are outlined in Table 5.1.

Component Type	Description
Account navigation	Provides the customer with access to self-service functionality, as described in Chapter 7.
Category navigation	Displays the product categories and/or other items that you have added to your core storefront navigation, as described in Section 5.3.5.
Footer navigation	Displays the footer content, usually including static links to contact information, frequently asked questions, and so on. This content is considered part of navigation and is covered in Section 5.3.5.
Image map	An image with a link embedded in some or all of its pixels, configurable via HTML.
Link	The component is nested under navigation nodes to provide connections to other parts of the storefront, as described in Section 5.3.5.
Mini cart	Summarizes the current contents and total value of the customer's cart.
Paragraph	A flexible component, editable via SmartEdit or any other content management interface in SAP Commerce, that can contain plain text, rich text, tables, images, hyperlinks, and so on.
Product carousel	Displays a set of products, with the attributes of those products (such as name, price, and image) being drawn directly from the product catalog.
Product reference	Shows products related to one another, in manners such as cross-selling, upselling, and accessories, as described in Chapter 3 and Chapter 4.
Search box	The component that allows customers to search your indexed search data for keywords.
Simple banner	Shows an image and can link to a URL when clicked. These components also contain metadata and, like all media in the SAP Commerce system, can be protected using security rules.
Simple responsive banner	Serves the same function as a simple banner but includes image files and parameters for each of your responsive breakpoints.

Table 5.1 Component Types

5.3.4 Restrictions Management

Restrictions mark a piece of content as being conditional—that is, being shown or not shown based on some specific parameter. *Time restrictions*, for example, mean that the component will only appear within a specific time range. *Category restrictions* mean that the component will show only if the user is currently viewing a certain category, thereby allowing bespoke content to be added to otherwise system-built pages, such as product listing pages.

In SmartEdit, users can add restrictions to components by selecting the appropriate component and then clicking the button, as shown in Figure 5.9. (For a more detailed understanding of restrictions, see Chapter 9.)

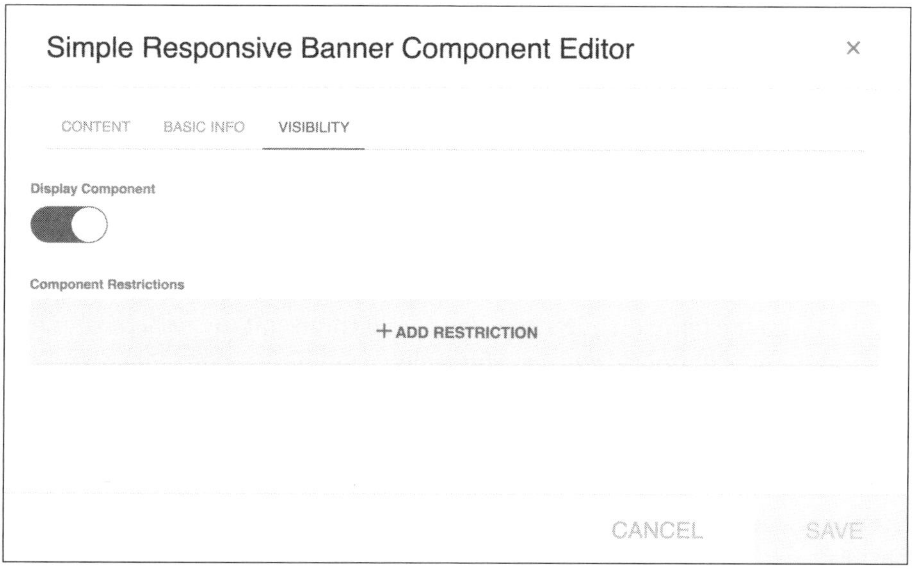

Figure 5.9 Adding Restriction in SmartEdit

One specific restriction type that bears mentioning in this context is the CMS action restriction, which, as its name implies, adds a CMS action to the component. This means adding some behavior to a component, over and above linking to some other part of the storefront via a click. The most commonly used CMS actions are as follows:

- `PickUpInStoreActionModel`, which initiates a buy online, pickup in store checkout process (as described in Chapter 3)

- `ShareOnSocialNetworkActionModel`, which opens an interface for sharing a product or page on one or more social networks
- `AddToCartActionModel`, which instantly adds a product to the customer's cart

`SimpleCMSActionModel` acts as the base for all CMS actions, and allows you to create your own new ones. You would begin doing this by defining a new item type, which we'll call `MyNewAction`, as shown in Listing 5.16.

```
<itemtype code="MyNewAction" jaloclass=
"de.hybris.platform.acceleratorcms.jalo.actions.MyNewAction" extends=
"SimpleCMSAction"autocreate="true" generate="true">
</itemtype>
```

Listing 5.16 Defining MyNewAction

To test this, wire it a simple visual element, a button that says **Click Me!** To do so, add the following to your storefront extension:

```
<%@ page trimDirectiveWhitespaces="true" %>
<button type="button">Click Me!</button>
```

You can, of course, wire your new action to a more sophisticated component than that. Listing 5.17, for example, shows how you would connect it to `ProductAddToCartComponent` in the accelerator storefronts via ImpEx.

```
# this relation is used by CMSActionRestriction, by adding
ActionRestriction to your action
INSERT_UPDATE ApplicableCmsActionsTypeForCmsComponent;target(code)[unique=
true];source(code)[unique=true];
;ProductAddToCartComponent;MyNewAction;

# CMS ACTION Restrictions
INSERT_UPDATE CMSActionRestriction;$contentCV[unique=true];uid[unique=
true];name;
;;ActionRestriction;A CMSAction restriction;

# CMS ProductAddToCart Components
INSERT_UPDATE ProductAddToCartComponent;$contentCV[unique=true];uid[unique=
true];name;actions(&actionRef);&componentRef
;;AddToCart;Product Add To Cart;PickUpInStoreAction,AddToCartAction,ShareOnSoc
ialNetworkAction,MyNewAction;AddToCart
```

```
# My New Action,
INSERT_UPDATE MyNewAction;$contentCV[unique=true];uid[unique=
true];url;name;restrictions(uid,$contentCV);&actionRef
;;MyNewAction;/mynewaction/act/
{productCode};My New Action;ActionRestriction;MyNewAction
```

Listing 5.17 Connecting New Action to ProductAddToCartComponent

Finally, you need to add your new action to the appropriate component view, using the syntax shown in Listing 5.18 (which comes from the example in the *ProductAddToCartPanel.tag* SAP Commerce accelerators file).

```
...
<%@ taglib prefix="action" tagdir="/WEB-INF/tags/desktop/action" %>
...
<div id="actions-container-for-${component.uid}" class=
"productAddToCartPanelContainer clearfix">
<ul class="productAddToCartPanel clearfix">
<action:actions element="li" styleClass="productAddToCartPanelItem span-
5" parentComponent="${component}"/>
</ul>
</div>
```

Listing 5.18 Sample Syntax from ProductAddToCartPanel.tag

5.3.5 Navigation

Navigation components are unique insofar as they are specific to menus, usually shared across pages, that allow the customer to move around the site. Although banners and other components will frequently include links to other pages, navigation components exist primarily for linking; as such, they should be designed with some intention. We generally recommend linking to your most important product categories and to any important nonproduct pages that you might have, from learning resources to (especially in the case of highly regulated industries) policy information. Product and product-related links typically go in your header, whereas **Contact Us**, **Frequently Asked Questions**, and copyright boilerplate typically go in your footer.

Navigation components can be edited only from the advanced edit perspective, as shown in Figure 5.10.

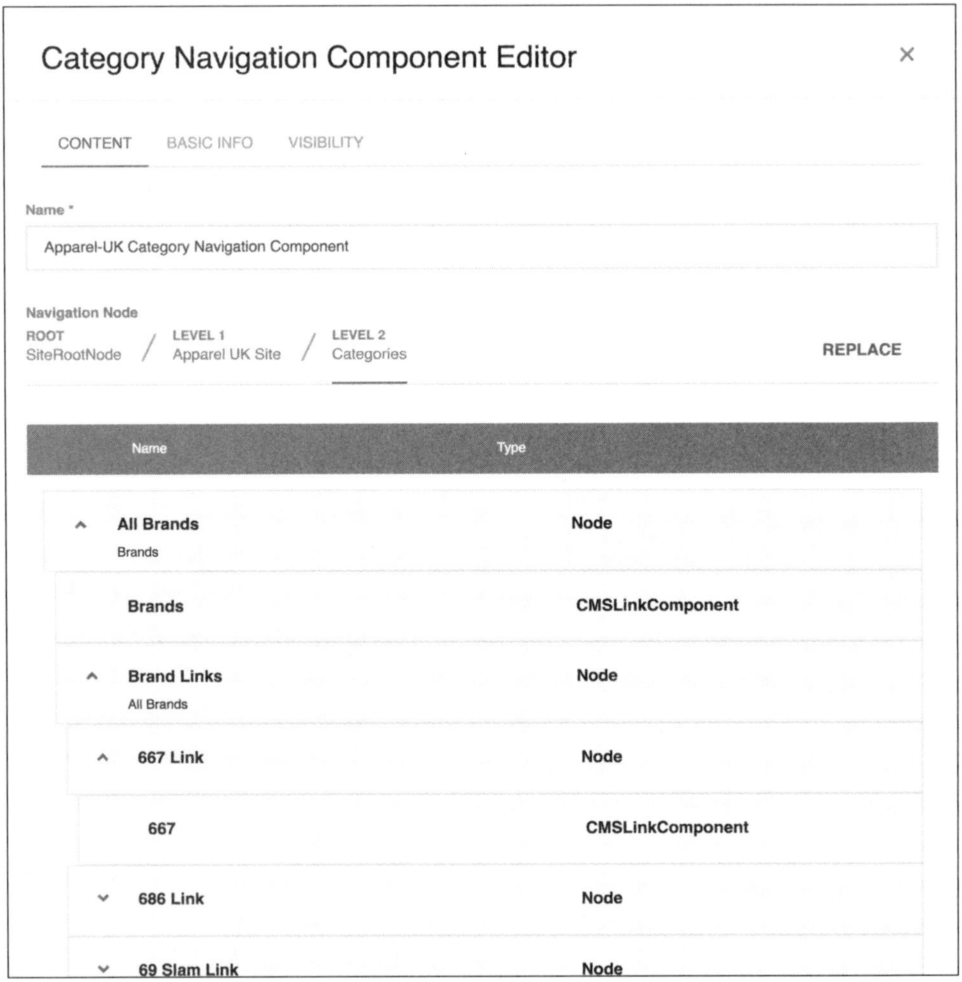

Figure 5.10 Editing Navigation Components in SmartEdit

In addition, the onsite search bar is itself a configurable component. Employees in the CMS Cockpit or SmartEdit can determine how long the search engine will wait for before making suggestions, as well as the kinds of suggestions it will then offer—suggesting keywords or specific products or both if autocomplete is turned on and, after the search is executed, following up with "Did you mean?" functionality if spell check is turned on. For a more thorough discussion of these features, as well as the search functionality attached to them, see Chapter 8.

There are some settings that are unique to the search bar component, however. Product reccomendations are handled at the SAP Commerce level rather than the search engine level, so they can be enabled only from the content managament side; likewise, the settings for delaying before returning results can only be set here. The system allows you to set the number of characters that the search bar will wait for (three by default) and the number of milliseconds (500 by default) that the storefront will then wait before returning results.

You might be wondering why anyone would *want* to intentionally delay autocomplete results. After all, reducing your response time for search can be key to providing a good customer experience, and long load times tend to greatly increase bounce rates. But, perhaps counterintuitively, these delay settings can help to improve performance and increase customer engagement.

This is because returning autocomplete results as quickly as possible, after every single keystroke, generally results in verbose, unwieldy suggestions, while also requiring the storefront to query the search engine after every single keystroke. It's generally better, then, to wait for a better idea of what the customer is looking for and also to wait for some indication that they are no longer typing. This feature allows you to account for both of those factors and to fine-tune the delay time based on your search engine's base response time and your customers' specific expectations. (For more on both these topics, once again, see Chapter 8).

5.3.6 User Accounts and User Groups

User groups are just what they sound like: groups of users organized in the SAP Commerce system. As we discuss in Chapter 9, user groups can contain employees or customers—but in the context of SmartEdit, we're concerned with customer-facing user groups. By adding user group restrictions to specific pieces of content, from a single banner to an entire page or section of your storefront, you can provide customers with a highly personal experience even if you have yet to set up automation.

In the personalization perspective, users can choose to view a page in the context of one or more user groups, each representing a category of customers to which you want to tailor your storefront experience: customers who are loyal to some specific brand, big spenders, deal hunters, or any other group that, in your view, drives (or should drive) customer behavior.

Most importantly, this view allows you to see what the page would look like to a customer who is a member of multiple user groups. As shown in Figure 5.11, the content that appears as a result of membership in each applicable user group will be color-coded, providing users with a transparent view of what customers will experience, why, and where the content might potentially clash.

Figure 5.11 Personalization in SmartEdit, Showing Components for Two Customer Segments

5.4 Personalization

A storefront, however well-designed, only goes so far if the content is not relevant to the customers using it—and because customers are not identical, the content that you serve to them shouldn't be, either. The *personalization module* helps you to tailor your experience to customers' preferences, expectations, and needs quickly and effectively. We'll start by going through the overall architecture of personalization in SAP Commerce before going into more detail on both basic and advanced configuration of those features.

5.4.1 Personalization Architecture

Personalization relies primarily on two extensions, personalizationservices and personalizationfacades, with the former handling core functionality and logic and the latter exposing those functionalities by providing appropriate facades and exposing POJOs for integration purposes.

The key objects used by the personalizationservices extension are as follows:

- CxSegments, which acts as the main object for customer classification, bridging the gap between customer-facing user groups (as discussed above, as well as in Chapter 9) with SmartEdit-specific *segments*
- CxAbstractAction, which is the main class for executing behavior, but which does not itself define that behavior, relying instead on other classes to extend it
- CxCustomization, which groups restricted components for the appropriate segment, such as SummerSale2019
- CxVariation, which defines variations on the customizations defined in CxCustomization—for example, SummerSale2019MensWear
- CxVariation, which stores the segments assigned to a user so that the system will remember which customers belong to which segment

The personalizationfacades extension then converts segments to storefront content, using the following converter and populator types, as defined in the *personalizationfacades-beans.xml* file:

- populator, which defines the source values the target object
- populatorList, which groups the relevant populators
- configurableConverter, which uses the populatorList to define the populators that will be invoked
- configurableSubtypeConverter and configurableSubtypeAwareConverter, which extend configurableConverter, defining the parent type of the object(s) to be converted and sorting those objects as actions or triggers

The relations among these objects, then, are as shown in Figure 5.12.

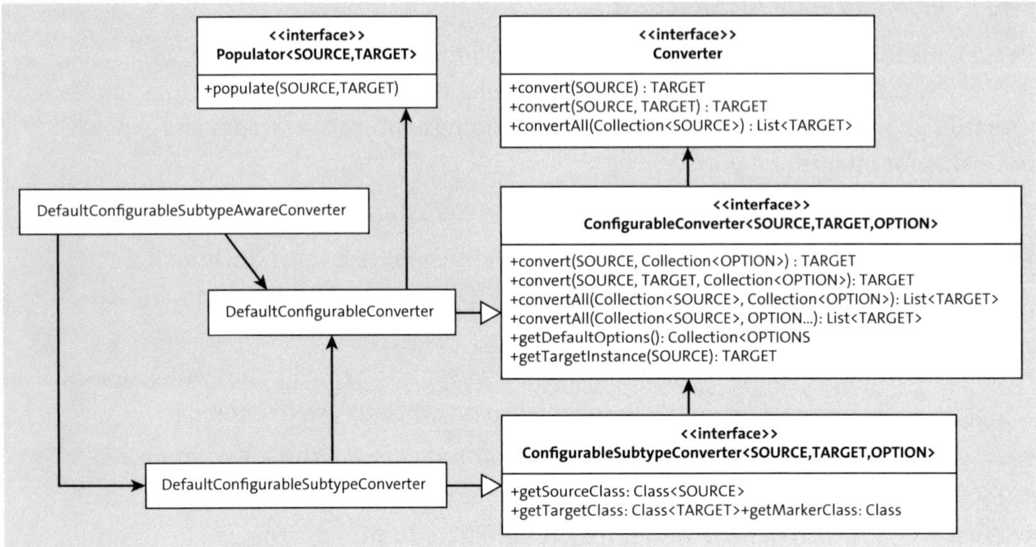

Figure 5.12 Data Model for personalizationfacades Extension

5.4.2 Configuring Personalization

As alluded to earlier, triggers activate variations for specific user groups. `CxTriggerService` executes the `CxTriggerStrategy` element registered in the system. `CxDefaultTriggerStrategy` uses `CxDefaultTrigger` to deploy a default variation—in other words, your storefront without personalizations—and `DefaultSegmentTriggerStrategy` then maps other variations to the appropriate customer segments.

`DefaultSegmentTriggerStrategy` also sets a threshold for customer affinity so that only truly appropriate segments will be considered. You can set this threshold using the `personalizationservices.segment.trigger.strategy.min.affinity` property.

Finally, `ExpressionTriggerStrategy` handles cases wherein multiple segments need to be combined and defines the logic for grouping operators (*and* as opposed to *or*), element negation, and segment definition. A JSON expression of this logic might look like Listing 5.19.

```
"expression": {
  "type": "groupExpression",
  "elements": [
    {
      "type": "segmentExpression",
```

```
      "code": "Men"
    },
    {
      "type": "groupExpression",
      "elements": [
        {
          "type": "segmentExpression",
          "code": "Women"
        },
        {
          "type": "negationExpression",
          "element": {
            "type": "segmentExpression",
            "code": "HatsFan"
          }
        }
      ],
      "operator": "AND"
    }
  ],
  "operator": "OR"
}
```

Listing 5.19 Logic for Combining Multiple Segments, as Expressed in JSON

5.4.3 Extending Personalization

If you want to extend the logic of personalization converters, you can do so in the beans for `configurableSubtypeConverter` and `configurableSubtypeAwareConverter`, as shown in Listing 5.20.

```
<bean id="defaultCxTriggerConfigurableConverter" parent=
"cxSubtypeAwareConverter">
    <property name="defaultOptions" ><value type=
"de.hybris.platform.personalizationfacades.enums.TriggerConversionOptions">BAS
E</value></property>
    <property name="markerClass" value=
```

```
"de.hybris.platform.personalizationfacades.trigger.converters.TriggerConverter
" />
</bean>
```

Listing 5.20 Extending Personalization Converter Logic

Using these beans, you can define one or more of your own `configurableSubtypeConverter` elements, as shown in Listing 5.21. (Be sure to use the same marker class here and in `configurableSubtypeAwareConverter`.)

```
<bean id="defaultCxSegmentTriggerConfigurableConverter" parent=
"cxSubtypeConverter" >
    <constructor-arg name="markerClass" value=
"de.hybris.platform.personalizationfacades.trigger.converters.TriggerConverter
" />
    <constructor-arg name="sourceClass" value=
"de.hybris.platform.personalizationservices.model.CxSegmentTriggerModel" />
    <property name="targetClass" value=
"de.hybris.platform.personalizationfacades.data.SegmentTriggerData" />
    <property name="populators">
        <map key-type=
"de.hybris.platform.personalizationfacades.enums.TriggerConversionOptions">
            <entry key="BASE" value-ref="cxTriggerPopulators" />
            <entry key="FOR_SEGMENT" value-ref=
"cxSegmentTriggerForSegmentPopulators" />
            <entry key="FOR_VARIATION" value-ref=
"cxSegmentTriggerForVariationPopulators" />
            <entry key="FULL" value-ref="cxSegmentTriggerFullPopulators" />
        </map>
    </property>
</bean>
```

Listing 5.21 Defining configurableSubtypeConverter

5.4.4 Advanced Personalization Module

The legacy CMS Cockpit includes an advanced personalization module, allowing SAP Commerce to segment customers into behavioral targeting groups (BTGs), which act as customer-facing user groups built on the fly and without necessarily having to persist past a single session. BTGs also can be configured in the administration perspective in the backoffice if you're running a compatible SAP Commerce version.

The advanced personalization module creates BTGs using *rules*—in essence, if/then statements that can contain one or multiple conditions and one or multiple results when those conditions are met. These conditions fall into four main categories (shown as they appear in the backoffice interface in Figure 5.13):

1. **Customer rules**
   These check for account-level information, such as the customer's country, postal code, gender, or current user group membership.
2. **Order rules**
   These check for details in the customer's order history, such as the products, categories of products, or total value of previous orders.
3. **Cart rules**
   These check the customer's currently active cart for certain products, categories of products, or quantities of products—or can simply check whether the cart is or is not empty or check its value.
4. **Website rules**
   These check for the customers' browsing behavior on the SAP Commerce storefront, including what products or categories they have viewed and what pages they have visited—or can check for affiliate links or URL parameters (in the form of keypairs, such as `?emailpromotion=true`).

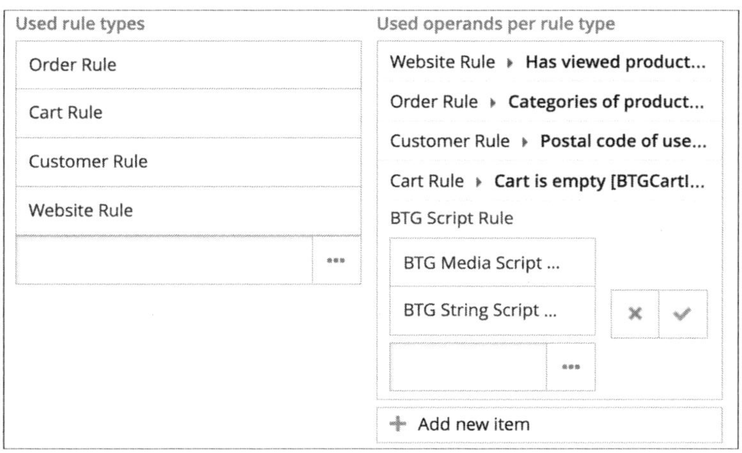

Figure 5.13 BTG Rules in Advanced Personalization Module

Note that the first two categories require you to know which customer you're dealing with because they refer to past orders and customer profile information. Cart rules and website rules, however, do not require a known user. You can extract relevant information about the cart and/or browsing session of an anonymous customer just as effectively as a known one.

It's also important to note that the values we're checking for do not need to be absolute. You could, for example, create a customer rule that checks whether the customer's postal code starts with 606, effectively checking whether they are in the greater Chicago area, rather than zeroing in on one specific zip code.

After evaluating some combination of these conditions, the advanced personalization module then performs one or more actions—adding the customer to one or more user groups and/or showing, hiding, or replacing a page component.

Advanced personalization relies on the btg and btgcockpit extensions, with the former handling the logic of BTGs and the latter governing the UI elements with which employees can manage BTGs and associated rules. BTGs run on a proprietary technology stack, entirely different from the Drools-based rules engine discussed in Chapter 8.

Because the advanced personalization module does not connect to SmartEdit, and because SmartEdit's personalization features serve a similar function with more flexibility, the older advanced personalization module is considered deprecated functionality. It is also less performant than user-group-based personalization and generally should be used only in earlier versions of SAP Commerce that are incompatible with SmartEdit.

5.5 Context-Driven Services

SAP Commerce Cloud's context-driven services is a cloud-based personalization and conversion optimization solution for commerce customers. It's offered as an add-on to SAP Commerce Cloud as well as SAP Commerce on-premise solutions. The context-driven services solution provides real-time customer experience personalization by capturing and analyzing contextual and behavioral data across each customer's commerce journey. The analyzed data intelligently creates individualized customer experiences, which results in an improved conversion rate, raises order value, and increases customer satisfaction and loyalty.

Combined with SmartEdit, customers are provided with relevant, valuable content at every stage of their shopping journey. With every click, the understanding of the customer is reassessed, enabling SmartEdit to show content that is relevant in that exact moment.

There are four components in context-driven services to start with: foundation, merchandizing, customer recovery, and segmentation and analytics. The capabilities are being rolled out in an incremental pattern over 2018 and 2019. Foundation and segmentation are available at the time of writing (September 2018) and are discussed in this section. Merchandising and customer recovery and other additional components have yet to be released.

All components are available when the option is included in the license. However, because context-driven services is a multitenant offering, you will be able to access these features automatically as they become available. These services can be implemented independently at any time based on customer timeline. However, the underlying foundational data layer needs to be implemented first before any other services can be implemented.

5.5.1 Foundation

Context-driven services foundation allows businesses to create, maintain, and continually extend customer profiles from a range of data sources. The context-driven services foundation uses short-term and long-term contextual data from SAP Commerce behaviors and interactions to drive the SAP Commerce experience. The current solution captures data from digital channels originating on the web, clickstream data, and commerce data.

It provides attributes, scores, and real-time metrics per customer, from anonymous to fully identified customers. Customer consent is always respected. The context-driven services foundation platform is extensible and leverages a schema-less, flexible data structure to capture new data and insights to enrich and extend customer profiles. The Lambda enricher framework provides full extensibility to utilize information from other SAP data sources such as SAP Customer Profile (formerly, Gigya Profile) and any external third-party systems and channels to create new insights.

Let's look at the architecture of foundation, different components of foundation, and how it integrates with the rest of context-driven services.

Foundation Architecture

The foundation data journey consists of four main steps: data capture, identity management, context processing, and consumption.

The incoming data is referred to as *context* and can be either streaming data or transactional data. The clickstream data from web events is mapped to the foundational extensible data model by a profile tagging solution. Transactional data like customer master data, orders, returns, and so on is passed on to SAP Commerce with prebuilt integrations.

Foundation starts to identify the customer from the first interaction. The anonymous user's context is captured via cookies and known user context via the login information. If the captured context matches an existing profile, it combines the data; otherwise, a new identity is created. Session matching, cross-site matching, and cross-device matching all contribute to building the context, and if the two profiles are identified for the same customer, then they are merged, leveraging the fully automated merge service.

Once the context is built, it's then processed and analyzed in real time and added as observations, transactions, or insights to the customer profile. Foundation can be extended via additional services to meet specific customer requirements.

The analyzed context can be consumed in two ways:

1. Through the foundation API that allows real-time access to a complete individual customer profile or parts of it
2. Through the foundation's real-time reporting service that allows you to query the customer data on multiple aggregation levels

Figure 5.14 summarizes the foundation architecture, showcasing the flow from data capture to identity management and context processing to consumption.

Customer profile data such as sessions, interactions, insights, and other relevant data is stored in the document database. The document database has various advantages compared to the traditional relational database, like providing flexibility to extend without redefining the database structure, allowing easy data augmentations to profiles, storing customer data in one place within a single JSON document, and making all customer profile data able to be retrieved with one request.

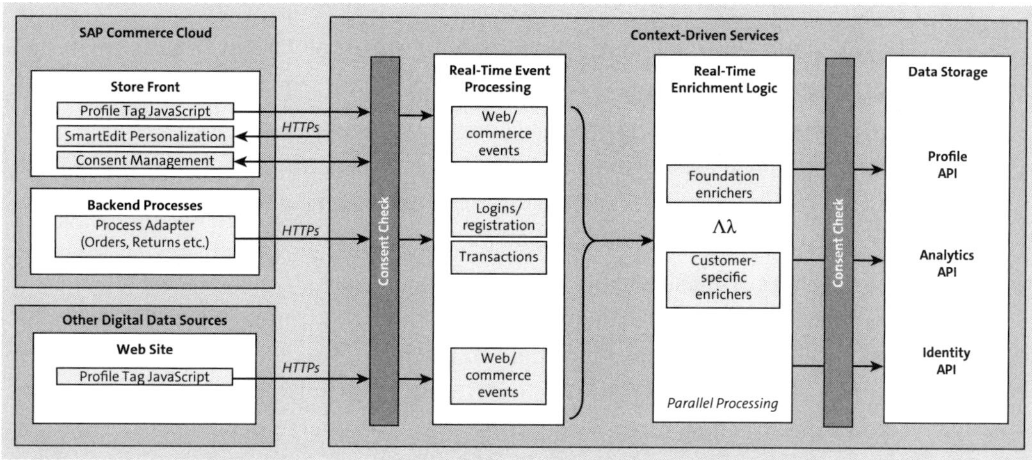

Figure 5.14 Context-Driven Services Foundation Architecture

Foundation Components

Foundation is built up of multiple components, as follows:

- **Profile tag**
  The profile tagging solution is a website tagging solution that is included with context-driven services to effortlessly capture data. It consists of a graphical user interface and JavaScript library.
- **Context service**
  This is a big data cluster that stores all raw events in the context service. Each enricher microservice can query the context service to access all the message details (context) for further processing.
- **Enricher microservices**
  Enricher microservices process data that flows through a context adapter. Enrichers usually analyze the data then persist insights and observations in the profile document.
- **Data privacy and consent management**
  Customer data cannot be collected or used without a customer's consent. The brand or store owner exposes consent management using context-driven services foundation consent services to customers at any level of data granularity, from global control to fine-grained control of data types and sources.

- **Consent service**
  The consent service manages all tenant- and user-specific consents. It creates and returns consent references, which can be used for all requests and operations.
- **Profile service**
  Context-driven services foundation provides a dedicated service to manage and retrieve profile documents. Consuming applications use the profile service to retrieve either full profile data or partial profile data.
- **Real-time reporting service**
  In parallel to the regular data processing through the context service and enricher microservices, the system sends data to the real-time reporting service. The real-time reporting service of context-driven services foundation allows you to process large event streams (such as clickstreams or commerce data) in real time. Data aggregation happens continuously and allows you to query data on different aggregation levels, from a raw event (single click) to aggregated calculations spanning multiple months or years. You can use the real-time reporting service either standalone or combined with enricher microservices—for example, to create additional insights, such as average cart value, total order volume, referrer analysis, and so on.
- **Identity service**
  All identities of a user are clustered in a single profile by the identity service clusters. It provides service endpoints to create, read, alter, and delete identities, profiles, and their relations.

Foundation Integration

Context-driven services foundation provides several prebuilt integrations, which allow it to set up and use pre-defined scenarios with low effort. It captures and analyzes customer interactions, contexts, and behaviors to create a continually evolving intelligent profile, enabling a deeper understanding of a customer's motivation and intent in real time. This enables customer-facing touchpoints like commerce and marketing to react and interact in more personal ways.

Foundation has prebuilt integrations with SAP Commerce and SmartEdit for personalization and the assisted service module, as follows:

- **Integration with SmartEdit for personalization**
  The prebuilt integration of context-driven services foundation with personalization allows for mapping of the customer data from foundation to segments and

using it in personalization via SmartEdit. The integration with personalization is based on three extensions:

- The `personalizationintegration` extension translates data from foundation to commerce with two mappers, `CxScriptProfileMapper` to interpret the context-driven services foundation data and `CxFixedSegmentsProfileMapper` to return fixed segments defined in a segmentation.
- The `yaasconfiguration` extension provides data models to hold required configurations to communicate with services to retrieve data.
- The `personalizationprofile` extension has mappers that navigate the foundation data and convert it; it can also resolve product and category affinities.

- **Integration with SAP Commerce**
  The prebuilt integration between SAP Commerce and foundation facilitates the data exchange between the two. The system is configured to retrieve the foundation data synchronously during login. Upon user login, an event is triggered that executes the following steps:
  - Calls context-driven services foundation to retrieve the user profile
  - Maps the context-driven services foundation data to segment data for personalization
  - Updates the segments for the users in the database
  - Calculates the personalized experience for the storefront

  Figure 5.15 depicts the data integration with SAP Commerce to create a meaningful customer experience.

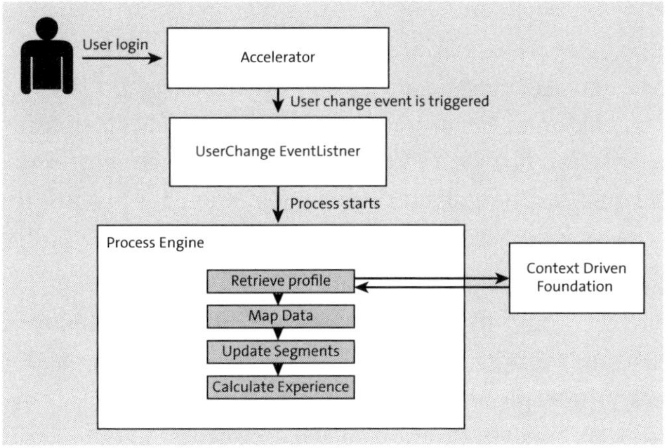

Figure 5.15 Sending Data to SAP Commerce System

- **Integration from SAP Commerce**
  The data from SAP Commerce is sent to foundation for the events like registration/login, page views, adding items to the cart, order placement, and banner clicks. The data is sent through `profiletagaddon`, the `yprofileintegration` module, and `hybrisanalyticsaddon`, as shown in Figure 5.16.

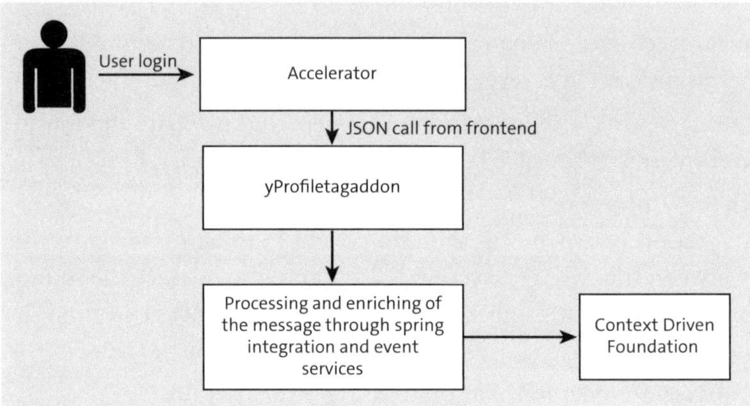

Figure 5.16 Getting Data from SAP Commerce

5.5.2 Segmentation

The aim of segmentation is to provide a personalized shopping experience to the customer when she interacts with the storefront by grouping customers into predefined segments in real time. This functionality is available for anonymous users as well as registered users, aligned with their consent preferences.

Real-time segmentation supports personalization from the customer's first interactions on site, if she has consented. Business users can quickly understand the segments that are driving various customer experiences and leverage that information to increase conversion. Segmentation functionality helps personalize web storefront content, promotions, and search. Segmentation drives conversion by placing the right products at the right time to deliver customer-specific experiences.

The process begins when the customer begins interactions with the storefront and storefront sends event data to context-driven services foundation. The context-driven services builds the customer profile and, based on the storefront interaction events, assigns the customer to the appropriate segment. The segment data is transferred to SmartEdit for meaningful personalization of the storefront layout. Figure 5.17 summarizes the segmentation process.

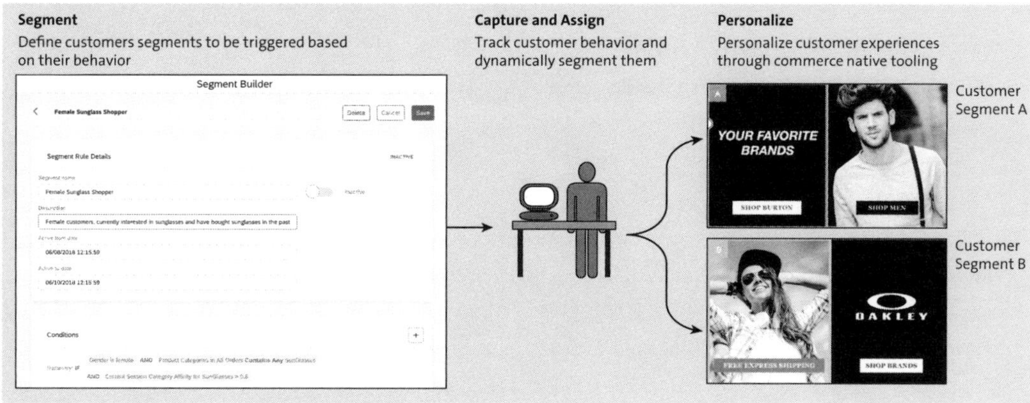

Figure 5.17 Segmentation Process in Real World

Let's look at how to create a segment and how to match customers with the right segments.

Segment Creation

Segment Builder is a tool in which you can define groups to segment customers by different attributes and conditions. The customer data may come from various sources and channels. To begin, follow these steps:

1. In Segment Builder, to add a new segment, click **Segmentation** and then **Segment Builder**; this will take you to the screen shown in Figure 5.18.

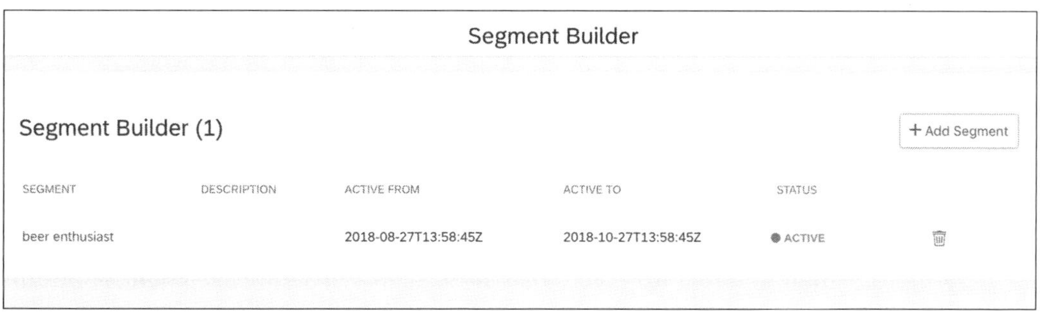

Figure 5.18 Create New Segment

2. Click the **Add** button and a window for defining the new segment and conditions will appear, as shown in Figure 5.19.

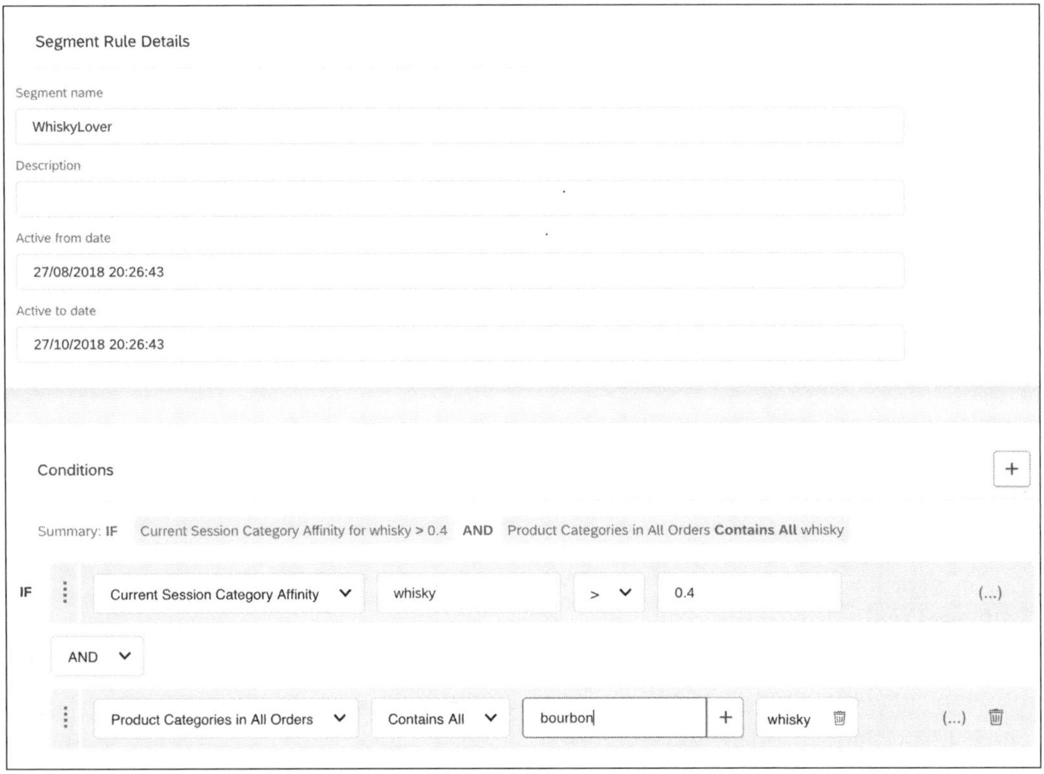

Figure 5.19 Define New Segment Details and Activate Segment

3. Provide the segment rule details, like **Segment Name**, **Description**, and **Active** period.
4. Define the conditions a customer must meet to be part of this segment.
5. Save the segment and toggle the **Active** button to activate the segment.

When a customer meets the required criteria, the segment service will place the segment in that customer's profile.

There are multiple condition types that are available to define a segment. For example, order conditions (like order value, order count, last order value, etc.), cart conditions (cart value, products in the cart, product value in the cart, etc.), customer conditions (customer zip code, gender, brand affinity, locations, etc.), and website conditions (URL matches and funnel level). In addition, custom conditions can be defined as well.

Segment Calculation

Context-driven services segmentation ships with a segment calculation service that assigns customers to the segments defined in Segment Builder in real time. It has a number of attributes, as follows:

- As the customer browses the web storefront, the customer profile document is updated by the enricher via the profile service.
- The profile service notifies you of the change in the profile document.
- The segment calculation service gets the segment information from the backend and recalculates the segments.
- The segment calculation service stores the calculated segments in the profile service.

This process continues for recalculation of segments in real time based on the customer's browsing activity. The segment calculation process is shown in Figure 5.20.

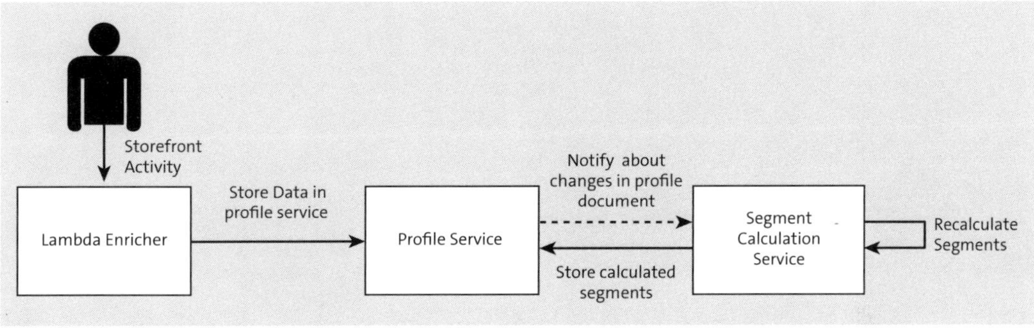

Figure 5.20 Segment Calculation Process

5.6 Summary

Customer experience is what expresses your brand's identity to your customers, leads them through their journey, and leaves them with a lasting impression of what you offer. It's the bridge between your offerings and your customers, your business, and the people it serves.

SAP Commerce provides multiple toolsets for managing your customer experience, from the overall layout, look, and feel of your site to rules and permissions associated with individual components and slots to the properties and contents of the components themselves. Personalization is built into all these toolsets, but most visibly into

SmartEdit and most robustly into context-driven services, the combination of which can help you craft a fresh, relevant, and effective experience for your customers.

One key outcome of a solid customer experience is, of course, an increase in the volume and value of orders—so in the next chapter, we'll look at how to manage orders, from acceptance to fulfillment to repeat business.

Chapter 6
Order Management

Delivering on the promise of omnichannel order management requires that you can take an order from anywhere and fulfill it from anywhere in turn. Your silos should not be your customers' problem, as we'll discuss in this chapter.

You can have the best storefront with the best user experience on any platform, but what does that get you if you can't actually deliver what your customer wants? Most likely it gets you fewer customers. If you can't provide a consistently good experience at every step of the customer journey, someone else will.

That journey needs effective marketing and a contextual user experience, as well as excellent customer support should something go wrong. In the end, this means that products and services need to be delivered on time and profitably. For this, you need to be able to manage orders and fulfill them.

In this chapter, we'll look at the key components of SAP Commerce's order management solution and how you can use them along with other SAP Commerce modules to provide an omnichannel bridge from your frontend to your backoffice.

For our purposes, order management consists of several modules. Included in this chapter will be SAP Commerce modules that take an order from before it's created through fulfillment and even through its return. The sales organization and quotations management capabilities are part of the core capabilities of SAP Commerce. Cart and checkout include much of the basic order structure, with the cart and order submission process that your storefront will use.

Built on top of this is the actual order management product that may be deployed as part of SAP Commerce or standalone. SAP Commerce order management consists of both a UI that you can see in the backoffice cockpits and many underlying services, such as the business process workflow, sourcing and allocation logic, and inventory availability. These factors together contribute to managing and fulfilling orders.

6.1 Sales Organization

The sales organization feature allows you to manage your sales force from within the backoffice. You can use it to create and modify sales organizations, set them up within a hierarchy, and assign sales representatives to customer accounts and buyers.

Although the sales organization feature is most commonly used in the B2B context, it can be used with any responsive accelerator storefront.

You can access the sales organization from the backoffice by logging in with the correct credentials for sales organization administration. Once you are logged in, if you do not find yourself in the Sales Organization Cockpit, then select it from the drop-down at the top of the screen.

You will now see **Sales Units** in the left navigation panel (see Figure 6.1). If you click it, you will see a list of sales units in the results panel that you are assigned to or that are child units of one you are assigned to. You can also search for a specific sales unit via the **Search** bar.

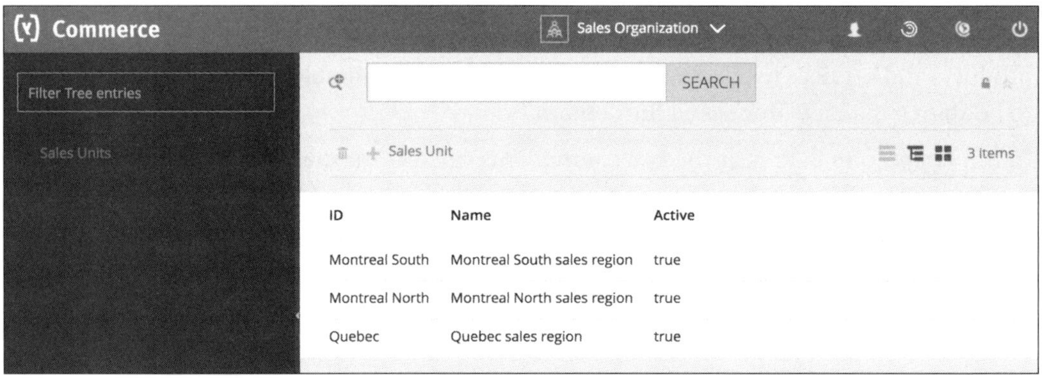

Figure 6.1 Sales Organization Showcasing Various Sales Units

Depending on whether you select the **List View** or **Tree View** icon, you will see the results either as a simple list or as one you can expand for more details about the hierarchy.

When you select one of the sales units, you will open the edit view and have access to three tabs: **General**, **Employees**, and **Accounts**.

Each account can contain a list of *customers* (employees who act as buyers for the account). This information populates the ASM customer list so that a sales rep can see the buyers they are responsible for, as we will discuss in the following sections.

6.1.1 General Tab

The **General** tab (see Figure 6.2) contains information pertaining to the sales unit itself.

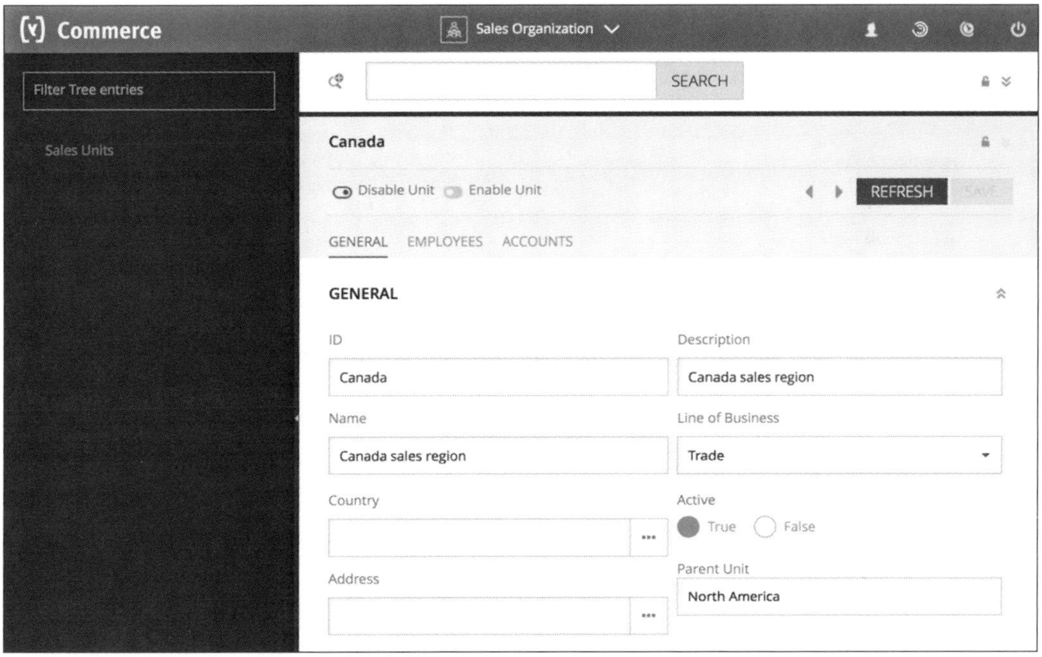

Figure 6.2 Sales Organization General Tab

You can create a new sales unit by clicking on the **+ Sales Unit** button. You will be prompted to add an **ID** and **Name** and optionally a **Description**, **Line of Business**, and **Parent Unit** within the hierarchy.

Above the **General** tab, there is an option to enable or disable the unit entirely. If you choose to disable the unit, a warning appears, stating that disabling the sales unit will disable all subunits and that undoing this action must be done manually for every descendant.

6.1.2 Employees Tab

Within the **Employees** tab, you will see a list of assigned employees (if there are any) and a **Search** bar underneath, as shown in Figure 6.3.

Figure 6.3 List of Employees in the Sales Organization with Their Assigned Roles

For each employee, you will see an **ID**, **Name**, and **Organization Role** (sales employee, approver, manager, administrator).

When you click in the **Search** bar, you can either type to search or select the **Create New Employee** option that will appear. The resulting **Create New Employee** wizard, as shown in Figure 6.4, will prompt for **ID** and **Name** and then allow you to assign a role and sales units.

You can edit an employee by searching and then selecting the **Options** button (three vertical dots) to bring up the **Edit Details** option. From there you can modify as required.

To add an employee to a sales unit, you need only search for him from within the unit. Select him from the search results and select **Save**.

To remove an employee from a sales unit, select them and from the **Options** button (three vertical dots) and select the **Remove** option.

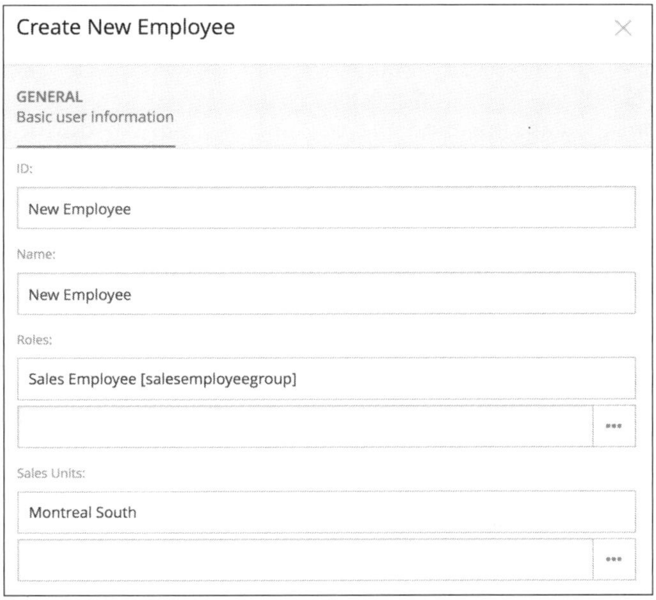

Figure 6.4 Wizard to Create Employees in the Sales Organization with Specific Roles

6.1.3 Accounts Tab

The **Accounts** tab (see Figure 6.5) is where you can view which accounts are assigned to a given sales unit and add or remove them.

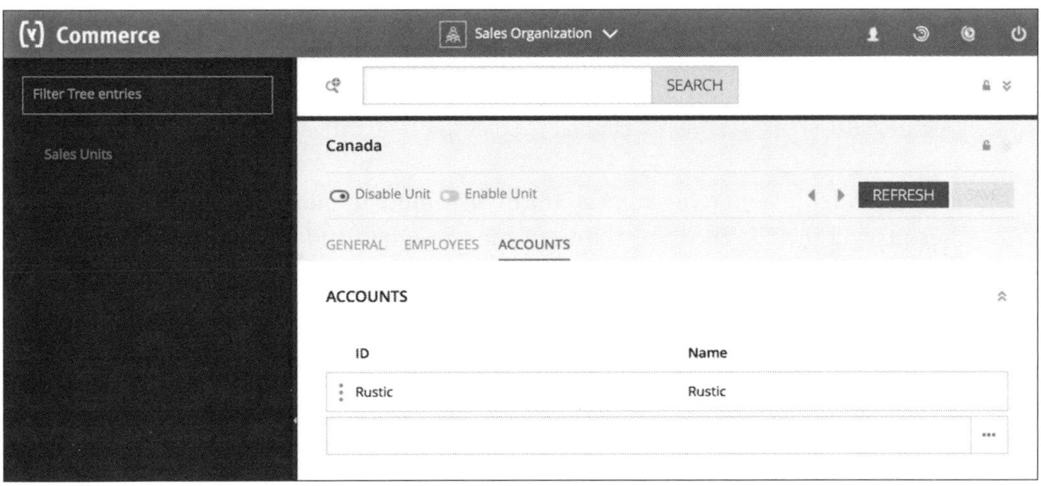

Figure 6.5 Sales Organization Accounts Tab

Similar to employees, to add an account to a sales unit, within the **Account** tab, type the name of the account you are looking for in the **Search** bar. Once you see it, select it and click **Save**.

To remove an account from a sales unit, find the account you want within the **Account** tab, select it, and from the **Options** button, select the **Remove** option.

6.1.4 Assisted Service Module Customer List

The assisted service module (ASM) customer list feature provides a sales representative who is logged in to ASM and a list of customers that are assigned to him in the sales organization module (see Figure 6.6). This gives the sales representative a convenient way to access his or her customers and start an ASM session on their behalf.

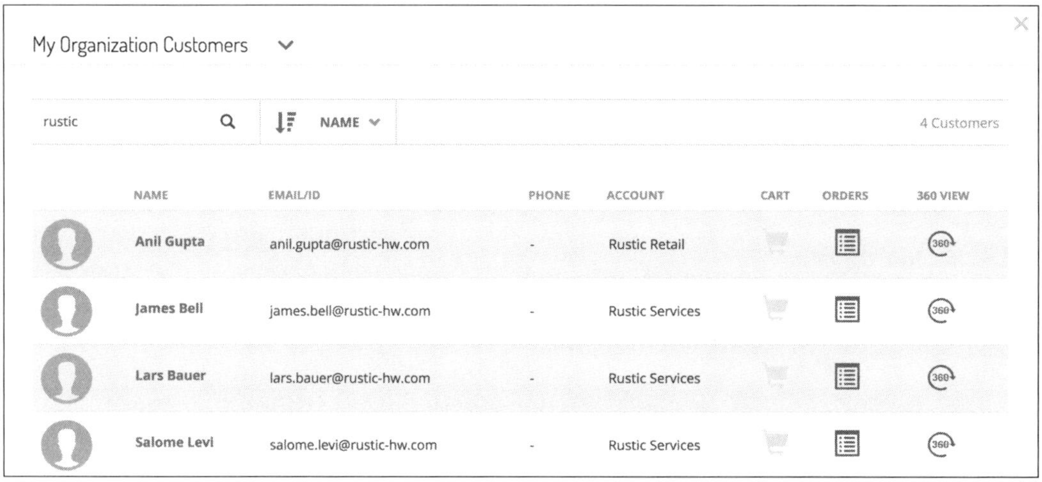

Figure 6.6 List of Customers Assigned to Sales Representative in Sales Organization

The sales representative can search for customers by name or account. The search results will include those accounts directly assigned and child sales units and child buyer units.

6.2 Quotation Management

Quotations in commerce facilitate order price negotiations between buyers and sellers. This feature was introduced in release 6.3. Quotations can be initiated by either buyers or sellers. Once the quotation is finalized/accepted, it turns into a session cart and the buyer checks out the cart in the usual way. In the following sections, we'll explore the overall quotation life cycle from a buyer perspective and sales person perspective, look at reactivating quotes that were dormant, figure out how to get a list of all quotes, and look at how email notifications play a role in negotiations.

6.2.1 Quotation Lifecycle

Buyers use the storefront to create quotes, and sellers create quotes using the assisted service module. If the quote exceeds a sales representative's authorized threshold, additional approval may be required. An additional seller approver role is supported for this purpose. The seller approver accepts or rejects a quote using the assisted service module.

Buyer Quote Process

A buyer creates a quote using the session cart on the storefront. The buyer can add products to his cart from the storefront using the quick order feature, by restoring a saved cart, or from a CSV file. The buyer can only request a quote if the cart reaches the minimum threshold amount (the usual threshold is set to $25,000, but it can be changed). The buyer must be logged in to create a quote. After creating the quote, the buyer can either save the draft quote, submit it, or cancel it. When the quote is submitted, its status changes to submitted, the session cart is cleared, and the buyer cannot modify it any further.

Once the seller receives the quote, she must log in to ASM to respond to the quote. She can accept the quote as is, modify it by adding products and incentives to make the offer more attractive and send it back, or reject the quote. The quote can be sent back and forth unless an agreement is reached between the parties.

If the quote exceeds the approval threshold, after the sales rep makes modifications to the quote it's sent for internal approval to the seller approver. Once the quote is approved, it becomes a legally binding document.

Once the buyer receives the quote from the sales rep, the buyer can accept the quote and create an order to complete the transaction, reject the quote and resubmit for negotiations, or cancel the quote. A diagram representing a buyer-initiated quote process is shown in Figure 6.7.

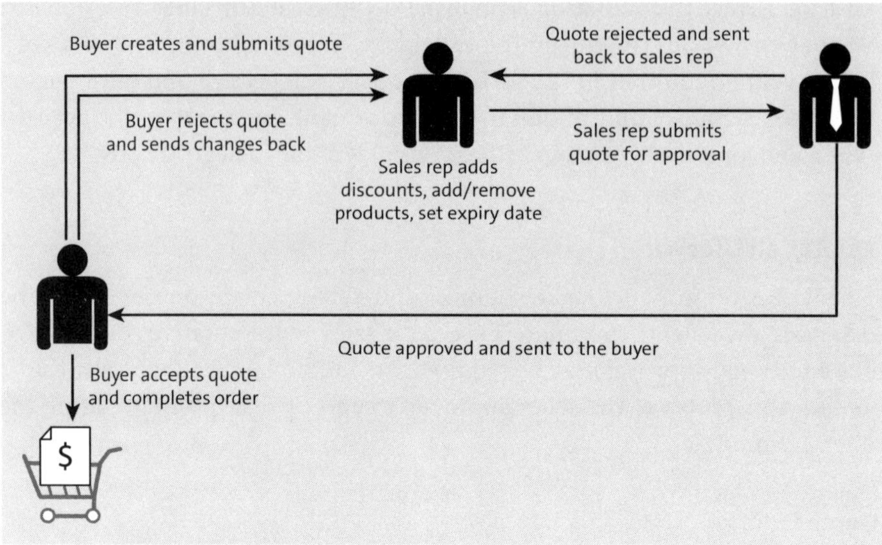

Figure 6.7 Buyer-Initiated Quote Process

Seller Quote Process

A sales rep can also initiate a quote using ASM. A seller-created quote might have to be approved if it's above a certain threshold before it can be sent to the buyer. The default threshold is set at $75,000 and it can be changed. The internal approval turns the quote into a legally binding document that the vendor must honor.

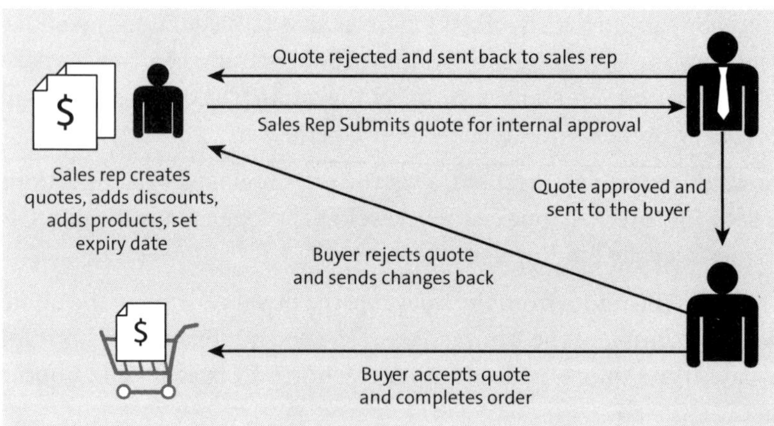

Figure 6.8 Seller-Initiated Quote Process

Once the buyer receives the quote from the sales rep, the buyer can accept the quote and create an order to complete the transaction, reject the quote and resubmit it for negotiations, or cancel the quote. A diagram representing a seller-initiated quote process is shown in Figure 6.8.

6.2.2 Requoting Inactive Quotes

Buyers can use inactive quotes to create a new quote. The new quote inherits all the products from the inactive quote, making it easy to requote items that are ordered frequently. When a new quote is created from an inactive quote, discounts, expiry dates, estimated totals, and comments are removed from the quote.

Buyers can view all inactive quotes by clicking on **My Account • Quotes**. A list of all the quotes is displayed, and by selecting an inactive quote and clicking on the **Requote** button (see Figure 6.9), a new quote is created from an inactive quote.

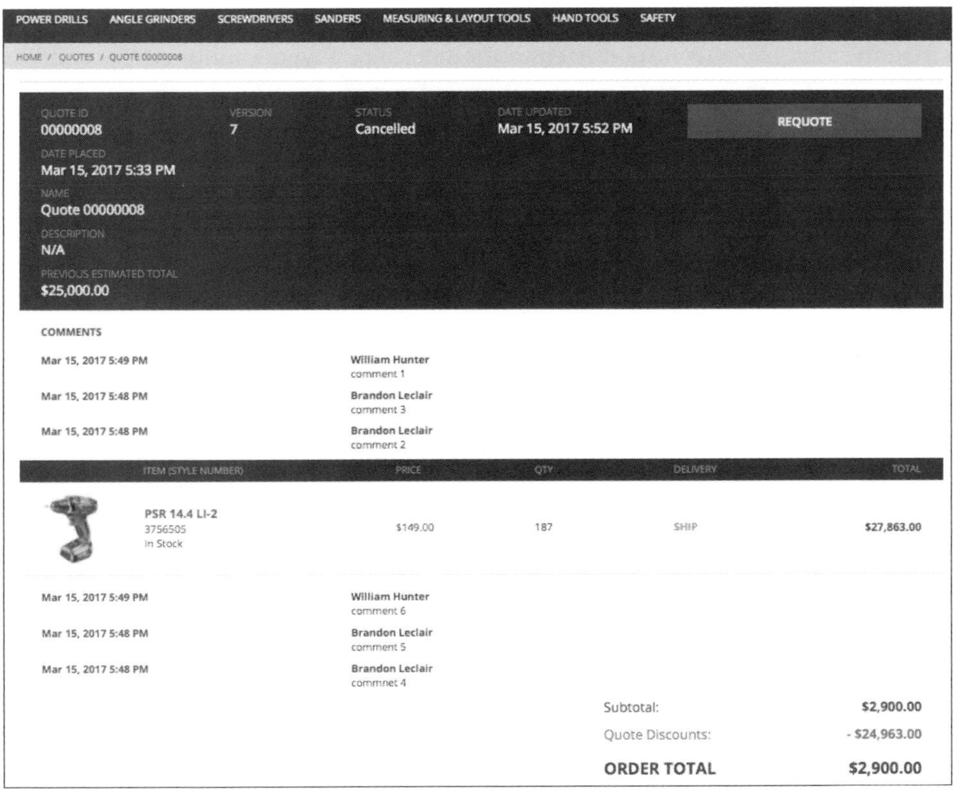

Figure 6.9 Requoting from Existing Quote

Note

The cancel quote feature can be used to create quote templates for items purchased often. A buyer can create a draft quote and cancel it without submitting it to the sales rep; the cancelled quote then is displayed in the quotes list.

6.2.3 Viewing Quotes

Buyers can view the list of quotes at any time. They can access the quote list from **My Account • Quotes** in the storefront. The list displays all the quotes that were created by the buyer and their statuses. The different quote statuses are as follows:

- **Draft**
  Quote that is created by the buyer but not yet submitted to the sales rep. The buyer can edit, submit, or cancel the quote.
- **Submitted**
  Quotes that have been submitted to the sales rep. Buyers cannot edit or cancel a submitted quote and must wait for the vendor response.
- **Ordered**
  Vendor quotes that were accepted and ordered.
- **Canceled**
  Quotes that were canceled by the buyer.
- **Vendor Quotes**
  Legally binding vendor quotes from the sales rep. Buyers can accept the vendor quote and order, cancel the vendor quote, or modify the vendor quote, which then puts the modified quote in draft status.

Figure 6.10 shows a list of quotes with different statuses.

Clicking a quote in the list displays the following quote details:

- Quote code and name
- Quote status
- Date created
- Expiry date
- Quote version
- Order number

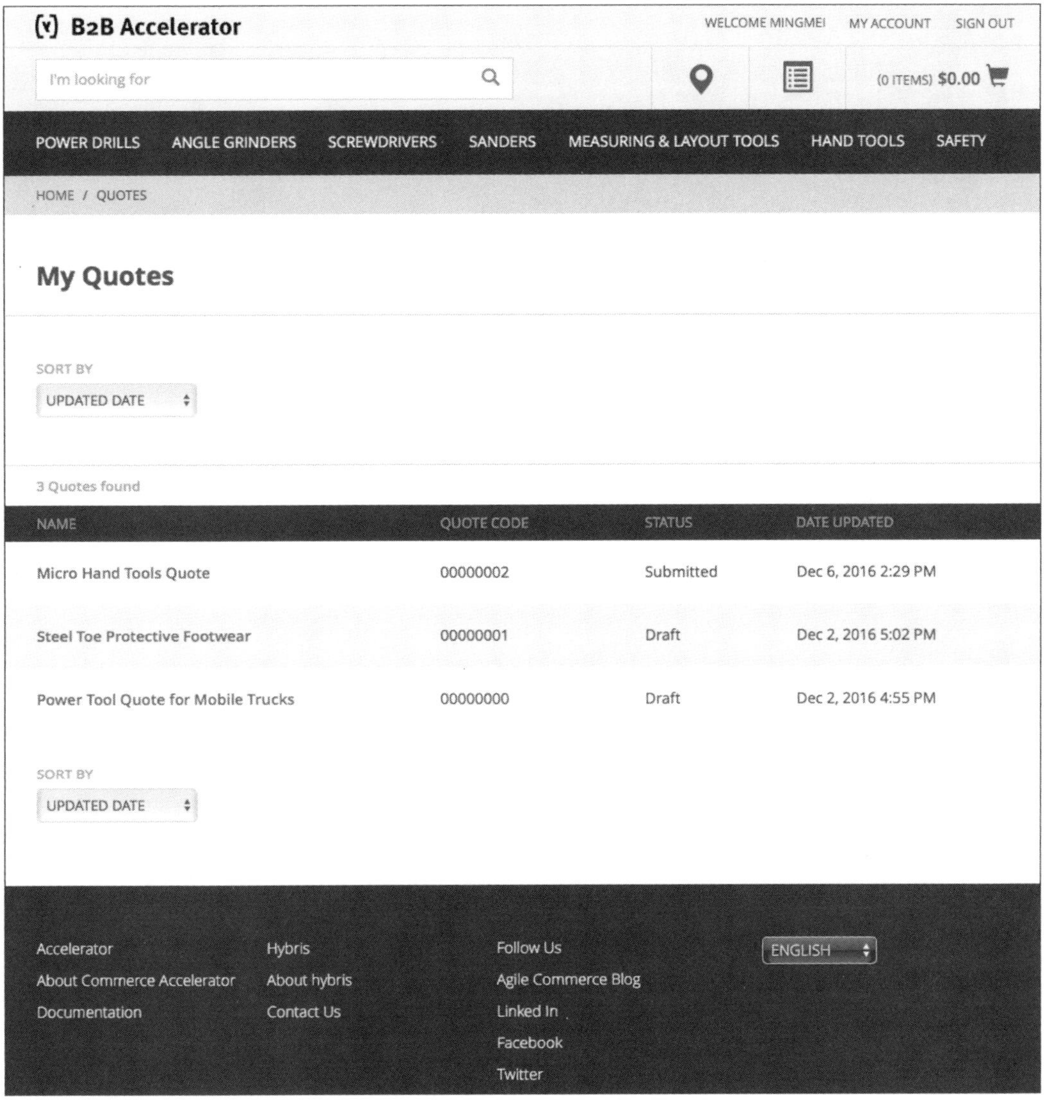

Figure 6.10 Quote List from Web Storefront

All the line items are displayed below the header. Figure 6.11 shows an example of the quote detail screen.

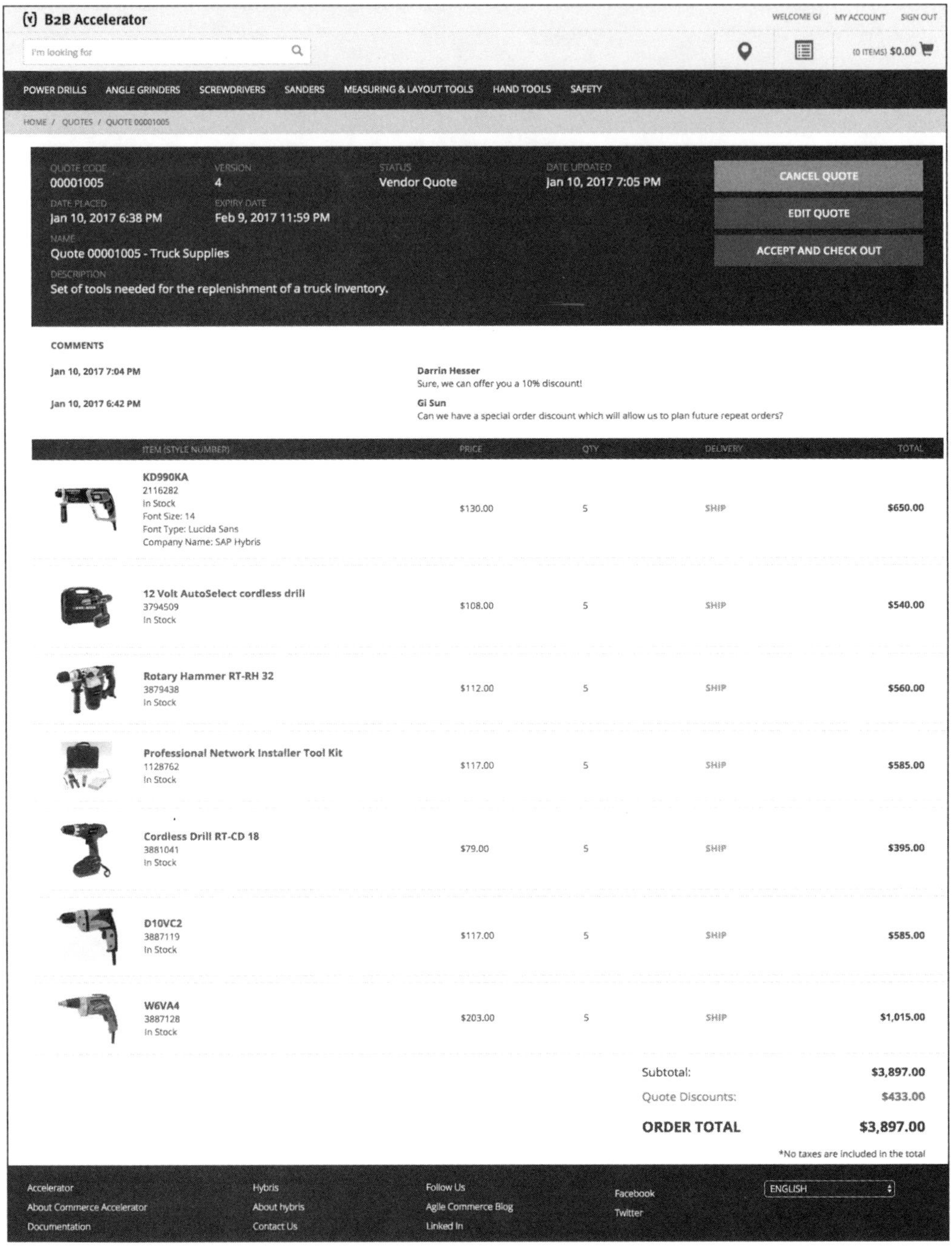

Figure 6.11 Quote Details Page Showing Quote Header, Comments, and Line Items

6.2.4 Email Notifications

A buyer receives email notifications throughout the negotiations phase. The email notifications include the list of all the items in the quote. The notifications are sent when the following happens:

- Buyer submits the quote
- Buyer accepts the quote and submits an order
- Buyer cancels the quote
- Quote is about to expire
- Quote has expired

The default email templates are available in the system, and the templates are improved from release to release. Figure 6.12 shows an example of an email notification generated by the quotes process.

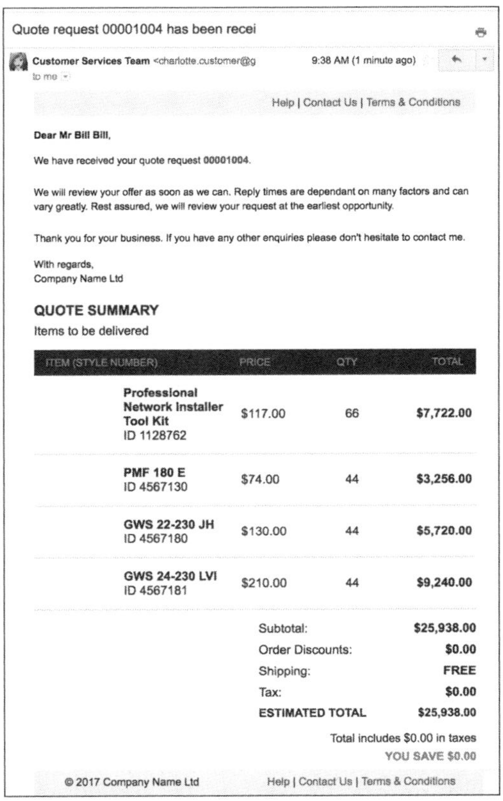

Quote request 00001004 has been recei

Customer Services Team <charlotte.customer@g 9:38 AM (1 minute ago)
to me

Help | Contact Us | Terms & Conditions

Dear Mr Bill Bill,

We have received your quote request 00001004.

We will review your offer as soon as we can. Reply times are dependant on many factors and can vary greatly. Rest assured, we will review your request at the earliest opportunity.

Thank you for your business. If you have any other enquiries please don't hesitate to contact me.

With regards,
Company Name Ltd

QUOTE SUMMARY
Items to be delivered

ITEM (STYLE NUMBER)	PRICE	QTY	TOTAL
Professional Network Installer Tool Kit ID 1128762	$117.00	66	**$7,722.00**
PMF 180 E ID 4567130	$74.00	44	**$3,256.00**
GWS 22-230 JH ID 4567180	$130.00	44	**$5,720.00**
GWS 24-230 LVI ID 4567181	$210.00	44	**$9,240.00**

Subtotal:	**$25,938.00**
Order Discounts:	**$0.00**
Shipping:	**FREE**
Tax:	**$0.00**
ESTIMATED TOTAL	**$25,938.00**

Total includes $0.00 in taxes
YOU SAVE $0.00

© 2017 Company Name Ltd Help | Contact Us | Terms & Conditions

Figure 6.12 Email Notification Generated by Quote Process

6.3 Capturing an Order

An order combines all the information required to bring the seller and buyer from quote to cash. It contains customer information such as identity and delivery address, payment and tax information, and products, prices, and promotions.

In SAP Commerce, an order is created by checking out a cart. That may be done via customer interaction on the accelerator storefront or via other channels by using the Omni Commerce Connect (OCC) API.

Several features are provided to support the process of turning a shopping cart into an order. In this section, we'll look at four features that contribute to capturing an order: Cart and checkout handles the actual shopping cart and order submission processes. Store locator lets a customer find local stores for shopping or pick up. The buy online and pick up in store process lets consumers manage their shopping online while retrieving their goods themselves from a local store within hours or minutes. Finally, payment and tax integrations allow a vendor to collect the right taxes and charge the appropriate amount to the payment method of choice.

6.3.1 Cart and Checkout

Cart and checkout (formerly called the order management module) is a set of services and a framework for defining your business process steps for submitting an order and handing it off for fulfillment.

Although a template business process is included for steps such as payment authorization, fraud check, and fulfillment integration, the template also offers open interfaces to allow implementation of custom integrations with payment, tax, and fraud service providers, warehousing and financial systems, and others to provide coverage of the complete ordering process.

> **Note**
>
> Note that cart and checkout consists of a set of framework services to support implementation of order submissions and management. For the out-of-the-box implementation of order management capabilities, see Section 6.4.

Some benefits of cart and checkout functionality are as follows:

- Provides an aggregated view of all orders placed by customers, independent of channel

- Provides a single view of orders so that customer experiences are consistent from one channel to another
- Process and control all orders in an organization in one place
- Centralized hub for integration with other parties such as SAP ERP, SAP CRM, warehouse systems, interactive voice response (IVR) systems, and phone and other offline order systems

The key features of cart and checkout are as follows:

- **Order business process**
  The order business process will define an order's passage through each step in the system once it has been placed. The process will understand which stage an order is in and define what stage it should be passed onto next. Third parties can integrate with the system to react to or cause status changes. The business process can be customized by extending it to add additional process steps as required.
- **Order versioning**
  During the order lifecycle, an order's status may change any number of times. Reasons for an order status to change include the following:
  - Items not in stock
  - Items on backorder
  - Order partially or fully shipped
  - Payment rejected
  - Fraud detected

  The order business process records such changes to an order, compiling an order version history. The order business process will track those changes not only on the order level but for consignments as well. This provides greater visibility of the status of an order to both customers and customer service agents.
- **Order splitting**
  Orders may combine purchase orders for different vendors, need to be shipped to different addresses, use different shipping methods, or ship from different fulfillment centers on different dates. To support this, a single order can be split up into multiple consignments.

  Each consignment needs to be routed to the correct location or system for fulfillment (e.g., a certain warehouse or store location for click and collect/pick up in store). Orders may also be split when part of an order is not available for immediate shipping (backorder or presale items, etc.). Consignment sourcing or routing is handled by SAP Commerce order management, by custom code, or through integration with a third party.

- **Order cancellation**
  This process provides functionality to set an order state to canceled. Individual line items can also be canceled and removed from an order. This will require recalculation of the order value and defining additional calls to the payment provider. The calculation can be done with the default service or extended with custom cart calculation.

  More advanced order cancellation capabilities are included in order management.

- **Hub for warehouses**
  Third-party warehouse management systems can integrate with cart and checkout's API, fetching orders (or parts of orders) and reporting fulfillment status and stock levels of items back to SAP Commerce. Warehouses may report additional information such as order tracking and carrier details once an order has been shipped. Cart and checkout provides interfaces to query information such as stock levels, restock, tracking details, and so on to display information on a website or wherever it's required.

- **Hub for fraud service providers**
  Cart and checkout makes it possible to check orders for fraud attempts. Fraud checking can take place in two stages—first through the SAP Commerce fraud detection extension, which does a basic scoring of various symptoms (such as blacklists, whitelists, and thresholds). Additional, more sophisticated checks can be done by third-party providers. Cart and checkout provides an interface to integrate such commercial products.

  If an order fails a fraud check, the business process places it into a fraud queue step to be brought to the attention of a customer service agent (CSA). This step prevents the order from being further processed until a CSA releases or cancels/rejects the order.

- **Stock information**
  To support websites displaying product stock information for specific warehouses or aggregated over all online stock, the stock service in cart and checkout makes it possible to manage stock information such as product delivery lead times, allowed overselling quantities, and always in stock or always out of stock items. The stock service can be fed easily by integration with existing warehouse systems.

Note

See Section 6.4.1 for more details on available-to-promise in order management.

6.3.2 Store Locator

Store locator functionality helps customers find nearby stores and provides directions to the selected store.

Using the SAP Commerce store locator functionality can save money and increase sales by allowing the customer to self-serve instead of calling customer service. Directing customers to a store for rapid purchase or even supporting them in placing an order online for later pick up in store can remove a barrier to sale.

Customers search for a store using postal codes, addresses, or GPS coordinates (provided by a mobile device). The store locator uses third-party services along with provided store location data to provide consumers with available store locations. The data can be input using the administration console or via a dedicated service. A CronJob can check for any new or updated locations in order to update the GPS coordinates.

From there, you may present customers with directions or available stock for purchase or order.

By default, this service is configured to work with Google Maps API and has a built-in adapter. This requires a Google account and an API key to use. By implementing a suitable adapter, you also can use the store locator with any custom third-party service that provides this functionality. Usually services of that type have limitations based on daily amount or request frequency. The store locator configuration enables you to avoid exceeding this limit.

The store locator supports display of mapplets by following the KML standard, which keeps the map information well-structured for easy display.

6.3.3 Buy Online, Pick Up in Store

One of the key use cases for omnichannel is allowing online customers to place orders online for pick up in store. For brick-and-mortar organizations, the ability to use store locations as "same-day delivery" warehouses for local customers is a very real competitive advantage over online-only competitors.

To use this feature out of the box, you can use the SAP Commerce, B2C accelerator storefront along with cart and checkout and order management.

The storefront (or a mobile application using the related services) can show consumers product availability at a store (or stores) they have selected from the store locator feature. From there, they can check out the order as they normally would, apart from defining the pickup location. This has the effect of overriding the order routing logic explained in Section 6.5.4 and sending the order (or consignment) to a specific store for pick up.

Fulfillment of a pickup order is done using the backoffice Order Fulfillment Cockpit. See Section 6.6.3 for information on the preparation and handover of the order in the store.

6.3.4 Payment and Taxes

In an online shop, payment, and often taxes, is always handled through integration with a third party. Cart and checkout includes a payment extension that allows an implementation team to build a custom payment gateway adapter to integrate with the payment service gateway of its choice.

For taxes, there are a variety of options. By default, cart and checkout includes tax calculation based on stored tax rows. This can work quite well in a VAT jurisdiction, but for more complicated tax systems such as those found in the United States, the best practice is to integrate with a specialized tax service that can provide an estimate or quote for your shopping cart and then record those taxes upon fulfillment.

An alternative way to implement integrations such as tax, payment, and others is to use the CIS framework, which offers template integrations for implementers, as well as a model for third parties to provide their own integrations with SAP Commerce that simply require plugging in those prebuilt integrations.

6.4 Distributed Order Management

The key to buy and fulfill from anywhere is to be able to have visibility of your products across your entire network. An item that sits on a shelf on the other side of the country doesn't help your customer who's in another store or looking at her phone, unless you can show her you have it and that you can get it to her.

Distributed order management is what makes "commerce anywhere" possible. If you can define what you have available and where it is, you can give every customer an endless aisle to shop in while reducing stale inventory that needlessly takes up space in the wrong location, waiting to be marked down for liquidation.

Distributed order management is a key capability of SAP Commerce order management, providing support both online and in store to cross over and sell from a common pool of available inventory.

In the following sections, we delve into the four key distributed order management capabilities of SAP Commerce order management. We'll start with the Order Fulfillment Cockpit, in which you can manage setup and execution of order fulfillment. Then we'll explain how inventory at different locations and in different states of availability lets you expose information about how much can be ordered and from where to your customers and the fulfillment system itself. This full visibility is what creates an endless aisle of all your available stock, independent of location.

6.4.1 Order Fulfillment Cockpit

SAP Commerce order management has two main user interfaces. There is the order management part of the Customer Support Cockpit, and there is the Order Fulfillment Cockpit. Both are accessed from the SAP Commerce backoffice application.

For setup of distributed order management, access the Order Fulfillment Cockpit. Once logged in with appropriate credentials—as a user with access to these cockpits—then you can select the cockpit you desire from the top navigation.

To set up the users with appropriate credentials to access the Order Fulfillment Cockpit and see various options, assign each user to a user in the backoffice Administration Cockpit. By default, order management uses roles such as administrator, warehouse manager, warehouse agent, and store agent, but you can configure others.

Once logged in to the cockpit with appropriate credentials, you will see in the left navigation panel choices such as **Inbox**, **Consignments**, **Fulfillment Locations**, **Inventory**, and **Returns** (see Figure 6.13).

There are also preset filters on the bottom of the left navigation that can help you find consignments in a specific status, such as **In Process**, **Complete**, or **Canceled**. There is also an option to save your advanced searches if you create them in the **Advanced Search** widget. This can save you time when looking for a common set of consignments.

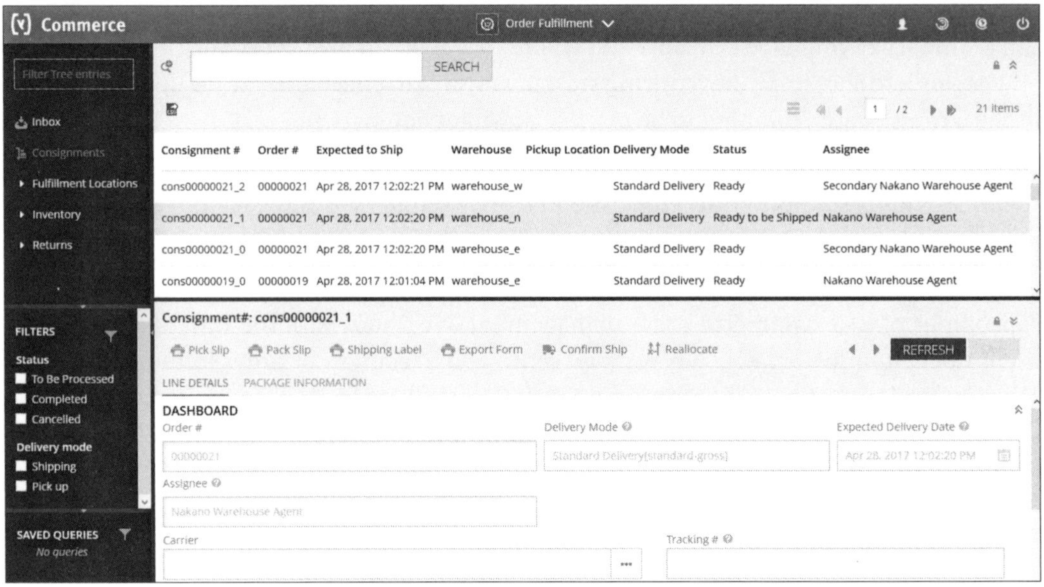

Figure 6.13 Order Fulfillment Cockpit Showing Consignments

For distributed order management setup, we're interested in the **Fulfillment Locations** (Section 6.5.1) and **Inventory** screens, as well as the Backoffice Administration Cockpit.

6.4.2 Stock and Availability

To determine what you can sell, you need to differentiate between what's in stock and what's available. What's the difference? Well, you might have 100 units of inventory in stock, but if you already sold 80 of them, then you only have 20 remaining that are available to sell.

The way that SAP Commerce order management determines your available-to-promise (ATP) stock is by combining stock levels with a configurable set of inventory events to produce a specific value for a specific base store.

Stock levels represent physical inventory as objects that include product code or SKU, quantity, a warehouse (the logical grouping of stock, not necessarily a physical location; Section 6.5.1), the bin location in which this particular unit can be found, the delivery date for the items to arrive at the location, advanced shipping notice ID, release date on which the items will be available to be shipped, and the in stock status (for which you can force the item to be in stock or out of stock, overriding the **Quantity** field).

These values can be seen and edited in the backoffice Order Fulfillment Cockpit under **Inventory/Stock Levels**, as shown in Figure 6.14.

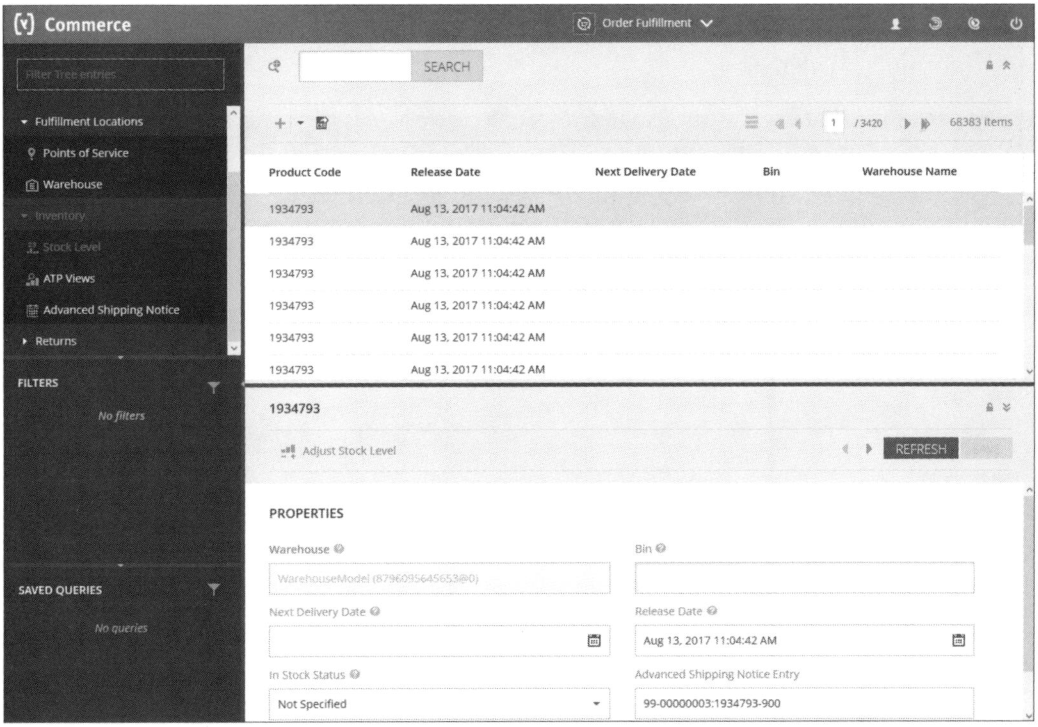

Figure 6.14 Order Fulfillment Cockpit Showing Stock Levels

In the left navigation, under **Inventory**, there is also a node for **Advanced Shipping Notices**. This is where a user can view advance notification of future inventory deliveries and then receive that stock into inventory.

Inventory events describe movements in your inventory. Examples include an increase in inventory, a shrink, an allocation to an order, or a reservation. There are several such events, and additional ones can be added during implementation.

Available-to-promise (ATP) is defined as the sum of stock levels for an item, adjusted by inventory events. By providing you with the ability to decide which inventory events are added to or subtracted from stock levels, you have the flexibility to define your ATP in a way that specifically suits your business.

ATP configuration is done in the backoffice admin. After selecting the **Administration** cockpit, in the left navigation panel select the **Order Management** node and then the **ATP Formulas** subnode.

Here, you can create or edit an ATP formula, give it a name, associate it with a specific base store or base stores, and define which events to include in that formula, as well as whether each event adds to or subtracts from the total. Figure 6.15 shows the ATP formula builder.

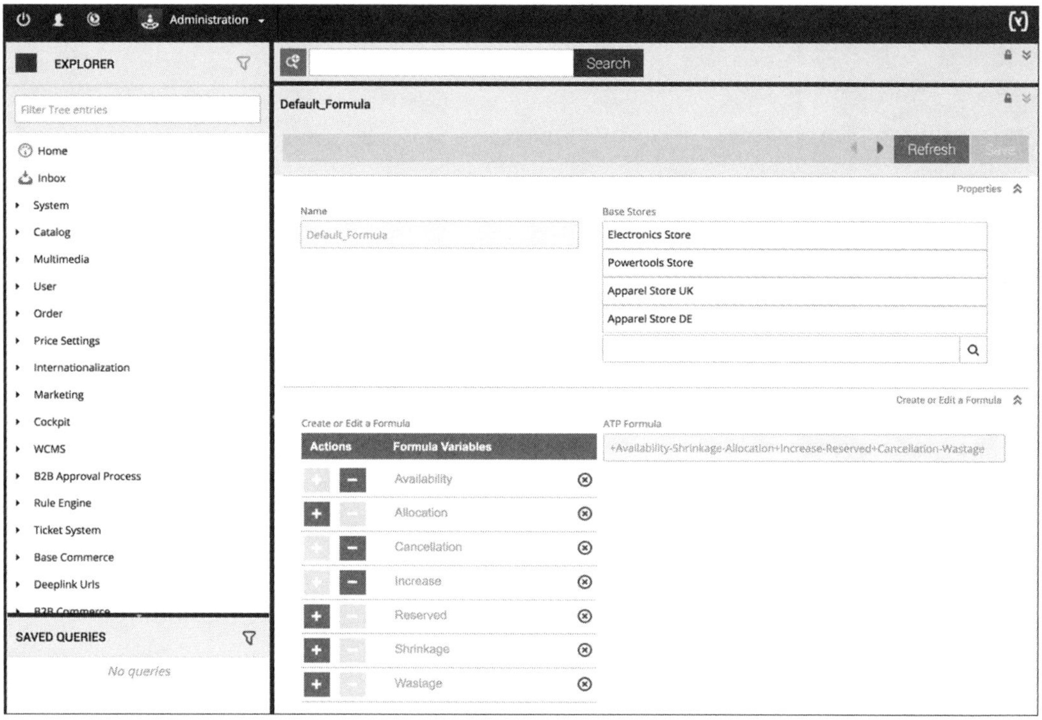

Figure 6.15 ATP Formula Builder in Backoffice Admin Cockpit

Alternatively, you can import the formula using ImpEx or set it using the ATP Formula Service API.

6.4.3 Enterprise Inventory

There are two main levels of inventory availability that are used by order management: global and local. Order management uses this information for allocating orders to fulfillment locations, whereas the storefront uses it to let a customer know what he can purchase.

By selecting a specific fulfillment location, you can get the available stock for that location. For a customer looking to buy online and pick up in store, this lets him see what you have available at him preferred location.

Knowing the availability globally and locally serve different purposes, but both contribute to a better customer experience. The information can be exposed on the storefront simply by showing available or not, how much is available, low, medium, or high, next available date for out of stock items, or the same information at the local level.

Within the Order Fulfillment Cockpit, the availability information can be viewed in the **ATP Views** page found under the **Inventory** option in the left navigation panel (see Figure 6.16).

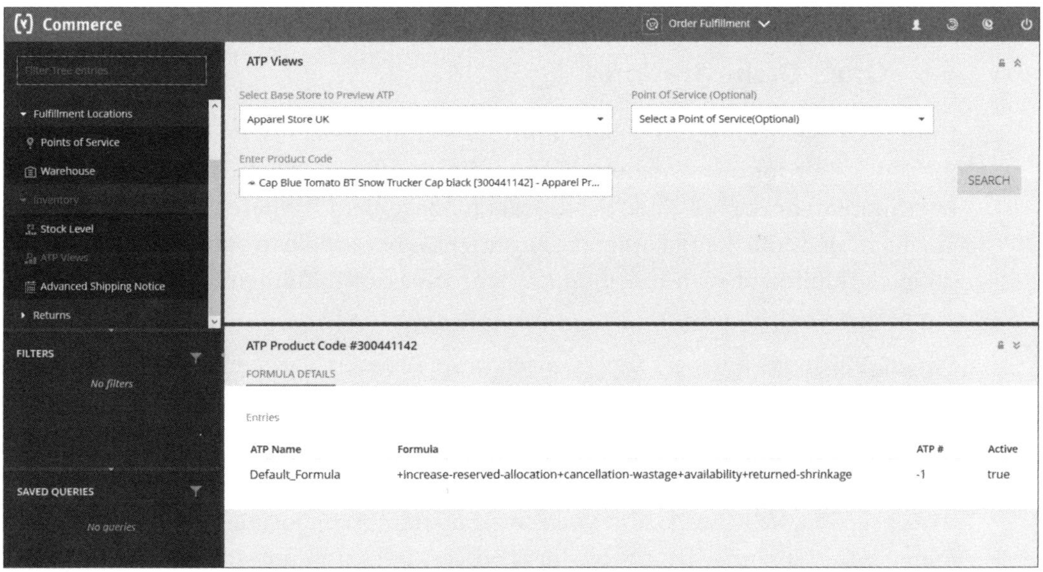

Figure 6.16 Order Fulfillment Cockpit Showing ATP View

This view lets you search for ATP information by entering the product code (SKU), selecting the base store, and deciding whether to filter the results by location. In addition to the available quantity, the actual formula used to calculate the value is shown.

6.4.4 Endless Aisle

By default, if you do not limit the results by selecting a point of service (Section 6.5.1), then a call to ATP returns (or shows in the UI) your global enterprise inventory (at the base store level). This represents what you have available across your entire fulfillment network, including internal warehouses and stores, as well as drop ship vendors and suppliers. For online orders this is useful because the specific location is less important than the fact that the product can be delivered to the customer.

The business value of showing all your product available as an endless aisle is that your customers can buy from you even if there's a great distance in between. The customer gets the product he wants, and the vendor isn't stuck with product in the wrong place, slowly going stale.

With this information, the next step is to identify the best source for the products that your customer wants.

6.5 Order Orchestration

Once you have the inventory availability data available in distributed order management, it's time for order orchestration to determine what to do with the order. This key differentiator of SAP Commerce order management is where the magic happens. The heart of omnichannel order management is being able to split orders apart and define a fulfillment plan based on an optimal set of fulfillment locations and systems.

Depending on the business logic in place, orders and consignments may be routed to warehouses, stores, third-party drop-ship vendors, externally managed locations, your own fulfillment cockpit, or backend systems like your ERP (be it SAP or non-SAP) or warehouse management system.

In this section, we'll look at how you can set up fulfillment locations with warehouses and points of service, what the business process is for fulfilling an order or a consignment, and how you can split orders into multiple consignments. We'll then look at how sourcing and allocation works to define which locations should fulfill orders and how the orders can be orchestrated and sent to one or multiple backend systems.

6.5.1 Warehouse and Points of Service

Fulfillment locations represent places or systems that can fulfill orders and parts of orders and either ship them to the customer or hold them for customer pickup.

In the backoffice Order Fulfillment Cockpit, under **Fulfillment Locations** in the left navigation panel you will see **Points of Service and Warehouses**.

In SAP Commerce, a point of service represents a physical address. There are different types of points of service, such as stores and warehouses, and each type may have additional attributes, such as store hours, that are specific to that type of location.

Configure a point of service in the backoffice in the **Points Of Service** section where you see and edit details like **Name**, **Address** and **Coordinates** (for use in calculating distances), **Type**, **Associated Base Store**, and **Associated Warehouses** (see Figure 6.17).

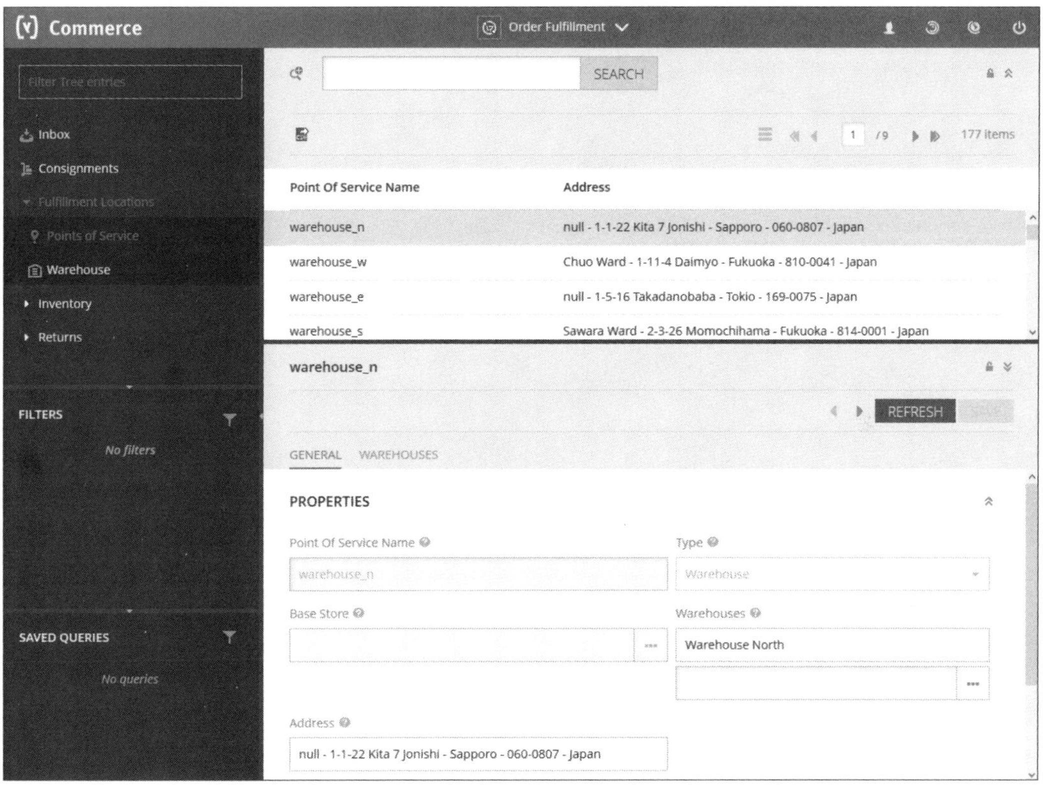

Figure 6.17 Order Fulfillment Cockpit Showing Fulfillment Locations

In SAP Commerce, a warehouse does *not* necessarily represent a physical location. It is a logical grouping of stock levels or pools of inventory. It's possible to associate multiple warehouses with a point of service and vice versa. By default, order management uses 1:1.

To configure a warehouse, in the backoffice Order Fulfillment Cockpit, navigate to the **Fulfillment Locations** node and then the **Warehouse** subnode. The **Warehouse Details** tab, shown in Figure 6.18, lets you see and edit details like **Warehouse Name** and **Code**, associated **Points of Service** and **Base Stores, Delivery Modes** supported by that warehouse, as well as information used for sourcing, such as **Priority** and **Score** and **Vendor Information** (if it's external).

There are also tabs for **Stock Levels** and **Consignments** allocated to the warehouse being looked at.

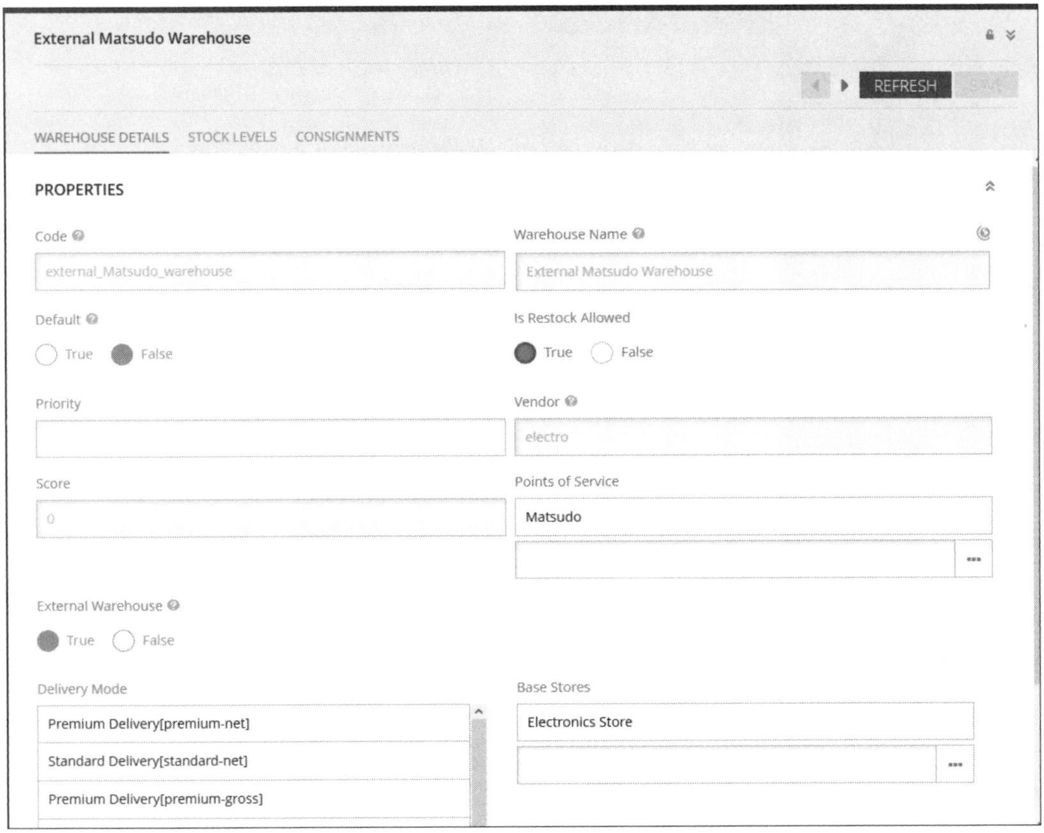

Figure 6.18 Warehouse Details

It's the combination of warehouse and point of service information with inventory availability that lets order management identify the optimal routing of orders and partial orders in order to fulfill them.

6.5.2 Business Processes and Order Status

The SAP Commerce process engine enables you to define business processes and runs these processes in an asynchronous way. It guarantees that actions are performed in the right sequence under the right conditions. A new process can be created for each process definition, allowing for a separate workflow for orders, consignments, and returns.

The process engine lets you define a series of steps (e.g., order states) with related actions for each step, such as waiting for events, notifying users and groups, and firing actions and events followed by flow decisions based on action results.

Order management includes specific implementations of the business process to handle orchestration of orders, shipments, returns, and email notifications. The order workflow includes steps that pertain to the order itself such as fraud validation, geolocation of the shipping address, sourcing, cancellation, and order update.

The consignment (shipment) workflow includes steps for the fulfillment process, including ship versus pickup, decline, reallocate, and confirmation. Also Section 6.6.2 for the consignment task assignment workflow that defines the specific pick, pack, and ship steps that can be assigned to a user. The return workflow includes steps for waiting for approvals, label generation, cancel, auto/manual refund, tax reversal, and inventory update. The send return label email process is a subprocess of the return workflow that simply generates and sends an email.

These processes (and others) can be defined using the dynamic process definition feature. The processes are defined in an ImpEx file that allows for changes without any need to rebuild or restart the application.

6.5.3 Order Splitting and Consignments

As discussed in Section 6.3.1, orders may need to be split to fulfill different items from different locations or systems. Order management will make the decision to split an order into as many consignments as needed to fulfill the entire order. Depending on how you set up your sourcing strategies (Section 6.5.4), you may prefer to keep orders together and ship in one parcel (this would be a no-split strategy), or you may choose to split an order apart if needed and fulfill according to other preferences.

See Figure 6.19 for a simple view of how a submitted cart becomes a single order before being split into multiple consignments.

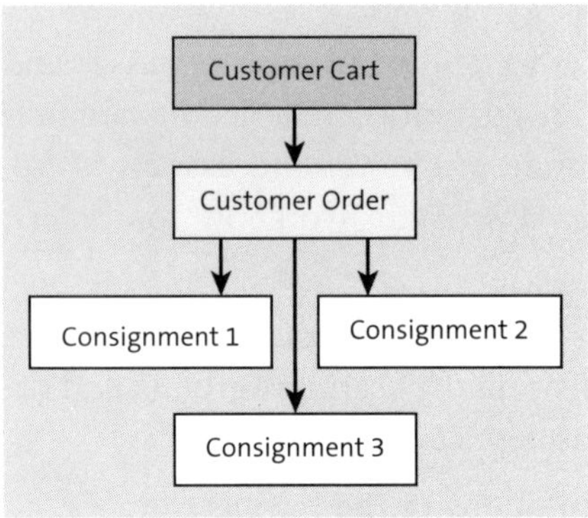

Figure 6.19 Customer Order Splitting and Consignments

The decision to split an order is made as part of the sourcing of the items in the order. The optimal source for each unit must be selected, and then these items can be grouped together as consignments. How is the location selected for each item?

6.5.4 Sourcing and Allocation to Fulfillment Locations

The process of fulfilling an order consists of three main steps:

1. Sourcing the order's items or deciding where to fulfill from (also called defining a fulfillment plan)
2. Allocating (or routing) the consignments to a fulfillment location
3. Picking, packing, and shipping the items

Sourcing can be a complex process by which a customer order, containing requested quantities for various products, is broken down into consignments. Each consignment indicates which fulfillment location or backend system will be responsible for shipping or providing each portion of the customer's order.

For example, let's say that a customer places an order to purchase a mobile phone and several accessories to benefit from a promotion. After the order has been submitted, it's sent to order management for fulfillment. In this case, there is no sourcing location that is capable of sourcing the entire order at once, so the order is split up into multiple consignments. Each consignment represents a subset of the order that will be shipped from a single sourcing location. How do we know the best way to split the order?

The sourcing service evaluates the best way to source orders using some defined sourcing strategies. The results collected during sourcing will determine the number of consignments to create.

This is done as follows (see Figure 6.20):

1. Filter the sourcing locations to obtain a minimal working subset.
2. Split an order into groups of order entries based on a collection of matchers.
3. Analyze the order to determine the sourcing strategies suitable for the order.
4. For each sourcing strategy, use the defined sourcing factors to rank and select the best locations and see if the order can be completely sourced. If not, then repeat these steps for the remaining products.
5. Return the sourcing results and allocate the consignments to fulfillment locations accordingly.

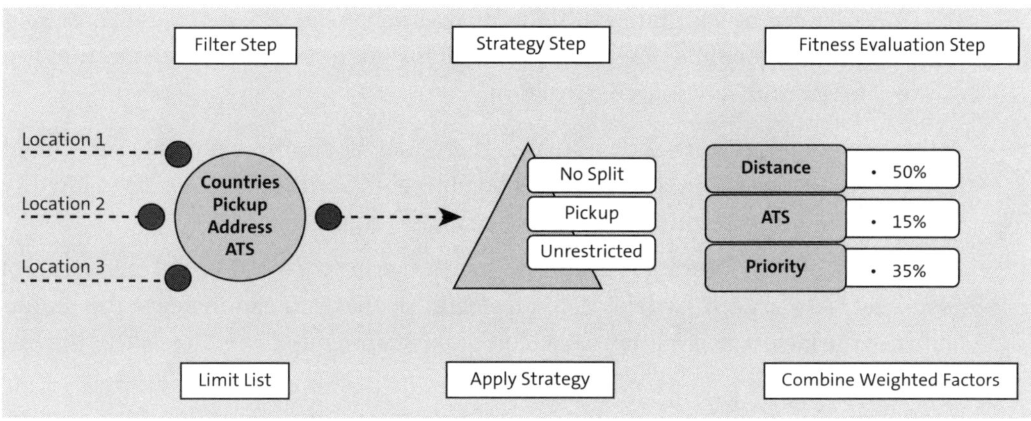

Figure 6.20 Order Sourcing Process

The filtering step allows us to indicate which subset of fulfillment locations or systems should be considered during sourcing. To qualify to be a sourcing location, a point of service must meet all qualification criteria. For example, it should be in a given country/region, be able to ship/pickup items, and meet a minimum stock availability.

The order analysis step allows us to determine which sourcing strategies should be executed and in which order. This is done by defining a series of business rules that, if matched, will recommend the sourcing strategies to use for a given order. For example, an item that is to be picked up will use the pickup strategy; an oversized item could have an oversized strategy.

The sourcing strategy will evaluate the best sourcing locations to use with the best consignment configurations given the strategy's constraints. During the sourcing process, multiple sourcing strategies can be applied until the order is completely sourced.

Some provided sourcing strategies include the following:

- **No splitting**
  The order must be completely sourced from a single sourcing location as one consignment.
- **Pickup**
  Similar to no splitting, the order must be completely sourced from a single sourcing location (store address chosen for pickup) as one consignment.
- **No restrictions**
  The order can be split into multiple consignments and order entries can be split across multiple points of service, such that any quantities of any order entries can be sourced from any sourcing location.

After applying the filters and strategies, there may be multiple possible fulfillment locations to choose from. This result set is subjected to a fitness evaluation to identify the optimal source according to specific business requirements.

The fitness of each location is evaluated by comparing each one based on a series of sourcing factors. Each factor is given a weight so that you can increase the importance of the factors that matter most to your business. Out-of-the-box factors include the following:

- The distance between the sourcing location and the shipping address
- The priority of the sourcing location (e.g., you may want to prioritize a warehouse above a store or an internal site above an external drop shipper)
- The amount of stock the sourcing location has available
- The score a fulfillment location has achieved based on previous results, which can be populated from a hot folder with results from an analytics solution

After passing through each of these steps, the sourcing results are collected and saved. The sourcing results will contain information about which order entries and quantities are to be fulfilled from a given point of service.

At the end of the sourcing process, the sourcing service analyzes the sourcing results and determines if the order is completely sourced or not. If the order is completely sourced, the sourcing results will serve to create the consignments and allocate them to the locations selected. Otherwise, a failure action will take place.

The weighting of sourcing factors can be configured from the backoffice **Administration** screen. From the left navigation panel, select **Order Management • Sourcing Configuration**. Here you can create a new configuration or edit an existing one. Each sourcing factor requires a weight. The weights are a percentage and must sum to 100.

You must then select which base store to apply this configuration to, as shown in Figure 6.21.

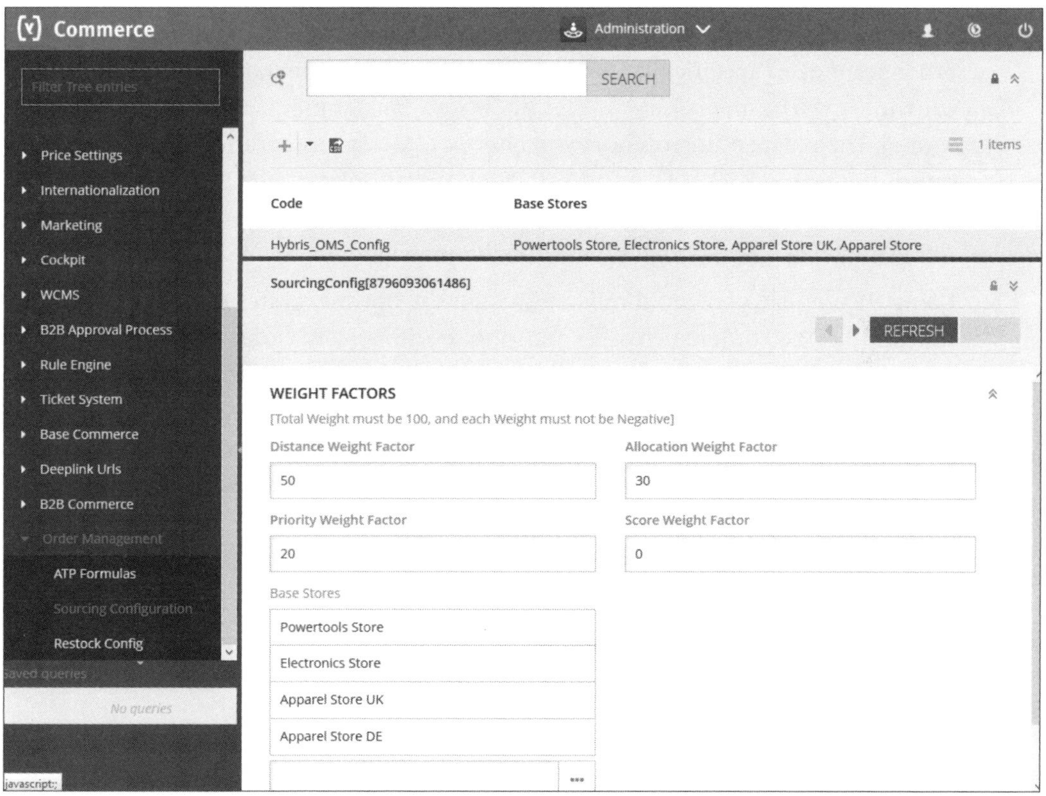

Figure 6.21 Sourcing Configuration with Weight Factors

6.5.5 Orchestrating Multiple Backends

The results of sourcing do not simply define a physical fulfillment location. Although they do provide this information, they can also provide an option for splitting orders across multiple backends. For example, an order could be split between two or three (or 16) ERP systems. Order management can be simply determining which system gets which order lines, or it can involve dynamic plant determination and informing the ERP (or warehouse management system or external order management system) which location it should be routing to.

Why is this necessary? Running complex landscapes with seemingly redundant software systems can come about because of mergers, acquisitions, and expansion into new geographies. It can be very difficult to have your commerce system integrate simply with all these different backends. Order management provides a lightweight orchestration layer that sits between the order system and those other systems.

Order management can orchestrate these various systems precisely as it does with physical fulfillment locations. By defining warehouses (logical stock pools) as either other systems or specific plants in an ERP system, order management sourcing will use the same data and rule set to identify where consignments should be allocated or routed. Then, depending on how you choose to do the integration, you can use the out-of-the-box SAP S/4HANA and SAP ERP integrations, provide custom integrations to other systems, or simply call the order management API to get the allocated information and then feed updates back to order management.

Using this model, you could mix and match the optimal systems to fulfill an order. Imagine a mixed order such as a smartphone with a plan. Order management could route the fulfillment of the SIM card for pick up at a local store within order management itself, the handset may be shipped from a warehouse managed by SAP ERP, some accessories may be ordered from external drop ship vendors, and the actual service plan could be routed to a subscription service such as SAP Subscription Billing.

See Figure 6.22 for a visual representation of how data can be fed to or retrieved from order management at each step of the order business process. At the beginning, different systems such as SAP ERP and vendors feed location and inventory information to order management. That information is used to allocate orders and consignments back to those systems for fulfillment purposes. In return, as the status changes they feed updates back to order management.

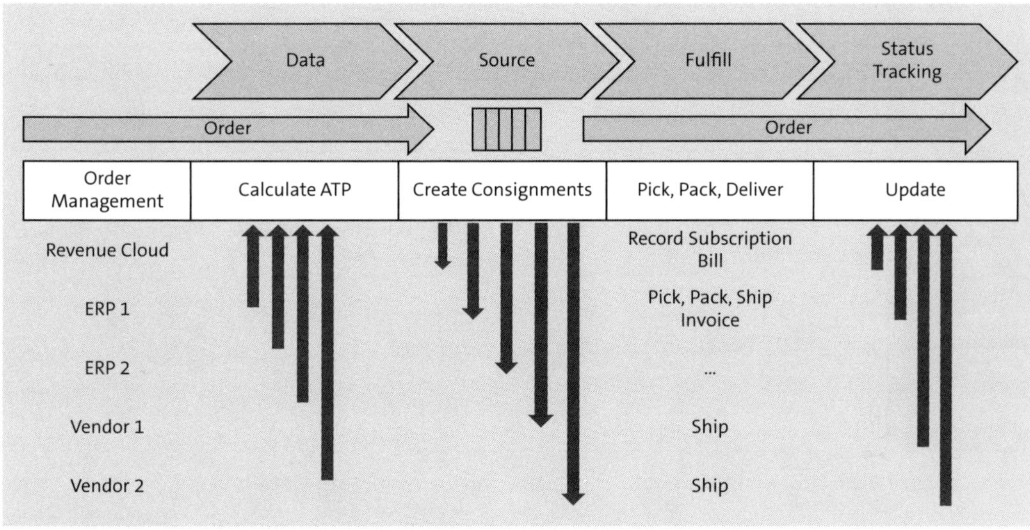

Figure 6.22 Multiple Backend Orchestration

6.6 Fulfillment Execution

Once order management's orchestration layer has routed orders to fulfillment locations, it's time for the crucial step to happen: preparing products for customers.

SAP Commerce order management has two main user interfaces. There is the order management part of the backoffice Customer Support Cockpit, and there is the backoffice Order Fulfillment Cockpit. Both are accessed from the SAP Commerce backoffice application. Once logged in with appropriate credentials—as a user with access to these cockpits— you can select the cockpit you desire from the top navigation.

For management of order and consignment fulfillment, access the Order Fulfillment Cockpit. Once there, you will see choices such as **Inbox**, **Consignments**, **Fulfillment Locations**, **Inventory**, and **Returns** in the left navigation panel, as shown in Figure 6.23.

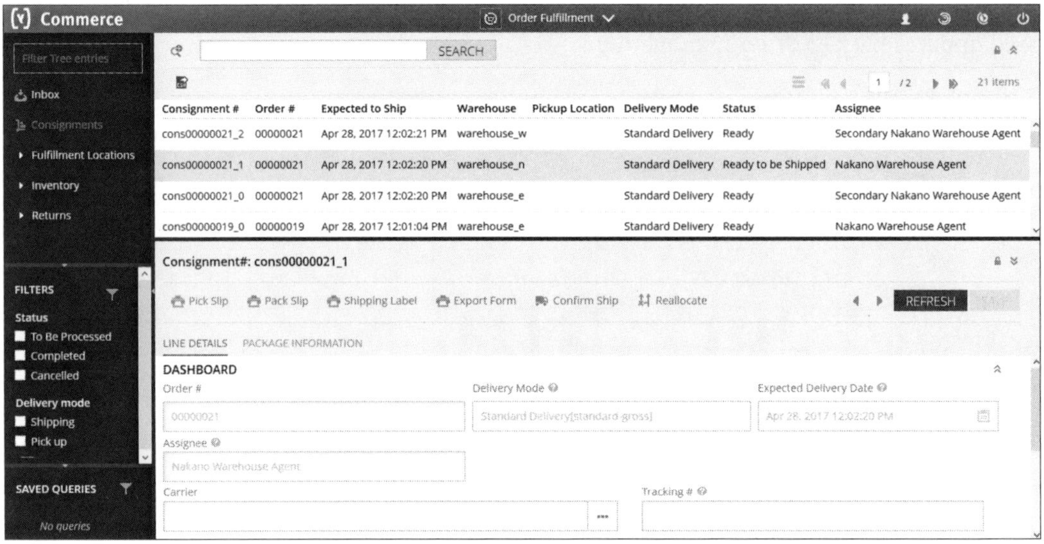

Figure 6.23 Order Fulfillment Cockpit Showing Consignment Details

The **Consignments** view provides you a list of consignments, as well as the details of a selected consignment in the lower half of the page. You can search for a specific consignment or group of consignments using the **Search** bar or the **Advanced Search** widget. In the list view, you will see the order number for the consignment, as well as the ship date, allocated warehouse, status, assigned employee, and the pickup location if it's a pickup item.

In addition, there are preset filters on the bottom of the left navigation that can help you to find consignments in a specific status, such as in process, complete, or cancelled, or to filter for orders to be shipped as opposed to those to be picked up. There is also an option to save your advanced searches if you create them in the **Advanced Search** widget. This can save you time when looking for a common set of consignments.

In the following sections, we'll explain using this view to work with consignments in need of fulfillment. That could be simply checking on the status of consignments that have been sent out for external fulfillment or picking and packing for shipping or for in-store pickup. This view also provides for handling fulfillment failures that require declining order lines and sending them back to be fulfilled elsewhere. Finally, there is a separate view for tasks that have been assigned to the logged-in user, allowing for different activities to be parceled out to specific people.

6.6.1 External Fulfillment

As discussed in Section 6.5.5, some orders or parts of orders may be allocated to systems external to order management for fulfillment. These may include SAP ERP, warehouse management systems, or even other order management systems, such as those at vendors.

In this case, the SAP Commerce order management backoffice fulfillment cockpit will serve mostly to provide consignment-level status information as those other systems feed updates back to order management. Should a reallocation be required, it could be handled manually here.

6.6.2 Pick, Pack, and Ship

When fulfillment is being handled within SAP Commerce order management, the Order Fulfillment Cockpit provides several features.

The standard flow of events is for a fulfillment agent to select a consignment, print a pick slip, find the item, print a packing slip and invoice, pack the items, and print a shipping label before confirming shipment. These printable documents are built from templates and can include specialized media such as images and barcodes using the document generation service.

In the **Consignment Details** widget, once you have selected a consignment, you will see buttons for each action you may want to take. You can also edit consignment information such as **Shipping Method**, **Carrier**, **Tracking Number**, and **Package Information** (which can be found in the **Package Information** tab).

After selecting a consignment, click the **Pick Slip** button (see Figure 6.24) to print a pick slip with the information required to find the items, SKUs, descriptions, images, quantities and bin numbers (if applicable), as shown in Figure 6.25.

Figure 6.24 Order Fulfillment Cockpit Showing Pick, Pack, Ship Buttons

Dec 12, 2016 3:23:59 PM

Order ID	**Order Date**
00000019	Mon Dec 12 13:03:06 EST 2016

Ship to
Jerome Gaileur

Address Line 1	1234 drive
Address Line 2	
City	Los Angeles
Postal Code	90210
Phone	613-537-5896

Customer Order

Shipment Details

Line #	Product Code	Product Image	Product Name	Bin Code	QTY
1	325414		EASYSHARE Z730 Zoom Digital Camera	bin111	1

Figure 6.25 Pick Slip Details

If you want to pick multiple items at once, you can select multiple consignments and click the **Consolidated Pick Slip** icon (see Figure 6.26). This will generate one document with products grouped together to simplify the picking process.

Once your picked items are ready to be packed, the packing slip process is very similar. You select the consignment you want to pack and then click the **Packing Slip** icon in the **Details** pane. This provides a document to put into the box, confirming for the customer what she is receiving. Once this is done, the consignment is considered either ready for shipping or ready for pickup.

For an order that is to be shipped, you follow the same process to generate a shipping label for the parcel. Clicking the **Consignment Details** icon for **Shipping Label** will print a document with the parcel information, address, and barcode provided by your shipping service integration, as shown in Figure 6.27.

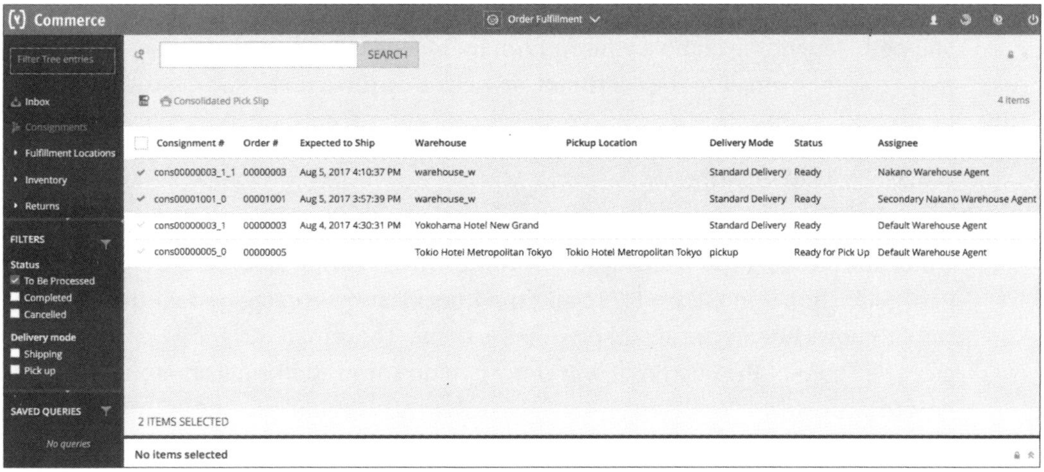

Figure 6.26 Selecting Multiple Consignments for Picking Multiple Items

If required, you can also print export forms when documentation is required to send parcels internationally.

Figure 6.27 Sample of Shipping Label

Once you're done, you can select the **Confirm** button to set the consignment status to **Shipped**. Depending on how your fulfillment business process workflow is set up, this may trigger an email to the customer, as well as confirm taxes and capture payment.

6.6.3 Pick Up in Store

If a customer has selected buy online, pick up in store, there is no shipping label step. Otherwise, picking and packing are the same. Once packing is complete (after clicking **Pack Slip**, shown in Figure 6.28), an email notification is triggered so that the customer knows he can come and pick up his items. This email is a good opportunity to cross-sell so that the customer will choose to do some additional shopping when he gets to your store.

When the customer receives his parcel, simply click the **Confirm Pickup** button (see Figure 6.28), which will change the status of the consignment to **Pickup Complete**.

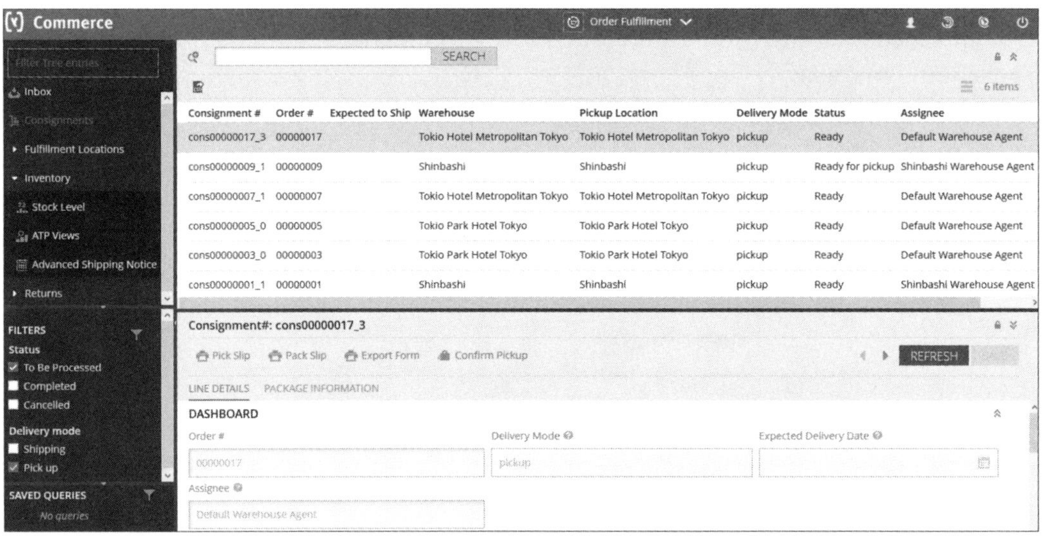

Figure 6.28 Confirm Pickup Status after Customer Receives Package

6.6.4 Declining or Relocating Consignments

There may be times when an allocated consignment cannot be fulfilled. This may be due to inaccurate data; some available products may be damaged or may have just been purchased by another customer. In such cases, rather than printing the packing slip, the employee will need to decline some or all of the allocated consignment.

In this case, he can select the consignment from his search results list view and then click the **Reallocate** button. This will bring up a new window to manage reallocation, as shown in Figure 6.29.

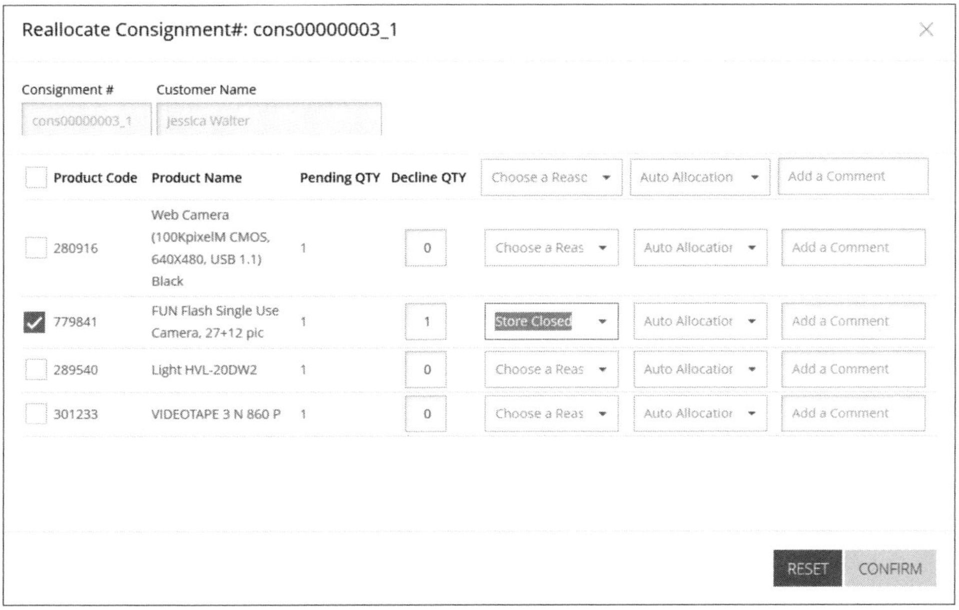

Figure 6.29 Consignment Reallocations

If the entire consignment must be declined, select the **Global** checkbox at the top left. This will multiselect all the items and set the same values for each of them until edited.

Then proceed to fill in the information for either the entire consignment or individual lines if some can be fulfilled. This information can be as follows:

- **Decline QTY** is the number you cannot fulfill.
- Add a **Reason Code**, such as out of stock or store closed.
- **Location** can be explicitly set if you know where you want to route the consignment to. Normally, you will leave this as an autoallocation so that the system can determine the best choice by sending these items back to sourcing.
- Add a comment in the free-text field

When you confirm your declines, those items will be sent elsewhere for fulfillment and you can continue to fulfill the remainder of the consignment if applicable.

6.6.5 Task Assignment Workflow: Inbox

As an alternative to using the consignments view in the Order Fulfillment Cockpit, there is also a section called **Inbox**.

The inbox shows a user consignment tasks assigned to her so that she can process shipments and avoid consignments that should be worked on by another employee at the same location.

By default, the consignment assignment workflow will choose the employee with the lowest workload (lowest number of assigned tasks) to assign the consignment to.

The advantage of using the inbox view is that you can easily take bulk actions by selecting multiple consignments at once and optimizing the task assignments among employees. The available bulk actions are the same ones you would expect from the consignment view and depend on the current state. You can print documents and reallocate using the three dots on each line and mark a step as complete by selecting it and clicking **Done**, as shown in Figure 6.30.

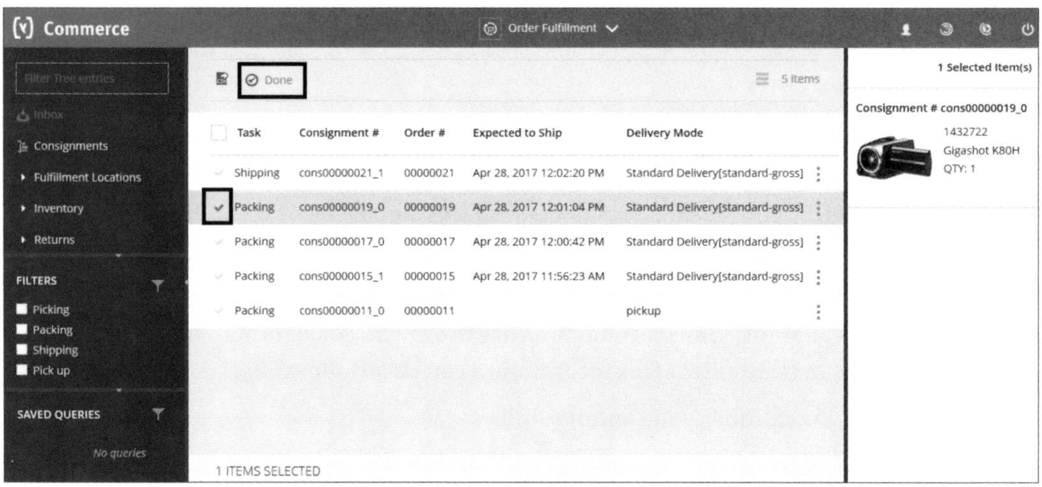

Figure 6.30 Task Assignments via Order Fulfillment Inbox

6.7 Order Lifecycle

The customer experience does not end with the receipt of the product. There is (or should be) an ongoing relationship between you and the customer you want to keep for life. Sometimes that involves changes to an order that is already in flight or even return of an order that has already been completed.

How that is handled is the key to keeping your customer happy. SAP Commerce order management provides capabilities to both your customer service agents and to the customers themselves by supporting self-service through the storefront.

In some cases, both elements are required as a customer request in turn needs to be processed by customer service.

In either case, as you will see in the following sections, the backoffice Customer Support Cockpit gives your team the tools to review orders and modify details, act on fraud checks, place orders on hold, or handle tickets. From there you can manage return requests and cancellations. The ability to make these requests or open help tickets is also part of the storefront order management self-service capabilities.

6.7.1 Backoffice Customer Support Cockpit

SAP Commerce order management has two main user interfaces. There is the order management part of the backoffice Customer Support Cockpit and there is the backoffice Order Fulfillment Cockpit. Both are accessed from the SAP Commerce backoffice application. Once logged in with appropriate credentials—as a user with access to these cockpits—you can select the cockpit you desire from the top navigation.

For scenarios like managing cancellations and returns or looking up order statuses in order management, use the backoffice Customer Support Cockpit (shown in Figure 6.31).

This view contains sections in the left navigation panel for **Tickets**, **Product Reviews**, and **Customer** for standard customer support scenarios. There are also sections for **Orders** and **Returns**. These are the ones we will discuss here.

Within the **Orders** section, you can choose from **Open Orders**, **Completed Orders**, or **All Orders** as an easy way of filtering what you want to see rather than searching. As in the Order Fulfillment Cockpit, you can do an advanced search and save it for reuse from the **Saved Queries** section.

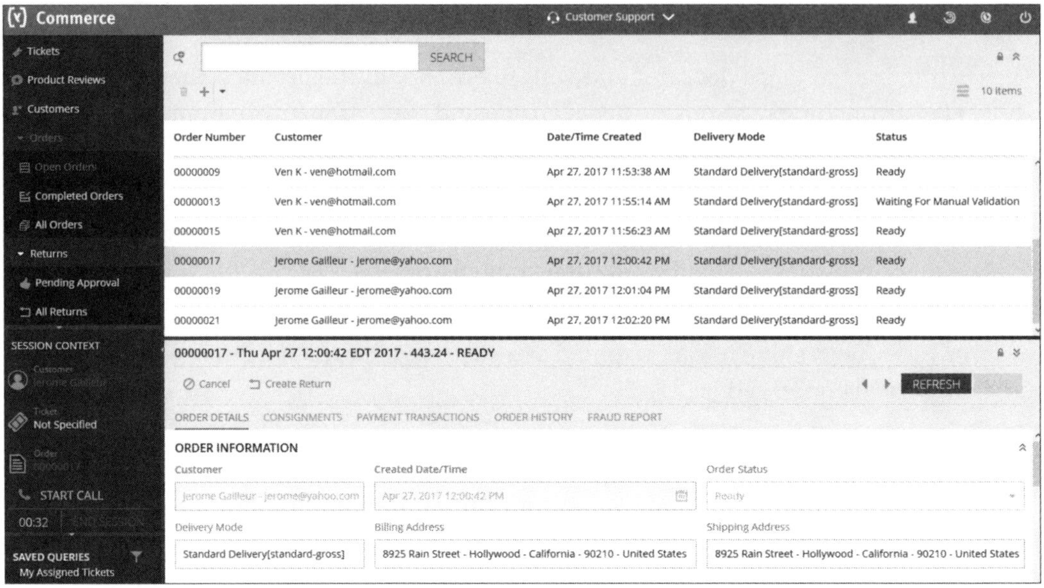

Figure 6.31 Customer Support Cockpit in Backoffice

As is common in the backoffice, you can select an order from your list view and see details in the detail pane below. The list view shows you high-level information such as order number, customer name, data, and order status.

The detail pane contains multiple tabs with additional information. From here you can view and edit information related to the order.

The **Order Details** tab (see Figure 6.32) contains the following information:

- **Order Information**
  Customer, billing and shipping addresses, delivery mode
- **Order Line Details**
  Information about the product and its status
- **Order Totals**
  Currency, discounts, taxes, and totals

The **Consignments** tab (see Figure 6.33) contains the following information related to fulfillment:

- **Consignment Number**
- **Tracking ID**
- **Delivery Mode**
- **Status**

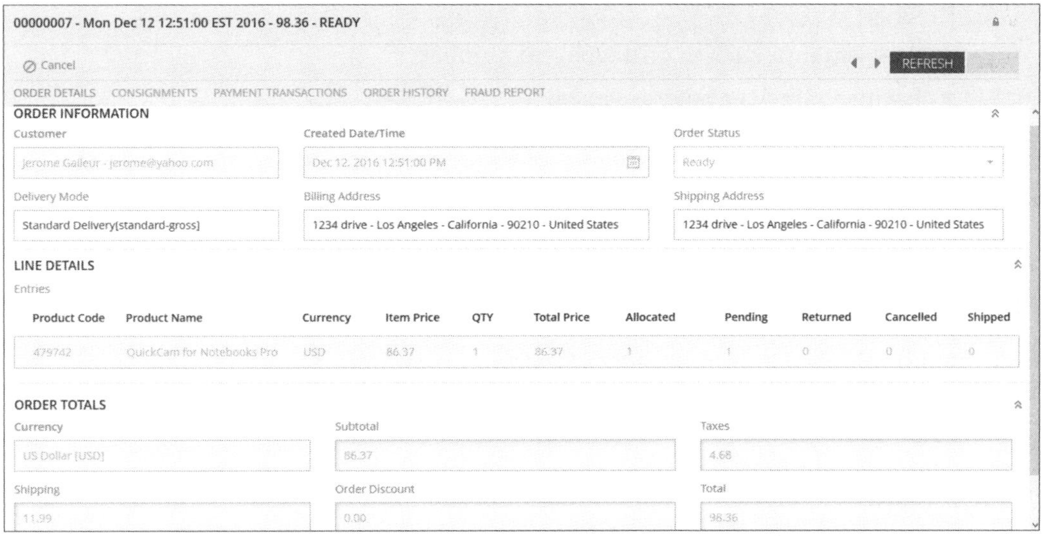

Figure 6.32 Order Details with Customer, Delivery, and Line Item Information

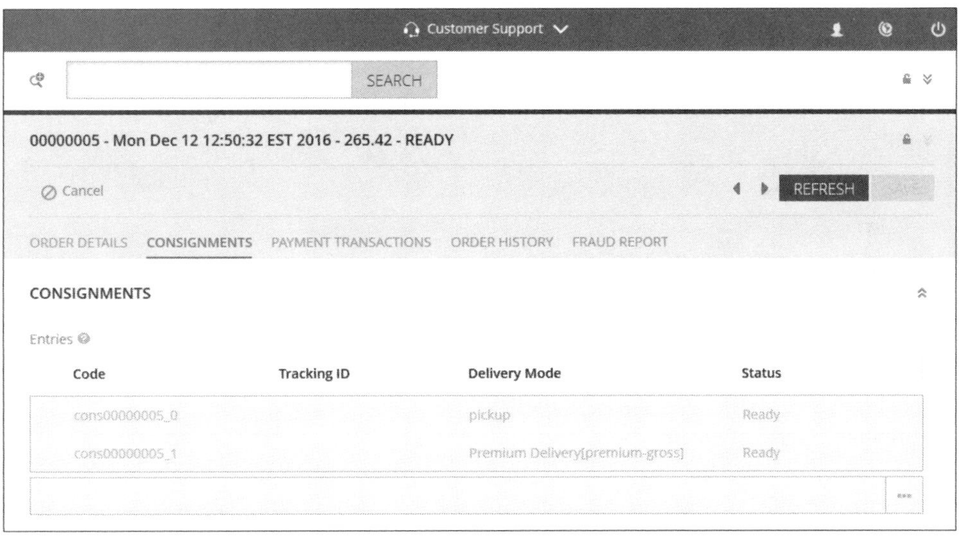

Figure 6.33 Consignment and Delivery Information

The **Payment Transactions** tab contains all the information for each payment on the order:

- **Code**
- **Payment Info**, such as card type and number
- **Payment Provider**, such as PayPal
- **Planned Amount** or amount authorized
- **Request ID**
- **Transaction Entries**, such as authorizations and captures

For a look at the payment transaction details pane, see Figure 6.34.

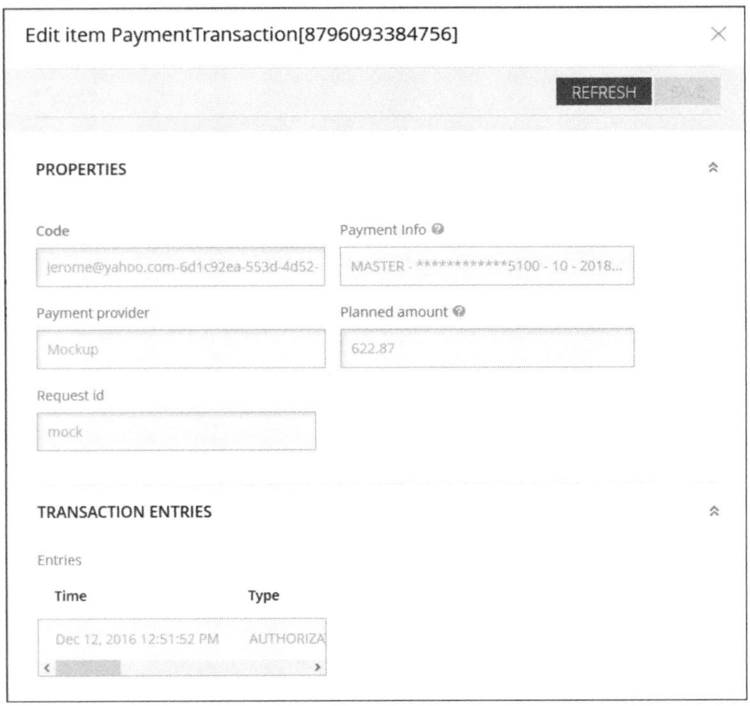

Figure 6.34 Payment Information

The **Order History** tab (see Figure 6.35) shows the versioning of the orders as various actions modify the order. Included in each entry is the following information:

- Date and time of the event
- The event itself (**Cancellation**, **Fraud Check**, etc.)
- A description

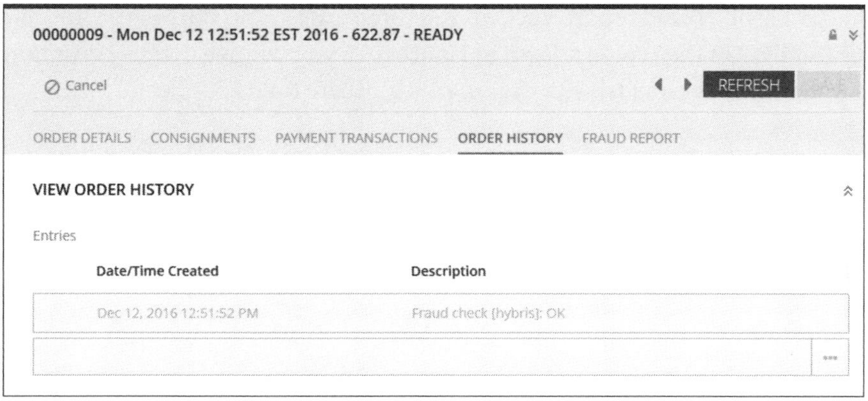

Figure 6.35 Order History Tab

The **Fraud Reports** tab allows you to view and manage fraud reports for customer orders. Some orders are potentially fraudulent, and a user must accept or reject the order. Upon selecting the tab, you will see a list of fraud reports for the order. The information included on this tab is as follows:

- **Code**
- **Provider** (SAP Commerce internal mechanism or via third-party integration)
- **Status**
- **Explanation**
- **Timestamp**

From here, you can use the thumbs up and thumbs down icons to accept or reject the order, as shown in Figure 6.36.

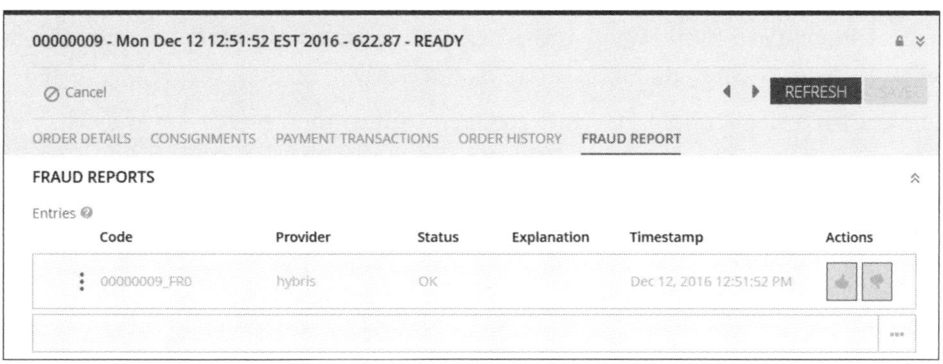

Figure 6.36 Fraud Management Screen

To see the details of a fraud report, click on the three dots at the start of the line and select **Edit Details**. On the screen shown in Figure 6.37, you will see details pertaining to which fraud rule has been triggered, along with a score for each rule.

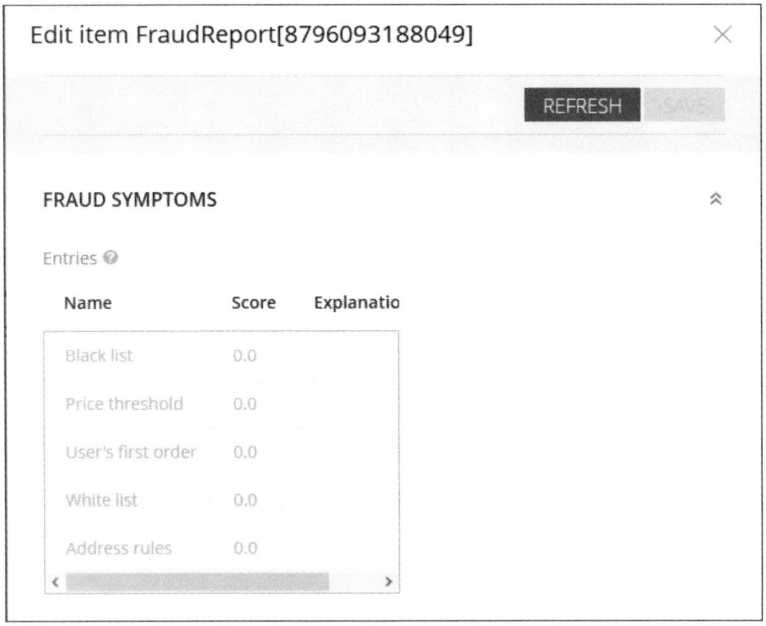

Figure 6.37 Fraud Report Example

6.7.2 Additional Order Actions

A customer support agent also can place an order on hold and then release it. This is normally done either due to a customer request or while trying to resolve a problem such as inability to fulfill. While the order is on hold, no fulfillment actions can be taken.

To place an order on hold, navigate to **Open Orders**, then search for and select an order. In the details pane, select the **On Hold** button, as shown in Figure 6.38.

The order now has button options to either **Cancel** the order or **Release** it back into the fulfillment process, as shown in Figure 6.39.

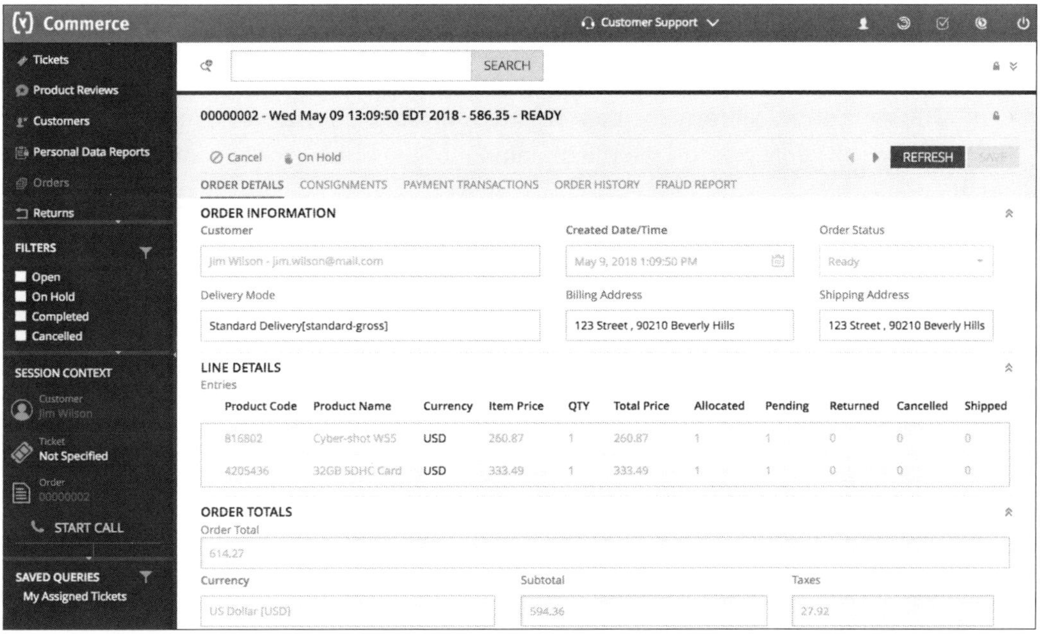

Figure 6.38 Placing Order on Hold

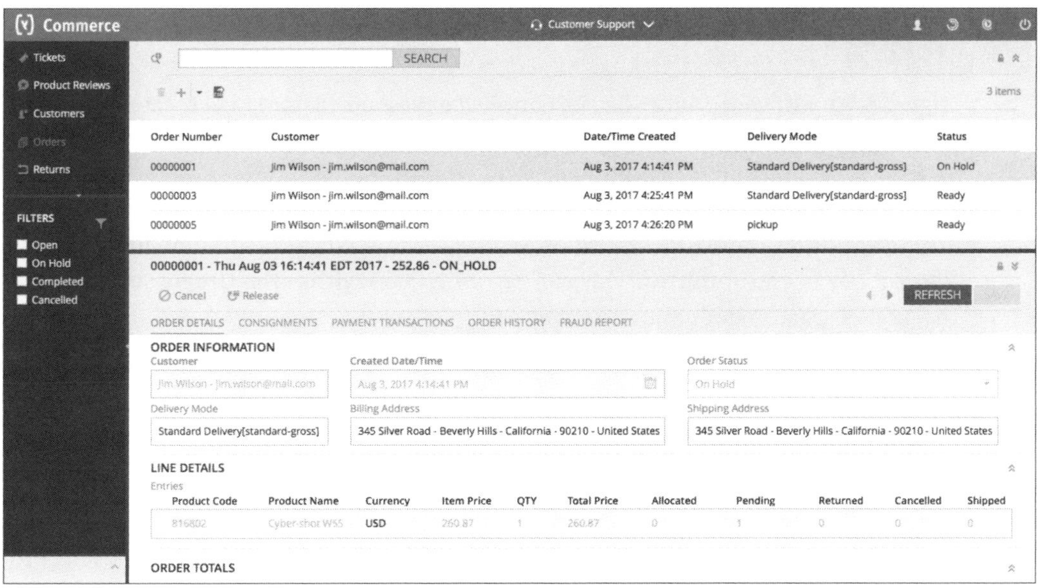

Figure 6.39 Cancel or Release Order on Hold

If an order is not completely sourced due to some failure, such as lack of available stock, then it is possible to manually trigger a rerun of sourcing. Such an order will be in a suspended status. Search for suspended orders in the **Open Orders** section. You will see button options for **Cancel** and **Source**, as shown in Figure 6.40. Clicking **Source** will allow you to send the remainder of the order back to sourcing.

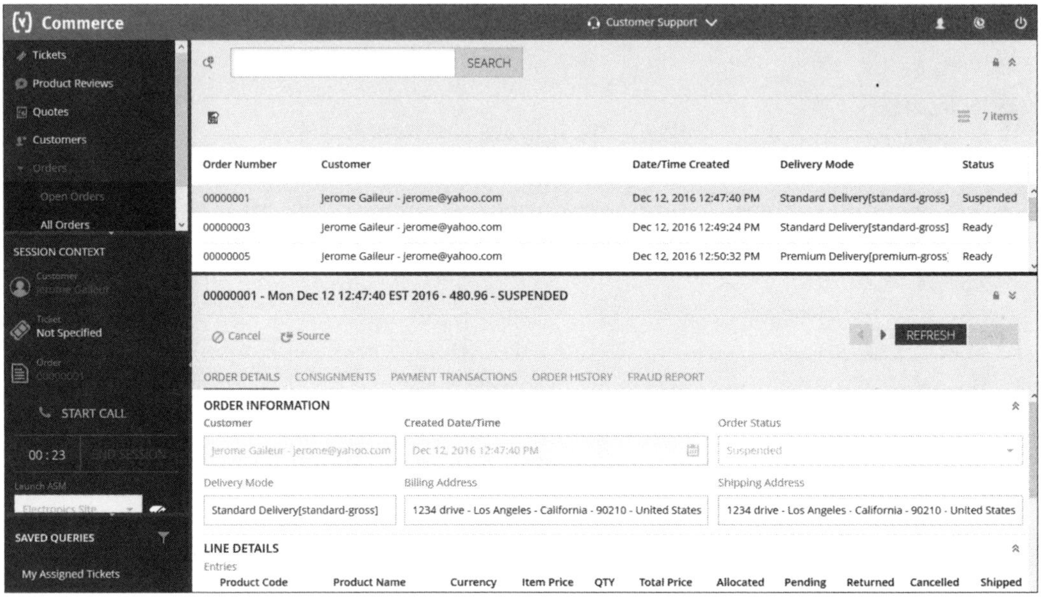

Figure 6.40 Suspended Order Can Be Canceled or Resourced from New Locations

6.7.3 Order Cancellations

There are times unfortunately when it is necessary to cancel some or all of an order after it has been submitted. This can be done from within the **Orders** section of the backoffice Customer Support Cockpit.

From the left navigation menu, select **Open Orders** and use the **Search** box to bring up the order you wish to cancel. Select it in your list of search results. In the details pane, you will see a **Cancel** button. Selecting that will bring up the **Cancel Order** window shown in Figure 6.41.

Select either individual order lines or the full-order checkbox, as well as the **Cancel QTY** (if different from all) and a reason, and add a comment if desired. Then select the confirmation button and answer **Yes** to the confirmation question. All selected lines will be set to canceled and the order price will be updated accordingly.

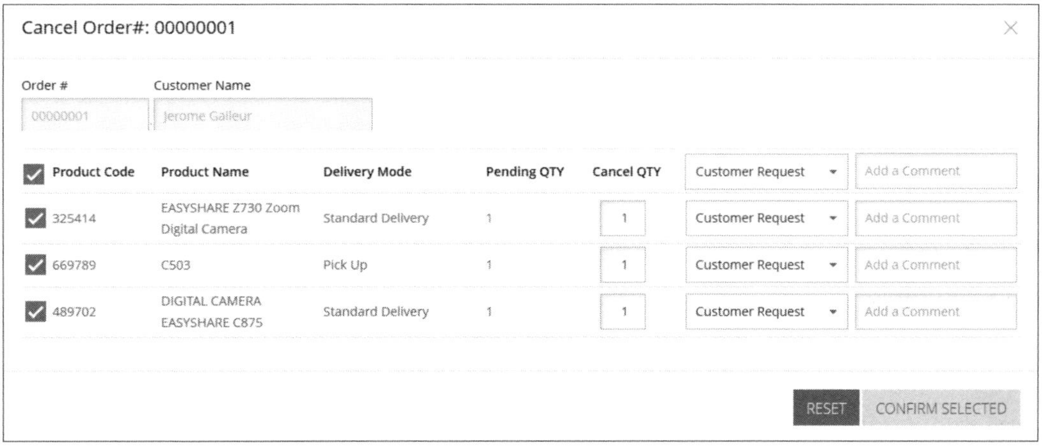

Figure 6.41 Cancel Order Screen

6.7.4 Order Returns

There are times when a customer may want or need to return some or all of an order after it has been delivered. This can be done from within the **Orders** section of the backoffice Customer Support Cockpit, as well as from the **My Account** storefront page using order management self-service.

Returns are managed from the **Returns** section of the backoffice Customer Support Cockpit. There are options such approving and rejecting return requests, manual refunds, and cancellations. First, you will need to create a return (or return request).

To create a return request, navigate to **Completed Orders**, search for the order you wish to return, and select it from the list of search results. In the details pane (see Figure 6.42), you will see a **Create Return** button.

After selecting this button, the **Create Return Request** window will appear, as shown in Figure 6.43. From here, you can select which (already shipped) items the customer wants to return along with how many, what the reason is, and a comment. There are also options to globally select all items from the order, modify the refund amount for appeasement purposes, and refund delivery costs.

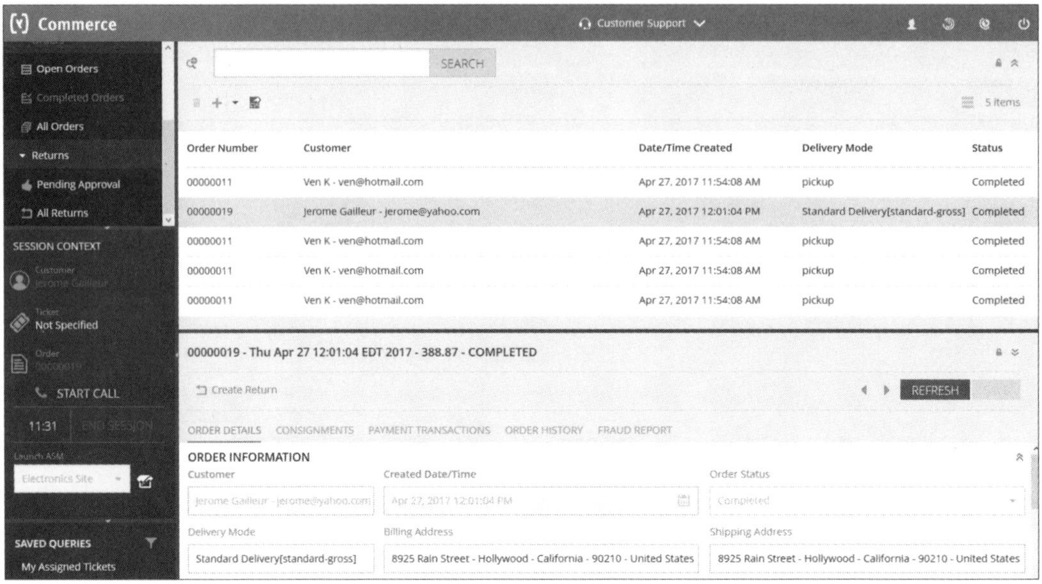

Figure 6.42 Search for Orders Eligible for Return

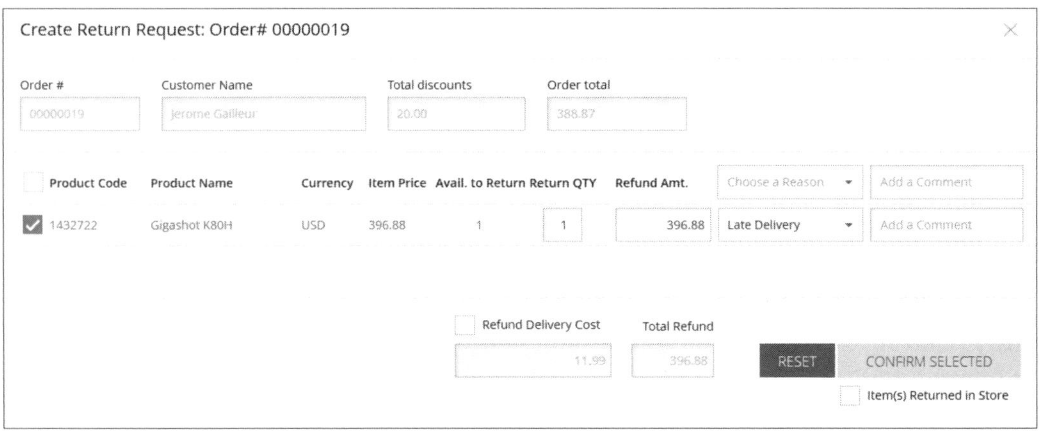

Figure 6.43 Create Return Request for Customer with Reasons and Refunds

If the process is being done for an in-store return, there is a checkbox for that too. In-store returns bypass the approval stage and move directly to **Completed**, triggering refunds and tax reversals.

The next step in the returns workflow is accessed by navigating to the **Returns** section in the left navigation panel. There are two subsections to choose from: **Pending Approval** or **All Returns**.

The **All Returns** section (see Figure 6.44) lets you search for any return in any status and view the following information:

- **RMA**
  Return merchandize authorization
- **Order Number**
  The identifier of the order
- **Customer**
  The first and last name of the person who placed the order
- **Created Date/Time**
  The date and time when the order was placed
- **Status**
  The status of the return—for example, **Completed**, **Pending Approval**, or **Wait**

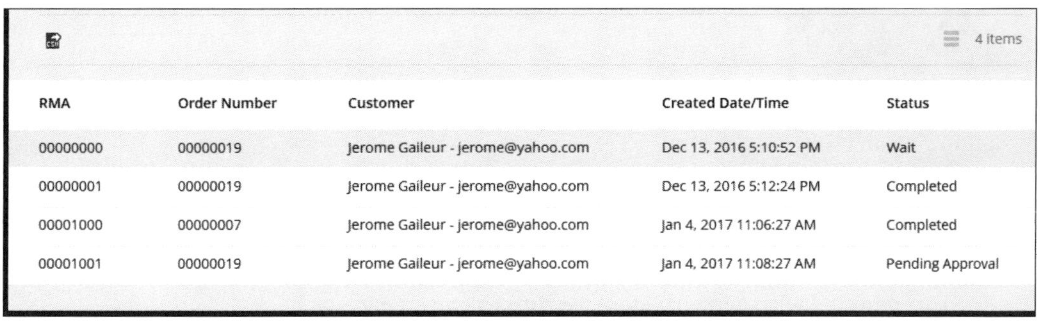
4 items

RMA	Order Number	Customer	Created Date/Time	Status
00000000	00000019	Jerome Gaileur - jerome@yahoo.com	Dec 13, 2016 5:10:52 PM	Wait
00000001	00000019	Jerome Gaileur - jerome@yahoo.com	Dec 13, 2016 5:12:24 PM	Completed
00001000	00000007	Jerome Gaileur - jerome@yahoo.com	Jan 4, 2017 11:06:27 AM	Completed
00001001	00000019	Jerome Gaileur - jerome@yahoo.com	Jan 4, 2017 11:08:27 AM	Pending Approval

Figure 6.44 Return Order List by Status

The **Returns Pending Approval** section lets you approve or reject and cancel a return request, as well as manually modify refund amounts (with appropriate permissions).

First, search for the return you want to address. In the details pane, you will see the return merchandise authorization (RMA) details, as shown in Figure 6.45.

From here, you have the following options:

- Approve the request
- Cancel the request (reject)
- Modify details such as refund amount and refund of delivery cost

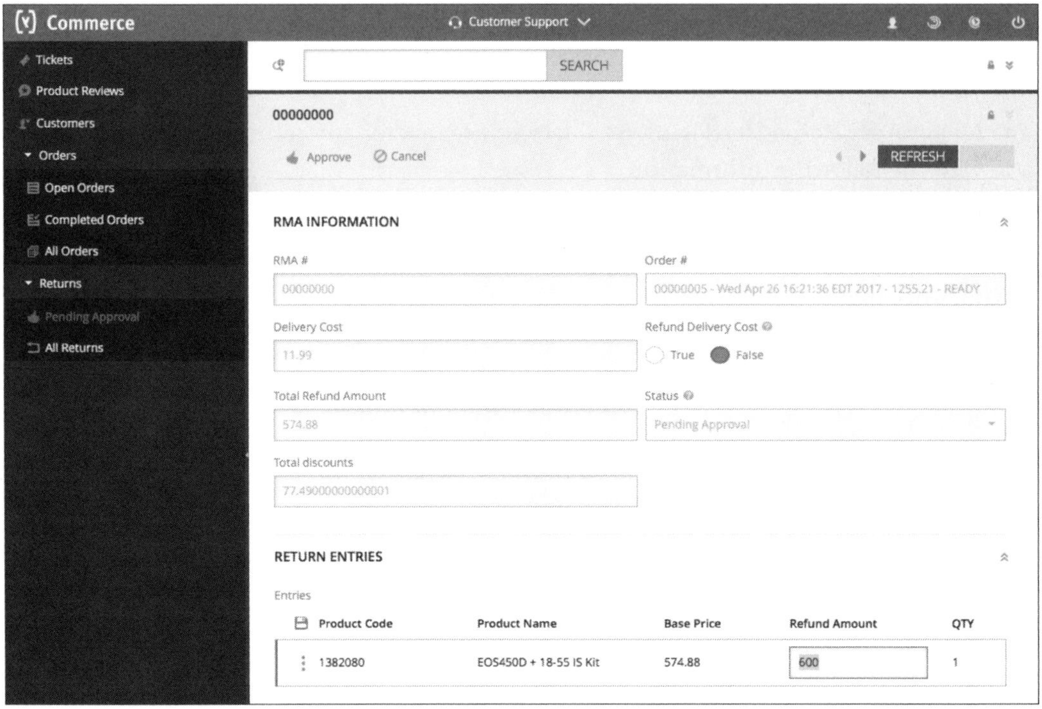

Figure 6.45 RMA Details

If you cancel the RMA, you will be able to enter a reason and a comment in the **Cancel RMA** window. If you approve the request, you will see a confirmation window, the return will move to a state of **Waiting for Goods**, and an email will be sent to the customer along with a return label for him to ship the items back.

The next step in the returns process takes place in the backoffice Order Fulfillment Cockpit in the **Returns** section of the left navigation panel. From this screen (see Figure 6.46), the user has the choice of accepting goods that have been received or cancelling the return if the goods have not been received.

The **Accept Goods** button will trigger a status change, a refund, and a tax reversal (where appropriate). The **Cancel** button will generate the **Cancel RMA** window (see Figure 6.47), in which you can add a **Cancellation Reason** and **Comments** if desired.

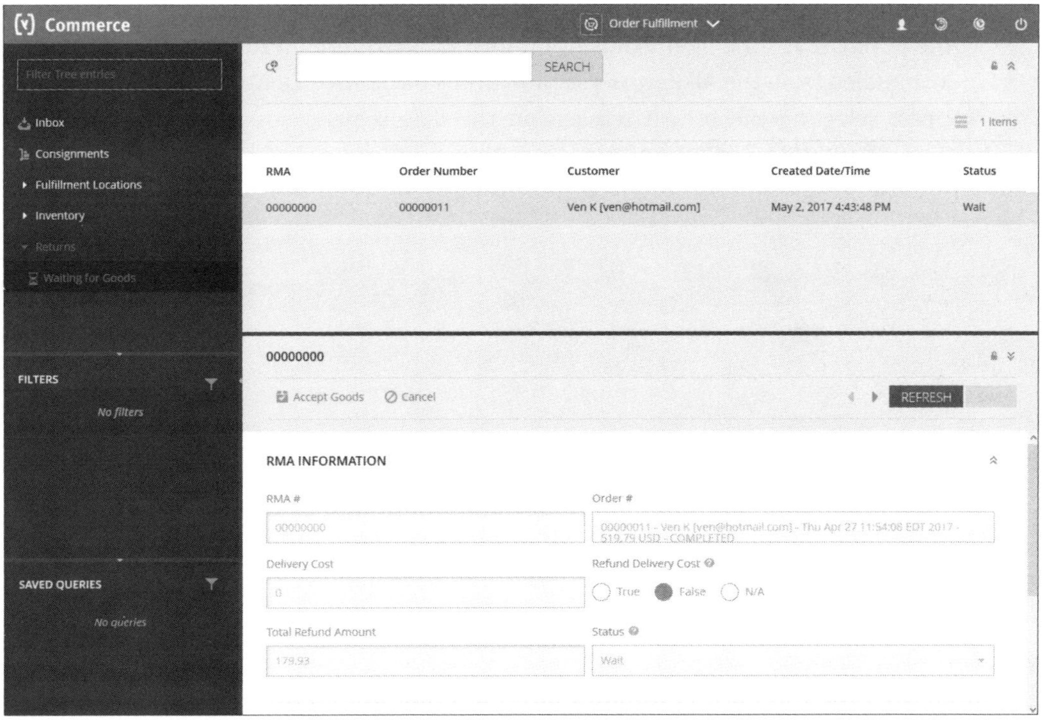

Figure 6.46 Accepting Returned Goods or Cancelling Return Request

Figure 6.47 Cancel RMA and Add Comments

Should either the refund or tax reversal fail—for example, if the original card used for the purchase is no longer valid—then manual (or offline) refunds and reversals can be handled from the **All Returns** section of the backoffice Customer Support Cockpit. Upon selecting the return request, in the details pane you will see **Manual Tax Reverse** and **Manual Refund** buttons, as shown in Figure 6.48.

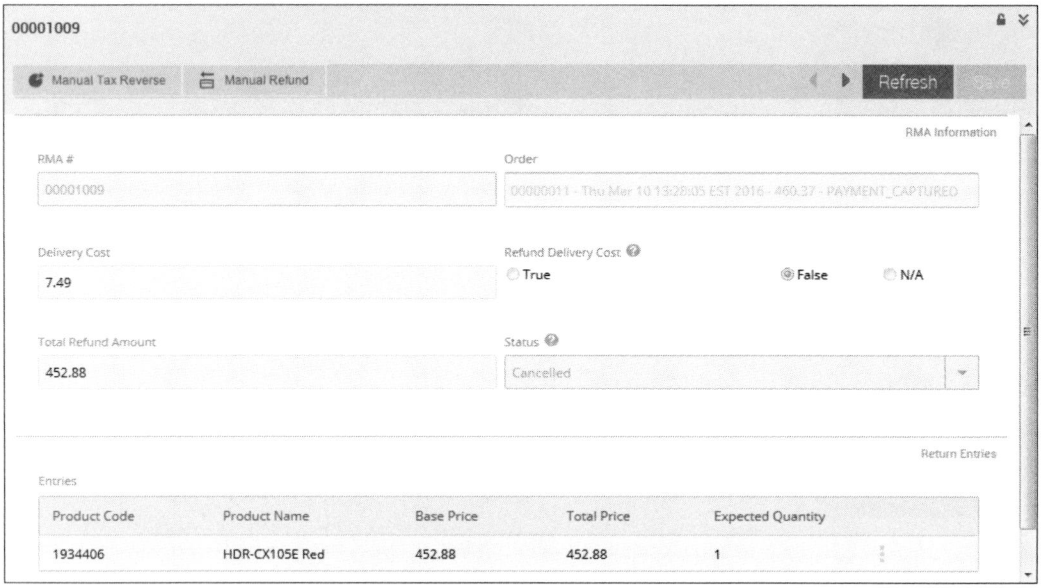

Figure 6.48 Manual Refund or Tax Reversal

After selecting an option, you'll see a confirmation window and the result will be recorded. Note that the manual processes simply mean you are recording that this is being resolved offline.

6.7.5 Order Management Self-Service

Although there is a place for a customer service agent to interact with a customer, there is also significant value in allowing a customer to do things for herself. This allows your agents to focus on the real value-added tasks while letting your customers get the results they want without waiting in a phone queue.

Order management supports self-service changes to orders via an API (which can be used to implement a custom application), as well as with a default implementation on the accelerator storefronts.

Accessed through the **My Account** section of the storefront, a user can bring up her account profile, see her order history, and then take self-service actions. Those possible actions include cancellations and return requests, as we will discuss in the following sections.

My Account

From the top navigation, on the right-hand side, you can select the **My Account** option. This will bring up a series of options, including **Order History** and **Returns History**, as shown in Figure 6.49.

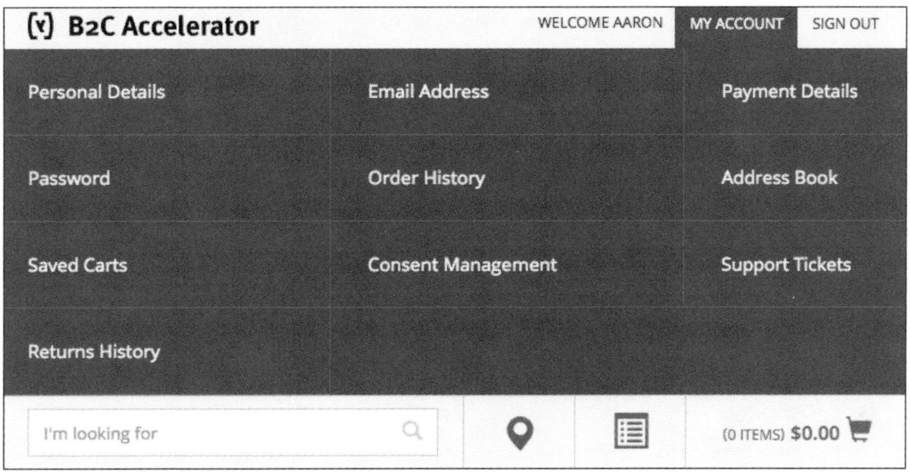

Figure 6.49 My Account Tab from Web Storefront

Order History

If you select **Order History**, you will see a list of your orders (see Figure 6.50), which you can sort. You can then select the desired order to view its details (see Figure 6.51).

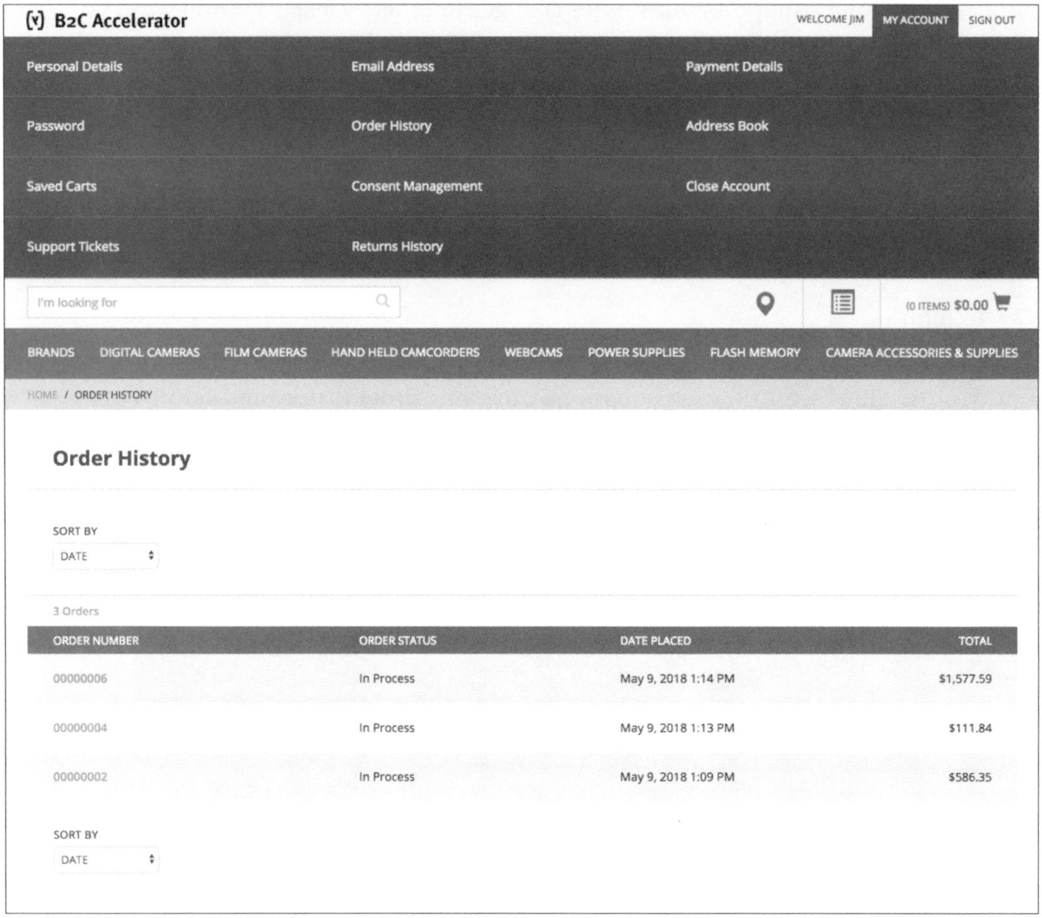

Figure 6.50 List of Orders in My Account

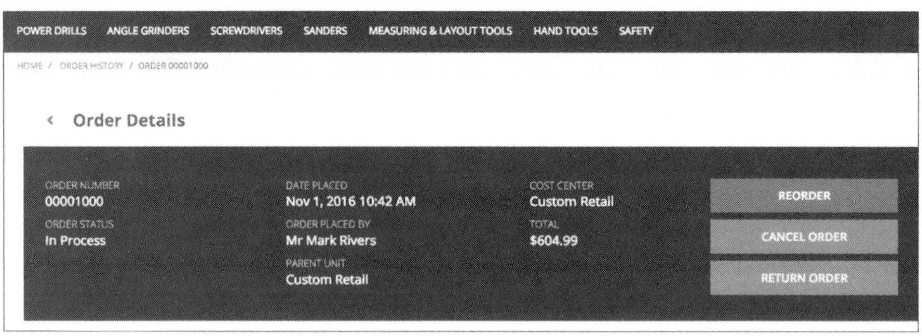

Figure 6.51 Order Details

Cancellations

From the **Order Details** section, if the order has not yet shipped, you can choose **Cancel Order**. Once you do, the **Cancel Order** window displays, as shown in Figure 6.52.

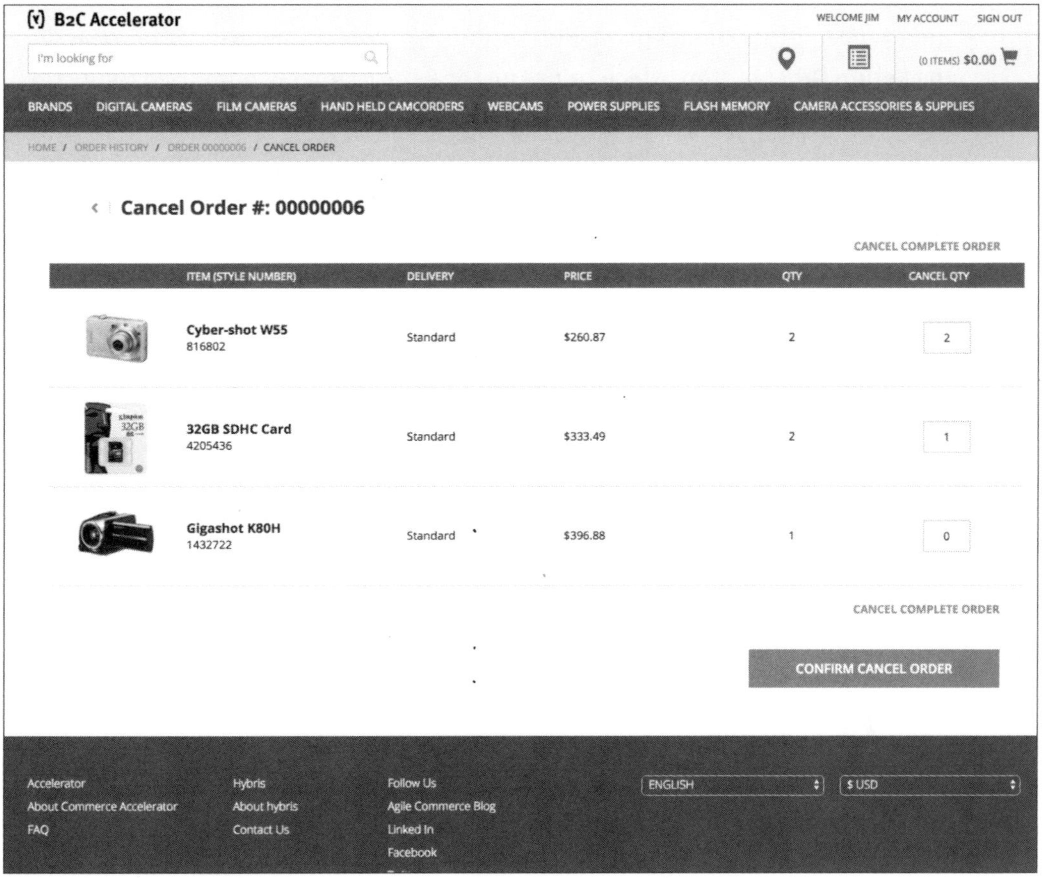

Figure 6.52 Cancel Order Screen

You can choose to set a specific quantity to cancel for each line item or to simply select **Cancel Complete Order** to have all lines automatically populated with the full amounts. Next, click the **Confirm Cancel Order** button. This will bring up a confirmation window. Once you select the **Submit Request** button, each item you chose to cancel will have its status set to **Canceled**.

Returns

The self-service returns process is very similar to the self-cancellation returns process. You access it from the **My Account • Order History** page and can choose from partial or complete order returns.

After selecting the (shipped) order you want to return (see Figure 6.53), you can select the **Return Order** button, which brings up the **Return Order** window (see Figure 6.54).

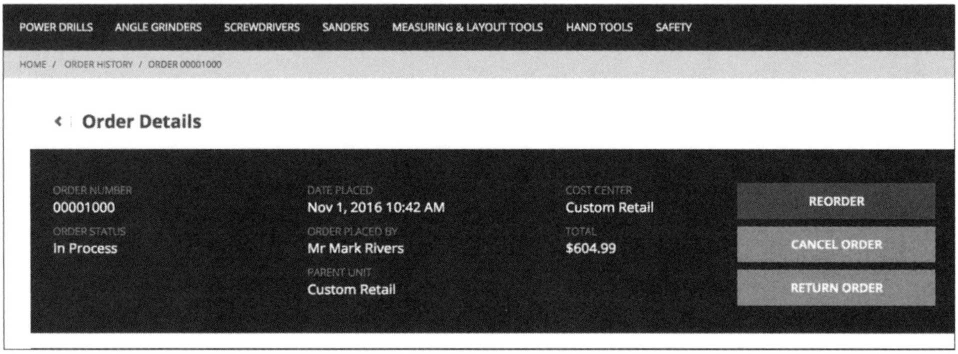

Figure 6.53 Return Order from My Account

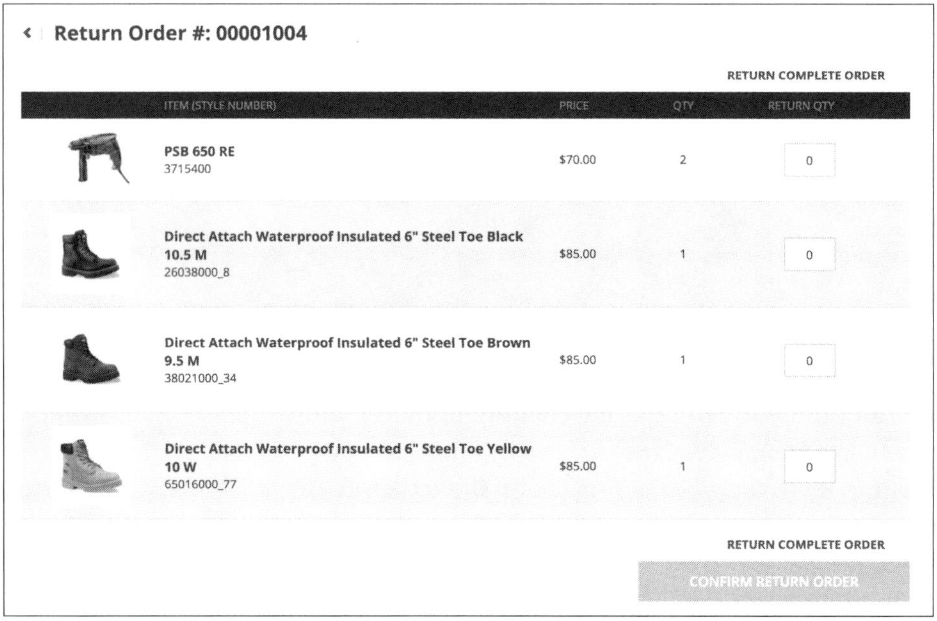

Figure 6.54 Return Order Window

You can choose to set a specific quantity to return for each line item or to simply select **Return Complete Order** to have all lines automatically populated with the full amounts. Next, click the **Confirm Return Order** button. This will bring up a confirmation window. Once you select the **Submit Request** button, a return request is generated and can be seen in both the **My Account Returns History** and in the backoffice Customer Support Cockpit under **Returns Pending Approval**. From there, as shown in Section 6.7.4, the return workflow can be followed for approval and modification or rejection of the request.

6.8 Summary

SAP Commerce order management serves as a bridge between the frontend order capturing systems, such as your web storefront or mobile applications, and backend systems such as SAP ERP and SAP EWM that take care of fulfillment.

By providing a consistent view of your orders and your available inventory, it can route orders to both internally managed fulfillment locations and external enterprise systems.

The backoffice includes two main order management cockpits—one for simple fulfillment such as in-store fulfillment and another for managing orders for returns and cancellations.

As a key component of your commerce solution, order management lets you balance built-in functionality with the ability to integrate with other enterprise solutions and is the tool that enables your omnichannel, buy anywhere, fulfill anywhere journey.

For more on how to service your customers by using the backoffice Customer Support Cockpit, see Chapter 7.

Chapter 7
Support and Service

You want your customers to be able to help themselves; when that's not sufficient, not efficient, or not practical, you want to be able to help them. Support and service are central to your identity as a business and your relationship to your customers, which in turn are central to commerce.

A customer journey neither begins nor ends when an order is placed. As we have discussed throughout this book, you should be crafting an experience that keeps your customers engaged throughout their decision-making process (as well as when they're not thinking about purchasing decisions at all) across all channels. We've talked about the vital role of personalized content and of automation—that is, the value of serving your customer a tailored experience without relying on a human being to tailor it, by hand, in real time.

Later in this chapter, we will discuss *self-service*, or those parts of account, order, or communication management that customers can complete (or at least initiate) on their own. This too is a form of automation, insofar as it allows a customer to check the status of an order, reset a password, or generate a return merchandise authorization (RMA) while interacting only with *the system*, as opposed to a human agent.

But what about those times when a customer *does* require direct intervention? That's what we'll be discussing for the bulk of this chapter on service and support: any interaction between one of your customers and your employees, whether that means order placement, account management, quote negotiation (in the case of B2B), general inquiries, or returns, replacements, and refunds.

Once a customer case has reached the point of requiring real-time human intervention, there are three general principles to keep in mind: you want the interaction to be efficient, effective, and auditable. Efficiency is generally the easiest to measure. How many orders is an agent able to take in a single shift? How many tickets are they able to create or complete? How many returns can they process? If you measure efficiency without focusing properly on effectiveness, however, then the results can be deceptive. An agent might be helping customers to complete their orders quickly, but missing opportunities to upsell, cross-sell, or capture relevant customer profile details—and this last point leads us to the importance of auditability, by which we mean the ability of managers and administrators to see which agent did what for whom, as well as the ability of the business to collect actionable customer data.

In short, you want to quickly identify your customer's needs, and then use the interaction as an opportunity to meet or exceed their expectations; along the way, you want to glean as much important information as you can about this customer specifically (as an individual) and about your customers more generally (as a group or a series of groups). You want to continually get better at meeting and exceeding expectations, and that means taking the time to learn—but without ever losing sight of the customer's immediate request, which is after all the reason they've initiated contact in the first place. This does not mean, then, that you should keep the customer on the phone for an in-depth demographic study every time they call with a question about an order. But it does mean that you should equip your agents to know what kinds of issues are common and to have information about the customer's previous orders and other interactions at the ready.

Deciding what information you want to be able to audit and by what criteria you determine effectiveness is tremendously business-specific. For some businesses, the sheer volume of calls means that cross-selling and upselling is impractical. For other businesses, especially traditional B2Bs, these concepts are not necessarily even applicable, and customer groups will be based on contracts and organization membership rather than demographic information or other emergent patterns. In these cases, when you already know who the customers are and they already know what they want, efficiency and effectiveness might be one and the same.

SAP Commerce has two employee-facing interfaces for service and support: the *assisted service module* (for helping customers build and place orders, manage their accounts, and navigate the storefront) and the *Customer Support Cockpit* in the backoffice (for servicing orders after they have been placed, and customer accounts once they have been created). In this chapter, we will discuss both—from the point of view of day-to-day use, and from the perspective of configuration, development, and underlying technology. We will also discuss the customer-facing self-service tools built into the SAP Commerce accelerator storefronts.

These tools allow you to provide efficient, effective, and auditable support to your customers and to continuously improve your interactions with them. Now, let's get into the details of what the tools include and how you can configure them for your business.

7.1 Backoffice Customer Service Cockpit

The Customer Support Cockpit in the backoffice is the central interface for servicing customer accounts, orders, returns, and product reviews as the home of the ticketing system. It is designed as a single point of entry for anything *other than* assisting customers with order placement and onsite assistance. (Those processes are handled in assisted service mode, which we will discuss in the next section.)

Access to these features is controlled by employees' membership in role-specific user groups (a concept which we describe in more detail in Chapter 9), with the key roles as follows:

- Customer support agents (CSAs), who can create and edit accounts, orders, reviews, and tickets
- Customer service managers, who can do everything that CSAs can do and, by default, also can export product reviews to CSV files
- Customer support administrators, who can do everything that customer service managers can do, and who also have access to administration, pricing, and personalization in the Customer Support Cockpit, as well as to the separate administration perspective in the backoffice, where they can manage other data, such as employee account settings

Most of the employees who use this interface will use it as CSAs, with only a select few being designated as managers or administrators. The features enabled for this basic group are those that are most commonly necessary for core service and support functionality; the other groups are intended for those who manage such teams or who have a higher level of authorization system-wide.

You can add additional authorizations to the CSA or manager roles if there are members of your customer support team who need more access than an agent, but less than an administrator.

In this section, our approach will be to start from the most restricted and protected forms of support and service information, then work our way out to data that can be created, edited, and removed by customers themselves. We will begin by looking at an administrator's view of customer and order data, both within the customer support perspective and beyond it, in the administration perspective. We will then discuss ratings and reviews functionality, customer data in general, and (with an eye toward auditability) the reporting functionality built into support and service. We will then take a closer look at the data and processes behind orders and returns, as well as the support and service ticketing system.

7.1.1 Administration and Unbound Customer Attributes

Before we dive into the core functionality of the Customer Support Cockpit, let's take a moment to discuss those features that are unique to administrators or other employees who have explicitly been given more access than agents, as well as the mechanisms for extending these permissions.

In addition to the customer information available to agents and managers, administrators have access to the **Administration** tab of customer information, shown in Figure 7.1, which shows attributes that are not otherwise visible to employees and may not even be visible to customers themselves.

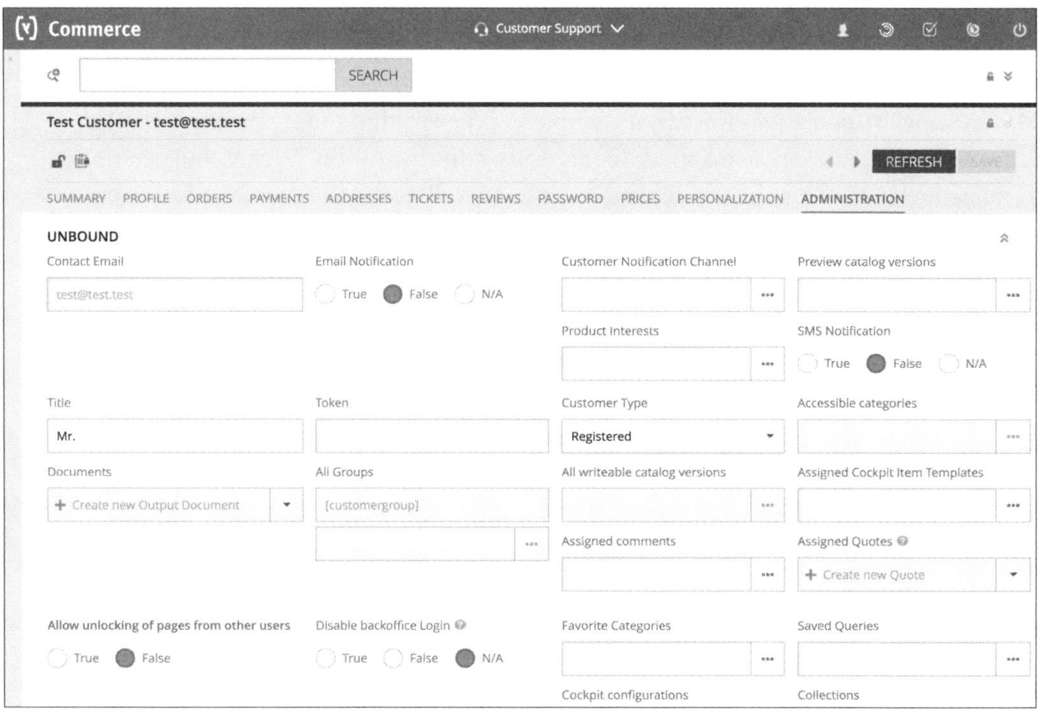

Figure 7.1 Administration Tab of Customer Account

This could include information collected for personalization and marketing purposes, account numbers from integrated and/or legacy systems, alternative contact information, or any other unbound or hidden attributes.

Administrators also have access to the **Personalization** tab, where they can view any rules currently driving personalized storefront elements (as discussed in more detail in Chapter 5) and the **Prices** tab, which shows the customer-specific **Price Groups**, **Tax Groups**, **Discount Groups**, and **Global Discount Rows** (discussed in more detail in Chapter 3 and Chapter 9). From a service and support perspective, this information generally is not necessary for ordinary agents; indeed, it may clutter their interfaces with unnecessary tabs and options. However, if customers are seeing a strange or broken combination of content on the frontend or are having a difficult time accessing a price or discount to which they should be entitled, then diagnosing the problem may require an administrator to take a look at the product and web content to which they have access.

As we've said, some businesses will want to change these permissions or define other roles. The appropriate settings live in the *customersupportbackoffice-backoffice-config.xml* file, as shown in Listing 7.1.

```
<context merge-by="type" parent="User" type="Customer" component="cs-editor-
area" principal="CustomerSupportAdministratorRole">
<editorArea:editorArea name="">
<editorArea:essentials>
<editorArea:essentialSection name="hmc.essential">
<editorArea:attribute qualifier="name" position="1"/>
<editorArea:attribute qualifier="uid" position="2"/>
<editorArea:attribute qualifier="customerID" position="3"/>
<editorArea:attribute qualifier="originalUid" position="4" readonly="true"/>
</editorArea:essentialSection>
</editorArea:essentials>
<editorArea:tab name="hmc.tab.common" position="1" />
<editorArea:tab name="hmc.addresses" position="2" />
<editorArea:tab name="hmc.password" position="3" />
<editorArea:tab name="hmc.customerpayments" position="4">
<editorArea:section name="hmc.customerpayments.method.section">
<editorArea:attribute qualifier="paymentInfos" label=
"hmc.customerpayments.method.details"/>
</editorArea:section>
</editorArea:tab>
```

```
<editorArea:tab name="hmc.orders" position="5" />
            <editorArea:tab name="hmc.tab.community" position="7">
                <editorArea:section name="hmc.user.sections.customerreviews">
                    <editorArea:attribute qualifier="customerReviews"
                                          editor=
"com.hybris.cockpitng.editor.extendedmultireferenceeditor">
                        <editorArea:editor-parameter>
                            <editorArea:name>listConfigContext</
editorArea:name>
                            <editorArea:value>customerReviewsListConfig</
editorArea:value>
                        </editorArea:editor-parameter>
                    </editorArea:attribute>
                </editorArea:section>
            </editorArea:tab>
<editorArea:tab name="hmc.customerprices" position="8">
<editorArea:section name="hmc.customerprices">
<editorArea:attribute qualifier="Europe1PriceFactory_UTG" />
<editorArea:attribute qualifier="Europe1PriceFactory_UPG" />
<editorArea:attribute qualifier="Europe1PriceFactory_UDG" />
<editorArea:attribute qualifier="europe1Discounts" />
</editorArea:section>
</editorArea:tab>
<editorArea:tab name="hmc.tab.personalization"
position="9" />
<editorArea:tab name="hmc.administration" />
</editorArea:editorArea>
</context>
    <context type="CustomerReview" component="customerReviewsListConfig">
        <list-view:list-view xmlns:list-view="http://www.hybris.com/cockpitng/
component/listView">
            <list-view:column qualifier="rating"/>
            <list-view:column qualifier="creationtime"/>
            <list-view:column qualifier="approvalStatus"/>
            <list-view:column qualifier="product"/>
            <list-view:column qualifier="headline"/>
        </list-view:list-view>
    </context>
<context merge-by="principal" parent="CustomerSupportAdministratorRole" type=
```

```
"Customer" component="cs-editor-area" principal=
"CustomerSupportManagerRole,CustomerSupportAgentRole">
<editorArea:editorArea name="">
<editorArea:tab name="hmc.administration" merge-mode="remove"/>
<editorArea:tab name="hmc.tab.personalization" merge-mode="remove"/>
<editorArea:tab name="hmc.customerprices" merge-mode="remove"/>
</editorArea:editorArea>
</context>
```

Listing 7.1 Permissions and Roles in customersupportbackoffice-backoffice-config.xml

Here you could, for example, give another role access to the **Administration** tab by removing the following line:

```
<editorArea:tab name="hmc.administration" merge-mode="remove"/>
```

You can use this same syntax to make different attributes accessible to different roles. The Customer Support Cockpit runs primarily on the `customersupportbackoffice` extension, and its settings will determine these visibility parameters. As we discuss additional tabs and features, keep in mind that you can control what employees can and cannot access at a granular level by these same means and, more broadly, by means of user groups and permissions.

7.1.2 Product Ratings and Reviews

In the SAP Commerce accelerator storefronts, customers can submit ratings and reviews for products. It is up to the individual business whether customers need to be logged in and/or need to have purchased the product in question before submitting ratings and reviews. Product review functionality in the Customer Support Cockpit (shown in Figure 7.2) allows agents to view these reviews, edit them, and approve them for public visibility (or not).

This process of manual review ensures that even if there are no automated checks on customer reviews in place, businesses are nonetheless able to block spam or other forms of offensive or unhelpful content. In addition to showing the reviews, SAP Commerce can use product ratings, via Solr, to locate and reorder product search results (as discussed in Chapter 8) and will do so using only approved ratings. By submitting user-generated content to manual review, you can maintain an editorial standard for what shows up on your product detail pages—and by incorporating this content in the Customer Support Cockpit, you can also quickly disable any bad content that does get through.

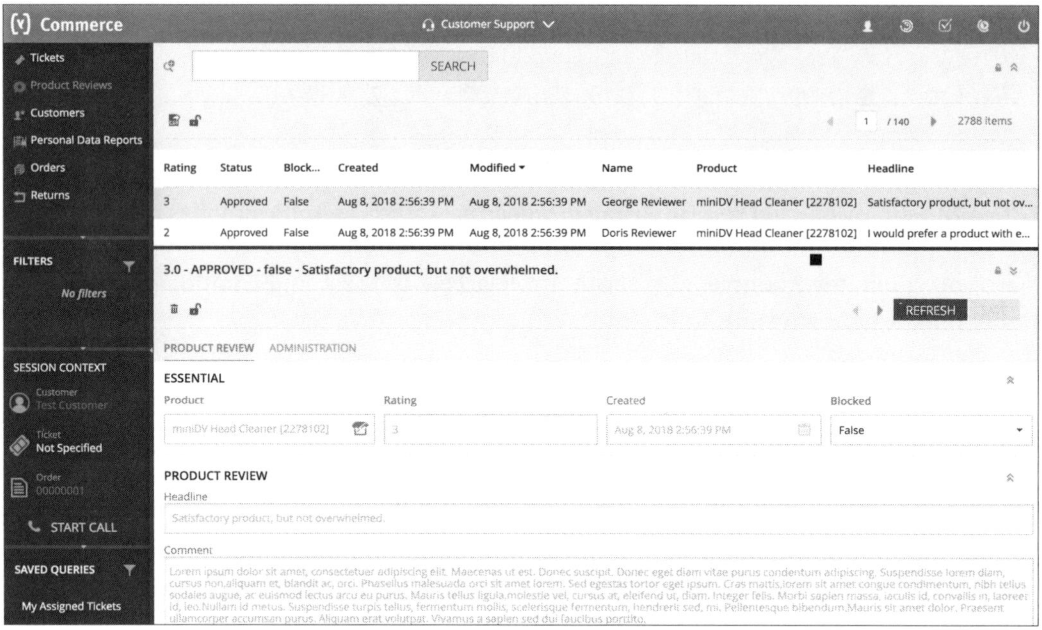

Figure 7.2 Product Review Approval in Customer Support Cockpit

Agents will see **Pending** reviews, which they can then set to a state of **Approved** or **Rejected**. If reviews are tied to customer accounts, they can also quickly find any other reviews submitted by the same account and block them all (which is especially useful in the case of spam).

If assigned the proper permissions, agents can also edit the content of reviews. To what degree you *want* to do this will vary. There is no objectively correct balance between maintaining the transparency and integrity of customers' unedited comments (showing their thoughts on the products, exactly as they entered them) on the one hand and maintaining a high editorial standard (displaying only clear, reasonably polished content) on the other. Many businesses find a middle ground, fixing capitalization and obvious keystroke errors, but leaving word choice and grammar as is. Certainly, you generally do not want to change the *intent* of the review, and keeping that intact is necessarily a subjective process.

In *customersupportbackoffice-backoffice-config.xml*, product review data are represented as shown in Listing 7.2.

```
<!-- Customer Reviews -->
 <editorArea:section name=
"customersupportbackoffice.customer.section.reviews">
                <editorArea:panel colspan="2" rowspan="2">
                    <editorArea:attribute qualifier="customerReviews" label=
"customersupportbackoffice.customer.section.reviews" editor=
"com.hybris.cockpitng.editor.asmdeeplinklisteditor">
                    <editorArea:editor-parameter>
<editorArea:name>selectedItemsMaxSize</editorArea:name>
<editorArea:value>5</editorArea:value>
</editorArea:editor-parameter>
<editorArea:editor-parameter>
                                <editorArea:name>referenceSelected/editorArea/
editorAreaConfigCtx</editorArea:name>
                                <editorArea:value>cs-editor-area</
editorArea:value>
                            </editorArea:editor-parameter>
                    </editorArea:attribute>
                    </editorArea:panel>
                </editorArea:section>
            </editorArea:tab>

<editorArea:tab name="hmc.tab.community" position="6" tooltipText=
"customersupport_backoffice_customer_tab_reviews_desc">
    <editorArea:section name=
"customersupportbackoffice.customer.section.reviews">
        <editorArea:panel colspan="2" rowspan="2">
            <editorArea:attribute qualifier="customerReviews" label=
"customersupportbackoffice.customer.section.reviews">
                <editorArea:editor-parameter>
                    <editorArea:name>selectedItemsMaxSize</editorArea:name>
                    <editorArea:value>15</editorArea:value>
                </editorArea:editor-parameter>
                <editorArea:editor-parameter>
                    <editorArea:name>referenceSelected/editorArea/
editorAreaConfigCtx</editorArea:name>
```

```
                    <editorArea:value>cs-editor-area</editorArea:value>
                </editorArea:editor-parameter>
            </editorArea:attribute>
        </editorArea:panel>
    </editorArea:section>
</editorArea:tab>
<context merge-by="module" parent="GenericItem" type=
"CustomerReview" component="cs-editor-area" module=
"customersupportbackoffice" principal=
"customersupportadministratorrole,customersupportagentrole,customersupportmana
gerrole">
        <editorArea:editorArea>
            <editorArea:essentials>
                <editorArea:essentialSection name="hmc.essential">
                    <editorArea:attribute qualifier="product">
                        <editorArea:editor-parameter>
                            <editorArea:name>disableDisplayingDetails</
editorArea:name>
                            <editorArea:value>true</editorArea:value>
                        </editorArea:editor-parameter>
                    </editorArea:attribute>
                    <editorArea:attribute qualifier="rating"/>
                    <editorArea:attribute qualifier="creationtime" label=
"customersupport_backoffice_reviews_creationTime"/>
                    <editorArea:attribute qualifier="blocked"/>
                </editorArea:essentialSection>
            </editorArea:essentials>
            <editorArea:tab name=
"customersupportbackoffice.customer.section.reviews">
                <editorArea:section name=
"customersupportbackoffice.customer.section.reviews">
                    <editorArea:panel rowspan="2" colspan="2">
                        <editorArea:attribute qualifier="headline"/>
                        <editorArea:attribute qualifier="comment" xmlns=
"http://www.hybris.com/cockpitng/component/editorArea">
                            <editor-parameter>
                                <name>rows</name>
```

```
                                <value>5</value>
                            </editor-parameter>
                        </editorArea:attribute>
                        <editorArea:attribute qualifier="alias"/>
                        <editorArea:attribute qualifier=
"approvalStatus" label=
"customersupportbackoffice.customer.section.reviews.approvalStatus"/>
                    </editorArea:panel>
                </editorArea:section>
            </editorArea:tab>
            <editorArea:tab name="hmc.administration">
                <editorArea:section name="hmc.section.metadata">
                    <editorArea:attribute qualifier="creationtime"/>
                </editorArea:section>
            </editorArea:tab>
        </editorArea:editorArea>
    </context>


<context merge-by="principal" type="CustomerReview" component="cs-editor-
area" principal="customersupportadministratorrole">
        <editorArea:editorArea name="customer reviews">
            <editorArea:tab name="hmc.administration" position="99"/>
        </editorArea:editorArea>
</context>
```

Listing 7.2 Product Reviews in customersupportbackoffice-backoffice-config.xml

7.1.3 Customer Account Information

Agents, managers, and administrators can also access data about customers' orders (which we will discuss in Section 7.1.5) and about customer accounts more generally. By clicking on the **Customers** tab (shown in Figure 7.3), agents can view customers' contact information, profile information, saved addresses or payment methods (or at least the characteristics of those that are exposed), transactions, support tickets, saved carts, and current active cart.

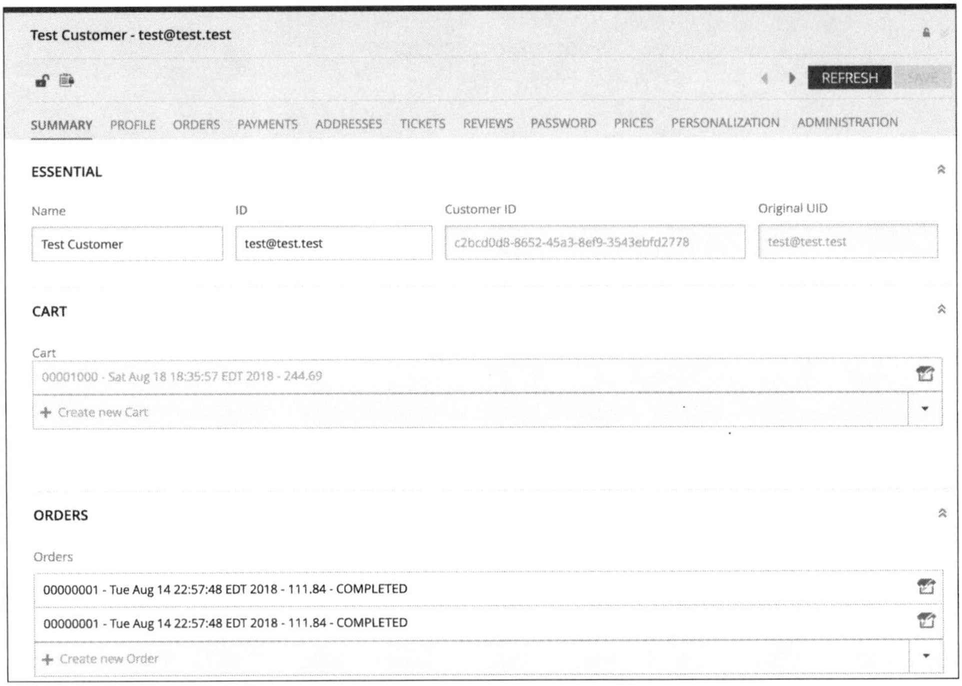

Figure 7.3 Summary Tab of Customer Listing

Customer information in the Customer Support Cockpit can be configured and customized using a series of XML files, all of which end in *backoffice-config.xml*. First, there is *platformbackoffice-backoffice-config.xml*, which covers general backoffice properties and functionality, the relevant portions of which appear as shown in Listing 7.3.

```
<editorArea:tab name="hmc.tab.common" position="1" />
<editorArea:tab name="hmc.addresses" position="2"/>
<editorArea:tab name="hmc.password" position="3" />
<editorArea:tab name="hmc.customerpayments" position="4">
<editorArea:section name="hmc.customerpayments.method.section">
<editorArea:attribute qualifier="paymentInfos" label=
"hmc.customerpayments.method.details"/>
</editorArea:section>
</editorArea:tab>
<editorArea:tab name="hmc.orders" position="5" />
<editorArea:tab name="hmc.customerprices" position="8">
```

```
<editorArea:section name="hmc.customerprices">
<editorArea:attribute qualifier="Europe1PriceFactory_UTG" />
<editorArea:attribute qualifier="Europe1PriceFactory_UPG" />
<editorArea:attribute qualifier="Europe1PriceFactory_UDG" />
<editorArea:attribute qualifier="europe1Discounts" />
</editorArea:section>
</editorArea:tab>
<editorArea:tab name="hmc.tab.personalization"
position="9" />
<editorArea:tab name="hmc.administration" />
</editorArea:editorArea>
```


Listing 7.3 Properties for Backoffice Representation of Support and Service Data

Next, there is *customersupportbackoffice-backoffice-config.xml*, which covers the elements specific to the Customer Support Cockpit but not specific to any single tab within in, as shown in Listing 7.4.

```
    <context component="cs-listview" type="User" module=
"customersupportbackoffice">
        <list-view:list-view>
            <list-view:column qualifier="name" label="customersupport-
backoffice_customers.customername"/>
            <list-view:column qualifier="uid" />
        </list-view:list-view>
    </context>

    <context merge-by="type" parent="User" type="Customer" component="cs-
listview" module="customersupportbackoffice" >
        <list-view:list-view>
            <list-view:column qualifier="creationtime" sortable="true" label=
"customersupport-backoffice_customers.creationtime"/>
            <list-view:column qualifier="type" sortable="true" label=
"customersupport-backoffice_customers.type"/>
        </list-view:list-view>
    </
```

Listing 7.4 Visual Elements Specific to Customer Support Perspective

The *customerview-backoffice-config.xml* file covers the properties and functionality specific to the **Customer** tab, as shown in Listing 7.5.

```
<context merge-by="module" parent="auto" type="Customer" component="editor-
area">
        <editorArea:editorArea xmlns:editorArea="http://www.hybris.com/
cockpitng/component/editorArea">
            <editorArea:tab name="hmc.tab.community" position="9">
                <editorArea:section name="hmc.user.sections.customerreviews">
                    <editorArea:attribute xmlns="http://www.hybris.com/
cockpitng/component/editorArea" qualifier="customerReviews" editor=
"com.hybris.cockpitng.editor.extendedmultireferenceeditor"/>
                </editorArea:section>
            </editorArea:tab>
        </editorArea:editorArea>
    </context>
```

Listing 7.5 Elements of Customer Tab in customerview-backoffice-config.xml

Properties and functionality specific to the ticketing system are represented in *customerview-backoffice-config.xml*, which we will discuss in a moment when we turn our attention to ticket data.

7.1.4 Personal Data Reports

Customer support administrators can also generate personal data reports when viewing a customer's account and then view a list of reports from the appropriate node in the Customer Support Cockpit (Figure 7.4). These reports contain the same information that appears to employees in the Customer Support Cockpit and the customer 360° view but can be easily exported for use in other systems or general reportability.

Support teams can periodically export this information to surface customer information outside of SAP Commerce and to take periodic snapshots of historical data. Note that if customers delete their accounts (as described in Section 7.3), then the default terms (in accordance with the law in the European Union) will require you to delete your records of this information, both current and historical.

By default, personal data reports are stored in the **auditreports** folder, which is secured via the permissions-based secure media access in the SAP Commerce system.

You can change this location by overriding the default attribute of the `reportFolderName` bean property in `de.hybris.platform.auditreport.service.impl.DefaultAuditReportDataService`. If you do so, you will then need to secure the new folder according to the conventions of secure media access as well, using the `media.folder.<folderName>.secured=true` property.

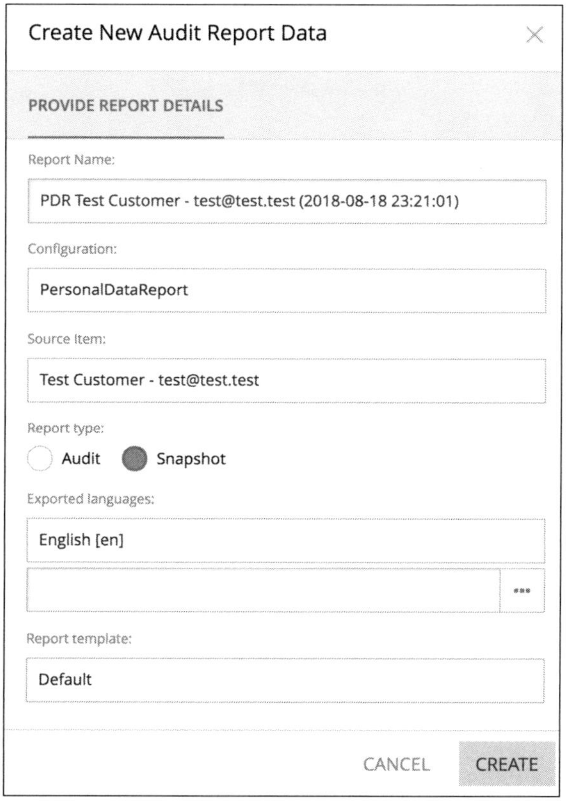

Figure 7.4 Creating New Personal Data Report

If you want to configure reports to be automatically removed after customers have deleted their accounts and after a retention period has elapsed, then you can do so in the two relevant CronJobs, `customerWithoutOrdersRetentionCronJob` and `customerWithOrdersRetentionCronJob`. As their names imply, these two CronJobs will remove customer accounts without any order history, and remove customer accounts *with* order history along with their associated order records, respectively.

If you want to remove reports periodically whether or not customers have deleted their accounts (which, once again, will help you to align your practices to the privacy laws of, say, the European Union), then you can do so by injecting a retention rule in this same file, as shown in Listing 7.6.

```
#RETENTION RULE
insert_update AfterRetentionCleanupRule;code[unique=
true];retirementItemType(code);itemFilterExpression;actionReference;retentionT
imeSeconds;retirementDateAttribute(enclosingType(code),qualifier)
; AuditReportDataRule; AuditReportData; 1=
1; basicRemoveCleanupAction; 2592000; AuditReportData:creationtime
```

Listing 7.6 Example Retention Rule

In addition, you can customize the content and format of these reports using report converters. You can do this by adding your strategies to the bean used to implement the interface, `de.hybris.platform.auditreport.service.ReportViewConverterStrategy`, as shown in Listing 7.7.

```
<alias name="defaultReportViewConverterStrategies" alias=
"reportViewConverterStrategies"/>
<util:list id="defaultReportViewConverterStrategies">
    <ref bean="reportViewConverterStrategy"/>
</util:list>
```

Listing 7.7 Settings for Report Converters

7.1.5 Orders

CSAs can access order history in two key ways. First, as explained in the previous section, they can access a customer record and view all the orders associated with that customer. Alternately, they can view a listing of orders by selecting the **Orders** tab on the left-hand menu in the Customer Support Cockpit. Both routes will result in a similar view, showing the current status of the order and providing access to its status and its contents (Figure 7.5).

If the CSA is searching for orders by some means other than beginning from a customer record, then they can filter the list of orders in the system by status—**Open**, **On Hold**, **Completed**, or **Canceled**—or can perform a search for the specific order number, or search by date, site, or store (if there are multiple) or sales application (if some orders have been placed by customers themselves through the storefront and others have been accepted via the assisted service module, imported from legacy systems, or transacted in-store).

CSAs can also search by applicable promotions, thereby showing all the orders that qualified for or received a specific offer if, for example, they want to follow up with customers who received it or if something has gone wrong with the offer and the goal is now to make it right.

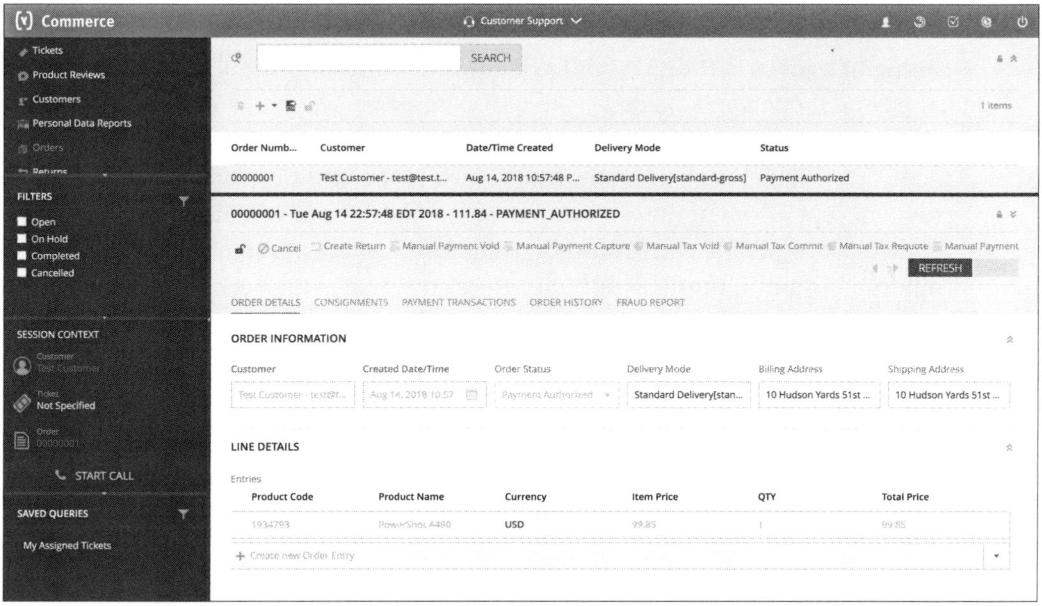

Figure 7.5 Orders Screen in Customer Support Cockpit

The view of an order in the Customer Support Cockpit is divided into tabs, and these tabs are divided into sections. The **Order Details** tab, for example, begins with the **Order Information** section, which includes the name of the customer whose account the order is associated with, the date of the order, its current status, the selected delivery mode, and the shipping or billing address—all of which often needs to be confirmed with a customer during communication. Next is the **Line Details** section, which shows each individual item that the customer purchased as part of the order, including quantity and price paid. Finally, this tab includes the **Order Totals** section, which displays the total cost of the order, the currency used to pay, and a breakdown of taxes, shipping charges, and order-level discounts.

The next tab shows **Consignments**. As we described more thoroughly in Chapter 3, consignments are simply the individual shipments or boxes into which an SAP Commerce order is divided for the purposes of fulfillment. An order may contain only one consignment, but if it needs to ship at different times, or from two different warehouses, or if part of it is shipped while another part is picked up in store, then the system will divide the order into multiple consignments automatically. In these cases, CSAs may need consignment-level information about tracking and about whether payment has been captured (which usually takes place on shipment).

This point leads us to the next tab, **Payment Transactions**. This will show each individual payment operation made by the SAP Commerce system when communicating with the payment gateway (a process that is, once again, explored in Chapter 3). Typically, this will include a preauthorization when the order is placed, and then a full payment capture when the relevant consignment ships. If you are in a testing environment, you will likely see other transaction types (or request IDs), such as "mockup." In any of these cases, CSAs can use this screen to check on the status of an order's payment or payments, all without seeing sensitive information unmasked.

The next tab contains general **Order History**, including any support or return requests associated with the order, and the status of any fraud checks, which are also shown on the following tab, **Fraud Checks**. Payment gateways typically include their own fine-grained fraud checking that will look for potentially invalid or stolen payment methods or other signs of invalid activity—but they typically charge per transaction for this process, so SAP Commerce includes its own onboard form of coarse-grained fraud-checking.

This system is designed to play nice, so to speak, with more detailed, payment gateway-level fraud checking and to catch the invalid activity that is either glaringly obvious or, on the other side of the same coin, so specific to your business that it might be too esoteric for a generic fraud engine.

Built-in fraud checks in SAP Commerce check every order placed against a series of symptoms that, when tripped, add to a fraud score. Should this score reach a set level, the order will enter a "check" status and will need to be reviewed by a CSA, a warehouse manager, or some other employee before the order proceeds.

So that CSAs, or at least their managers, will understand what these fraud reports mean, we will briefly discuss the default fraud symptoms:

- `BlackListSymptom`
  This checks that the customer's email is not on a list of unapproved addresses

- **WhiteListSymptom**
  This checks that the customer's email is on a list of approved addresses (sometimes used in B2B to double-check that the user placing the order is approved to do so)
- **FirstTimeOrderSymptom**
  This checks whether the customer is placing an order on the storefront for the first time
- **DifferentAddressSymptom**
  This checks whether the customer is shipping or billing to an address for the first time
- **OrderThresholdSymptom**
  This checks whether the total value of the order is over a certain amount
- **OrderEntriesSymptom**
  This checks whether the customer has ordered more of a certain product than the maximum specified in the maxNumberPerOrder property

These symptoms are stored in `FraudService`, which communicates responses via the `FraudServiceResponse` Java object.

You can add your own symptoms to the fraud detection process by appending a new symptom check to the standard configuration, which always extends from the `AbstractOrderFraudraudSymptomDetection` class. Your new class, which for the moment we will refer to as `MySymptom`, would be added to the code, as shown in Listing 7.8.

```
public class MySymptom implements OrderFraudSymptomDetection
{
   public FraudServiceResponse recognizeSymptom(FraudServiceResponse
fraudResponse, AbstractOrderModel order)
   {
      if (... positive ... )
      {
         fraudResponse.addSymptom(
            new FraudSymptom(
               "...explanation...",
               100d, // score
               "MySymptom" // symptom code
            )
         );
```

```
      }
      else //
 optionally we may even add a symptom to result if test was negative
      {
         fraudResponse.addSymptom( new FraudSymptom( 0d,"MySymptom") );
      }
      return fraudResponse;
   }
}
```

Listing 7.8 Adding New Symptoms for Fraud Detection

The related Spring configuration then would be as shown in Listing 7.9.

```
<bean id="mySymptom" class="MySymptom">=
<!-- replace definition of default hybris fraud provider -->
<bean id="defaultHybrisFraudServiceProvider" class=
"de.hybris.platform.fraud.impl.DefaultHybrisFraudServiceProvider">
   <property name="providerName" value="Hybris"/>
   <property name="symptomList">
      <list>
         <ref bean="blackListSymptom"/>
         ...
         <ref bean="mySymptom"/>
      </list>
   </property>
</bean>
```

Listing 7.9 Spring Configurations for New Fraud Symptoms

You can use this same file to change the order and importance of existing symptoms, deciding by what amount they will increment the total fraud score (50 points each, unless you specify otherwise for a specific symptom). The code to do is shown in Listing 7.10.

```
public abstract class AbstractOrderFraudSymptomDetection implements
OrderFraudSymptomDetection
{
public static final double DEFAULT_INCREMENT = 50;

private double increment = DEFAULT_INCREMENT;
```

```
private String symptomName;

protected FraudSymptom createSymptom(final boolean positive)
{
return createSymptom(null, positive);
}

protected FraudSymptom createSymptom(final String explanation, final boolean
positive)
{
return new FraudSymptom(explanation, positive ?
 getIncrement() : 0, getSymptomName());
}

public String getStrategyName()
{
return getSymptomName() + STRATEGY_SUFFIX;
}

public String getSymptomName()
{
return symptomName;
}

@Required
public void setSymptomName(final String name)
{
this.symptomName = name;
}

/**
 * @return the value to be used as score in case the symptom has been tested
positively.
 */
public double getIncrement()
{
return increment;
}
```

```
public void setIncrement(final double increment)
{
this.increment = increment;
}
}
```

Listing 7.10 Weighting Fraud Detection Symptoms

To provide an example of altering this evaluation, the code in Listing 7.11 would decrement the fraud score by 500 (or, more exactly, increment the score by -500).

```
<bean id="whiteListSymptom" class=
"de.hybris.platform.fraud.symptom.impl.WhiteListSymptom">
<property name="symptomName" value="White list" />
<property name="increment" value="-500" />
<property name="favoredEmails">
<list>
<value>goldMember@gmail.com</value>
<value>silverMember@gmail.com</value>
</list>
</property>
<property name="favoredUserIDs">
<list>
<value>goldMember</value>
<value>silverMember</value>
</list>
</property>
</bean>
```

Listing 7.11 Reducing Fraud Score by 500 for Customer on Whitelist

Most CSAs will never need to know how to do this, of course, nor even how it works behind the scenes. Most businesses set their fraud rules in place during development and then more or less leave them alone as they grow. But in the event that you identify a pattern of suspicious orders that you need to block, or if you notice too many legitimate orders getting marked for review, then you may want to take a look at these configurations.

Having gone through the functionality of orders in progress and the CSAs' view of those orders, let's turn our attention to returns.

7.1.6 Returns

In general, there is a point in the order fulfillment process when a given order can no longer be canceled and must be returned instead. Typically, this dividing line is shipment or pickup, if you are selling finished physical goods—but in the case of custom order, cancellation may not be allowed at all or may be disallowed after a set remorse period or after the customization process reaches a certain step behind the scenes. Still other businesses may disallow returns entirely or as a rule with occasional exceptions, as is common in the case of groceries and other perishable goods. In these cases, however, the business will still generally offer refunds in some cases and will therefore still have some use for the returns processes and tooling present in SAP Commerce.

These sorts of rules are generally set as part of commerce management and order management, both of which we covered in Chapter 3 and Chapter 6. From a service and support perspective, it is important simply to remember that different product types or categories, or different order types, can have their own rules attached for refunds and returns. To expand on the grocery example, if you sell some perishable goods and some nonperishable goods—produce and paper goods, say—then you will almost certainly have different return rules for one than for the other.

These rules will be reflected both in the Customer Support Cockpit and in the customer-facing self-service UI. Customers will be able to initiate a cancellation or a return based on these rules, and unless they are logged in as an administrator or some custom role with expanded permissions, members of your customer support team will be subject to this same business logic.

Customers can initiate returns from their self-service interface, as shown in Figure 7.6. When they do so, they will able to request a *full return* of the order (meaning that they are then expected to return all the items that they have received) or a *partial return* (meaning that they are then expected to keep some of the items but return others). A partial return can include only part of a line—so, for example, if a customer orders two of the same shirt, the interface allows them to initiate a return for one of the two.

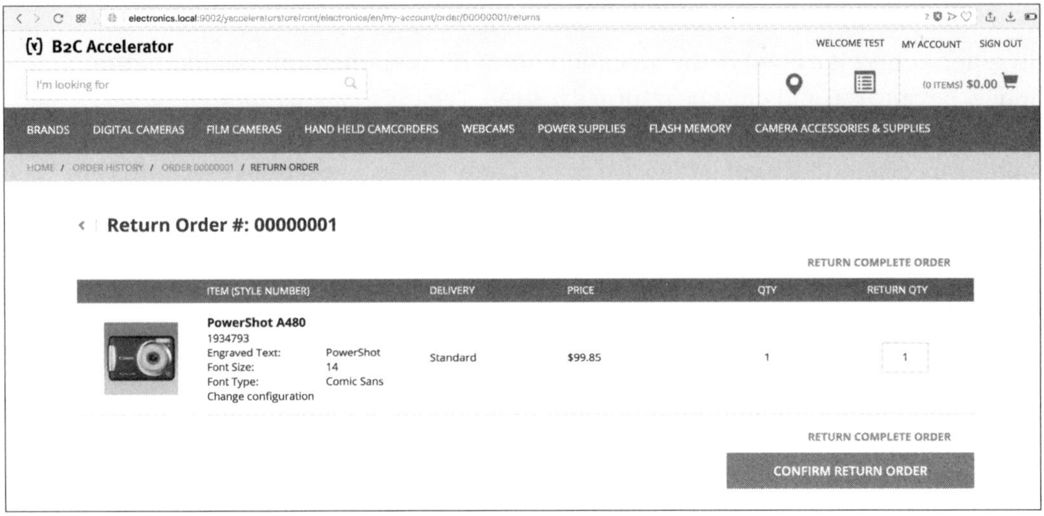

Figure 7.6 Creating Return in Customer Self-Service

When the customer initiates a return, this creates a return associated with the original order number. In general, the system will also kick off an RMA process, wherein the customer may receive a return shipping label to send back the goods. Warehouse managers can then confirm that they have received the goods, and CSAs can then confirm that the goods are received and that the return is therefore approved.

In the case of expired produce, damaged electronics, or torn apparel, the return or refund process may not actually involve taking the goods back. There still may, however, be a good case for leveraging something like an RMA process. In some cases, businesses will accept damaged goods claims on the honor system—after checking that this is not the twentieth such request from the same customer within a short time, at least—but in other cases, the business will opt instead to have the customer send images of the damaged goods or provide some other form of proof. The ticketing system's built-in messaging and file attachment comes in handy in such cases, and this may mean that your business may use a so-called return process that, behind the scenes, is more of a ticketing, documentation, and refund process.

CSAs can also kickoff return processes, whether because of direct contact from the customer or because of a product recall or because the customer has created a generic support ticket rather than kicking off a return in the system. Regardless of whether a customer or a CSA initiated the return, it will appear in the **Returns** tab of the Customer Support Cockpit, as shown in Figure 7.7.

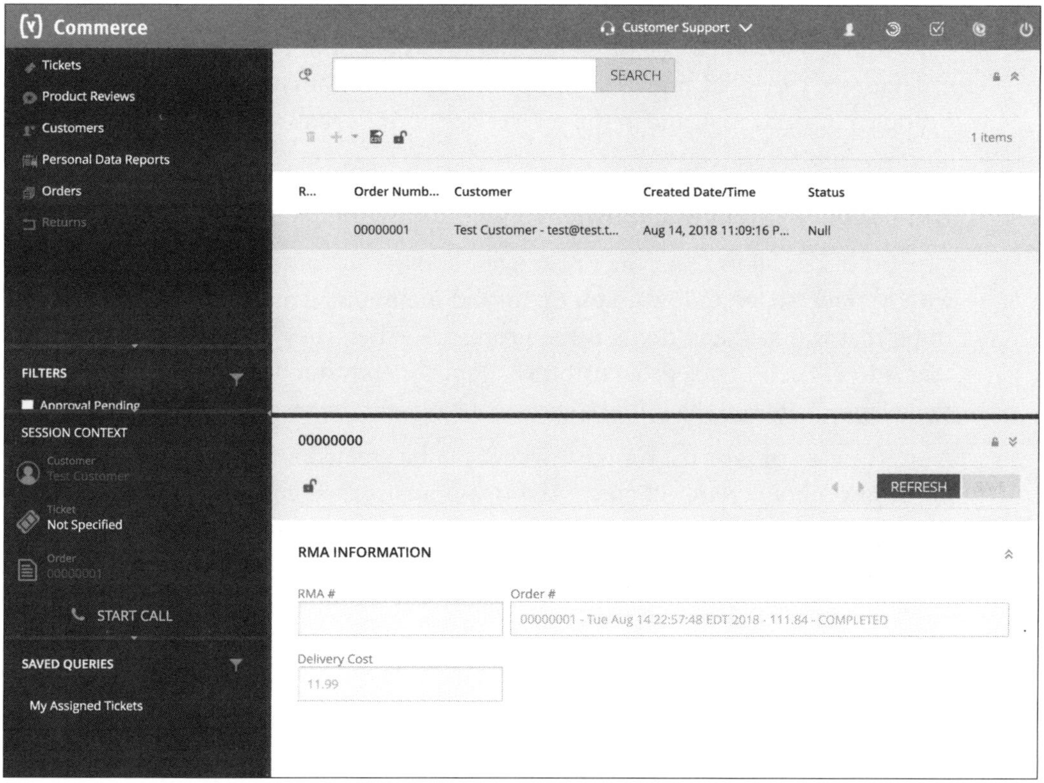

Figure 7.7 Returns Screen in Customer Support Cockpit

CSAs can filter returns by those that are currently in progress or by those that are already completed (and more specifically, by those that have been accepted or those that have been rejected) and can also search by customer account, RMA number, original order number, or comments on the order. This ensures that CSAs can locate the order in question if the customer initiates contact, even if that customer does not have a registered account and/or does not provide complete information or context about the request.

It is generally someone on the warehouse side who confirms that the items have been received—so for a more detailed explanation of the warehouse management side of this process, see Chapter 6. Once this has been confirmed, however, it's generally the CSA who communicates with the customer, if necessary, marks the return as complete, and, if appropriate, issues a refund. If they have permission to do so, CSAs can initiate manual voids and manual captures on saved methods of payment. This is useful not only for refunds but also for replacements, which will sometimes require CSAs to not only cancel the original order (in whole or in part) but also place a new order for the corrected, replaced, or substituted items. The customer will receive notification, both via email and in the self-service portal, for all such changes.

7.1.7 Support Ticket Management

Support tickets allow CSAs, their managers, and the customers that they are working with to track issues, follow up on them, and maintain an auditable record of everything that was said and done in the process. Further, they allow customer support teams to efficiently delegate customer inquiries and to reduce the amount of time that elapses between the initial communication and the resolution of the issue.

As in the case of returns, support tickets can be created either by customers or by CSAs. In general, CSAs will create the tick if a customer initiates contact by some means other than the self-service portal—in other words, *most* support tickets will exist as a result of customer contact of one kind or another—but when this feature is being used proactively as well as reactively, CSAs might create tickets simply to log communication that *they* initiated with a customer. Perhaps they were following up on an order, or on an abandoned cart. Perhaps the business contacts any customer who has placed large orders in the past but has not placed one in some time. These are cases that *can* be handled through automation and often should be. But the support ticket system allows for a white-glove approach to customer contact, which can be preferable in businesses that tend toward small numbers of high-value transactions.

Regardless of who created it, a support ticket acts as a log of all communications between one CSA (or several) with a customer regarding a specific issue. This could mean issues related to an order or return, and tickets can be associated with specific order numbers, but it could also mean issues with managing a customer account or inquiries about products that are not currently available on the storefront. The categories of contact available to a customer (and to a CSA) are entirely configurable and extensible, so they can and should reflect whichever cases most frequently require direct communication between your customers and your support staff.

The *ticketsystem-backoffice-config.xml* file covers the properties and functionality specific to the ticketing system, as shown in Listing 7.12.

```
<context merge-by="type" parent="User" type="Customer" component="editor-
area">
        <editorArea:editorArea>
            <editorArea:tab name="hmc.tab.customer.tickets" position="6">
                <editorArea:section name="hmc.section.customer.tickets">
                <editorArea:panel colspan="2" rowspan="2">
                    <editorArea:attribute qualifier="tickets" />
                    </editorArea:panel>
                </editorArea:section>
            </editorArea:tab>
        </editorArea:editorArea>
    </context>
```

Listing 7.12 Ticketing System Elements in customerview-backoffice-config.xml

These settings control the attributes that will be shown in these different tabs of the Customer Support Cockpit, as well as the size and position of elements within the UI. The values shown here are the defaults that ship with the standard accelerators, but it is common to move or remove sections based on the practices of individual businesses. If you are using a ticketing system outside of SAP Commerce, for example, and therefore do not want to use the one built into the Customer Support Cockpit, then you could suppress the **Ticketing** tab here without losing the other core functionality related to order and customer account management.

Note that, in this example, you would also need to remove the buttons related to ticking from elsewhere in the employee-facing UI and wire the ticket creation in customer self-service to your other ticketing system, or else remove those tools as well. In other words, these settings files are useful and efficient for showing or hiding customer data in this interface, but they should not be mistaken for a pervasive on/off switch for broadly defined support and service features. These settings concern what agents are empowered to do *here*, not what is possible in the system as a whole.

We will return to the topic of support tickets as in-app messaging later in Section 7.3, when we discuss the range of self-service options available to customers. For the moment, we will focus on the management of tickets from the Customer Support Cockpit, from the moment a ticket is created (as shown in Figure 7.8) to the moment it's closed (and, as we will see, potentially on to the moment when it is reopened, and beyond).

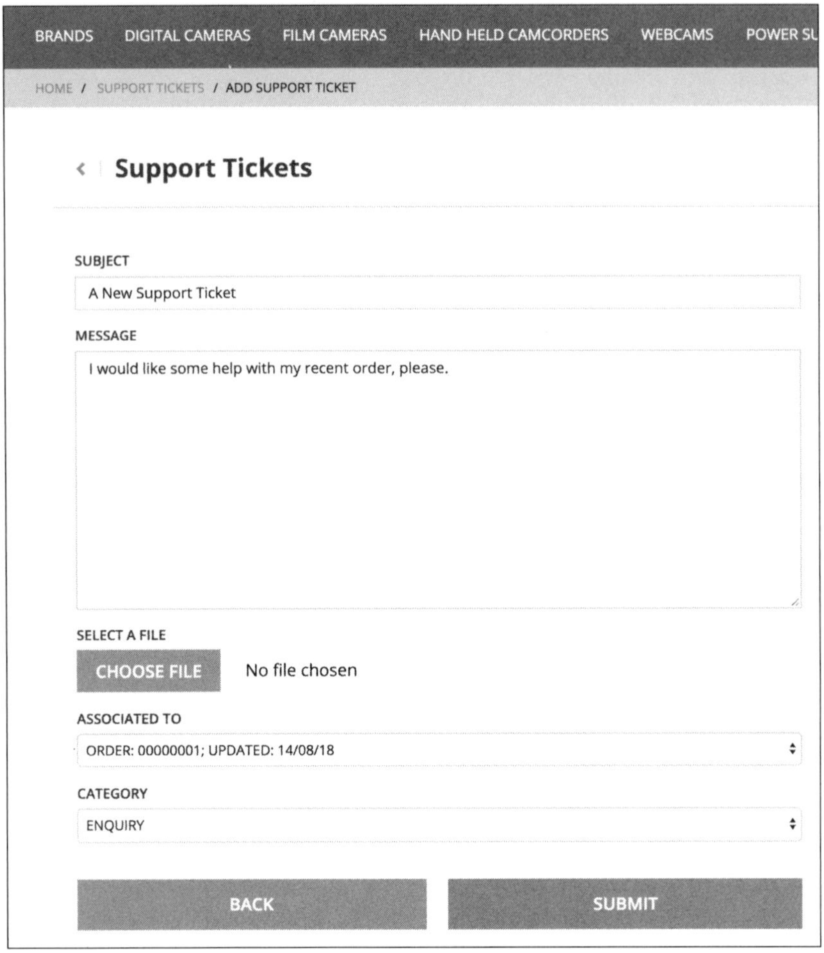

Figure 7.8 Creating New Ticket in Customer Self-Service Interface

A support ticket always includes a subject line, a message, and a category (enquiry, problem, or complaint by default, though once again, this list can be changed). It must be attached to a customer account, can optionally be attached to a customer's specific order, and it can optionally include a file attachment as well. If a CSA is creating it, a ticket can also be assigned to someone at the time of creation. This can mean assigning the ticket to some specific agent or group of agents, or it can mean CSAs assigning newly created tickets to themselves, taking ownership of the issues for which customers contacted them.

Upon logging into the Customer Support Cockpit, an agent generally will see the current list of open tickets that are assigned to the them, tickets assigned to the group to which they belong, or tickets that are unassigned (Figure 7.9). Unassigned tickets can be picked up by any agent at any time and generally represent issues that customers have reported but that have not yet been addressed by the customer support team.

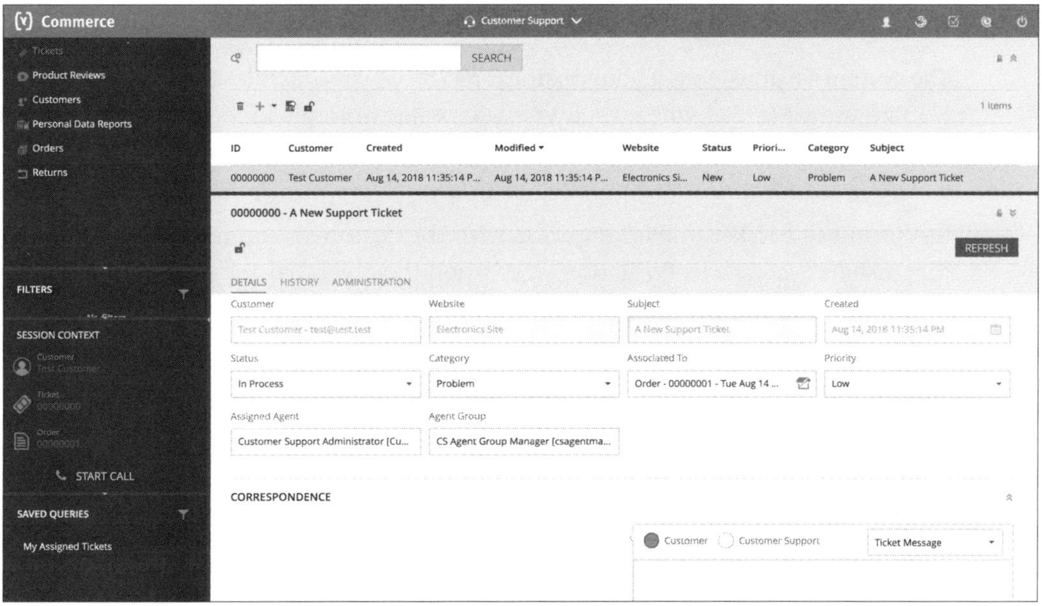

Figure 7.9 Open Ticket in Customer Support Cockpit

The system will show the amount of time each ticket has been in the system, thereby giving agents the ability to take care of customer cases that have already been going on for a while before moving on to those that have only recently been added to the system.

There is one other attribute that tickets must have when created, and it is one that CSAs will frequently search or sort on: priority. Tickets can be marked as high, medium, or low priority (generally by CSAs or their managers, rather than by customers themselves), and higher-priority tickets can then be addressed before lower-priority ones. Issues with payment or security, for example, should generally take precedence over general inquiries about unavailable items or site functionality, even if those more general, less urgent questions have been in the system longer.

By default, the Customer Support Cockpit will not enforce any of these priorities on users. The system will not stop a CSA from, for example, picking up a low-priority ticket even though there is currently a high-priority ticket that they could take on instead. There are, after all, some situations where a specific CSA *should* knock out three simple, low-priority tickets quickly, rather than spend a large amount of time on a single, more complicated issue. (In such a case, another agent would likely be working on that lager issue concurrently.)

The system assumes that if your business has more specific rules for who ought to be working on what and when, then you will build this logic in via agent groups and rules for assigning tickets, whether those rules are enforced systemically or simply by a manager looking at each incoming ticket.

CSAs can use a ticket to communicate with the customer, can reassign the ticket if they need assistance or escalation, and, when they feel that they have resolved the issue, can close the ticket. Should the issue then turn out not to be resolved after all, the CSA can return to the closed ticket and reopen it, as can another CSA, a manager or administrator, or the customer.

Tickets may not be necessary for all customer support interactions; some businesses do not use them, for example, for order placement or returns because in those cases the order or return itself acts as the auditable data object for the communication between employee and customer. Other businesses do create tickets for these sorts of interactions, or even take the notion a step further and keep one or more open tickets on a customer's account at all times simply to log any and all communications with the customer, regardless of whether they involved issues in need of resolving, or to let CSAs share notes on a customer account.

Again, these latter uses assume that the Customer Service Cockpit is being used a bit more proactively—not simply to identify issues, resolve them, and collect useful data from doing so, but to then use that data to engage better and more efficiently. This does not work for every business, because of both scale—often, customer support teams are overwhelmed simply by direct support requests and do not have time to branch out beyond that—and expectations: not every customer wants unsolicited contact from a CSA; some would prefer to be the one to make the contact, rather than being the one contacted.

Our point is simply that the toolset enables both styles of customer support interaction, as well as anything and everything in between. As you find yourself achieving your initial support goals and satisfying customers in the short term, it's worth considering whether there may be better ways to improve customer happiness in the longer term.

The core idea is simply to encourage your customer to associate your support and service practices with success and satisfaction rather than problems and delays. This can mean the kind of white glove service mentioned earlier, but it can also be as simple as following up on issues that have already been resolved after a set period. Customers who make large purchases from you are often more willing to purchase accessories or service for those big-ticket items if they feel that you are there for them *even if they don't purchase anything else*. If you have the bandwidth, and if your customers are receptive, periodic check-ins can sometimes work wonders.

Before we move on, let's take a moment to recognize the portions of *customersupportbackoffice-backoffice-config.xml* that govern the tabs displayed on a ticket. These tabs are represented as shown in Listing 7.13.

```
<widget id="csBackofficeSpaceManagement" widgetDefinitionId=
"com.hybris.backoffice.spaceManagement" slotId=
"cockpitWidgetChildrenInvisible" template="false">
<setting key="widgetStyleAttribute" type="String"></setting>
<setting key="widgetStyleClass" type="String"></setting>
<virtual-sockets/>
</widget>
<widget-connection sourceWidgetId="csAdvancedSearch" outputId=
"searchData" targetWidgetId="csBackofficeSpaceManagement" inputId=
"searchData"/>
<widget-connection sourceWidgetId="csBackofficeSpaceManagement" outputId=
"collapseState" targetWidgetId="csCollapsibleContainer" inputId=
"collapseState"/>
<widget-connection sourceWidgetId="csBackofficeSpaceManagement" outputId=
"collapseState" targetWidgetId="csCollapsibleContainer" inputId=
"collapseState"/>
<widget-connection sourceWidgetId="csCollectionBrowser" outputId=
"selectedItem" targetWidgetId="csBackofficeSpaceManagement" inputId=
"listSelectedObject"/>
```

Listing 7.13 Ticket Properties in customersupportbackoffice-backoffice-config.xml

By altering these parameters, you can easily provide a more recognizable and on-brand ticket layout to your CSAs and customers alike.

7.2 Assisted Service Module

When a customer needs assistance placing an order—or doing anything else on the frontend that they could in theory do for themselves but are having difficulty doing unassisted—the assisted service module (ASM) allows your support team to help them to do so. Fundamentally, ASM is an overlay for your web frontend that allows agents to take over a customer's session and therefore their cart (Figure 7.10). The support agent working via ASM, usually called an *assisted service agent* (ASA), can in principle do anything that a customer can do, from browsing to purchasing.

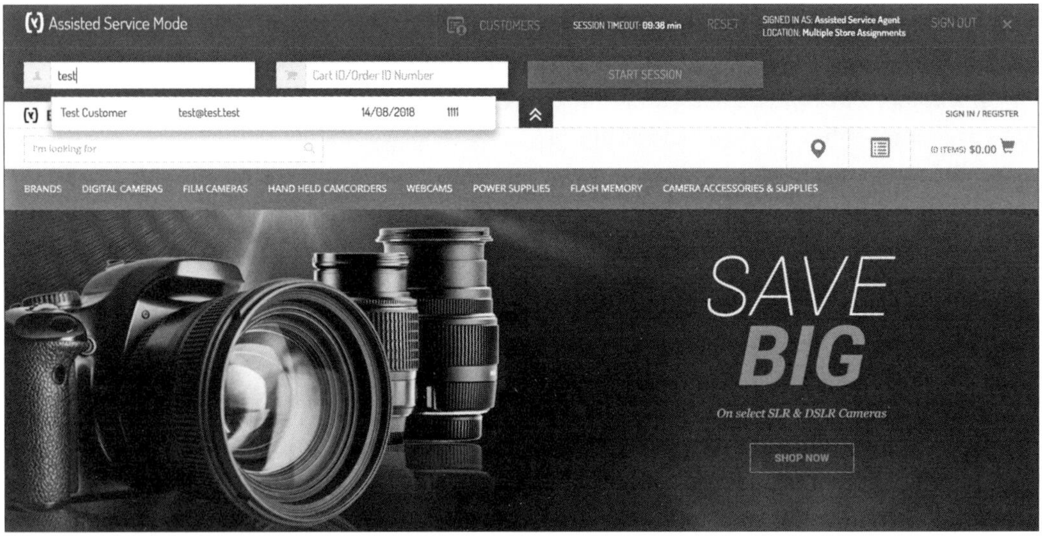

Figure 7.10 ASA Searching for Customer Account in ASM

Behind the scenes, the ASA has a combination of the customer's permissions and her own. This means that if the customer has access to special prices or personalized web content, the ASA will see that experience reflected—but if there are prices, promotions, products, or features that the ASA can access on the customer's behalf, the ASA will see these as well. (We will discuss this mechanism at the end of the chapter, and you can refer to Chapter 9 for a more complete explanation of user group permissions and system-wide restrictions.)

The advantages of this approach should be fairly obvious: The SAP Commerce accelerator storefronts already have a great deal of careful CX design built into them, and over the course of your project you will tailor this experience to your business and your customers. A great deal of work will have gone into making your searching, browsing, and purchases processes intuitive and efficient—so why not give your support team access to this same flow?

It is true that support agents can become remarkably quick with dedicated order entry screens, often completing orders faster than a user could possibly place one in a customer-friendly UI. But as discussed earlier in this chapter, that may not maximize the opportunity for cross-sells, upsells, and data gathering. And just as importantly, dedicated order entry UIs can require a steep learning curve for new employees, whereas your customer-facing checkout process is, by definition, intuitive to anyone who has ever shopped online, which is to say just about everyone.

In addition, this approach means that ASAs are able to help customers with issues not necessarily related to order placement. If a customer is having a difficult time setting a new default payment method or initiating a password reset, an ASA can complete such tasks on their behalf. And because the ASA is seeing essentially what the customer would see, she can talk the customer through the process, thereby making a second call about the same issue far less likely.

This does, however, raise two important caveats. First, you do not necessarily *want* ASAs to be able to do *everything* that customers can do. Some businesses do not actually let ASAs check out on customers' behalves, for example, because they do not want anyone but the customer to have access to the payment entry forms, shipping addresses, or other sensitive information. Other businesses consider this risk minimal, so long as they only allow ASAs to use saved payment methods (meaning that they never see any information other than the type of card and the last four digits). Still others do allow ASAs to enter addresses and credit card information.

Which leads us to the second caveat: ASM is not a true impersonation or "spoofing" tool. It does not, in other words, take over the customer's browser session. ASAs cannot move a mouse pointer or tab between fields on the customer's behalf, and any changes made by the ASA will be visible to the customer only after refreshing the page or clicking to another. ASM is true *cobrowsing*, meaning that the ASA and the customer share not the browser session but rather the user session in SAP Commerce. The two can in fact collaborate on the same cart, with an ASA adding or removing some items and the customer doing likewise, as we will discuss later in this section.

In this section, we'll look at the core features of ASM and how to extend them. We'll begin with the customer 360° view, then move on to order placement support, promotions functionality, and the process of integrating ASM with context-driven services.

7.2.1 Customer 360° View

When speaking to customers, to be efficient and effective, your CSAs need context. They need to know not only what the customer is telling them, but also what information you have collected from previous interactions. This means seeing the customer's order history and support tickets, but it also means seeing broader profile information, from their favorite brands and colors to their preferred in-store pickup locations. The customer 360° view allows an agent in assisted service mode to see all of this without jumping to a separate interface.

Naturally, the more information we know about the customer, the more context we can offer the agent using the customer 360° view. We don't need to stop at information generated in SAP Commerce; we can also include marketing insights or demographic information gleaned from social media. These broader uses of the tool generally require some integration, however, as well as some additional due diligence for customer privacy. As such, if this is the first time your support and service team has ever had access to something like the customer 360° view, we generally recommend starting with the data that we can collect simply from SAP Commerce (which is already quite a bit, and an example of which is shown in Figure 7.11) and then working outward from there.

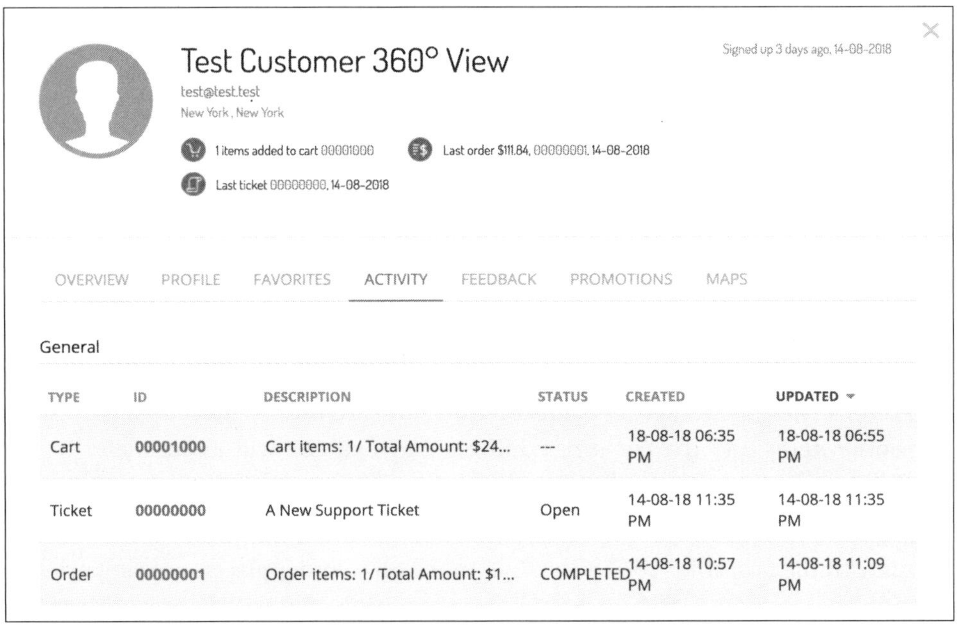

Figure 7.11 Customer History in Customer 360° View in ASM

The first tab in the customer 360° view is **Overview**, which can include the sorts of rich persona and profile information mentioned earlier, but also can offer a considerable amount of useful context simply from the customer's browsing and buying behavior. We can, for example, view a customer's last cart, any products or categories he has recently viewed or purchased, and any pages he has recently visited.

Beyond this, agents can see calculated data about the customer's preferences (as in the example of favorite colors), as well as the customer's interests or notifications that the customer has requested about products coming back into stock or changing in price. (We will go deeper into the underlying functionality of interests in Section 7.3.) Agents can see what products the customer is interested in but has not yet bought, add new notifications, edit existing ones, or remove ones that are no longer relevant—which may be causing the customer to receive more email than he wants, if he doesn't fully understand how to update his notification preferences.

Next, there is the **Profile** tab, which shows saved billing addresses, delivery addresses, phone numbers, and saved payment methods. After that is **Favorites**, which integrates with context-driven services to retrieve a list of the products or categories in which the customer has shown the most interest. (We will discuss this integration more in a moment.)

The next tab is **Activity**, which shows all the customer's most recent orders, carts, saved carts, and tickets in a single convenient view. After that is **Feedback**, which shows any support tickets that the customer has submitted, along with the status of each and the most recent time at which the ticket was updated. This tab also shows any product reviews that the customer has written, thereby providing an extra layer of insight into what he has purchased and, perhaps even more importantly, what he thought of those products.

The next tab is **Promotions**, which we will discuss in a moment, followed by **Maps**, which shows any brick-and-mortar store locations, for example, that are relevant to the customer's past or intended purchases and overall preferences.

In combination, these tabs allow an agent to better anticipate a customer's requests, intentions, and preferences and, just as importantly, avoid asking the customer to repeat himself. Even if different agents have to jump in and out of various customer accounts, and they often must, none of them will have to start from scratch.

ASM appears when the agent appends a markup to the end of the storefront URL. By default, this markup is the `?asm=true` keypair. This brings up the collapsible ASM header, which is configured in the *assistedservicesstorefront.js* file, as shown in Listing 7.14.

```
function saveCollapseBtn(){
            var pos = $(".js-ASM-collapseBtn").offset().left
            var parentWidth =  $(".js-ASM-collapseBtn-wrapper").width();
            var obj = {
                position: pos/(parentWidth/100),
                state: $("#_asm").hasClass("asm-collapsed")
            };

            document.cookie = "ASMcollapseBtn=
" + encodeURIComponent(JSON.stringify(obj))+"; path=/";
        }

function readASMcollapseCookie() {
            var nameEQ = "ASMcollapseBtn=";
            var ca = document.cookie.split(';');
            for (var i = 0; i < ca.length; i++) {
                var c = ca[i];
                while (c.charAt(0) === ' ') c = c.substring(1, c.length);
                if (c.indexOf(nameEQ) ===
 0) return jQuery.parseJSON(decodeURIComponent(c.substring(nameEQ.length,
c.length)));
            }
            return null;
```

Listing 7.14 ASM Header in assistedservicesstorefront.js

If you enter these parameters correctly, they will be reflected in *assistedservicesstorefront.css*, as shown in Listing 7.15.

```
#_asm
#_asm .collapseBtn-wrapper
#_asm .collapseBtn-wrapper:before
#_asm .collapseBtn-wrapper.active:before
#_asm .collapseBtn
#_asm .collapseBtn svg
#_asm .collapseBtn svg path
#_asm.asm-collapsed .collapseBtn svg
#_asm.asm-collapsed .ASM_header
```

Listing 7.15 ASM Header in assistedservicesstorefront.css

The key extensions of the assisted service module are as follows:

- assistedservicefacades, which provides and exposes the data model
- assistedserviceservices, which connects the facades to services
- assistedservicepromotionfacades, which adds promotions functionality
- assistedservicewebservices, which exposes ASM to webservices
- assistedservicecustomerinterestsfacades, which connects **Favorites** and **Advanced Overview** in ASM to customer interest data
- assistedservicestorefront, an add-on that exposes this functionality to the accelerator storefronts

Each of these extensions uses providers to retrieve data from elsewhere in the system and connect it to ASM. For example, to register the start and end of an ASM session, the CustomerSupportEventService class is referenced, alongside the amusingly named AssistedServiceService class in the *assistedserviceservices/resources/assistedserviceservices-spring.xml* file, as shown in Listing 7.16.

```
<alias name="defaultAssistedServiceService" alias="assistedServiceService"/>
    <bean id="defaultAssistedServiceService" class=
"de.hybris.platform.assistedserviceservices.impl.DefaultAssistedServiceService
">
        <property name="modelService" ref="modelService"/>
        <property name="userService" ref="userService"/>
        <property name="baseSiteService" ref="baseSiteService"/>
        <property name="cartService" ref="cartService"/>
        <property name="sessionService" ref="sessionService"/>
        <property name="flexibleSearchService" ref="flexibleSearchService"/>
        <property name="pagedFlexibleSearchService" ref=
"pagedFlexibleSearchService"/>
        <property name="commerceCartService" ref="commerceCartService"/>
        <property name="customerAccountService" ref="customerAccountService"/>
        <property name="commonI18NService" ref="commonI18NService"/>
    </bean>

    <alias alias="commerceCustomerSupportService" name=
"defaultAsmCommerceCustomerSupportService"/>
    <bean id="defaultAsmCommerceCustomerSupportService" class=
```

```
"de.hybris.platform.assistedserviceservices.impl.DefaultCommerceCustomerSuppor
tService">
        <property name="assistedServiceService" ref="assistedServiceService"/>
```

Listing 7.16 ASM Providers in assistedserviceservices/resources/assistedserviceservices-spring.xml

The `assistedservicefacades` class, meanwhile, contains some key settings for ASM behavior. For example, ASM sessions will time out after a set number of seconds to prevent agents from leaving sensitive information on their screens should they walk away from their desks, and this timeout can be set in *assistedservicefacades/project.properties*, as shown in Listing 7.17.

```
# Defines the time after which the asagent is logged out of the ASM
                        assistedservicefacades.agentsession.timeout=660
                        #
 Defines the time which the timer counts down from in the storefront
                        assistedservicefacades.agentsession.timer=600
```

Listing 7.17 ASM Settings in assistedservicefacades

In addition, ASM offers *deep links* functionality, meaning that a URL can log an agent in with a customer and/or a cart already loaded. This is achieved using suffixes such as these in storefront URLs:

- */assisted-service/emulate?customerId=customerID*
- */assisted-service/emulate?customerId=customerID&cartId=cartID*
- */assisted-service/emulate?cartId=anonymousCartID*

Settings for this feature can be found in `assistedservicestorefront`, where the default implementation of the `AssistedServicesRedirect` strategy (called `DefaultAssistedServicesRedirect`) holds the following values, found in the *local.properties* file:

```
assistedservicestorefront.redirect.customer_and_cart=/cart
assistedservicestorefront.redirect.customer_only=/my-account
assistedservicestorefront.redirect.error=/
```

7.2.2 Order Placement Support

ASM allows agents to check out on a customer's behalf. After selecting a customer account and beginning a session, the agent will immediately have access to the customer's current cart. Anonymous customers, meanwhile, can give the agent a cart ID, which the agent can then enter to pick up the session. Either way, the contents of the cart will be available for checkout, and the agent can begin that process immediately, potentially carrying it all the way through to order placement (see Figure 7.12).

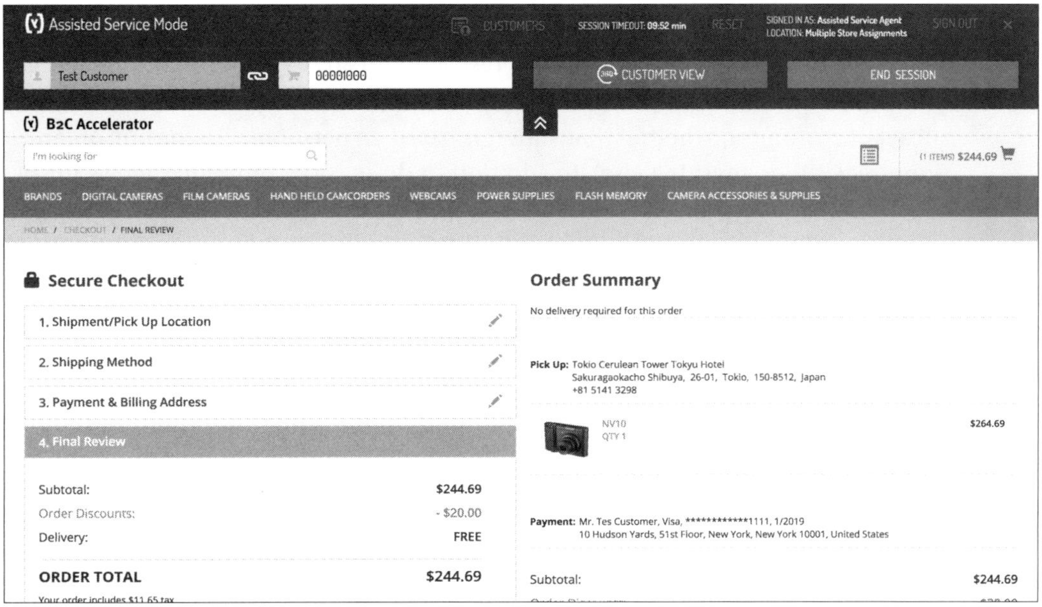

Figure 7.12 Checkout Process, as Viewed by ASA

In the cased of a logged-in customer, ASM also allows the agent and the customer to effectively collaborate on a cart. That is already happening, in a sense, when the agent picks up an existing cart—but they can then add to it, remove from it, or change quantities, and the customer will see these changes reflected in their own browser upon refreshing the page. Likewise, on refresh, the agent can see any changes that the customer makes to the cart.

This means that one can pass the checkout process to the other at any time. Just as the customer can pass a cart to an agent for checkout, so too can an agent prepare a cart for a customer and then allow the customer to place the order.

As discussed earlier, this line may be drawn for security reasons—namely, not wanting the agent to deal with credit card information or, conversely, not allowing customers to purchase limited, regulated, or free items for themselves. If such rules are in place, they can be different per storefront or per agent group, such that checkout is only available to more experienced agents or within lines of business in which there is a clear business case for doing so.

7.2.3 Promotions

As discussed in Chapter 9, *restrictions* can assign prices, web content, or promotions to specific browsing experiences. Time restrictions can restrict promotions to a certain time, for example, or user group restrictions can restrict promotions to a certain subset of customers (whether that subset is based on personas, purchasing organizations, regions, or anything else). In addition to these, SAP Commerce allows for two other restriction types: `AssistedServiceSessionRestriction` and `ASMCMSUserGroupRestriction`.

These restriction types are based on whether an assisted service mode session is currently in progress, thereby allowing assisted service agents access to special content, promotions, and prices. Agents can view the promotions available to add to the customer's cart in the customer 360° view, as shown in Figure 7.13.

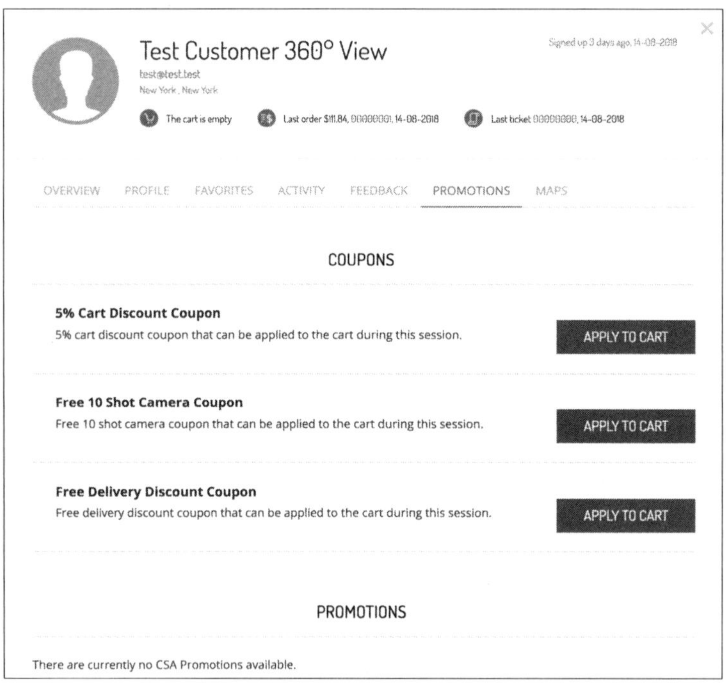

Figure 7.13 Promotions Available to Customer, as Viewed by ASA

Beyond that, agents can have access to products or categories. If you sell regulated goods that customers cannot buy for themselves, or if you offer free samples or appeasement products, then these restriction types will allow assisted service agents to add these items to the customer's cart and/or order them on the customer's behalf.

`AssistedServiceSessionRestriction` simply restricts something to any ASM session, whereas `ASMCMSUserGroupRestriction` restricts something to a specific group of assisted service agents. Used individually or in combination, these retraction types can provide highly targeted toolsets to your support team, and can empower them, in turn, to provide highly targeted experiences to your customers.

Notably, these restriction types do not need to be used only on products, prices, and so on. They can also be used to surface new actions entirely to assisted service agents, above and beyond the standard out-of-the-box actions such as adding products to carts. That statement is necessarily open-ended, but after reading this chapter, you should be in a position to begin experimenting with the possibilities that ASM enables.

The `assistedservicestorefront` holds the logic for ASM user groups and restrictions, and where you would go to add your own restriction. You do this by first adding a custom restriction bean to *assistedservicestorefront-spring.xml*, as shown in Listing 7.18.

```
<bean id="customRestrictionListMergeDirective" depends-on=
"assistedServicePathRestrictionsList" parent="listMergeDirective">
    <property name="add" ref="yourCustomRestriction"/>
</bean>
```

Listing 7.18 ASM User Groups and Restrictions in assistedservicestorefront

Next, add the definition for that custom bean, as shown in Listing 7.19.

```
<bean id="yourCustomRestriction" parent="assistedServicePathRestriction"
class=
"de.hybris.platform.assistedservicestorefront.restrictions.YourCustomRestricti
on">
<property name="paths" ref="asmSalesGroupRestrictedPathsList" />
</bean>
```

Listing 7.19 Definition for New Custom Bean Defining New ASM Restriction

Finally, create a new class for your restriction and define its behavior in the `de.hybris.platform.assistedservicestorefront.restrictions` package, as shown in Listing 7.20.

```
public class YourCustomRestriction extends AssistedServicePathRestriction
{
private final static Logger LOG =
 Logger.getLogger(YourCustomRestriction.class);
private List<String> paths;
@Override
public boolean evaluate(final HttpServletRequest httpservletrequest, final
HttpServletResponse httpservletresponse)
{
if (getPaths().contains(httpservletrequest.getServletPath()))
{
if (getAssistedServiceFacade().isAssistedServiceAgentLoggedIn())
{
final UserGroupModel managerGroup = getUserService().getUserGroupForUID(
AssistedservicefacadesConstants.AS_MANAGER_AGENT_GROUP_UID);
final UserModel agent = getAssistedServiceFacade().getAsmSession().getAgent();
// restrict access in case agent is not in manager group
if (!getUserService().isMemberOfGroup(agent, managerGroup))
{
try
{
final String previousPage =
 (String) ObjectUtils.defaultIfNull(httpservletrequest.getHeader("referer"), "
/");
httpservletresponse.sendRedirect(previousPage);
getAssistedServiceFacade().getAsmSession().setFlashErrorMessage("asm.action.re
stricted");
LOG.debug(String.format("Agent [%s] is not allowed to proceed with page [
%s], has been redirected to [%s]",
agent, httpservletrequest.getServletPath(), previousPage));
}
catch (final IOException e)
{
LOG.error("Failed to send redirect from AssistedServiceCheckoutPathRestriction
 class.");
```

```
}
return false;
}
}
}
return true;
}
/**
 * @return the paths
 */
protected List<String> getPaths()
{
return paths;
}
/**
 * @param paths
 *          the paths to set
 */
@Required
public void setPaths(final List<String> paths)
{
this.paths = paths;
}
}
```

Listing 7.20 Defining New Class for New ASM Restriction

7.2.4 Integrating with Context-Driven Services

To make full use of the **Favorites** tab in the customer 360° view, you will need to integrate ASM with context-driven services, an advanced set of content management and personalization tools that we explore in more detail in Chapter 5. Here, we will briefly go through the steps necessary to make this connection and make use of the data from one tool in the other.

The extension that enables interests is called `customerinterestsservices`. It implements the following methods:

- getProductInterest, which retrieves the article number of a product in which the customer has expressed interest, as well as the customer's ID, the notification type, and the associated storefront
- removeProductInterestByProduct, which removes the customer's notifications for a given product
- getProductByCustomerInterest, which retrieves all the products in which a given customer has expressed interest
- getProductsCountByCustomerInterest, which retrieves the total number of products in which a given customer has expressed interest

The customerinterestaddon extension then surfaces these methods to the frontend so that customers can add, remove, and edit their interests via self-service. Finally, the customerinterestsfacades extension returns the customer's interests, making them visible and accessible to agents using the ASM interface.

The CustomerInterestsDataProvider class facilitates communication between customerinterestsfacades and another extension, assistedservicecustomerinterestsfacades, which surfaces the customer's interests as favorites and enhanced overview data.

To enable this communication, however, you will need to add the assistedserviceprofileaddon extension to your build recipe. In this example, we'll add it to the recipe b2c_acc_plus, which you can find in your Hybris directory under *installer/recipes/b2c_acc_plus*.

In this directory, begin by adding your new extension to the *build.gradle* file, as follows:

```
extensions {
extName 'assistedserviceyprofileaddon'
```

Next, add your new add-on to the list of add-ons in the recipe, as shown in Listing 7.21.

```
pl.project.addons {
names "assistedserviceyprofileaddon,captchaaddon,liveeditaddon,commerceorgsamp
lesaddon,promotionenginesamplesaddon,hybrisanalyticsaddon,
eventtrackingwsaddon,assistedservicestorefront,assistedservicecustomerinterest
saddon,customerticketingaddon,privacyoverlayeraddon,textfieldconfiguratortempl
ateaddon,
smarteditaddon,consignmenttrackingaddon,consignmenttrackingmockaddon,notificat
ionaddon,customerinterestsaddon,stocknotificationaddon,orderselfserviceaddon"
```

```
template "yacceleratorstorefront"
storeFronts "yacceleratorstorefront"
platform pl
}
```

Listing 7.21 Adding New Add-On to b2c_acc_plus Recipe

After that, find the `customerinterestsfacades` definition and set the following properties, with your own storefront addresses replacing the accelerators values listed here:

- Set `piwik.tracker.url` to `http://electronics.local:9001/yprofileeventtrackingsws/events`
- Set `piwik.tracker.https.url` to `http://electronics.local:9002/yprofileeventtrackingsws/events`
- Set `eventtrackingwsaddon.events_endpoint.enabled` to `true`
- Set `yprofilecommons.automatic.consent-reference.generation.enabled` to `true`
- Set `yprofileeventtrackingws.events_endpoint.enabled` to `true`

Finally, add your new configuration via ImpEx, as shown in Listing 7.22.

```
INSERT_UPDATE YaasOrganisation;identifier[unique=true];basePath[unique=true];
;ORGANIZATION_IDENTIFIER;path;;

INSERT_UPDATE YaasProject;identifier[unique=
true];yaasOrganisation(identifier);baseSite(uid)
;PROJECT_IDENTIFIER;ORGANIZATION_IDENTIFIER;electronics;

INSERT_UPDATE YaasClientCredential;identifier[unique=
true];clientId;clientSecret;pubsubClient;yaasProject(identifier);oauthURL
;CLIENT_CREDENTIAL_IDENTIFIER;CLIENT_ID;CLIENT_SECRET;;PROJECT_
IDENTIFIER;https://api.yaas.io/hybris/oauth2/v1;

INSERT_UPDATE YaasService;identifier[unique=true];serviceURL;serviceScope
;ProfileClient;https://api.yaas.io/hybris/profile-edge/v1;' '
;ConsentServiceClient;https://api.yaas.io/hybris/profile-consent/v1;' '
;AsmProfileDataServiceClient;https://api.yaas.io/hybris/profile/
v1;hybris.profile_consent_view hybris.profile_context_view
hybris.profile_catapult_view hybris.profile_metamodel_view hybris.profile_view
hybris.profile_manage hybris.profile_identities_view hybris.profile_
identities_manage hybris.profile_graph_view
```

```
;AsmProfileIdentityServiceClient;https://api.yaas.io/hybris/profile-identity-
service/v1;hybris.profile_consent_view hybris.profile_context_view
hybris.profile_catapult_view hybris.profile_metamodel_view hybris.profile_view
hybris.profile_manage hybris.profile_identities_view hybris.profile_
identities_manage hybris.profile_graph_view

INSERT_UPDATE BaseSite;uid[unique=true];yaasProjects(identifier)
;electronics;PROJECT_IDENTIFIER

INSERT_UPDATE BaseSiteServiceMapping;baseSite[unique=
true];yaasService(identifier)[unique=true];yaasClientCredential(identifier)
;electronics;AsmProfileIdentityServiceClient;yprofile.client
;electronics;AsmProfileDataServiceClient;yprofile.client
;electronics;ProfileClient;yprofile.client
;electronics
```

Listing 7.22 ImpEx Script for Adding Context-Driven Services Configuration/Integration

You can also set how long interests will persist in the system in the `pcustomerinterestsservices` extension by setting the `customerinterestsservices.expiryDay` parameter.

7.3 Self-Service

Before, after, during, and sometimes *instead of* working with customer support agents, customers in the SAP Commerce accelerator storefronts can do a significant amount for themselves (Figure 7.14). Customers can of course edit their **Personal Details** (name and title) and their email addresses and passwords (the latter of which they can reset either by entering a new one while logged in or by initiating an email-based reset process). They can also manage their saved addresses and payment methods and change which of each is the default during express checkout (which we explored in more detail in Chapter 3).

Beyond that, customers can view their order and returns history and either request an order cancellation or initiate a return. In general (as discussed in Chapter 3), the available options are based on order status, with orders that have not yet shipped being eligible for cancellation and then, once they have been fulfilled, no longer being eligible for cancellation and instead being eligible for return, replacement, or refund. Customers can also see pending and past returns, as well as any saved carts (sometimes called *wishlists*) for future orders (also discussed in Chapter 3).

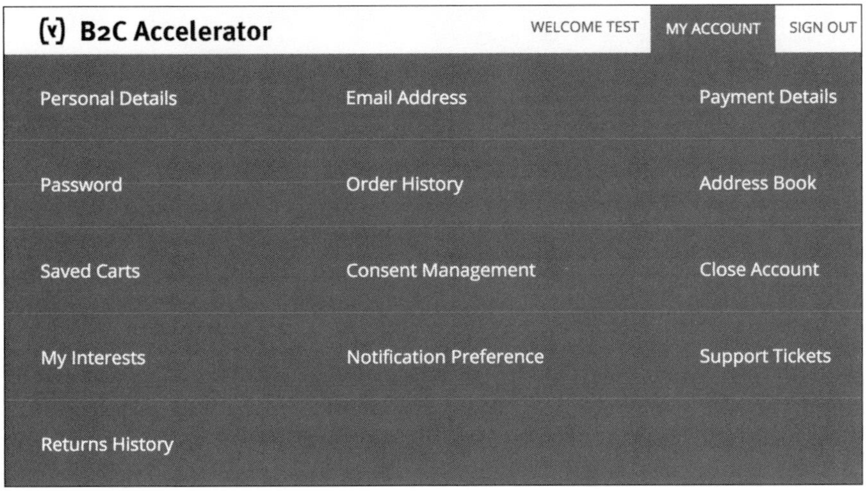

Figure 7.14 Self-Service Menu in Electronics Store

In addition, there are some self-service screens introduced in direct response to the European Union's General Data Protection Regulations (GDPR) that are important for any business concerned with assuring their customers' privacy (and with assuring customers that they are concerned with assuring their privacy). Customers can set their communication and profile tracking preferences (with the latter falling under consent management, which is shown in Figure 7.15, and which is discussed in more detail in Chapter 10) and, if they would like to, they can close their accounts.

Closing an account immediately prevents the customer from logging in but saves key account information for a set retention period. After the retention period, this data is deleted. Here we are talking about the customer's email address(es), contact information, shipping details, delivery preferences, consent management settings, account history, payment details, and order history.

Finally, customers can view the current status of active customer support tickets and add additional messages to them. This screen can act as a hub for correspondence between customers and agents, almost working as a form of in-app messaging that allows for logged, asynchronous communication without having to reply via email.

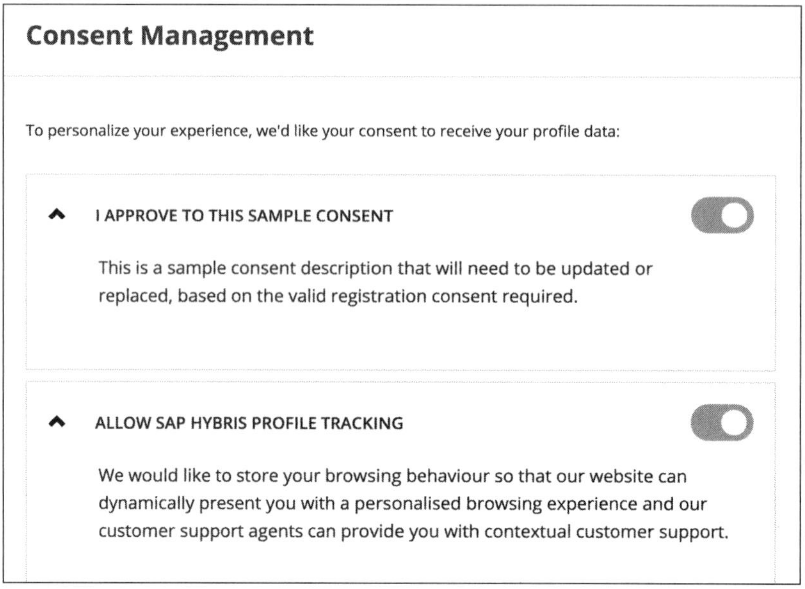

Figure 7.15 Consent Management in Self-Service

Customers will be notified when a ticket is closed, and if the agent included a message when closing the ticket, the customer will see this message as well. The customer can still communicate with the CSA after the ticket is closed and can reopen the ticket if they would like to do so. When reopening, they too can include a message, as well as an additional file attachment.

Customers can also use self-service to create new support tickets, rather than having a CSA create one on their behalf, including a subject line, a description, and, optionally, a file attachment and an associated order. Further, customers can categorize their newly created tickets (which will other otherwise simply fall into your default ticket category, usually *enquiry*). Customers can also use self-service to view and manage their interests in the **My Interests** area, as shown in Figure 7.16.

Customers can express interest in a product from the associated product detail page by clicking, for example, **Notify Me When In Stock** for an out-of-stock product. They can then remove this interest by clicking the **Do Not Notify Me** button that will then replace the old one; alternately, they can use the **My Interests** page in self-service to remove the interest. This too will disable notifications for that product and will allow the customer to do likewise for any products for which the customer no longer wants notifications.

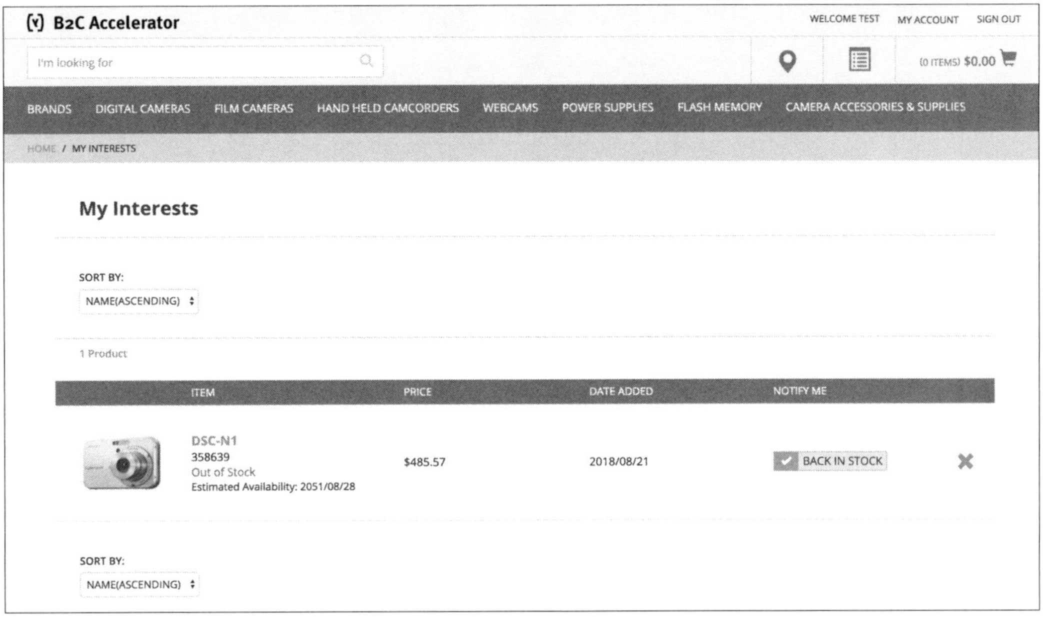

Figure 7.16 Customer's View of My Interests Area in Self-Service

Used in combination, these self-service features can enable customers to take care of minor or common issues for themselves, allowing your support and service team to focus on the issues that most require their attention, radically reduce repetitive inquires, and prevent simple issues from lingering unsolved for long periods of time. Used in combination with the manual support and service features in SAP Commerce, these features give you the tools you need to ensure that all customer issues are solved efficiently, effectively, and with thorough data collection.

7.4 Summary

Customers can perform a wide range of activities for their own accounts and orders using the self-service tools provided in SAP Commerce accelerator storefronts, and these activities tie directly into the support and service tools available to customer support agents, managers, and administrators in the backoffice toolsets. Agents can also assist customers with order placement, account management, special promotional activities, and general inquiries using the assisted service module view, which itself can contain a wide range of customer information from within SAP Commerce and beyond.

All these functionalities are tuned to be relevant to a wide range of businesses and business operations with minimal configuration, but they are also highly extensible. ASM in particular offers tremendous latitude of functionality, and the ticketing system can act as a central hub both for internal record-keeping and for communication between your support team and your customers. This allows you to forge a strong relationship with your customers and to connect with them directly.

As we've said, however, you will need to start crafting your identity as a business and your customers' impression of you well before a customer ever reaches out for service or support. In the next chapter, we will discuss what is perhaps the single most important way of doing so and of guiding your customers to the best of what you have to offer—namely, search and navigation.

Chapter 8
Search and Navigation

Your products are loaded and looking fantastic. Your customer experience strategy is aligned perfectly to your business goals and your customer's expectations. That's great, but it doesn't mean much if your customers can't find your products or navigate your storefront—so let's discuss how to configure your search and navigation experience.

Broadly, the terms *search* and *navigation* refer to the paths that your customers will take to find the products and/or content that they are looking for in your web storefront—and your goal in designing this experience is to make those paths as efficient, engaging, and effective as possible. The first step toward being able to do that is understand how your customers will use your storefront: What are they looking for? Where do they start? When might they want to be surprised with an unexpected option or recommendation? When do they definitely *not* want to be slowed down or sidetracked?

The answers to these questions will of course differ wildly from vertical to vertical, region to region, business to business, and, indeed, customer to customer—but there are some key principles to navigation generally, and to search more specifically, that can be broadly applied to almost any use case.

In this chapter, we'll take a close look at the under-the-hood configurations of search within SAP Commerce, as well as the employee-facing tooling that makes it accessible to both technical and nontechnical users. We'll also share some best practices for tuning your onsite search engine to keep your storefront performant and your results relevant.

We'll then talk about configuring search within the backoffice tooling—and finally, we'll talk about how this somewhat broader use of SAP Commerce's search technologies can open your mind to nonstandard uses of onsite search, with a special focus on how search works when finished goods or standard selling models are not in play.

8.1 Overview

On paper, navigation and search are often thought of as separate routes, perhaps even separate solutions: search happens when customers type in a keyword or SKU and navigation when they move through the experience in any other way. In practice, the line is considerably blurrier than that, as we will discuss in a moment, but to a certain degree there *is* a separation between managing search and managing navigation in SAP Commerce accelerator storefronts.

For example, the category names usually embedded in the top menu are driven by *navigation nodes*, containers for web content. Because these nodes are web content, they offer all the same possibilities for personalization that we discussed in the context of banners in Chapter 5: they can be shown only at certain times or only to certain segments of customers, for example.

But this also means that, although it is common for your navigation nodes to mirror your top-level product categories, the nodes themselves are independent of those categories and indeed of all product data. They are managed separately, through SmartEdit or the backoffice. These nodes are generally thought of as being part of search, but from a content creation and maintenance perspective they are distinctly navigation.

On the other side of that same coin, there are some pages on your storefront that might be considered part of the navigational experience but are in fact driven by search. As we discussed in Chapter 5, whereas a content page (such as a homepage) is built primarily from web content and a product detail page is built primarily from product content, a product listing page is built primarily by the search index. (If you are seeing inconsistency between the data displayed on your product listing and product detail pages, the first thing to check is the frequency and accuracy of your indexing process.)

It is the search side of search and navigation that will require us to learn some new terminology and master some new technologies—so before we go much further, to understand how we arrive at a product listing page like the one shown in Figure 8.1, let's take a moment to define our terms and discuss the architecture of search in a standard SAP Commerce deployment.

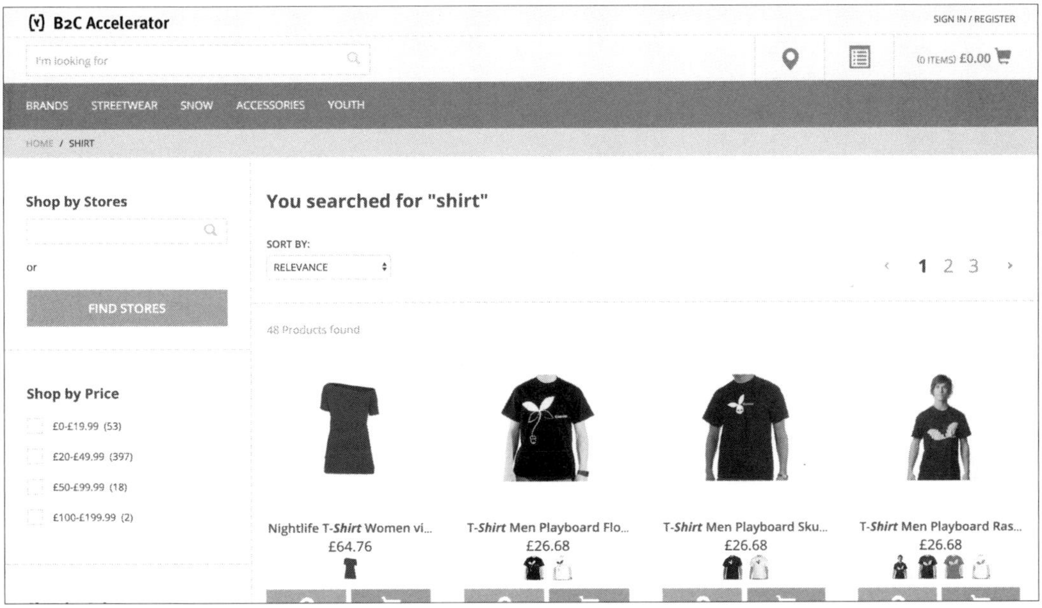

Figure 8.1 Product Listing Page, with Search Results and Facets, in Apparel Store

8.1.1 Search and Faceted Search

The product search on an SAP Commerce website is driven by a search engine: not one of the public-facing search engines, such as Google, but an internal onsite search engine that works in a similar way—namely, by building an index of content. Google wants to create an index of the entire public internet, whereas you, of course, will be creating an index of whatever your customers are searching for, usually beginning with (and sometimes ending with) products.

Although it would be technically possible to have your storefront directly query your database for, say, all your products that are blue, doing so would not be performant. At the very least, it would not be performant at the scale of frequent, near-constant searches on the frontend. Search engines provide a considerably lighter-weight process, segregating search to its own dedicated system architecture rather than querying a database that is busy with other tasks and, just as importantly, performing search operations on a dedicated index of data rather than the full product data set. (Google works in this same way, albeit with a vastly larger index.)

SAP Commerce comes tightly integrated with an open source search engine called Solr. It is based on the older Lucene search engine, and it natively supposed multilanguage, multicurrency, and multicatalog scenarios, much like SAP Commerce itself. Solr is highly configurable in its own right, and the full range of its abilities is outside the scope of this book. However, where appropriate, we will be highlighting the aspects of Solr that are most frequently tweaked for the purpose of product search in SAP Commerce.

The most important feature that differentiates Solr from standard Lucene search is *faceting*, which simply means filtering by clicking on an attribute value common to some, but not all, of the search results. For example, if a customer were to search for "TV" and then click on the facet for "4K," the product listing page would update to show only the 4K TVs in the original result set.

Faceted search is powerful because it allows the customer to quickly clarify her request in a few clicks, or perhaps even a single click. It acknowledges that a customer who performs a keyword search and doesn't find what she's looking for is unlikely to scroll through page after page of irrelevant results. More likely, she will refine her search or search again—or, if she's already taken these steps and still hasn't found what she was looking for, she will most likely abandon the process.

To prevent *that* from happening, we want to make sure that the search results are as relevant as possible and that the most prominent facets are in fact the ones most important to your customers. Most customers don't mind a few additional clicks, especially if their initial search was as vague as "TV" or "shirt." But they won't put up with *more* than a few clicks, or with the results failing to become more relevant to them even as they refine their results. This brings us to our next introductory topic: indexing.

8.1.2 Indexing

The first step in any process of onsite search engine configuration is to decide which of your product attributes belong in your index. Your search index can contain any number of attributes from your product data. On the extreme end, you could index every product attribute in your system of record. At the other extreme, you could index only your canonical SKUs. In practice, of course, you probably will not do either of those things. Rather, the attributes that you choose to index should be as follows:

- Attributes that your customers will search on (such as product names, category names, and potentially long descriptions)
- Attributes that your customers will use to sort of facet search results (such as prices, colors, and sizes)

- Attributes that you want to use for spell-checking and/or autocomplete (which vary wildly from project to project)
- Attributes that will need to be shown on the product listing page (such as short descriptions and thumbnail images)

Any attribute that falls into at least one of these categories probably should be indexed, and any attribute that falls into all four categories (as product name often does) *definitely* should be indexed. Again, remember that this is a functional best practice, not a technical limitation or requirement. Solr can handle large indexes, as can SAP Commerce. But you never want your index to be any larger than it needs to be.

Keep in mind as well that you are marking *attributes* for indexing, but it is the values within these attributes that Solr will actually search on. Color, for example, is an attribute. Blue is one possible value for that attribute, one possible facet into which to drill down, and one possible keyword for Solr to look for when it is performing its primary keyword search, its spell-check, and its autocomplete.

One additional note on the preceding terminology: in Solr, there is a hard distinction between spell-check on the one hand and auto-complete on the other. *Autocomplete* is the predictive text that customers are presented with when they start typing something that looks like an indexed keyword, sometimes called type-ahead functionality (shown in Figure 8.2).

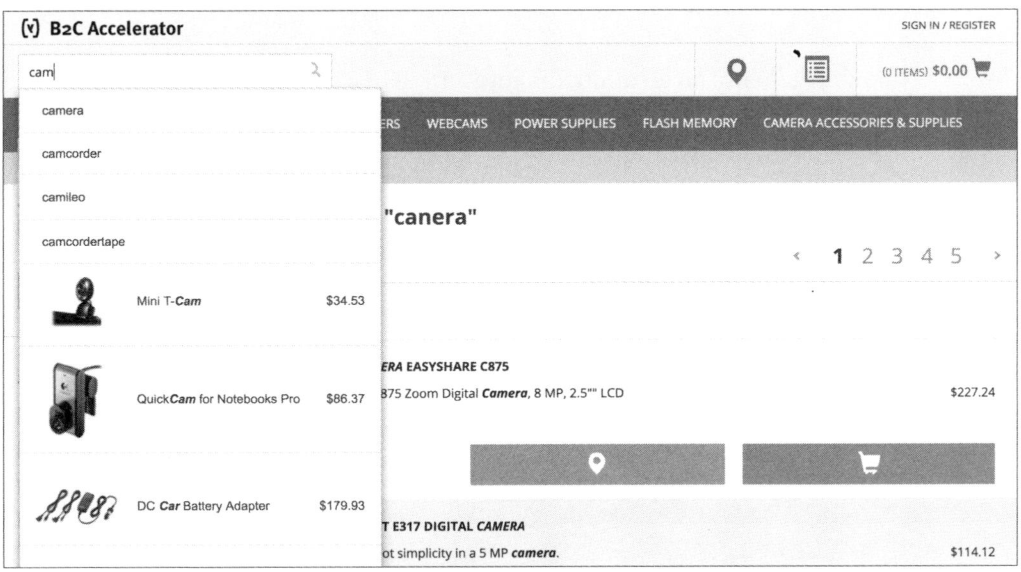

Figure 8.2 Autocomplete Functionality in Electronics Store

Spell-check refers to the suggestions made after a search is executed, if the search is close to an indexed keyword but not an exact match. This is sometimes referred to as "did you mean?" functionality (shown in Figure 8.3).

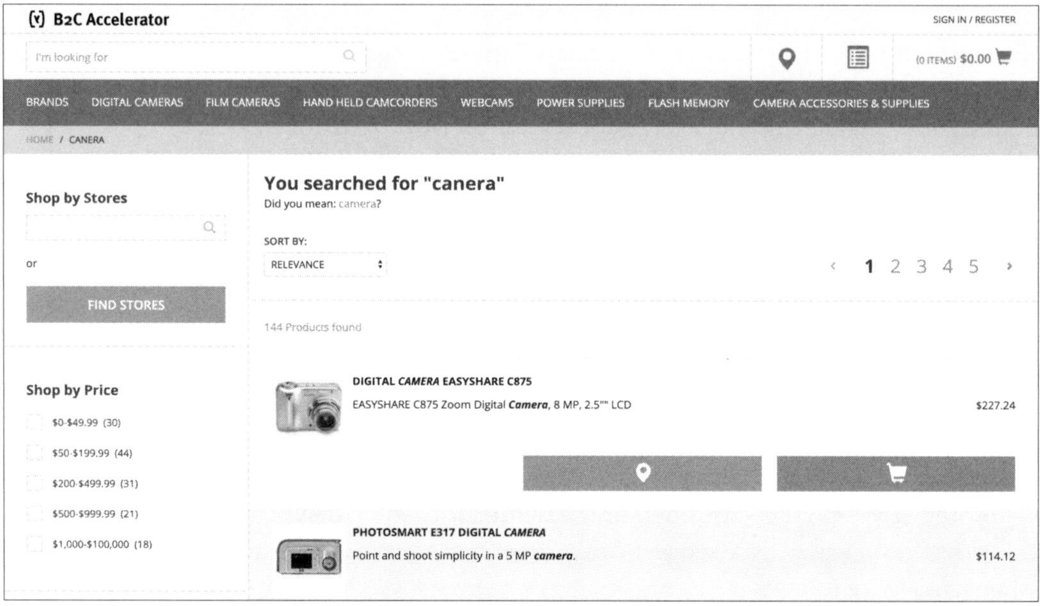

Figure 8.3 Spell-Check Functionality in Electronics Store

Solr allows you to use an attribute for autocomplete without using it for spell-checking, or vice versa. This is especially useful in verticals in which misspellings are common: spell-check is naturally better at catching those sorts of mistakes than autocomplete is. Solr will not suggest "shirt" if the customer types "sirt," for example, but spell-check *will* respond to an executed search for "sirt" by asking, "Did you mean *shirt*?"

When the customer searches for a keyword, Solr looks for that keyword in the values of the indexed attributes—or rather, it looks for a *filtered* version of the searched term, a *query*, the configuration of which we will discuss in the next section. Based on the assigned weight of each attribute and the frequency with which the query shows up within the values, Solr then assigns each result a score and sorts the results accordingly, as we'll discuss in the next section.

8.1.3 Scoring

Scores generally are not visible to end customers, but behind the scenes they are the core mechanism by which Solr determines inclusion, exclusion, and relevance-based sort order. You can adjust these scores at a fine-grained level using commerce search and adaptive search in the backoffice, as we will discuss later in this chapter—but this base score will determine your base search results at a coarse-grained level, and you should always get that right before zooming in and performing specific tweaks.

When Solr calculates the score of a product, it actually does so three times, and the importance of each of these scoring schemes can itself be adjusted. First, there is *exact*, which looks for the precise keyword that the customer has typed into the search box. Second, there is *fuzzy*, which looks for words that are close to the terms entered, within a configurable range of tolerance. Finally, there is *wildcard*, which will ensure that *some* results show up in almost any search, thereby avoiding null search result pages.

Behind the scenes, the core scoring mechanism is carried over from Lucene, a combination of vector space model (VSM) and Boolean scoring. In simple terms, fuzzy and wildcard matching narrows down the list of possible fields, and then the search engine looks for the query within those fields. The more times the term appears in a given product's relevant fields, the higher the score of the product.

The relative importance of exact and fuzzy matches will vary from business to business. If customers commonly misspell product or category names—or if the official names contain trademark symbols or other special characters that customers are highly unlikely to type—then fuzzy search will be vital for guiding them to the product. With that said, however, you will almost always want to privilege an exact match over a fuzzy one. If the customers know what they want, then it is in your interest as well as theirs to show it to them as quickly as possible. You can see an example of the process for configuring attribute-level exact and fuzzy weights in Figure 8.4.

This is why weighting attributes is so important. It ensures that, for example, a search for "Christmas tree" will show Christmas trees above sweaters with images of Christmas trees on them. In that example, you would want to weight product categories more highly than product names or descriptions, because while other seasonal products might contain the phrase *Christmas tree* in these secondary attributes, presumably only Christmas trees will belong to the category called *Christmas Trees*.

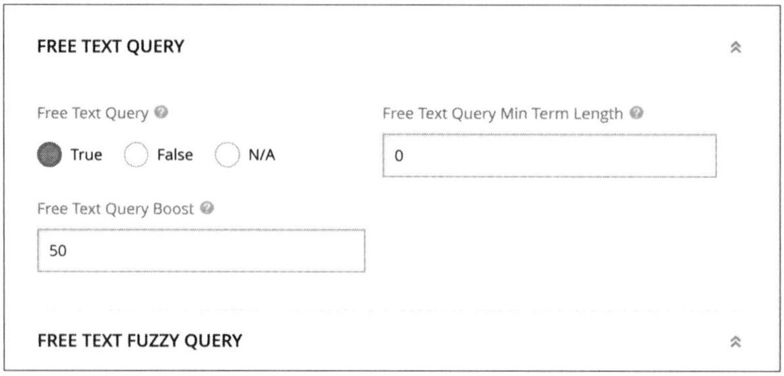

Figure 8.4 Configurations for Exact and Fuzzy Matches

Relevance score, we should note, is simply the default sort in Solr. When customers search for a product, then by default they will see the results that Solr determines to be relevant, in descending order of relevance. If the customer then sorts the products by price or name or rating, however, the relevancy rules will no longer apply to that particular search.

This is not only the default but also a best practice: a customer who wants to see the least expensive product first will likely lose confidence if he sees another, more expensive product above the least expensive one for marketing purposes.

Sort provider configuration lives in the `solrfacetsearch` extension and, according to the parameters shown in Listing 8.1, uses the `de.hybris.platform.solrfacetsearch.config.impl.DefaultFacetSortProvider` single base class.

```
<bean id="facetNameSortProviderAscending" class=
"de.hybris.platform.solrfacetsearch.config.impl.DefaultFacetSortProvider">
<property name="comparator" ref="facetDisplayNameComparator"/>
<property name="descending" value="false"/>
</bean>

    <bean id="facetCountSortProviderDescending" class=
"de.hybris.platform.solrfacetsearch.config.impl.DefaultFacetSortProvider">
<property name="comparator" ref="facetCountComparator"/>
<property name="descending" value="true"/>
</bean>
...
```

Listing 8.1 Sort Provider Configuration in solrfacetsearch

You can add your own sorts by registering them here, after implementing them in the `de.hybris.platform.solrfacetsearch.search.FacetValue` class.

Relevance sorting can, of course, take price, name, or rating into account. These are attributes in the Solr index, so they can be used to weight search results—but that once again falls into the category of fine-grained adjustment. Before we get there, let's take a closer look at the coarse-grained search configurations available in the SAP Commerce tooling.

We'll discuss how to build your index, how to set it to update automatically, and how to set a given attribute as a facet, as well as how to use it for spell-check and autocomplete later in this section and in Section 8.2. Some of this configuration will take place in XML settings, and a little of it will even take place in the code—but as you will see, a tremendous number of key settings can be manipulated directly through the admin and adaptive search perspectives in the backoffice.

All these ways of working are, in the end, ways of configuring, managing, and usefully interpreting a Solr query. So before we move on to the topic of configuration, we will first take a moment to dig deeper into how Solr queries are composed and how they translate to an SAP Commerce frontend.

8.1.4 Solr Queries

With all that in mind, we can understand what the system actually sees when an end customer types something into a search box on a storefront, so now let's look at how to read the different parts of a Solr query, how (and why) the customer's initially searched terms are transformed in the querying process, and what additional steps and options SAP Commerce itself adds to the search process. Once we've done that, we will be able to take a closer look at how to configure and customize those options in the next section.

Let's begin by looking at a Solr query (with the expectation that you will understand what we're looking at much better in just a moment). If a customer searches for the word *camera* in the electronics store, with default settings, the query would look something like Listing 8.2. We will explain this query throughout this section.

```
q=(ean_string:(camera^200.0 OR camera*^100.0)) OR (code_
string:(camera^180.0 OR camera*^90.0)) OR (name_text_
en:(camera^100.0 OR camera*^50.0 OR camera~^25.0)) OR (manufacturerName_
text:(camera^80.0 OR camera*^40.0 OR camera~^20.0)) OR (keywords_text_
en:(camera^40.0 OR camera*^20.0 OR camera~^10.0)) OR (categoryName_text_en_
```

```
mv:(camera^20.0 OR camera*^10.0 OR camera~^5.0))
&spellcheck=true&spellcheck.dictionary=en&spellcheck.collate=true
&spellcheck.q=Camera&defType=edismax&bq=
&fq=(((catalogId:"electronicsProductCatalog") AND (catalogVersion:Online)))
&start=0&rows=20
&facet=true&facet.field={!ex=fk1}Colour of product, 1766_en_string&
facet.field=Mounting, 1867_en_string&facet.field=allCategories_string_mv&
facet.field=brand_string_mv&facet.field={!ex=fk5}price_usd_string&facet.field=
{!ex=fk8}Megapixel, 63_string&facet.field={!ex=fk6}allPromotions_string_mv&
facet.field={!ex=fk7}Lens type, 472_en_string_mv&facet.field=Resolution, 80_
string&facet.field=categoryPath_string_mv&facet.field={!ex=
fk11}availableInStores_string_mv&facet.field=category_string_mv&sort=
score desc,inStockFlag_boolean desc,score desc&facet.mincount=1&facet.limit=
500&facet.sort=count
```

Listing 8.2 Solr Search Query

Now, let's break this query down. The first part of the query is the most important, specifying the term being searched for, as well as the fields being searched for that term, and the weights of each. In this example, Solr is searching for the term *camera* in the EAN (European Article Number), code (article number), name (identifier), manufacturer name, keywords list, and category fields, with different weights for exact, fuzzy, and wildcard matches. You can recognize these by their syntactical conventions, which are as follows:

- ^ for exact (as in `camera^200.0`)
- *^ for fuzzy (as in `camera*^50.0`)
- ~^ for wildcard (as in `camera~^10.0`)

This is the heart of the query, and understanding its syntax is critical to understanding what we will be adjusting in the rest of the chapter. Take another look at it, now that you understand what the symbols and numbers indicate (see Listing 8.3).

```
q=(ean_string:(camera^200.0 OR camera*^100.0)) OR (code_
string:(camera^180.0 OR camera*^90.0)) OR (name_text_
en:(camera^100.0 OR camera*^50.0 OR camera~^25.0)) OR (manufacturerName_
text:(camera^80.0 OR camera*^40.0 OR camera~^20.0)) OR (keywords_text_
en:(camera^40.0 OR camera*^20.0 OR camera~^10.0)) OR (categoryName_text_en_
mv:(camera^20.0 OR camera*^10.0 OR camera~^5.0))
```

Listing 8.3 Portion of Query that Shows Weighting for Exact, Fuzzy, and Wildcard

The next part of the query indicates whether spellcheck is currently active and, if so, what dictionary Solr should be spell-checking against, as follows:

```
&spellcheck=true&spellcheck.dictionary=en&spellcheck.collate=true
&spellcheck.q=Camera&defType=edismax&bq=
```

After that, the next part (Listing 8.4) applies some additional filters and pagination rules. In this case, there will be 20 rows returned; most importantly in an SAP Commerce context, we specify the catalog version in which we are searching: in this case, the online catalog version. This layer of specificity in the query means that we can test our search functionality in the staged catalog version without running into live data and that customers searching in the online catalog version will not run into data that is not yet ready for the live site.


```
&fq=(((catalogId:"electronicsProductCatalog") AND (catalogVersion:Online)))
&start=0&rows=20
```

Listing 8.4 Portion of Query that Invokes Catalog Version

The final part of the query (Listing 8.5) contains information on faceting, which will determine which facets are available to the customer and the order in which they will be listed. Here the facets being displayed are the color of the product, mounting, brand, price, applicable promotions, megapixels, lens type, screen resolution, whether the product is available for pickup in stores, and whether it is available for order online.

```
&facet=true&facet.field={!ex=fk1}Colour of product, 1766_en_string&
facet.field=Mounting, 1867_en_string&facet.field=allCategories_string_mv&
facet.field=brand_string_mv&facet.field={!ex=fk5}price_usd_string&facet.field=
{!ex=fk8}Megapixel, 63_string&facet.field={!ex=fk6}allPromotions_string_mv&
facet.field={!ex=fk7}Lens type, 472_en_string_mv&facet.field=Resolution, 80_
string&facet.field=categoryPath_string_mv&facet.field={!ex=
fk11}availableInStores_string_mv&facet.field=category_string_mv&sort=
score desc,inStockFlag_boolean desc,score desc&facet.mincount=1&facet.limit=
500&facet.sort=count
```

Listing 8.5 Remaining Portion of Query

These queries can be viewed in the Solr console, as we will discuss later in this section, or in the log of queries run on the SAP Commerce frontend, which is located in the *hybris/logs/solr* directory.

Now, *camera* is a fairly straightforward search term, insofar as it probably matches exactly with a keyword in the search index. (It does, in fact, in the example of the electronics store, which sells cameras.) But what about longer, stranger, or otherwise less straightforward searches?

Customer search behavior can be quirky, counterintuitive, and domain specific. Google users tend to phrase their searches as questions, to cite one famous example—leading to snarky articles about the absurdity of European Union citizens searching for "What is the EU?" when in fact that is roughly how anyone might perform a search about their own country (for an article describing their branches of government, or their electoral system, or even simply their borders and boundaries). People interact with machines in odd ways, and that's perfectly fine so long as we account for that fact and prevent it from interfering with the machines' functions.

This is why search engines tend to eliminate the parts of the query that make it look and feel like natural language; "what is" provides little or no specificity about what the user is looking for. In this aspect, Solr is no exception. It uses filtering to transform what the customer types into a leaner and more digestible string. By way of example, let's imagine that instead of typing "camera," our customer types, "I'm looking for Cameras." Solr would apply four different *analyzers* to this search:

1. `MappingCharFilter`
   Removes special characters such as the apostrophe in "I'm." (This filter will also remove accent marks.)
2. `WhitespaceTokenizerFilter`
   Divides the query into individual words so that each can be searched separately. This ensures that Solr is looking for the word *camera* on its own, rather than trying to find the entire clump of text.
3. `StopFilterQuery`
   Removes any words generally considered useless in a Solr search, also known as *stop words*. These words typically include articles such as *a* and *the*, and conjunctions, such as, in this case, *for*.
4. `LowercaseFilterFactory`
   This would remove any uppercase letters, transforming *Cameras* into *cameras* because we almost certainly do not want to make a distinction between those two searches.

By the time Solr is ready to interpret "I'm looking for Cameras," therefore, the query is actually for "looking cameras." This is much simpler and much more likely to produce relevant results—but it's still less than ideal, in two ways. First, the word *looking* is not especially useful and may even push irrelevant results to the top of the results page. If Solr is searching products' long descriptions, for example, and a phone is described as *great-looking*, then we might get great-looking phones that the customer wasn't looking for alongside the cameras that they were. (And of course, if a camera is described as "looking" some way or other, then it will be boosted above the other cameras, whether or not it's a camera we want to feature.)

This can be a tricky problem to solve, but if you are seeing your customers frequently using specific words for which Solr has no particular use, then you may want to adjust your search configurations accordingly. If customers are searching for a feature that simply isn't represented in your indexed data, then you may want to add whatever it is they're searching for. If they are simply searching in some syntactically odd way—like by starting a search with "I'm looking for"—then you may want to explicitly tell Solr to ignore the irrelevant words, in this case by adding "looking" to the list of stop words.

In this case, let's say that we've gone ahead and done exactly that. The word *looking* is removed from the query, just like the words *I* and *for*. What we're left with is the query "cameras." But there is still one inefficiency here.

As you might have guessed, if you're paying very close attention, the final issue is the *s* at the end of the word. Just as we want to ignore capitalization, rendering "Cameras" and "cameras" effectively identical searches, so too do we probably want to ignore pluralization. We will want a search for "cameras" to produce identical results to a search for "camera."

Solr achieves this through a process called stemming. In the same way that the analyzers listed above can reduce a sentence such as "I'm looking for Cameras" down to the useful unit of information for an electronics store—namely, "camera"—stemming can reduce a single string or word down to its useful part. At its simplest, this means removing pluralization, such that our string would come full circle and become simply "camera."

Depending on the stemming algorithm being applied, however, considerably more might be removed. The Porter algorithm, for example, uses the Solr dictionary to drill the searched words down to what it considers their roots. *camera* would remain *camera*, but *television*, for example, would become *televis*. This can be useful when customers aren't sure what they're looking for or when they frequently misspell the values being searched.

Indeed, Porter is the default stemming algorithm for Solr search in SAP Commerce. Depending on version, the parameter invoked will be `solr.EnglishPorterFillerFactory` or something similar. Many customers continue using this setting without any issues, and some prefer it even after trying other options.

But the Porter algorithm is right for every situation, and if customers are getting strange results, then a good place to start as far as finding out why is the stemming process. Take a look at the query, and see whether customers are actually seeing a search for what they think they are. If not, then you may want to use a less aggressive stemming strategy, such as KStemmer.

This, of course, gets us into the topic of configuration. Having walked through the basics of search in general, of Solr in particular, and of the construction of a Solr query, we can now talk about how Solr will work differently in different SAP Commerce rollouts: how users both technical and nontechnical can configure coarse- and fine-grained search behavior and, most importantly, which improvements can be made and which problems solved by doing so. For each way of working, we will provide a brief overview of what business users can do in the tooling and what technical users can configure behind the scenes.

8.2 Configuring Solr Search

Most configurations of the SAP Commerce accelerators ship with a default configuration for Solr. This configuration is a great place to start, but it should not necessarily be considered a best practices guide; more to the point, it may not be right for your business. At the same time, you'll want to avoid reinventing the wheel or discarding aspects of Solr configuration that *are* widely accepted best practices. Let's take a moment, then, to walk through some guidelines for finding the right balance—not just how to configure Solr, but also, on a more basic level, *how much* to configure Solr.

8.2.1 Deciding How to Configure Solr

Very broadly, most Solr-related issues on SAP Commerce projects are the result of configuring Solr either too much or too little. This may seem like an oversimplification, and of course the details do vary wildly from case to case, but the patterns are consistent enough that they are well worth understanding.

Under-configuration occurs when organizations deploy Solr with the default settings that ship with the SAP Commerce accelerators or else something very close to them.

Some customers with single-country, single-language deployments, for example, will nonetheless leave all the default languages from the SAP Commerce accelerator storefronts enabled.

In the case of the standard SAP Commerce, B2C accelerator, this would mean that the electronics store's four languages (English, German, Japanese, and Chinese) would all be included in the Solr index, as shown in Figure 8.5, thereby increasing the size of the index and slowing down the indexing process. Any default languages that you are not using should be removed from the index configuration, not only because they could be causing problems, but also, more simply, because they are not serving any clear purpose in the index.

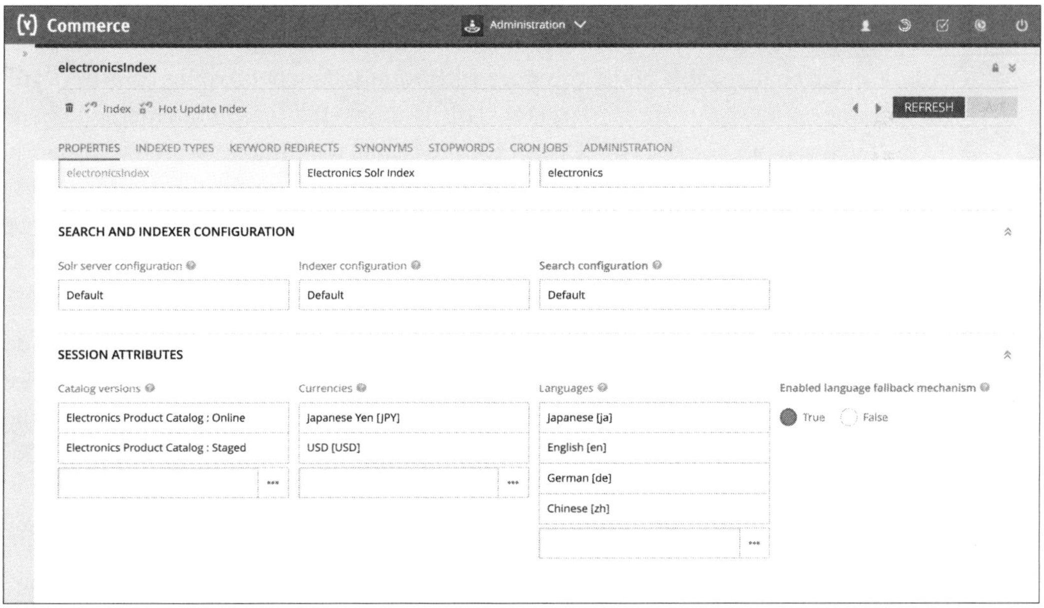

Figure 8.5 Language and Currency Settings in Search Index

Over-configuration, by contrast, generally means using many highly specific configuration changes or customizations when a smaller number of broader ones could achieve the same goals more efficiently. This might mean using a large number of redundant boost rules rather than simply adjusting the weight of a few key attributes, or it might mean creating an enormous library of synonyms and/or keyword redirects (which we will discuss shortly) when the real issue is that the search query is being filtered too aggressively.

Most commonly, customers avoid the broader and more effective option because it would involve data cleansing, with all the upstream impact to the system of record that data cleansing implies. For example, we have seen electronics customers boosting their highest-value products not because they necessarily want their most expensive items at the top, per se, but because they want devices (televisions, phones, smart watches) to sort above accessories (digital antennae, phone cases, smart watch straps), and they simply have no product category for devices defined in their data.

This workaround works well enough until a manufacturer releases an unusually expensive accessory or an unusually inexpensive device, at which time the order no longer looks at all like the customer wanted it to. Far better to categorize deceives as such, if that's the reason the products in question are being boosted.

Over-configured rules tend to create brittle configurations, wherein one marketer cannot make changes to a given category without effectively breaking another category, as set up by some other marketer. This is more of a team management issue than a technology issue: it is important for the teams working on search to be working from a shared understanding and a shared set of clearly defined goals; if the data or the configuration is insufficient to meet those goals, then the problem has to be solved a single time, upstream at the source, rather than multiple times at the end of the data flow.

You should be thoughtful, in other words, about what you change and what you do not. The settings in the SAP Commerce accelerators are meant to be a starting point and to enable the quick setup of a demo or testing environment—but they should not be considered best practices, certainly not across the board, and certainly not for all businesses. Now, let's take a closer look at how to change these settings.

When configuring your Solr search for an SAP Commerce deployment, there are four ways of working. Business users, such as marketers, will most often make changes using the adaptive search perspective in the backoffice, which provides functionality for boost rules, hero products, and search profiles. More technical users may also use the backoffice search and navigation node, where they can configure the indexed attributes and the weights thereof, as described in the previous section.

These same users may also use Solr's own management console, which lives outside of SAP Commerce. Finally, developers can make configuration changes directly in the XML-based settings for Solr and for SAP Commerce.

Anything that falls outside of these four ways of working generally will be considered customization, as opposed to configuration. Where appropriate, we will point out which extensions, beans, and so on would need to be customized to make a deeper change—but step-by-step instructions for doing so are necessarily outside the scope of this book. We will discuss some common customizations and the business benefits they can provide, but our main focus will be on those changes that you can make *without* customizing as such.

8.2.2 Adaptive Search

Adaptive search (shown in Figure 8.6) is the primary tool for marketers and merchants to adjust onsite search results on a fine-grained level. Here you can apply boost rules, promote or exclude products, and show, hide, and reorder facets. Furthermore, these rules can be applied globally or at a category level, and these settings can be specific to a given search profile.

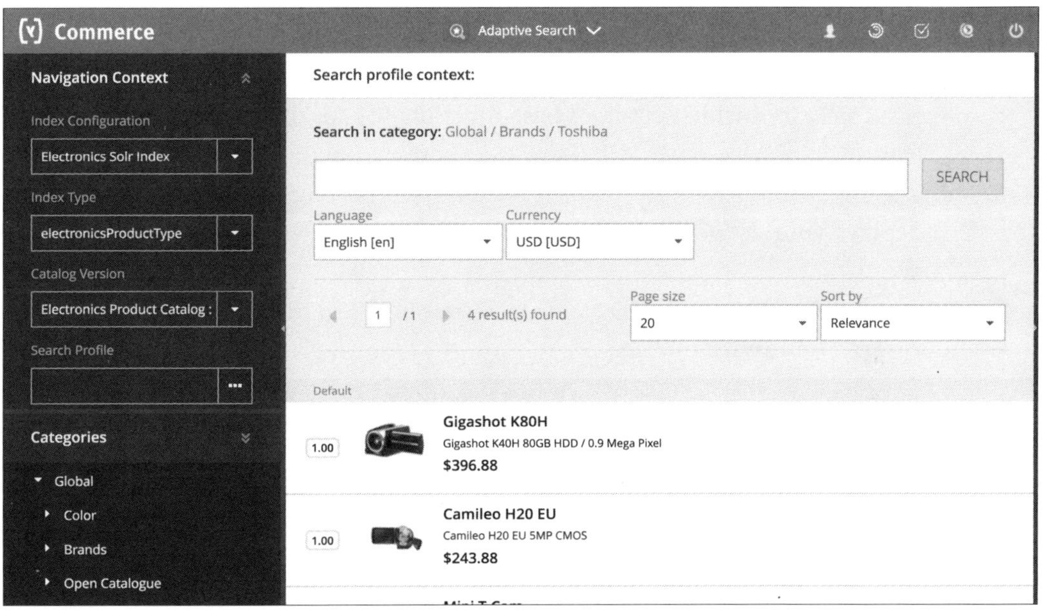

Figure 8.6 Product Category in Adaptive Search Perspective

Once again, before business users make any of the tweaks described in this section, you will want to be sure that your search is already providing reasonably relevant results—and if it is not, you will want to make coarse-grained adjustments first. Fine-grained over-configuration is an enormously common cause of poor search results, employee frustration, and customer confusion. But once the coarse-grained settings are in good order, day-to-day adjustments will take place here in adaptive search, for the most part. Let's take a moment to understand the underlying functionality of adaptive search—namely, search profiles.

Search profiles can be *simple* (meaning that they apply regardless of the category being browsed or searched) or *category-aware* (meaning that they apply boosts and preferences that are local to a specific product category). Customers can fall into multiple search profiles and, when they do, they can merge, with marketers deciding at the per-boost rule level whether a given profile should supersede the others in terms of order of activation.

We highly recommend creating search profiles for your key customer personas (the identification of which we discuss more thoroughly in Chapter 5 and Chapter 9). Because most customers experience your product catalog by way of search, tweaking this experience for customers is an especially evident, configurable, and effective mode of personalization.

Search profiles run on the following extensions:

- `adaptivesearch`, which provides base functionality for the implementation of the feature
- `adaptivesearchwebservices`, which exposes Search Profiles to the API layer and deploys your active profiles to *localhost:9002/adaptivesearchwebservices/swagger-ui.html*
- `adaptivesearchfacades`, which acts as a layer between `adaptivesearch` and `adaptivesearchwebservices`
- `adaptivesearchbackoffice`, which holds configurations for wizards and actions in the backoffice
- `adaptivesearchsamplesaddon`, which contains sample data for the SAP Commerce accelerator storefronts
- `adaptivesearch`, which communicates the parameters of your search profiles to Solr, appending the query and effectively adding profile-specific parameters to your searches

8.2.3 Search and Navigation

The search and navigation node can be found within the admin perspective in the backoffice. (In earlier versions of SAP Commerce, these functions lived in the hybris

Management Console [hMC], an older developer-facing interface that has been phased out throughout the 6.x release cycle.)

Each storefront that you have configured will, in most cases, have its own search index with its own set of configurations, as well as a single configuration for the Solr search in the Backoffice Product Cockpit (which we will return to later in this chapter, and which we already discussed somewhat in Chapter 4).

Some projects use multiple indexes on a single storefront due to strict divisions between (usually B2B) lines of business, siloed internationalized rollouts, or frequent updates and heavy testing on staged data—and if you have nonproduct content indexed, as described at the end of this chapter, then you will probably have at least one additional index to account for that content. In most cases, however, your search index configurations will match one-to-one with your web storefronts.

Once you have selected a configuration, the first tab shows base properties, such as the name of the index, the catalog versions included in it, and the currencies and languages it contains. In addition, this tab allows you to toggle the **Language Fallback Mechanism** settings on or off. If this option is set to **true**, then any fields or media items not available in the user's local language will be displayed in the fallback language (English, let's say) instead. If it is set to **false**, then those spaces will be left blank.

The next tab shows the **Indexed Types**. This shows exactly what it sounds like it shows: the SAP Commerce type or types that Solr is converting into searchable documents to create the index. This is usually a single type per index: product in most cases, and some other single type in most other cases. Even in implementations with multiple subtypes for the `product` type, it is usually this base type that the index should invoke.

This view will also allow the user to view and edit the settings for reindexing. Solr generally performs an `UPDATE` operation frequently to refresh values that update throughout the day, such as stock levels, and then performs a `FULL` reindex less frequently to catch larger changes to the product data set, such as additional categories. The system can also perform a `PARTIAL_UPDATE`, which updates only certain selected attributes rather than performing a full DIF, for improved performance.

Full reindexing also removes from Solr those items that have recently been removed from the database, ensuring consistency. Solr also offers an option that *only* removes items, called a `DELETE` operation. This is usually run as-needed, rather than on a regular schedule as with `FULL`, `UPDATE`, or `PARTIAL_UPDATE`.

Under **Indexed Properties** (shown in Figure 8.7), you can view the individual attributes included in the index of the selected type and quickly see which of them are currently being used for faceting, spell-check, and autocomplete.

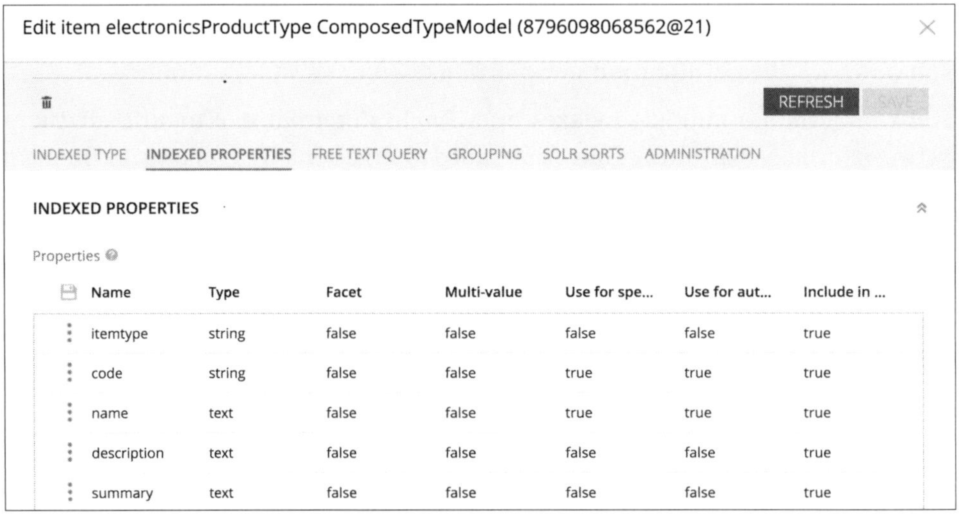

Figure 8.7 Indexed Properties in Search and Navigation Settings

You can also see the attribute type. The valid types for indexing are as follows:

- `boolean`
- `int`
- `string`
- `sortabletext`
- `text`
- `float`
- `double`
- `date`
- `long`

Note that none of these are rich-text fields and that not all of them are appropriate for all of Solr's features. You would not, for example, want to use a long piece of text (such as the long description of a product) for autocomplete; doing so could surface odd-looking chunks of natural language to a customer.

In this context, it is worth mentioning briefly that the search bar on the storefront is itself configurable. Users in the CMS Cockpit or SmartEdit can change the number of characters that the system will wait for before making an autocomplete suggestion, as well as how many keyword suggestions and/or product suggestions to make (with the keyword recommendations being straightforward Solr autocomplete, and the product recommendations being an SAP Commerce feature layered on top).

By default, the system will withhold suggestions until the user has typed three characters and then wait half a second before showing the results. This saves on performance while also preventing a jittery user experience wherein every character typed results in an instantaneous avalanche of probably irrelevant recommendations. These precise settings, however, may not be right for you. Perhaps your customers generally type longer strings before expecting recommendations. Perhaps they don't mind a shorter delay, or perhaps they only want to see product recommendations, not keyword recommendations. All of this is configurable within the CMS UIs in SAP Commerce.

Back in the search and navigation perspective, you can also view and edit information for each attribute's *value provider*, as shown in Figure 8.8. The important thing to understand here is that the value stored in Solr for a given attribute is not necessarily matched one-to-one with the value stored in the SAP Commerce product catalog. In such cases, the indexing process will transform the value.

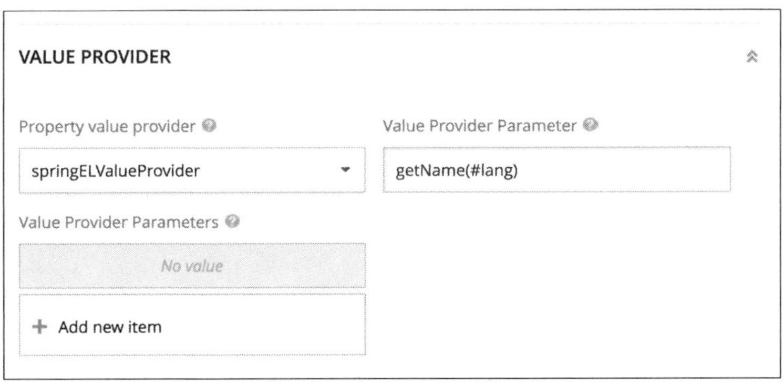

Figure 8.8 Value Provider for Name Attribute Name

Figure 8.8 shows a very simple example, meant to account for localization. Because the attribute `name` can hold values in every language active in the system, you need to specify that Solr will retrieve it in the local language. Do this by invoking the **Property Value Provider** `springELValueProvider` and providing the **Value Provider Parameter** getName(#lang) to specify that the name of the product should appear in whatever language the customer is currently using to search.

The transformations can, of course, be considerably more complicated than that. SAP Commerce ships with numerous value providers for indexing default data types, such as the productBundleTemplatesValueProvider property value provider for product bundle data. SAP also provides some new *value resolvers*, which generally work more efficiently and should be employed where possible. These include the following:

- ProductAttributesValueResolver, which looks for variant products' attributes in the equivalent attributes for their base product
- ProductClassificationAttributesValueResolver, which does likewise for attributes based on classification rather than typing
- ProductImagesValueResolver, which will locate and retrieve the first gallery image for a product and use it on the search results page
- ProductKeywordsValueResolver, which retrieves the full list of a product's keywords
- ProductUrlsValueResolver, which resolves and retrieves a product's URL location on the storefront
- ProductPromotionAttributesValueResolver, which retrieves a list of the promotions for which a given product qualifies

The next tab for index settings allows you to create *keyword redirects*. These allow the storefront to send customers somewhere other than a natural search results page when they search for a specific term. You might, for example, redirect the customers to their cart summary page when they type "cart" into the search bar (which some customers do, odd though it may seem). Likewise, you might want to redirect customers who search for the word "help" to your **Frequently Asked Questions** or **Contact Us** page.

Keyword redirects (shown in Figure 8.9) also are useful for sending customers to promotional or informational pages if they type the name of a product or category for which you have created a large amount of content. You might want to send customers to a brand landing page if they search for the name of one of your top brands, or you might want to send them to a page counting down to the release of an upcoming product for which they've searched. You can set keyword redirects to check for any string, looking for an exact match, or check for a search that starts with, ends with, or contains the specified keyword.

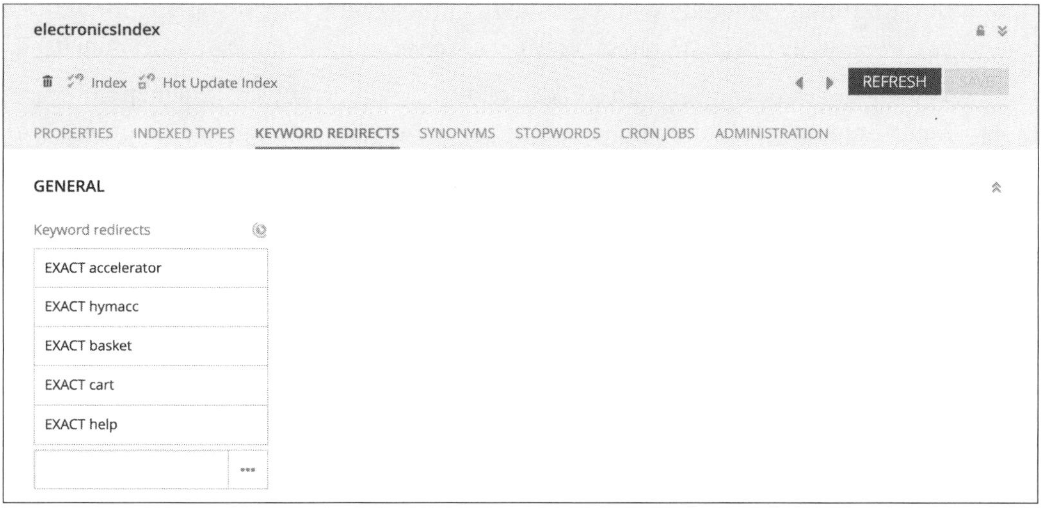

Figure 8.9 Default List of Keyword Redirects

Because keyword redirects are a step added by SAP Commerce, they are evaluated *before* other forms of Solr filtering. This means that they can circumvent more complicated rules (which can improve response time), but it also means that if you have a very long list of redirects, the system will have to churn through it on every single query (which can have the opposite effect).

You do want to be careful not to be *too* broad with your use of keyword redirects, as doing so can constitute over-configuration. Customers do *generally* expect to see a search results page when they search and, once again, frustrating a customer's expectations with search results is always a bit risky. You want the results to feel relevant and personalized, not arbitrary and semi-randomized.

The next tab allows you to configure *synonyms*, or words that Solr will understand to mean the same thing as other words. Although Solr does a good deal of internal spell-checking, it is always possible to stump it. Searching for "cmera" or "canera" will show results for "camera" (via the "Did You Mean?" functionality), but typing something way off, such as "kamyra," may not show results for "camera." The trickier your product set is for your customers—especially your first-time customers—to spell accurately, the more useful synonyms can be.

Synonyms are also enormously useful when the customer really is typing a *synonym*, whether it's a regionalism or an abbreviation. Mapping "trousers" to "pants" or "af" to "autofocus" can guide your customers to the results they're looking for without you necessarily having to build every possible variation into the product data itself.

Synonyms can be configured as unidirectional (where typing "af" will map to a search for "autofocus") or bidirectional (where "af" or "autofocus" map to each other). With a unidirectional synonym, the system is actually searching for both words, performing a search for both "af" *and* "autofocus." This means that a direct search for "autofocus" will result in somewhat different results, which may not be the desired behavior. If it is not, then a bidirectional synonym might work better, since it makes the results for the two words truly identical.

SAP Commerce provides **From** and **To** fields for unidirectional synonyms, and this same interface can be used to create bidirectional synonyms, albeit in a slightly counterintuitive way. Users can simply enter both terms in the **From** field, separated by a comma, as shown in Figure 8.10. The two terms will show as mapping to "null," but in fact will map to each other.

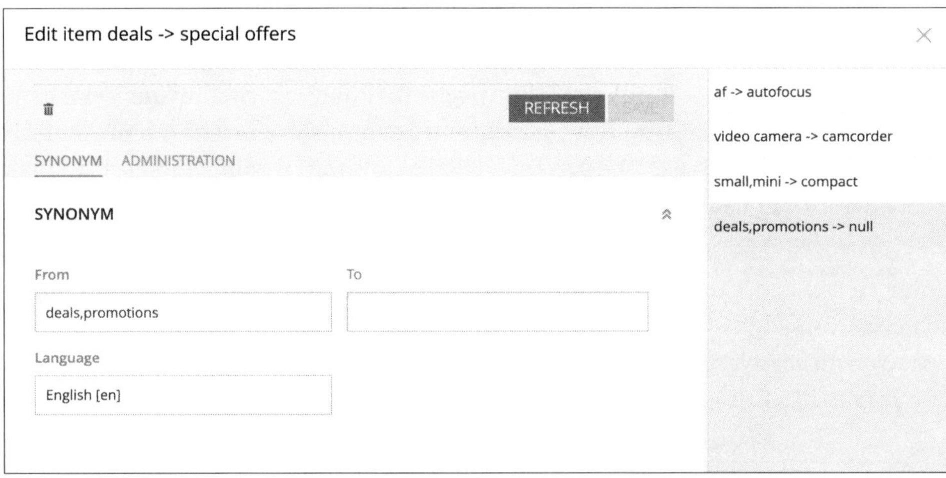

Figure 8.10 Bidirectional Promotion and List of Unidirectional Promotions

The next tab allows the user to add stop words to Solr's internal list. As we discussed earlier, Solr will ignore some words, such as *and*, *the*, and *a*, by default—but here users can add words that should be ignored within a specific storefront. These settings are, by their nature, highly business-specific, which is why there is no default list of SAP-Commerce-specific stop words in the system. Most typically, these are used to remove words from the query that are so broad as to apply to *every* product, or something very close to that. A business that only sells shoes might choose to ignore the word "shoe," for example, or may want to ignore their own brand name if theirs is the only brand that they sell online.

The next-to-last tab lists the CronJobs associated with the Solr index. You can easily access the settings for your `FULL` and `UPDATE` operations and see the schedules on which they are set to run. (Most SAP Commerce accelerators run an `UPDATE` every minute and a `FULL` reindex once per day.) You will also be able to see logs of the previous times these operations have run and what errors they encountered, if any. You will see your `DELETE` operation here as well, but again, by default it does not run on a regular schedule.

The final tab is **Administration**, a catch-all for the general settings attached to your index and for any feature that does not fit neatly into the previous tabs. Notably, this is an easy way to view your *value range sets*—attribute-specific settings that group values into ranges rather than displaying each value individually. These are used for numerical values, most commonly price (though also, commonly, technical attributes, such as megapixels).

After all, customers almost always want to facet on price, but they do not want an option for $10, an option for $11, and so on. Rather, they generally want a set of *ranges*: Less than $10, $10 to $50, and so on. Here you can see both the numbers being evaluated and the phrasing with which these ranges are described: "Less than $10," distinct from "$0–$9.99." These can be adjusted in the pop-up shown in Figure 8.11.

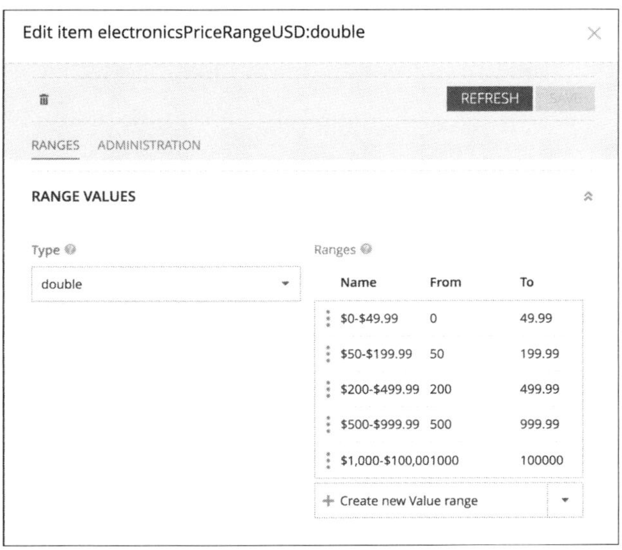

Figure 8.11 Value Range Sets for Prices in Electronics Store

As you can see, a great deal can be done from the adaptive search and search and navigation perspectives—but next let's focus on what requires us to go outside of the backoffice entirely.

8.2.4 Solr Console

Solr has its own management console, located at *:8983/solr/*, in which you can adjust resource allocation settings, view logs, and test queries—even going so far as to see a breakdown of which value in the indexed attributes contributed which score value to the total relevancy score of a given product. Because this level of visibility is not currently available in the SAP Commerce tooling—adaptive search shows a given product's boost and bury multiplier, but not its total score—developers and other highly technical users should expect to spend some time in the Solr console (see Figure 8.12).

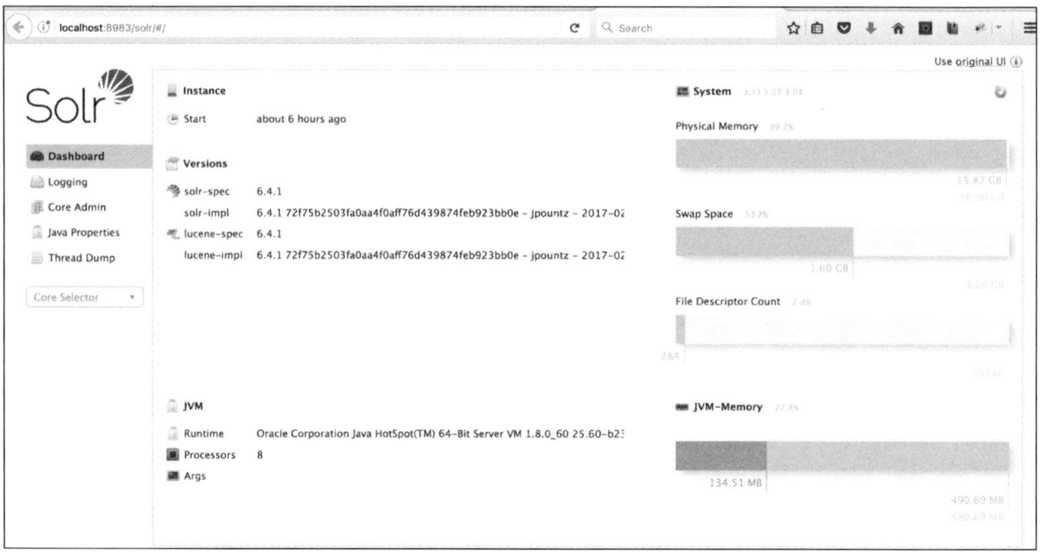

Figure 8.12 Standalone Solr Console

Beyond information about queries, this console is important for viewing the performance of the Solr cluster. This is where you would come to perform a Solr-specific thread dump, for example, or view memory and processor allocation.

Because the Solr console lives outside of the framework of the SAP Commerce UIs, access to its various features cannot be set at a fine-grained level per user or user group (as outlined for other UIs in Chapter 9). Authorization is handled at the Solr server level and generally should be restricted to those who thoroughly understand Solr on a technical level.

Once again, the full range of Solr's solution-agnostic abilities is outside of our scope here; refer to Solr's own technical documentation for detailed instructions.

8.2.5 XML and Spring Configuration

Some of the basic logic of Solr's faceted search can be configured in SolrSearchQueryData and, more specifically, in SolrSearchFilterQueryData. A FilterQueryOperator example in this configuration is shown in Listing 8.6.


```
<!-- FilterQueryOperator -->
    <enum class=
"de.hybris.platform.commerceservices.search.solrfacetsearch.data.FilterQueryOp
erator">
        <value>AND</value>
        <value>OR</value>
    </enum>

    <bean class=
"de.hybris.platform.commerceservices.search.solrfacetsearch.data.SolrSearchFil
terQueryData">
        <property name="key" type="String"/>
        <property name="operator" type=
"de.hybris.platform.commerceservices.search.solrfacetsearch.data.FilterQueryOp
erator" />
        <property name="values" type="java.util.Set&lt;String>"/>
    </bean>
```

Listing 8.6 FilterQueryOperator in SolrSearchFilterQueryData

SearchFiltersPopulator, as its name implies, populates the data for SearchQuery and adds it as filter queries. By default, the populator will apply AND logic to the lists of SolrSearchQueryData. Any indexed property that has OR logic applied or that is not configured as a facet will be ignored by the populator and treated as an ordinary attribute.

Most implementations will use the configuration called `DefaultFacetSearchStrategy`, which allows query conditions and parameters to be set at the query object level. In this default mode, the system will use the `FacetSearchListener` interface and at least one implementation of the `FreeTextQueryBuilder` interface.

Free-text query builders allow oddly formatted keyword searches, and even some degree of natural language, to be transformed into a query that Solr can more readily understand. There are two free-text query builders available:

1. `MultiFieldFreeTextQueryBuilder`, which divides the text into several *subqueries* and then calculates a relevancy score based on the combined scoring of those subqueries.
2. `DixMaxFreeTextQueryBuilder`, which works similarly to `MultiFieldFreeTextQueryBuilder` but has the following additional logic for grouping the subqueries, with the score for each group being the highest score of any of its subqueries (rather than the sum of the scores of all the subqueries in the group):
   - You can configure the grouping disjunction logic using the `groupByQueryType` key, which also allows you to group queries by their type (the possible types being free text, free text fuzzy, and free text wildcard).
   - You can use the `tie` key to determine whether the final score will take lower-scoring subqueries into account in the case of two maximum subquery scores being equal.

Earlier versions of SAP Commerce were, for obvious reasons, compatible with earlier versions of Solr, and SAP maintains some compatibility with these earlier versions (and, by extension, with the configurations created for projects that ran them) using search process settings. These older versions used what is now called `LegacyFacetSearchStrategy`. Although enabling this legacy mode is not generally recommended, it is necessary when working with older versions of the SAP Commerce system (most particularly version 6.2) and therefore bears mentioning.

In this mode, query configurations and parameters are established at the configuration level rather than at the query object level. Although this enables most of the functionality of Solr search in SAP Commerce, it does make it difficult to make any of the search settings contextual: dynamically including or excluding facets from a search response, for example.

As a result, running Solr in legacy mode means removing the following features from the instance:

- Default query operators (for specific queries)
- Query filtering
- Free-text search
- Facets (as opposed to facet values)
- Fields to be included conditionally in the response
- Boosts

Legacy mode is not compatible with the `FacetSearchListener` interface and will require you to use the `SolrQueryProcessor` and `SolrResultPostProcessor` interfaces instead.

8.3 Boost and Bury

Boost and bury functionality refers to the ability of a user—generally a marketer or other nontechnical user—to raise or lower the position(s) of one or more products in a search result set such as a product listing page.

In the left-hand menu of the adaptive search, users can select the **Index Configuration**, **Catalog Version**, and **Search Profile** that they would like to edit. When these have been selected, the user can then promote or exclude products, apply faceting or boost rules, and change the order in which facets will appear on the product listing page. Promoted products will always show up at the top of their category or, in the case of a globally promoted product, any search in which they appear.

Recall the example of the search query for *camera* from earlier in this chapter. Solr is excellent at taking a potentially ambiguous phrase such as "I'm looking for cameras" and whittling it down to its most important part from a document recall perspective. But *camera* is also an excellent example of a search term that might be *too* simple, or too broad, to be useful in and of itself. A customer probably has a fairly clear idea in her head of what sort of camera she's looking for, and she probably needs guidance to find her way to it.

As such, boosting and burying is especially important for category pages. As discussed in Chapter 5, category listing pages are essentially just product listing pages built by Solr, showing all of the products in a given category—which means that by default all of the products on the page have the same Solr score. We're only scoring on category membership, and every product present is a member of the category on which we're filtering, so the order will be effectively random unless you set some boost rules and/or manually promote at least one product. You can see some of these settings from the backoffice side in Figure 8.13.

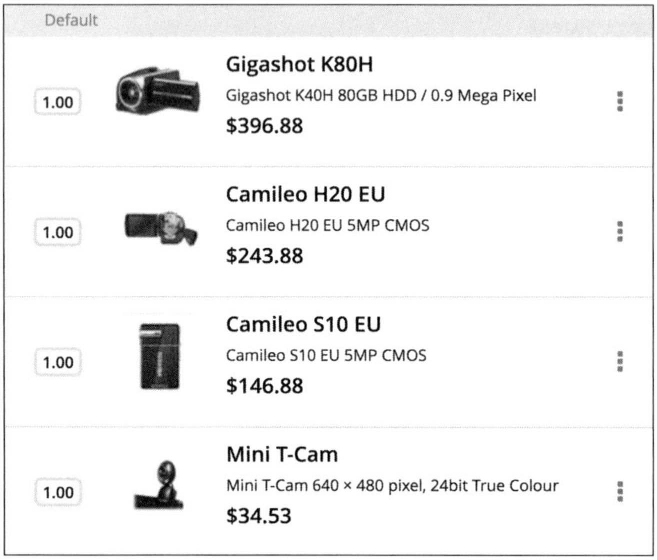

Figure 8.13 Products from Single Category with No Boost and Bury Logic Attached

For keyword search results, boost and bury functionality is a way to guide customers to the results that you would most like them to find—and/or the ones that you think they are most likely looking for, and ideally the products that overlap customer interests and business preferences—without them even necessarily knowing that's what's going on.

With search profiles, the recommendations can be highly relevant to identified customers, with big spenders seeing big-ticket items prominently, brand-loyal customers seeing their preferred brands front and center, and all customers being subtly guided toward the products that you want to promote in order to raise margin or order velocity or clear stock. (For a more thorough discussion on how to decide which products should be promoted, see Chapter 3, Section 3.5.)

8.4 Commerce Search and Adaptive Search

The most important functional difference between commerce search and adaptive search is that the latter supports *search profiles*, which apply personalized search configurations—and therefore personalized search results—to specific user groups. (See Chapter 9 for more information on user groups and user group restrictions.) This means that any defined customer segment can receive a personalized search experience, with big spenders seeing big-ticket items boosted toward the top of their search results, for example.

Another important difference, however, is that commerce search does not have explicit *burying* functionality. It does not have the **Exclude** option available in adaptive search, nor any other mechanism for hiding a product other than boosting other products above it so that it is less likely to be seen. You could, for example, boost in-stock products to effectively suppress out-of-stock products or boost some promoted brands to effectively suppress some others. Although this technique can in many cases achieve the same result as an explicit exclusion, it is generally considered less convenient and is more prone to human error or unforeseen consequences, as described in Section 8.3.

Commerce search runs primarily on four extensions, all of which are currently considered deprecated:

1. `commercesearch`
2. `commercesearchbackoffice`
3. `commercesearchsamplesaddon`
4. `commercesearchatddtests`

These use an older version of boosting, based on `BoostRule` objects, each of which is itself composed of an `operator`, a `PropertyValue`, and a `boostFactor`. For example, a rule might add 50 boost points if the name of the product contains *camera*.

The user experience in adaptive search is quite similar, but with two important differences. First, boosts in adaptive search can be applied to search profiles rather than being applied to all users. Second, boosts in adaptive search can optionally be applied in a *multiplicative* fashion, whereas commerce search always combines its boosts in an *additive* fashion.

Commerce search also uses an older framework for boost rules, the data model for which is shown in Figure 8.14.

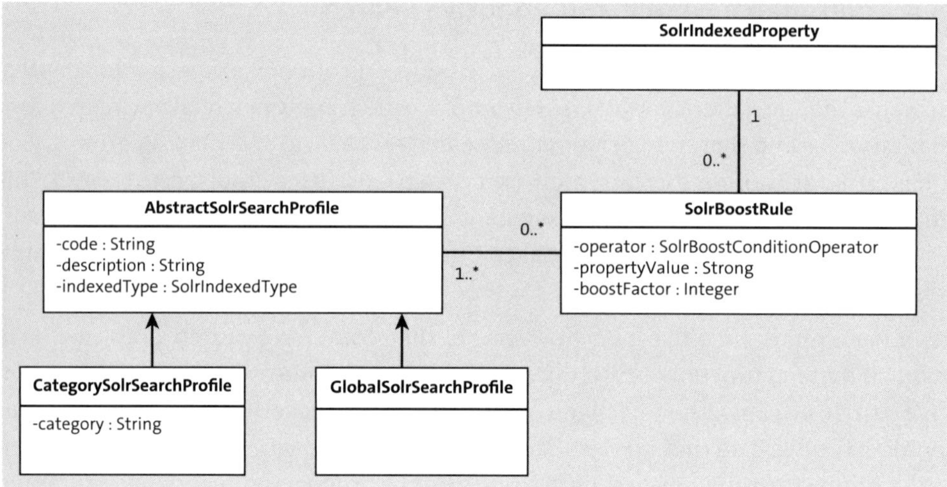

Figure 8.14 Legacy Data Model for Boost Rules in Commerce Search

8.5 Solr and PCM in Backoffice

For the settings that are not contained in the commerce search or adaptive search perspectives, there are two additional locations in the backoffice that are worth mentioning: the **Search and Navigation** node in the administration perspective; and the Product Cockpit perspective. We discuss the latter in more detail in Chapter 4, as far as its effect on product data, which in turn affects the search index built from that data—but the Product Cockpit perspective also uses Solr search in another way entirely.

When logged into the Product Cockpit perspective, users can search for products and refine those search results using facets, similarly to how customers can do so in an SAP Commerce storefront, as shown in Figure 8.15. This search does not simply look like a Solr product search; it *is* one, built from an additional Solr index configured specifically for backoffice users.

This index is typical considerably lighter-weight than the one used on the frontend, specifically *because* the process of selecting attributes for each is roughly the same: What will users be searching on? What will they use to filter that search? And what attributes should be shown in the search results? This data set is typically more limited for backoffice users, who have a detailed knowledge of the product data, or at least of the portion of the product data for which they are responsible. For similar reasons, this Product Cockpit perspective search index typically does not use boost rules. Your merchants and marketers tend to be the ones doing the promoting, not the ones who need to be cleverly promoted to.

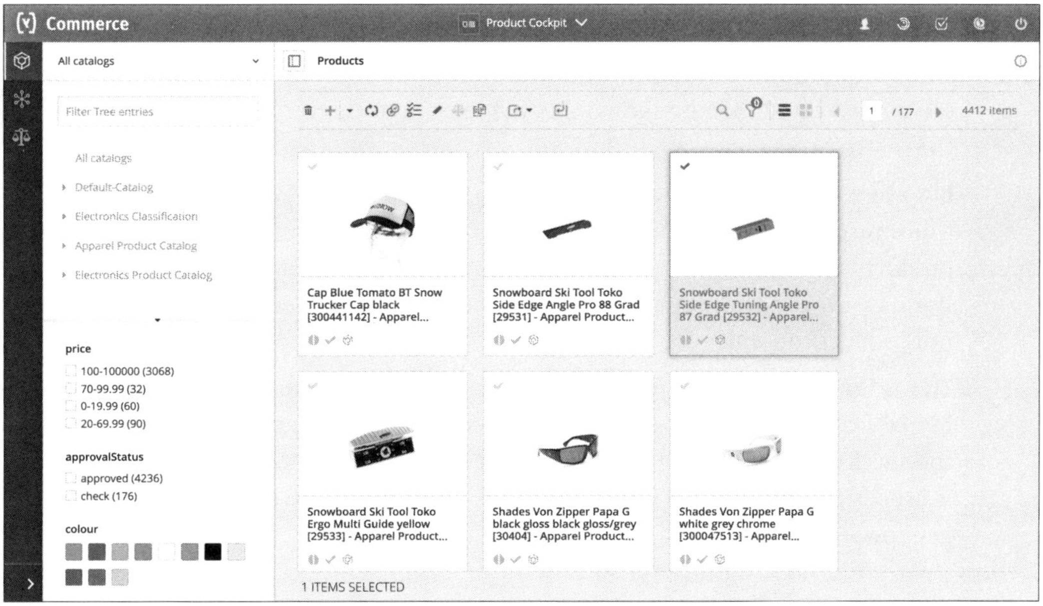

Figure 8.15 Faceted Search in Backoffice

This backoffice Product Cockpit search can be configured in the `backofficesolrsearch` extension, via `SolrFacetSearchConfig` and integrating with the `solrfacetsearch` extension. When `backofficesolrsearch` is active, the system will have the additional `BackofficeIndexedTypeToSolrFacetSearchConfig` type. When a user performs a search invoking this composed type, the system chooses a `FieldSearchFacadeStrategy` and will generally choose the `DefaultSolrFieldSearchFacadeStrategy`.

8.6 Indexing Nonproduct Content

Not every SAP Commerce implementation will include an index for product data. After all, not every SAP Commerce implementation has a product catalog—and even those that do often house data that is not related to products, or at least not related to any specific product or category. This content could include learning materials, manuals, event information, and perhaps even press about business, whether in the form of text, video, or audio.

If your customers search *primarily* on product information, then the simplest way to add these kinds of content to your search is to associate them with product data. A fashion retailer, for example, might keep an archive of videos from New York Fashion Week and tag those videos with the products or categories featured in the videos. Customers could then be shown these videos (or at the very least, links to them) on the search results page.

But as we alluded to earlier, this is not the right approach for every situation. Sometimes customers truly aren't searching for products, or even content that is related to products in any clear or predictable way, when they perform a keyword search. In these cases, you will want your onsite search engine to keep a searchable index of nonproduct content.

This is fundamentally no problem for Solr, which after all was not built for SAP Commerce searches specifically. As discussed earlier in this chapter, Solr simply indexes the specified attributes on a specified type in SAP Commerce—and though this type is usually `product`, it could just as easily be `page` or `component`, or something even more generic, such as `document`.

8.7 Summary

Configuring your onsite search properly is, for most businesses, the single most effective way of giving your customers a strong first impression of your storefront and a positive experience interacting with it. Even for those business that do not place search and navigation quite so firmly at the core of their SAP Commerce experience, there are enormous benefits to indexing your relevant data properly and empowering your team to maintain and configure it strategically. In SAP Commerce, these settings can be robust, appropriate to your goals, and highly personalized.

Search and navigation are fairly pervasive notions in SAP Commerce, but some concepts are *so* pervasive that we simply couldn't fit them comfortably into any individual chapter. When we talk about personalization, for example, what are the core functionalities that allow us to sort users into groups, and then to divvy up content and access based on those group memberships? When we talk about localizing content, how does the system define the differences (and similarities and overlaps) among regions?

In the next chapter, we will discuss these broader cross-module topics, providing a closer look at concepts and features that are crucial to some aspects, and relevant to *all* aspects, of SAP Commerce.

Chapter 9
Cross-Module Topics

In the previous chapters of this book, we've referred extensively to concepts such as restrictions and permissions, as well as to the platform's strategies for internationalization. These are pervasive concepts throughout the SAP Commerce suite. In this chapter, we'll take some time to explain each in greater detail.

In this chapter, we will discuss topics that don't fit neatly into any of the previous or preceding topics but that are key to any SAP Commerce implementation. There is no clearer example of this than the SAP Commerce accelerators—which, even in projects that don't use their codebase, is critical to consider as a sample deployment, a set of best practices, and a set of default configurations and sample data.

First, we will take a deep dive into users, user groups, and permissions—the heart and soul of customer accounts, employee roles, and authorizations throughout SAP Commerce. Next, we will discuss the SAP Commerce approach to internationalization and other forms of localization, including the management of multiple languages and currencies within a single selling experience and some key best practices for multi-country rollouts. Finally, we will discuss search engine optimization (SEO) and crafting your approach to making your site or sites as prominent, discoverable, and accurately represented as possible on external search engines such as Google.

9.1 Users, User Groups, and Permissions

As discussed in Chapter 1, restrictions are used pervasively throughout SAP Commerce to present data conditionally. Time restrictions determine when a given promotional banner might show up on the storefront or when a certain product or promotion might become available to a given customer, for example. The scope of restrictions goes well beyond that, however. They do drive customer segmentation and personalization, as well as content scheduling, but they also drive backoffice permissions for employees and the conditional display of internationalized or localized content (both on the storefront and in the backoffice).

For this reason, restrictions present a unique and useful opportunity to discuss SAP Commerce functions that do not fit neatly into any single module and, more importantly, to discuss how these modules fit together.

In this section, we will focus on user group restrictions, which allow users or groups of users to view (and in the case of employees, create, edit, or delete) data within the SAP Commerce system. User group restrictions are the heart and soul of employee authorization and provisioning *and* customer segmentation in SAP Commerce, and in this section you will learn how to use them effectively, efficiently, and in accordance with best practices. We'll begin by defining our terms.

9.1.1 What Is a User?

A *user* is, simply, anyone with access to any part of the SAP Commerce system, whether that means the storefront, the internal toolset, or some combination of the two.

Within the SAP Commerce type system, there are two subtypes of users by default: customers and employees. Customers generally have access only to the frontend and the ability to place orders on their own behalf. Employees generally have access only to the backoffice tooling.

It is possible for a user account to blur the lines between these two categories, as in the case of someone shopping on the web storefront and receiving an employee discount. The user in question would need either two accounts—one a customer account, the other an employee account—or a single account with some of the permissions of each.

In general, however, there will be a fairly firm separation between customer accounts on the one hand and employee accounts on the other, as is the case in the sample data. SAP Commerce accelerator storefronts come packaged with sample customers and employees for testing. Most of these should be deleted before go-live, on the off chance that a malicious user might guess the user IDs and passwords. There is, however, one default customer and one default employee that cannot be deleted: the anonymous user and the admin.

The *anonymous user* is a customer built to have the minimum possible storefront permissions: this is what someone sees when they come to your site and you don't know who they are yet. Some businesses will not show prices or will only show default prices to this customer, for example. In guest checkout scenarios, an automatically generated guest user account will be attached to the customer's session once they initiate checkout—but until then, and unless analytics are being collected on the user's session via SAP Marketing Cloud, the user is considered generic and anonymous.

The *admin* (shown in Figure 9.1) is an employee with complete, across-the-board access to the backoffice, the SAP Commerce administration console, and just about everything else. This account is enormously useful for development and debugging and cannot be deleted because it offers a failsafe in the case of functional admins getting locked out of the system—but this role should not be used day-to-day in production, and any security audit should ensure that the admin's default password (nimda) has been changed to a unique and considerably stronger one.

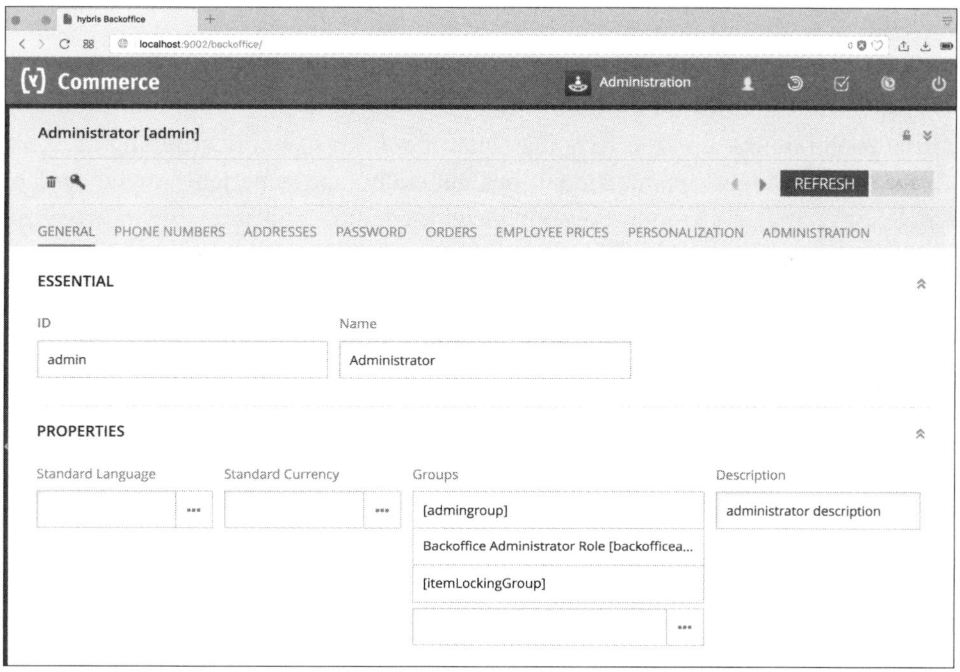

Figure 9.1 Built-In Admin Account

Access rights can be applied at the individual user level, but this is not recommended. This approach can result in scattered permissions, the source and intent of which are unclear, which is far from ideal from a security auditing perspective. Furthermore, if an employee changes roles or leaves the company, the transition process becomes a scavenger hunt for both the permissions that should be removed from that employee's account and those that should be added to it.

Instead, rights should be applied at the user group level. This makes the process of recategorizing customers, onboarding new employees, changing employee roles, or removing an employee from the system much more auditable and scalable. In the case of the default admin account, for example, the pervasive permissions actually come from the (also default) admin group.

User groups are the heart and soul of access and authorization in SAP Commerce, and mapping them to the project's own internal roles and processes should be the next step after settling on a data model. User groups really are that important, both from a security perspective and from a project planning perspective. Let's dive into how they work.

9.1.2 What Is a User Group?

A *user group* in SAP Commerce is just what it sounds like: any grouping of users. These can be purely organizational, but generally, and especially in the case of employee-facing user groups, they will have restrictions and access rights attached. Access rights apply read, write, create, and delete permissions to specific types and attributes of types within the SAP Commerce system.

Although they share an underlying framework and can be managed from the same interface, customer-facing and employee-facing user groups do serve different functions and should be considered somewhat separately when designing and building an SAP Commerce implementation—so before we go much further, we'll take a moment to consider them individually.

Employee-Facing User Groups

Employee-facing user groups are about access and authorization. They determine which employees are able to access which data and what they can do with that data, at both coarse-grained and fine-grained levels.

User groups establish permissions not only for types, but also for attributes of those types. Because you can apply permissions at the attribute level, and because you can establish read/write/create/delete permissions for each of these attributes, you can achieve a high degree of granularity in your employee roles—creating, for example, a merchant team that can see prices but cannot change them or an internationalization team that can see English-language values but can only change French-language values.

User groups can be nested. In every configuration of the SAP Commerce accelerators, for example, there is a user group called `EmployeeGroup`, under which there is a group for product content users, under which there is a group for product content creators and another distinct one for product content approvers and administrators. One such subgroup for product managers is shown in Figure 9.2.

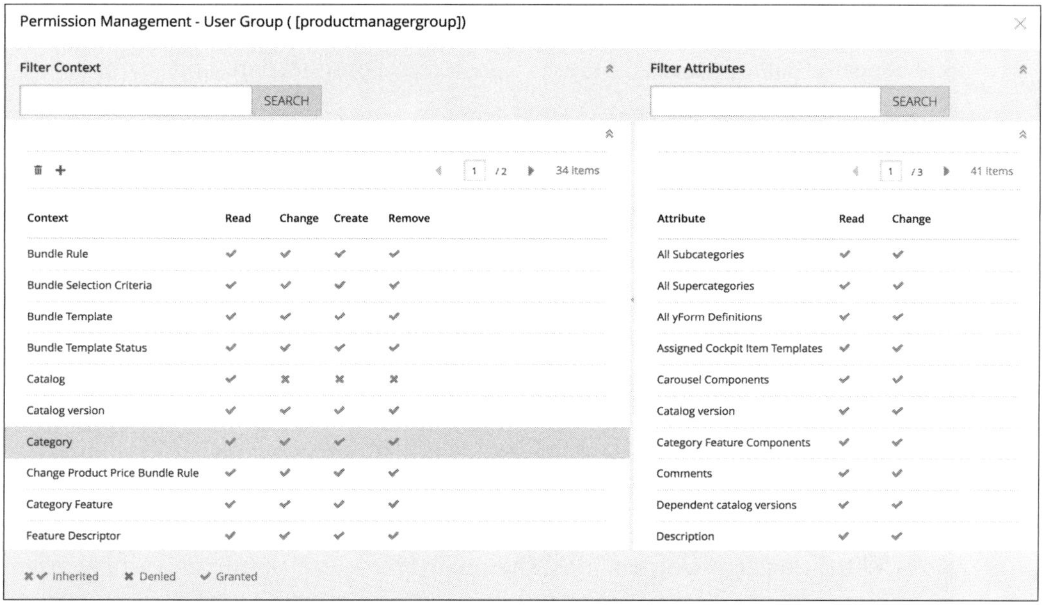

Figure 9.2 Permission Management Pop-Up in Admin Perspective of Backoffice, Showing Permissions for ProductManagerGroup

Because any or all of these groups may have permissions attached, the system has some built-in logic for resolving potential access conflicts. In short, the system will always privilege an explicit *no* over an implicit *yes*, generally defaulting to the most restrictive option available.

This means that, when nesting user groups, there are some best practices to keep in mind. First and foremost, be certain to avoid creating loops. If user group B is a member of user group A, then user group A should not also be a member of user group B. The system will not stop you from creating these loops.

Nor will the system prevent you from applying permissions directly to users rather than to user groups. There is no technical reason that permissions cannot be applied at the individual user level. This is against best practices, however, because it can easily result in "rogue" permissions that were not intended for product managers, say, but were applied selectively to one specific product manager. For the sake of security, compliance, and sanity, permissions should always be applied at the user group level.

As in the example of `EmployeeGroup`, you should begin by modeling a basic set of permissions that will be applicable to most, if not all, of your relevant users—all employees might need to be able to log into the backoffice, for example—and then nest more specific groups beneath: one for all employees who work with product data, one beneath that for those employees who *approve* product data, and so on.

This is the simplest way to ensure that employees in other departments or lines of business are not inadvertently granted access to data that should be able to view or edit. This approach also makes troubleshooting far more efficient if an employee's permissions are not behaving as expected: there should be one specific user group that is likely to be causing the issue and only a handful of user groups that possibly could be causing it.

User groups also have some high-level settings that live outside of the **Permission Management** screen, most notably read and write access to any catalog versions (both product catalogs and content catalogs) currently active in the system. Typically, few if any users and user groups will have direct write access to the online catalog versions because these should be updated through the synchronization process, as described in earlier chapters—and most content creators will only have write permissions for the staged catalog versions. These same high-level permissions apply to languages, as we'll discuss in Section 9.2.

Now that we've covered some key techniques (and pitfalls) for employee-facing user groups, let's turn our attention to customer-facing user groups.

Customer-Facing User Groups

Customer-facing user groups are for segmentation. They group your customers into whatever categories are most important to your business, thereby allowing SAP Commerce to service those customers with different products, prices, promotions, or content.

Very commonly, this means grouping customers by region. Businesses that serve both the United States and Canada will frequently create a user group for each country, sometimes with groups beneath the Canadian customer group for those customers who prefer to browse in English and those who prefer to browse in French.

Customer-facing user groups are equally useful for product catalogs that include multiple lines of business. B2B companies that sell to multiple buyers who should not see one another's product arrays can leverage user group restrictions to show or hide products or categories on a per-group basis. B2C companies can create products or categories that are exclusively for loyal customers. You can see an example of overlapping visibility, as viewed in SmartEdit, in Figure 9.3.

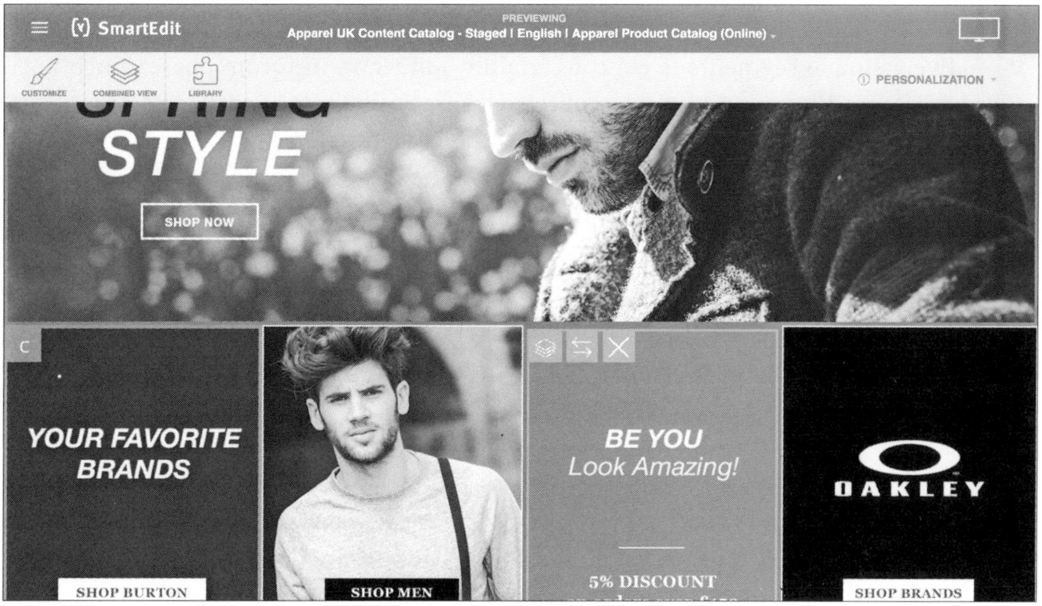

Figure 9.3 Personalization in SmartEdit, Showing Segment-Specific Content

Indeed, user groups are also useful for implementing customer loyalty. The SAP Commerce, B2C accelerator storefronts have three loyalty tiers modeled out of the box—`bronzeloyalty`, `silverloyalty`, and `goldloyalty`—tied to some default promotion templates and web content.

In an SAP Commerce-only installation, these groups are built manually. However, they can be tied to SAP Loyalty Marketing, a microservices-based solution that introduces point accumulation and spending, as well as automatic tier advancement, to the SAP Commerce accelerator storefronts. In this case, customers can accumulate points from orders and then pay for future orders in whole or in part using points.

Similarly, user groups themselves are built manually, or else via CronJobs, by default—but if you are running SAP Marketing Cloud or SAP Customer Profile, then you can leverage the golden record of your customers to build and enhance your customer-facing user groups. SAP Marketing Cloud, for example, incorporates data from outside of the SAP Commerce experience, including social media sentiments and orders from other channels, and continually generates customer segments via machine intelligence.

To what degree customer segments *should* be automated depends on the project. For a business that is still collecting customer information, still building a golden record, and/or still acclimating its customers to shopping online, a small number of relatively simple segments is almost certainly sufficient. In future phases, such businesses can then use their newly collected transactional data to enrich their segments, create new ones, and plan additional promotional initiatives.

User group restrictions also can be applied to prices, either on an individual basis or grouped together as *price lists*, which are exactly what they sound like: a list of prices on at least one (but usually several) products, mapped to a user group. Similarly, user groups can be associated with *discount groups* and *tax groups*, which group and assign promotions and tax rates, respectively.

Price lists are commonly associated with B2B loyalty groups, as described, but they are even more important in a B2B context.

9.1.3 B2B Customers and B2B Business Units

You might notice that the strict division between employees and customers—one group for the frontend, one for behind the scenes—somewhat assumes a traditional, B2C-focused flow, in which customers can place orders for themselves without the intervention of approvers, either within their own organization or within the organization from which they are buying. This is standard for retailing finished goods to customers, but not all businesses sell finished goods or sell directly to customers.

The standard customer type is, by default and in effect, a B2C customer; though that's not always obvious to those working on B2C projects, B2B customers tend to notice it almost immediately.

For this reason, there is a subtype of customer called B2B customer. This type contains all the attributes of a standard B2C customer, including user ID, password, email address, and user group membership, but adds attributes associated with the customer's role within the purchasing organization, as well as their approval flows.

This is the most important thing to understand about the user and customer types, and indeed about most types in SAP Commerce: the core attributes are functionally vital and designed to be used across verticals, but the types themselves are designed to be extensible. B2B is the cleanest and most commonly used example of extending this particular type, but it's far from the only real-world application of the concept. The same idea aligns user accounts with existing SAP ERP or SAP CRM data or creates roles for merchants and suppliers in a marketplace (B2B2C) scenario.

Just as a B2B customer extends the concept of customers, organizations and B2B business units extend the concept of user groups, offering the kind of mapping necessary in a purchasing organization that includes approvals, budgets, and cost centers. Organizations and B2B business units are fundamentally kinds of user groups. As such, their relationship to one another is highly customizable, as we will discuss in a moment.

With that said, the default structure of an organization in SAP Commerce mirrors a typical B2B purchaser, with an organization representing the company and B2B business units nested below the organization, representing different offices, regions, or lines of business. Cost centers are generally mapped to the B2B business unit level, as are addresses, so that only approved options for payment and shipment appear to a B2B customer during checkout.

As shown in Figure 9.4, in addition to being a member of at least one B2B business unit, a B2B customer will be a member of at least one user group associated with his role, the standard organizational roles being purchaser, approver, manager, and administrator. Purchasers can place orders, approvers can approve (or reject or negotiate) those orders, managers can set budgets and assign cost centers, and administrators can create users and assign roles within their organization. B2B price lists are typically assigned at the unit or cost center level, thereby providing a tailored list of prices to specific purchasers.

Some B2B businesses hide pricing from users without fully verified accounts (or simply do not let such users onto their site in the first place), but others maintain a list of default, base prices that appear to anonymous or provisional purchasers.

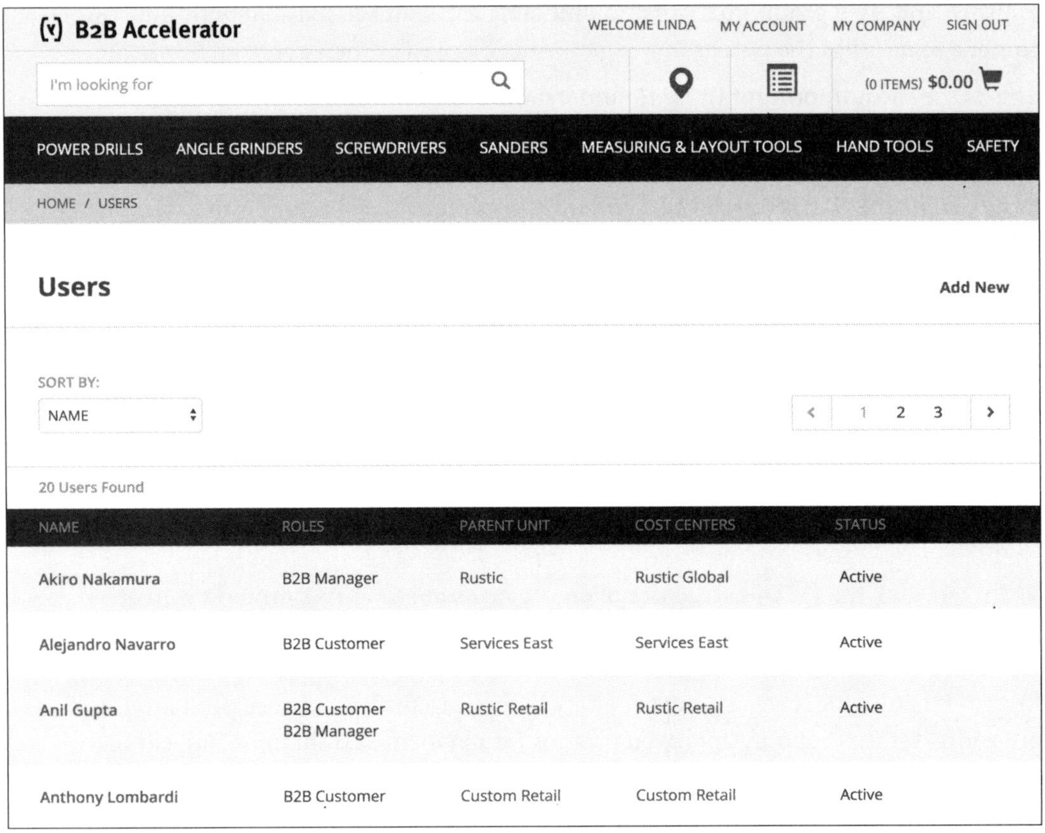

Figure 9.4 B2B Admin Self-Administration in Powertools Store in SAP Commerce, B2B Accelerator

9.1.4 Extending the User and User Group Types

The types `user` and `usergroup`, as well as their primary sub types, `employee`, `customer`, `organization`, and `business unit`, are core to SAP Commerce and generally should not be heavily altered during development. Adding attributes to these types is expected, but *removing* core attributes or changing their overall role in the system architecture is not recommended.

However, it is common practice to create subtypes of these types to accommodate business-specific logic.

For example, customers who purchase from different lines of business sometimes have very different attributes from one another on their accounts. This comes up frequently with businesses that work in both the B2C space and the B2B space, but it also occurs when companies simply sell in a wide variety of ways as a result of acquisitions or expansions.

Customers who buy flooring and customers who buy T-shirts may end up using the same interface but may need to see very different data and may need to have very different attributes attached to their user accounts. In this case, it would be common practice to create two new customer types, perhaps called `flooringcustomer` and `apparelcustomer`.

Even without that element of bifurcation, it might make sense to create a subtype of customer called `[businessname]customer` so that customizations made to the customer experience do not conflict with native functionality.

If during the foundational phase of your project you see many differences between the native SAP Commerce customer type and your own goals and requirements, consider mapping out a subtype of this sort early on to avoid having to alter the type system later on in development, when doing so can cause significant disruption.

9.1.5 User Groups in the SAP Commerce API

By exposing SAP Commerce user groups, customer segments can essentially be syndicated to other systems—taking the work you've done in SAP Commerce and beyond to get to know your customers and using those insights across channels. This is also of tremendous use if you plan on exposing your customer segments to other channels, such as native apps, in-store kiosks, or points of sale, in real time. If certain customer groups should receive certain special offers or special pricing, then using the API is the best way to make that segmentation omnichannel without relying on asynchronous sync.

Invoking user groups via the API is also necessary if you plan to leverage customer-facing SAP Commerce user groups in a nonaccelerator environment, so we will briefly discuss how to do so.

To retrieve a user group, use the following format of the `GET` method in the API. A request for a single user group would look like this:

```
GET /usergroups/{userGroupId}
```

A GET request for the bronzeloyaltygroup, then, would look like this:

```
GET ../usergroups/bronzeloyaltygroup
```

In addition to this getUserGroupById search method, you can use the findUserGroups method to search through your user groups using a text string. The latter is preferable when invoking specific user groups for SAP Commerce logic, but the latter can be useful when the consuming service needs to display or page through multiple groups. For example:

```
GET /usergroups?text={text}&pageSize={pageSize}&currentPage={currentPage}&
sort={sort}
```

This example shows every possible parameter that you can set when using the GET method for this purpose, including pagination, sorting, and the values that will be returned.

In line with the model-view-controller principle, the user group API declares three Spring beans: defaultCmsUserGroupFacade, defaultCmsUserGroupDataConverter, and defaultCmsUserGroupDataPopulator, the parameters for all of which can be set in the cmsfacades-usergroup-spring.xml file.

9.2 Internationalization and Localization

Localization is a native feature of both product and web content in SAP Commerce, and the platform is remarkably flexible in terms of the relationships among various territories, languages, and currencies. This is one of the platform's greatest strengths, but the sheer number of potential configurations also can be daunting.

In this section, we'll look at your options for localizing and internationalizing content in SAP Commerce, with an eye toward mapping these options to the problems that they solve and the scenarios that they best serve.

9.2.1 Data Structure

Any attribute can be multilingual in SAP Commerce, just so long as that attribute does not require a single, canonical, unique value. Article numbers and validity periods, then, cannot be internationalized—but product identifiers, short and long descriptions, prices, media, and SEO metadata can.

As database entries, internationalized values are marked with a language marker. These markups retrieve either strings or resource bundles to present the localized values to the proper users.

The English-language value for a product's description, for example, would be listed as `descripton_en`. This is the convention when there is a single version of each language, but in the case of more specific regionalization, a second underscore and second code is generally included. So businesses that sell to both the United States and the United Kingdom might have both `descripton_en_us` and `descripton_en_uk` to account for differences in vocabulary and spelling.

In the backoffice, end users can immediately recognize a localizable field by the globe icon next to it. Clicking this icon will expose a list of fields for the localized value of this attribute. As discussed in the previous section, these fields can be readable or writeable for only certain employees, based on their user group permissions, as shown in Figure 9.5.

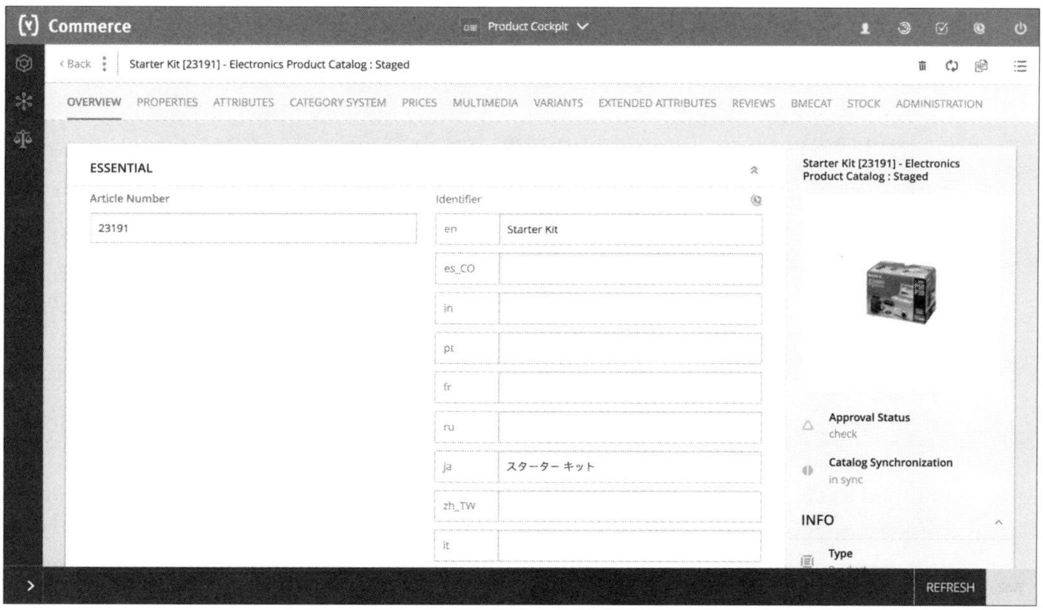

Figure 9.5 Product in Backoffice Product Cockpit Perspective, Showing Globe Icon for Attribute's Identifier and Description

In SAP Commerce, `ServiceLayer` includes a package called `i18N`—an abbreviation for "internationalization," referring to the 18 letters between the *i* and the *n*. Here you can alter both Java platform objects (such as `Currency` and `TimeZone`) and SAP Commerce objects (such as `LanguageModel`, `CurrencyModel`, and `CountryModel`). The relationships among these objects is not always one-to one, even when the terminology overlaps.

The `Locale` Java object is of particular note because there is no single SAP Commerce type that corresponds to it directly. Instead, locales are built as a combination of the SAP Commerce objects `LanguageModel`, `CountryModel`, and `RegionModel`.

This is because countries/regions, languages, and currencies are uncoupled by default, providing maximum flexibility. Let's look at each, with specific attention paid to what makes them distinct, how they interact, and why some projects might need to heavily configure or customize while leaving the others relatively close to default settings.

9.2.2 Countries and Regions

SAP Commerce differentiates between a *country* and a *region*, with the latter being a subset of the former, but they do serve similar functions—namely, providing tags with which to associate tax groups, warehouses, and other highly geography-specific elements to the correct user sessions and transactions on the frontend.

A business might establish a single fallback distribution center for the Midwestern United States, but then have additional distribution centers for Illinois, Wisconsin, and so on. In this case, the Midwest would be set as a region, with the states nested beneath it as additional regions. All of this would, naturally, be nested under the United States as a country, as shown in Figure 9.6.

It is important to keep in mind that most restrictions on the accelerator storefronts do *not* take country or region directly into consideration. Prices can be associated with currencies, as discussed ahead, and products, categories, and content can be mapped to catalogs or user groups, but the SAP Commerce system does not support country or region restrictions out of the box. They are intended to be lightweight parameters associated with transactional objects, rather than being pervasive to the frontend experience in the way that catalogs or user groups are.

With that said, we have seen organizations create their own country or region restriction types, with some success. If the techniques described in Chapter 3, Section 3.5 do not provide adequate localization for your project, then creating a custom restriction type might be worth considering.

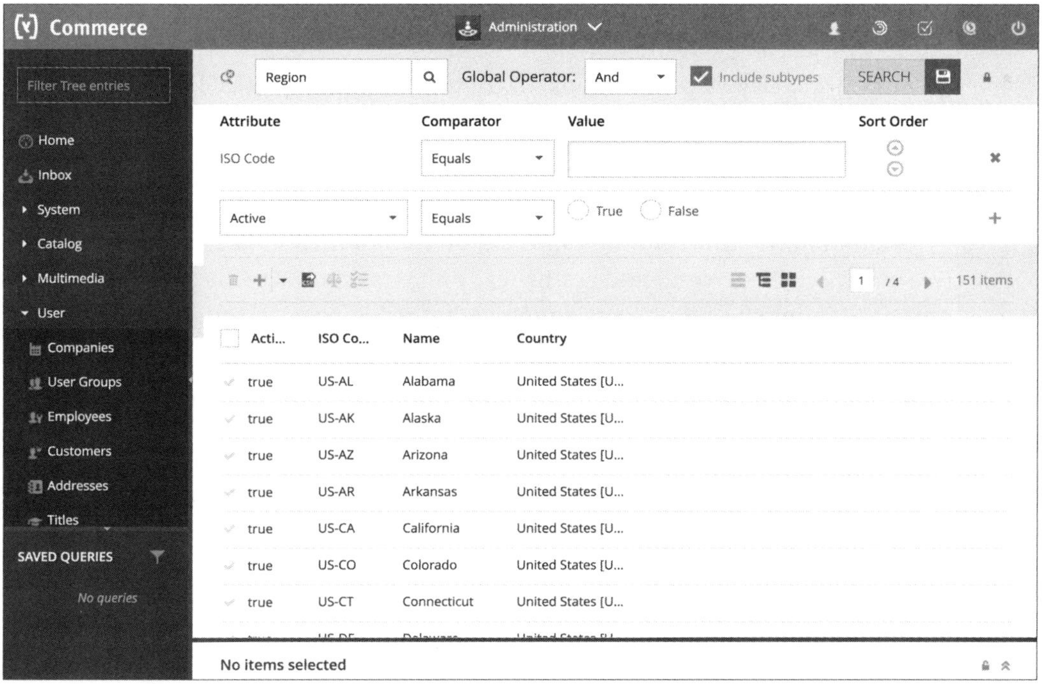

Figure 9.6 United States of America: Example of Regions in Accelerator Sample Data

If you do take this approach, be sure to leverage the existing country and/or region objects in SAP Commerce rather than creating your own. Otherwise, you could end up with two sets of objects with overlapping functionality—one set of regions for transnationality, one for catalog restrictions—and significant confusion can result during testing.

9.2.3 Currencies

The simplest way to achieve multicurrency pricing in SAP Commerce is to create price rows in a single base currency, then dynamically populate values for other currencies using a conversation rate. In the backoffice admin perspective, users can simply navigate to the **Internationalization** node, select the target currency, and establish that, for example, one Euro equals 1.25 US dollars. Although this approach is the simplest, it is not right for every project.

Currencies in SAP Commerce can also have their own prices and price lists associated with them. To achieve this, in the admin or Product Cockpit perspectives of the backoffice, users can navigate to the **Prices** tab of a product's information, then add prices with currency restrictions. Like user group or time restrictions, currency restrictions display data conditionally—in this case, tying a specific price for a specific product to a specific currency.

Most businesses find this approach preferable to a flat conversation table for two reasons. First, on-the-fly conversion can result in numbers that do not conform to the convention of whole dollars, or 49, 50, 95, or 99 cent increments, which some businesses (especially in retail) find aesthetically displeasing and some customers (again, especially in retail) find off-putting. Assigning prices to each product for each currency in which it can be purchased prevents this problem.

Second, it is not necessarily the case that your products will cost the same (even after currency conversion) in each currency. Your price in US dollars, converted directly to Mexican pesos, might be higher than the local market expects. So again, it can be advantageous to give regional merchants more control, as opposed to allowing a single equation to determine all international pricing based on a single primary price. You can see some of these parameters in Figure 9.7, which shows a Backoffice Product Cockpit user adding a new price row to an existing product.

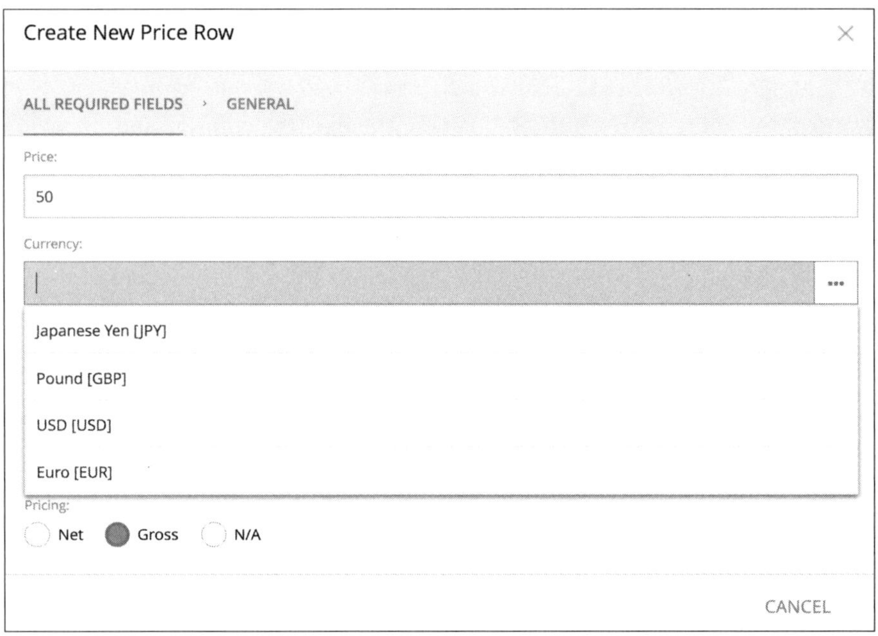

Figure 9.7 Adding Price Row with Currency Restriction for Euros in Product Cockpit Perspective of Backoffice

Now, you might be thinking, what about different regions that share a currency but should not necessarily have the same prices? Couldn't the discrepancy issue we just described apply to Germany and Hungary as well as to the United States and Mexico?

It most certainly could, and indeed the European Union is a part of the world where different regions might share a currency without necessarily sharing prices. In this case, prices would probably not be assigned at the currency level but rather by user group, storefront, or catalog. Some businesses that sell through the European Union maintain separate web storefronts or different product catalogs within a single web storefront for their different European customers, which makes good sense when the product assortment, search behavior, and/or promotions are different for each country or region.

If these different European countries see most or all of the same products, however, then the most common solution is to sort customers into user groups, divided up in whatever way the prices themselves are divided up. If Western Europe has one set of prices and Eastern Europe has another, for example, then two customer-facing user groups are sufficient and there is no need to further divide the customers up by country or territory.

But if each country has its own prices, then it may make good sense to create a user group for each country. Users might be initially placed into these groups based on a menu selection on the frontend or based on the location service in their browser. If and when they create customer accounts, their regional user group membership should be confirmed and finalized based on their shipping and/or billing addresses (though shipping address is generally the better choice because in most countries it is the shipping address that determines tax rates and other fees that may affect the final price).

9.2.4 Languages

In the SAP Commerce suite, the term *language* refers both to a discreet written language, such as English or French, and to a national or regional variation on one of those languages, such as US English, UK English, Canadian French, or France French. As already discussed, these languages are stored in the system and represented in attributes using underscores and two-letter codes: `_en` for English, `en_us` for US English, and so on.

If you set a *default language*—usually English for US customers—then fields without localized values will show the default values instead. This is useful in line of business, such as manufacturing, in which some highly technical attributes will not benefit from translation. Those values that need to be localized can be, and the rest will be global by default (see Figure 9.8).

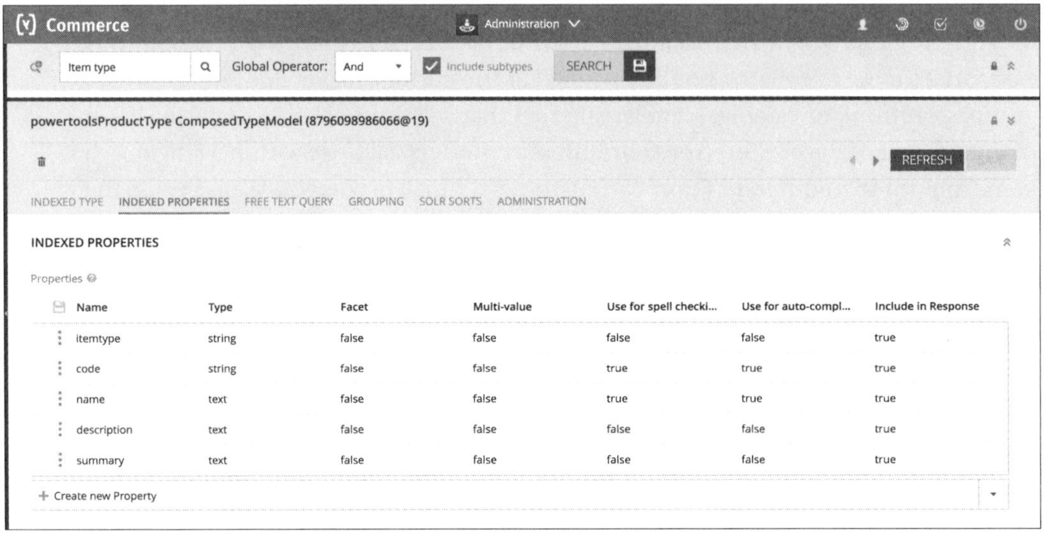

Figure 9.8 Internationalized Attribute in Search Index, as Seen in Backoffice

The SAP Commerce accelerator storefronts ship with sample data in English, German, Chinese, and Japanese, but SAP Commerce supports far more languages than that out of the box, with native support for Spanish (both Latin-American Spanish and Spain Spanish), Portuguese, (both Brazilian Portuguese and Portugal Portuguese), French, Italian, Polish, Russian, Korean, Bahasa Indonesia, Hindi, and Czech. The basic buttons and navigation of the backoffice are natively available in all of these languages, even though UI elements for the end customer frontend are not.

It is important to consider that these languages may not be native in all the technologies with which you are integrating. Solr, for example, does not currently have native support for Spanish—so if your project requires Spanish as one of its languages, you will need to build in time for additional configuration and installation, even though Spanish is one of the out-of-the-box languages in SAP Commerce itself.

Languages in SAP Commerce can alter currency display conventions regardless of the currency itself. For example, European storefronts tend to use commas in place of decimal points (and vice versa) and place the currency symbol after the number rather than before it—so a product in the electronics store that costs $99.95 will display its cost as 99,95$ if the user is browsing in German but paying in US dollars.

As described in the section on user groups, employee roles can be mapped to read or write permissions for a given language to regionalize teams or, for example, allow the team translating into French to write to French-language fields while only being able to view English-language values.

9.2.5 Multicountry Rollouts

For implementations that serve a wide variety of countries, there are some important architectural choices to make, and they should be made as soon as possible. In short, how connected do you want your different regions to be?

The electronics store is an example of the most unified approach, in which there is a single product catalog, a single content catalog, and a single set of promotions for all four of the countries served by the site. There are several assumptions reflected in this setup.

First and foremost, it assumes that customers browsing in Japan, China, Germany, and the United States should all have access to most, if not all, of the same products. As discussed previously, this does not necessarily mean that these products are offered at the same prices or in the same quantities—and if there are *some* products that should be available in China but not Japan, say, then this can be achieved via currency restrictions or user group restrictions. But a single-site, single-catalog architecture generally does operate on the assumption that there is significant overlap among the products available in different regions.

Second, and perhaps just as importantly, the setup in the electronics store assumes that the merchants and marketers for these different regions are working very closely together, or else that there is a single, global product team approving their work holistically before it goes live. This is because in an architecture in which regions share a single product catalog, a full catalog version synchronization would synchronize *every* region's products. If the regional teams are not working closely, or if there is no global team giving the entire product data set a final pass, the Japanese could accidentally send incomplete data from China live, for example.

You could mitigate this issue by creating selective synchronization jobs, thereby allowing Japan to sync only those product or categories that are ready for launch. But remember that *a single product* is the smallest unit that can be synchronized at a given time. Without significant customization, you cannot sync a single attribute *on* a product. So if the products or categories because of their Japanese values also have new values in Chinese, those new values will be almost certainly included in the sync, whether or not they are ready to be.

In scenarios in which the regional reams require greater autonomy, you might consider something closer to what is demonstrated in the apparel store. Here there is still only one product catalog—though its contents are localized, just like the product and category content in the electronics store—but there are two separate content catalogs, one for the United Kingdom and one for Germany.

To the end customer, the difference between these two approaches might be, and probably should be, invisible. But to any team that works on web content, the difference in autonomy can be immense. With two separate content catalogs, UK marketers or merchandizers can launch a new page or promotion, update the layout of the homepage, or make some other eye-catching change, without having to inform the German team.

The setup in the apparel store, would not remove any of the complications described earlier in the context of *product* data because there is still only one product catalog active. But the design principle it demonstrates could easily be inverted, with two regions sharing a content catalog but each having its own product catalog.

This can be a powerful approach in any project in which teams operate autonomously. Even for businesses for which data always begins in a primary region and in a canonical primary language, it is common practice to send that base data to each region for translation, region-specific merchandizing and marketing, new photography of local packaging, and so on. This process does not always involve checking back with the global headquarters because it is after all the local team's responsibility to know what will work in the team's region. In this particular scenario, it may be wise to consider the *master catalog* design principle, as shown in Figure 9.9.

None of the current SAP Commerce accelerator storefronts demonstrate the idea of master catalogs, but the premise is simple enough: All products that would be sold in *any* region (or by any line of business or to any purchasing organization) live in a single catalog. This catalog is built and maintained by the global team, or else by all regional teams collaboratively. All attributes that are common to all these products will be added at this master catalog level, probably via the type system, and any values that are the same for every region (such as article number) should be filled in at this level, or else during initial data load from SAP ERP, SAP S/4HANA, or another source system. Future changes to these attributes and values will always take place at the master catalog level.

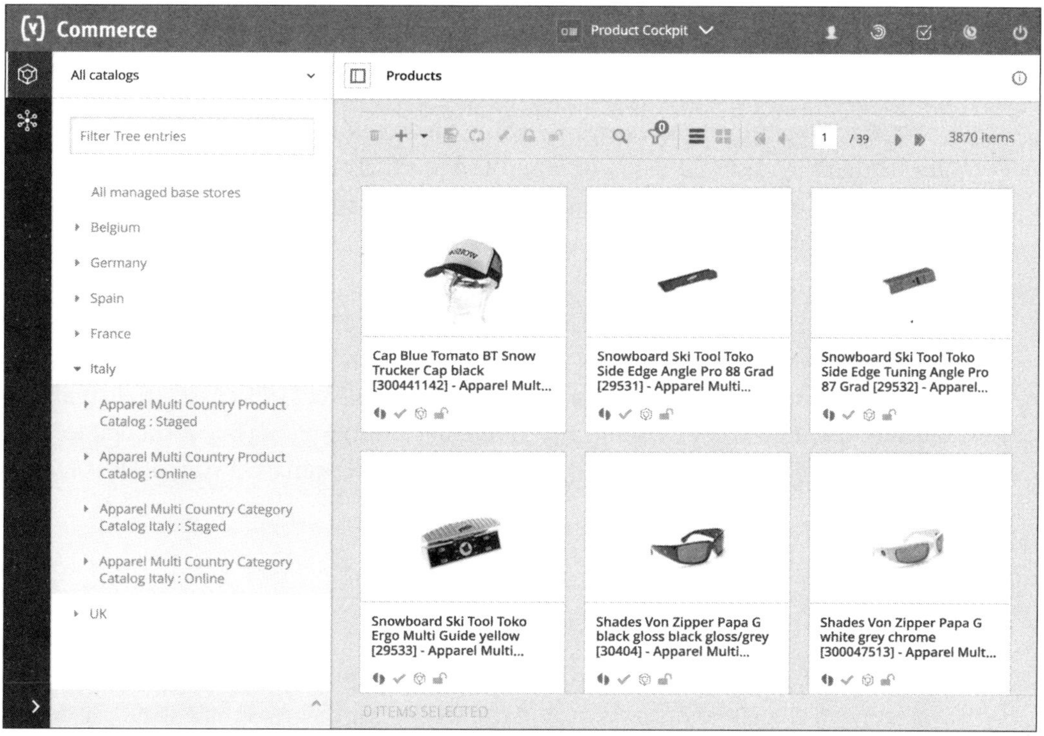

Figure 9.9 Product Cockpit Perspective of Backoffice, with Master Catalog and Several Country-Specific Base Stores Enabled

Using selective synchronization, these products and categories will then populate multiple regional catalogs. Any attributes that are specific to these regions will be added here, probably by the classification system, and any values that are specific to localities (such as translated identifiers and descriptions) will be added in each regional catalog. Any changes to these attributes or to product pricing or availability will be made at the regional catalog level.

You can then repeat this process, dividing up the content of the regional catalog into multiple country-specific catalogs. You might have a regional catalog for Europe, say, with catalogs for France, Germany, and Italy beneath it. Each of these catalogs could be managed by separate teams, with all the benefits thereof, without the central, global leadership team giving up the ability to create content at the global or broader regional level.

This approach offers each region the freedom to reorganize, synchronize, merchandize, and market without the intervention of a central approver or admin while also maintaining a single source of truth within SAP Commerce for base product data.

Master catalogs are unnecessary when only a few regions are in play, when all regions are handled by a single team, or when the product data set is the same across all regions and mostly static once deployed. But in faster-moving or less centralized business, master catalogs can mitigate risk significantly and increase efficiency markedly.

The core question throughout this section has been: How do you want your content to be seen? In the last section of this chapter, we will discuss the equally important goal of making sure that your content gets seen at all. Let's discuss a topic that concerns every project, goes beyond any individual module of this book, and indeed goes well beyond SAP Commerce—but that SAP Commerce can help you tackle. Let's talk about SEO.

9.3 Search Engine Optimization

There is no way to fully automate your search engine optimization, by which we really mean Google optimization, and the reason for that is Google itself. By design, the algorithm by which Google ranks pages and sites is secret and constantly in flux.

Of course, to say that the rules are constantly changing is not to say that there are no rules, and acknowledging some measure of inconsistency is not the same thing as giving up on consistency. All of Google's ever-shifting SEO preferences stem from a few key principles.

For example, Google will always reward a site for having a lot of legitimate links to it; conversely, it will consistently ding a website for repetitive content. These two rules are related. Some sites attempt to game the system by spamming links in a circular fashion, hundreds or thousands at a time, back to a single source. Google therefore uses repetitive content as a red flag for illegitimate linking.

These two principles have wide-ranging effects. Legitimate links to your site are good, which is all the more reason to maintain a social media presence. Repetitive content is bad, which is all the more reason to leverage the variant system within SAP Commerce, storing the description of a product family at the base level rather than copy-pasting it to each variant.

Some of the knock-on effects are stranger and harder to account for, however. In 2016, Google decided somewhat arbitrarily that responsive websites would be preferable to adaptive ones, partially because of the repetitive content rule. Then in 2017, it backtracked on this somewhat, providing guidelines for mobile site SEO regardless of responsiveness.

All this is to say that the specific rules are essentially their own field of study and outside the scope of this book—but the general, evergreen principles of good SEO will outlast those microlevel changes, and indeed may well outlast the search engine dominance of Google, if we can imagine that far ahead.

In this section, we'll focus on how SAP Commerce enables SEO content injection, with the full understanding that the content itself can never be fully automatic or algorithmic because your content will always be specific to your business—and content will always be king.

9.3.1 URL Construction

SAP Commerce builds its URLs for products and categories out of three primary parts. First, there is the base URL of the website, as defined in the backoffice. Second, there is the category tree, as the URL will show the path from a top-level category down to the product or category currently being viewed. Third, there is the unique identifier for the product or category, shown at the end of the URL after */p/* in the case of products and */c/* in the case of categories.

The advantages of this approach are twofold: it means that SEO-friendly category names will automatically lead to SEO-friendly URLs, and it means that URLs will appear in the user's current language without the need for repetitive content. In a product page URL, German-language users will see the German value for the name of each category and for the product, even though they're seeing the same unique category that an English-language user would.

These rules are governed by `DefaultProductDataUrlResolver` and the `DefaultCategoryDataUrlResolver`, with anointed bindings to `ProductPageController` and `CategoryPageController`.

The SAP Commerce accelerators offer a default configuration for these resolvers, and this default can be used as is or taken as a sample or template in the *commercefacades-spring.xml* file, as shown in Listing 9.1.

```
<alias name="defaultCategoryDataUrlResolver" alias=
"categoryDataUrlResolver" />
<bean id="defaultCategoryDataUrlResolver" class=
"de.hybris.platform.commercefacades.url.impl.DefaultCategoryDataUrlResolver">
<property name="commerceCategoryService" ref="commerceCategoryService"/>
<property name="pattern" value="/{category-path}/c/{category-code}"/>
</bean>

<alias name="defaultProductDataUrlResolver" alias="productDataUrlResolver" />
<bean id="defaultProductDataUrlResolver" class=
"de.hybris.platform.commercefacades.url.impl.DefaultProductDataUrlResolver">
<property name="commerceCategoryService" ref="commerceCategoryService"/>
<property name="productService" ref="productService"/>
<property name="pattern" value="/{category-path}/{product-name}/p/{product-
code}"/>
</bean>
```

Listing 9.1 Default Resolver in commercefacades-spring.xml

Again, these default settings are based on best practices and are broadly applicable—but SEO is a moving target, and it is by customizing these readily available properties that you can achieve other, preferred URL constructions. Maybe you prefer a "flat" URL with only a product identifier after your root URL. In that case, you can remove the CategoryDataUrlResolver from the URL construction process and have the ProductDataUrlResolver retrieve only the product's identifier. The process of URL construction is modular, in that sense, and therefore easily tweaked to the particularities of your project.

It bears mentioning that URLs are not purely for machine consumption. Customers do see them, and, especially in the case of B2Bs, customers may even frequently type them—so it is perfectly reasonable for businesses to consider URLs from an aesthetic point of view as well as a purely functional one. Even if the default SAP Commerce accelerators URL construction is entirely adequate from a pure SEO perspective, implementation teams should still expect to at least tweak the settings described.

9.3.2 Sitemaps

We're probably dating ourselves by so much as mentioning HTML sitemaps, which were a common practice for showing users the structure of a website in the earlier days of the web. Nowadays, customers are extremely unlikely to seek out an HTML sitemap, preferring to browse top-level categories or, increasingly, to begin their commerce experience with a keyword search.

But sitemaps still serve an important function. It's just that the audience for them is no longer human users but rather the "spiders" that search engines use to "crawl" your website and index its content. These bots aren't looking for HTML sitemaps. They're looking for crisp, unambiguous XML.

This is especially important in an SAP Commerce context. A product that exists in multiple categories does not have a canonical URL as such—because, as we've discussed, the URL is constructed on the fly, based on category structure, language, and article number—and though that does *not* count as repetitive content by Google's definition, it can easily create the *appearance* of repetitive content.

To address this potential problem, SAP Commerce generates XML sitemaps automatically, clearly spelling out the uniqueness of products and the many-to-many relationships of products to categories. These are located after the root URL of the SAP Commerce accelerator storefronts, at */sitemap.xml*. If you are running the electronics store locally, for example, you will find the sitemap at *http://electronics.local:9001/yacceleratorstorefront/sitemap.xml*.

Depending on how often your products appear, disappear, and change, you may want to generate a sitemap as often as hourly or as seldom as annually, and you can make these sorts of changes in the `acceleratorservices` extension by assigning one of the following values to the `SiteMapChangeFrequencyEnum` attribute: `always`, `hourly`, `daily`, `weekly`, `monthly`, `yearly`, or `never`. A product catalog—and more specifically and perhaps more importantly, a category structure—that is more or less static after go-live will not require frequent sitemap generation; a product catalog that changes often or a content catalog that is heavy on important and timely content will.

Likewise, you can select the page types invoked in the sitemap in the `acceleratorservices` extension by assigning one or more of the following values to the `SiteMapPageEnum` attribute: `homepage`, `product`, `category`, `categoryLanding`, `store`, `content`, and/or `custom`.

If you change your URL construction or if you have specific requirements for your sitemap that are not covered in the default settings, then you will need to change your sitemap settings accordingly.

In this case, you would extend the `de.hybris.platform.acceleratorservices.sitemap.generator.impl.AbstractSiteMapGenerator` abstract generator, which itself implements the de.hybris.platform.acceleratorservices.sitemap.generator.SiteMapGenerator interface.

Each SiteMapPageEnum has its own generator bean in Spring, and each of these has its own populator bean, as shown in Table 9.1.

SiteMapPageEnum	Bean ID	Bean Class
HOMEPAGE	homePageSiteMapGenerator	de.hybris.platform.acceleratorservices.sitemap.generator.impl.HomePageSiteMapGenerator
PRODUCT	productPageSiteMapGenerator	de.hybris.platform.acceleratorservices.sitemap.generator.impl.ProductPageSiteMapGenerator
CATEGORY	categoryPageSiteMapGenerator	de.hybris.platform.acceleratorservices.sitemap.generator.impl.CategoryPageSiteMapGenerator
CATEGORYLANDING	categoryLandingPageSiteMapGenerator	de.hybris.platform.acceleratorservices.sitemap.generator.impl.CategoryLandingPageSiteMapGenerator
STORE	pointOfServicePageSiteMapGenerator	de.hybris.platform.acceleratorservices.sitemap.generator.impl.PointOfServicePageSiteMapGenerator

Table 9.1 SiteMapPageEnums and Associated Bean IDs and Classes

These generators are listed in the de.hybris.platform.acceleratorservices.cronjob.SiteMapMediaJob CronJob, which then generates and posts the sitemap on the schedule you've set.

Finally, the populators for these generator beans are shown in Table 9.2.

Generator Bean ID	Populator Bean ID	Populator Bean Class
homePageSiteMapGenerator	homepageToSiteMapUrlDataPopulator	de.hybris.platform.acceleratorservices.sitemap.populators.ContentPageModelToSiteMapUrlDataPopulator
productPageSiteMapGenerator	productModelToSiteMapUrlDataPopulator	de.hybris.platform.acceleratorservices.sitemap.populators.ProductModelToSiteMapUrlDataPopulator
categoryPageSiteMapGenerator	categoryModelToSiteMapUrlDataPopulator	de.hybris.platform.acceleratorservices.sitemap.populators.CategoryModelToSiteMapUrlDataPopulator
categoryLandingPageSiteMapGenerator	categoryModelToSiteMapUrlDataPopulator	de.hybris.platform.acceleratorservices.sitemap.populators.CategoryModelToSiteMapUrlDataPopulator
pointOfServicePageSiteMapGenerator	pointOfServiceModellToSiteMapUrlDataPopulator	de.hybris.platform.acceleratorservices.sitemap.populators.PointOfServiceModellToSiteMapUrlDataPopulator
contentPageModelSiteMapGenerator	contentPageModelToSiteMapUrlDataPopulator	de.hybris.platform.acceleratorservices.sitemap.populators.ContentPageModelToSiteMapUrlDataPopulator
customPageSiteMapGenerator	customPageToSiteMapUrlDataPopulator	de.hybris.platform.acceleratorservices.sitemap.populators.CustomPageToSiteMapUrlDataPopulator

Table 9.2 Populator Bean IDs and Classes for Each Generator Bean ID

9.3.3 Metadata: Descriptions and Keywords

SAP Commerce provides fields for metadata keywords and metadata descriptions. These elements are generally referred to as *metadata* in SEO because they are not so much the content of the page (or product or category) as they are content *about* that content. The values of these attributes are generally passed to the header of the page on which the content in question displays and, as with the XML sitemap described in the previous section, the audience for this metacontent is not human customers but search engines.

SAP Commerce provides metadata keyword and metadata description fields for every product and category and, in the case of SAP Commerce accelerator storefronts, every content page. Product and category metadata can be edited from the Product Cockpit perspective in the backoffice, and metadata for content pages (such as the homepage, **Contact Us** page, and **FAQ** page) can be edited in the CMS Cockpit or in the admin perspective in the backoffice.

It might seem odd to divide SEO metadata content, which is usually managed by a single team or even a single individual, between the product catalog and the content catalog. However, this quirk is a consequence of the way in which pages are generated in the SAP Commerce accelerators and, more broadly, of the way that data is segregated in SAP Commerce generally to serve omnichannel or non-SAP Commerce accelerators projects.

As discussed in Chapter 5, only content pages (such as the homepage) are static in SAP Commerce. This does not mean that content on such pages cannot be personalized or made dynamic, but simply that the pages were built and laid out by hand at some point during the content development cycle. Someone has to build a content page; by the same token, the assumption is that someone will build the SEO content for it.

Product and category pages, as you will recall, work differently. They are truly dynamic, with the most important parts of the pages not living on a *page* per se. On a product detail page, the body is generated from the product catalog, grabbing current values in the local language from the appropriate product record on the fly. On category pages, as discussed in Chapter 8, the content you're seeing is another step removed from the page itself—generated not from the product catalog directly, but primarily from the Solr index of the appropriate product content.

Because product and category pages are built on the fly from product data, so too is the SEO content pulled on the fly from the product catalog.

That said, by default these fields will still need to be filled in within the product catalog. Either a user or group of users will need to enter it by hand, or it will need to be bulk imported—unless, that is, you would like these fields to populate on a truly automated basis directly from your existing product data. Some customers, especially those with a robust SEO practice, prefer to manage their descriptions and keywords manually (as shown in Figure 9.10), favoring human decision-making and knowledge at every step of the process, while others prefer the convenience and machine intelligence of a CronJob.

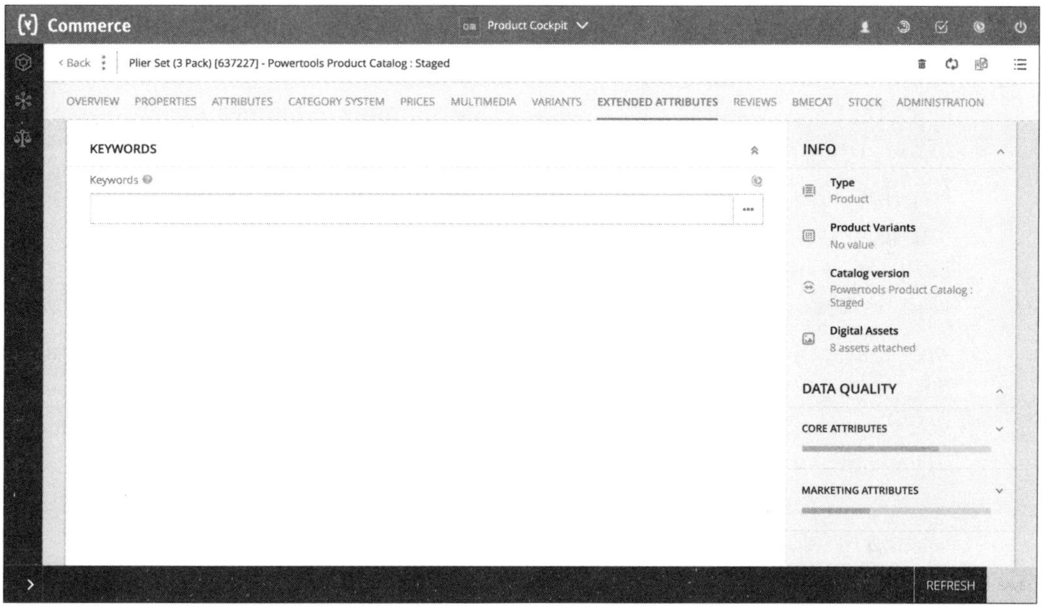

Figure 9.10 Product Cockpit Perspective of Backoffice, Showing Fields for Metadata Keywords

Those who want the latter will have to make a few small changes in `ProductPageController`, the Spring controller that initiates actions when a customer loads a page on the frontend. When the site calls the `productFacade.getProductForCodeAndOptions` function, it does so with a series of parameters, each called `ProductOption`. By adding the desired attributes to `ProductPageController` as `ProductOptions`, you can push whichever product attributes you'd like into the header of a product page.

The appropriate parameters would be added to the line in `productFacade.getProductForCodeAndOptions` that begins with:

```
final List<ProductOption> extraOptions =
```

The added parameters would look like this:

```
ProductOption.KEYWORDS, ProductOption.DESCRIPTION);
```

9.4 Summary

In this chapter, we have discussed some functionalities and ideas that, despite not being the focus of any specific module in SAP Commerce, permeate every discussion of the platform and of what you can build on it.

Hopefully this has gotten you thinking about how the pieces fit together and, more importantly, how they fit into solutions in the real world. This technology doesn't exist for its own sake, after all. It exists to enable your vision and help you realize your project's objectives.

Now that we've covered these cross-module topics, in the next chapter we'll take a deeper dive into the architecture of the SAP Commerce system. Keep in mind what you've learned about users and user groups, about localization, and about data flow in general as we explain how those parts form a working whole.

Chapter 10
SAP Commerce Platform

This chapter introduces the main concepts of the SAP Commerce platform within the SAP C/4HANA suite. We'll cover topics such as architecture, data model, import and export, workflows, and security to give you a solid understanding of the fundamentals of the platform.

In this chapter, we'll introduce the main architecture topics of the platform and other core components. This chapter is mainly focused on the extensibility of the platform. Understanding the main architecture components and how to extend the platform considering best practices for architecture data models and security can help you design a solution to attend to your organization's business needs with SAP Commerce, a solution that is scalable, upgradeable, and secure.

In Section 10.1, we'll go deeper into the architecture layers of SAP Commerce and how to work with the concept of extensions and the operation mode of the solution from an architectural perspective. Section 10.2 will further elaborate on how the data model works within the platform and how it's used to manage data within the platform. In Section 10.3, we'll examine how to import and export the data used in the platform and what kind of mechanisms can be used to manage data. Section 10.4 will explain the workflow collaboration tools that exist for users within the platform and how to enable and manage these. Finally, in Section 10.5, we'll cover important security topics like permissions, how to set and manage them, and password encryption to secure the application, as well as data protection topics, like consent and how to set up and manage the website user's consent within the SAP Commerce platform.

10.1 Architecture

The architecture of the SAP Commerce platform is flexible and modular. The flexibility comes from several layers of abstraction and modularized functionality. Functionality is built on top of the SAP Commerce platform, which includes all core functionality. To successfully customize the platform, you must understand its various layers. In this section, we'll discuss the different architecture layers of the platform, as well as extension options and how to set up the architecture to run SAP Commerce.

10.1.1 Architecture Layers

The SAP Commerce platform is divided into individual packages, such as commerce, content, channels, and orders. These packages consist of individual modules referred to as *extensions*.

The SAP Commerce suite contains several layers, each of which has different functions and data abstraction levels, as shown in Figure 10.1.

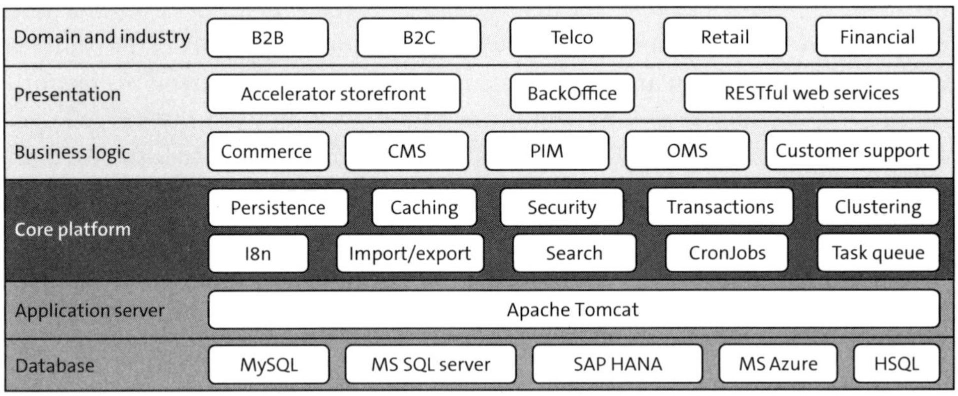

Figure 10.1 SAP Commerce Layer Architecture

The domain and industry layer has specific extensions for predefined business models (e.g., B2B, B2C, retail, etc.). Below that is the presentation layer with the accelerator storefronts, backoffice, and RESTful web services. Below that is the business logic layer. On top of the core extensions, the platform contains several pieces of SAP Commerce software, such as the build framework and third-party software such as prebundled Apache Tomcat.

SAP Commerce runs in Java virtual machine (JVM) and connects to external databases (with an on-premise scenario, these can include SAP HANA, MySQL, etc.). The platform layer abstracts data from the storage structure on the database using the persistence framework and provides functionality such as clustering, CronJobs, internationalization, and more.

10.1.2 Extensions

The SAP Commerce platform consists of a set of modules that are composed of extensions. These extensions provide standardized functionality and are supported and maintained by SAP. Extensions that are part of the SAP Commerce platform are also referred to as *core extensions*. Project-specific customizations are implemented as new extensions, also referred to as *custom extensions*. A well-designed extension will improve code readability and reuse, which is important to help avoid increased complexity during future upgrades to newer versions.

When creating extensions, we recommend keeping the logic and storefront-related features in separate extensions. That's why extensions are organized into the following four groups:

1. SAP Commerce accelerators project extensions
2. SAP Commerce accelerators cockpit extensions
3. SAP Commerce accelerator storefronts API extensions
4. SAP Commerce accelerators sample data and test data

Add-ons are a type of extension that extend the functionality of an SAP Commerce accelerator storefront. The add-on is primarily intended to customize frontend logic and allow customization of the storefront without modifying the storefront files directly. With add-ons, upgrading SAP Commerce accelerators is easier because no customizations need to be merged from the old implementation. Features can be more easily switched on and off without refactoring the storefront; customers with multiple storefronts especially benefit from this. Using add-ons also facilitates the implementation of multiple features in parallel instead of working directly within the SAP Commerce accelerators.

A full SAP Commerce solution can consist of a large number of extensions. For clarity, it's important to use clear and appropriate naming conventions for custom extensions. A recommended practice is to add a specific prefix to custom extensions to make it easier to identify where an extension comes from. In this way, custom extensions can be distinguished easily from, for example, third-party extensions. As with all naming in software design, naming conventions must be carefully defined. They must scale and accurately describe what the extension is implementing.

The following recommended practices for extensions can be considered:

- Place all functionality related to a particular feature into one extension.
- Depending on the size of the feature implementation, splitting the extension into several smaller extensions should be considered. This keeps the extension more maintainable.
- Avoid cyclic dependencies between extensions. When there is a cyclic dependency, extension A depends on extension B, which in turn depends on extension A. This means that modifying one extension can lead to modifications in other parts of the implementation.
- Consider placing APIs in separate extensions from their implementations. This will make it easier to switch to another implementation in the future.
- Minimize coupling (creating dependencies) between extensions for better maintainability. Only create couplings when necessary.
- Exclude unused extensions.

For a full list of all recommended practices for extensions, visit *help.hybris.com* or *wiki.hybris.com*.

10.1.3 Modes of Operation

Three different operation modes are available to run SAP Commerce:

1. **Single operation node**
   This is the most basic operation mode, in which a single machine runs one instance of the SAP Commerce installation, as shown in Figure 10.2.

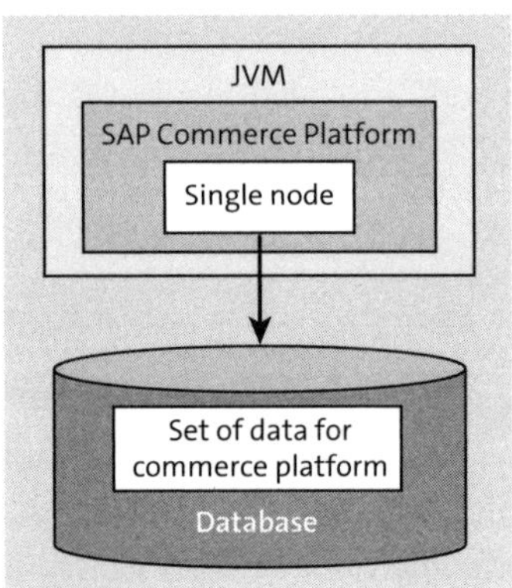

Figure 10.2 Single Node Setup

- **Cluster mode**
  When running in cluster mode, several individual nodes are considered. All these nodes are connected to a common database and communicate with each other via the Transmission Control Protocol (TCP) or User Datagram Protocol (UDP), as shown in Figure 10.3.

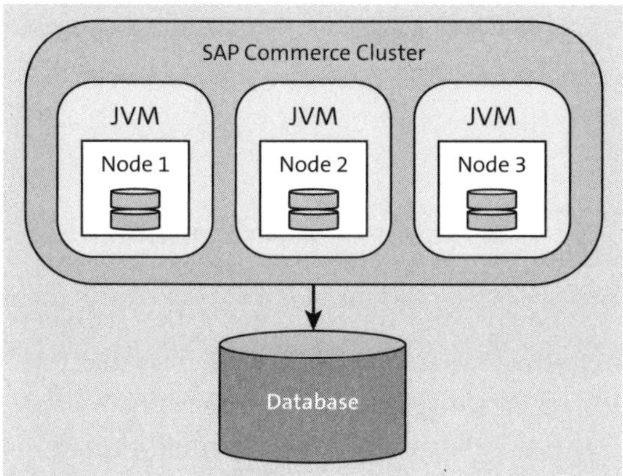

Figure 10.3 Cluster Mode

- **Multitenant mode**
  When SAP Commerce runs in multitenant mode, several individual, distinguished sets of data separated by database table prefixes are allowed, as shown in Figure 10.4. Multitenant mode can be used for either single node or cluster mode operation.

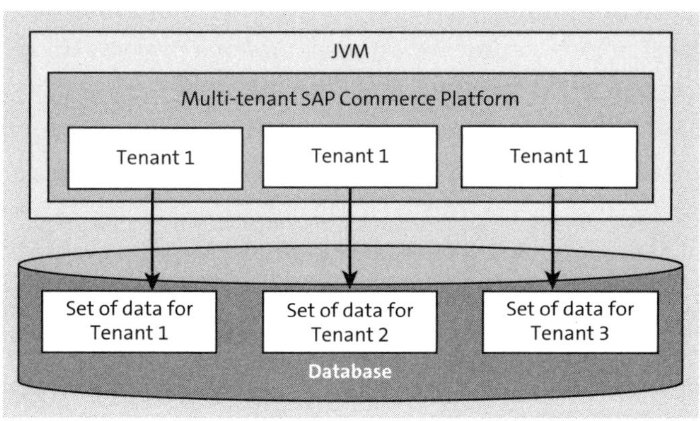

Figure 10.4 Multitenant Setup

10.2 Data Model

The data model that underlies the SAP Commerce platform is defined in XML files. Within SAP Commerce, the type system is used to organize all kinds of data (e.g., product information, customer data, and orders). The concept of the data model is based on the concepts of system types, core data types, and extensions. In this section, we'll cover these topics and discuss how they're used when extending the platform.

10.2.1 System Types

A *type* is considered the template for objects in the SAP Commerce platform. Every object that is stored in the platform is considered a type instance. The types define the product data that objects may carry and specifies the relations between objects. Types make data persistent as they categorize the data and relate the data into database fields. Product information, customer data, order data, and other data is organized by using types in the platform. Types are meant for persisting objects, and the attributes of a type manage and store the data for the object; at deployment, a database table structure is defined to store an object.

The object instance of a type is called the item and we identify two major type families. The system-related types and the business-related types.

The system-related types make up the type system itself or extend the type system and deal with internal data management like:

- **Infrastructure types**
  `ComposedTypes` set up type definitions and may carry attributes to hold information. Every persistent object in SAP Commerce is an instance of a `ComposedType` or one of its subtypes.
- **Data types**
  These types are used to describe attributes by either carrying attributes values or representations for these values or by creating relationships between objects. The following are considered data types: `CollectionTypes`, `MapTypes`, `EnumerationTypes`, and `AtomicTypes`.

The business-related types (e.g., `Order`, `Discount`, `bike`) allow for management of product and/or customer information to run the business. Figure 10.5 shows an example of an overview of the type hierarchy defined within an out-of-the-box installation.

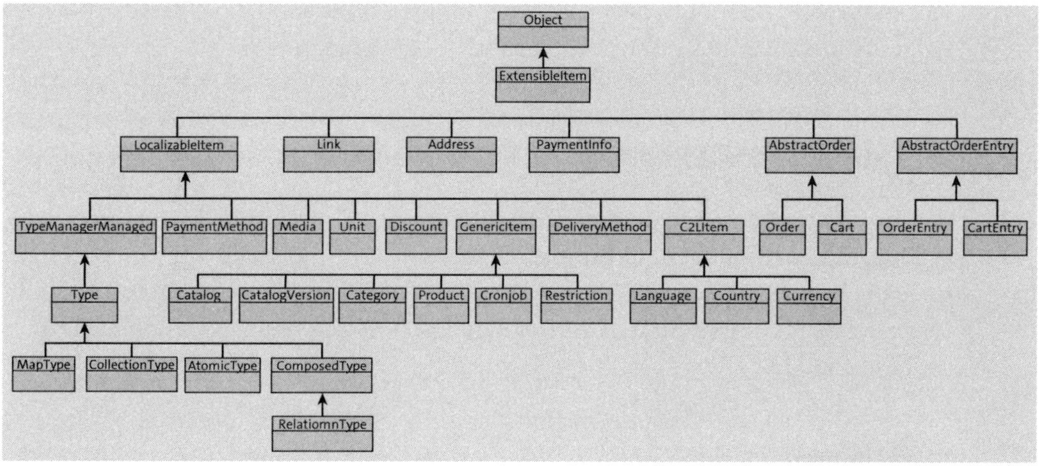

Figure 10.5 Type Hierarchy Example

10.2.2 Core Data Types and Extensions

The *icore-items.xml* file contains all basic definitions of the types that are fundamental for the platform and relations provided and used by the platform. Among the entities in the icore.items.xml file, definitions can be found for different kinds of users, products, invoices, orders, and more.

When new functionality is added to the platform, additions might be needed to the data model. These new data types for extensions (called *item types*) are defined in *<extension-name>-items.xml* files. If an extension or add-on includes new item types or extends existing item types, this must be done in a file named *<extension-name>-items.xml*. Also, if relationships to the overall data model are changed or new relationships are added to the overall data model, this also must be done in a file named *<extension-name>-items.xml*. This file is located in its own top-level resource directory. SAP Commerce refers to data types as item types, and each item type is defined in an item type XML element. By adding a new `itemType` element to the *<extension-name>-items.xml* file, a new item type is defined. In the same way, SAP Commerce refers to the relationships between item types as relations, and new relations are defined by adding a relation XML element to the *<extension-name>-items.xml* file.

At build time, and when the database is initialized, the platform will combine all XML declarations for the extensions that are being used and Java classes, and a database schema is created.

To extend the data model, new data types and relations should be created, and data types declared by other extensions need to be extended.

10.3 Import and Export

Various types of data are used on the SAP Commerce platform, like customer data, product data, or catalogs, for example. All this data is imported into or exported from the SAP Commerce platform. In the following sections, we'll discuss three important topics related to import and export of data into and out of SAP Commerce: ImpEx, CronJobs, and hot folders.

10.3.1 ImpEx

SAP Commerce comes out of the box with an integrated text-based import and export extension called *ImpEx*, which allows for the creation, update, removal, and export of platform items such as customer, products, order data, and so on to and from comma-separated values (CSV) data files. The import and export of data can be done both during run-time and during initialization or update processes.

The ImpEx extension can be used via the SAP Commerce API, the backoffice, or the SAP Commerce administration console.

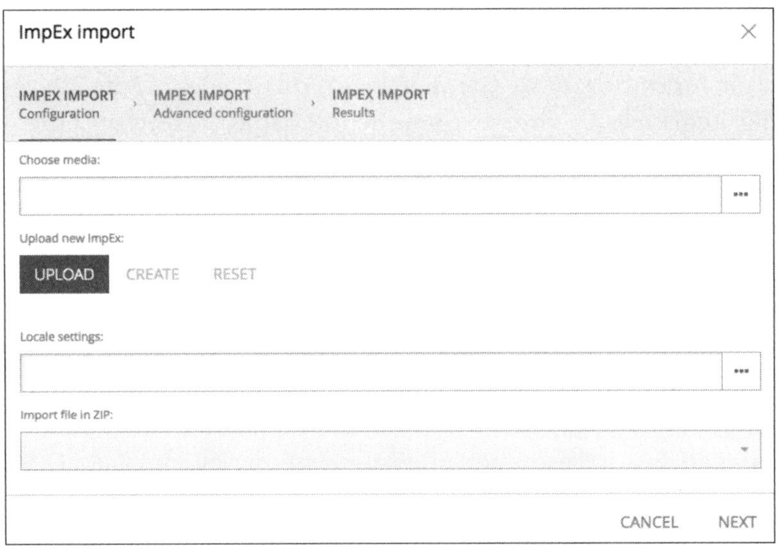

Figure 10.6 Import Wizard (Backoffice), Configuration Tab

To start an import within the backoffice, use the import wizard to set basic parameters for a CronJob that imports data into the platform. Figure 10.6 shown the **Configuration** tab of the import wizard. Navigate to the import wizard via **System • Tools • Import**.

Within the main tab, the source media are defined, as well as the locale settings, which are important when importing data for which the separator symbols might be different per locale. A ZIP archive can be used when the media are in a ZIP file.

10.3.2 CronJobs

The SAP Commerce platform provides mechanisms to plan and execute regular tasks. This is called *CronJob* functionality, and it's used to execute tasks (called CronJobs) regularly at specific points of time. CronJobs usually are used to create backup data, update catalog contents, or recalculate prices—processes that can take a long time and/or have to be executed frequently. CronJobs are used to start these long, periodic processes in the background. CronJobs execution makes it easy to log and check the results.

The key idea of applying CronJobs is to start a long or periodic process in the background, with the ability to log each run and to check its result easily. A CronJob consists of four types that interact with one another: `CronJob`, `Job`, `Trigger`, and `CronJobHistory`, as well as the `JobPerformable` class, which is related to the `Job` type:

- **`Job` type**
  The `Job` type describes the logic to be executed.
- **`CronJob`**
  The `CronJob` type contains the setup for a single run of a `Job`, as well as the protocol information, like logs.
- **`Trigger`**
  The `Trigger` type is the schedule mechanism for executing a `Job`.
- **`CronJobHistory`**
  The `CronJobHistory` type contains the `CronJob`'s execution information like start and end time.

Figure 10.7 illustrates the CronJob concept.

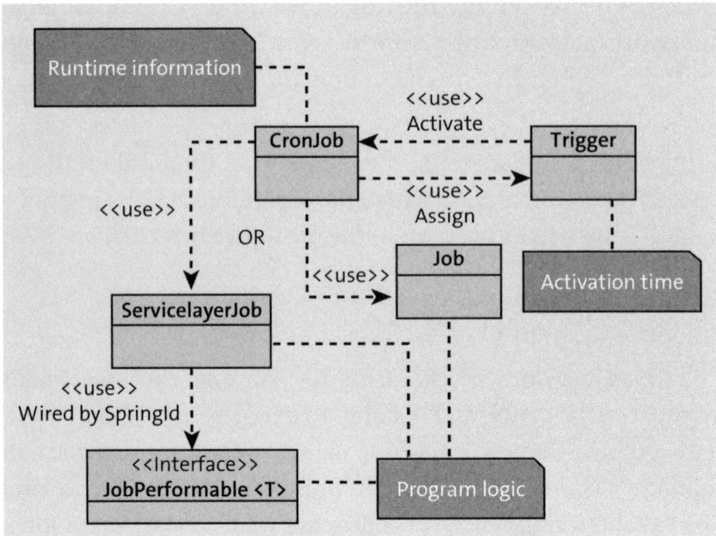

Figure 10.7 CronJob Concept

10.3.3 Hot Folder

The SAP Commerce template comes with a batch package that enables the automated import of data from hot folders into the platform. This means that simple CSV files are internally translated into fast, multithreated SAP Commerce ImpEx scripts that can import content directly into, for example, product catalogs. The hot folder is scanned periodically by the system to identify the moment to import new data. Certain files might be grouped into batches to spread the data load across multiple files and have less impact on performance when importing large amounts of data. This feature is used for automated updates for stock levels, prices, and product catalog feeds that might be imported from external systems.

Spring integration is used to provide a pluggable, highly configurable, service-based design that enables you to extend the service easily to attend to your organization's specific requirements. The system will process any files encountered in the hot folder. Figure 10.8 shows the integration mechanism using a hot folder for importing data.

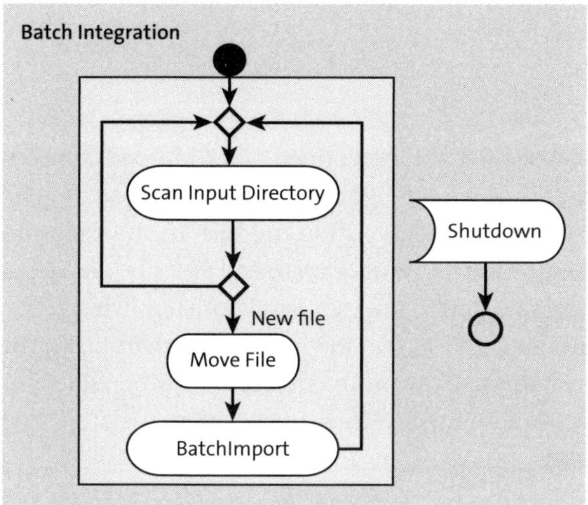

Figure 10.8 Hot Folder

10.4 Workflow

SAP Commerce offers workflow functionality to facilitate sequential (team) processes like product creation and review, the handling of customer complaints, or the publication of certain content or marketing banners on the website. These in-house business and collaboration processes can be modeled using SAP Commerce's workflow and collaboration functionality. In this section, we'll discuss the workflow concept and explain how to use workflows within the SAP Commerce backoffice (e.g., creating, managing, and executing workflows).

10.4.1 Overview

In this section, we'll cover workflow concepts (where workflows can be used and how they function within the platform), as well as introduce how to create, manage, and execute workflows within the backoffice.

The following functionalities can be executed with the workflow and collaboration functionality:

- Workflow creation
- Workflow tracking
- Creation of new workflow templates

- Assigning specific users and user groups to specific tasks
- Real-time notification emails
- Adding attachments to tasks

There are two types of workflows available: the predefined workflow for complex processes and ad hoc workflows for single tasks. Figure 10.9 shows how a complex process can be handled using the workflow collaboration module. In the example, Peter, who is in charge of creating new products, wants Paul to add descriptions to the product and Mary to polish the images related to the product before publishing it on the company's web shop. After both Paul and Mary have performed their tasks, the changes are sent to Tobias, who must approve the products before they're published. If Tobias rejects the changes, the workflow will return to the previous step (and Tobias can add comments as needed).

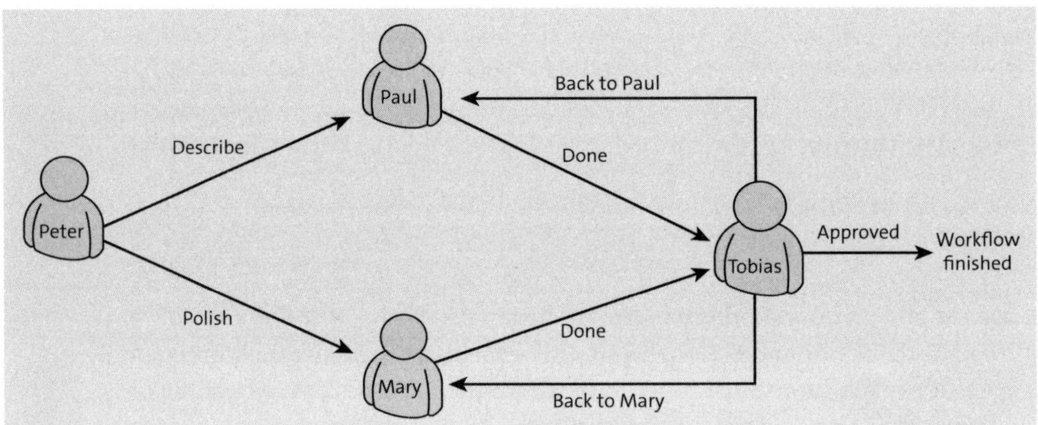

Figure 10.9 Workflow Process

When working with workflows, the following key concepts should be considered:

- **Workflow templates**
  These templates are made of multiple workflow action templates and define the sequence of the workflow in the form of options.
- **Workflow action templates**
  Workflow action templates define steps in a workflow and are linked to other workflow action templates via options.

- **Options**
  Options define a possible result of the workflow action template and define the next steps after the current workflow action template.
- **Workflow**
  This is the actual workflow created from the workflow template.
- **Workflow action**
  The workflow action is the individual step within a workflow. It can have the following statuses: pending, in progress, completed, disabled, or ended.
- **Decision**
  The decision is the actual choice and stores the results of an action.
- **Comment**
  The user can leave comments on a workflow action, and they can contain information pertinent for the next workflow action.
- `VisibleForPrincipals`
  This attribute is assigned to specific users that can create or see workflows in an assigned template.

There are three types of user roles defined within the workflow extension:

1. Workflow modeler/designer, who sets up and defines the workflow templates
2. Workflow manager, who creates the actual workflows from within the workflow templates
3. Workflow assignees, who are employees that are assigned to execute specific steps in the workflow

10.4.2 Workflows in the Backoffice

As mentioned previously, templates are used to work with workflows. The templates are managed within the backoffice by authorized users. In this subsection, we'll discuss how to create, manage, and execute workflows using the backoffice.

Managing Workflow Templates

In the backoffice, a workflow modeler/designer with the right access can create or change workflow templates by going to the administration console and clicking **System • Workflow Administration • Workflow Templates**. After clicking an existing template, the details are shown in the lower part of the screen for that specific template. Figure 10.10 shows an example of the general information in a template where **Essential** data such as **ID** and **Owner** is maintained, **Properties** such as **Name** and **Description** are stored, and **Actions** are assigned to the template. Furthermore, CronJobs can be defined or restrictions assigned and advanced attributes allocated to the workflow template. On the **Administration** tab, you'll see administration data such as creation date, ID, name, and last changed date.

Figure 10.10 Workflow Template Details

In the backoffice, the modeler/designer can create new templates by clicking on the **+** icon above the existing templates. A pop-up will appear to create the new workflow template, as shown in Figure 10.11.

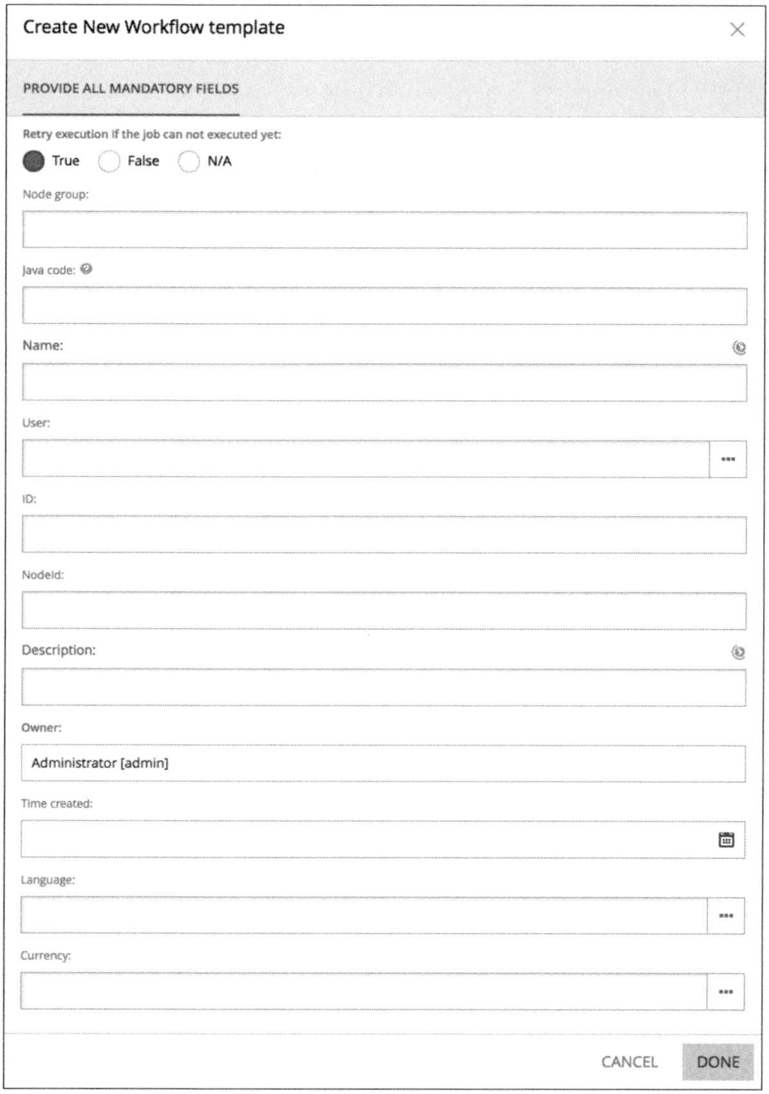

Figure 10.11 Create New Workflow Template Screen

Creating Workflows from a Template

In the backoffice, the workflow manager who creates the actual workflow from the template can create new workflows. To do so, follow these steps:

1. Click the **Collaboration** icon in the top-right corner of the browser section of the screen.
2. The **Collaboration** widget appears where workflows or tasks are shown. In the lower part of the screen, click to create a new workflow.
3. A **Create Workflow** widget appears. Select the template to create the workflow from the **Workflow Template** dropdown list, and define the name of the new workflow within the **Essentials** tab, as shown in Figure 10.12.

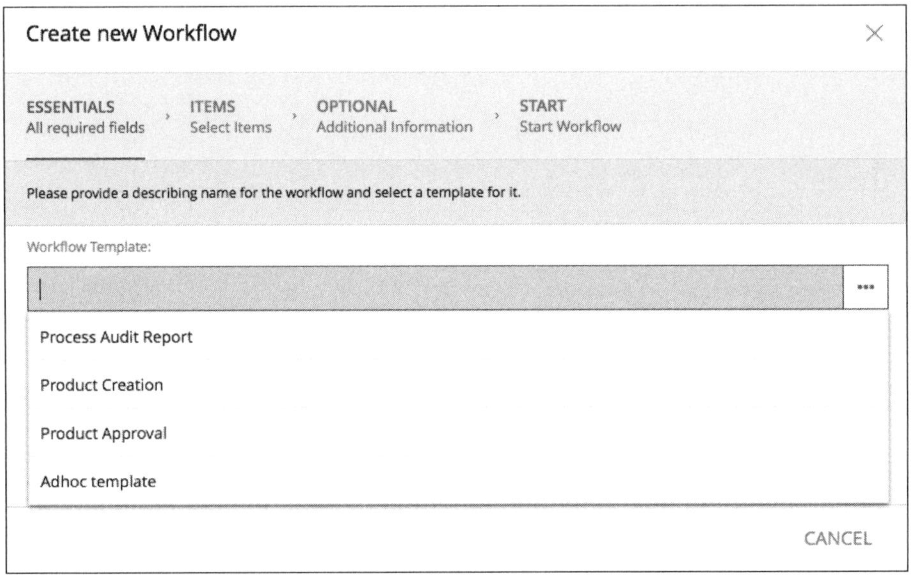

Figure 10.12 Workflow Template Selection for Workflow Creation

4. On the next tab, **Items**, select the **Attachment Type** from a dropdown list (e.g., products, audit reports, category), and select the items that will be edited in the workflow, as shown in Figure 10.13.

In the **Optional** screen, you can provide a description for the workflow. You can choose to start the workflow immediately or save it.

Executing Workflows

The workflow assignees receive the workflow items in the **Collaboration** widget and select the task associated with the profile to execute it. Figure 10.14 shows the area to add a new description to the product in the **Edit Product** screen in the backoffice.

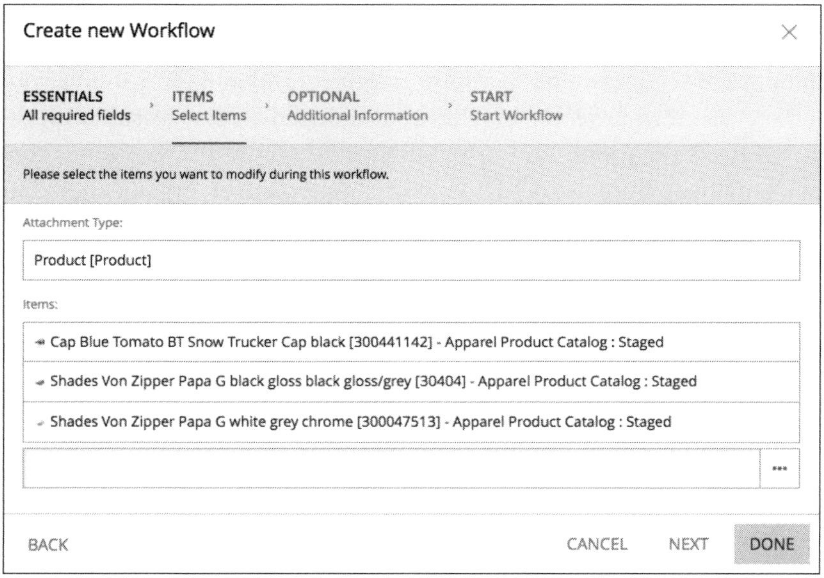

Figure 10.13 Select Items for Workflow Creation

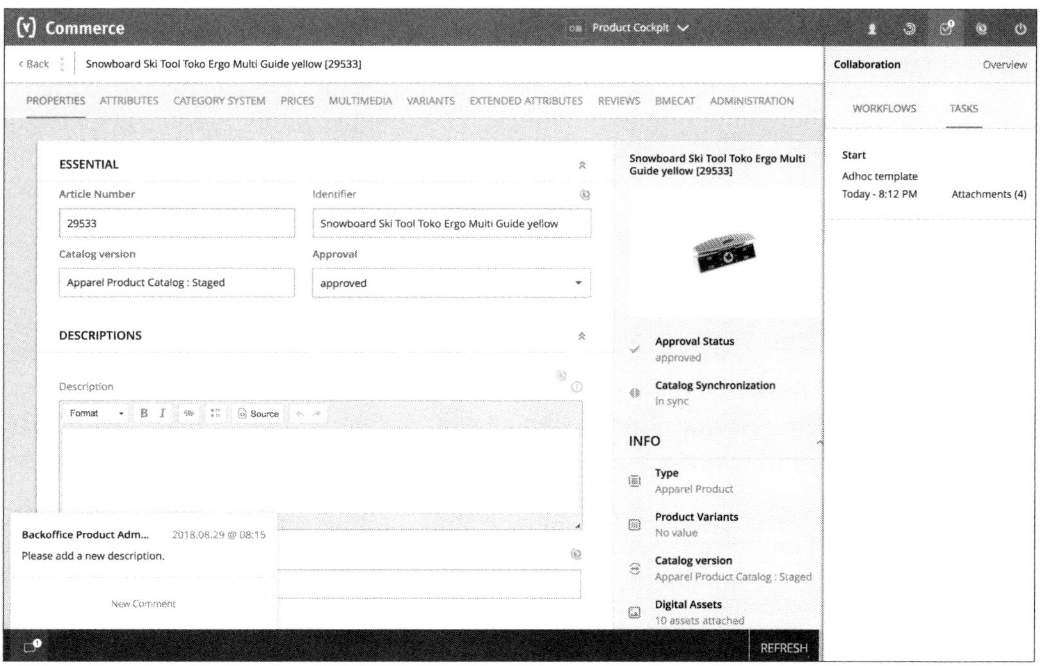

Figure 10.14 Workflow Execution Screen

10.5 Security

When installing the SAP Commerce platform, we recommend reviewing various security aspects to secure your platform from unauthorized access or users with the wrong access rights for their jobs. An important tool for security is the *permissions* concept, which provides a framework to define and implement an organization-specific access rights policy. By using the permissions services, specific access rights for users and user groups can be defined.

Permissions is an abstract concept, sometimes also referred to *as user rights*. The meaning of permissions in the SAP Commerce context goes beyond user permissions and must be defined as a security policy; it also includes topics like data encryption, type of credentials, security auditing, and so on.

In this section, we'll cover various concepts that are part of the platform or need to be defined to guarantee the security of the platform. First, we'll talk about permissions, how they're defined, and how they're checked within the platform. After that, we'll introduce specific security mechanisms that are part of the platform, like the cross-origin resource sharing (CORS) and HTTPS certificates. Then, we'll introduce the concepts of password protection and customer data policies and what SAP recommends on these topics. Consent management is described in detail, and we'll show you how to manage the consent templates that come out of the box with the SAP Commerce platform. Finally, we'll review recommended practices for security management throughout a project life cycle.

10.5.1 Permissions

The permission services provided do not automatically restrict access to the items or types in the system but provide a framework to implement a security policy that reflects the organizational access rights security policy. Within a permissions framework, a very detailed level of access restrictions can be assigned, and access rights can be assigned on a hierarchical level. This means that access rights might inherit down through several hierarchy levels, and the permissions system determines how this is set up.

Permissions can have various stages (e.g., read, change, create, and delete). The following stages are not limited to this specific list because the framework can handle any created and implemented permissions:

- **Read**
  This permission specifies if the user account is granted access to the respective type at all. All type's attributes will be shown (unless explicitly overridden), but no other actions than read are possible at this access level. When the permission is set to deny, the user won't be able to see instances of the type or read the value for the type's attributes.
- **Change**
  The change permission defines if the user account is allowed to modify attributes of the type. Users with this access right can only change (edit attribute values) and not create or delete instances of a type. When the change access right is set, read is also required to get access to the type.
- **Create**
  When the user is allowed to create instances of the type (e.g., create products or customers), the create permission is assigned to the specific type. If the user has create rights but no change rights, he can create instances of a type without being able to set any attribute values (which is not a common use case). Usually, a user with create rights also has change rights.
- **Delete**
  Users with the delete permission are allowed to delete items of the type (e.g., delete products of a certain type). Just delete rights on a type level might not be enough to delete items of that type. It might be that other required access rights might not be granted, or the user account might not have sufficient overall rights. For deleting a product from the catalog, the user needs delete and change access rights for the catalog version.

Some of the most important ways in which access rights can be managed are as follows:

- **Global permissions**
  Global permissions are related to a user or user group and are meant to be of the lowest priority. As these rights do not relate to any specific type, object, or attribute, they provide the most basic access rights. Any specific permission overrides the global permissions (type, item, or attribute permissions).
- **Type permissions**
  The type-related permissions define user access rights to the type level. A user that has type permissions assigned has access by default to all type attributes unless

specifically defined differently. Because these permissions are simple to define and evaluate in the system, they are a good starting point in building security policy (there isn't a high impact on performance when checking for type permissions).

- **Item permissions**
  The use of item permissions allows for very detailed access control because it's possible to grant or deny permissions for item instances. Managing and verifying permissions on the item level can significantly degrade performance, so we recommend assigning permissions on a type level and to user groups, rather than to individual users. Usually a huge number of items is involved, which makes permission checks performance-intensive. For specific scenarios in which the security of important item instances needs to be guaranteed, this can be a useful tool to override default security permissions.
- **Attribute permissions**
  Attribute permissions can be assigned to explicitly grant or deny access to individual attributes holding the international content of a type or an item. This is an even more refined access control than item permissions. Attribute permissions do not override type-related permissions, so if there is a type-related permission to deny <change>, then no change permissions can be granted to any attributes of that type. A good example of when to use this option is when <change> is granted, on attribute level the attribute permission can be set to grant or deny change for that specific attribute.

When creating access policies, it's important to consider the priority and in which order permissions should be applied to users and user groups. As described earlier, certain permissions can override others, and certain combinations can cause performance issues or cancel certain permissions set on a specific level. The idea is that the most general permissions have the lowest priority and the most specific permissions have the highest priority. If a user has two opposing permissions (grant and deny) for a specific type because the user belongs, for example, to two different groups, the deny setting ranks higher in priority than the grant setting.

Users can belong to user groups, and when a user group is assigned to specific permissions, all users in that group inherit the same permissions. When users belong to various user groups and have several (sometimes mutually exclusive) permissions, the user will inherit all these permissions. Usually permissions are set on the user group level. Therefore, these inherited permissions can be overridden by assigning additional permissions on the user level or subgroup level. For more on user groups and permissions, see Chapter 9, Section 9.1.

10.5.2 Managing and Checking Access Rights

One tool to manage permissions is the permission management service. Use this service to set permissions and assign them to user groups for the security policy to function. In addition, the permission checking service lets you check the existing permission assignments for specific users or user groups.

The framework used to manage and check user access rights is called *permissions services*, and it can be used to implement an access rights system on the SAP Commerce platform. The permissions services can be used to assign, modify, or remove permissions related to the users of a website, like employees and customers. The framework consists of separate services to manage access rights and check what kinds of access rights are applied. Ahead, we'll discuss the most often used services of this framework.

Permissions services focus on permission assignment, which in most cases is the relations among a permission (distinguished by its name), the principal (a user or user group), and the object (item, type, or attribute to which the permission is assigned). The only exceptions are global permissions that are assigned to users only. Permissions services can be used to assign permissions to both individual users and user groups, as well as to check permissions for users or user groups. The method in permission services takes a `PrincipalModel` argument, which can be either a user or user group. In most cases, permissions are assigned to user groups or checked against specific users. The most important services are as follows:

- `PermissionManagementService`
  This service is used to create and manage permissions and permission assignments. Some of the operations supported by this service are as follows:
  - Creation of new permissions (`Void CreatePermission (String permissionNoname);`)
  - Returning a list of all defined permissions (`Collection<String> getDefinedPermissions();`)
  - Assigning permissions
  - Replacing permissions
  - Removing permissions

- **PermissionCheckingService**
  This is used to check the effective user rights. This service provides the answer to the following questions:
  - Is a permission for an object granted to a principal?
  - Is a permission granted for a principal globally?

  The answers are returned for the given permission, principal, object and item. The answers are calculated from the existing permissions created with PermissionManagementService using the permission checking rules.
- **PermissionCRUDService**
  This service is used as a wrapper over PermissionCheckingService and provides checks for the four main platform-defined permissions (create, read, update, and delete).
- **PermissionCheckResult**
  This service determines whether the permission is granted or denied.
- **PermissionCheckValue**
  This service shows the number of defined permissions used by other services. The result of the checking permission can be as follows:
  - ALLOWED, meaning permission is granted for the principal
  - DENIED, meaning permission is denied for a principal
  - NOT_DEFINED, meaning no actual permission assignment was encountered for the operation
  - CONFLICTING, meaning there are both DENIED and ALLOWED assignments for a principal
- **PermissionConstants**
  This is a list of predefined permissions.
- **PermissionAssignment**
  This is an object used by PermissionManagementService to return information regarding the permission for a particular user's user group.

When working with permissions and user permissions, the following best practices should be considered:

- Code must invoke methods from PermissionCheckingService because permissions are not automatically enforced.
- When nothing is defined, the default behavior is denied.

- Use global permissions as a fallback or default assignment. These permissions have the lowest priority and are always overridden by the item, type, or attribute permission assignments.
- Permissions assigned to user groups are inherited by all members of the group.
- Permissions for types apply to every item of that type.
- Attribute permissions assignment should be used for detailed control of specific attribute values.

10.5.3 Cross-Origin Resource Sharing Mechanism

SAP Commerce supports the cross-origin resource sharing (CORS) mechanism. This security mechanism helps a web browser and server decide which cross-origin requests for restricted resources should or should not be allowed.

By default, web browsers do not allow JavaScript requests from servers other than the current site you're visiting; this is the well-known by same-origin policy. One way to bypass the same-origin policy is to use a CORS HTTP header, which is one of the most common methods of relaxing server security.

10.5.4 HTTPS Certificates

HTTPS certificates are a secure way of sending data between the browser and what that the browser is connected to.

When you request an HTTPS connection to a website, the website will initially send its SSL certificate to your browser. This certificate contains the public key needed to begin the secure session. Based on this initial exchange, your browser and the website then initiate the SSL handshake. The SSL handshake involves the generation of shared secrets to establish a uniquely secure connection between yourself and the website. When a trusted SSL digital certificate is used during an HTTPS connection, users will see a padlock icon in the browser address bar. When an extended validation certificate is installed on a website, the address bar will turn green.

The SAP Commerce platform handles HTTPS traffic using a certificate signed by a self-signed root certificate authority. Because the SAP Commerce platform trusts this root certificate authority by default, the HTTPS resource can be accessed from SAP Commerce itself, as illustrated in Figure 10.15.

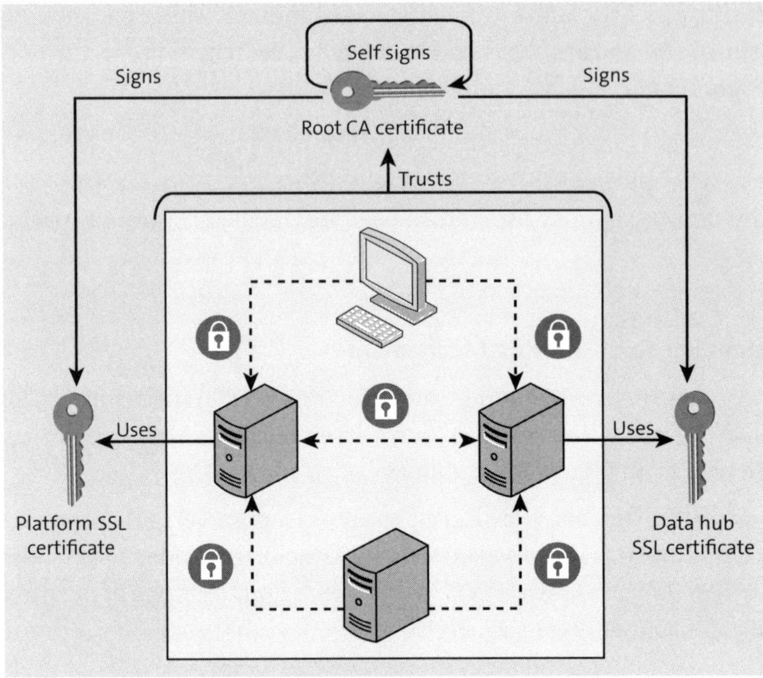

Figure 10.15 HTTPS Certificate Usage

10.5.5 Password Security Policies

It's important to set password security policies to define requirements that passwords must meet to be set or changed. The SAP Commerce platform provides customizable extension points to fine-tune password handling. This feature tremendously contributes to increased platform security. The two out-of-the-box password security policies that are delivered with the SAP Commerce platform are regex and blacklist. The regex solution prevents users from using passwords that are too easy to hack, and the blacklist bans the most commonly used passwords. Beyond these, organizations can implement their own password policies.

10.5.6 Data Protection

In a commerce solution like SAP Commerce, both customer and (organizational) employee data is shared within the platform. The protection of personal data therefore is a priority for any commerce solution. Whether this means storing customer data or limiting employee access or data sent to other parties, data protection should be of the utmost importance. SAP purchased Gigya in 2018, which was added to the SAP Customer Experience portfolio as SAP Customer Data Cloud. SAP Customer Data Cloud helps businesses securely identify consumers across devices and channels. With three integrated products (SAP Customer Identity, SAP Customer Consent, and SAP Customer Profile), SAP Customer Data Cloud helps drive customer registrations and engagement and manage customer permissions and customer consent across the entire customer life cycle. Further, it helps business to transform their customer data into unified customer profiles that are governed, orchestrated, and analyzed from a central and secure environment.

SAP Commerce comes with out-of-the-box mechanisms to facilitate data protection, like consent management, which will be discussed next.

10.5.7 Consent Management

Customers that are browsing your site and being tracked (e.g., through cookies, order entries, etc.) need to be informed and consent to such tracking. This applies for all users (registered and anonymous), and the solution must be designed to be able to not track the user if consent is not given. Local laws must be taken into account when it comes to customer data and consent management.

Consent on retaining personal data needs to be an option for a customer to agree to every time data will be collected, and this means the solution must have consent entry points implemented in the appropriate section. Usually this arises the first time data is being collected (e.g., registration process) or whenever the customer decides to have her personal data collected (e.g., in **My Account** settings), as shown in Figure 10.16.

But organizations are not limited to these moments and can create entry points on other pages. Another moment in which consent must be managed is when the user decides data should not be collected anymore after consenting to it previously. This means that you need a mechanism that shows what the user has consented to, and an option must be given to the user to remove that consent.

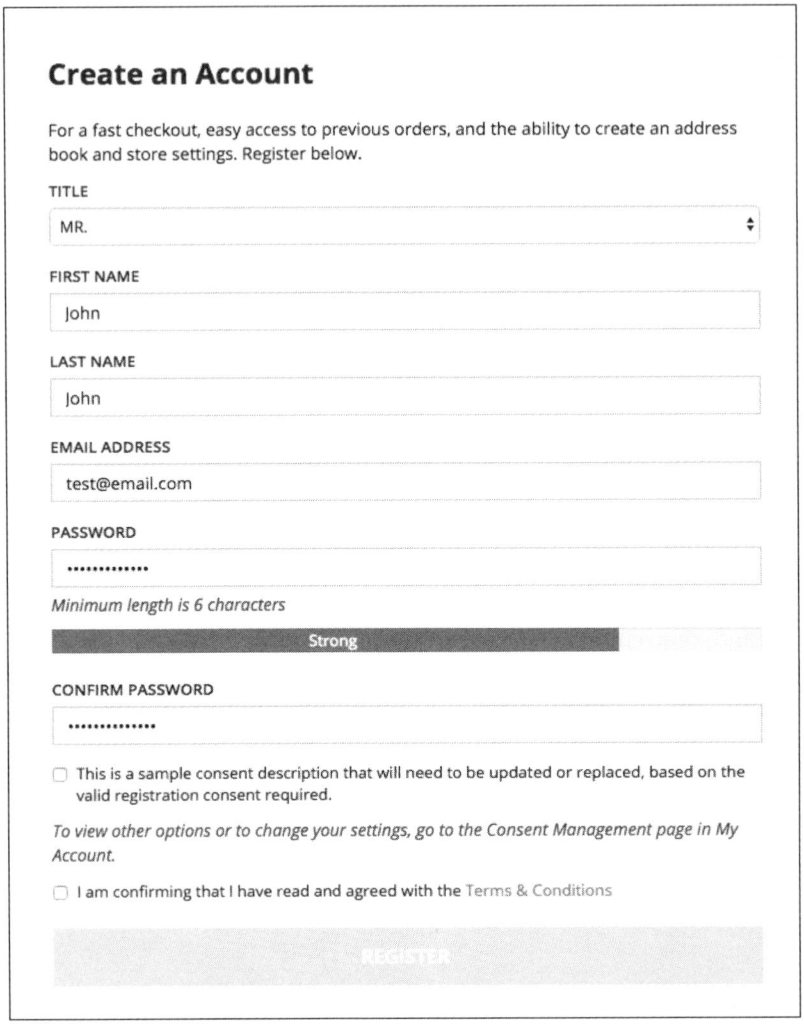

Figure 10.16 Customer Consent to Collection of Data at Registration

The SAP Commerce accelerators provide functionality for data subjects (customer, contact, or account) to give consent to collect or transfer their personal data. This means there are consent mechanisms during, for example, the account registration process, but users can also change their consent settings at any time from the **Consent Management** page. A logged-in user can click on **My Account** and will find the **Consent Management** widget on the screen to access and change consent settings, as shown in Figure 10.17 and Figure 10.18.

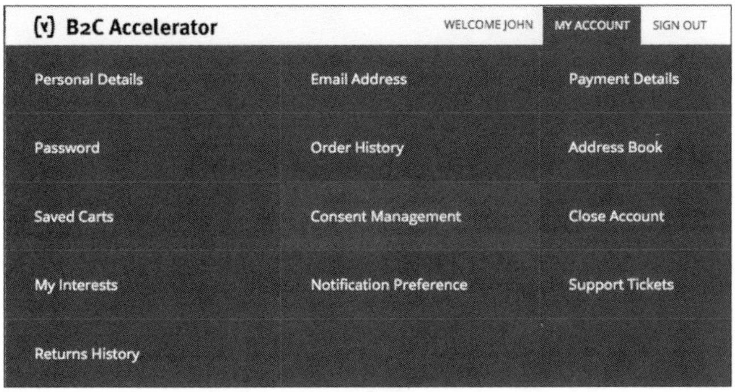

Figure 10.17 Consent Management in My Account Section

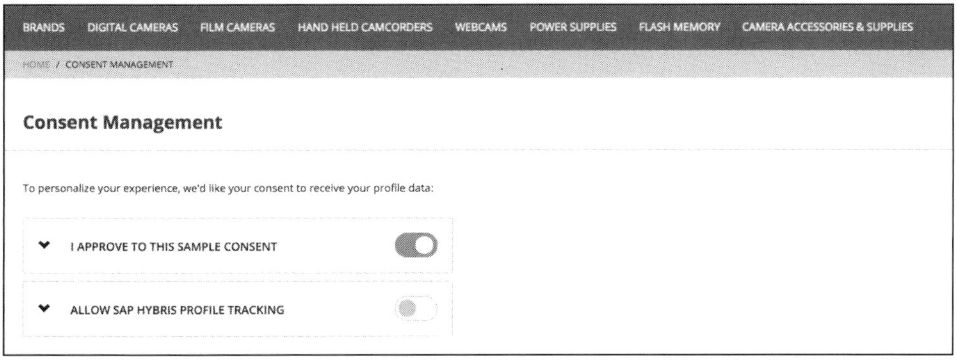

Figure 10.18 Change Consent Management Settings

Consent request templates have been incorporated into the **Registration** and **My Account** pages, and the consent template examples are included as part of the code of the storefront in the `b2c_acc` recipe. New templates can be created, modified, and removed as needed.

As of SAP Commerce 6.6, anonymous consent management is available, which gives anonymous users control over the tracking of their data. Anonymous users can decide whether they want their data to be tracked by clicking **Accept** or **Decline** on the consent pop-up shown in Figure 10.19.

In the backoffice, a user with the right access rights can manage consent templates by going to the administration console and then to **User • Consent • Consent Template**. Here a user can create new templates or change existing templates. A consent template consists of an ID, a name, a description, a site, and a version. Figure 10.20 shows this functionality in the backoffice.

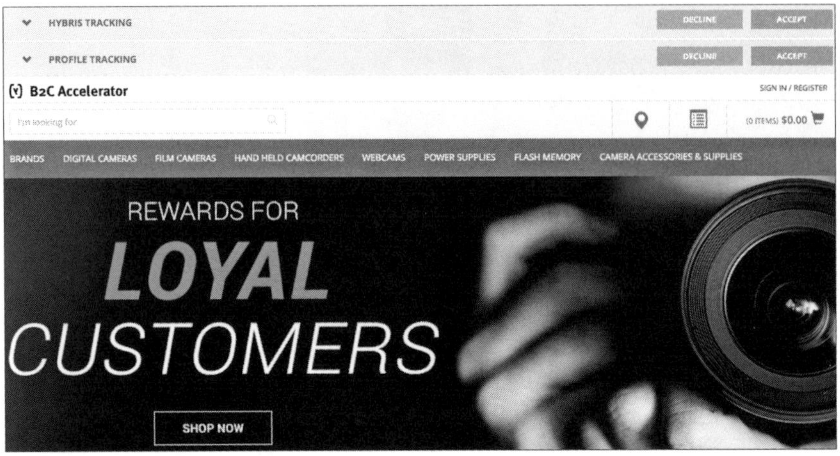

Figure 10.19 Anonymous Consent Pop-Up

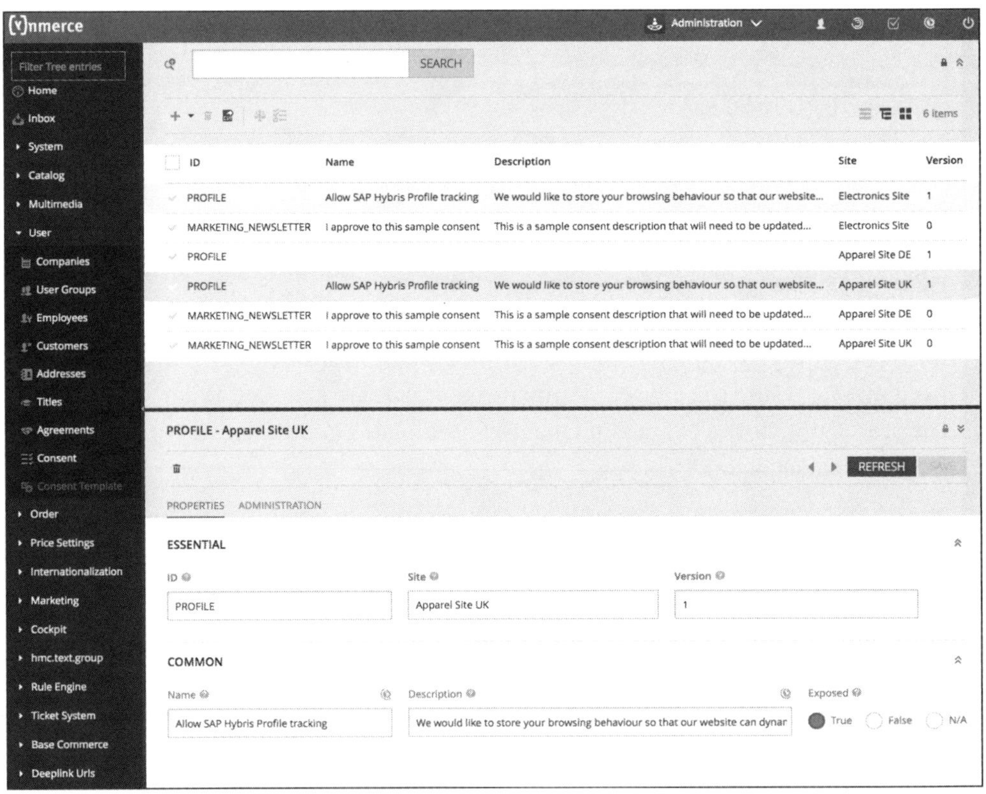

Figure 10.20 Manage Consent Templates in Backoffice

10.5.8 Security Recommended Practices for Projects

Throughout the life cycle of a platform, application security should be considered one of the most important nonfunctional requirements. In addition to design activities that help set up security policies (like user groups, permission definitions, etc.), there are security practices to be considered per each phase of a development project, as follows:

- **Development phase**
  During the development phase, there are different practices to be considered to guarantee application security:
  - **Coding practices**
    In accordance with coding standard guidelines, secure coding practices should be followed during the development phase. The recommended practice is to follow secure coding practices provided by the Open Web Application Security Project (OWASP). In the application lifecycle framework for SAP Commerce on the wiki, there is a cheat sheet available with the top ten recommend OWASP practices for SAP Commerce.
  - **Static code analysis**
    In line with coding best practices, we recommend executing static code analysis using tools such as PMD, FindBugs, and so on. These tools include rules to identify common security pitfalls in code. The feedback these checks provide to the development team cab help reduce security vulnerabilities during the coding phase. As a standard best practice, developers should invoke PMD and Sonar during local builds.
  - **Continuous integration/continuous delivery**
    These processes should be set up during the setup sprint, and the build and deployment pipeline should include steps to execute static code analysis and security checks. The SonarQube Quality Profile tool is delivered with SAP Commerce 6.6 and includes critical rules covering security vulnerabilities. SonarQube provides a central place for analyzing the quality of the code, including a view to see trends from build to build and identify possible bugs in the custom code.
  - **Security testing**
    During the development phase, security smoke test tools should be used to make sure potential security issues are caught early in the process. Security smoke tests are automated test cases that cover a set of security scenarios to be passed before going to a production environment.

- **Testing phase**
  During the testing phase of a project, the solution is tested to attend to functional and nonfunctional requirements. During testing, it's important to test the security of the application before going to deployment. Internal security audits consist of an exploratory information-gathering exercise in which information is gathered that can help you understand the application and architecture information available, and sequential execution of testing is run by simulating attacks to the platform. The information to be gathered in the first exploratory phase is as follows:
  - The database used, software versions, and operation systems
  - The search engine characteristics
  - Fingerprinting of the web application
  - Identifying the application entry points
  - Gathering and analyzing any error codes that are generated

  When testing for attacks, it's important not to attack the platform without a structured and carefully executed plan in place. There are specific areas to spend time and attention on. The following are these areas of attention and possible activities for each:
  - **Infrastructure and architecture**
    Activities such as penetration testing of the platform infrastructure by using spiders and crawlers to unveil the application tree and nodes should be considered. During the testing, old, backed up, or unreferenced files, as well as access to the administration interface, should be tested.
  - **Authentications and testing of authorizations**
    In these tests, topics like credential transport and encryption and vulnerable login and logout features should be tested.
  - **Session management**
    Topics like cookie management, session token generators, and cross-site request forgery (CSRF) should be tested and verified.
  - **Testing business logic**
    Business logic can be tested by trying to bypass it and by executing cross-site scripting (XSS) attacks or testing buffer overflow.

10.6 Summary

In this chapter, we introduced the basic components of the SAP Commerce platform. Because an SAP Commerce solution needs flexibility to attend to the business needs of an organization, it's important to understand the concept of architecture layers and extensions and what benefits and flexibility they bring to the solution without losing scalability and upgradeability. We also discussed how data is managed within the architecture and how custom extensions need to be addressed within the data model using the type system. Import and export mechanisms were another key factor discussed; these mechanisms flow data into and out of the platform. We then covered the collaborative workflow tools that are in place to manage tasks and activities within teams (e.g., product management teams working on the approval process for new products and marketing attributes).

We ended by discussing security and various aspects of security. Security is closely tied to the data model and type system principle, which provides mechanisms to easily restrict access on the global, type, item, or attribute level of an item. We shared best practices for how to do this without affecting performance, for example, and how to avoid misconfigured access that can affect the overall security of the platform. Also, we covered data protection and consent management options provided by the platform and offered recommended practices for how to test security.

In the next chapter, we'll discuss integrating SAP Commerce with other SAP C/4HANA systems and non-SAP systems.

Chapter 11
Integration

Digital platforms unconnected to the rest of the IT landscape are like beautiful floating islands unconnected to the rest of the world. Creating a comprehensive customer experience requires seamless integration of the frontend applications with the enterprise landscape, as we'll discuss in this chapter.

The journey of prebuilt integrations for SAP Commerce started with the acquisition of hybris by SAP in 2013. At this time, two trends converged: SAP's strength, being a business process company (and consequently having integration with various capabilities in its DNA), on one hand, and the requests of SAP customers for prebuilt integrations, which help to decrease project costs (integration efforts are still a significant cornerstone of SAP Commerce implementation projects) and which provide integration best practices at the same time, on the other hand. Consequently, prebuilt integrations between SAP ERP and SAP Commerce for order management and order fulfillment, respectively, were included in SAP Commerce 5.3, which was released after acquisition.

Since the 5.3 release, the SAP Commerce integration portfolio has evolved many times and now includes a comprehensive set of prebuilt integrations. In this chapter, we'll discuss the details of these, starting with the core categories of integrations—namely, master data, process data, and functional data integrations. For master data, we'll look at the details of the customer data and product and pricing data integrations between SAP Commerce and SAP ERP, SAP S/4HANA and SAP CRM systems; for process data, the focus will be on order management.

Then we'll discuss the details of integration with SAP Marketing Cloud, SAP Sales Cloud, SAP Service Cloud, SAP Subscription Billing, SAP Customer Engagement Center, SAP Jam Communities, and the SAP Digital Payments add-on. Last but not least, we'll look at SAP Commerce integration strategies and technologies.

11.1 Basics

Following the idea of always looking at business processes and providing seamless integrations for them, SAP Commerce builds its integrations on three major pillars, regardless of the affected business process and regardless of the affected backends. The first pillar is master data because consistent master data along the value chain and along with the implemented business processes is an absolute prerequisite and foundation for all process integrations. With consistent master data, you can achieve the first level of integration between systems. Only if you have consistent master data can you look at business processes.

All SAP Commerce integrations include similar sets of master data. First and foremost are customer and consumer master data. In almost all integrations of SAP Commerce, you'll see either a prebuilt integration for customer and consumer master data or a recommendation on how to deal with this master data. Next to customer and consumer data, you'll find prebuilt integrations for product or material master data, for catalog data, and for prices. As noted, once you have consistent master data, you can start looking into business processes—and one of the most important process for SAP Commerce is order management or order fulfillment. Here we're looking at how orders captured in SAP Commerce are fulfilled in various backends. Linked to orders and their fulfillment is the management of returns, which customers carry out through digital channels. These two processes are complemented by customer service processes.

The first two pillars in the prebuilt integrations offered by SAP Commerce, consistent master data and process integration, give you a jump start into your integration projects to save costs. This frees up funds to build features, which at the end of the day move the needle and help you differentiate you're your competitors. At the same time, the prebuilt integrations for master data synchronization and process integration provide you with a set of best practices for integrating SAP Commerce, which reduces the risk in implementation projects.

With master data synchronization and process integration as the foundation, SAP Commerce offers a third pillar of integrations: the functional pillar or the pillar of features. This is driven by the intent to offer features out of the SAP portfolio that enrich the SAP Commerce offering and enable its users to offer experiences to their customers that they could not offer if they relied on SAP Commerce features only. One example of this feature enrichment is product recommendations, a feature invoked from SAP Marketing Cloud that allows you to create algorithms to retrieve relevant product recommendations in real time based on customer browsing behavior in the SAP Commerce accelerator storefronts.

All prebuilt integrations follow the SAP Commerce architecture guidelines and are provided as SAP Commerce extensions. These extensions are either part of the SAP Commerce delivery or can be downloaded and provisioned separately.

Table 11.1 shows a summary of the three integration pillars provided by SAP.

Master Data	Processes	Features
▪ Products ▪ Prices ▪ Stock levels ▪ Customer ▪ Consumer	▪ Order management ▪ Return management ▪ Ticket processing ▪ Customer service	▪ Price calculation ▪ Available-to-promise (ATP) information ▪ Credit check ▪ Personalization with SAP Marketing Cloud, segmentation option ▪ Product recommendations with SAP Marketing Cloud, recommendation option ▪ Self-service using SAP CRM ▪ Configure, price, and quote ▪ Customer engagement with SAP Jam communities

Table 11.1 Three Pillars of Integration: Master Data, Process, and Features

With the described master data synchronization, process integration, and feature integration, the prebuilt integrations cover all components of the SAP frontend, as well as the products of SAP's digital core. This starts with SAP ERP, which was the first prebuilt integration SAP Commerce offered and which includes integration with SAP Marketing Cloud. Over time, integrations with SAP S/4HANA, SAP CRM, SAP Sales Cloud, SAP Service Cloud, SAP Subscription Billing, and SAP Customer Engagement Center were added. As a result, several SAP products can be used to cover the relevant commerce-related business processes, as shown in Table 11.2.

Commerce Process	Product
Order management/order fulfillment	SAP ERP, SAP S/4HANA, SAP CRM
Return management	SAP ERP, SAP S/4HANA, SAP CRM

Table 11.2 List of Commerce Business Processes and Corresponding SAP Products

Commerce Process	Product
Customer service	SAP CRM, SAP Service Cloud, SAP Customer Engagement Center
Payments	SAP Digital Payments add-on
Service fulfillment	SAP CRM
Communities	SAP Jam communities
Variant configuration	SAP Product Configuration
Subscription management	SAP Subscription Billing

Table 11.2 List of Commerce Business Processes and Corresponding SAP Products (Cont.)

Let's now take a closer look at master data synchronization and selected process integrations in the next sections.

11.2 Master Data Management

The foundation of integration begins with master data. Master data types consist of customer data, product data, and pricing data to begin with. Master data integration flows can be inbound, outbound, or both. They can be full uploads or incremental updates based on requirements. In this section, let's look at the master data mappings and data models in different systems, as well as the common settings required for integrations, followed by customer data integrations, product integrations, and, last but not the least, pricing data integration.

11.2.1 Data Models and Objects Overview

SAP Commerce and the SAP backend (SAP S/4HANA, SAP ERP) use different data models for customer information. The applications also use different terminology to describe their entities. Understanding how data is mapped for customers, contact persons, product pricing, and stock levels will help clarify how replicated data is organized in the receiving system. Figure 11.1 showcases the mapping between SAP Commerce and SAP ERP or SAP S/4HANA.

The master data is asynchronously replicated via intermediate documents (IDocs) with Application Link Enabling (ALE). When data is changed, pointers are activated and IDocs are generated for sending. IDocs are then sent to SAP Commerce, data hub, which provides mapping from specific IDocs to raw, canonical, and target models. SAP Commerce, data hub generates the ImpEx data that is imported by SAP Commerce. Figure 11.2 showcases the data flow from the backend system to SAP Commerce.

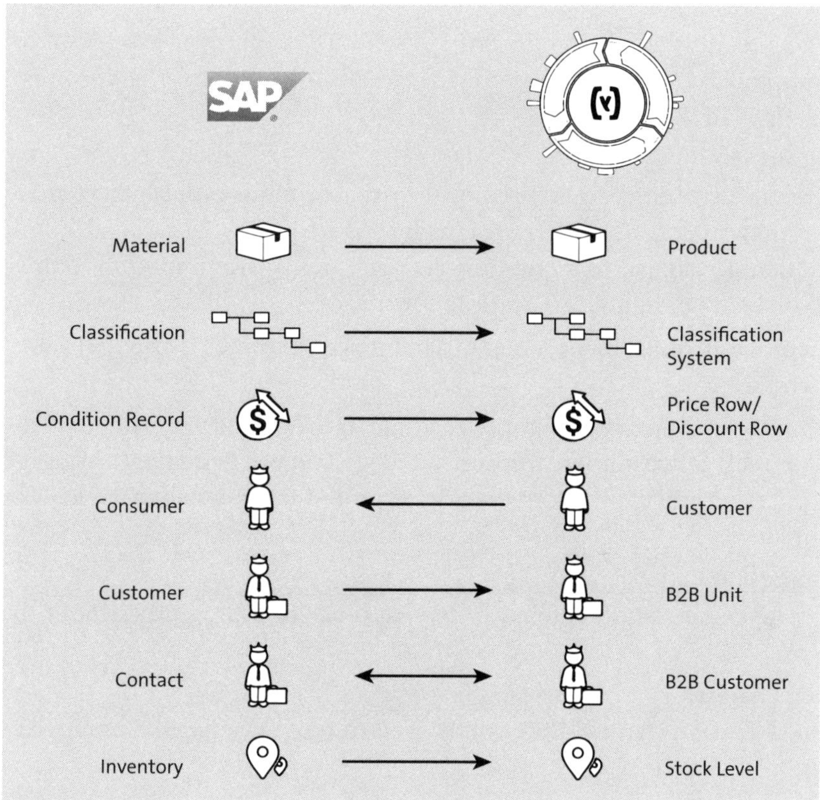

Figure 11.1 SAP Commerce Master Data Mapping with SAP Fulfillment Backends

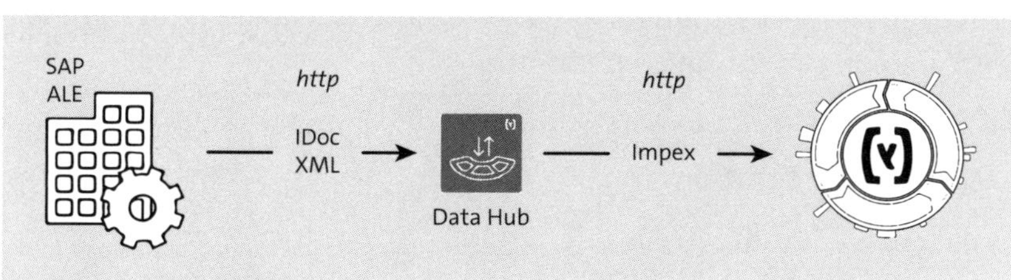

Figure 11.2 Data Flow from SAP ERP or SAP S/4HANA to SAP Commerce

Some of the common configurations are required and they are set up in the SAP Commerce backoffice Administration Cockpit. These settings are applicable for multiple integration scenarios. Under the SAP Commerce common settings (**SAP Integration • SAP Base Configuration • Common Settings**), provide values for the following objects:

- **Order**
  Enter the document type used in the SAP backend. The order type is relevant for synchronous and asynchronous order management integrations. The document types are defined in the backend.
- **Reference Customer**
  Enter a reference customer to be used in the asynchronous order management and synchronous pricing. The reference customer is created in the backend (Transaction VD01) and assigned to a one-time account group. Two important points, depending on your configuration, are as follows:
  - In asynchronous order management, a reference customer is used as a one-time customer.
  - In synchronous pricing, the reference customer is used to calculate prices in the catalog and cart for customers who are not logged on yet. Once they are logged on, the prices are calculated from the pricing procedure assigned to the logged-in customers.
- **Sales Organization**
  Enter the sales organization defined in the backend for selling products in the online store.
- **Distribution Channel**
  Enter the distribution channel that will be used to route products to online customers.
- **Division**
  Enter the sales division in the backend for selling products in the online store.

Basic settings like the RFC destination for SAP Commerce, data hub, a port, and a logical system are a prerequisite for data replications.

11.2.2 Customer Data Integration

The customer data in SAP Commerce is referred to as a customer or contact person in a B2B scenario and a consumer in a B2C scenario. The customer master data is essentially the data required to conduct business and provide service to the customer.

The data replication between SAP Commerce and SAP ERP or SAP S/4HANA will be discussed in the following sections.

Business to Business

Company data translates to a B2B customer in SAP Commerce terms. In B2B scenarios, the respective backend system is usually the leading source system for customer data. SAP Commerce receives all account/customer data from an SAP backend. The replication of account data from SAP ERP and SAP S/4HANA takes sales-area-dependent data into consideration. This happens by creating a B2B unit hierarchy with a subnode for each sales area. Partner roles such as sold-to and ship-to are considered, and related addresses are created in SAP Commerce.

B2B customer data can be transferred from SAP Commerce to the SAP backend or from the SAP backend to SAP Commerce. This supports the following scenarios:

- Replication from the SAP backend to SAP Commerce (see Figure 11.3) makes sense if the contact data along with the account data are maintained in the SAP backend.

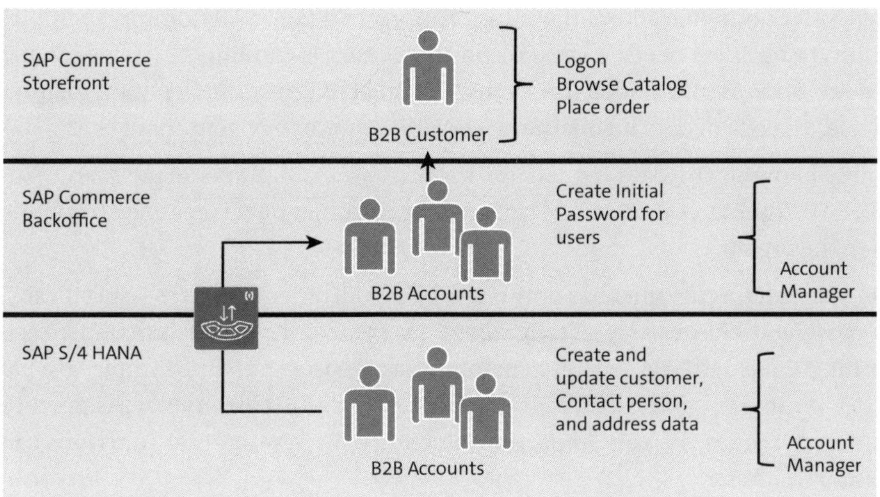

Figure 11.3 B2B Customer Data Flow from the SAP Backend to SAP Commerce

- Replication from SAP Commerce to the SAP backend (see Figure 11.4) applies in cases in which the SAP Commerce capabilities for B2B customer self-registration or the delegated user administration capabilities in SAP Commerce are used. In the latter case, a special admin user creates the user for his or her company through the storefront.

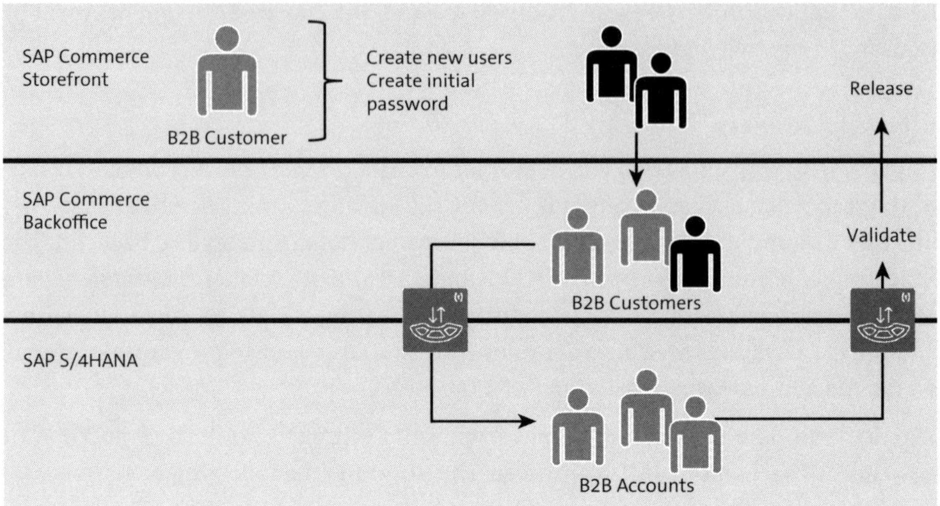

Figure 11.4 B2B Customer Data Flow from SAP Commerce to the SAP Backend

Although SAP Commerce allows these two options to adjust SAP Commerce implementations to business needs, a good recommendation is certainly to decide on one of the given options and not to use both in parallel. Bidirectional contact maintenance raises the risk of data inconsistencies caused by cross-system changes.

Differences between the data models for the SAP backend (SAP S/4HANA and SAP ERP) and SAP Commerce data models affect how customer data is mapped from one system to the other.

In the SAP backend, a customer has only one address. All other addresses—specifically, ship-to party and bill-to party—are assigned by means of partner functions. Each partner function exists as a separate customer in the backend; for example, a separate customer master record contains an address, and this customer is assigned to the main customer as the ship-to partner function. Different partner functions can use the same address.

Figure 11.5 shows the Display Customer transaction (Transaction VD03) in the backend, where you can view the partner functions assigned to a customer.

Although several partner functions are available in SAP ERP, only ship-to party and bill-to party are replicated to SAP Commerce. In SAP Commerce, the B2B unit is equivalent to a customer in the backend, which means that customer addresses in the backend are replicated to SAP Commerce as B2B unit addresses. A B2B customer in SAP Commerce is equivalent to a contact person in the backend.

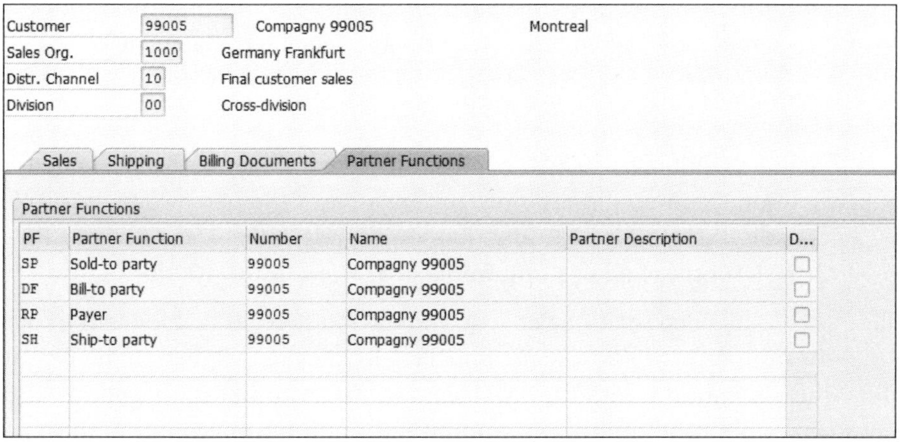

Figure 11.5 Customer Information Screen in SAP Backend

For every SAP backend partner function replicated to SAP Commerce, a new address is created for the B2B unit. You can view the replication results in the backoffice Administration Cockpit, under **B2B Commerce • B2B Unit** in the **Addresses** tab. In addition to the standard address details in the backoffice, SAP-specific information is included in the **Administration** tab for replicated addresses. The **SAP Address Usage** field indicates whether the address is for a ship-to or bill-to partner function in the backend.

The **SAP Customer ID** field provides the ID of the customer in the backend, and this ID is used to resolve a specific technical issue in SAP Commerce. Although the same address can be used by different partner functions in the backend, the same address cannot be used more than once in a B2B unit in SAP Commerce. For this reason, a new address is created for every partner function address replicated from the backend, even if this results in duplicate addresses for a B2B unit. For example, if the ship-to and bill-to partner functions for a customer in the backend both use the same address, they are replicated as separate, identical addresses in SAP Commerce. When an address is updated and saved in either the backoffice or the online store, SAP Commerce checks the SAP customer ID and automatically updates any identical addresses that are assigned to that SAP customer ID.

The SAP backend also accommodates sales area dependencies in SAP Commerce with parent and child B2B units.

In the SAP backend, partner functions, price groups, and discount groups are sales-area-dependent. A customer with multiple sales areas replicates from the backend to

SAP Commerce. The customer maps as a parent B2B unit with child B2B units for each sales area. The parent B2B unit contains sales-area-independent data. The child B2B units contain sales-area-dependent data, including ship-to party and bill-to party addresses, price groups, and discount groups.

The ID of a child B2B unit consists of the ID for the parent B2B unit, the sales organization, distribution channel, and division. For example, if the parent B2B unit ID is 1234567, sales organization ID is 1000, distribution channel ID is 10, and division ID is 00, the resulting ID of the child B2B unit would be 1234567_1000_10_00.

An online store is mapped to one sales area, and the sales area is defined in the base store. In SAP Commerce, when B2B customers log in, they're assigned to the parent B2B unit. When integrating with the SAP backend, the customer is assigned also to the appropriate child B2B unit. The assignment is based on the sales area of the base store.

Figure 11.6 shows the relations between sales areas and customers in the backend and how they are mapped in SAP Commerce.

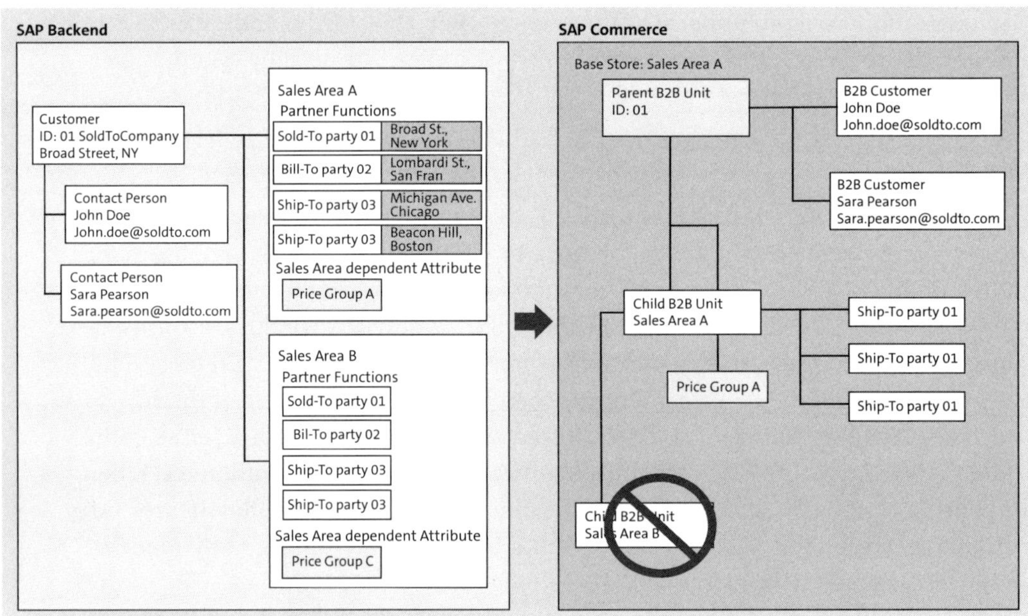

Figure 11.6 Sales Area Mapping from SAP Backend to SAP Commerce

Taxation Classification Information for Customer Data

Some customers may have unique taxation classification information. For example, educational institutions may be taxed at a lower rate than other customers. When you replicate customer data from the SAP backend, taxation classification information is not included. As a postreplication step in SAP Commerce, maintain taxation classification information manually. In the base store, you can assign a default taxation classification attribute that applies to all customers. Then, once replication is complete, you can maintain taxation classification information manually for exceptional customers only.

Business to Consumer

The leading system for B2C customers or consumers is SAP Commerce because the end customer registers himself and owns and maintains his data in SAP commerce. Consumer data is treated in two ways:

1. **Registered consumer**
   In this scenario, the consumer data is present in both the commerce system and the backend system (SAP ERP or SAP S/4HANA). For every customer who registers, their data is replicated back to SAP ERP or SAP S/4HANA and they are replicated to the backend as a consumer in account group 0170.
2. **One-time consumer or guest user**
   In this case, the user conducts all transactions as a guest user, and the consumer information resides only in SAP Commerce and isn't replicated to the backend. The backend will get the order information but not the consumer info. The order will have the embedded consumer information in it but no separate consumer record.

The registered consumer in SAP Commerce can replicate consumer data to the affected SAP system (see Figure 11.7). This replication is valid for an SAP ERP or SAP S/4HANA integration, in which a customer of type consumer is created from SAP Commerce consumer data. It is also valid for integrations with SAP CRM, SAP Sales Cloud, SAP Customer Engagement Center, and SAP Marketing.

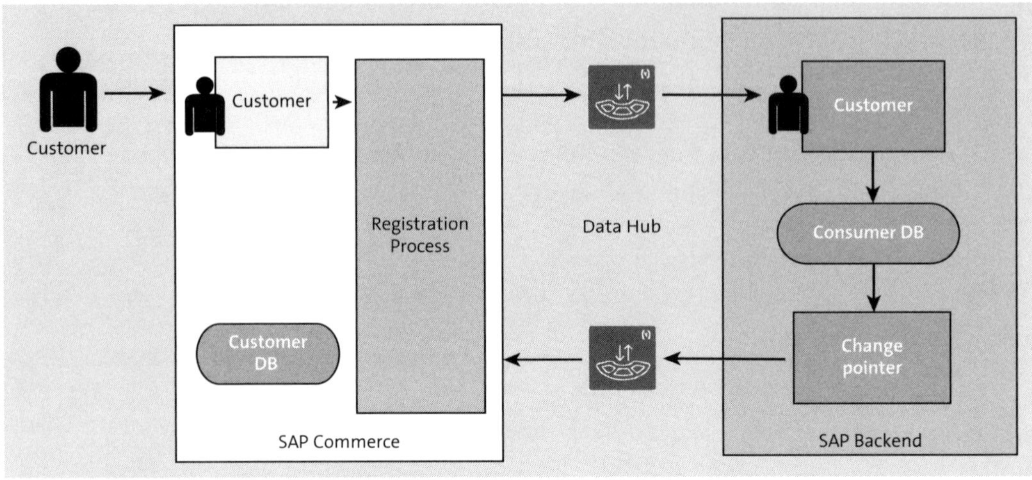

Figure 11.7 Consumer Data Integration between SAP Commerce (as the Leading System) and SAP ERP or SAP S/4HANA

The sequence of steps to replicate the consumer data from SAP Commerce to SAP ERP or other backend systems is as follows:

1. The B2C consumer registers online. Once registered, the administrator can see the record in the backoffice administration cockpit.
2. Once the replication is complete, the admin can check the correct account group with an SAP ID via Transaction VD03 (Display Customer).
3. The SAP backend sends notification that the replication was successful.
4. In the **My Account** section, consumers can create new addresses, change existing addresses, add or edit a title, first name, or last name, and so on.

From a business perspective, customers and contact persons belong to the B2B scenario, and consumers belong to the B2C scenario. The SAP backend needs both a customer ID and contact ID to create a consumer from the replicated data. Even if a consumer is created directly in the backend, a contact person is created automatically along with the consumer. Due to this requirement from the backend, both the starting customer ID and the contact ID are specified in the local.properties file.

11.2.3 Product Data Integration

For product or material data, prebuilt integrations rely on a process in which the SAP backend—namely, SAP ERP, SAP S/4HANA, or SAP Master Data Governance (SAP MDG)—is the leading system. This follows an understanding that the decision to sell a material via digital channels is reflected in the master data maintenance of the SAP backend first, so materials or products are replicated to SAP Commerce. SAP Commerce uses data that controls the business process, like the ID, the product name, the base unit of measure, and the sales unit of measure, as a foundation for catalog maintenance.

In SAP Commerce, the basic data is then complemented with information that is needed to present a product in the digital channels—like description, specification, categorization, and images. Again, the prebuilt integrations offer a concept for sales-area-dependent data. Every level on which product data can be maintained is linked to a configurable catalog version; that is, each sales area can be assigned a catalog version. As a result, the default catalog contains the basic data, whereas the configured catalog version contains the sales-area-dependent data, such as units of measure and delivering plants. During subsequent catalog maintenance, the data can be used accordingly.

Note

Integration of SAP Commerce with SAP Marketing Cloud supports a case in which SAP Marketing Cloud is served with product master data not from an SAP backend but from SAP Commerce.

Let's look at the possible components of product data integration:

- **Product master replication**
  When replicating the initial load from SAP S/4HANA or SAP ERP, you execute the transfer using the standard method for replicating product master data to an external system. The source SAP system must process the full object, including both changed and unchanged data. Delta loads require custom enhancements. SAP Note 1966001 provides instructions to create a report to force the delta load to retrieve the full object. The standard delta load, which is based on ALE change pointers, only distributes changed values. Ensure that change pointers are properly configured and activated (Transactions BD50 and BD61) in the source system.

- **Classification data replication**
  Along with the product data, classification data can be synchronized with SAP Commerce. Classification data maintained in the SAP backend can be used for faceted search in SAP Commerce. Classification data from the SAP backend can also be used as a foundation for adding content data for consumption by SAP Product Configuration. The product master data synchronization is a good example of how the SAP backend capabilities and the capabilities of SAP Commerce complement each other by focusing on their individual strengths: SAP backend for data that controls the business processes, and SAP Commerce product content management for information relevant for digital channels.
- **Inventory data replication**
  The prebuilt integrations of SAP Commerce with SAP ERP and SAP S/4HANA master data synchronization include a replication of inventory data. As part of this replication, unrestricted stock information is extracted from the SAP backend. This information is used either for showing the stock information on the storefront or as a foundation for sourcing and availability calculation capabilities of order management for SAP Commerce.

  The product master must be uploaded before uploading the inventory data, and the corresponding warehouse data in SAP Commerce must match corresponding plant data in the SAP backend. In the SAP backend, execute program RMCPAMRP with the message type value set to `LOISTD`, along with the correct receiving system, material, and plant information.

11.2.4 Pricing Data Integration

Pricing data is a critical part of master data synchronization. The replication of SAP condition records to SAP Commerce price and discount rows is a prerequisite for pricing scenarios and is supported by the prebuilt integrations. Similar to product master data synchronization, the exchange of pricing data supports sales area dependency for use in catalog versions.

Pricing data is replicated to SAP Commerce from the SAP backend to make prices and discounts from SAP available in online stores. The online stores can operate without being connected to the SAP backend when the pricing data is replicated and is available for use.

Note

When prices and discounts sent from the SAP backend are valid only during a specific time frame, the resulting price and discount rows remain in SAP Commerce even after the prices and discounts are no longer active. You can remove expired price and discount rows by scheduling a CronJob.

In the SAP backend, prices and discounts are assigned to sales areas. For the purposes of catalog mapping, each sales area consists of a sales organization and a distribution channel. (The division is not relevant when mapping prices and discounts to catalogs.) Sales areas are equivalent to catalog versions in SAP Commerce and should be mapped as such in the backoffice. This mapping ensures that all prices and discounts assigned to sales areas are automatically replicated to corresponding catalog versions. Only one sales area can be mapped to one catalog at a given time.

In the backoffice, use a mapping table to indicate which sales areas are mapped to specific catalog versions in SAP Commerce via **SAP Integration • SAP Global Configurations • Pricing Replication**.

In the **Pricing Replication** tab, use another mapping table to indicate which sites are mapped to specific catalog versions and promotion groups in SAP Commerce. Once this data is saved, it becomes part of the overall data mapping set.

To specify the systems used in the data distribution, message dispatching, and sending and receiving systems, a model view needs to be created in the SAP backend.

In the distribution model display (Transaction BD64) in the SAP backend, choose **Create Model View** in the edit mode and provide details like **Short Text**, **Technical Name**, and validity dates. Choose **Add Message Type** and provide values for **Model View Name**, **Sender**, **Receiver**, and **Message Type**; the value of the latter should be **COND_A**.

For replication discounts and pricing conditions from the SAP backend, go to the **Display Condition Records** screen (Transaction VK13) and enter the condition type to be viewed—for example, PROO—and then select **Condition Information**. Enter values for the **Sales Organization**, **Distribution Channel**, and **Material**, and then choose **Execute**. Select the applicable rows from the table, and then choose **Send Condition**. Make sure the **Message Type** is **COND_A** and that **Logical System** shows the correct receiving system name.

The replication results can be viewed in the corresponding catalog in the backoffice. Under **Catalog • Products**, search for the corresponding product, then check the price information in the **Pricing** tab.

In general, the SAP Commerce prebuilt integrations use the APIs offered by the backend system. For example, SAP ERP and SAP S/4HANA integrations use ALE and IDocs for both getting data from the SAP backend and sending data to the SAP backend. SAP Commerce uses ALE because customers know how to use ALE—how to operate it, administer it, and extend it.

Independent from this, HTTP is used as communication technology. Only the XML payload is defined by the IDocs. The IDocs are mediated between the SAP backend and SAP Commerce via a middleware layer. Here either SAP Commerce, data hub or SAP Cloud Platform Integration is used. The IDocs listed in Table 11.3 are used in the SAP ERP and in the SAP S/4HANA integration.

Data Type	IDocs
Company and account data (B2B unit)	DEBMAS, ADRMAS
Contacts (B2B customer)	ADR3MAS (always combined with DEBMAS for company data)
Consumer (B2C customer)	DEBMAS, ADR2MAS
Products	MATMAS
Classification	CHRMAS, CLFMAS, CLSMAS
Prices	COND_A
Inventory	LOISTD
Orders	SALESORDER_CREATEFROMDAT2
Order confirmations, returns, cancellations	ORDERS
Shipping notifications	DELINF
Invoices	INVOIC

Table 11.3 IDocs for SAP ERP and SAP S/4HANA Integrations

Nevertheless, SAP Commerce will migrate from IDocs to SOAP interfaces for the SAP S/4HANA integration over time. In the latest integration, released in August 2018, you will see that the prebuilt integrations consume SOAP interfaces for customer data exchange (`BusinessPartnerSUITEBulkReplicateRequest_Out` and `BusinessPartnerSUITEBulkReplicateRequest_In`).

Integrations with other SAP products use OData (e.g., the integration for SAP Marketing Cloud) or REST interfaces (e.g., the integration with SAP Subscription Billing) in the backend.

11.3 Order Management Scenarios

Order management or, better, order fulfilment for physical products provides a good example of how SAP Commerce gives customers a way to choose the scenario that best fits their business requirements instead of following a one-size-fits-all approach.

All the scenarios that will be explained in detail in this section follow a common pattern. The customer starts by browsing the catalog to discover products to purchase. Subsequently, the customer adds the products to the cart and checks out. At this point, the integration for order fulfillment kicks in. The order that was created in SAP Commerce is sent to an SAP backend (SAP ERP or SAP S/4HANA). Here the order is transferred to logistics; that is, one or more deliveries are created for the order. The deliveries are picked, packed, and shipped using the capabilities for warehouse management and distribution. Once the delivery is shipped, an invoice is created for the customer. During this process, status information is sent back to SAP Commerce to allow for status tracking by the customer. This is the foundation of the financial execution.

There are two considerations for order management scenarios: to what degree native SAP Commerce features are used and how tightly SAP Commerce is integrated with the SAP backend. Keep in mind that the end user will not be able to identify which of the scenarios is used for a given storefront.

In the following sections we will have a look at asynchronous order management integration, synchronous order management, and other scenarios like distributed order management and order orchestration.

11.3.1 Asynchronous Order Management

Asynchronous order management is the simplest integration scenario. In asynchronous order management, only the cart functionality of SAP Commerce is used. This means that until the user submits the order, only SAP Commerce functionality is consumed. Upon order submission, the order is sent to the backend asynchronously. For decoupling SAP Commerce from the SAP backend, SAP Commerce business process functionality is used, which sends the data to the middleware. Status updates are received from the SAP backend asynchronously as well.

With this architecture, SAP Commerce stays fully operational even if there is (at least for a limited period) no backend connectivity available. Further, scaling the load from a high number of users is managed purely in SAP Commerce.

Asynchronous order management is the best fit for customers who meet the following criteria:

- Find available SAP Commerce capabilities for order capture (including price calculation, availability, and other features) sufficient or can customize these capabilities accordingly
- Prefer decoupled infrastructures
- Prefer to manage the load purely in the SAP Commerce layer

We see this integration scenario very often in pure B2C scenarios, in which the business requirements as such are less complex and the challenge scaling the load resulting from managing a high number of users.

Another option is asynchronous order management with real-time integration, which is still basically asynchronous order management. This means that primarily the cart functionality of SAP Commerce is used. The order synchronization with the backend works in the same way as for asynchronous order management.

The difference is that for selected services or, better, for selected features, the capabilities of the SAP backend are used. A related offering is available for the following:

- **Price calculation**
  Interestingly, SAP Commerce, in contrast to most custom integrations, does not use order simulation in the backend. Instead it consumes a still rather new API, which was optimized for price calculation (and only for price calculation; other price-related features such as free goods are not supported). This makes this API incredibly fast (in comparison to order simulation).

  For implementation projects, consider that SAP Commerce passes a limited set of pricing attributes to the backend. When this is not sufficient (which will most probably always be the case), related enhancements either in SAP Commerce or in the backend (by implementing the related BAdIs) are necessary.

- **Available to promise (ATP)**
  Strictly speaking, SAP Commerce gets ATP information. It doesn't initiate an ATP check (which would include management of related reservations, requirements, and confirmations).
- **Credit check**
  Credit check is available with SAP ERP only.

From a technical perspective, SAP Commerce calls the related APIs directly and synchronously in the backend. As of today (release 1808), the APIs are RFCs. Consequently, SAP Commerce leverages Java Connector (JCo) to communicate with the ABAP backends. Note that these calls are made using a service user in the backend, so backend authorizations do not apply.

JCo comes bundled with SAP Commerce and does not have to be installed separately. Further, SAP Commerce provides additional features that make consumption of JCo easier.

These capabilities come at a price: they cannot be used when the connection to the SAP backend is, for whatever reason, not available. Fallbacks are certainly feasible, but they are not implemented out of the box as part of the prebuilt integrations. The APIs listed in Table 11.4 are used for this.

Feature	Main API	Notes
Price calculation	PIQ_CALCULATE	Offered as of SAP ERP EHP 7 and higher only.
ATP information	BAPI_MATERIAL_AVAILABILITY	
Credit check	BAPI_CREDITCHECK	Available with SAP ERP only; not supported for SAP S/4HANA.

Table 11.4 List of APIs

Real-time integration is largely intended for companies that have complex implementations for the affected services and consequently want to reuse existing SAP backend functionality. This provides consistency and leverages the work done in the backend. The strength of this scenario is that the complete backend functionality runs in frontend SAP Commerce, including, for example, pricing requirements, user exits, and even custom modifications.

With these characteristics, this scenario provides a good balance between the pure asynchronous order management scenario and synchronous order management. We see this scenario often in B2B cases, in which the SAP backend functionality is needed at least to a restricted degree, but either strong decoupling is still required or other SAP Commerce functionality (e.g., B2B approvals) is needed.

11.3.2 Synchronous Order Management

In this scenario, the UI runs in SAP Commerce and the cart is completely managed by the order functionality of the SAP backend; there is literally no persistence for the order in SAP Commerce.

This scenario is completely based on the ABAP backend concept of stateful RFCs. As soon as either the cart is displayed or the first product is added to the cart, the first RFC call is made to the backend. At this time, the backend session is created and the order management context is initialized. Every subsequent call to the backend is connected to the same session in the backend, and only the related deltas are added to the order management context. Between two calls, the order data is not persisted but is kept in the session only.

Nonetheless, with every call, all order functions in the backend are executed, including the ATP check, product substitution, listing/exclusion check, and all user exits. As a result, the SAP Commerce UI behaves from a purely functional perspective very similarly to the create order functionality of the backend. Of course, SAP Commerce makes a significant effort to hide the complexity of the backend from the user—for example, by offering the message mapping feature, which "translates" backend messages to messages that can be understood by SAP Commerce storefront users.

At the point, when the user submits the order in the storefront, the order is persisted. Also, the order history is based on RFCs to the backend, so it shows all orders that were created, regardless of whether they were created through the storefront or through other channels (e.g., EDI or native backend applications). This approach differentiates synchronous order management from other approaches often seen in custom implementations and based on order simulations. It is certainly faster than order simulations in every round trip.

Synchronous order management offers the highest possible degree of consistency with the SAP backend because only the business logic of the SAP backend is leveraged, but it comes at a price: the load needs to be managed to a large degree in the backend. This is certainly possible, but the use case needs to be considered for the backend.

Another important point to consider is that SAP Commerce (at least where it affects carts and orders) is almost not operational when the backend is not available. The available fallback feature addresses this issue only to a limited degree.

Note that selected SAP Commerce functionality is not available if synchronous order management is used, such as saved carts, quotations, and some of the SAP Commerce B2B features. In addition, SAP Commerce's functionality for personalization is restricted. Keep in mind that all SAP Commerce features that rely on carts and orders are affected and hence are not supported. Due to the nature of the RFC scenario, the usage of the assisted service module is restricted.

From an API perspective, synchronous order management is based on the so-called Lean Order (LORD) API family. For selected functions, SAP Commerce uses wrappers for some LORD functions, which might be changed in the future.

We see that synchronous order management is often used by SAP ERP-savvy customers with B2B scenarios who heavily invested into their backend implementations and need to reuse these investments. With its strong focus on order capture, it works well as a tactical solution for customers who migrate from earlier (sunset) SAP e-commerce products.

The prebuilt integration supports B2B only. Although it works with customization for B2C as well, using it for B2C scenarios is certainly an exotic case.

11.3.3 Leveraging Order Management for Commerce

The order management integration for SAP Commerce shows how SAP Commerce not only connects to and uses the capabilities of the SAP backend but also enriches the complete offering beyond the usual SAP Commerce use cases. Embedded into asynchronous order management integration scenarios, order management for SAP Commerce can be used to add features related to distributed order management and order orchestration in the SAP backend. With this integration, order management for SAP Commerce is responsible for *sourcing* the order; that is, it decides from which location(s)/warehouse(s) the order is fulfilled. It does so based on the inventory information provided by the SAP backends and based on the ATP calculation and sourcing algorithms, which are part of order management for SAP Commerce.

Let's consider a use case for the default plant determination in SAP ERP. Plant determination in SAP ERP is static to a large degree; it depends on customer master data, product master data, or on a combination of both. In contrast, the sourcing algorithms in SAP Commerce can be dynamic; they can depend on availability, on inventory, on priorities, and on other factors. If a given location/warehouse doesn't fit, the next location is checked according to the algorithm. The asynchronous order management integration with SAP Commerce now lets SAP Commerce make the sourcing decision and simply forwards the determined location/warehouse as SAP ERP plant to the order, which is created in SAP ERP. With this capability, SAP Commerce provides features to the SAP backend that are otherwise not available.

At the same time, this integration supports use cases in which multiple deliveries are created per each order in the SAP backend.

On the SAP ERP side, once the sourcing plant is finalized and the delivery is created, the consignment/order is updated with the delivery information. This information can be accessed in the SAP Commerce accelerator storefront by the customer and in the backend by the service support representative. After delivery creation, the product is shipped and invoice gets created. The invoice information is added to the customer account summary in SAP Commerce.

This entire process from inventory and ATP check to source plant/warehouse determination to delivery, shipping, invoicing is shown in Figure 11.8.

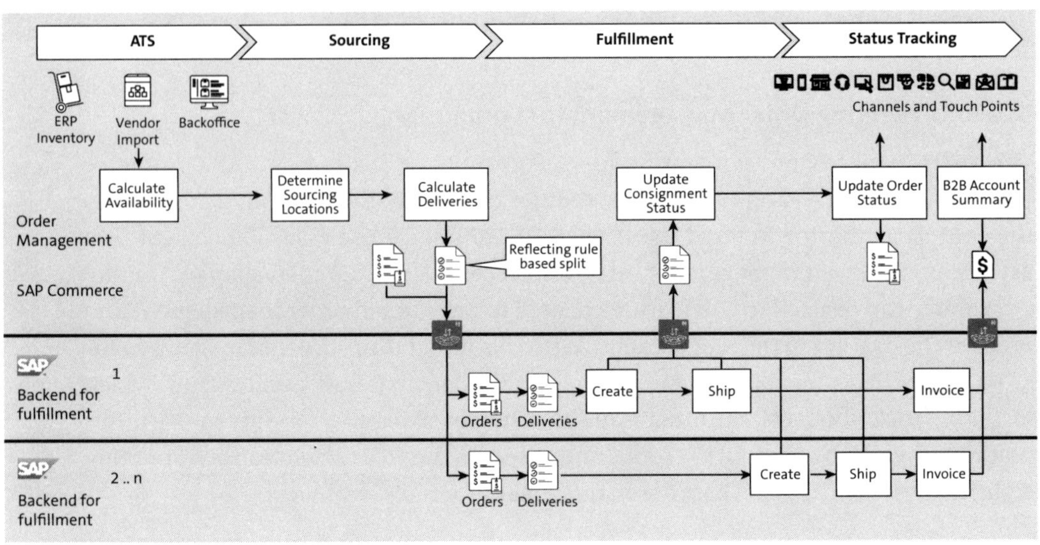

Figure 11.8 Asynchronous Order Management with Dynamic Plant Determination

11.3.4 Multibackend Integrations

The logic described in Section 11.3.3 provides the foundation for multiple backend support in SAP Commerce. The starting points are the sourcing algorithms of order management for SAP Commerce and the order consignments that are created based on the sourcing result. The integration now uses an assignment between SAP Commerce warehouses and SAP backends to split the order among the backends. Figure 11.9 shows the basic configuration screen in the backoffice where you can map the SAP plant to the logical system.

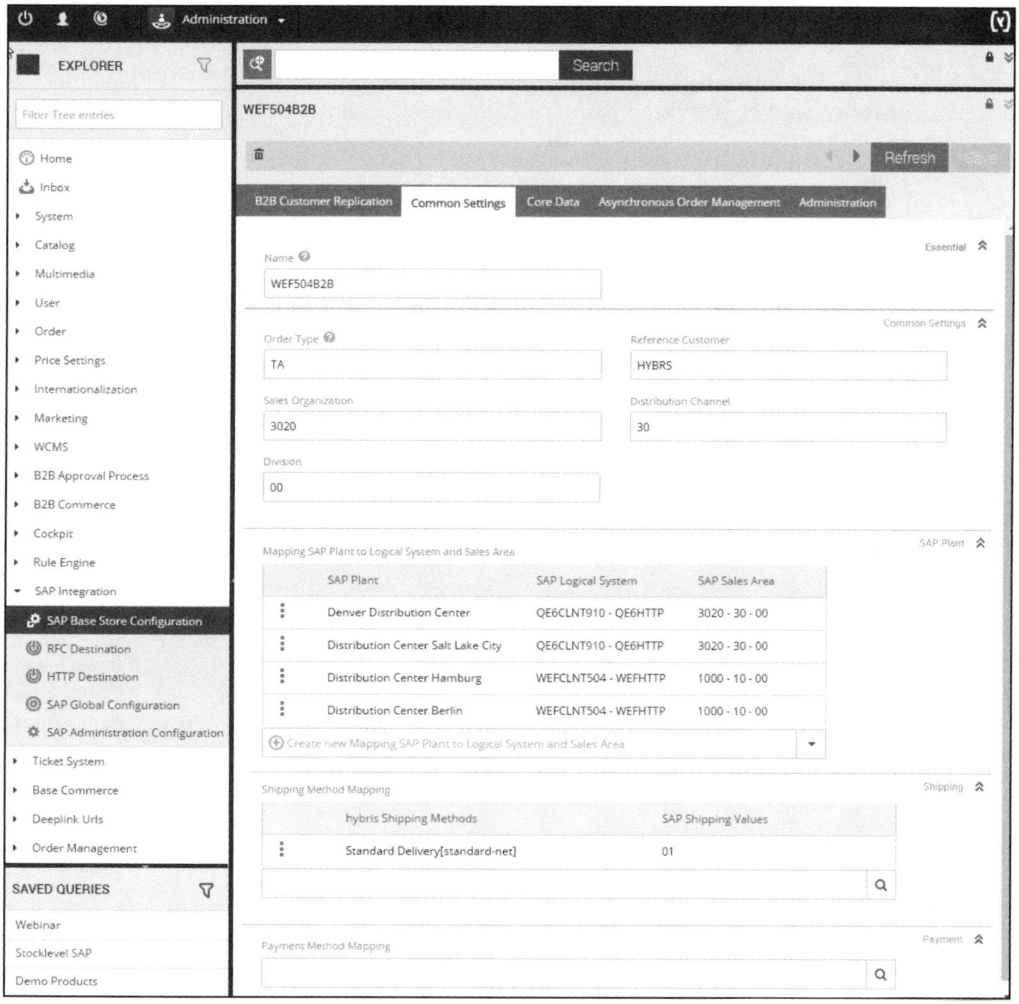

Figure 11.9 Configuration Settings for Mapping SAP Plant to the SAP System

All consignments for a given location/warehouse are forwarded to the assigned SAP backend. As a result, the logistics can be managed in a distributed manner on one hand, but SAP Commerce keeps a 360° view of the order for the customer on the other.

Note that this integration assumes delivery-related billing in the SAP backend—that is, that the customer gets at least one invoice from each backend. In addition, multiple backend integration requires special attendance to master data management because it doesn't provide capabilities for master data consolidation.

This scenario fits especially in cases in which, for example, different product lines are managed by different backends (either SAP backends or non-SAP backends). However, the complexity in the logistics should be hidden from the customer, and the customer should be provided with a consistent experience in the storefront.

Another example is a setup in which a company acquires other companies that have their own backends. SAP Commerce is supposed to provide a consistent brand experience across all acquisitions. Instead of waiting until a potential backend consolidation project is delivered, SAP Commerce can provide a holistic experience to the customer and hide the organizational complexity. Figure 11.10 showcases multiple backend systems connected to SAP Commerce.

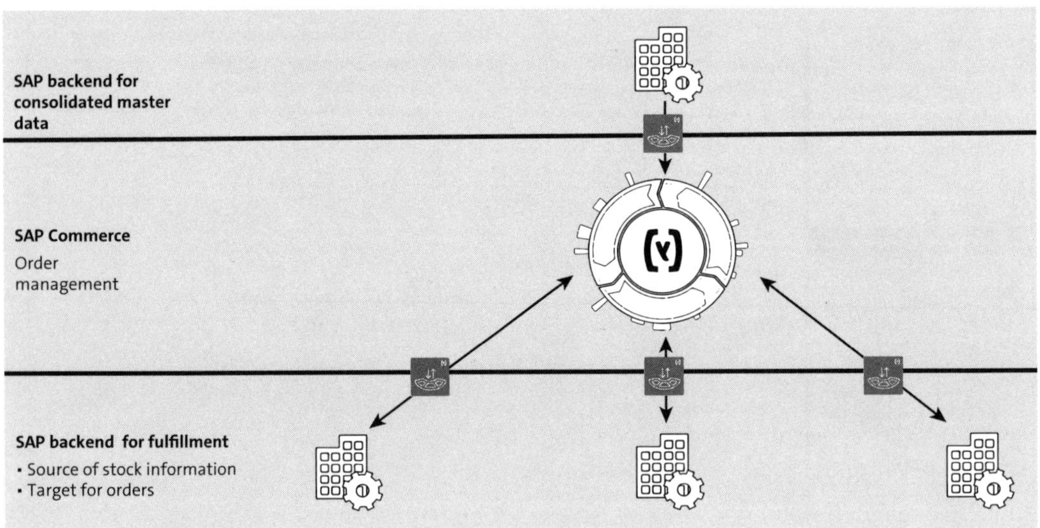

Figure 11.10 Fulfillment in Multiple SAP Backends

11.4 Price Calculation in an Integrated SAP Landscape

Another discussion, which is a subject of almost every asynchronous order management integration project, centers on the best approach for price calculation. Instead of following a one-size-fits-all approach, SAP Commerce offers two different scenarios that cover different requirements. Both scenarios have a way to create orders in the SAP backend in common.

11.4.1 Price Calculation Based on Consistent Master Data

This scenario showcases the SAP Commerce price calculation capabilities based on the pricing master data replicated from the SAP backend. PriceRows and DiscountRows are replicated as per the master data synchronization described previously. This means that PriceRows and DiscountRows in SAP Commerce are based on condition records from the SAP backend. As a result, although different pricing "engines" are used in SAP Commerce and in the SAP backend, both engines follow the same logic and use consistent data.

This price calculation option is a good fit for organizations who meet the following criteria:

- Prefer decoupled infrastructures
- Prefer to manage the load purely in the SAP Commerce layer

We see this option used often in B2C scenarios or in combination with the second option, when the prices in the catalog are calculated using one option and the cart pricing is calculated using the other price option.

11.4.2 Price Calculation Based on SAP Pricing Engine

This option was described briefly previously when we discussed real-time synchronous integration. Every call for price calculation is replaced with a synchronous JCo/RFC call to the backend. With this, SAP Commerce needs to be connected to the SAP backend to return results, and it provides a high level of consistency with the SAP backend because the same pricing engine is used.

This price calculation option fits for customers who require the following:

- Industry-specific pricing
- Highest possible consistency between SAP backend and SAP Commerce
- Protection of their investments in ABAP-based SAP backend pricing

We see this option used often in B2B scenarios with companies that have also chosen to use asynchronous order management with real-time integration.

11.5 Integration with SAP Marketing Cloud

SAP Commerce and SAP Marketing Cloud have many synergies that can help engage the customer in the way customer wants to be engaged by offering a personalized experience while respecting consent guidelines. Valuable data can be gathered from the customer activity on the web storefront that can provide valuable insights to create effective marketing strategies. To make that happen, there are prebuilt integrations between SAP Commerce and SAP Marketing Cloud that help to seamlessly move data between the two systems. The integration flow between the two systems is detailed in Figure 11.11.

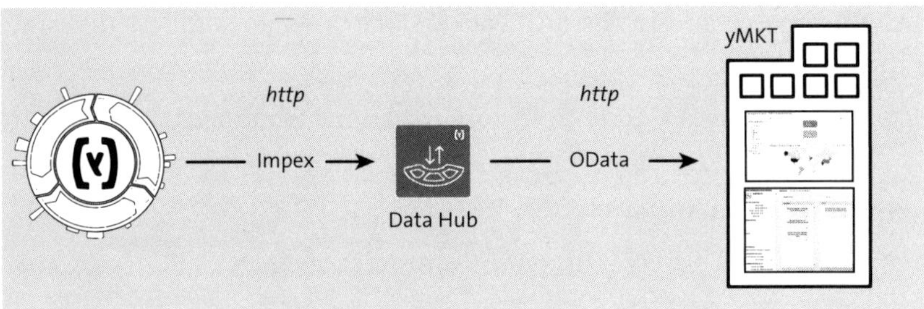

Figure 11.11 SAP Commerce Data Integration with SAP Marketing Cloud

The following integration scenarios are supported between SAP Commerce and SAP Marketing Cloud:

- **Master and transactional data replication to SAP Marketing Cloud**
  Replicate data from SAP Commerce to the SAP Marketing Cloud system. Various data types can be replicated, including product, order, customer, cart, and review data.
- **Product and offer recommendations (B2C)**
  Retrieve product and offer recommendations from the SAP Marketing Cloud for display in the storefront. Determine the visibility and success of recommendations by tracking how many times they are seen and clicked on by customers. Thanks to storage within SAP Commerce, the exchange of product recommendation data between systems is uncompromised even when the SAP Marketing Cloud system is unavailable.

- **Segmentation (B2B and B2C)**
  Seamlessly leverage data from the SAP Marketing Cloud system to configure personalized shopping experiences for your customers. You can access marketing data directly from SmartEdit when creating restrictions and customizations.
- **Clickstream data transfer to SAP Marketing Cloud**
  This allows you to analyze how the consumer interacts with the storefront, including what products were viewed, what products were added to the cart, and what products were purchased.

Figure 11.12 summarizes the data integration and flow between SAP Commerce and SAP Marketing Cloud.

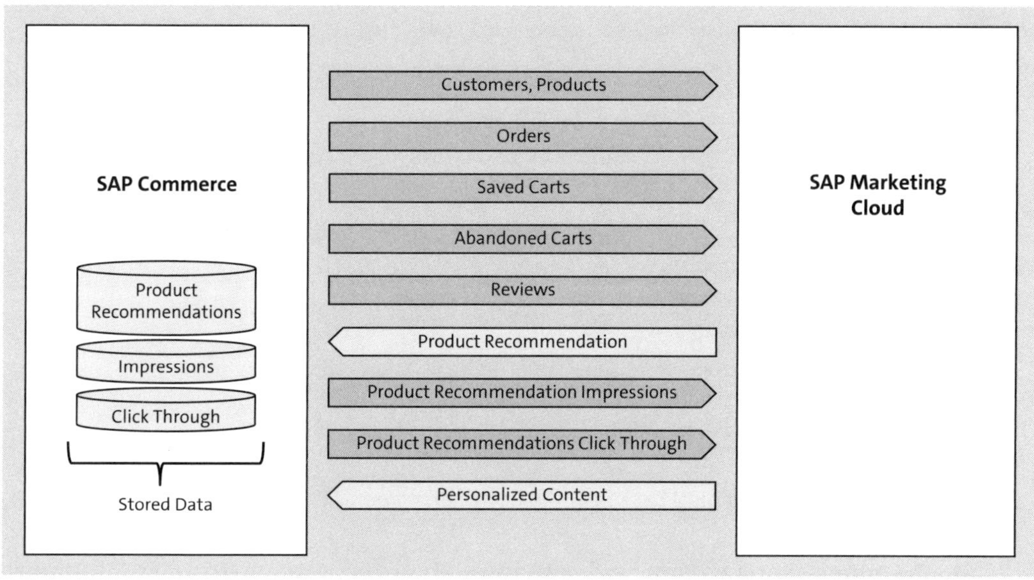

Figure 11.12 SAP Commerce and SAP Marketing Cloud Integrations

In the following subsections, let's look at the core data (e.g., customer data, product data, cart data) exchange, see how intelligent product and offer recommendations are generated, see how personalization is created with campaign and segmentation data, and discuss transfer of clickstream data from the SAP Commerce storefronts to SAP Marketing Cloud.

11.5.1 Data Replication to SAP Marketing Cloud

Master and transaction data is replicated to SAP Marketing Cloud via export jobs and SAP Commerce, data hub. Different master data and its mappings are shown in Figure 11.13.

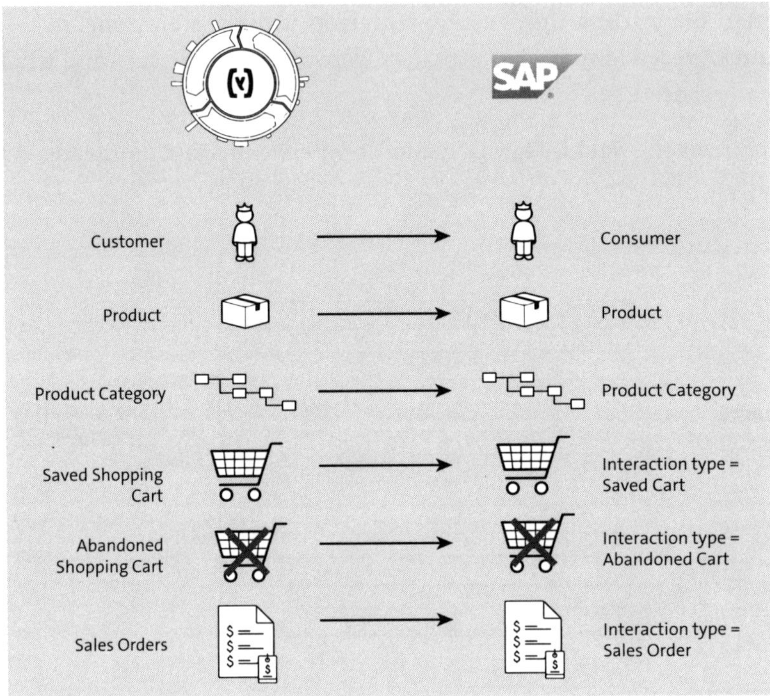

Figure 11.13 Data Mapping between SAP Commerce and SAP Marketing Cloud

Sales orders, shopping carts, and abandoned shopping carts are stored in SAP Marketing Cloud as *interaction types*. If the sales orders or shopping carts are associated with a campaign, respective campaign information is replicated to SAP Marketing Cloud.

The product reviews and ratings are also replicated to SAP Marketing Cloud. The reviews that are approved and not blocked are replicated. Ratings are transferred as whole numbers. If a rating is a fraction, it's rounded up.

11.5.2 Product and Offer Recommendations (B2C)

The SAP Marketing Cloud recommendation engine makes it possible to generate product and offer recommendations in real time. These recommendations are based on information from the storefront about what products were added to the cart, what products were viewed, what products were taken out of the cart, and what product were purchased, to name a few. Figure 11.14 showcases the data exchange and direction of data flow.

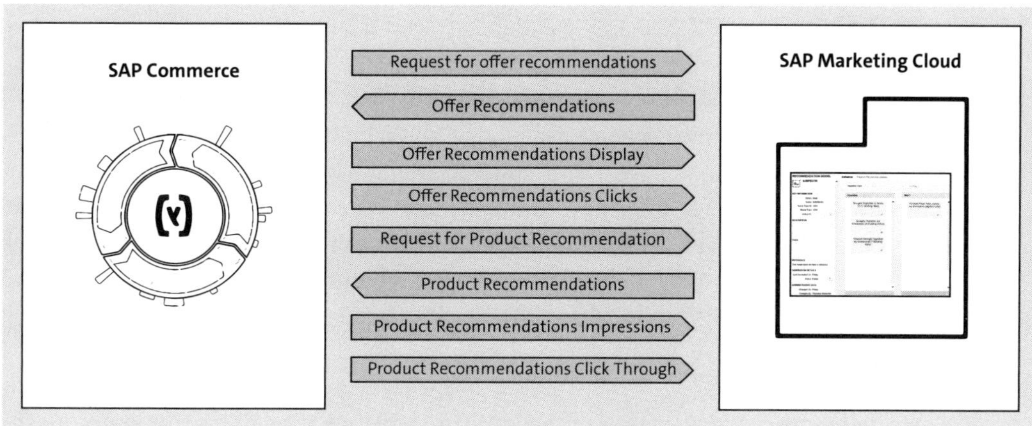

Figure 11.14 Product and Offer Recommendations Integration

SAP Commerce requests the recommendations by sending information about the products viewed and what products are in the cart. Once this information is replicated in SAP Marketing Cloud, the recommendation engine generates offers in real time to be displayed on the storefront. Availability and inventory levels are considered when generating the recommendations and they are updated as the products are added into a cart or purchased. The process works as follows:

1. Product recommendations are provided to known and anonymous users.
2. The web storefront determines the success of the recommendation data by tracking how many times a recommendation was viewed, clicked, and converted to an order.
3. The recommendations received from SAP Marketing Cloud are stored in the SAP Commerce system for accessibility and to reduce the number of calls made to SAP Marketing Cloud.

Figure 11.15 shows an example of how product recommendations appear in the storefront.

Figure 11.15 Product Recommendations

The various settings for offer and product recommendations can be configured in either SmartEdit or Web Content Management System (WCMS) Cockpit. Most of the settings are identical for both offer and product recommendations.

11.5.3 Personalization with Segmentation

Customer segmentation plays a critical role in identifying the right candidates for the right campaigns in all channels. Integrating marketing systems with SAP Commerce can seamlessly match customers with the right products and offers to improve sales and create a personalized shopping experience for storefront consumers. Figure 11.16 shows the data integration and flow between SAP Commerce and SAP Marketing Cloud.

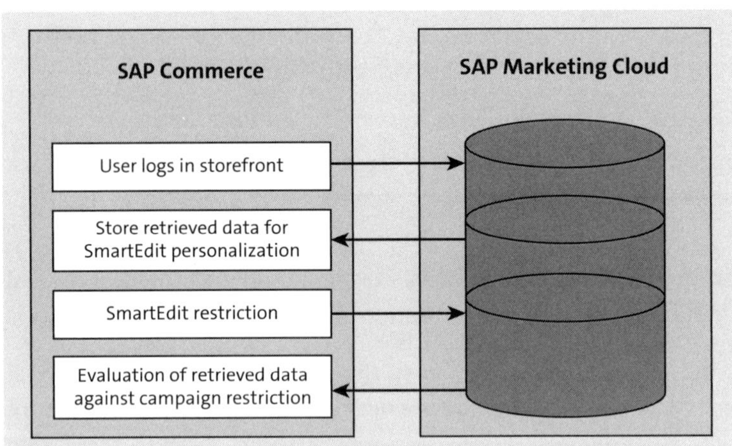

Figure 11.16 Segmentation and Personalization Data Integration and Flow between SAP Commerce and SAP Marketing Cloud

When a user logs on to the storefront, SAP Commerce retrieves all campaigns associated with that customer from the SAP Marketing Cloud system. The campaigns and target groups from the SAP Marketing Cloud system lay the foundation for defining personalization for customers targeted by specific campaigns.

Note

Personalization based on SAP Marketing Cloud data is only applicable for registered customers who have consented to receive personalized content and offers.

Email campaigns are an effective way to reach customers and track the success of the campaign. The success of an email campaign can be determined from order, saved cart, and abandoned cart data sent from SAP Commerce to the SAP Marketing Cloud system.

Email campaigns are created in SAP Marketing Cloud with a URL that contains an `sap_outbound_id` parameter, which identifies the contact and campaign ID and is sent to specific customer segment(s). When the customer clicks the URL and navigates to the SAP Commerce online store, the campaign ID stays in the user session; depending on the result, the campaign ID is sent with the order or saved cart or abandoned cart data. Campaign information associated with an order or saved or abandoned cart helps determine the success of the campaign.

Shopping cart abandonment is a known issue that impacts customer retention, cost per acquisition, revenue per email, and traffic. Customer recovery campaigns are designed to remind the customer to come back, continue shopping, and complete a purchase.

The abandoned shopping cart scenario is an end-to-end process involving SAP Commerce and SAP Marketing Cloud. The goal of the process is to convert abandoned shopping carts into sales.

When the status of the shopping cart is determined to be abandoned (no activity for two hours by default), abandoned cart information is sent to marketing and a follow-up email campaign is triggered. This campaign email has a URL to identify the abandoned cart. If the customer clicks on the URL and the action results in a sales order, the sales is attributed to the campaign, thus completing the end-to-end process.

11.5.4 Clickstream Data Transfer to SAP Marketing Cloud

Customer behavior in the storefront is tracked, aggregated as events, and sent to SAP Marketing Cloud. The most common event types are view product detail page, add to cart, remove from cart, successful checkout, and read review.

Insights gained from the data can be used as additional input for recommendation engines, for customer segmentation, or for campaign planning.

The integration supports approximately 200 events per second. If large amounts of data accumulate at peak times, try limiting the event types to those that provide the most valuable information. Figure 11.17 shows examples of the clickstream data being transferred from SAP Commerce to SAP Marketing Cloud.

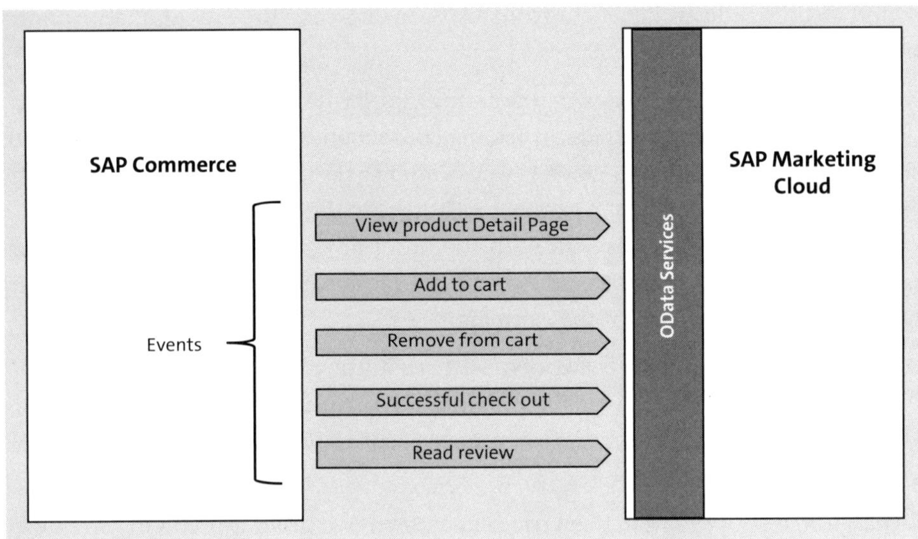

Figure 11.17 Clickstream Data Integration between SAP Commerce and SAP Marketing Cloud

11.6 Integration with SAP Sales Cloud and SAP Service Cloud

SAP Commerce integration with SAP Sales Cloud and SAP Service Cloud enables large enterprises to provide best-in-class sales and service support to their customers and assist them in the best way possible throughout their buying journey, regardless of channel or touchpoint.

The SAP Commerce and SAP Cloud for Customer integration provides a standard integration between the commerce and customer support solutions in the SAP product portfolio. The customer master data is replicated from SAP Cloud for Customer to SAP Commerce to ensure the customer can be served effectively from either system. One of the systems could be defined as the leading system for the customer master.

The product catalog data is accessible from SAP Cloud for Customer to ensure the sales and service agents can search and browse the online catalog to look up product information, configure product bundles, add products to carts, create quotes, or even check carts out for customers on their behalf.

The integration synchronizes service ticket data from SAP Commerce with SAP Cloud for Customer to connect customers with customer support agents. Once connected, agents can communicate with customers and resolve their needs via the SAP Commerce ticketing system or in real time via the phone.

An agent can click on a link in the SAP Sales Cloud system that seamlessly opens the assisted service module using single sign-on to allow the agent to provide interactive support to the customer in real time or offline. He can also help a customer with her account information, payment details, existing orders, cancelled orders, split orders, and delivery address, to name a few.

The quotations created by the customer or a sales personal in SAP Commerce are replicated to the SAP Sales Cloud system for further processing and actions. The sales representative can update and accept the quote in SAP Sales Cloud, and updates in SAP Sales Cloud are replicated to SAP Commerce. The customer can then edit, accept, or reject the quote in the SAP Commerce storefront.

Figure 11.18 summarizes the supported integration scenarios between SAP Commerce and SAP Service Cloud and SAP Sales Cloud.

In summary, the following integration scenarios are supported between SAP Commerce and SAP Sales Cloud and SAP Service Cloud:

- Synchronization of customer master data from SAP Commerce to SAP Cloud through SAP Commerce, data hub
- SAP Commerce catalog and storefront access for sales agents from SAP Sales Cloud and SAP Service Cloud
- Integrated SAP Commerce ticketing system
- Integrated SAP Commerce assisted service module for providing real-time and offline sales and service support

- Single sign-on to quickly connect from SAP Sales Cloud to SAP Commerce storefront
- SAP Commerce quote replication from SAP Commerce to SAP Sales Cloud

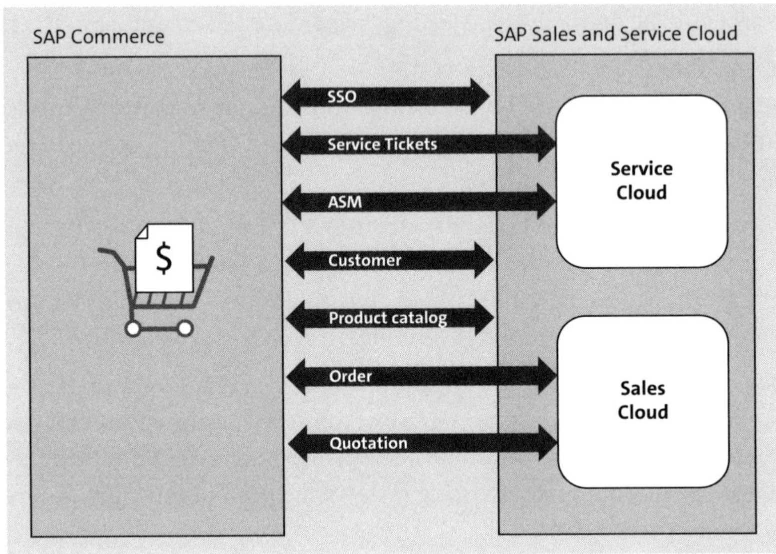

Figure 11.18 Integration Scenarios Supported for SAP Sales Cloud and SAP Service Cloud

Some customers have one or more SAP ERP backend solutions, and those are usually the leading systems for customer and material master data. In that case, the SAP ERP backend will be integrated with SAP Commerce and SAP Sales Cloud and SAP Service Cloud. All customer data and material data will be replicated from SAP ERP to SAP Commerce, SAP Sales Cloud, and SAP Service Cloud. This will ensure that there is a single source of master data across all the systems. Figure 11.19 shows an example of the multisystem data integration.

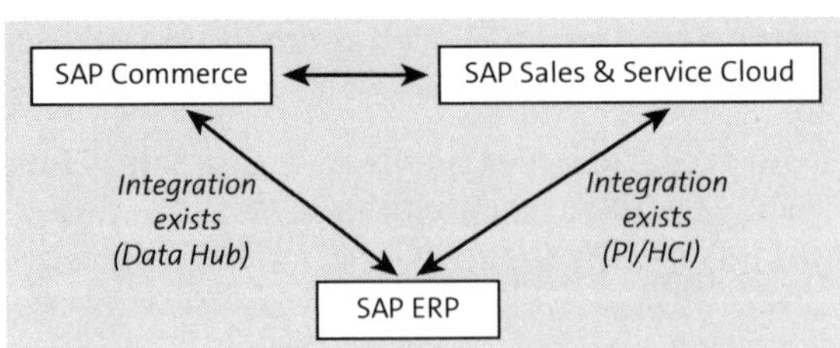

Figure 11.19 Multisystem Integration with SAP ERP, SAP Commerce, and SAP Sales Cloud and SAP Service Cloud

11.7 Integration with SAP Subscription Billing

SAP Commerce integration with SAP Subscription Billing using SAP Cloud Platform helps to monetize subscription and usage-based services, sell them across channels and touchpoints, bill for them, and collect and recognize revenue.

The details of the customers who register on the SAP Commerce storefront are replicated to SAP Subscription Billing. Subscription product master data is replicated from SAP Subscription Billing to SAP Commerce using SAP Cloud Platform Integration. Only products of the commercial subscription type are replicated. Bundled products currently are not considered.

Once the customer and products are replicated, customers can place orders for these products, and the order details are replicated to SAP Subscription Billing to create subscriptions. Customers can then manage their subscriptions from the SAP Commerce storefront. There are three main types of replication, as follows:

- **Customer replication**
  B2C customers registered in SAP Commerce are replicated to SAP Subscription Billing. Customers can be replicated to SAP S/4HANA and then to SAP Subscription Billing. Any updates made to the customer data in SAP Commerce are also replicated to SAP S/4HANA or SAP Subscription Billing.
- **Subscription product replication**
  Subscription products are replicated from SAP Subscription Billing to SAP Commerce using SAP Cloud Platform Integration. A *subscription* is a contractual agreement between a customer and the enterprise and entitles the customer to access specific products and services for a certain period. Product billing is handled by the attached rate plan. The product details are replicated asynchronously to SAP Commerce by running a CronJob at the SAP Commerce end. The rate plans associated with the product are also replicated.
- **Subscription order replication**
  Subscription orders are replicated from SAP Commerce to SAP Subscription Billing. Customers can then view and manage their subscriptions from SAP Commerce by making synchronous calls to SAP Subscription Billing. Subscriptions are created for the individual line items in the order. The customer can view the subscription bills for a given date range and view the unbilled usage details of the subscriptions. The customer can also extend or cancel the subscription.

Figure 11.20 summarizes the SAP Subscription Billing integration scenarios with SAP Commerce for customer data, product data, and order data replication. The replication leverages SAP Cloud Platform Integration. After order creation, if a subscription is created, the SAP Subscription Billing API takes over the subscription management with SAP Commerce.

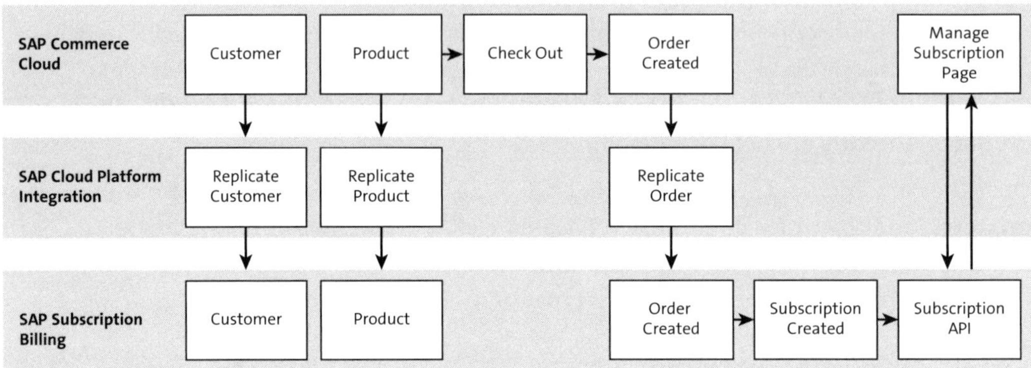

Figure 11.20 SAP Commerce Integration with SAP Subscription Billing

11.8 Integration with SAP Customer Engagement Center

Integration of SAP Customer Engagement Center with SAP Commerce provides a single service and support solution before and after sales across all areas of business to create a unified experience. This integration focuses on managing accounts, managing sales orders, service ticket management, launching the assisted service module, and text or video chats.

Account integration with SAP Customer Engagement Center enables account creation and updates in SAP Commerce using SAP Customer Engagement Center in the backend. The accounts created in SAP Commerce are replicated to SAP Customer Engagement Center, and accounts deleted in SAP Commerce are marked for deletion in SAP Customer Engagement Center.

The sales order integration between SAP Commerce and SAP Customer Engagement Center enables viewing and searching through sales orders from SAP Customer Engagement Center. The sales order details are replicated to SAP Customer Engagement Center once a sales order is created, and data is retrieved synchronously from SAP Commerce.

SAP Commerce customers can manage their tickets residing in SAP Customer Engagement Center from SAP Commerce storefronts. From **My Account**, a customer can access all ticket actions: view a list of existing tickets, view the details of a specific ticket, create a new ticket, or update an existing ticket.

Figure 11.21 shows the list of support tickets in the SAP Commerce frontend.

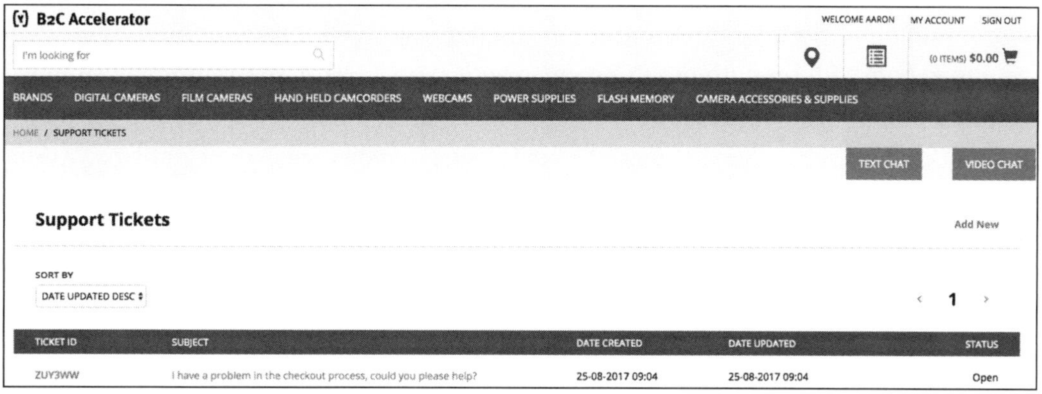

Figure 11.21 List of Support Tickets

Agents can launch the assisted service module from SAP Customer Engagement Center if they have appropriate access in SAP Commerce. The assisted service module launches the SAP Commerce storefront on behalf of the customer for performing various tasks, such as creating a sales order or creating a service ticket, thus helping the customer close the transaction successfully.

SAP Commerce is integrated with SAP Customer Engagement Center live text chat and video chat widgets. This allows an SAP Commerce customer to chat via text or video with an agent in SAP Customer Engagement Center. The chat and video widgets are launched with floating modal pop-up windows that overlay the storefront UI.

11.9 Integration with the SAP Digital Payments Add-On

Customers' IT teams have to offer connections to payment service providers (PSPs) for standardized processing of credit cards and other digital payment methods. In the past, these were point-to-point connections from multiple SAP systems to multiple PSPs. The SAP Digital Payments add-on enables SAP sales processes (e.g., order to cash, internet sales, retail sales) to support credit cards and other real-time payment methods (e.g., Venmo, Google Wallet, PayPal, Apple Pay, Bitcoin, Alipay) in a secure and efficient way. It offers an integration hub approach: SAP manages central operation, maintenance, and support of interfaces in one place, giving companies an increased choice of payment service providers and payment methods. It also ensures secure, PCI-compliant card processing and easier cash reconciliation in follow-on finance processes.

SAP Commerce provides out-of-the-box integration with the SAP Digital Payments add-on, with ready-to-use PSP connectivity as an alternative to current custom PSP integrations.

During checkout, payment can be made using a credit card. By integrating SAP Commerce with the SAP Digital Payments add-on, the user can register a card using the add-on, and SAP Commerce will use the tokenized card information to make the payment during order placement.

Integration of SAP Commerce with the SAP Digital Payments add-on is implemented using RESTful API calls.

11.10 Integration with SAP Jam Communities

SAP Jam Communities redefined how communities drive value to the business and engage customers. They bring customer-driven reviews and information seamlessly into SAP Commerce to drive informed decision-making, discover related products, and build lasting relationships with customers to improve conversion rates and enhance customer experience.

SAP Jam Communities help visitors review the content created by other customers. Customers also can share product recommendations on social networks. The community content is search engine optimized and integrated with commerce search.

Figure 11.22 shows an example of integrated SAP Jam Communities content in SAP Commerce storefronts.

Community content is seamlessly integrated with SAP Commerce product catalog information and vice versa. SAP Jam communities provide engagement opportunities to encourage conversations and help customers in their buying journeys. Customer reviews and Q&As are visible in the SAP Commerce storefronts. By providing relevant content, the community encourages members to return and ultimately lowers the total customer acquisition cost.

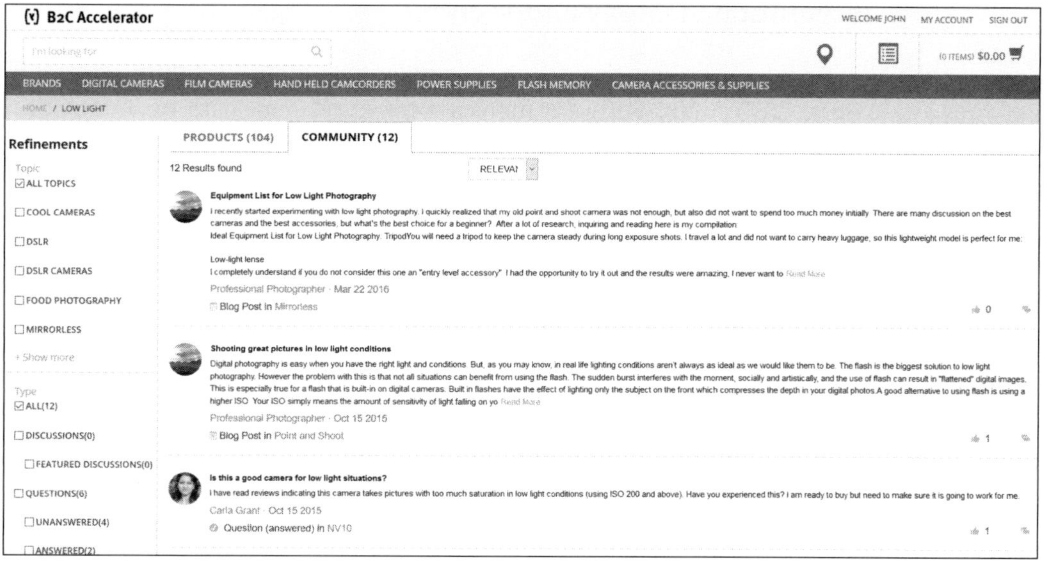

Figure 11.22 SEO-Friendly SAP Jam Communities Content Integrated with SAP Commerce Search

Figure 11.23 shows an example of customer reviews in SAP Commerce accelerator storefronts.

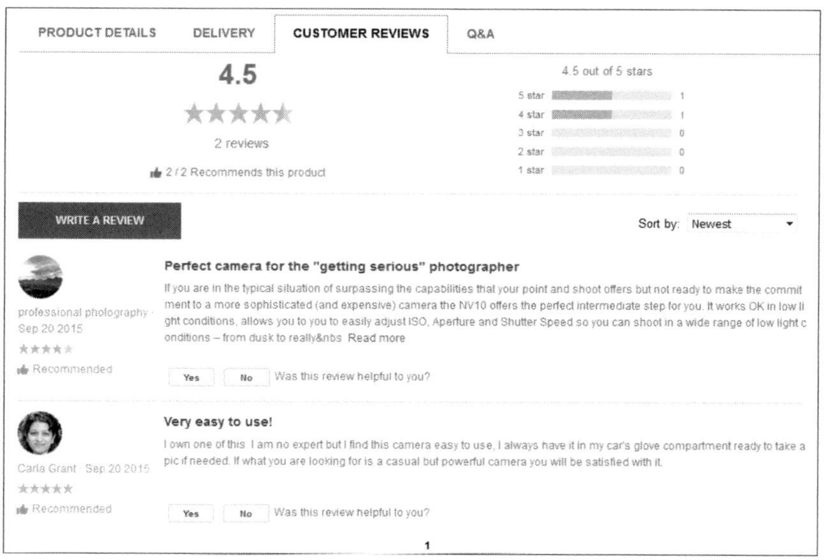

Figure 11.23 Customer Reviews from SAP Jam Communities in SAP Commerce Storefronts

11.11 Integration Strategy and Technology

The SAP integration strategy focuses on the public APIs and routes through middleware integration content. Both are managed by SAP Cloud Platform Integration. Future public APIs will be the basis on which SAP and its customers and partners will build integrations.

SAP is establishing guidelines for its future integration scenarios across its solution portfolio. There are three cornerstones to consider in the future vision of integrations:

1. **SAP Cloud Platform Integration**
   This is the strategic integration service within SAP Cloud Platform. It facilitates the integration of business processes among different departments, organizations and companies. It's like a broker between the connected systems and arranges for technical communications between the components and correct translation of data.
2. **Public APIs**
   New applications will expose their business functionalities via public APIs. Customers and partners will be able to take advantage of these, and SAP will build these public APIs. The preferred protocols will be REST and OData.
3. **SAP API Business Hub**
   As SAP publishes more integration content for hybrid and cloud integrations, this will be used for reference templates for customizations. This new content will be available in the SAP API Business Hub. It will combine existing business APIs and available integration content in one place.

SAP Commerce is fully aligned with the overall SAP integration strategy. The first set of public APIs were released in the 1808 release of SAP Commerce. In the following subsections, we'll look at SAP Commerce, data hub and at SAP Cloud Platform Integration.

11.11.1 SAP Commerce, Data Hub

Although SAP Commerce is getting ready for the future state of integration, SAP Commerce, data hub still plays a critical role in integration and will continue to do so for the immediate future.

SAP Commerce, data hub is an ETL integration platform provided by SAP Commerce that facilitates data loads from one or multiple sources and uploads them to the target systems. It is the original integration layer and is built on the Java Spring framework.

SAP Commerce, data hub works primarily asynchronously, which means the data transformation process is independent of external systems. Removing this reliance on the availability or responsiveness of backend systems allows for quicker response to the customer. SAP Commerce, data hub offers collection, aggregation, correlation, consolidation, and quality assurance as primary features of its integration layer. It acts as a staging platform by processing the uploaded data and preparing it for delivery to target systems.

SAP Commerce, data hub moves data from the source system to the target system in three phases: load, compose, and publish. Figure 11.24 shows the data flow in SAP Commerce, data hub, as follows:

1. The data from the source system is loaded as raw data. It is then moved to a data pool, where it is ready for the composition phase.
2. In the composition phase, the raw items are converted to canonical items, which represent a master data type view that is different from the source and target systems. During this stage, SAP Commerce, data hub is like a staging platform. In this phase, the data can be consolidated from multiple sources, the data quality and integrity are checked, and issues are fixed. Once the data is composed, it is ready to be published.
3. In the publication phase, the canonical data items are transformed into target system items and are delivered to a target system using the target adapters.

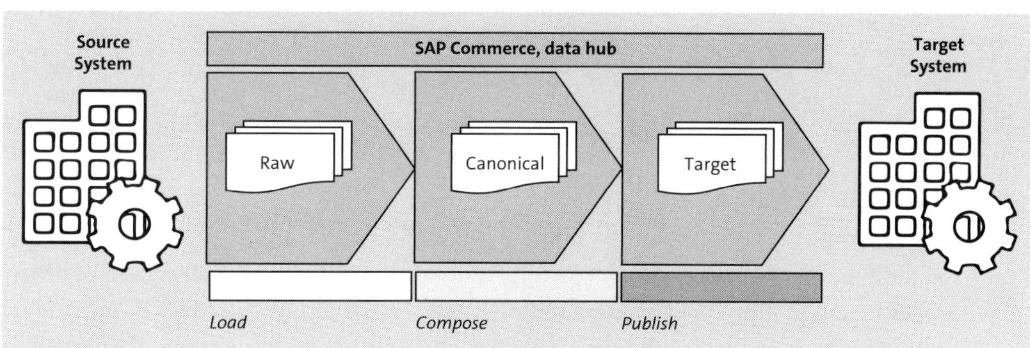

Figure 11.24 Data Flow in SAP Commerce, Data Hub from the Source System to the Target System

Careful planning is required to undertake a successful data integration project using SAP Commerce, data hub. Understanding what components are required for the needs of your project is the first step in this planning. Certain components are mandatory, and for some SAP Commerce provides an out-of-the-box solution. These out-of-the-box components are shipped together with the SAP Commerce software package. Other components are purely optional, their inclusion being dictated solely by the needs of your project.

SAP Commerce, data hub provides an interface to perform SAP Commerce, data hub workflow tasks like viewing item and status counts, creating named pools, creating new feeds, assigning feeds to pools, initiating load, composing and publishing actions, analyzing errors, and more.

SAP Commerce, data hub can be accessed by logging into the backoffice and going to **Administration • Administration • Data Hub**.

Figure 11.25 shows an example of the SAP Commerce integration with SAP ERP using SAP Commerce, data hub. In this scenario, the SAP Commerce system is the lead for customer and order data and SAP ERP is the leading system for delivery, order status, products, and pricing data.

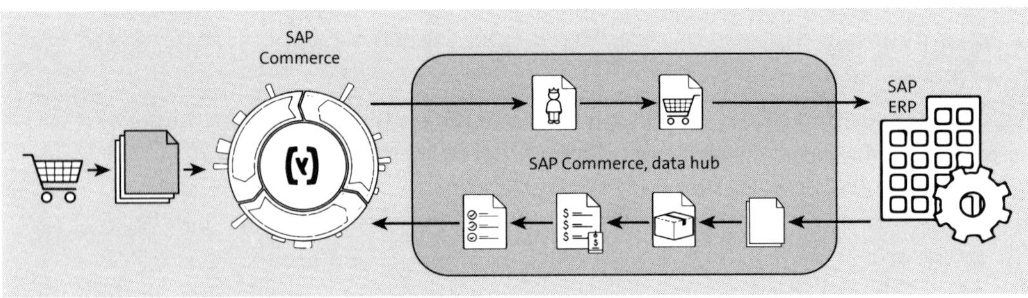

Figure 11.25 SAP Commerce Integration with SAP ERP

11.11.2 SAP Cloud Platform Integration and Integration Objects

SAP Cloud platform is an open platform as a service (PaaS) that offers core platform services, in-memory capabilities, and microservices to build and extend cloud applications. The SAP Commerce integration strategy is based on using SAP Cloud Platform Integration, which facilitates integration using publicly available APIs and manages data transfer using industry-standard protocols like REST and OData. SAP Cloud Platform Integration supports integration with SAP and non-SAP systems in cloud-to-cloud and cloud-to-on-premise scenarios. A few other points to note about SAP Cloud Platform Integration are as follows:

- Supports diverse integration scenarios, like integrating processes and data for application-to-application and business-to-business scenarios
- Prepackaged integration content helps to jump start the integration process
- Customizable SAP integration scenarios provided to include your custom requirements
- Customizable access to SAP Cloud Platform Integration available via public OData APIs

With the newly exposed OData v2 APIs, you can dynamically expose services by defining integration objects in the backoffice or via ImpEx. With the introduction of integration objects, SAP Commerce Cloud provides a new way of defining the structure of a business-level entity used for process integration and master data synchronization. Integration objects facilitate the creation of API services.

The new Integration APIs module has a backoffice perspective in which administrators can model integration objects at runtime. There is an option to monitor the inbound data flow and filter the search results as needed. Once the integration object is modeled, the generated EDMX definition can be imported into SAP Cloud Platform Integration or another OData-based tool.

All inbound data loaded via OData services is tracked in the backoffice. When an integration object is loaded, a corresponding `InboundRequest` item is created and associated with it. Administrators can track the status of the request and filter by type, date range, and integration key. The payload of the request is also available for viewing. The monitoring data remains in the system for seven days and is controlled via a configurable data-retention setting. All monitoring is configured or disabled at runtime via properties and CronJob UIs available in the platform.

The integration of SAP ERP and SAP S/4HANA is based on the integration flows (iFlows) deployed in SAP Cloud Platform Integration.

11.12 Summary

In this chapter, we focused on SAP Commerce integrations and the evolution from point-to-point custom integrations to prebuilt integrations leveraging the public API framework with SAP Cloud Platform Integration. We discussed out-of-the-box SAP

Commerce integrations for master data synchronization, process integrations, and functional integrations.

We started with the customer, product, and pricing data integrations, followed by asynchronous and synchronous order management integrations. We looked at the details of integrating with SAP Marketing Cloud, SAP Service Cloud and SAP Sales Cloud, SAP Subscription Billing, SAP Jam communities, and more.

Last but not least, we covered SAP's integration strategy and current integration technologies in play, like SAP Commerce, data hub, APIs, and SAP Cloud Platform Integration.

SAP Commerce integrations enable an end-to-end seamless experience for customers, from storefront browsing to cart management, order, and service management complimented by offer management. An integrated landscape creates complete transparency, and prebuilt integrations reduce implementation time.

In the next chapter, we'll explore the self-service capabilities of the SAP Commerce cloud portal.

Chapter 12
Cloud Portal

Cloud portal is like a window into the world of SAP Commerce Cloud, providing transparency into the workings of operations, technology management, security, and monitoring all rolled together. It's accessible from anywhere at any time, empowering you to take control of your system even though it is hosted in the cloud.

Having round-the-clock access to your system and full visibility into operating activities is critical to the success of your business. The cloud portal for SAP Commerce Cloud provides a cloud-delivery platform to accelerate, simplify, and derisk commerce implementation. The cloud portal provides not only critical self-service accessibility but also the ability to operate a commerce site with full transparency and control it with round-the-clock access. Basically, it is an end-to-end cloud operating model built on a public cloud infrastructure, the cloud automation engine, and the self-service portal.

The cloud portal is powered by the cloud automation platform, which manages cloud operations. It is mainly designed to manage infrastructure, operate commerce software to the best of its abilities, self-manage commerce development cycles, and give insight into how the commerce platform is performing via centralized logging and monitoring.

The cloud portal allows for the deployment of commerce environments on dedicated public cloud infrastructure. It gives you options to validate a build, perform quality checks to meet best practices guidelines throughout the application lifecycle, and ensure a successful implementation, deployment, and ongoing operation. Cloud development automation saves customers countless hours of custom build process development and ongoing maintenance.

The cloud portal uses the SAP Cloud Platform for high availability and scale, and the automation engine that manages deployments leverages Microsoft Azure for seamless management of SAP Commerce Cloud subscriptions. Figure 12.1 depicts the architecture of the cloud portal, showcasing its components, the automation engine, and the data centers.

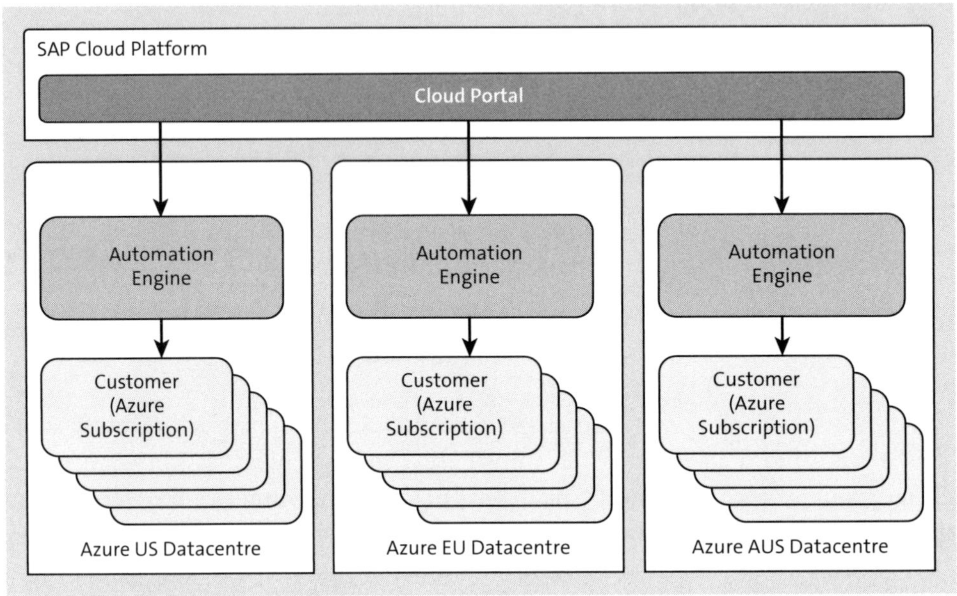

Figure 12.1 Components of Cloud Portal

In this chapter, we'll look at how to get started and what setup needs to take place first. We'll examine cloud operations from deployment, configuration, and management perspectives. We'll also discuss the infrastructure services that are part of the offering and look at security and monitoring options that come with the territory.

12.1 Getting Started

Cloud portal is the user interface for SAP Commerce Cloud and is available for customers and/or nominated partners. If you are on SAP Commerce Cloud, you must use this self-service portal and are responsible for different tasks, including:

- Connecting the code repository to the SAP Commerce Cloud (e.g., configure and enable access and connectivity)
- Triggering the build process and configuring/initiating the deployment of builds to the environment

- Management of environments, including creation, configuration, and termination
- User management
- Configuring firewall rules and VPN configurations

Within one business day of signing a contract, you will be provided with access to a self-service portal that includes dev and staging environments, as well as a default sample store with the latest edition of the software.

The cloud portal was part of special release in June 2018, based on SAP Commerce Cloud 6.7, which is the earliest supported version. Thus, 6.7 is the required release for cloud portal and, in addition, users should have an account with SAP Cloud Platform Identity Authentication, an up-to-date version of a standard internet browser, and a publicly accessible Git repository.

Let's look at how the portal access works, how to set up the code build access, and how to set up the code build specifications with manifests.

12.1.1 Portal Access

The cloud portal is created with an initial system admin user to get started. To create additional access to the portal, user identification has to be verified through SAP Cloud Platform Identity Authentication. Once a user ID is confirmed, access to the portal can be requested at *https://portal.commerce.ondemand.com*.

Two-factor authentication is available for cloud portal access and is recommended when logging in for an additional layer of security.

12.1.2 Code Repository Setup

For automated code building, the code repository must be connected with the SAP Commerce Cloud subscription configured in the cloud portal. The corresponding code repository must have access to information from the cloud portal as well; the two need to be connected to define the application building process. The steps to configure the automated code build are as follows:

1. You might have already created a Git-based code repository. Here we will use Bitbucket, but you could also use something like GitHub or GitLab. To get the URL of the Git repository, click the **Clone** button. Copy the SSH URL, as shown in Figure 12.2.

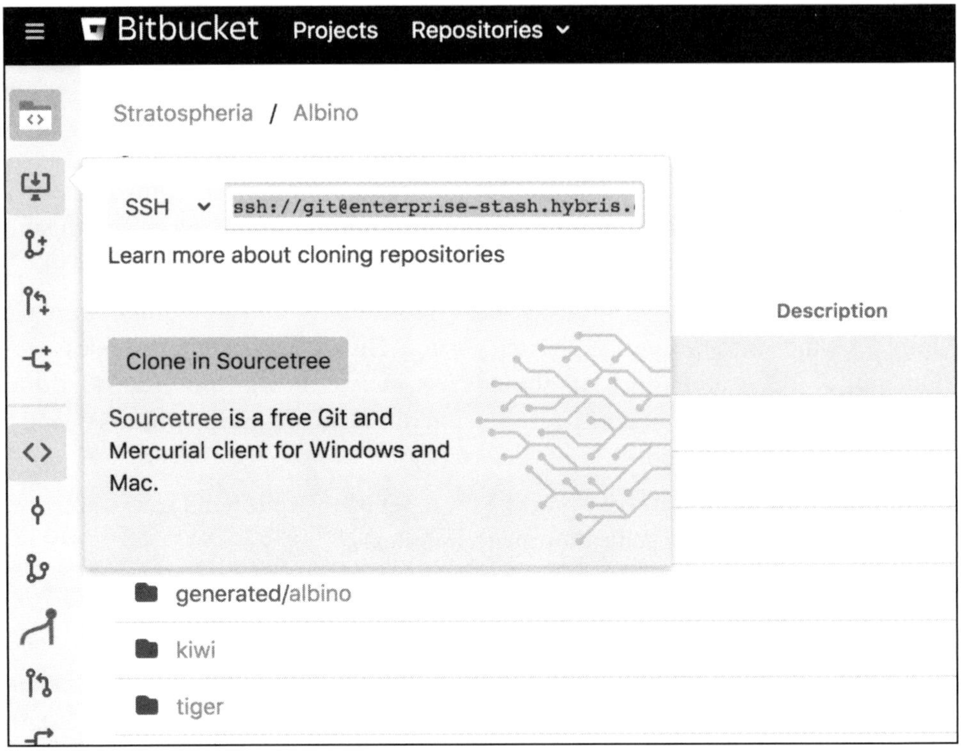

Figure 12.2 Capturing SSH URL from Code Repository

2. In the SAP Commerce cloud portal, open the configuration screen from the tabs on the main screen.
3. Once in the configuration screen, click **Repository**, paste the SSH URL link into the **Repository URL** field, and click **Create SSH Keypair**. This will generate an SAP Commerce Cloud–specific key for the code repository; copy this key.
4. Next, open the code repository and click the **Settings** button, then click on **Access Keys**. Click **Add Key**, which will open an **Add Public Key** window. In this window, paste the access key from the SAP Commerce cloud portal and click the **Add Key** button. In Figure 12.3, we're adding the access key in Bitbucket.

This establishes the setup between the code repository and the SAP Commerce cloud portal.

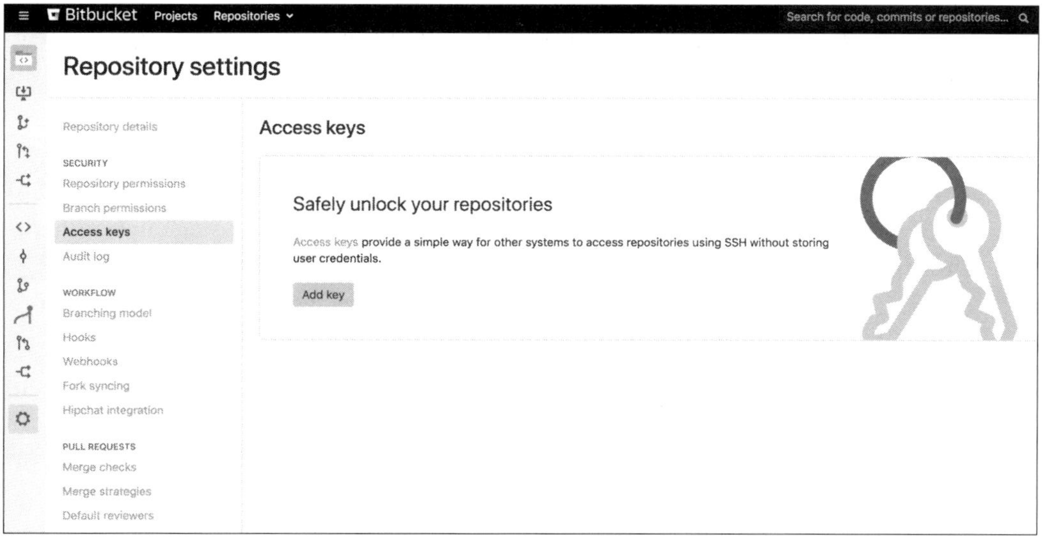

Figure 12.3 Adding Access Key in Bitbucket from Cloud Portal

12.1.3 Building Manifests

To configure SAP Commerce Cloud to exact specifications, build manifests are used. The build process is defined at the root level of the code repository via the manifest.json file.

Various components of the manifest help configure build properties with extensions, properties, aspects, and tests. As part of the manifest, the exact version of SAP Commerce Cloud is defined. This is a mandatory aspect of the manifest. An example is as follows:

```
{  "commerceSuiteVersion": "6.7.0.1",
```

The extension adds to the SAP Commerce functionality and is enabled in the SAP Commerce Cloud deployments. The SAP Commerce properties should be set up in the *local.properties* file.

12.2 SAP Commerce Cloud Operations

There are many tasks included in SAP Commerce Cloud operations: cloud environment deployment, frontend configuration security, user management, and more.

These are essential to ensure the system is running optimally and resources are managed properly. We'll describe these tasks in this section.

12.2.1 Deployment

Now that the initial cloud portal setup has been highlighted, let's look at the SAP Commerce Cloud deployment. The deployment consists of creating environments, forming the builds, and deploying code to the right environments.

Provisioning Environment

Three environments are provided by default (development, staging, and production), and additional environments can be purchased as add-on services. You'll use the cloud portal as the sole interface for managing the SAP Commerce Cloud environments.

Available environments are listed in the **Environments** tab, and a new environment can be created by clicking the **Create Environment** button, as shown in Figure 12.4.

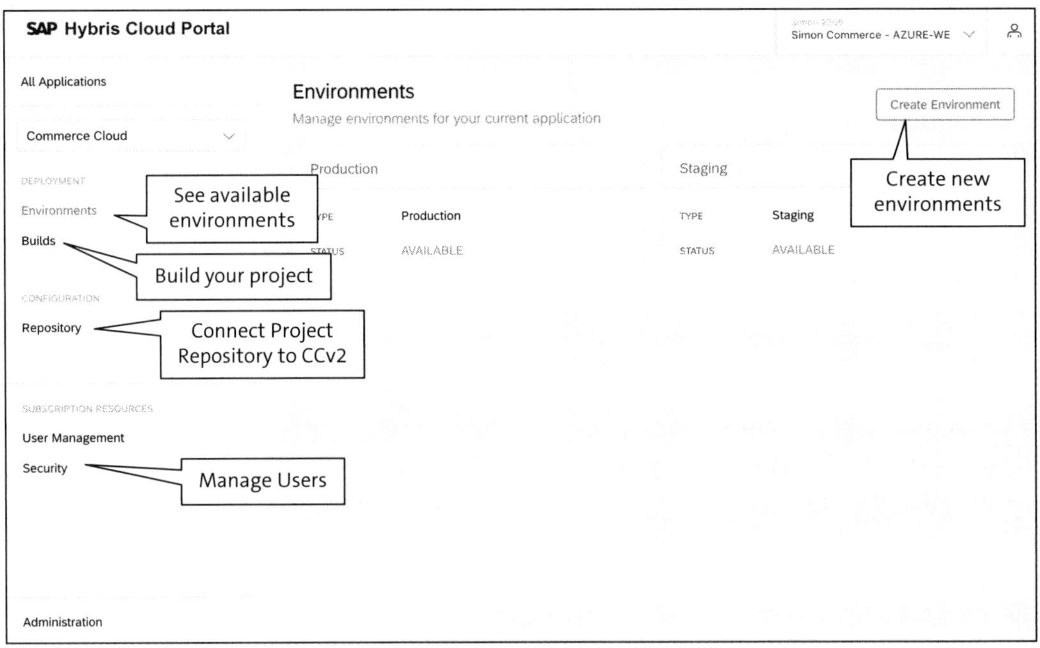

Figure 12.4 Environment Overview Screen

Once the **Create Environment** button is selected, another screen will pop up. It will prompt you to provide the name of the new environment and to specify what type of environment needs to be created: development, staging, or production. Once you're finished, click **Save**.

After creating the new environment, it will appear in draft status. Once it is fully ready, it can be provisioned.

Figure 12.5 shows the created environment.

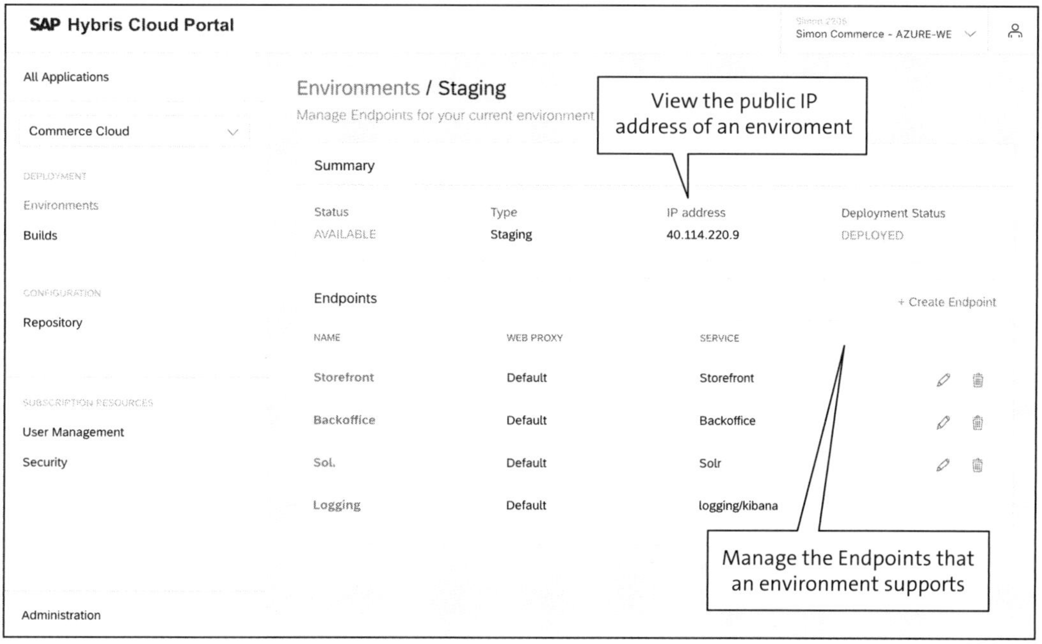

Figure 12.5 Overview of Deployed Environment

After deploying the environment, the performance log activity can be viewed via the Kibana dashboard. Kibana is an underlying performance management plugin that is seamlessly integrated with the cloud portal to provide performance activity logs for each deployed environment.

Creating a Build

The purpose of the build process is to get code ready so that the code can be deployed to an environment. To start this process, click the **Create Build** button. On the **New**

Build screen, provide a build **Name** and **Git Branch Name**, then **Save** the build, as shown in Figure 12.6.

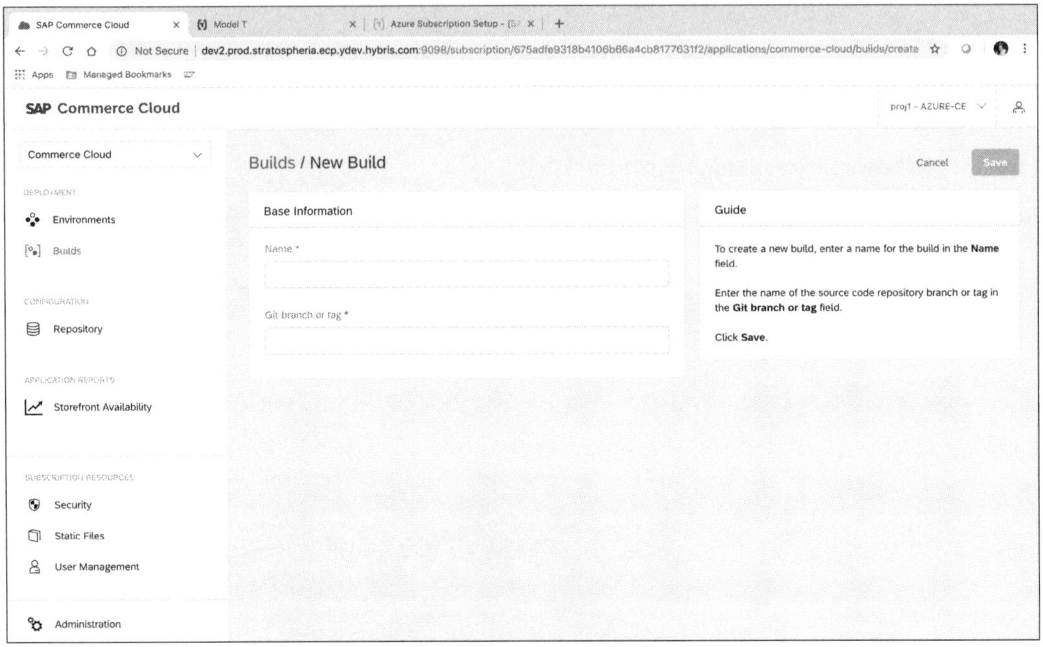

Figure 12.6 Specify Build Details in Create Build Screen

Once the build is created, select it to see its status and build log. The build log shows all the steps taken to create a build.

Deploying a Build

Once the build is ready, it can be deployed to an environment, as shown in Figure 12.7.

In the **Deploy Build** screen, select the target environment and database actions: initialize, update, or no action. The **Initialize Database** action will overwrite the database tables, which is the right action if you are performing the initial setup. The **Update Database** action will update the changed tables, so be mindful of which action is chosen. Once the deployment environment and database action are selected, click the **Deploy** button to deploy the build to the final environment.

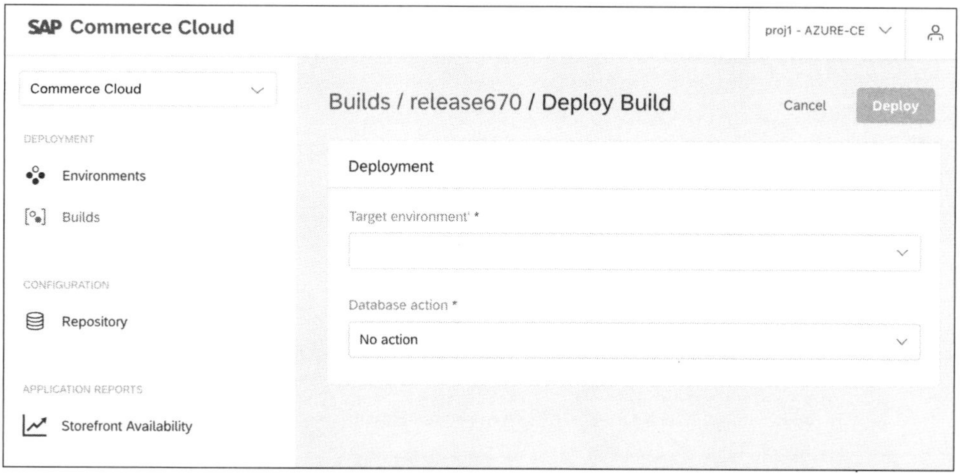

Figure 12.7 Deploy Code Build to Environment

12.2.2 Configuration

Next, you will prepare SAP Commerce Cloud by configuring various endpoints that connect to various services, defining the alternate landing pages, and providing storefront accesses.

Endpoint Management

Endpoints configure the web tier of the application to control web traffic and secure access to SAP Commerce Cloud, as shown in Figure 12.8.

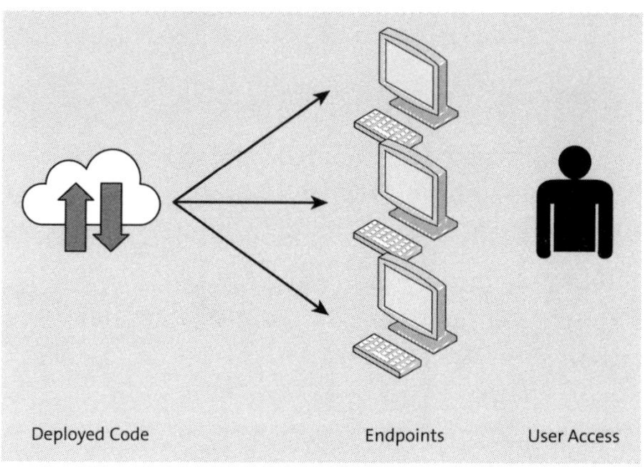

Figure 12.8 Accessing SAP Commerce Cloud Storefront via Endpoints

Endpoints can be managed from the **Environments** screen (see Figure 12.9), where all the existing endpoints are listed and new ones can be created.

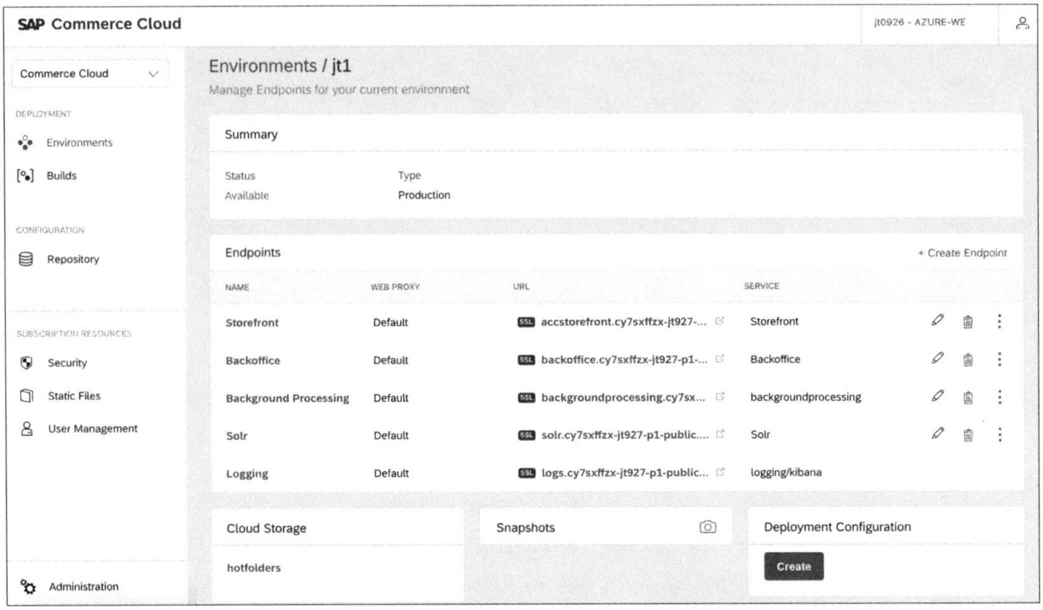

Figure 12.9 Endpoints Overview Screen

To create a new endpoint, click the **Create Endpoint** button, which will take you to the **Create a New Endpoint** screen, as shown in Figure 12.10. Enter the **Name** of the endpoint and provide the **Domain** and URL. Set up the **Web Proxy** and select an **Application** using the endpoint. Add an **SSL Certificate** if using HTTPS, and click **Next**.

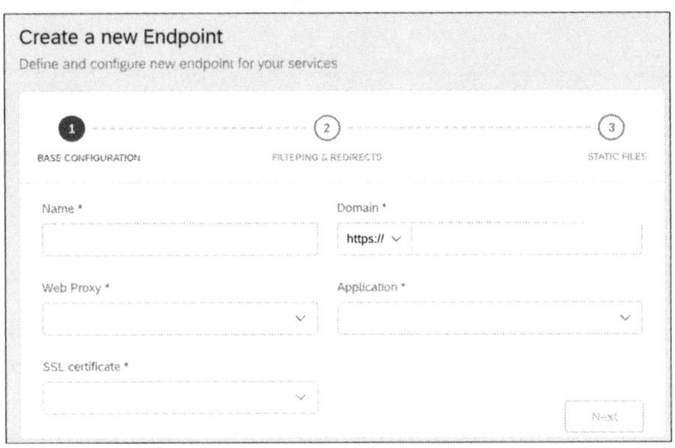

Figure 12.10 Define Endpoint Details

On the next screen, shown in Figure 12.11, define the IP filtering criteria.

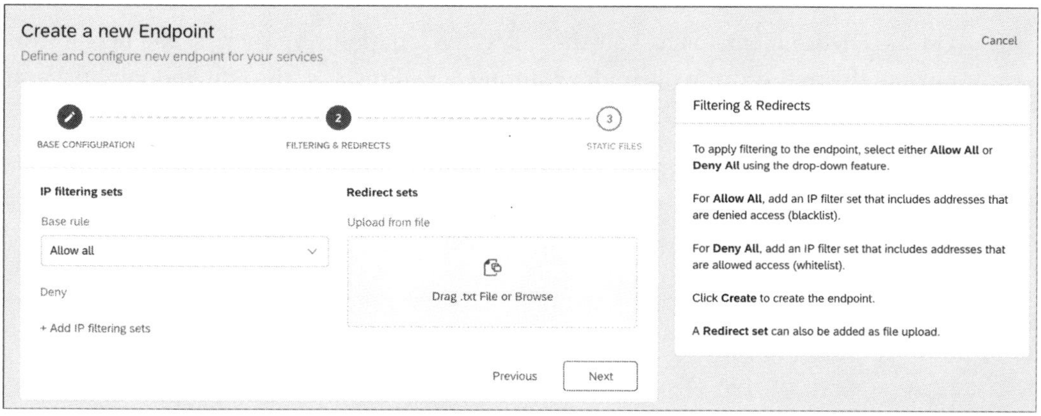

Figure 12.11 Define IP Filter Sets for Endpoint

You can select either **Allow All** or **Deny All**. If you select **Allow All**, you can select the IP addresses that are not allowed access. If you select **Deny All**, you can select the IP addresses that are allowed access. Once finished, click the **Create** button to create the endpoint. This completes IP address accessibility setup via an endpoint.

Website Redirect Configuration

For a seasonal promotion, wouldn't it be nice to redirect your customers to the seasonal promotions page directly rather than modify the original webpages? The website redirect provides the configuration to do just that.

Website redirect has a set of rules that defines the new location that visitors will see. To create a redirect set of rules, define the desired redirect rules in a plain text file with Apache syntax, as shown in Listing 12.1.

```
# Redirect rules for autumn campaign
# @author Testi Testmann
Redirect "^gloriousleaves$" "campaign/98323/index.html"
Redirect "^autumn/(.*)$" "campaign/98325/$1"
Redirect "^autumn/(.*)$" "campaign/98325/$1"
Redirect "^products/leafblower-5662.*$" "campaign/98399/leafblower-
special.html"
```

Listing 12.1 Example of Defining Redirect Rules

Once the rules are defined, they can be attached to the endpoints by uploading the text file in the cloud portal.

On the **Environments** page, edit the respective endpoint by clicking the pencil icon. Upload the redirect rule file under **Filtering & Redirects** on the **Edit Endpoint** page, as shown in Figure 12.12. Each endpoint supports one redirect set.

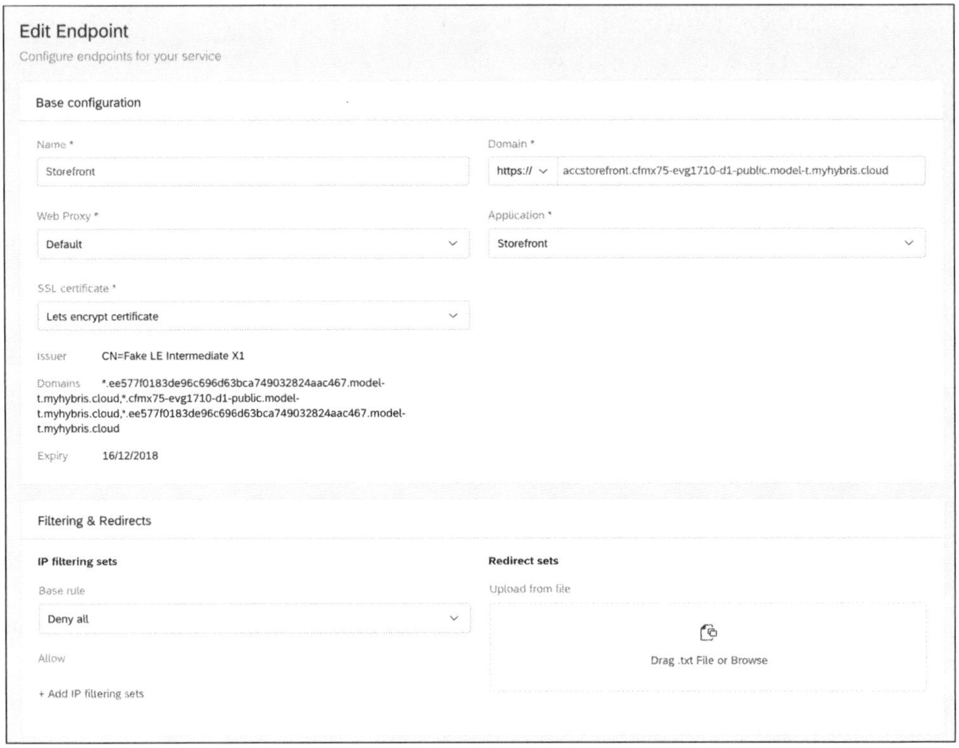

Figure 12.12 Upload Website Redirect Rules in Filtering and Redirects Section

When the redirects are no longer required, they can be deleted from the **Edit Endpoint** page by clicking the trashcan icon next to the redirect.

Frontend Configuration

Your storefront must be configured to be accessible by anyone, be they your employees or consumers. Let's look at some guidelines to do so.

Storefront access is granted via a storefront endpoint that can be configured in the **Environments** page. If your storefront is configured to the root web path, the endpoint will route you to the storefront. If it is not, then it needs to be appended in the URL to include the root path.

For example, if your storefront is configured to the */USstorefront* path, the URL to the storefront is as follows:

https://accstorefront.<your-site-path>.cc.commerce.ondemand.com/USstorefront

To enable user-friendly website addresses for your storefront, you can configure the address at the context root by adding a value and `contextPath` in the build manifest.

In the build manifest, follow these steps:

1. In line 22 (bolded for convenience) of Listing 12.2, set the value for `"key":"storefrontContextRoot","value":""` in the properties section of `accstorefront`.
2. In line 32 (bolded for convenience) of Listing 12.2, set the value for `"name":"yacceleratorstorefront","contextPath":""` in the `webapps` section of `accstorefront`.


```
{
            "name": "accstorefront",
            "properties": [
                {
                    "key": "spring.session.enabled",
                    "value": "true"
                },
                {
                    "key": "spring.session.yacceleratorstorefront.save",
                    "value":"async"
                },
                {
                    "key": "spring.session.yacceleratorstorefront.cookie.name",
                    "value": "JSESSIONID"
                },
                {
                    "key": "spring.session.yacceleratorstorefront.cookie.path",
                    "value": "/"
                },
                {
                    "key":"storefrontContextRoot",
                    "value":""
                }
            ],
```

```
        "webapps": [
            {
                "name": "mediaweb",
                "contextPath": "/medias"
            },
            {
                "name": "yacceleratorstorefront",
                "contextPath": ""
            },
            {
                "name": "acceleratorservices",
                "contextPath": "/acceleratorservices"
            }
```

Listing 12.2 Storefront Configuration in Build Manifest Code

To configure base site URLs, you can either use a properties file (the default method) or you can configure a database property. This enables features such as password reset, email links, and payment provider redirects at runtime. To begin, follow these steps:

1. In the backoffice, click **Data URL Resolution • Data URL Resolution**, as shown in Figure 12.13.

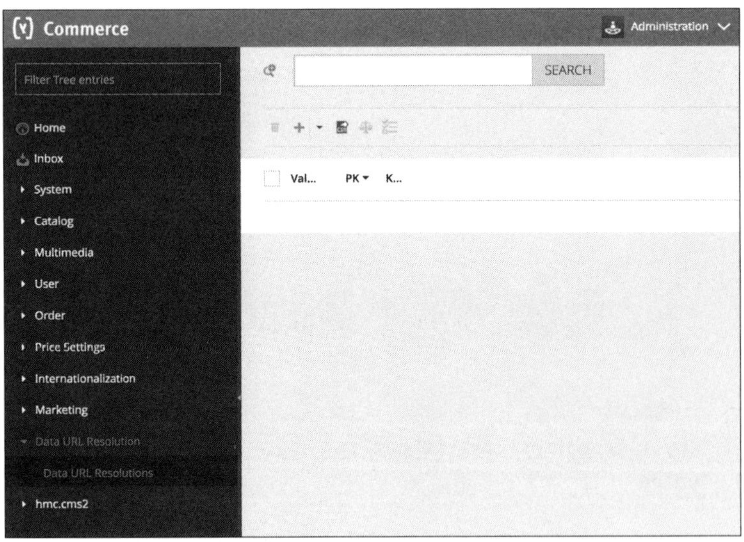

Figure 12.13 Overview Screen for Data URL Resolution

2. On the next screen, click the plus (+) button to open the **Create New Data URL Resolution** page. Here enter the **Value** and the **Key**, then click **Done**, as shown in Figure 12.14.

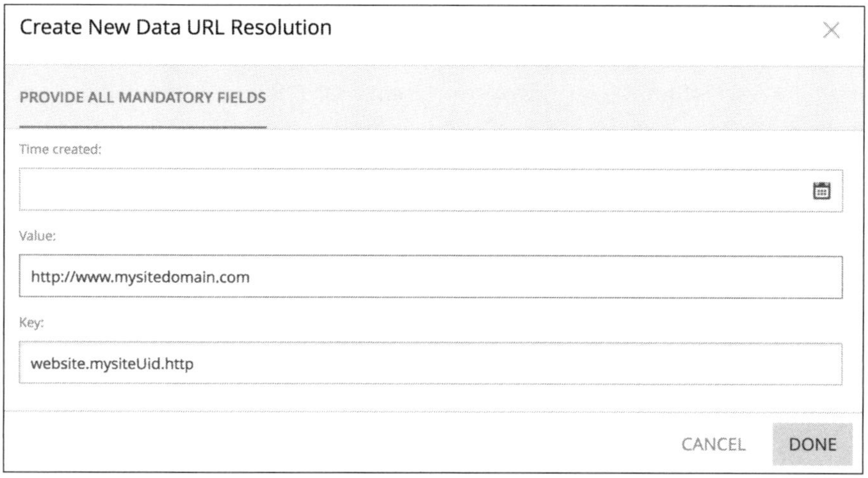

Figure 12.14 Creation of New URL Resolution

3. The new URL resolution will appear in the URL resolution screen, as shown in Figure 12.15.

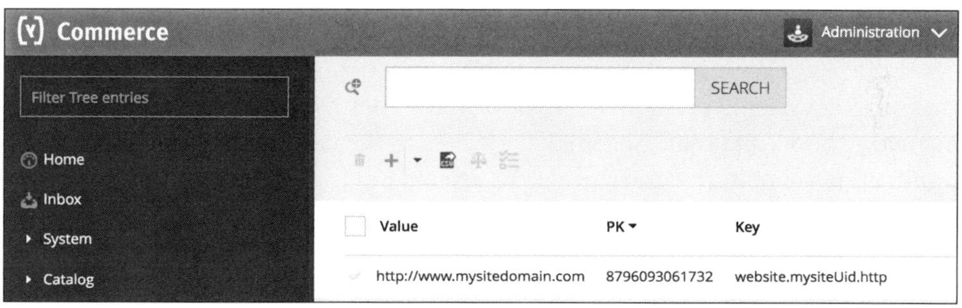

Figure 12.15 URL Resolution Overview Screen Showing Newly Created URL Resolution

12.2.3 User Management

As part of the cloud portal for SAP Commerce Cloud, you can manage user access and user rights via the user management functionality. A user with the system administrator profile can manage users. The system administrator role is granted to the user

ID provided by you during the account onboarding process. The system administrator is responsible for managing the users, permissions, and security configurations.

Cloud portal provides the ability to manage user access by adding, deleting, and modifying the access. User management is the responsibility of the customer.

Users must have authorized S-user numbers before they can be invited to access the cloud portal. To request an S-user, logon to the SAP ONE Support Launchpad and request a user ID. You can access the support portal at *https://launchpad.support.sap.com/#/user/management*.

To add users for the cloud portal, the system admin can click the **Invite Person** button. On the **Add User with Role** page, provide the user's **S-Number**, **Email**, and **Role**, then click **Save**, as shown in Figure 12.16.

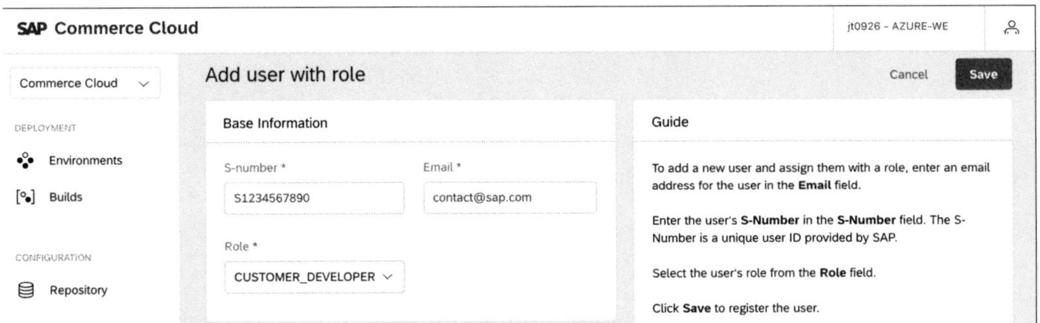

Figure 12.16 User Details Provided in Add User Screen

Once the new user is saved, it will appear in the user list on the user management overview screen, and that user will have access to the cloud portal according to the profile assigned to it. The user can also be deleted by clicking on the trashcan button next to it in the user overview screen.

12.3 Infrastructure Services

SAP Commerce Cloud provides many infrastructure services, such as scalability, monitoring, maintenance, and database services for efficient operations and managing cloud environments. The infrastructure services can be automated, planned, or manual. The hosting platform of SAP Cloud Commerce resides in cloud infrastructure operated by Microsoft Azure. Let's look at these services.

12.3.1 Scalability

During the year, various planned or unplanned events occur that require increased platform capacity. The initial sizing is based on the business metrics provided by the customer. Planned marketing campaigns or a specific event like Black Friday can increase website traffic and therefore require additional resources. To meet an additional capacity requirement, the scaling event can be triggered either manually or automatically. We recommend notifying SAP in advance when increased traffic is expected to ensure that adequate resources are provisioned. Ideally, customers should inform SAP at least three business days in advance.

Automated scaling can be triggered when the SAP Commerce Cloud platform detects that an operational metric (such as CPU load or inbound request volume) is outside of standard operating boundaries.

Increased capacity in SAP Commerce Cloud is achieved via horizontal scaling—that is, adding additional servers to deal with more traffic. Multiple servers are connected to work as a single unit.

12.3.2 Monitoring

SAP's Network Operation Center (NOC) monitors systems on a 24/7 basis and reacts to the alerts that may be triggered by system checks. Basic monitoring is available for all environments, and advanced monitoring is available for staging and production environments.

A range of monitoring checks are performed by the SAP Commerce Cloud teams, providing information on system health and trends (e.g., load average, CPU, RAM, database). You'll receive a monthly report detailing the performance of the previous month, including information on the following:

- Website and infrastructure availability
- Bandwidth
- Service fulfillment
- Environment sizing
- Database health
- Security updates
- Application performance information

12.3.3 Maintenance

SAP performs regular scheduled maintenance activities to sustain optimal performance, reliability, and security of the SAP Commerce Cloud application. SAP is responsible for ensuring your system's continuity during ongoing patching activities related to the infrastructure and database. Any noncritical activity that will not affect system availability might be carried out during business hours.

Any maintenance activity scheduled by SAP that will impact service will be coordinated with your team to ensure the least disruption to business. Maintenance and patching of the Azure database service and network infrastructure are performed automatically and transparently. The patching and system upgrades required for the customer environments are scheduled in advance with customers. In case of emergency maintenance, when a critical security patch needs to be implemented urgently to ensure environment protection or SAP's service delivery, SAP may reserve the right to implement a patch in accordance with the SLA.

12.3.4 Database Services

SAP Commerce Cloud includes a dedicated database for each of your provisioned environments. The database services include all capabilities related to infrastructure, patches, snapshots, restores, high availability, and global redundancy, supported and maintained by SAP.

Standard Database Operations

You are responsible for standard database operations, all of which can be initiated from the cloud portal. Some of the functions within the portal that you'll initiate are as follows:

- Data snapshots and restores. Before deploying to a production environment, it is highly recommended to make data snapshots to enable data restore if a rollback is required.
- On-demand database backup and restore services.

A ticket must be raised in the support portal if manual database updates or modifications are required. Other standard database procedures that can be requested through a ticket are as follows:

- Database operations to support application deployment (e.g., backup and restore services)

- Support for production, staging, and development environments
- Emergency triage of application query problems

Database Health and Performance Monitoring

SAP proactively monitors databases to ensure optimal health and performance, and any application-related performance issues are reported to customers. Monitoring includes (but is not limited to) topics such as database transaction units, data space usage, large tables, application queries, and so on.

Service Recovery

In the event of data loss or data corruption, an SAP Commerce Cloud provides data recovery mechanisms.

On the database level, different mechanisms exist for backup on the following schedule:

- Weekly full database backups
- Hourly differential database backups
- Transaction log backups every 10 minutes

All database backups are stored in geographically redundant storage for 35 days. Files saved to cloud storage are persisted multiple times across primary and secondary datacenters. Application servers do not require backup processes because they can be recreated from a Docker image.

Disaster Recovery

Disaster recovery planning is a critical part of the SAP Commerce Cloud infrastructure. In case of a natural disaster or a human-induced disaster, there is set of processes and tools in place to get systems back up in time to minimize the impact on business.

The SAP Commerce Cloud infrastructure provides very competitive disaster recovery offerings. SAP provides full offsite database and system backups and restoration of service from the backups as part of its disaster recovery service. Standard disaster recovery service restores the database from a georeplicated backup, so the recovery time is subject to database size, network latency, and database restore time. Depending on the offering you have, your recovery point objective (RPO) and recovery time objective (RTO) may vary, as follows:

- The standard service RPO is one hour and RTO is 24 hours.
- The premium service RPO is five minutes and RTO is four hours.

In case of a disaster, SAP provides data recovery services that include full database and system backups. The disaster recovery services include a fully functional replica of the production environment, an IPsec VPN (fully encrypted) tunnel to the customer site, and conceptual network information, to name a few.

12.4 Security

Security controls are in place for infrastructure components including network firewalls, intrusion detection systems, and hardened configurations in standard servers. Network devices, servers, and applications all have intensive log management processes in place.

Cyberattacks, such as distributed denial of service (DDoS) attacks, are monitored, and mitigation service is also offered to protect customer websites from volumetric attacks.

Change management processes are in place for effectively managing access, changes to your systems, and any other information. SAP staff can access the systems and any other information only with correct access authorization.

Security processes and procedures related to the development and deployment of custom-implemented code are the responsibility of the customer. The SAP Commerce Cloud security provides guidance and details in compliance with SAP's cloud security framework.

SAP Commerce Cloud services provides firewall management. Firewalls are highly available with no single point of failure to allow only approved traffic inbound and outbound. Firewall audit logging is in place with 90-day online retention periods and one-year offline retention. Internal and external firewalls are used to create trust domains between the public and individual landscapes.

Firewall rules and SSL certificates are applied in the **Security** section of the portal. The security management is linked with endpoint management. The default setup in the endpoints is to deny all IP addresses. The file with the allowed IP addresses can be uploaded to allow access.

SSL certificates can be added or deleted in the SSL tab endpoint, as shown in Figure 12.17. From the main cloud portal screen, click the **Security** like in the left menu. Then select the **SSL Certificates** tab and click **Create**. The **Name**, the **Description**, the certificate text (in the **Certificate File** field), and the info needed to generate the certificate (in the **Key** field). Click **Save**, and the new certificate is generated and ready for use.

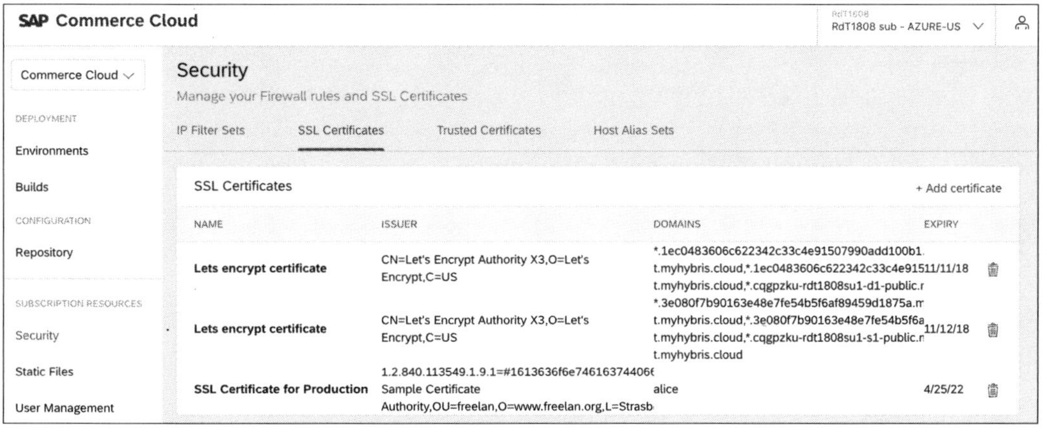

Figure 12.17 Adding SSL Certificates

Adding trusted certificates is a critical part of the security setup. To add a trusted certificate in the **Security** screen, click the **Trusted Certificate** tab, then click the **Add Certificate** button to add a new trusted certificate, as shown in Figure 12.18.

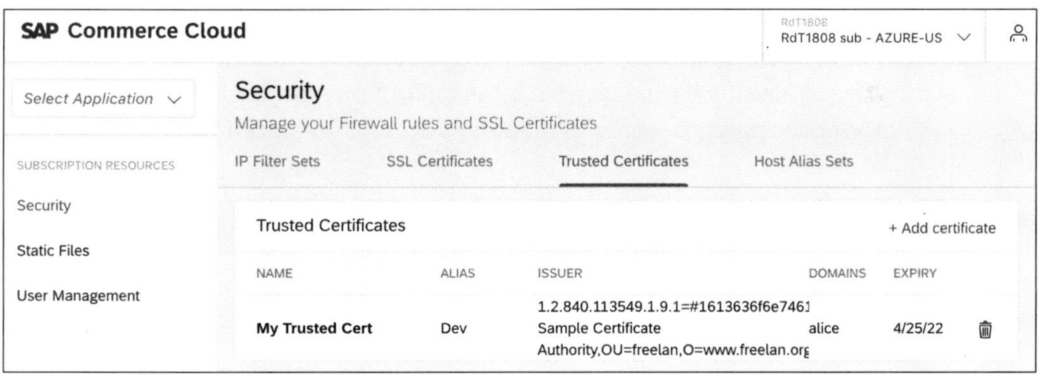

Figure 12.18 Adding Trusted Certificates

IP Filter Sets (see Figure 12.19) define the IP addresses that are allowed or denied access to the storefront. These IP addresses are stored in a file that can be uploaded for referral to—by the endpoints, for example.

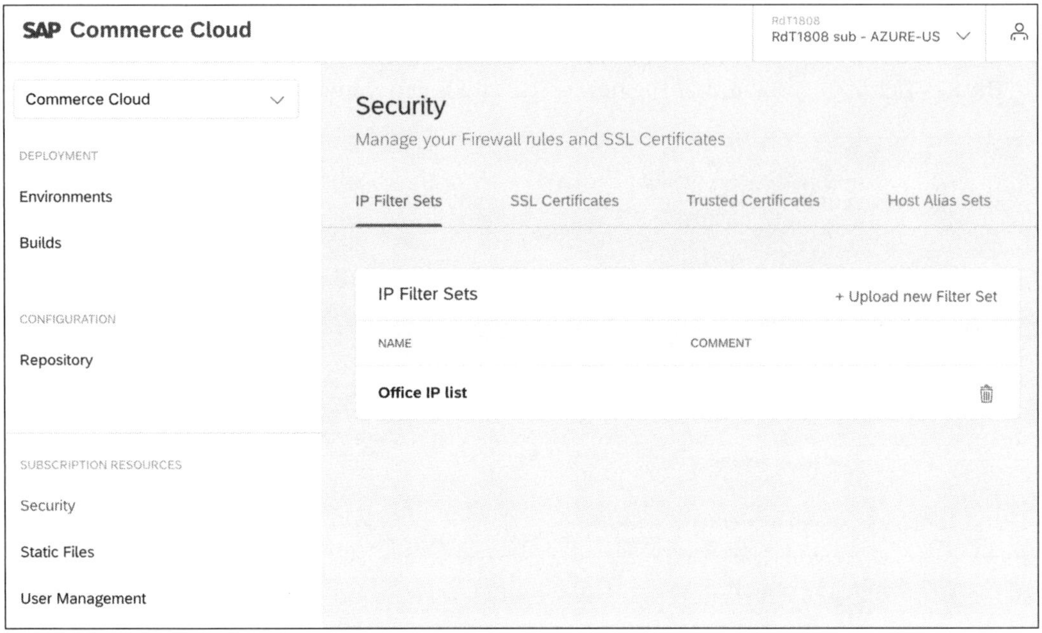

Figure 12.19 Uploading IP filter Sets

12.5 Support

There might be times when you need to contact SAP for support. How you go about setting it up and using it when needed is the topic of this section. It all begins with the system administrator, the super user, in the customer organization.

12.5.1 User Creation

The company system administrator will initiate the process of setting up other users who will be able to create tickets, monitor the status of the tickets, and look for resolutions in the SAP knowledge base.

The system administrator will start by requesting an S-user or D-user who might need to report an incident or request service from the SAP support portal. To request an S-user, go to *http://support.cap.com/user-admin*.

On this site, click **Manage Users and Authorizations**, followed by **Request User**. On the next screen, add details like **First** and **Last Name**, **Email**, **Language**, and so on.

Authorization will need to be assigned for the user to create and monitor incidents, report incidents, display incidents, display all incidents, send incidents to SAP, and close incidents.

12.5.2 How to Create an Incident

To create an incident, go to *https://launchpad.support.sap.com/#incident/create*.

Enter the customer number and S-user ID. If requested, enter the product and installation number. Then select the required environment for which the ticket needs to be created.

On the next screen, enter the incident details, like priority, subject, and description of the issue at hand. Select the CEC-HCS component so that the ticket is assigned to SAP Customer Experience Cloud Services.

Provide as much detail as possible, including a screenshot of the incident, so that the support team can recreate the incident. Also give your contact details so that the SAP team members can reach you in case they have questions. Once finished, submit the ticket.

12.6 Summary

In this chapter, you learned about the self-service components offered by the cloud portal. We started with a look at portal access via the link that is received soon after the contract is signed and how to connect the code repository to the cloud portal to enable an automated SAP Commerce build. We looked at provisioning environments, creating and deploying SAP Commerce builds, and configuration and user management. We then reviewed the infrastructure services, security, and support.

By offering most of the cloud deployment, operations, and development capabilities via self-service, the cloud portal is intended to empower you to operate and execute your own vision.

The Authors

Seema Vishnoi is the head of SAP Commerce market development and go-to-market activities in Latin America. Seema is passionate about innovation and adoption of the SAP C/4HANA portfolio as well as helping customers succeed in their digital transformation journey. She has played key roles in solution management, sales operations, and innovative business solutions and has successfully lead various CRM initiatives for customers within SAP. Outside of SAP, Seema is an adjunct professor at Villanova University.

Sietse Verhoog is the director of SAP Customer Experience Expert Services for Latin America and the Caribbean at SAP. He came to Latin America from the Netherlands in 2011 and joined the SAP Hybris team in Latin America in 2014. He is responsible for the team of customer experience experts, architects, developers, and industry specialists based out of Mexico, Colombia, and Brazil who provide support focused on customer success to the SAP C/4HANA customers and partners throughout the region.

Drew Messinger-Michaels co-created the CX Business Consulting and Functional Consulting groups within SAP Commerce, along with SAP Customer Experience Expert Services offerings such as the Commerce Capabilities Workshop, Solr Workshop, Roles and Permissions Workshop, Hybris Health Check, and Functional Analyst Certification. He writes and podcasts about arts, culture, and technology, online and elsewhere.

Index

A

B

Q

R

S

T

U

V

W

Y